SCENOGRAPHY

SCENOGRAPHY
An Indian Perspective

SATYABRATA ROUT

NIYOGI
BOOKS

Published by
NIYOGI BOOKS
Block D, Building No. 77,
Okhla Industrial Area, Phase-I,
New Delhi-110 020, INDIA
Tel: 91-11-26816301, 26818960
Email: niyogibooks@gmail.com
Website: www.niyogibooksindia.com

Text and images © Satyabrata Rout

Editor: Arkaprabha Biswas
Design: Shashi Bhushan Prasad

ISBN: 978-93-91125-29-5
Publication: 2022

All rights are reserved. No part of this publication may be reproduced or transmitted in any form or by any means, electronic or mechanical, including photocopying, recording or by any information storage and retrieval system without prior written permission and consent of the Publisher.

Printed at: Niyogi Offset Pvt. Ltd., New Delhi, India

CONTENTS

Foreword	7
Author's Note	15
Introduction	19
Space that Exists in Time	45
Manipulation of Space in Ancient India	65
Space and Scenography in Popular Indian Theatres	111
Conventions of Space	157
Alternative Performance Spaces	199
Multiplicity of Art: Perception, Interpretation, Aesthetics	235
Understanding Scenography: Exploring Ideas	263
Representing Design Ideas: Paper Works	343
Elements of Design	379
Principles of Design	459
Scenographic Dramaturgy: The Space Game	519
Interviews	543
Acknowledgments	564
Index	568

FOREWORD

WRITING OF THE STAGE SPACE

Scenography—the art of writing of the stage space from ancient Greece—is the international term for describing the visual images in a stage space. This includes costumes, props and accessories, light and any scenic element needed to tell the visual story—the supporting player of the narrative—so that the eyes of the spectator see what they are *not* hearing with their ears. The art of scenography brings together the two spectatorial senses—vision and sound—so that the spectator may experience not only the narrative movement, but also the context in which it is being performed. Scenography tells the story behind the text, just as looking at a painting tells more than its title. It is a sublime and subtle art that takes a lifetime to acquire. Each piece is a new challenge and venture into an unknown territory. There is not one method or answer, but only universal principles of art to give support to the work, and crucially the development of a personal aesthetic that will ultimately inform all the choices made. Without this personal aesthetic, it is impossible to make decision and choices. The colour of a material for a costume, the height of a wall, the roughness of a texture—everything is the result of an informed decision that is led by personal choice. And thus, fine art and scenography are close partners.

To establish this personal aesthetic is the main point of study, and it is a lifelong learning activity. How to achieve it and where to begin? At first, it seems bewildering as there are so many possibilities.

Has it to do with reading plays?—Knowing history?—Having a Fine Art vocabulary?—Is it the technical competency?—Is it different in every country?

So many questions, but the answers are relatively simple, at least to start with. All drama is about people, their joys and sorrow, their situations, hopes and desires. Writers and creators select these universal patterns and present them in the stage space so that the spectator may recognise and see them anew. The scenographer must, first and foremost, be a compulsive observer of human nature to know how to transform that reality into the heightened experience on a theatre space. But, it's no good just looking. The scenographer, the visual artist of the theatre, must develop a facility for remembering, and nothing is better than keeping a little sketch book in a bag or a pocket with a small pencil ready to note down the shape or stance of a person; the fall of a piece of cloth, the texture of a wall and all the fascinating minutiae of daily life. And then, the scenographer has to develop good organisation to actualise them to a fine art, for a multitude of drawings are useless if they can't be quickly retrieved when needed for reference. These references can then serve as the start for making the essential scale figures that are always needed when the proposed idea becomes a three-dimensional model of the performing space.

The scale model is a way of taking the actual space home in its miniature form and playing with it to try and tell the story clearly, and to let the imagination wander. This 'play time' is very crucial, where ideas have to be rigorously tested against one's personal aesthetic. There is such a long journey from conception to production, with so many people and interventions, that the scenographer has to be very sure of the quality of the scenographic proposal and at the same time, remain flexible enough to let all the other collaborators in the team take part in the creation. Only the combination of all these seemingly disparate elements will make a coherent visual statement. And it is very important to *feel* the performing space by walking through it, looking out at where the spectators will sit, study the sightlines and find where the *strong points* of the space are sited, for that will tell where furniture should be placed.

More and more scenographers from all over the world are being concerned about the unnecessary wastes of the props and about making more sustainable sets in these days when our planet is in danger. The days of constructing large pieces of scenery and throwing away those after the production because of the high expenses of storage are nearly gone and in many productions, the performer and their costumes become the main scenographic elements. Scenic pieces that add to or enhance the performance have to justify their occupation of the space and of course, can enchant and add to the spectators' experience. Finding the appropriate props and accessories is equally important. A production should tour more and more so that theatre and stories can reach people even if they do not have an access to a formal theatre building, and this flexibility in art and feasibility in production have opened a new vista of innovation and imagination for a scenographer. Scenography, therefore, unites the performer and the stage space into a three-dimensional sculptural form. No longer do performers simply perform in front of a painted two-dimensional background that they cannot see, unaware of the environment in which they will perform. Scenography has become the composite description of this visual theatre activity and distinguishes itself from the ever-growing number of theatre consultants, who design interiors of theatres often without consulting the very people, who have to work in them. Theatre design, to many people, means buildings rather than the space in which stories of life and death are imagined and retold for generations after generations.

LOOKING INTO THE EAST

For many years, Western theatre practitioners have travelled to the East to observe and learn the art of storytelling—how to retell, with the simplest and most dramatic means, the epic tales that resonate through so many cultures. For many decades, the influence of Indian, Japanese, Chinese, Greek theatre techniques has been absorbed into the modern-day Western theatre vocabulary.

Yukio Ninagawa in his seminal production of Shakespeare's *The Tempest* showed us that Titania's bower could be evoked just with a beautiful floral silk kimono. Ariane Mnouchkine explored Kathakali dance and costume to tell the Greek myth *Les Atrides* by creating a perfect synchronicity of word and vision. Peter Brook's retelling of the *Mahabharata*, in association with the French scenographer Chloé Obolensky, was seen all over the world and her reinvented devices have become part of our visual theatre language.

In the mid-1970s, I made my first visit to India as a young designer for a production of George Bernard Shaw's *Candida* with a company comprising of actors from the National Theatre of Great Britain, directed by a Shakespearean scholar, John Russell Brown. I was sent seven weeks in advance with my ½" – 1'0" accurate three-dimensional scale model to the National School of Drama in New Delhi, where the setting—a Victorian clergyman's house backing on to a park in the north-east suburbs of London—was to be built. The costs were to be paid by the company in England. Shaw specifies very precisely exactly how the house should look, its fireplace, the stained-glass front door, the bookcases—every little detail requiring a naturalism that now we would think only appropriate for a film location. *Candida*, originally written in 1894, is a dialectic between the clergyman, a Christian socialist and a visiting poet, both of whom love Candida in very different ways. I had constructed a three-dimensional backcloth of houses and trees in an effort to make an integrated stage picture. My arrival in the drama school in Delhi at that time was a huge shock. There were no workshops at all to construct this. There was a large yard in the open air, and one elderly man with a saw. My visit was sponsored by the British Council, who wonderfully provided me with a translator who accompanied me everywhere. But nothing could hide my dismay and inexperience. There was a great deal of staring and looking at the model, much admiration and much shaking of heads. As all this was going on, out of my control, I was looking at people passing, noticing their wonderful textiles and embroideries. In the building I saw several beautiful wall hangings and an idea came into my head; 'Why be in India trying to do what we do in London? Why not try and capitalise on the strengths of the local artists and artisans?' I hesitantly asked my British Council colleague if it might be at all possible to interpret the three-dimensional, built backcloth of North-east London as a huge embroidered textile, possibly a series of silk hangings that I had seen on the walls. Then I proposed that finding the Victorian furniture and just creating the simplest structure of the clergyman's house would suffice and do justice to the text, as the proposed embroidered backcloth would provide the description of the rest of the things.

Everyone smiled. Heads stopped shaking and within a very short time I was in a British Council car going up a steep hillside somewhere outside Delhi to a women's cooperative, where they were sewing to commission. Though the hand-sewing machines operated on the floor of a huge rooftop with little dogs running around, I saw this was wonderful work. There I met an Indian textile designer who immediately offered her services as the coordinator of the project. And so with huge excitement the work began. White silk was obtained for the base of the seven pieces that would be eventually joined together, and sample stitches, autumn colours of embroidery silks were found and I showed them how to scale up from my model. They were so skilled and inventive, it was a lesson in itself. I went up several times to see work in progress, but nothing prepared me for the final moment when it was brought to the theatre and hung from the flies to stretch out. It was just beautiful and still remains in my memory as a great lesson I learned: Be flexible.

There are many ways to achieve and interpret the work, and it is so important to respect the interpretive artists by giving them a carefully thought out and beautiful template to work from. Look to see what the unique qualities a workshop can offer and how a real collaboration can take place, for however brilliant the concept or idea is, if it is not translated with love and care onto the stage, all will be lost. I must admit, it was slightly unnerving to see my linoleum floor covering being dragged along the road to the National School of Drama by a camel, but that was all part of an unforgettable experience and a big learning curve. I returned to London while *Candida* was performed in Delhi and then went on tour and came out again to meet it in Bombay for the end of the tour. It had done well over the months—a few things lost, a few things added, but nothing untoward. A few days later, on the way to the airport, in the long slow queue on the single road, instructed by my British Council colleague, the driver suddenly diverted and we entered a small shantytown. There was the set for *Candida* with a blue tarpaulin roof stretched across. The fireplace, the clergyman's bookcases, the front door with the stained-glass windows, the linoleum floor and a smiling family of four. Here I learned the greatest lesson of all, years before such things were spoken about in the West—nothing needs to be wasted and theatres are not exempt. Later, I received a photograph of the silk-embroidered hangings depicting Victoria Park and the houses in Hackney of North London, hanging in the atrium of the British Council in Delhi.

LET ART BE YOUR AMBASSADOR

It is an honour to introduce readers to this book. Professor Satyabrata Rout draws together all the diverse threads of scenographic philosophy with practical explanations of useful techniques and systems. There are clear diagrams and illustrations designed to enhance the experience of creating art that speaks to so many people and enhances their theatrical experience. We live in an age where our art and culture travel with us beyond many oceans and skies and influence our global colleagues.

The historical backgrounds and explanations of different forms of theatre and their magical effects provide an important reference point for all readers. In fact, this is almost 'several books in one'! And one of the astonishing revelations, which Peter Brook observed in his many Indian travels, is the complicity of the spectators who know what the tricks are and at the same time, enjoy the ritual of being tricked into believing the reality of what they know is fake. The Mobile Theatres of Assam set a good example to Brook's observation. Scenographers are like the greedy magpie birds that pick things up that attract them and store them and recycle them for future use. There are many instances of Indian artists, both literary and visual, bringing their own sensibility and aesthetics to plays by Brecht, Federico Garcia Lorca, Nikolai Gogol and of course, Shakespeare, and making them seem as though they truly belonged in India. It is an important part of the scenographer's work to be well read and to know the international dramatic repertoire, as discussions with directors on a collaborative project are often made up of references and quotations.

In this age, scenographers, armed with design skills and knowledge, are often taking the lead in creating productions, especially in site-specific work, or collaborating with colleagues who practise physical or other visual skills. Barriers and demarcations are fast dissolving, but with this come the challenge and responsibility for each theatre discipline to thoroughly understand the process of the other. For the visual artist, the medium is a drawing, painting and scale model, the use of colour and texture, scale and proportion. Suggestions of how to do this are well explained in this book, but of course each artist has to go on their own journey and find their own personal signature. Practice and fluency are vital. There is a famous saying: 'A drawing a day keeps the devil away!' Finding the right medium to express the quality of the drama is another challenge, as is considering the kind of surface to work on. Indian handmade papers in different thicknesses offer many possibilities to work with inks and acrylics, and create immediate textures that can give a simple drawing a very particular atmosphere. However, one thing that I am sure about is that art speaks louder than words, even to the extent that many people over the centuries have been afraid of the power of art. When presenting a scenographic proposal, nothing is as powerful as good visual images that inspire the team and make people want to do the work.

Let art be your ambassador! As this book shows, art knows no boundaries, barriers or borders and needs no passports. It is a universal currency with different values. An Indian perspective may be the context of this book, but its rich history is a gift to the world that is hungry for all the ideas and inspirations.

Pamela Howard OBE
London, United Kingdom

(Prof. Pamela Howard is one of the few important scenographers who have revitalised the concept of scenography and visual design in the perspective of the world theatre. As an internationally acclaimed theatre maker, Howard has penned the most discussed book on scenography; What is Scenography? *She is Professor Emeritus at the University of the Arts, London and a frequent visitor the famous Carnegie Mellon University at Pittsburgh, USA, Department of Drama. She has been awarded OBE for her service to theatre in 2008 and is the mastermind behind the SCENOFEST; World Scenography Festival in London.)*

AUTHOR'S NOTE

With hardly any documentation available on scenography with an Indian orientation, Indian theatre has been craving for a practical treatise in this regard for quite a long time. Apart from a few interviews or memoirs of productions that pop up in the columns of a newspaper supplement or the pages of a magazine, nothing substantial has yet been brought out. Scenography, as perceived by the Western world, has largely redefined theatre by bridging the void between designers and directors. But it is a sad truth that such an ideology, which had a profound influence upon its immediate world, has not yet been re-modelled and chiselled to suit the Indian scenario. Despite having a considerable number of creative theatre makers and scenographers with international acclaim, Indian theatre lacks a proper documentation of the works of these masters; the reason lies in our artistic temperament. Even after possessing all the resources, we have failed miserably to theorise our practices till date. Among the many things that this book pioneers, the most prominent one is the analytical codification of the nature of scenography that the book offers by theorising the masterpieces of Indian theatre.

During the early 1980s, in the National School of Drama, the very term 'scenography' was missing from the academic scene altogether. Hence the students were left with nothing other than scenic design to perch on. There exists a big gulf between these two terms—while the former deals with the entire space and its visual vocabulary, inclusive of the actors and the audience, the latter emphasises on the spatial arrangement of the play and its technology. However, the similarities between the two terms can never be overlooked. The ideas complement each other and upon reaching a certain juncture, they intermingle to form a single entity. The lack of proper resource material kept us ignorant about the current trends of world scenography. All the study materials available in those days were based on Western concepts with references from Western productions and plays, something almost none of us had a direct access to. The longing for a book that reviews the themes from an Indian perspective thus became an overwhelming urge in me. I had always been dreaming of a book that talks about our theatre, narrates our productions, depicts the visual imagery that emerges out of our tradition and sketches out the forms and colours of Indian cultures and design. Perhaps, it is this impetus that provided momentum for bringing out this volume.

In the past, very few could dare to adopt theatre design as a fulltime profession, Alkazi being in the forefront. In Delhi, Nissar Allana, Bansi Kaul, Robin Das and in the far East, at Manipur, Ratan Thiyam started practising this new theatre discipline. The works of these masters had a profound influence upon me and inspired me in shaping my career in theatre design. I have learnt scenography by observing their works and sometimes involving myself in their productions. Even though I specialised in design and direction from the National School of Drama, one of the premier theatre institutions of the world, its training did not seem to be that much helpful when I stepped into practice. Doing theatre in India is different from that of the West. Indian theatre improvises more, depending on the situations. In India, creativity and execution solely depend on the socio-economical structure, and that makes the difference. It was during my days in Rangmandal, Bhopal, I understood the cultural disparities between the West and India that made it difficult to merge both. The quality of the Indian theatre always depends more on the commitment of the practitioners to work in diversified conditions than on intellectual theories. In India, each and every show would give us new theory, which blooms and fades away in each evening with the production. Each show brings new challenges that always poses a complicated question—how to theorise our practices with so much of diversity?

A contradiction has always been there over the importance of theoretical frameworks and the field works. Even though practice goes beyond the theoretical framework, the importance of theory cannot be ignored while practising theatre. Practice, beyond doubt, develops our skills but we have to learn the fundamental principles to understand the thoughts and concepts. At the same time, we have to go beyond these principles in order to stay with the contemporary times, since the concept in theatre depends on the psychology of people which is very much related to the social changes. But to build up and go ahead, a well-established foundation is also essential.

I do not know exactly when and how I stepped into this mesmerising world of theatrical visuals. But as a student of theatre, I opted for specialisation in design and direction because of my inability of speaking Hindi, which was not my mother tongue. Unfortunately, the National School of Drama orients its students to learn Hindi to be an actor. But can one imagine how difficult would it be to practise a language in which one is not familiar from the beginning! Honestly, I could not afford to invest the time and energy in learning a language at the drama school, nor did I have the intention to go to Mumbai to act in the commercial movies and serials. My disqualification as an actor because of the linguistic barrier compelled me to adopt design and direction as a specialisation. Slowly in due course of time, it grew into my passion and finally became my life.

When I opted for teaching design and direction in various theatre workshops in early 90s, I found it difficult, since most of my students were from remote corners of India with no background of theatre vocabulary. Western plays were alien to these peripheral practitioners and naturally, for them learning through Western methods were difficult and irrelevant. At the same time, to formulate a concept out of the popular Indian productions was a difficult task for me. Especially in design, no reference materials were available related to Indian theatre. So, I started teaching out of my personal working experiences. In the beginning it was arduous to develop a definite tone, but gradually over the period, the teaching methodology advanced into a systematic order.

In the process of teaching design and direction, I developed a passion to pen down various concepts and methods which I have come across in my profession. I started working on the first draft of this book when I joined in the Department of Theatre at University of Hyderabad in the year 2007. But soon I realised, my experiences and working knowledge were not adequate enough to bring out a good reference book that covers all aspects of theatre arts and design. A break was necessary to gain more ideas about the theatre history, architecture, art and design and Indian culture as whole. It was only after I revitalised myself by reading more seminal works, that I mustered the courage to restart this pioneering work.

Penning down such a massive book through a thorough research on scenography, performance design, traditions, cultures and different architectures across the times, visiting many ancient performance spaces to collect reference material and finally developing more than 100 illustrative drawings through CAD and collecting many photographs of different theatre productions from various Indian theatre groups, took me 12 long years. These years taught me to focus on the subject with a good deal of patience. More than writing a book, it is the knowledge and information that I received over these years, that I cherish more.

I hope this book will be an asset and a handy reference to the Indian theatre practitioners and students, and will certainly orient the young minds for scenography as a viable career.

Dr Satyabrata Rout
Hyderabad, India

INTRODUCTION

ACROSS CULTURES AND BOUNDARIES

Scenography, the visual lexis of 'performance', underwent a sea of changes in the beginning of the 20th century. The idea of visual imagery and theatrical ambience evolved according to the demands of time and space—a trend not prevalent in the ancient, medieval, or colonial times. In the early days of theatre in the West, plays were usually performed in open-air venues; indoor setup came into use only later. The gestures and gaits of the performers as well as the text came together to forge an imaginary world in the psyche of the viewers. But the quest for an ideal theatrical ambience persisted since the advent of theatre. The great Roman architects constructed magnificent multistoried playhouses, complete with ornate walls, pillars, arches and staircases, to lend grandeur to the performing arts. Much later, towards the end of the 17th and the beginning of the 18th century, the scenic masters of Italy and France introduced wings, cyclorama, curtains and borders to the stage, effecting significant developments in the art of stage design and scenography. Thus, architectural fantasies were achieved by employing painted sceneries as spectacular backdrops, contributing to the visual aesthetics of presentations.

The Italian designer Ferdinando Galli-Bibiena[1] redefined the art of stage design by introducing multi-point perspective or angled perspective in theatre through painted sceneries. On painted curtains, Bibiena

---

1 Ferdinando Galli-Bibiena (1657–1743) was an Italian architect, painter and stage designer. He introduced perspective in the design of painted sceneries.

Roman Theatre at Orange, Vaucluse, France. 1st century AD. Courtesy: Wikimedia Commons

Left: Painted sceneries showing angle perspective by Ferdinando Galli-Bibiena.
Centre: Painted curtain design for a semi-circular architectural ruins by Ferdinando Galli-Bibiena.

characteristically portrayed buildings, walls, statues and courtyards. These curtains could be rolled up or parted to reveal different settings and situations. But the quest for visual spectacles did not end there. Another famous Italian architect and stage designer, Filippo Juvarra,[2] also had a significant impact on the evolution of architectural fantasies and creating visual intrigue. Juvarra introduced wings to the stage, emphasising on curvilinear designs in his painted sceneries. The technique helped direct the audience's attention to the foreground, where the action takes place. By the end of the 19th century, spectacular displays in stage design had become an integral part of theatrical presentations, attracting large audiences to the theatre in Europe.

Gradually, the two-dimensional painted curtains were replaced by three-dimensional scenic visuals. This new approach in design came

---

2 Filippo Juvarra (1678–1736) was an Italian architect, active in the late-Baroque style. He also incorporated 'angle perspective' in his drawings. He had designed painted sceneries mostly for opera.

RIGHT: Painted Scenery: Courtyard of a palace—design for an opera by Filippo Juvarra (1714).
Courtesy: Scanned from the book *The Developement of the Theatre: A Study of Thearical Art from the Beginnings to the Present Day.*

into practice through the works of Adolphe Appia[3] and Gordon Craig[4], who revolutionised scenography. Their efforts ensured that stage design evolved into an integral expression of theatre aesthetics in the beginning of the 20th century, paving the way for psychological atmosphere to play a significant role in stage design.

But the legacy of Indian theatre, which greatly varies from that of the West, finds its roots in classical traditions. Indian classical theatre is

---

3   Adolphe Appia (1862–1928) is regarded as the father of modern lighting and scenic design. Born in Switzerland, he worked as a music composer and designer in Wagner's operas in Germany. Appia had contributed in defining theatre space in various ways, including eurythmics space in collaboration with the Swiss musician and composer Jaques-Dalcroze.

4   Gordon Craig (1872–1966) was a noted scenographer of English theatre. The son of famous actress Ellen Terry, Craig is known for the introduction of modern concepts of design and theatrical elements to the stage, such as three-dimensional stage props, masks, large puppets, etc. He designed *Hamlet* for the Moscow Art Theatre in 1912 in collaboration with Konstantin Stanislavsky. Craig and Appia are regarded as the architects of modern scenography.

Left top: Study of facade of Santa Cristina by Filippo Juvarra (1715).
Left bottom: Rhythmic space designed by Adolphe Appia (1912).
Right: Gordon Craig's drawings for *Hamlet*. Designed and directed by Craig for Moscow Art Theatre (1912).

based on the performative practices and principles, specified in the *Natya Shastra*. Spaces and scenic visuals in Indian classical theatre were expressed through the gaits and bearings of the actors which also became an integral part of the performance. The change of dramatic environments in classical performance was conveyed through a series of stylised movements known as 'parikramya'[5]. The entry and exit of performers to and from the stage was

---

5   'Parikramya' or 'parikrama' is a ritual associated with classical Indian theatre whereby the performer encircles the stage with the help of 'nritya'—dance—and music in order to change the locale. This was an integral part of the Sanskrit theatre.

A scene from the play *Shakuntala* by Kalidasa (5th century AD.). Hindi Translation: Mohan Rakesh. Design and direction: Satyabrata Rout. Courtesy: Department of Theatre, S.N.School, University of Hyderabad, India.

facilitated by a half-curtain, known popularly as 'rangapatti' or 'yavanika'[6]. By analysing scenography in Sanskrit theatre in the light of the West, it may be suggested that while scenic visuals in Western theatre evolved as an added expression to the presentations, in Indian theatre, it emerged out of the inner rhythm of the performance.

---

6   'Rangapatti' or 'yavanika'—the half-curtain—was a technical device used in the Sanskrit theatre to facilitate the entry and exit of the characters to and from the stage. The actors would take entry behind the half-curtain propped up by two dancers as a part of rituals in the performance.

SCENOGRAPHY IN COLONIAL INDIA

During the colonial period, European theatre found exposure in India as the new urban theatre in cities like Calcutta, Bombay and Madras. This was a new, hybrid form of theatre—an amalgamation of the cultures of East and West—and became the primary source of entertainment for the Indian elite. These theatres used painted sceneries as the backdrop to represent the scenes and the locals. These huge and intricate paintings were brought from England and other parts of the West to be used in the performances in colonial India, since no Indian stage-craft artist was aware of this method yet.

In the mid-19th century, a gifted Indian painter by the name of Raja Ravi Varma[7] left for Europe to study painting. Upon his return, and deeply influenced by the trends in Western realism, he made Indian women the subject of his paintings. His many illustrious works, largely dedicated to the myth and folklore through the characters of Draupadi, Saraswati, Lakshmi, Damayanti, Shakuntala, etc., garnered him wide acclaim both at home and abroad. His fusion of Indian traditions with the school of Western realism encouraged a great number of upcoming Indian scene painters, gradually turning him into the grandmaster of Indian scene paintings.

Towards the latter half of the 19th century, a number of commercial theatre companies were established in the present-day states of Maharashtra, Bengal and Gujarat. Influenced by the works of Ravi Varma and a selection of British painters working in India at the time, Indian scene painters took to creating realistic paintings on canvases for stage sceneries. These theatre companies presented their productions,

---

7 Raja Ravi Varma (1848–1906) belonged to the princely state of Travancore. He is considered one of the pioneers of realism in Indian painting and is known for popularising Indian deities, mythical characters and calendar images. His works hold the testimony of European techniques, fused with Indian sensibility.

Shakuntala (Oil on Canvas). A Painting by Raja Ravi Varma (1870).
Courtsey: Wikimedia Commons

Painted curtain for the play *Yayati and Devyani* (1970). Painted by V.V. Divkar. Courtesy: Dr Nissar Allana.

spectacular visuals, through the use of meticulously painted, hyperrealistic sceneries. Influence of the post-medieval, Elizabethan style of presentation was apparent in these productions, particularly in the costumes, props, ornaments and painted sceneries. In the beginning of the 20th century, a few Marathi stage painters—Anandrao, Baburao Mestry and P.S. Kale among others—developed a technique wherein the angled perspective was introduced to painted curtains. These painters became adept at establishing outdoor locales like streets, landscapes, forests, hills and mountains without compromising on the accuracy of the forms and colours. This style of scenographic design, employing painted sceneries, dominated the dominated the Parsi theatre[8] and company theatres for a few decades. Subsequently, 'cut-scenes', 'gaze scenes', and 'cut-outs' were introduced to enable the actors to interact with the created space. With the help of this innovation, one could go behind the curtains, explore the sceneries from various directions, suddenly appear on and disappear from the stage, etc. Such actions were not possible with painted sceneries. Theatre companies gained considerable popularity due to their spectacular designs and scenic splendours. Soon, similar theatrical companies started cropping up in India as the leading entertainment industry. Many of them built their own theatre houses to host regular performances, while a few preferred to stage their productions across the country, travelling with the entire paraphernalia of stage construction—sceneries, costumes, props and galleries, tents, chairs and benches. This trend of presentation continued for more than a century in India and the companies enjoyed widespread fame, riches and honours. Even today, some popular Indian theatre companies travel from village to village or from one town to another to present their art, following in the footsteps of their predecessors.

Indian theatre experienced a marked transformation during the fourth decade of the 20th century, primarily due to the influence of the Indian national movement. Inspired by the progressive art movement and its ideology—'art should fulfil the needs of the people and help in effecting change in the society'—intellectuals, artists and writers from across the country were drawn to theatre, leading to the formation of the IPTA[9]

---

[8] Parsi theatre is an Indian theatre genre that was influenced by the European theatre, especially Shakespearean dramas. It continued to serve as the most popular entertaining medium in colonial times till the Independence, for more than hundred years.

[9] The Indian People's Theatre Association (IPTA) is recognised as the cultural wing of the Communist Party of India (CPI). The 20th-century freedom movement compelled many sensitive Indian writers, artists and academicians to realise that art expressions can become relevant only through its association with the people's struggle movement and cultural reformation, resulting in the formation of the IPTA in 1943.

A scene from *The Marchant of Venice* by Shakespearean touring company (1953). Acted and Directed by: Geoffrey Kendal.
Courtesy: https://in.pinterest.com/pin/411094272227329233/.

in 1943. More than a theatre association, IPTA manifested a progressive cultural movement in the country. Prithviraj Kapoor, Ritwik Ghatak, Khwaja Ahmad Abbas, Salil Chowdhury, Kaifi Azmi, Balraj Sahani, A.K. Hangal, Sombhu Mitra, Utpal Dutt, Bijan Bhattacharya, Habib Tanvir and a number of artists, painters, poets, writers and thinkers joined hand in hand in IPTA to propagate socio-political awareness among the people of India. Gradually, numerous branches of the IPTA were established throughout the country. Social activists kept moving from one place to another, singing patriotic songs, organising poster exhibitions and performing street plays to motivate the people against British colonialism, effectively transforming theatre into a fundamental tool for political awareness rather than a leisurely pastime.

With a change in intent and ideology, new developments were seen in performance styles and theatre design. Concept and story attained renewed significance for the need to produce elaborate and spectacular presentations. Since IPTA usually conducted their plays and other art-related activities in improvised spaces like marketplaces, street corners, etc., additional scenic elements were deemed unnecessary. These street performances could rely solely on the underlying theme and the improvisation of space, characters, properties and costumes. Gradually, new ideas and progressive beliefs were adopted in the spheres of playwriting and stage design, setting the tone for modern Indian theatre in the post-colonial period.

BEGINNING OF THE EXPERIMENT

During colonial times, a number of theatre houses were founded in the metropolitan cities of India. The comfort and convenience provided by these newly built proscenium theatres led to the development of many unprecedented forms and techniques in theatre presentations. The Bengali actor-director Sisir Bhaduri[10] introduced interpretative visuals with the support of designers like Mani Gangopadhyay, Charu Roy and Anath Maitra. His production of Rabindranath Tagore's *Bisarjan* (1926) is believed to be one of the earliest plays to incorporate interpretative design elements. In the hands of Bhaduri, the play *Visarjan* got artistic acclamation and was appreciated for its design.

In the 1930s, the revolving stage was introduced at the Rangmahal Theatre in Calcutta by Satu Sen[11], who also introduced box sets to theatre.

---

10 Sisir Kumar Bhaduri (1889–1959) was one of the stalwarts of Bengali theatre. A teacher of English literature, Bhaduri joined Bangla theatre in 1923. He had acted in many plays with the lead roles such as, Chanakya in the play *Chandragupta*, (1911) written by D.L. Roy and *Alamgir* (1923) written by Kishori Prasad Vidyavinod, etc. He is considered as the 'Bal Gandharva' of Bengal theatre. He was awarded the Padma Bhushan by the Government of India in 1959.

11 Satu Sen (1902–1978) was an early Indian scenic designer. He went to Europe and USA

A number of older spaces in the city of Calcutta were soon converted to turntable. In 1943, the great famine broke out in the erstwhile province of Bengal (present-day Bangladesh and the Indian states of West Bengal, Odisha and Bihar). Thousands of people perished from disease and starvation owing to the negligence of the British imperial government. The Bengal IPTA reacted strongly to the tragedy through the presentation of Bijon Bhattacharya's[12] play *Nabanna* (*New Harvest*) in 1943. The play was directed by Sombhu Mitra[13], who invited Khaled Choudhury[14] to design the set and create the ambience for the presentation. The visual imagery of *Nabanna*, composed using symbolic set elements and painted curtains for backdrops, was able to convincingly convey the vicious and appalling circumstances of the famine. Subsequently, the production of

---

to study theatre technique and worked under Richard Boleslavski, a disciple of Constantin Stanislavsky. After his return to India, he engaged himself in reforming Bengal theatre and designed lights and sets for many plays. He became the founder-director of the Asian Theatre Institute (ATI), established in Delhi in 1957–58, now known as the National School of Drama.

12   Bijon Bhattacharya (1906–1978) was a prominent Indian theatre and film personality from Bengal. He was the pioneer of the 'navanatya andolan' (progressive theatre movement) and wrote plays depicting the plight, agony, pain and sufferings of the common man. He was a founder-member of Bengal IPTA and penned the famous play *Nabanna*. Sri Bhattacharya had also worked for the famous *Ananda Bazar Patrika*, published in colonial Bengal. He was the husband of the legendary Bengali writer Mahasweta Devi.

13   Sombhu Mitra (1915–1997) is considered as the pioneer of Bengali theatre. He literally redefined theatre of Bengal after Rabindranath Tagore and acted-directed most of his plays. He was a founder-member of Bengal IPTA and established Bohurupee, a theatre group, in Calcutta. He was conferred with many prestigious awards including the Padma Bhushan, Sangeet Natak Akademi award, Ramon Magsaysay award, etc. Shambhu Mitra became the synonym of Bengal theatre.

14   Khaled Choudhury (1919–2014) was one of the early scenographers of modern Indian theatre. Primarily a book illustrator and painter, Choudhury started his theatre career with IPTA. He had received the Sangeet Natak Akademi award and was conferred with the Padma Bhushan in 2012.

Set design for the play *Raktakarabi* (1954). Direction: Sombhu Mitra. Set design: Khaled Chaudhury. Courtesy: Shamik Bandopadhyay.

Raktakarabi (*Red Oleanders*) (1954)[15], also directed by Sombhu Mitra, established Khaled Choudhury as an important scenographer of modern Indian theatre. Describing design as total visual integration, Khaled Choudhury states:

> Stage design can never be an art in itself... The elements of stage design are static while everything else in the play is dynamic. Therefore the endeavour should be to give the stage props a quality that would create the impression of dynamism related to the movements of the actors. The director, the stage designer and lighting designer have to work closely together to make the stage design an organic part of the performance[i].

As a leading scenographer, Choudhury created history with his outstanding interpretative designs in various Calcutta-based productions,

---

15 *Raktakarabi* is a Bengali play written by Rabindranath Tagore.

such as Sombhu Mitra's *Raktakarabi* (1954) and *Putul Khela* (1958), Shyamanand Jalan's[16] *Shuturmurg* (1967) and *Pagla Ghoda* (1971) and Tripti Mitra's[17] *Gudiya Ghar* (1981). His work in these productions garnered him recognition as the foremost scenographer of modern Indian theatre. Before the advent of Khaled Choudhury, the theatre scene in Bengal was dominated by playwrights and actors; but with the introduction of design as a vital element of presentations, Bengali theatre got a breath of fresh air.

Utpal Dutt's[18] two major productions—*Angar* (1959) and *Kallol* (1965)—set the trend of naturalistic theatre movement in India, informed and enkindled by 19th-century European drama. In both productions, the visuals and the exploration of space were realised with such precision that the results dimmed even the original settings and locations. In *Angar*, Tapas Sen[19] created the palpable impression of a deluge with his creative stage lighting. It is said that the illusion of rising water in the coal mines was so naturalistic that a few audience members at the Minerva Theatre, Calcutta, fled in panic. The production was reminiscent of the famous

---

16 Shyamanand Jalan (1934–2010) was an Indian theatre director. He founded Padatik Theatre Group in 1972 and directed and produced plays in Hindi. In 1972 he received Sangeet Natak Akademi Award.

17 Tripti Mitra (1925–1989) was a famous Bengali actress and play director. She was the wife of Sombhu Mitra. Ms Mitra had been conferred with the Sangeet Natak Akademi award (1962) and Padma Shri (1971) by the Government of India.

18 Utpal Dutt (1929–1993) was a legendary theatre personality from Bengal and a member of IPTA. He started his career as an actor with the Shakespearean Theatre Company, founded by Geoffrey Kendal, and formed the Little Theatre Group in 1949. Dutta is known for his political affiliation for the Communist Party of India and presented many politically charged and socially relevant plays. He was awarded with the Sangeet Natak Akademi fellowship.

19 Tapas Sen (1924–2006) is arguably the best known lighting designer of India. He was the founder member of IPTA.

naturalistic simulation of the rain effect in David Belasco's[20] production of *The Tiger Rose* (1917).

The art of scenography gained new meaning and momentum in India after Independence, gradually becoming an integral part of theatre presentations, the legacy of the painted curtains of Parsi theatre not remaining so relevant anymore. Two-dimensional painted sceneries paved the way for three-dimensional set designs—ideal for representing life in its actuality. With the advent of European realism, scenography once again altered its form. Box sets, with a three-walled, covered setting, complete with doors, windows, arches, staircases and pillars, were introduced to theatre performances. In the second half of the 20th century, a number of amateur theatre groups emerged in various cities and towns, presenting an experimental form of theatre wherein design played a significant role.

THE TRENDSETTER

After Independence, as a policy of the Government of India and in recognition of the vison of Smt. Kamaladevi Chattopadhyay[21], the Sangeet Natak Akademi was established with a view to formalise education and to impart training in the area of performing arts. The academy aimed to preserve and promote India's heritage and traditions in the performing arts; to bring all kinds of folk, traditional, experimental and modern art forms under a single canopy. The Asian Theatre Institute (ATI), now

---

20 David Belasco (1853–1931) was one of the naturalistic theatre directors of 19th-century European and American theatre. He was born in California, shifting first to London and ultimately to New York City, where he established his own theatre.

21 Kamaladevi Chattopadhyay (1903–1988) was a freedom fighter, social reformer and artist of many folds. She was the driving force behind the upliftment of Indian culture and tradition after Independence. Institutions like the National School of Drama, Sangeet Natak Akademi, Central Cottage Industries Emporium and Craft Council of India are her brainchildren. She married to Harindranath Chattopadhyay, the noted poet-actor and the brother of Smt. Sarojini Naidu. She was honoured with Padma Vibhushan by the Government of India in 1987.

Set design for the play *Ashad Ka Ek Din*. Design and direction: E. Alkazi. Courtesy: National School of Drama, New Delhi.

known as the National School of Drama (NSD), was subsequently established in Delhi for conceptual theatre training and education under the aegis of UNESCO and the Bharatiya Natya Sangh in the beginning of 1958 and was subsumed by the Sangeet Natak Akademi in 1959.

Over the following years, imparting professional training on theatre, the National School of Drama emerged as a premier theatre training institution of modern India. The blueprint of the syllabus for a three-year practice-based programme was initially prepared by Ebrahim Alkazi[22], the architect of modern Indian theatre. Alkazi succeeded in establishing a balance between

---

22 Ebrahim Alkazi (1925–2020) is the most influential theatre director of 20th-century India. He studied theatre at Royal Academy of Dramatic Arts (RADA), London, in the early 1950s and became the director of the National School of Drama (1962–1977). Mr Alkazi had virtually redefined modern Indian theatre in the post-Independence period. He has been conferred with the Padma Vibhushan by the Government of India, and the Sangeet Natak Akademi award along with many other national and international honours.

Western and Eastern sensibilities in theatre practices, with a special emphasis on theatre technology and craft. Literary works of the proponents of Indian playwriting—Mohan Rakesh, Dharamvir Bharati, Surendra Verma, Vijay Tendulkar, Girish Karnad and others—and many Western authors were adapted for the stage by the students of NSD, replete with meticulously designed sets and properties. Scenic design and stage lighting was thusly included into the syllabus as courses of study and became an integral part of NSD productions. Plays such as, *Ashadh Ka Ek Din* (1958), *Aadhe Adhure*, (1969), *Mricchakatika* (5 AD), *The Lower Depths* (1901–02), *Danton's Death* (1902), *King Lear* (1606), *Antigone* (441 BCE), etc. prompted new trends in visual design and stagecraft during the 1960s–70s. While indicating Alkazi as the trendsetter of modern Indian theatre, Professor Kumara Varma states:

> With the establishment of the National School of Drama in 1959, the concept of scenic design in India underwent a sea of change. Under the directorship of Ebrahim Alkazi who, besides being a director, was also an able designer, the school established new aesthetic principles for the Indian theatre and its students carried these ideas to every corner of the country. Alkazi's interests were wide, ranging from classical Greek to Sanskrit plays, from Shakespeare to contemporary western and new Indian writing. As a result, his designs were not confined simply to the proscenium but extended into other spaces as well: ancient monuments, open courtyards, terraces. Ingeniously interpreting each space to the mood and atmosphere of the play, Alkazi managed to design widely varying sets even for the same play (as in his three different productions of *Tughlaq*).[ii]

MAKING OF THE 'VISUAL THEATRE'

While conventional theatre was engaged in interpreting 'text' and 'action', the attention of scholars, critics and spectators was drawn to a genre of

Manohar Sing in the role of Tughlaq in the play *Tughlaq* (1973). Design and direction: E. Alkazi. Courtesy: National School of Drama, New Delhi.

theatre, which India had never experienced before. This new form of theatre—the visual theatre—was introduced by E. Alkazi in the National School of Drama in the 1960s, which was manifested with the production of Dharamvir Bharati's phenomenal play *Andha Yug* (1953).

The visual movement of space served as the vocabulary of this new theatre. Unlike text-centric plays, this genre appropriated visual design as its primary language of expression. The actors' physical gestures and bodily movements, as well as the theatrical expression of scenic design, lights, props, masks and stylised makeup, combined to manifest 'visual' theatre. This unified expression of multiple visual elements as an integral aspect of theatre that accords the presentation with varied aesthetic qualities was hitherto an unknown phenomenon in India till the productions of *Andha Yug* in the year 1964 and *Tughlaq* in 1974. These plays were first presented in the 'found spaces' of Feroz Shah Kotla ground and then reproduced at the ruins of Purana Qila in Delhi. In India, the importance of space in a performance was realised for the first time with these pioneering productions. A new outlook on costumes, props, masks, makeup and other visual elements, along with the treatment of space, which could communicate the director's interpretation separate from literary sources, was also realised. A sensibility for visual culture and poetic imageries led to this neo-expression and laid the foundation of 'visual theatre' in India. Along with the characters of a play, design also functioned parallelly as a character of the production, making the designer a master visionary of this new lexicon. Elements borrowed from the fine arts—paintings and sculptures, as well as various other interdisciplinary visual expressions—were introduced for the creation of this vocabulary. Theatre became the scenographer's studio, where colours, lines and forms are experimented through visual compositions. This experimentation cleared the way for other art aesthetics, such as interacting with sound, music and the bodily expressions of the performers. However, the visual aesthetics of Alkazi's productions, though meticulously and magnificently designed to articulate innovative interpretations, often lacked theatrical flexibility. Theatre, which springs from social gestures and community life, was often overshadowed by the prescriptivism of Alkazi's productions. Ironically, his disciples, in the later years, tried to break away from the set conventions in this area, resulting in the widespread espousal of visual theatre in the mid 1970s with new interpretations and meanings.

Dr Nissar Allana[23], in continuation of Alkazi's visual sensibility, introduced contemporary scenography to Indian theatre through the productions *Aadhe Adhure* in 1976 and *Cherry Ka Bagicha (The Cherry Orchard)*, in 1981. A brilliant and gifted scenographer, Dr Allana, who relinquished his practice in medicine for the theatre, holds an important

---

23   Nissar Allana is the noted Indian scenographer who continued with the legacy of E. Alkazi through his own devised method and represented India as a scenographer in many international design festivals.

position in the Indian contemporary theatre scenario. Bansi Kaul[24] also emerged as one of the pioneers of scenography in the 1970s. His explorations of bold, striking lines along with rhythmic forms and bright colours through the use of costumes, elaborate makeup and scenic visuals formed the prime language of his productions—*Sharvilak* (1989), *Tukke pe Tukka* (1990), *Gadhon ka Mela* (1993), et al. Ratan Thiyam[25], another eminent director and scenographer of contemporary Indian theatre, drew on indigenous Manipuri traditions to explore the aesthetics of art via the interplay of colours, music and choreography. Robin Das[26] found possibilities in the 'irony in spaces' for his theatre design. His constant experimentation with the actors' physical expressions, coupled with intricately contrasting designed spaces for both the actors and the audience, created a new vocabulary in Indian visual theatre. Das's search for the sublime through substantial, sketchy compositions, much akin to a painter, established him as an artist of a different stroke.

Following the pioneering work of these visionaries, a new generation of Indian scenographers emerged in the contemporary theatre practices who are currently engaged in exploring 'visual theatre' and striving for new expressions. I, being a scenographer and director of contemporary practices, am exploring the potential of alternative theatre spaces. By blending the unique features of Chhau dance and the visual cultures of my native state Odisha, I aspire to create an alternative theatre expression, derived out of the interplay of actors, masks, objects, design and space in the domain of modern scenography and direction. Bapi

---

24 Bansi Kaul is a noted Indian theatre director and Scenographer.

25 Ratan Thiyam is the most influential Indian theatre director of the 21st century whose influence is felt globally.

26 Robin Das is one of a few gifted theatre designers and directors of India who has influenced a generation of young practitioners of this country. He was a professor of design at the National School of Drama.

Bose, a Delhi-based theatre director and scenographer, is also working on developing this vocabulary through the integration of space and design, but with a different approach which is meticulous, neat and functional. It is amazing to perceive the scenography, concealed underneath various meanings and interpretations, in his productions. Suresh Anagalli and C. Basavalingaiah of Karnataka are also pursuing this genre of theatre in an attempt to establish substitute expression in line with South Indian conventions. Sanchayan Ghosh from Santiniketan, a young and aspiring painter-turned-designer, has also undertaken a few experiments in the area of scenography by intermixing various art potentials and installations with theatre. Abhilash Pillai, a professor of theatre direction at the National School of Drama, and Deepan Sivaraman from the School of Culture and Creative Expressions, Ambedkar University, Delhi, are trying through a different approach to bring Western sensibility to Indian contemporary theatre design in the 21st century. In the productions of Sivaraman, one can interact with reflections of abstract ideology; while Pillai has been engaged in various collaborative projects, exploring the possibilities in paintings, jugglery, circus, traditional art forms and all kinds of allied arts, including digital media within the perimeter of performance design.

Nissar Allana's designs in *Aadhe Adhure*, *Cherry ka Bageecha* and *Nati Binodini*; Bansi Kaul's visual expressions in *Sharvilak*, *Tukke pe Tukka* and *Kahan Kabir*; Robin Das's scenography for *Barnam vana*, *Mricchakatika*, *Shila Sringar* and *Three Sisters*; Prasanna's productions *Laal Ghaas Par Neele Ghode* and *Fujiyama*; Bapi Bose's designs in *Dilli Chalo*, *Julius Caesar* and *Ashad Ka Ek Din*; Abhilash Pillai's experimental productions *Anth-Anant*, *Prometheus Bound*, *Midnight's Children* and *Clowns and Clouds*—a theatre-circus Project; Deepan Sivaraman's *Spinal Cord*, *Peer Gynt*, *Ubu Roi* and *The Legend of Khasak*; and my own visual expressions in *Rashomon*, *More Naina Rang Chade*, *Animal Farm*, *Evam Indrajit*, *Tumhara Vincent*,

August ka Khwab and *Shakuntala*, have undoubtedly opened new vistas in the field of Indian scenography and interdisciplinary art aesthetics.

THE POSTMODERN APPROACH

Indian theatre underwent radical changes in the first decade of the 21st century. Adopting a postmodernist approach, Indian theatre received worldwide recognition, in part due to the advent of globalisation. Design and direction merged to become a single entity. New theatre forms like, devised plays and site-specific performances emerged as the scenographer's space. The hegemony of the written word was disparaged, instead focussing on visual imagery to create this new theatre genre. Alternative visual elements, apart from the actors' physical expressions, became instrumental in this creative expression. Concept lighting, abstract expressionist approaches to scenic visuals, application of interdisciplinary stylisations in sets, costumes, masks, props and makeup, and many other creative elements were devised into a process that made theatre a complex expression.

Still from the play *Rashomon* (2005). Scenography and direction: Satyabrata Rout. Courtesy: Y.S. Gill, School of Communication, Faridabad. This is a prime example of environmental performance design.

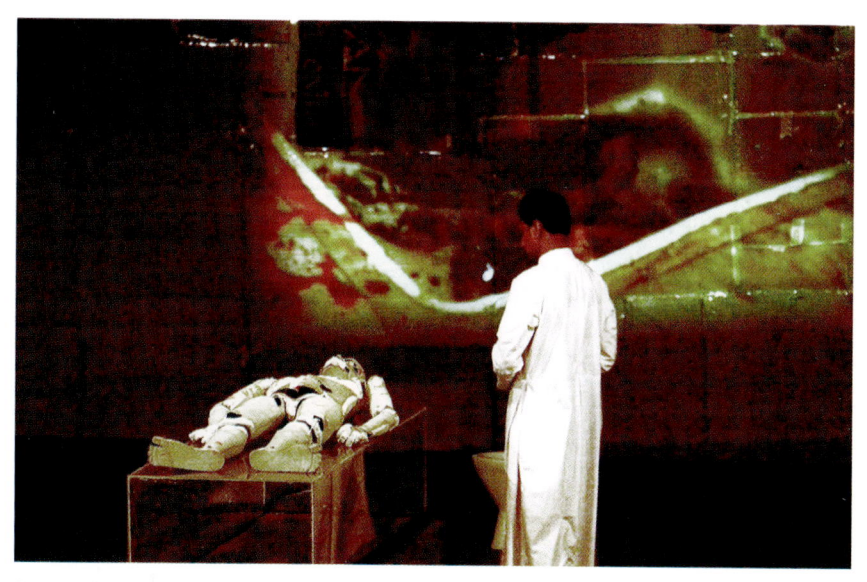

Still from the play *Spinal Cord* (2009). Scenography and direction: Deepan Sivaraman. Courtesy: Oxygen Theatre, Kerala.

The effects of modernism are constantly and rapidly changing the field of scenography in contemporary Indian theatre. Complex mechanisation, fragmented human lives and advanced digital technologies come together as the primary source of avant-garde theatre practices. The traditional conventions of scenography were brushed aside for this new approach that has broken all perceived boundaries between varied art forms. This new brand of theatre is gradually drawing attention of the world, and the Indian style of scenography is now being followed and appreciated across the globe.

References
i   http://www.indianetzone.com/29/khaled_choudhury_indian_theatre_personality.htm.
ii   Varma, G. Kumar. 1998. 'Design'. *The World Encyclopaedia of Contemporary Theatre*: Vol-5: Asia/Pacific, London: Routledge. p. 207.

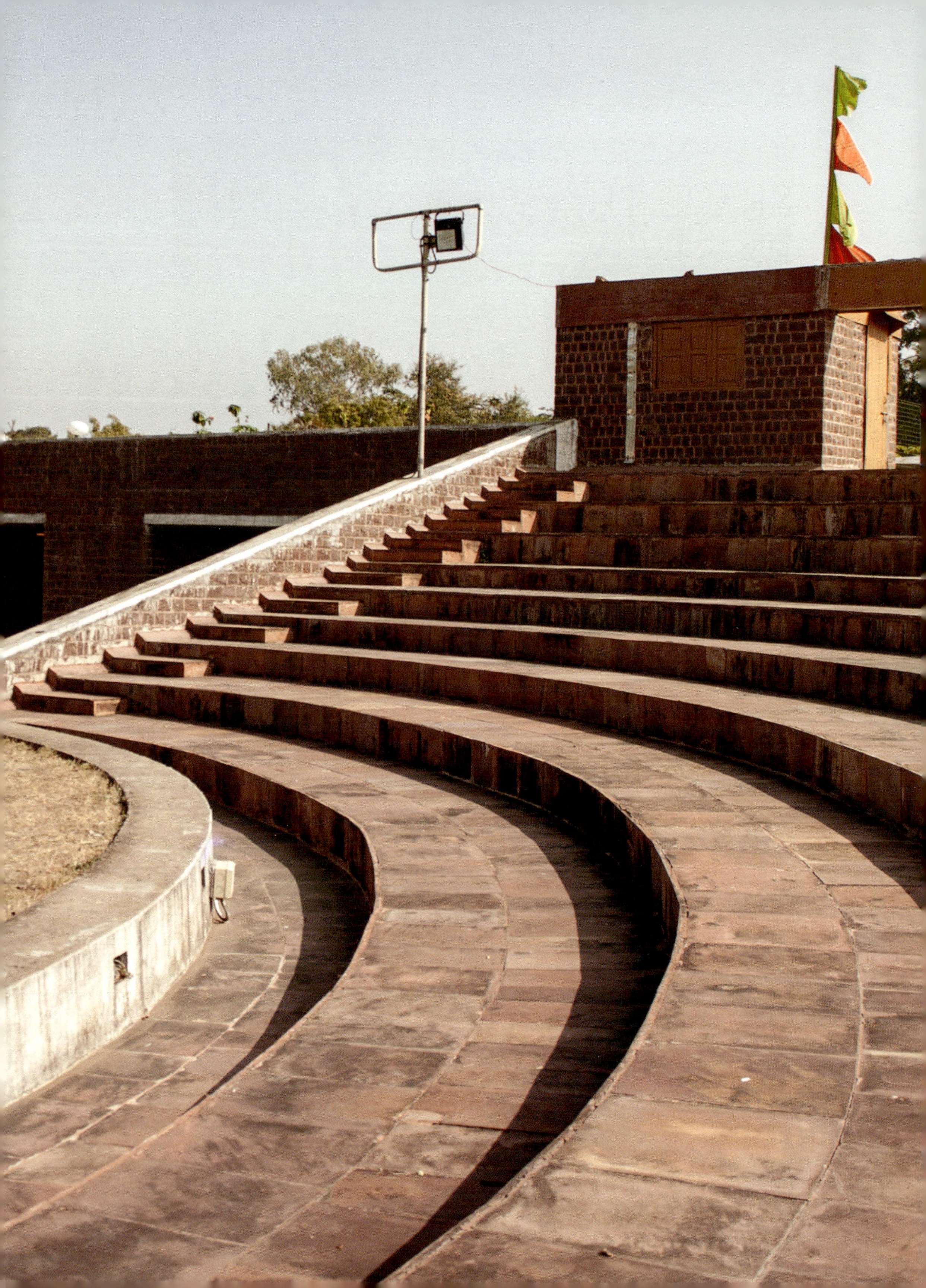

SPACE THAT EXISTS IN TIME

THEATRE: A NEVER-DYING ART FORM

Theatre has undergone radical changes since its genesis. With the passage of time, its form has continually been modified, and at times, even restructured. It has witnessed its fair share of highs and lows. While historically theatre has been used as a medium to promote communal harmony and propagate social awareness, it also provides a platform for the refinement of culture and the society at large. The past serves as a repository of the events that contributed to the reformation of theatre spaces and performances in the course of its long existence. With changing times, theatre has faced almost the same problems in both the East and the West. In the process of adapting to the changes in civil society, it had to accept modifications to its form and flavour, and thus it remains relevant even today in spite of remaining dormant for years.

The brilliance of theatre is in bringing together and uniting people, which has kept it in good stead for years together. Since this art form evolves through human gestures and social expressions, it has come to be the most potent channel for communicating to the masses. It articulates the current time and space, for theatre lives in the 'present'. Where all other art forms are displayed after completion, theatre is created simultaneously with its performance; it is immediate. For instance, a painter may display his work only after applying the final stroke to his creation, a writer publishes his manuscript when he is done with writing, but a performer showcases his art while he is engaged in its making. Thus, the time of creation is concurrent to the time of presentation in the context of performing arts, making it the ideal medium for the exchange of human experiences.

Theatre is essentially an activity involving two groups of people—the performers and the audience. These two groups, or even two individuals, come together in a common space, be it formal or informal, and theatre begins on the spot. A story unfolds in front of the spectators, with both groups sharing their experiences during the process of unfolding. The act is at once simple and instantaneous, and therein lies the beauty of theatre. From commonplace community activities to the most intricate performances of the world, from street presentations to sophisticated productions, each subscribes to a common phenomenon—the sharing of human experiences. Elaborate spaces and technological fripperies are inconsequential to this exchange. Even a well-plotted story with provocative dialogues proves trivial. Theatre can thrive without these aspects, but not without the presence of the spectators.

Jerzy Grotowski, a noted theatre practitioner of the 20th century, rightly argues: 'By gradually eliminating whatever proved superfluous, we found that theatre can exist without make-up, without autonomic costume and scenography, without a separate performance area (stage), without lighting and sound effects, etc. It cannot exist without the actor–spectator relationships of perceptual, direct, "live" communion.'[i] Analysing this revolutionary contention of Grotowski, we realise the importance of three essential elements in the making of theatre—actor, spectator and performance space (formal or informal). With these three fundamental ingredients, theatre has been able to serve societies across civilisations and times. This is and always has been the aim of theatre,

Meghdoot Open Air Theatre, Rabindra Bhawan Complex, Firoz Saha Marg, Delhi. (Est. 1967). The complex was designed by Ebrahim Alkazi, the then director of the National School of Drama, New Delhi, India. Courtesy: Author's personal collection.

and it will continue as a contemporary and relevant art form as long as it remains true to its purpose.

THE PERFORMANCE SPACE

A performance space is a distinctive space, physically and perceptually different from our understanding of the concept. Within this space, many direct and indirect transformations are affected. As Prof. Gay McAuley points out:

> What is presented in performance is always both real and not real, and there is constantly an interplay between the two potentialities, neither of which is ever completely realized. The tension between the two is always present, and, indeed, it can be argued that it is precisely the dual presence of the real and not real, that is a constitutive of theatre.[ii]

A story, a character, a concept, or even a physical being, during a presentation is allowed to pass through multiple spatial and temporal transformations without compromising its distinctive presence. Interactions between the performers and the audience are facilitated by the space itself. Such a space is both flexible and adaptive, allowing for a constant interplay between 'seeming' and 'being': the conflict between the fictive reality of character, plot and ambience, and the physical reality of the performers, the stage and objects. Art historian Joseph Roach[1] also emphasises this concept, opining that a 'Theatrical performance is the simultaneous experience of mutually exclusive possibilities: truth and illusion, presence and absence, face and mask.'[iii] This coexistence of contraries is only possible in a performance space. Enthusiasts, or those who have witnessed and experienced a theatrical presentation, must have perceived something unique and mesmerising happening in front of them, confined to the theatre space but distinct from any banal daily activity. The spectators and performers are well aware of the physical space they share during a performance. But within this physical time and space, both also experience a dramatic space—a fictional world of imagination. Facilitated by the performer(s), spectator(s) are able to visualise a different person in a separate time and space. This, in essence, is a simultaneous overlay of two different realities,

---

1   Joseph Roach is a theatre historian, stage director and performance studies scholar. He has chaired the Performing Arts Department at Washington University in St. Louis, the interdisciplinary PhD in theatre and drama at North-Western University and the Department of Performance Studies in the Tisch School of the Arts at the New York University.

possible only in a performance space. Ronald A. Willis of the University of Kansas observes:

> Spectators must thus deal with a dual-leveled encounter which trumpets the fact that in the theatre two modes of experience, two kinds of event, can and do exist in the same space at the same time. This fact, although seemingly counterintuitive, nurtures the essence of theatrical magic. Much that we regard as performance magic springs from a complex experience of immediate presence. Audiences and performers are in each other's presence as both real and imagined beings.[iv]

DEFINED SPACE

When appreciating a sculpture or any architectural monument, one may evaluate its form and structure from various angles by moving around the structure. But this may not hold true for a live performance; the visual range of a spectator is less than 180°. An audience may not move with the performers to appreciate the play since one's position in a theatre is almost fixed, though there are certain exceptions. At any given moment, one can see only a portion of the performance space and the activities in that space—the entirety of the visual composition evades a seated spectator. This configuration of 'seeing' dictates the visual compositions in a play. The art of theatre, in this respect, differs from that of a film, television and similar art form.

In general, a theatrical performance cannot shift the action into real space. All activities take place in a delineated space that is restricted and defined, limiting the performance area. Sometimes only one of its sides is open to the audience; in other kinds, the audience may encircle the performance space. Occasionally, in environmental theatres or site-specific performances, where the spectators move with the scenes, the action takes place in separate, preordained locales; spectators and

A scene from the play *Reth: Songs of the Sand*. (2016). An Indian adaptation of *The Merchant of Venice*. Playwright: William Shakespeare. Hindi adaptation: Kuldeep Kunal. Scenography and direction: Satyabrata Rout. Courtesy: Asvin Gidwani and AGP World, Mumbai.

performers share a common space. But, irrespective of the style of performance, this space is always defined, and the world of imagination has to be realised within its framework. This is the limitation of theatre, but in this limitation also lies its inherent strength. Such is the irony of this art form—since everything has to be visualised within a particular space, regardless of size and shape, theatrical performances become symbolic, imaginative and creative. Each performance creates its own grammar and vocabulary, and is expressed through the medium of metaphor. It resembles life, but not real life per se. Life is subject to interpretation in this art form.

Metaphor, the thrust of creation—or how 'life' is reimagined in a defined space—becomes essential in a theatre presentation in addition to its functionality. The purpose of this metaphorical space is best served when it is meaningfully played out by actors during a performance, which is further enlivened by dramatic developments. As the show progresses, the limited space breaks its barriers and penetrates into the psyche of the audience, allowing one to visualise unseen ideas and experience new events along with the dramatic action: a gamut of emotions thus flows through the audience gallery.

MAGICAL SPACE

A theatregoer may have experienced the magical transformation of space during a performance. When the third bell rings and the auditorium lights are dimmed, the world around us becomes obscure. With the rising curtain and growing intensity of onstage lights, another world begins to take shape in front of us. Gradually, we are drawn into this strange and unreal world, and begin to experience its quirks and idiosyncrasies. It permeates our imagination, such that we lose ourselves and breathe in tune with the dramatic events unfolding before us. These events then assume the form of real life: performers transform into characters, a plain wooden platform turns into a magnificent palace, an ordinary chair assumes a royal throne, a painted cut-out of a tree expands its foliage to become a dense forest.

To better understand the idea of magical space, let us discuss a few examples of such performances. In 2011, I directed *Matte*

A scene from the play *Matte Eklavya* (2013). Design and direction: Satyabrata Rout. Courtesy: K.D. Ramayah, Adima Ranga Tanda, Kolar, Karnataka.

Eklavya[2]. The acting area was segregated into two distinct parts—an outer and an inner space; it was the demand of the performance design. Generic actions were presented at the downstage while a psychological space—the inner space, demarcated by a black net curtain—was created at the upstage. The black net seemingly merged with the background, making the entire space appear as a single unit. On occasions, the audience could perceive an inner space magically developing in the empty performance area, exploring simultaneously a separate time and space. In this inner, psychological space, one could see Eklavya, a young tribal archer from the *Mahabharata*, practising archery in a dense forest—the forest, of course, existing only in the imagination of the audience. In another sequence, Maharishi Vyasa and Lord Ganesha are seen engaged in writing the great epic when Eklavya suddenly appears in the dreams of Ganesha, realised through the

---

2   *Matte Eklavya* is the Kannada version of Kuldeep Kunal's Hindi play *Eklavya Uvaach*. The play was designed and directed by Satyabrata Rout for Aadima Ranga Tanda, Kolar, Karnataka, in 2011. The play travelled to Colombia, South America, and participated in the international festivals at Bogota, Villa de Leyva and Pasto. The play was also invited in many schools at Bogota and was well received by the students. Back in India it was performed at the Bharat Rang Mahotsav theatre festival(2013), organised by the National School of Drama and also participated in the Mahindra Excellence in Theatre Awards (META) festival(2013) in Delhi where the play received five prestigious awards including the Best Director and the Best Actor awards.

psychological space upstage. In a subsequent scene, Vyasa asks Ganesha to reveal Eklavya's mental state after he has been rejected by Guru Drona as his disciple. To realise the drama and emotions, Ganesha invites Vyasa to walk into his dream and watch the event in person. With that, the scene materialises upstage, behind the net curtain, where Eklavya appeared practising archery in front of an effigy of Guru Drona. Both spaces, the outer and the inner, are juxtaposed in the performance area, where each space actually represents a different time and space, far removed from one another.

The segregation of space unlocks a fantastical world in the imaginations of the spectators. A single prop, an element of the set, a particular dialogue, or even a moment of thought-provoking silence may facilitate the viewers' entry into the magical space, enriched by their personal experiences. In the aforementioned play, the effigy of Drona guides the audience to visualise the rest of the scenic environment out of their experiences, as related in the great epic. Theatre transforms a real, physical space into a dramatic space. Through this process of transformation, it allows the spectator to relive the various layers of their own personal journey, such that they may relate to certain aspects of the characters within themselves. This is theatrics—the magic of theatre. Once the show is concluded, the imagined world vanishes with it. As light gradually floods the gallery, the audience is found to be spellbound, unable to break free as they move out of the performance area.

TIME AND SPACE

The originality and uniqueness of theatre lies in its evolution as it has further matured as a hybrid art form, assimilating elements from a variety of other disciplines. While theatre adopted the three-dimensional art forms in formulating the gestures, postures and the movements of characters by way of choreography and compositions, it has also embraced the picturesque beauty of painting in its visual design. The existence of theatre is based in the framework of time and space. The timeline in a theatre presentation remains firmly in the 'present', making it a live art form. It articulates in contemporary idioms such that every presentation appears fresh and new—yesterday's performance may vary from today's in terms of temperament, mood or the quality of the audience. Somewhat like the variance between the contemporary and the world of past events, situations, lifestyles and consciousness.

Scenography, though derived from spatial art forms, affords a unique spatio-temporal experience in the context of theatre. One is able to feel the harmony and rhythm of a performance as one experiences music, perceives the colours, lines and compositions of a painting or a sculpture, or appreciates the dimensions of space in an architectural edifice. Visual compositions such as costumes, lights, sets and props are experienced in a unique amalgamation of space and time. Features of other art forms are absorbed into the performance to create a composite expression. This makes 'theatre' unique, wherein the actors, scenic elements, choreography, music, lighting effects, etc. are seen and heard in tune with the performance.

INVISIBLE SPACE

As mentioned earlier, a theatre performance seldom recreates reality. Rather, it creates an imagined semblance of life onstage. Simultaneously, it appropriates the medium of metaphor for its expression. A spectator receives a play through the prism of his life's experiences. Any play would fall flat if weighed down by an attempt to show life's innumerable intricacies in the plot. Even extensive detailing of life's vast expanse is an outlandish notion. Alternatively, conveying specific nuances via codified expressions and symbolic gestures would succeed in making 'invisible space' a reality, visible only to the mind's eye. A successful production always aspires for an active participation from the audience instead of only a passive engagement. It merely alludes, coaxing the spectator to unlock a world of imagination. As a universal truth, the physicality of a performance space has certain limitations that may not be altered. Bringing the entire world inside a limited space for the presentation or recreation of life is also impossible. But Peter Brook's million-dollar question, 'How many trees make a forest?'[v], serves as eternal encouragement for scenographers and directors of the world. Can a forest be created in a performance space in its physical form? Or is it essential to recreate a forest with trees, bushes and creepers to present a scene? The answer is 'No'. A jungle can effectively be manifested even without a single twig. For a theatre presentation, the ambience and psychological atmosphere of the scene is more significant and convincing than fabricating a real one onstage. A performance space crammed with unimaginative decorations, thus leaving no room for actors to perform, may kill the performance. Meaningful and effective scenography must allow for the audience to participate in creating the desired ambience by way of imagining their own psychological spaces, empowering them to break the barriers of the physical performance space to a limitless, imaginary world. This space remains invisible but changes and moves with the journey of the performance. The following excerpt from a well-known Indian play illustrates the concept of invisible space. In the fourth scene of Girish Karnad's *Hayavadana* (1971), Padmini, Devadatta and Kapila pass through a dense forest en route to a fair in Ujjain. Seeing a flower-laden tree, Padmini asks Kapila:

PADMINI.   [...] Kapila, what's that glorious tree there? That one—covered with flowers?

KAPILA.   Oh that! That's called the Fortunate Lady's flower—that means a married woman...

PADMINI.   I know! But why do they call it that?

KAPILA.   Wait. I'll bring a flower. Then you'll see. [*Goes out.*]

PADMINI.   [*Watching him, to herself*]. How he climbs—like an ape. Before I could even say 'yes', he had taken off his shirt, pulled his dhoti up and swung up the branch. And what an ethereal shape! Such a broad back, like an ocean with muscles rippling across it—and then that small, feminine waist which looks so helpless.[vi]

In this particular situation, the characters, their dialogues and actions, replete with symbolism and analogy, help in achieving the desired impression in the given space. This eliminates the need for a physical forest in developing a spatial relationship. In the above example, the conversation among the characters is indicative of the space as a dense forest, which, though physically non-existent, is much more exciting and apparent in Padmini's soliloquy. Such dramatic action opens a gateway to the mind, enabling spectators to accept the imaginary as real— making an invisible space visible, complete with all details.

CONCEPT OF SPACE IN SANSKRIT THEATRE

Natya Shastra, the gospel of Indian dramaturgy, indicates 'make-believe space', being an important element of a performance. The gestures, postures, and mannerisms of performers in relation to the space and other elements of theatre, such as costumes, ornaments, makeup and visual imageries, are referred to as 'aharya abhinaya'. Quality of the space is unequivocally determined by the speech and gestures of the actors. A performance is thus revealed and circumstantiated through narrative verses and expository dialogues. This idea is better understood when analysed in the context of Sanskrit drama. In the Sanskrit play *Urubhangam*, one can visualise the horror of the battlefield at Kurukshetra through the text, narrated by the soldiers at the outset of the performance. Not only do these soldiers bring forth the story of the war through their gestures, speech and movements, but also, they detail the battlefield, thus helping create the desired visual in the psyche of the audience.

Soldier 1:   We have arrived at the ashrama of this battlefield...

　　　　　　Home of the warriors, witness to their strength and valour...

　　　　　　Their pride and glory assemble here in this hermitage...

　　　　　　To become bridegrooms of the nymphs of heaven.

Soldier 2:   You are right!

　　　　　　The hipbones of elephants immobile,

　　　　　　Make new life in the nests of vultures,

　　　　　　Chariots lie empty with no one to ride,

　　　　　　Gone are the heroes to the heaven, none alive.

Soldier 3:   Look, look!

　　　　　　Look at the sight...

　　　　　　As the woman helps the bridegroom down from the palanquin,

　　　　　　The jackals, dogs and wild beasts...

　　　　　　Are dragging the vacant bodies of soldiers from the chariots.

　　　　　　The battlefield of Kurukshetra patched with flesh, torn skins, bulging eyes and...

　　　　　　Distorted faces connected with veins of blood.[3]

The above is one of many instances of an imaginary space as developed in Sanskrit theatre. Since Sanskrit plays were performed in empty spaces, without any sets or props, playwrights made use of descriptive and narrative texts to create the ambience, suitable for the play. These texts were rendered with the help of 'angika' (physical) and 'vachika' (vocal) 'abhinaya' (enactment). Similarly, a multitude of invisible spaces and imaginary visuals are connoted in every dramatic text, to be unlocked and revealed to the audience by skilled performers.

'Parikramana' or circumambulation was yet another creative device employed in Sanskrit theatre that was unique in many ways. This

---

[3] Excerpt from *The Shattered Thigh*, an English translation of the Sanskrit play *Urubhangam*, by Mahakavi Bhasa in 2nd century BC. The play was translated by Steph Jones and Satyabrata Rout for East-15 Acting School, University of Essex, South End at Sea, England, in 2013.

performance technique came to be used when a performer needed to change the locale. By moving around on or encircling the stage, accompanied by relevant text and music, a performer could change the nuances of the space while remaining within the visible area. The act of 'parikramana' with the help of a 'yavanika' lent grandeur to the presentation. This unique method of utilising the available space made Indian theatre flexible, dynamic and vibrant.

Irrespective of the variety of performance spaces available, one factor shall remain constant in theatre—the power of magical transformation. The metamorphosis of actors into characters, of imagination into reality and of fiction into fact is possible only in a tangible performance space. This transformation germinates and develops with the action in a theatre space and passes through a series of experiences, both personal and universal, of the audience. A person's concept of the imaginary world of fiction leans on one's belief in real people, actual situations and existing spaces. The 'suspension of disbelief' is thus possible only in a theatre space.

PRACTISING SCENOGRAPHY

Scenography is not a new term in the lexis of theatre. It finds first mention in ancient Greece as 'skenographia' in Aristotle's *Poetics*. In the Indian context, however, the term did not enter common parlance till the last decades of the 20th century. In essence, scenography pertains to the visual vocabulary of a theatre performance and is different from the commonly used term 'scenic design'. It is indeed a much wider concept, encompassing techniques of scene-making and the visual aesthetics of a performance in entirety, including the integration of performers, spaces and spectators. The aesthetics of a performance, which was once the responsibility of the director, is now undertaken by the scenographer. In other words, scenography is a kind of visual text created through a performance; the scenographer becomes the interpreter of that text 'by drawing attention to the way stage space can be used as a dynamic and "kinaesthetic contribution" to the experience of performance.'[vii] Prof. Pamela Howard attempts to fathom the scope of scenography in her article 'Directors and Designers', which begins with the following lines:

> The visionary architect Adolphe Appia saw that 'creation' meant the synthesis of space, light and performance achieved by one total personal vision… In the twentieth century and twenty-first century the move out of playhouses into new spaces demands an exploitation of the architecture before relying on design. Logically this results in the work of designer and director merging to become a single and unique creator of text and vision.[viii]

The concept of space is expressed through the language of visuals. That is to say, in a performance, what we perceive through the sense of vision encompasses the ambit of scenography. In this way, it is closer to visual arts like painting, sculpture, architecture and installation art; the only difference being that while the visual arts are measured in the dimension of space, scenography has to be measured in the criterion of space and time. A performance space, no matter how beautifully designed, will remain defunct till an actor steps into it. Once an actor places himself in that performance area and begins interacting with the visual elements, the entire space comes alive in all its dynamism and vigour. This interaction is akin to translating the actors' speech into visual narrations that communicate with the audience like any another character in the play. The space then becomes an integral part of the performance and actively moves with the happenings in the play. Prof. Howard further discusses the significance of theatre design and designers:

SPACE THAT EXISTS IN TIME | 61

Modern theatre design has moved forward from the décor and decoration of the post-war years, and with it the responsibilities of the theatre designer have changed. Nowadays, the designer can expect to be consulted from the beginning of production planning, and choices have to be made at an early stage. This means that the theatre designer has to start from the first point of training to be much better informed and knowledgeable about all the theatre arts that are part of creating

A scene from *Evam Indrajit* (2010). Playwright: Badal Sircar (Bengali). Hindi translation: Dr Pratibha Agrawal. Scenography and Direction: Satyabrata Rout. Courtesy: Avartan, Hyderabad.

an integrated theatre production, and to understand that scenography describes being part of that whole, and not, as design now implies, an applied decorative art.[ix]

To know what scenography is, and to understand the visual vocabulary of theatre, one needs to interact with the performance space time and again so as to comprehend the potential of an empty space in converting verbal text into a visual one. One must discover the intrinsic mystery behind theatre vocabulary that transforms an empty space into an interactive platform. One must understand how the content of a play is translated into a theatrical form that unfolds slowly and steadily in an empty space, where colours, texture, lines and forms become reflections of real life. A space is thus cut, chiselled and modified by the performers as the story moves along.

CONCLUSION

Scenography, the art of transforming space into a visual experience, is increasingly being adopted in India in recent times as a major subject of study by theatre institutions, universities and other academic areas of research and practices. Student designers have started coming out of the spell of old, conventional theatre design and are increasingly exploring the potential of scenography in the contemporary context. This departure from conventional practices is apparent in the works of younger designers and directors. Looking at a sample of the novel initiatives in spatial practices in current times, one can be sure of a revolution in modern Indian scenography.

References

i   Grotowski, Jerzy. 2015. *Towards a Poor Theatre*. London: Bloomsbury Methuen Drama. p. 19.

ii McAuley, Gay. 2010. *Space in Performance: Making Meaning in the Theatre*. Ann Arbor: University of Michigan Press. p. 126.

iii Roach, J. 2004 'It', *Theatre Journal* 56: (4): 559.

iv Willis, Ronald A. 2012. *Fragile Magic: A Guidebook for Theatre Respondents*. Newburyport, MA: Focus, R. Pullins. p.6.

v   Brook, Peter. 2019. *The shifting Point: Forty Years of Theatrical Exploration, 1946–87*. London: Bloomsbury Academic. p.35.

vi Karnad, Girish. 1975. *Hayavadana*. New Delhi: Oxford University Press. p. 25.

vii Rewa, Natalie. 2004. *Scenography in Canada: Selected Designers*. Toronto: University of Toronto. p 120.

viii Howard-Reguindin, Pamela F. 2006. 'Directors and Designers: Is there a different direction?'. *The Potentials of Spaces: The Theory and Practice of Scenography and Performance*, edited by Alison Oddey and Christine White, Bristol: Intellect. pp. 25–31.

ix Howard-Reguindin, Pamela F. 2009. *What is Scenography?* Florence: Taylor and Francis. p. xxiv.

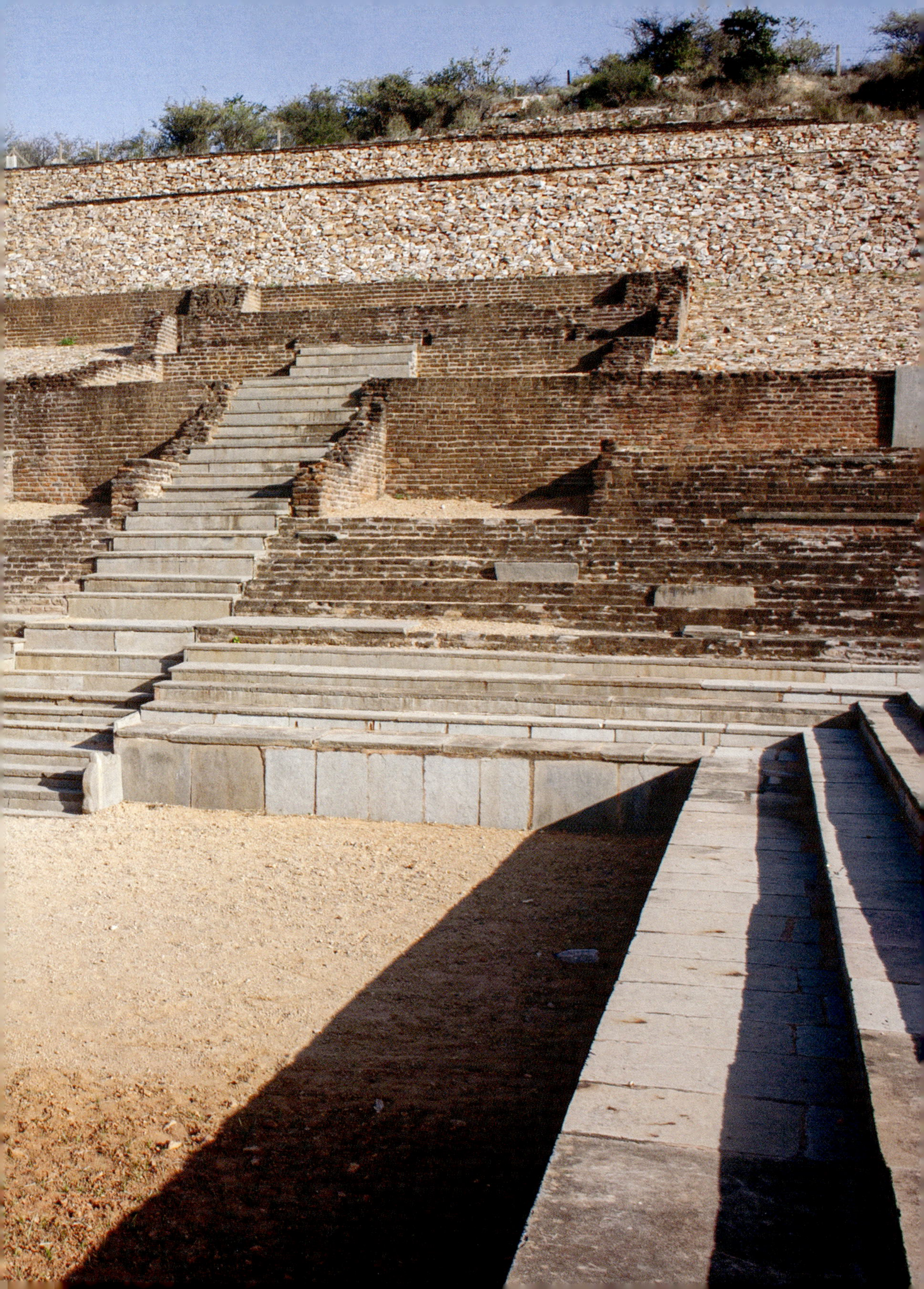

MANIPULATION OF SPACE IN ANCIENT INDIA

ORAL TRADITIONS

India's performance culture predates both classical Indian and ancient Greek theatre. There are evidences of a rich tradition of oral storytelling in ancient rock carvings dating back to the pre-Vedic period. In the post-Vedic era, however, the two great epics of Indian literature—the *Ramayana* and the *Mahabharata*—determined the socio-cultural fabric of Indian society as well as its artistic traditions. These epics also served as the source of the various performance cultures in ancient India. As narrated by Maharishi Valmiki in the *Ramayana*, the tale of King Rama was performed by the twin brothers Lava and Kusa in the royal court of the kingdom of Ayodhya. According to scholars, their rendering of the *Ramayana* formally codified the trend of 'oral storytelling traditions' in India. Patanjali's *Mahabhashya* (2nd century BC), a commentary on Sanskrit grammar and linguistics, mentions an oral tradition of 'granthika' and 'sobhanika'. The granthikas not only recited legends of the fight between Bali and Sugriva from the *Ramayana*, or the slaying of the demon King Kansa by Lord Krishna from the *Mahabharata*, but also performed them. Patanjali has described another oral and narrative style of presentation in his great discourse. Known as Mankha Vidha, presenters from the Ajivika cult, a beggar community, used to move

A page from *Kelieh va Demneh*, a Persian version of the *Panchatantra*. The 15th century manuscript is kept at the Topkapi Palace Museum in Istanbul, Turkey.
Courtesy: https://commons.wikimedia.org/wiki/File:Kelileh_va_Demneh.jpg.

around in groups narrating stories and displaying a series of painted scrolls, while seeking alms.

Vishnu Sharma's *Panchatantra*, written in the 3rd century BC, has had significant influences on India's storytelling traditions. Originally written in Sanskrit, the book comprises stories with roots in the oral traditions of antiquity, either performed or narrated by folk communities as part of age-old conventions. Some of these stories are believed to have been borrowed from the *Jataka Katha* (known popularly as *Jataka tales*)—Vishnu Sharma analysed and reinterpreted the stories for the wayward sons of King Amarshakti of Mahilaropya—though there is no conclusive evidence towards the same.

On taking all such sources into consideration, it becomes evident that the performance tradition in India is as old as its civilisation, and has continued for millennia in oral and physical forms, codified as 'natyam' in a later age. Paul Kuritz affirms:

> Archeological excavations revealed dance in India well over 5000 years ago. Dance and drama continued throughout India's Vedic, Epic, and Classical periods. [...] Before the Aryan invasion, Dravidian kings amused themselves with minstrels and festivals. [...] The *Rig Veda* suggests that dramatic theatre came into being around the eighth century B.C. In addition, Jataka stories depicting Indian life between 600 B.C. and 300 B.C. contain references to theatre.[i]

EARLY TRENDS AND PRACTICES

Early evidences of theatre at the Sita Bangira (Sitabenga) cave in Surguja district in the state of Chhattisgarh strengthen belief in the existence of dramatic performances during pre-classical antiquity. Inscriptions on the cave walls suggest that the performance of poetic renderings from 'Yadu Vansha' and 'Hari Vansha'—stories of the Krishna dynasty—was a usual practice. These performances were conducted in a small amphitheatre inside the cave. Similar performance spaces for ancient theatrical practices are found in the cave of Ranigumpha in the Udayagiri hills, near Bhubaneswar. Built by the famous emperor Kharavela during the 2nd and 1st centuries BC, Ranigumpha provides ample evidence of the existence of a 'rangamandapa' or performance space based on Indo-Greek theatre architecture. Inscriptions on ancient Indian temples, built subsequently during the reigns of various dynasties such as the Chalukya, Pandya, Ahira, Bhoi, etc., provide further testimony to such spaces. In the rock shelters of Bhimbetka in Madhya Pradesh, or at Nagarjunakonda in the Deccan plateau, one can find remnants of ancient performance spaces belonging to the classical era. With reference to the Nagarjunakonda amphitheatre, Professor H.V. Sharma opines that 'it is also probable that the excavated theatre is a relic of the degenerated form of the *caturasra* of the classical kind. In that state, the theatre might have gone to serve the purpose of the popular Buddhists' presentations.'[ii]

By analysing various such specimens, historical records and folklore, it becomes possible to delineate the trends in performance spaces in pre-historic, Vedic and ancient India. Theatre, practised as a communal activity, served as a carrier of religion and rituals, and also flourished as a social art among the populace. Indian culture was fostered and flourished under the patronage of the Vedic cult and Buddhism, wherein all activities and ritualistic practices led to offerings and prayers. Theatre as a medium for religious offerings came to be an integral part of worship. In the Vedic era, separate places were designated for dramatic activities inside temple complexes. These improvised performance spaces were often covered with canopies, though some did remain open to the sky and were perhaps also used for sacrifices. There are adequate instances of such type of performance spaces all over India—predecessors to the classical Indian theatre.

With the decline of Sanskrit drama, traditional and folk performances occupied the centre stage. Theatre, liberated from the control of temple authorities and royal patrons, became an essential part of common life, changing accordingly its colour and form. It subsequently adopted the language of the folk, replete with native dialects, indigenous costumes, folk music and dance. One could experience an eclectic variety of theatrical forms across the country, practised in a variety of dialects, costumes and approaches—an attribute for which Indian theatre is known to the world even today. Some of these folk forms emerged out of community activities while the rest were derivatives of temple culture and rituals.

Theatre practices and performance culture thus formed an integral part of the lifestyle of the natives. However, there is a dearth of authentic records of any such performance practices for further study or research. The reason for this is rooted in Indian philosophy, which recognises life as 'maya' or illusion—keeping a record of illusive activities would be naive to them. Most ancient Indian authors and playwrights thus thought it prudent to not affix their names or even dates to manuscripts. As a result, nothing is clear about their origins. No permanent architectural constructions of theatre houses or performance spaces exist in the country either. Some scholars therefore doubt their existence in ancient times. The *Natya Shastra* relates only methods and techniques sans practical or historical precedents. Yet, the post-*Natya Shastra* era witnessed performance traditions like Kootiyattam and Kathakali that still continue in India. The koothambalam, a permanent performance space inside temple complexes in Kerala, bespeaks the glorious performance tradition in ancient Indian theatre. It thus becomes possible to deduce the various ancient performance spaces by analysing Indian oral history and myth, the diverse traditional and folk forms, and the specifications of playhouses mentioned in the *Natya Shastra*.

Space is an integral part of a performance, irrespective of its nature or form. In the beginning of human civilisation, people may have used public spaces for social gatherings or rituals. They may have offered prayers and performances in music, dance and related forms, prompting perhaps the genesis of theatre. The parietal arts and cave paintings of pre-historic civilisations bear testimony to the existence of performance spaces for community-based activities. A few of these identified performance spaces exist in mountain valleys, within dense forests, inside caves, or in temple complexes, enabling us to conclude beyond doubt that India had a strong performance tradition comparable to ancient Greek and Roman theatres.

Bhimbetka Rock Arts. Courtesy: Author's personal collection.

HISTORICAL PERFORMANCE SPACES
Rock Shelters of Bhimbetka

The ancient rock shelters of Bhimbetka are situated in the Vindhya hills in central India, about 45 km south-east of the city of Bhopal. Spread over an area of 30 sq. km, the site features over 700 rock shelters that were inhabited by the prehistoric people more than 60,000 years ago. Rock paintings belonging to different eras and depicting various early human activities spread extensively across the walls and ceilings of the caves, with the earliest dating back to the Upper Palaeolithic period. These magnificent rock shelters were first discovered by noted archaeologist Dr V.S. Wakankar in 1957.

Murals of hunting, singing and dancing, childbirth and other communal activities serve as strong evidence towards the existence of ritualistic practices in this prehistoric settlement. Religious activities also find place in these murals, which scholars argue as evidences of early systemised religions. Though the nature of such community rituals is still not apparent, Dr Wakankar has pointed out certain tribal performance forms by analysing the extant rock art, related thusly by M.L. Varadpande: 'Dr Wakankar records two interesting Mesolithic cave paintings from

Bhimbetka with a ritualistic character. In one composition four dancers are seen, two standing, one sitting and one leaping in the air. The author calls this a wizards' dance in which 'one dancer has a bison-horn mask, one a feathered head-dress, a third a wolf's head mask and claws, and the forth seems to be taking off into outer space.'[iii]

By looking at all such paintings and built structures, and by analysing the subjects carved on the walls, one can assert the existence of open-air performance spaces in the outer courtyards of the caves at Bhimbetka in the pre-historic era.

SITA BANGIRA (SITABENGA) CAVE THEATRE

Sitabenga cave is the earliest known historical performance space in the Indian theatre tradition. Located in the Ramgarh hills near Ambikapur in Surguja district of the state of Chhattisgarh, the site also features an adjacent cave identified as Jogimara. Situated inside separate hillocks, the two spaces are connected by a huge natural tunnel, almost 60 metres in length, known as Hathipol. The site was first documented by J.D. Beglar and Alexander Cunningham in 1874–75. Beglar describes, 'The cave is a natural cavern, improved by art. In plan, the cave is an oblong, nearly 45

Place for human gatherings and community activity at Bhimbetka rock shelter.
Courtesy: Author's personal collection.

feet long, with straight ends and one straight side, the back wall being not straight, but curved. […] The roof is 6 feet high at the entrance and quite flat in front of the entrance, […]'[iv] According to T. Bloch, the inscriptions on the walls of the cave serve to describe the space—built by one Sutanuka, a devadasi (divine courtesan), for her lover during the 3rd century BC. One such inscription on the cave wall reads:

(11) adipayamti hadayam! Sabhava-garu kavayo. e ratayam…
(12) dule vasamtiya! hasavanubute! kudasphatam evam alam g. (*t*.)

(poets venerable by nature [who] kindle or illumine the heart...
they tie garlands thick with jasmine flowers around their necks)

Noted historian G.K. Bhat sheds some light on the use of the cave as a performance space:

> The archaeological discovery of an open-air theatre, the stage construction conforming to the *Natya Shastra* directions, in the Sitabenga cave of Ramagarh hills in Laxmanpur, in Surguja district of Madhya Pradesh by Bloch, who assigns it to at least 300 B.C., is yet another confirmation of the high antiquity of Sanskrit drama.[v]

Sitabangira cave theatre. The oldest theatre found in the caves which is 2500 years old.
Courtesy: Prof. Yogendra Chobey's personal collection.

It is believed that a grand festival known as 'Kaumudi-Mahotsava' was organised here every year during ancient times in the spring season. Similar to the modern-day festival of Holi, a celebration of colours by the Hindu community in India, the event was devoted to Kamadeva, the god of love. Music, dance, theatre and other allied activities were perhaps presented as part of the gala. Comparable to the ancient Greek festival of city Dionysia, artists from the eastern and northern parts of India would gather at Sitabenga for the *mahotsava*.

The cave manifests a small hall-like structure with the stage carved on the hill outside. The audience gallery features a semi-circular arrangement of rows of stone structures rising like staircases and could accommodate up to 50 distinguished guests. The interior assumes an oblong form—46 feet deep and 24 feet wide. The rock-cut seating area spans three sides of the cave, leaving one side open to view the performance. The performance space, positioned below and in front of the cave, resembles a miniature Greek theatre. A couple of holes are found cut into the floor at the entrance, meant for holding wooden posts to which curtains would be fastened in order to prevent cold air from entering on winter nights.

Jogimara, the smaller cave adjacent to Sitabenga, is just 9 feet long, 6 feet wide, and measures 6 feet in height. Jogimara is believed to have served as a greenroom or retiring place for the artistes during performances.

Ranigumpha Amphitheatre

A performance space that resembles a *Vikrista Madhyama rangamandapa*—a rectangular theatre of the classical period—is found in the cave structure of Ranigumpha in the Udayagiri hills near Bhubaneswar, Odisha. Constructed by Mahameghavahana Kharavela of the Chedi dynasty during the 2nd century BC, Ranigumpha provides ample evidence of the existence of an amphitheatre in the Indo–Greek architectural style. The structure featured a large wooden deck or platform, stretching out in front of the first floor,

A perspective view of the caves which includes Sitabangira and Jogimara caves.
Courtesy: Prof. Yogendra Chobey's personal collection.

which served as the 'rangapitha' or the main performance area. A vast open space in front of the structure would accommodate a large audience. Sri Dhiren Das, eminent scholar and exponent of Odia jatra, refers to it as a 'classical theatre' in his book *Jatra: People's Theatre of Orissa*. Historian M.L. Varadpande also indicates the architectural structure as a theatre with a quote by Percy Brown:

> This 'abbey church' is a double-storied production with its cell ranged around three sides of an open courtyard, the fourth side comprising the frontal approach. A broad terrace, projected from the upper story, was originally supported on structural pillars, either of wood or stone, and these formed the veranda of the ground floor.[vi]

ABOVE: Mattavarni of ranigumpha amphitheatre. Courtesy: Author's personal collection.

FACING PAGE ABOVE: The clear view of Ranigumpha stage. Note the Rangasirsha and Rangapitha as mentioned in the *Natya Shastra*. Courtesy: Author's personal collection.

FACING PAGE BELOW: The royal chair for the king to watch the performance. Courtesy: Author's personal collection.

The rangapitha on the first floor is accessed via a rock-cut staircase that leads up to the terrace, where a large throne with arms and a footrest is found—a seat of honour for the king carved into the rock. The rows of caves on the ground level were used primarily as accommodation for monks and priests. Many supplementary chambers and recesses, used as wardrobes, green rooms, tiring rooms, etc., were also built on this level for purposes related to rituals and other performance-oriented activities. On either end of the ground floor exists an ornate projected square area, slightly elevated from the ground and with roofed decorative pillars, to serve as 'mattavarani', in accordance with the principles of the *Natya Shastra*. These defined spaces housed musicians, who would use the

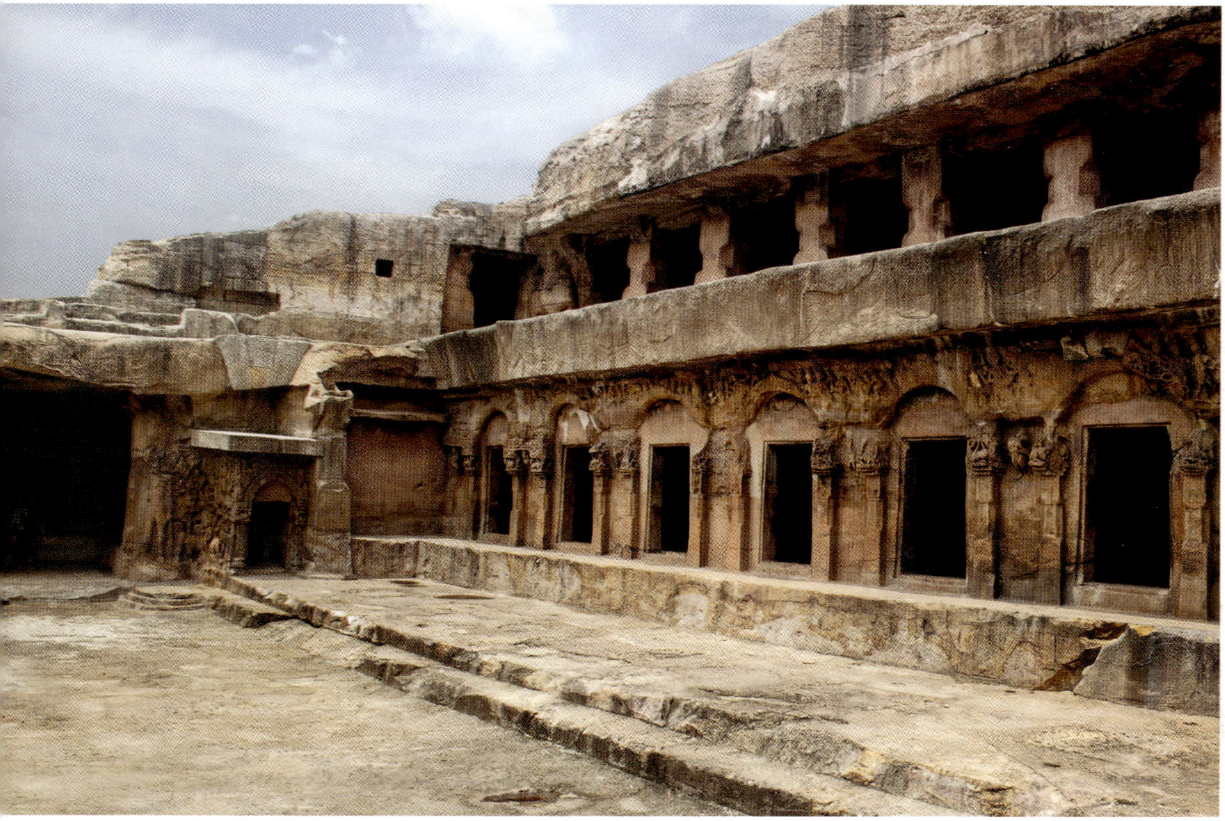

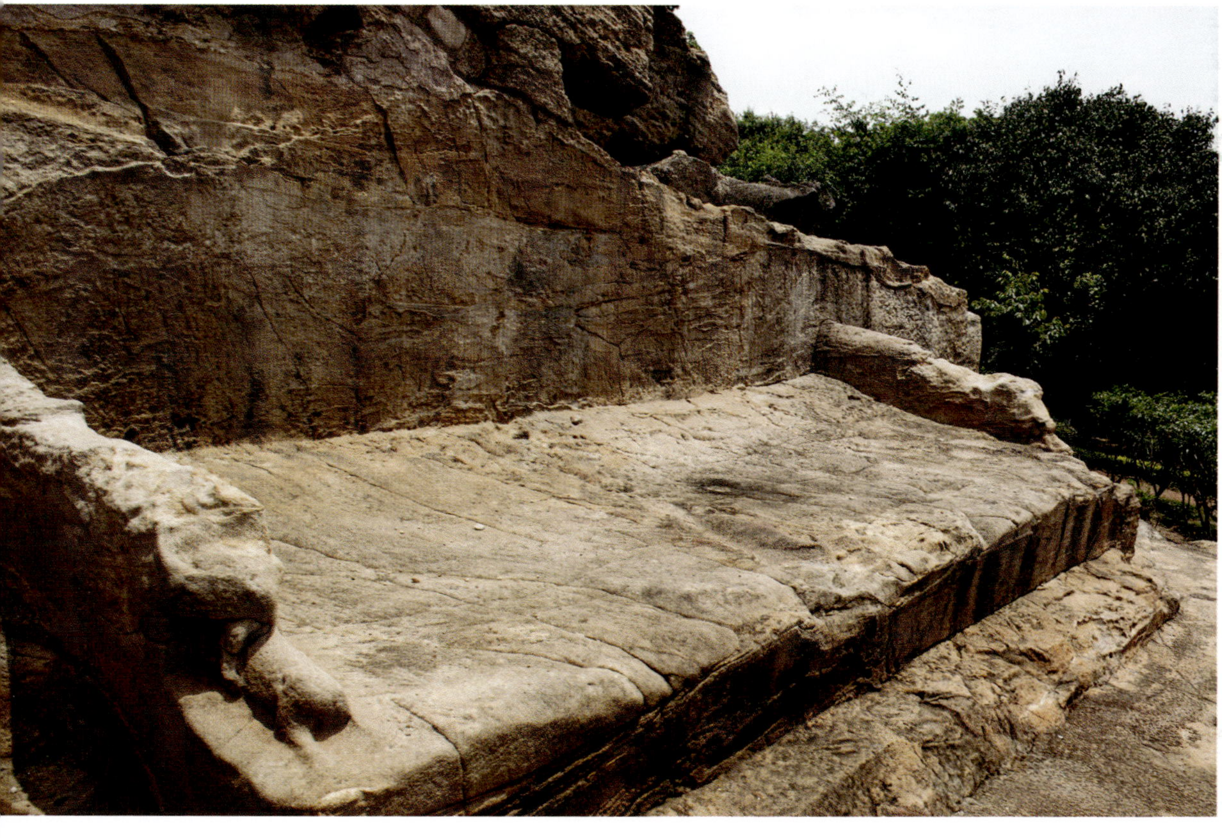

Panel figures in the upper story of the Ranigumpha Theatre.
Courtesy: Author's personal collection.

space to sit and play instruments or sing during performances. Intimate scenes could also have been performed here as part of the play if necessary, in the discourse. Varadpande relies on Percy Brown to further define the site:

> That the open courtyard and its overlooking terraces were especially designed for some spectacular kind of ceremonial seems fairly clear, and a clue to the form that it took is also provided. For around the walls of the upper story there is a long frieze containing figures engaged in a series of connected episodes of a distinctly dramatic character. As the same scenes are repeated in parts, in one or more of the other viharas on this site, they evidently represent some vivid epic in the heroic age of the people.[vii]

It therefore becomes evident that performances were held at Ranigumpha, which manifested a large open-air theatre along the lines of Indo–Greek architecture and in parallel to ancient Greek theatre.

Nagarjunakonda Amphitheatre

Nagarjunakonda, named after the Buddhist philosopher–monk Nagarjuna, is located 150 km south-east of the city of Hyderabad in the state of Andhra Pradesh. According to historical evidences, human activities began here as early as 20,000 years ago. The area was earlier known as Sri Parvata and was ruled by the Ikshvaku kings, who patronised dance, theatre and other ceremonial events during their reign. For conducting such affairs, they constructed a square-type theatre following the Indo–Greek architectural style on Nagarjuna hill.

The site was first discovered by archaeologist A.R. Saraswathi under the aegis of the Archaeological Survey of India (ASI) in 1926, while the amphitheatre, located on the right bank of the River Krishna, was excavated in 1954. By analysing the site's architecture in the light of the *Natya Shastra*, and by tracing the thread of panel paintings of the Jataka tales[1] inscribed on the walls and steps of the amphitheatre, one can recognise the space as a 'caturasra madhyama natyamandapa'—a square, medium-sized theatre. Prof. H.V. Sharma of the National School of Drama (NSD), New Delhi, has conducted extensive research and documentation on the site, and identifies it as a ritualistic theatre from the classical era:

> One is led towards the stage through a pathway of about 6 feet wide and about 15 feet long. As one reaches the stage one finds rows of seats all around the stage excepting at the entrance and a long flight of steps on the opposite side, leading to two open spaces, one above the other. These open spaces seem to have been two halls as a series of pillars, in two rows, facing each other, indicate. The top hall contains two shrines, one of Haritidevi, a Buddhist goddess, and the other of Pancika, her husband, again, a god.[viii]

---

1   Jataka-Katha (The jataka tales) is a large volume of ancient Indian literature, portrays the previous births of Gautam Buddha in animal as well as human forms. The tales are dated back to 300 BC–400 AD.

Top view of the Nagarjunakonda Amphitheatre (2nd Century AD), in the Krishna Basin, Dist. Guntur, Andhra Pradesh. Courtesy: Author's personal collection.

At the top of the aforementioned stairway were two enclosures that perhaps served as tiring rooms for performers. Presentations in the amphitheatre would include stories from the Jataka tales, as is affirmed in the panel paintings, along with other forms of entertainment such as acrobatics, small fights and games popular at that time.

The architectural design of this 'caturasra rangamandapa', for reasons unknown, did not completely adhere to the principles of 'Mandapa Vidhanam' outlined in the *Natya Shastra*, deviating from it in several aspects. The theatre was constructed with mud and bricks. Instead of rising upwards, the theatre sank down to form a pit-like structure. The square performance area measured approximately 32 cubit—*hasta*[2] or 48 ft on each side. The gallery forming the first row of seating was approximately 2 cubit in height, gradually rising upwards in a staircase arrangement. The auditorium encircles the performance area while a gangway provides access to the galleries between individual rows of seating.

Natamandira at the Sun temple of Konark
The Sun temple of Konark was built by the Odia king Narasingha Deva-I, popularly known as Langula Narasingh Deva of the Eastern Ganga dynasty in 1278 AD. According to historical accounts, the temple was built as a tribute to the Sun God. Facing the main shrine, directly in front of the 'mukhashala' or the entrance of the temple, stands the 'natamandira'—a massive square structure manifesting an open theatre. There is ample evidence of classical performances being held in this space as part of offerings to the deity. According to many scholars, Mahari Nritya[34], the ancestral form of Odissi dance, was also regularly performed here as a ritualistic practice. The 'natamandira' thus seems to have been specifically created for offering performances to the Sun god.

Another objective of creating this exotic masterpiece of architectural splendour was to promote the practice of rituals and theatrical activities. Though the main shrine was destroyed in the course of time, the 'natamandira' has been preserved and remains intact. Essentially an open-air theatre, embellished columns adorn the four sides of the stage. These life-sized pillars, carved with figures of dancers, musicians, courtesans,

---

2 One *hasta* measures approximately 18 inches or 1 feet 6 inch.

3 Mahari Nritya is a ritualistic dance form of Odisha, practiced in the temple of Lord Jagannath for more than thousand years. It is assumed that this dance or dances of similar kind (Gotipua) were performed in the Natamandira at Konark temple. The form became instrumental in the development of Gotipua and Odissi dance in Odisha.

animals, flowers and creepers, form an 8-foot-high square performance space with a side length of 48 feet. Steps on the eastern and western sides of the stage lead to the main performance area. There are two huge lion figures empowering over elephant flank the entrances on the east and the west.

The temple at Konark was built at a time when Sanskrit drama was already declined. It can thus undisputedly be stated that the space was not meant for classical Indian theatre performances. However, it is apparent that the 'natamandira' complex served as a local cultural hub for ritualistic and traditional activities in the pre-medieval period.

The Koothambalam at Thrissur

The Koothambalam, a vestige of classical Indian theatre, has existed since the post-classical period to modern times, and is found in various temple premises in the state of Kerala. It is kind of a closed auditorium built for the performance of Kutiyattam, a semi-classical theatre form, and is regarded as one of the most sacred places in a temple complex. The structure and the performance culture of the Koothambalam subscribe to the principles of the *Natya Shastra*—the theatre is designed like a huge hut, made of wood, mud and stone, and measures approximately 48 feet in length and 36 feet in breadth. The performance space is basically an elevated square wooden platform of 12 feet long on each side with a stage height of 3 feet. At four corners of this space stand four richly carved pillars that support the roof of the stage—a sort of false ceiling under the main roof of the auditorium. A separate level towards the back of the performance area houses a *mizhavu*, a drum-like instrument that accompanies presentations of Kutiyattam and Koothu. The outer structure of the Koothambalam is built entirely out of wood, with many openings to allow light and ventilation. Performances are presented in front of distinctive oil lamps while the stage is usually decorated with coconut and palm leaves and banana plants. The basic form of the Koothambalam, owing to the fact that each of its spaces and

The Lion gate of the Natamandira of the Sun temple at Konark (13th century AD). Courtesy: Author's personal collection.

activities is considered sacred and unique, has remained unchanged for centuries.

The Koothambalam at the Vadakkunnathan temple in Thrissur, an exotic masterpiece of Indian theatre architecture, was designed and built by the great architect Velanezhi Jathavedan Namboodiri in the 11th century. The then Maharaja of Kochi decided to have the existing Koothambalam, built during ancient times, demolished and a new one constructed at the same place while retaining the splendour and magnificence of the original. A renowned architect of the royal court, Jathavedan Namboodiri, scrupulously observed the ancient building but did not prepare a model or any floor plans. At the time of demolition, the engineers insisted on the preparation of a detailed model and drawings of the building so that the grandeur of the original could be replicated. But Namboodiri asserted that he had formed a complete mental picture of the marvellous Koothambalam and no paperwork was thus needed for the execution of

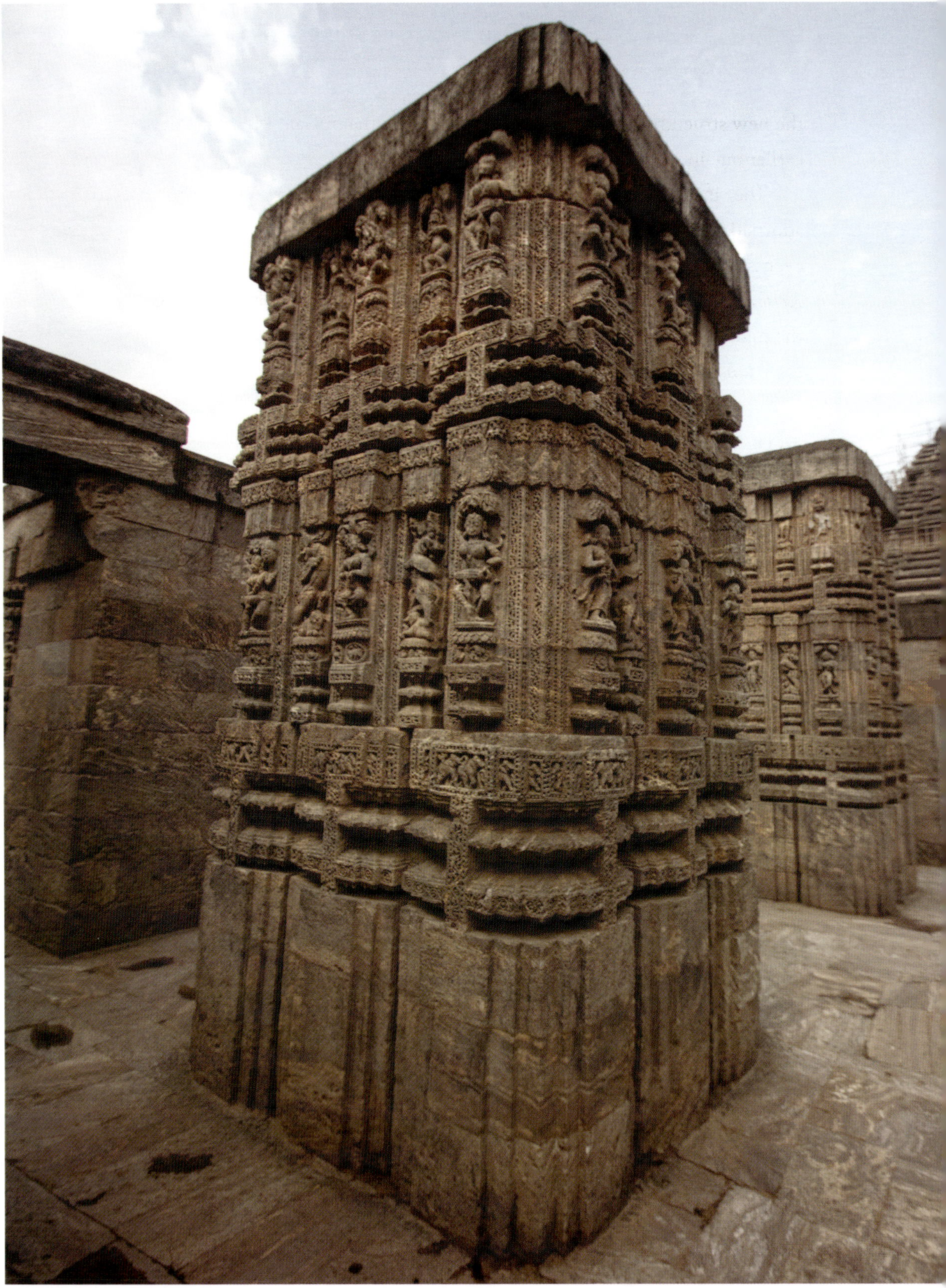

the new structure. Once complete, the new Koothambalam surpassed the earlier one in splendour, majesty and exuberance.

The interior embellishment of the Koothambalam at Thrissur, adorned with ornate sculptures, murals and wooden structures portraying events from the lives of gods, completes the design. Episodes from *Krishna Lila* are elaborately engraved on each of the panels encircling the main shrine. These panels also depict stories from the *Ramayana* and the *Mahabharata*.

THE ART OF SPACE-MAKING IN THE NATYA SHASTRA

Indian dramaturgy is attributed to the sage Bharata's *Natya Shastra*, which was written between the 2nd century BC and 2nd century AD, and is comparable to Aristotle's *Poetics*, written almost during the same time in Greece. Of the 36 chapters in this treatise, dedicated to various aspects of dramatic presentation, the second chapter, 'Mandapa Vidhanam' or the

Koothambalam at Kalamandalam Thrissur, Kerala. Courtesy: Wikimedia Commons.
FACING PAGE: The monumental design of the ornate pillars inside the Natamandira, Konark. Courtesy: Author's personal collection.

principles of a playhouse, provides a detail account of the various types of performance spaces used in classical Indian theatre.

Classical Indian theatre never included any external design or scenography in presentations except for a few stage props. Rather, emphasis was placed on the performance style to impart aesthetic pleasure. Instead of giving importance to the design of the stage for each scene, Bharata focuses on the splendour and architectural grandeur of the playhouse and its performance spaces. Unfortunately, there are no existing ancient playhouses as prescribed in the *Natya Shastra* for further research or study unlike the ruins and records of ancient Greek theatres. The few performance spaces from the classical period that have been unearthed in various excavations tend to deviate from the theories and principles of the treatise. This leads us to believe that classical Indian theatre houses may have been constructed with fragile materials such as clay or wood, which

Interior of Koothambalam, showing stage proper. Courtesy: Wikimedia Commons.

could not stand the test of time. Some scholars are also of the opinion that playhouses were used to be temporarily erected for performances and dismantled after each presentation. Nonetheless, the *Natya Shastra* provides for a clear theoretical understanding of the nature of playhouses used for classical performances. Projecting the types of theatre houses according to the treatise, Dr P.S.R. Apparao elucidates:

> The theatre mentioned in the *Natya Sastra* are of three kinds: *vikrstha* (oblong); *caturasra* (square) and *tryasra* (triangular). Again, each of them are in three sizes; *jyestha* (large), *madhyama* (middle) and *avara* (small). Thus, there are nine varieties of theatre in all. The dimensions of these theatres are measured in *hastadanda* units.[ix]

Although the *Natya Shastra* conveys nine different types of theatres, not all of them are practically viable for presentations—some of these prove to be too large or too small for any performance. Only the three following types are thus considered for practical use.

- *Vikrista Madhyama*—oblong theatre of the middle size (64 *hasta* by 32 *hasta*)
- *Caturasra Avara*—square theatre of the small size (32 *hasta* by 32 *hasta*)
- *Tryasra Avara*—triangular theatre of the small size (16 *hasta* on each side)

However, the treatise enables us to ascertain the types of playhouses considered suitable for the presentation of different genres of theatre in ancient times. Dhananjaya[4], author of the *Dasharupakam*, has methodically analysed different types of plays and their theatrical performances following the 10 distinct types as mentioned by Bharata in the *Natya Shastra*. Accordingly, plays with large numbers of characters and elaborate

---

4   Dhananjaya was a 10th-century Sanskrit scholar who has defined and elaborated the term 'rupakam' described by Bharata Muni in the *Natya Shastra*.

storylines are best presented in big performance spaces while smaller productions are better suited to more intimate performance spaces.

The 'jyestha natyamandapa', the largest of the prescribed theatre houses, was considered suitable for the gods; the 'madhyama', for kings and nobles, while the 'avara' or the small theatre was intended for the common folks. It is codified in the *Natya Shastra* that the *Vikrista Madhyama natyamandapa*—the oblong, middle-sized theatre—is the most suitable 'prekshagriha' (playhouse) for any kind of presentation. Dhananjaya also categorised plays according to their suitability to different types of theatres: 'natak', 'prakarana' and 'prahasana' to be presented in a *Vikrista Madhyama natyamandapa*, while the smaller *avara natyamandapa* was preferred for intimate performances like 'vana', 'dima', 'vithi', etc.

In contrast to the Greek and Roman theatres, the Indian treatise only recommends closed playhouses except for the presentation of *Amritamanthanam*[5]. As per the *Natya Shastra*, this 'samavakara'[6] *rupaka* was presented in a huge open-air theatre built on Kailasa Parvata, the abode of Lord Shiva in the Himalayas, for this purpose. The theatre was specially designed by Vishwakarma[7] to accommodate delegations comprised of gods, humans and ashuras (demons), who were invited to witness the first ever performance from across the three realms—Swarga (heaven), Martya (earth) and Patala (underworld). The play was presented for the distinguished audience by the 'one hundred sons and daughters' or disciples

---

5   In the history of Indian theatre, *Amritamanthanam* claims to be the first-ever written play which was presented in an open air theatre near the Himalayas. The play was written by the sage Bharata and belonged to the category of *samavakara*. The Sanskrit text has not been discovered till today.

6   Samavakara is a type of plays (rupaka), out of ten categories of Dasarupaka. It deals with stories from well-known legends. The characters of Samavakara are mainly gods and devils. It is of three acts. Its major emotions are excitement, love and deception.

7   According to Indian *vastu shilpa* tradition (architecture), Vishwakarma is the principal architect of the universe and the presiding deity of all craftsmen and architects.

Types of Indian Theatre

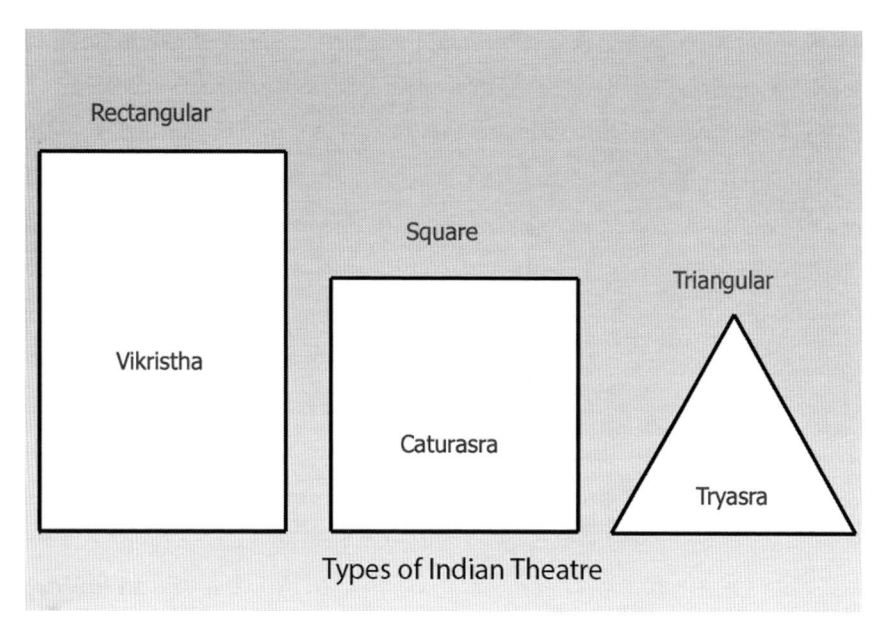

- Rectangular — Vikristha
- Square — Caturasra
- Triangular — Tryasra

Three types of Indian Classical 'natyamandapa'. (Drawing made by the author).

of Bharata Muni. In the play, Lord Vishnu, one of the three supreme deities in Hinduism, as a character, serves amrita (nectar) to the gods in the guise of Mohini, the enchantress, while depriving the demons of it. The demons in the audience gallery became annoyed at this partiality of Lord Vishnu and started creating a ruckus, which resulted in the stopping of the performance midway. Indra[8], the presiding deity of the event, consequently drove them from the auditorium by striking them with the Vajra[9] which was damaged in this act. He then placed that broken weapon in the middle of the stage as a mark of triumph of good over evil, and named it the 'jarjara-dhvaja'— the broken banner-staff. Jarjara-dhvaja sthapana[10] turned into a ritualistic

---

8 Lord Indra is regarded as king of the gods in Hindu mythology.

9 *Vajra*, meaning thunderbolt, is the weapon of Lord Indra.

10 Jarjara-dhvaja sthapana is a ritualistic activity included in the *purvaranga* or prologue, performed before the start of a Sanskrit play in Indian theatre.

activity and was immediately assimilated into the *purvaranga* or prologue of subsequent plays. As stated in the *Natya Shastra*, no performances were held in open-air theatres after this event.

The concept behind this fiction is as follows:

- Theatre is a strong and direct medium of communication.
- The medium is meant only for selective audiences, i.e. the *rasika*: one who can appreciate *rasa* (aesthetic flavour or sentiment) and understands the performance.
- There must exist a bond between the actors and spectators throughout the play so that the audience is able to interpret the gestures, postures and *mudras* of the performers with clarity. This helps the audience to identify with the subject of the play, which in turn leads to *rasa-prapti* or contendedness.

Since the aforementioned requirements are not achievable in an open-air theatre, an intimate and closed environment is preferred for presentations—perhaps the reason why Bharata Muni did not refer to any open-air performances in the *Natya Shastra*. Large gatherings like that in Greek and Roman theatres were also advised against in Indian dramaturgy.

> [Canto] 17. An [oblong] playhouse meant for mortals should be made sixtyfour cubits in length and thirtytwo cubits in breadth.
> [Cantos] 18–19. No one should build a playhouse bigger than the above; for a play [produced] in it (*i.e.* a bigger house) will not be properly expressive. For anything recited or uttered in too big a playhouse will be losing euphony due to enunciated syllables being indistinct [to spectators not sitting enough close to the stage].[x]

Since the expressions of the performers would not be discernible in a large theatre, a medium-sized playhouse is recommended by the sage. According to the treatise, the dimensions of the 'prekshagriha' should provide perfect visibility and audibility to the audience. The roof of the auditorium should also take the shape of a half-sphere dome, referred to as 'shailaguhakara' or like a cave in the mountains.

Though three varieties of theatres were considered for presentations, due to the practicality of the spaces, the *madhyama* or middle-sized theatre was considered the most appropriate. The other two types of spaces—*caturasra* and *tryasra*—can also be used but only occasionally.

Vikrista Madhyama Natyamandapa

Natya Shastra regards *Vikrista Madhyama* as the most appropriate theatre for performance. The dimensions for this particular type of theatre house were prescribed by Bharata Muni that provides suitable visual and aural aesthetics of the performance to the audience. As such, the architectural design of the theatre always remains in tune with the demands of the presentations. As indicated earlier in the discourse, the *Vikrista Madhyama* is a rectangular, medium-sized theatre with a length and breadth of 64 cubit-*hastadanda* and 32 cubit- *hastadanda* (96 feet and 48 feet) respectively. This closed theatre structure is supported by four large pillars, one in each corner, named after the 'chaturvarna' or the four castes in Hinduism—Brahmana, Kshatriya, Vaishya and Shudra. These pillars serve as the primary support for the roof.

Roof and walls. According to the *Natya Shastra*, the playhouse should be made like a mountain cavern and it should have two floors [on two different levels] and small windows; and it should be free from wind and should have good acoustic quality.'[xi] The roof of a theatre is to be shaped in such a way that it forms a rib at the centre. From this central point, the roof slopes down to rest on the walls. The structure has to look like a cave from the outside and a dome from the inside to afford uniform audibility to all the spectators. The walls need to be fabricated with wooden planks and plastered with mud and clay, with gaps in between for proper ventilation. Skylights should be provided on the walls to allow natural light to enter and aid visibility in daytime performances.

Rangamandapa—the performance space. The interior of the theatre is split down the middle, where each half forms a square with a side of 32 cubit. While one half becomes the 'rangamandapa' or the stage, the other one forms the 'darshak-dirgha' or audience gallery. The 'rangamandapa' is again longitudinally divided into two equal parts, each measuring 16 cubit by 32 cubit, forming the 'nepathya' or backstage towards the rear and the 'rangabhumi' or acting area in the front. The two areas are separated by a permanent wall, with a door at each end allowing the performers to enter and exit the stage. The 'nepathya' is varyingly used for make-up and costume and other backstage activities. The 'rangabhumi' is further split into two equal parts, constituting upper and lower areas of 8 cubit by 32 cubit. The upper area is elevated by about half a cubit or 9 inches from the lower area, thus forming two distinct levels. While the upper level is called 'rangasirsha' or upstage, the lower level is known as 'rangapitha' or downstage. In the middle of the 'rangasirsha' appears another square-shaped area, elevated by half a cubit and measuring 8 cubit on each side, known as *vedika* (similar to an altar). This area serves as a seating place for musicians during performances. While the 'rangapitha' functions as the main acting area, the 'rangasirsha' is used only for entry and exit unless the script demands otherwise.

Mattavarani. On either side of the 'rangapitha' exists a defined square space known as 'mattavarani'. As per the *Natya Shastra*: 'On [each] side

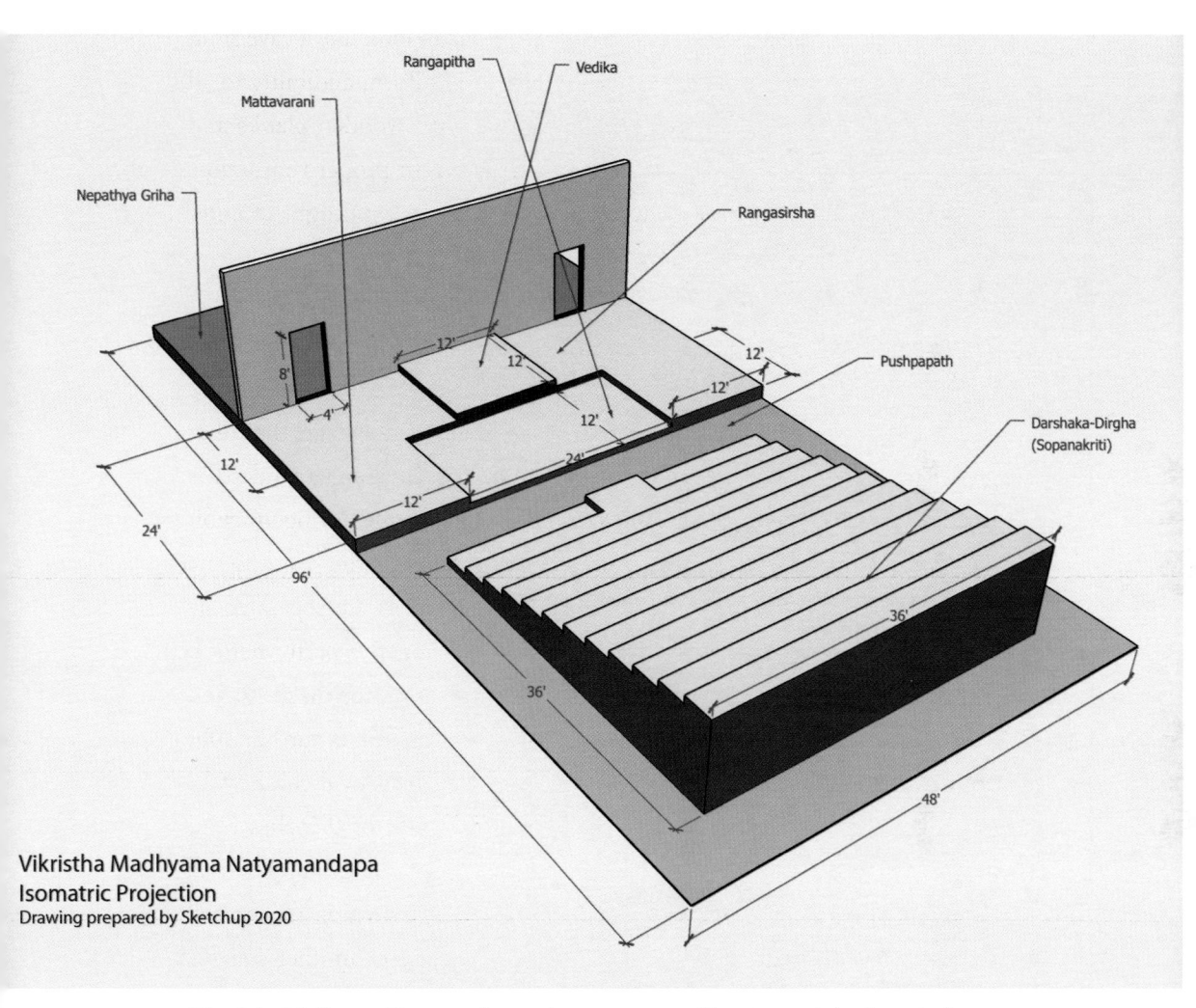

Vikristha Madhyama Natyamandapa
Isomatric Projection
Drawing prepared by Sketchup 2020

Vikrishtha Madhyama Natyamandapa with measurements. (Drawing made by the author).

of the stage (*rangapitha*) should be built the mattavarani and this should be furnished with four pillars and should be equal in length to the stage (*rangapitha*) and its plinth should be a cubit and a half high.'[xii] By analysing the above description, one can deduce the dimensions of the 'mattavarani' to be 8 cubit in both length and breadth and 1.5 cubit in height from ground level. As the name suggests—*matta* translates to 'mad' and *varani*

94 | SCENOGRAPHY

Descriptions

- **A-** Nepathya
- **B-** Vedika
- **C-** Rangasirsha
- **D-** Mattavarani
- **E-** Rangapitha
- **F-** Designated seat for king
- **G-** Prekshagriha
- **H-** Pushpapath
- **I-** Main entry to the auditorium
- **J-** Brahmin Pillar
- **K-** Sudra Pillar
- **L-** Kshatriya Pillar
- **M-** Vaishya Pillar
- **N-** Left entry to the stage
- **O-** Right entry to the stage

Ground plan
Vikristha Madhyama Natyamandapa
Measurement of various components

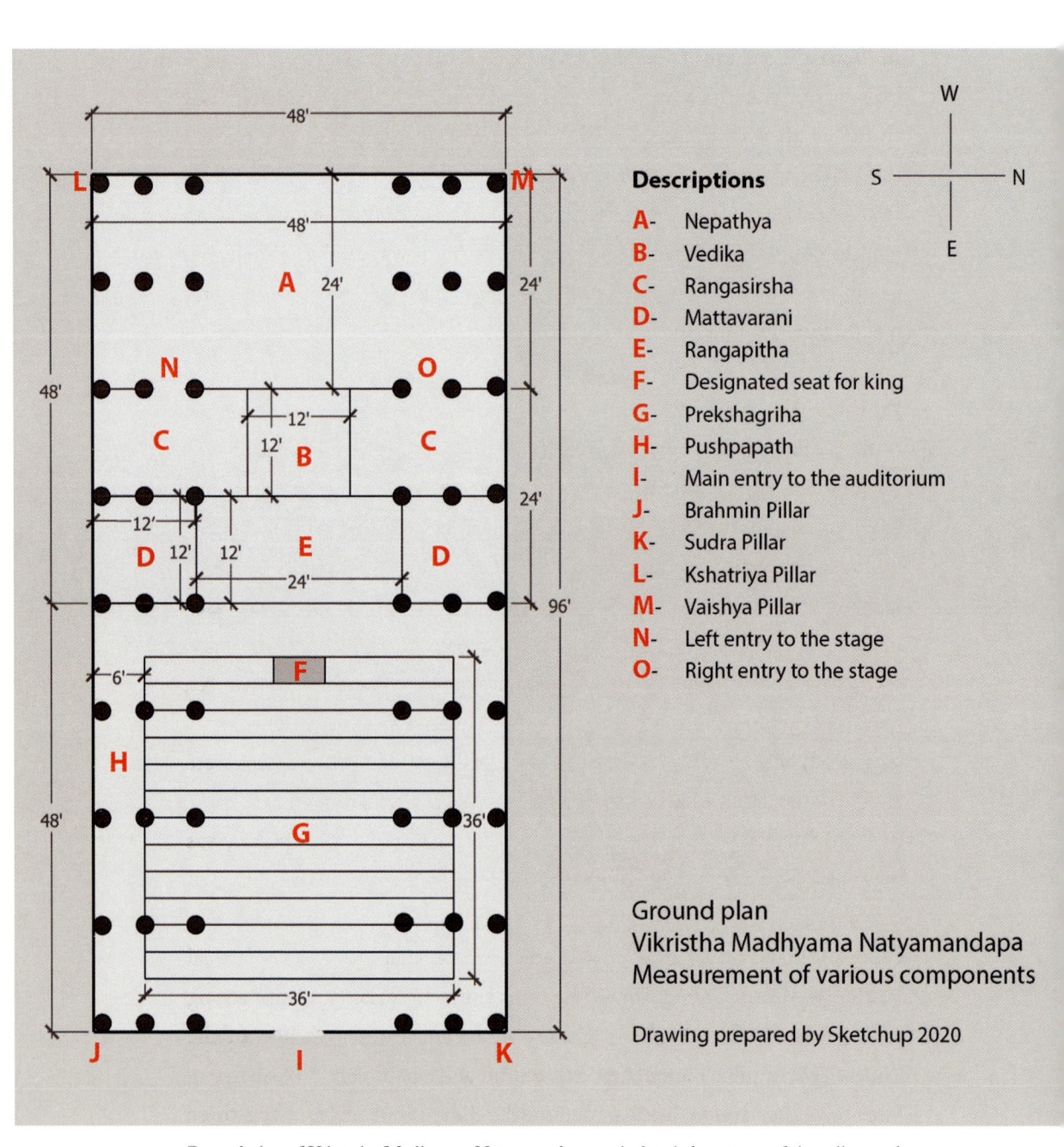

Drawing prepared by Sketchup 2020

Ground plan of Vikristha Madhyama Natyamandapa with detailed position of the pillars and descriptions. (Drawing made by the author).

to 'female elephant(s)'—reliefs of ecstatic female elephants would have been carved on the plinth to represent *sringara rasa*.[11] Pillars on each corner of the 'mattavarani' hold a separate roof within the structure of the playhouse, thus creating a dual-roof structure. The area is designed to provide aesthetic pleasure to the spectators, and although there is no mention of performances in the 'mattavarani', it is assumed that the space is supposed to be used for enacting intimate scenes—as a lovers' secret meeting point or a place for conspiracy, etc.

Prekshagriha. Half of the *Vikrista Madhyama natyamandapa* is dedicated to the 'prekshagriha' or auditorium, forming a square space with a side of 32 cubit. Passages encircling and permeating the space allow the audience to enter the gallery. These passages or aisles are referred to as 'pushpa patha' or flower-strewn paths, and are adorned with pillars of different colours in keeping with the name. The seating manifests a 'sopanakriti' or staircase-like arrangement to offer a clear view of the performance to each of the spectators. In the audience gallery during ancient times, the front rows, marked by white pillars, were dedicated to Brahmins; subsequent to them, marked by red pillars, were rows of seating for Kshatriyas; Vaishyas were assigned the level adjacent to yellow pillars on the north-western side; while the north-eastern side of the last gallery, marked by blue pillars, was meant for Shudras.

Pillars. Pillars are of great significance in the making of the classical Indian playhouse. The *Natya Shastra* recommends having four strong pillars, named after the four castes in Hinduism, on the corners of the theatre. These pillars should be erected on an auspicious day in keeping with *tithi* and *karana* (based in Indian astrology). After installing these

---

11   *Sringara* is one among the nine *rasa*s in the classical theatre arts of India, and is usually translated as romantic love or erotic sentiment.

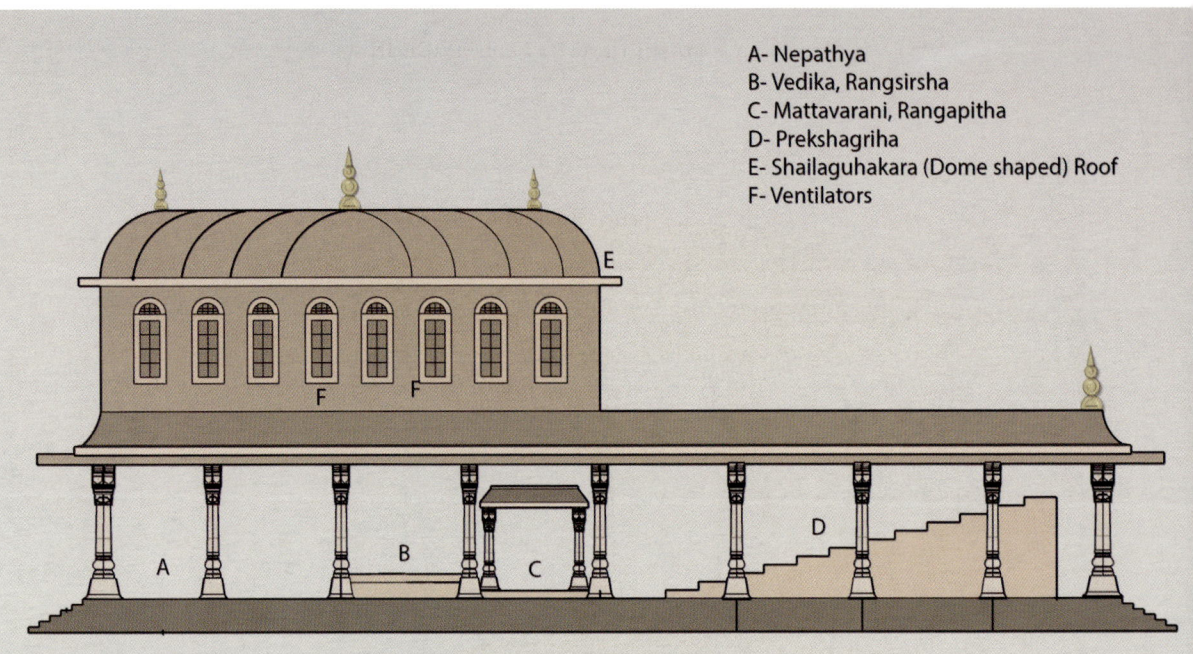

A- Nepathya
B- Vedika, Rangsirsha
C- Mattavarani, Rangapitha
D- Prekshagriha
E- Shailaguhakara (Dome shaped) Roof
F- Ventilators

Cross section of Vikristha Madhyama Natyamandapa
Drawing made by Sketchup 2020

Front Elevation of
Vikristha Madhyama Rangamandapa

Drawing made by Sketchup-2020
Not in Scale

Mattavarani

Drawing made by Sketchup-2020

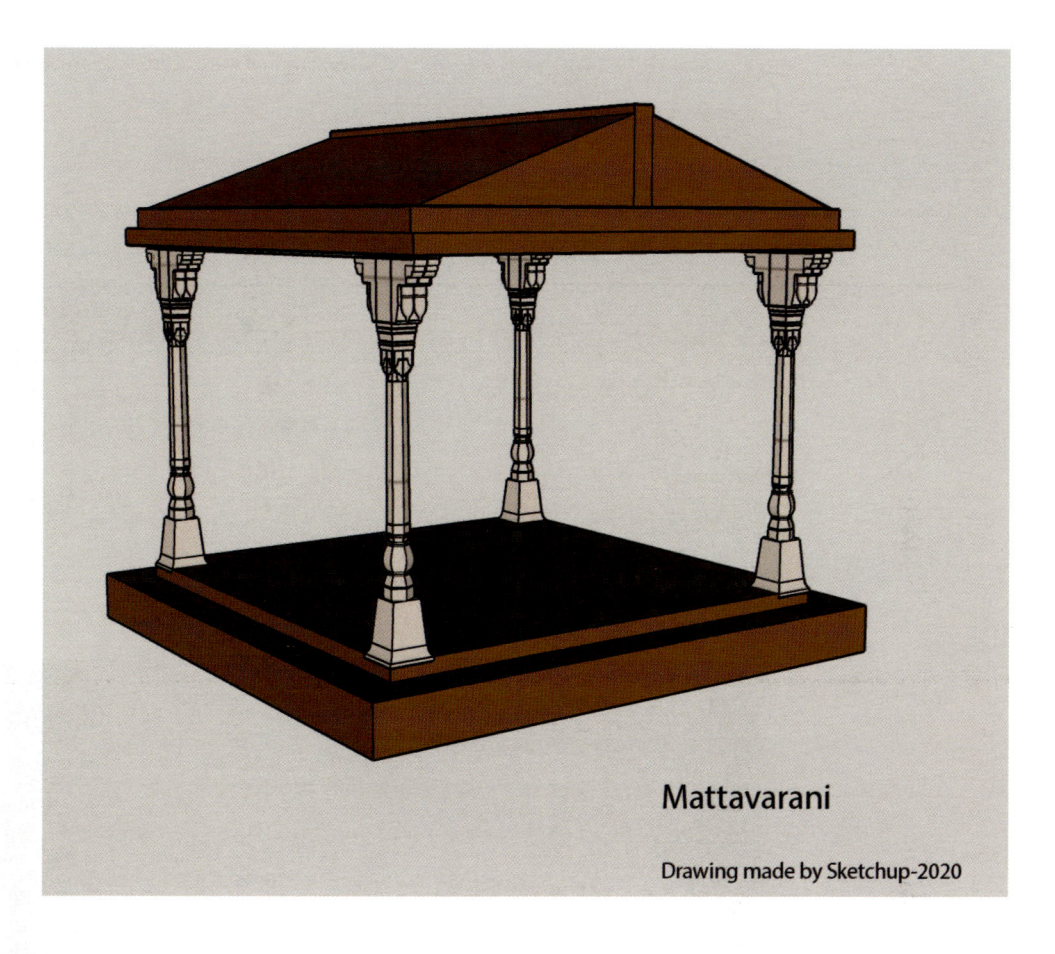

four pillars that hold up the roof, another set of seven pillars are placed on each side of the theatre in an equidistant manner. As such, there should be a total of 18 outer pillars along the periphery of the structure, nine along each length of the building including the four major pillars. Dr P.S.R. Apparao further elaborates:

> Then, pairs of pillars should be fixed at a distance of 16 h., added up between each pair on the western and the eastern edges. The distance between each pair of pillars should be 4 *h.*, Because of such an arrangement, on the western and the eastern edges, they add up to eight

pillars. Then, in keeping with the pairs of pillars at the back of the tiring room, seven such rows, each consisting of four pairs, should be fixed, so that together they make twenty-eight pillars in the remaining part of the entire theatre.[xiii]

It becomes clear from the above discourse that there should be a total of 54 pillars in the structure—the 4 main pillars on the 4 corners, 7 pillars each on the northern and southern sides, 4 pillars each on the eastern and western sides, and 28 pillars inside the theatre. The arrangement of the pillars can be well understood through the accompanying drawing.

Bharata Muni has meticulously drawn detailed pictures of the *Vikrista Madhyama natyamandapa*, beginning from concept to execution, in the *Natya Shastra*. Selection of a suitable space for the playhouse, types of wood for construction, the appropriate *tithi* or time to build, and various other details are clearly recorded in the treatise. But, unfortunately, Bharata does not provide such detailed descriptions of the other types of playhouses, indicating instead that the same principles are to be followed for all the types. Prof. H.V. Sharma, in his seminal volume titled *Caturasra Madhyama Natyamandapa*, tries to interpret and justify the principles of the various architectural plans as per his understanding. Similarly, other scholars have been and still are continually reinterpreting the three forms of theatre houses. As such, the preceding description of the *Vikrista Madhyama* playhouse may differ from that offered by other scholars as it is the author's own interpretation of the subject.

SCENOGRAPHY IN CLASSICAL INDIAN THEATRE

Bharata Muni has provided adequate resources to comprehend the various kinds of theatres mentioned in the *Natya Shastra*. He has also accordingly codified performances and their presentations—categorised as 'nataka', 'prakarana', 'prahasana', 'anka', 'vyayoga', 'bhana', 'vithi', 'dima', 'samavakara'

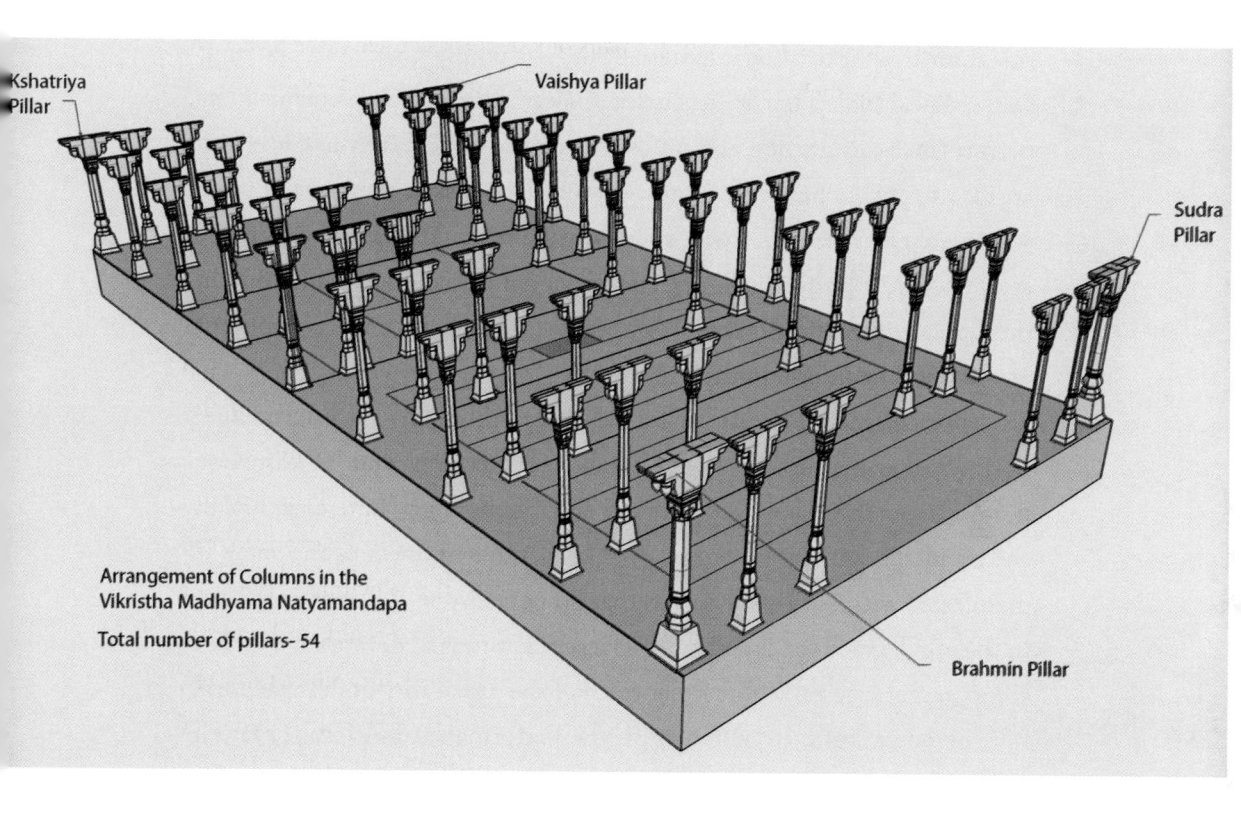

Arrangement of Columns in the Vikristha Madhyama Natyamandapa
Total number of pillars- 54

Labels: Kshatriya Pillar, Vaishya Pillar, Sudra Pillar, Brahmin Pillar

and 'ihamriga' (Ref. *Dasharupakam* by Dhananjaya)[12], the plays were presented in different playhouses as suitable for each genre. Of the four types of performances (*abhinaya*), one major aspect is dedicated to 'aharya abhinaya'[13]—performance with the help of design elements like makeup, hairstyle, costumes, ornaments, jewellery, etc. While he has discussed such technicalities in detail along with specifications for their usage, nothing is mentioned about the scenography or scenic visuals in a performance. In

---

12 As discussed with Prof. Mahesh Champaklal of M.S. University, Baroda: Bharatmuni has mentioned about different categories of plays and named them as 'rupakam' in *Natya Shastra*. But Dhananjaya has elaborately redefined them according to their nature—vastu, neta and rasa and authored his scholarly book *Dasrupakam* in 10th century.

13 A discourse on aharya abhinaya forms a major theme of the XXI chapter of the *Natya Shastra*.

this context, a theatre house represents only an empty space. As a matter of fact, classical Indian theatre has never allowed added scenic elements in its performance culture. Sets and props are deemed unnecessary in conveying an idea to the audience in a presentation. In Sanskrit theatre, the stage was treated as a neutral space where any scene could take place. But the space, which appears outwardly 'empty', is not actually so, as anything in the world may be imagined as an embodiment of a performance—without any physical manifestations.

Space in Indian theatre (classical and traditional) is a catalyst that portrays visuals through symbols, abstract gestures and atmospheric perspectives. These abstract gestures and symbols get into meaning in the mind-space of the audience. And thus, the emptiness of the space is manifested with imaginary visuals that do not exist on the stage space but in the mind-space or the collective subconsciousness of the viewers. Indian scenography is based on the inner truth of the physicality of the space and not the outer truth. It exists within the performance and is experienced only through it.

Contemporary theatre across the world now subsumes various disciplines—acting, stage-designing, costumes, stage-lighting, makeup, choreography, etc. However, such delineation is actually a western concept, adopted by Indian theatre in recent times. In the *Natya Shastra*, such compartmental divisions do not exist. Rather, it pleads for 'holistic theatre', something that can be achieved in its entirety. Scenography in classical theatre is an aspect of this holistic performance approach. The novelty of classical Indian drama lies in its genesis—it was conceived as an abstract 'presentational style', rather than a realistic 'representational form', as is a common practice in occidental art forms. The classical Indian performance style was never adept at the portrayal of life in its apparent form as it does not perceive life from an external viewpoint. In Indian theatre, life is presented through metaphor and symbolism;

stylisation is a common practice in Indian theatre. The principle of presenting a 'patra'[14] or character on the stage is inherent to spatial presentation and scene-making. The Aristotelian concept of 'unit of space' cannot be realised in the context of classical Indian theatre. A change of space and locale is integral to a performance, related directly to the actors' physical expressions and empowered by the text (literature). In a classical performance, an existing locale may easily be transformed into a different one through a ritualistic practice known as 'parikramana'[15], wherein a performer, with the help of a series of rhythmic physical movements as well as the tune of music, appears to reach his desired location, in full view of the audience, by circumambulating the stage. Furthermore, the performance never brings forth anything for a long period of time, be it space, character, emotion, or plot. For that reason, multiple locales, events and characters may exist simultaneously in a single space–time frame in a performance. Everything is expressed through abstract gestures as an allegory to the reality of life. As aptly analysed by Paul Kuritz:

> The makeshift nature of the performance required few scenic items; it exploited instead the Indian love for symbolism, imagery, and costume. Sanskrit texts did not even indicate scenery, though female stagehands may have changed the *yavanika* to suggest various *rasas*—white for an erotic setting, yellow for heroic, a dull color for pathos, multicolored for farce, black for tragedy, and red for violence.

---

14 The literal meaning of *patra* is container. A performer in Indian theatre is termed as *patra*, a medium that can carry any *ranga* (colours or emotions) and reflects the same in its purest form. Broadly speaking, a *patra* is comparable to a character in a play.

15 Parikramana refers to circumambulation of sacred places in the Hindu, Jain and Buddhist contexts. Indian Sanskrit theatre adopts *parikramana* as a technical means to change the locale through a series of stylised movements by a performer.

The Indian *ranga* was, like the world, a neutral place where many different locations existed simultaneously. Indian theatre thus aimed for even less illusory imitation than the Greek theatre.[xiv]

Scenography in classical Indian theatre emphasises on 'make-believe' space, in which the play text plays a crucial role. To achieve the desired imagery, performers would narrate the verses accentuated by physical gestures, expressed by the way of *chari*—stylised foot movement, and *mudra*—gestures, gait and mime. For instance, to establish a scene in a forest, the actor performs the forest and its various aspects—trees, birds, mountains, rivers, etc.—through their gestures and other physical movements. Through the presentation and the subsequent narration, the audience is able to visualise the unseen imageries required to appreciate the play.

As discussed, the performance space in classical Indian theatre remains neutral, where all the scenic visuals are pertained. This concept of 'performing the space' may be better understood by analysing a scene from the famous classical play *Abhijnanasakuntalam*[16], where King Dushyanta enters the stage on a chariot while chasing a fleeing deer through the forest. The actor, playing the role of Dushyanta, would enter the stage, performing 'natya'[17]. His *chari* would indicate that he is riding a chariot. He would then establish the horses and the cart through his hand gestures. After this scene, he creates the ambience of a jungle through his physical movements and the rendering of the text. In a similar manner, the deer would be established through hand gestures and movements of the performer. The nuances of the performance, in which scenography is achieved through choreography, thus becomes an integral part of the

---

16   *Abhijnanasakuntalam* is a well-known Sanskrit play, written by the great poet Kalidasa sometime between the 1st century BC and 4th century AD, dramatising the story of Shakuntala as narrated in the *Mahabharata*.

17   Natya refers to the enactment with the help of music, dance and text (speech) on a stage space.

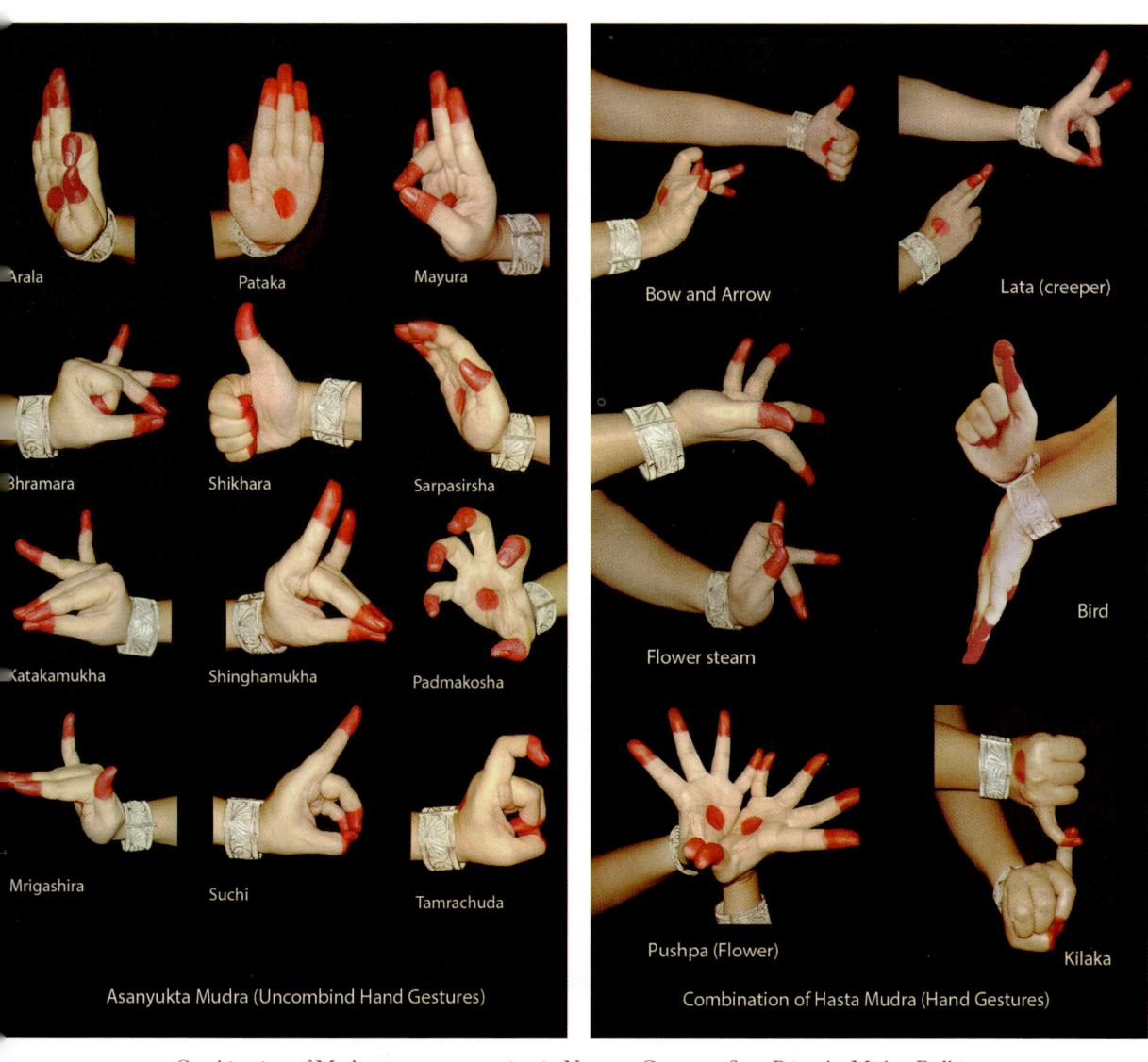

Combination of Mudras to create meaning in Natyam. Courtesy: Smt. Priyanka Mishra Padhi (Odissi dancer), Hyderabad.

presentation. Through the performance, the spectators would be elevated to the spiritual height of attaining the *rasa*. In the process of receiving *rasa*, the audience needs to realise the inner truth of the performance for which they are called 'rasika'—a person who receives and appreciates the essence or *rasa*. In the course of a play, the psychological participation of the audience, reciprocating the performance by imagining the ambience and scenes conveyed by the performers within a neutral space, becomes essential. In other words, scenography in classical Indian theatre is manifested in its choreographic visuals, enabling the audience to regard the experience through the efficacy of the performance.

Classical Indian theatre exclusively employed such imaginary visuals emerging out of the text and performance. In another example, in establishing the battlefield of Kurukshetra in the play *Urubhangam*[18], a group of three soldiers enters the stage and creates the atmosphere of the battlefield with their rendering of text, gestures and gaits as the play commences, thus sufficing the effect of scenography. In another play by Bhasa, *Madhyama Vyayoga,* the fight between Bhima and Ghatotkacha can be established through mime and the performance of 'natya'. Because of its rich performance tradition, Indian theatre never placed any emphasis on the physical embodiment of space. Instead, importance was given to costumes and makeup. A spectacular and intricate presentation style makes classical Indian theatre a unique performance tradition—one that has been instrumental in establishing the aesthetics of performance culture round the world. However, that is not to imply that classical Indian theatre entirely rejected the use of scenic elements. The use of selected properties, such as 'jarjara-dhvaja', 'yavanika', 'chamara,' etc., by actors indicates a conscious effort for visual aesthetics. In the ritualistic practice

---

18 *Urubhangam* was written by Mahakavi Bhasa in the 2nd century BC. Thirteen plays written by Bhasa have been discovered till date.

Still from the Sanskrit play *Shakuntala*. Courtesy: Department of Theatre Arts, University of Hyderabad.

Jarjara-dvhaja sthapana. Courtesy: Department of Theatre Arts, University of Hyderabad.

of 'purvaranga'[19] or prologue, performers enter the stage with the 'jarjara-dhvaja'[20] and place it upstage on the 'rangasirsha', near the 'vedika'. This multi-coloured, visually striking flag is placed on the stage to connote the performance as a celebration of life. The 'yavanika' (half-curtain) is another symbolic prop used by the performers to enter and exit the stage during the course of the play. The entry of the characters from behind this colourful curtain, held up by two dancers, elevates the visual grandeur of the performance. There is also evidence of the use of some hand props by other characters like the female attendants (paricharika) and the one who holds the royal parasol (chatradharini). Scenography in classical Indian theatre relies more on spiritual experiences than the physical embodiment of visuals. It has to be evaluated through the art of choreography and *natya*, providing *rasa* to the viewers.

CONCLUSION

Performance, as a ritualistic activity, continues in India from the ancient period to current times, and is not only confined to theatre but encompasses all social activities, be it tribal, folk, classical, rural or urban. Glimpses of India's rich performance traditions are apparent in the conduct of its various festivals, ceremonies, commemorations and even day-to-day activities. To observe and celebrate such occasions, entire local communities gather at stipulated places like panchayat ghar, namghar, temple-yard, etc. This enduring legacy substantiates the fact that performance culture has come to be an integral part of the people's lifestyle. Most Indians have some memory of celebrating certain occasions by presenting plays and other such performances. Occasions such as Holi, Diwali, Dussehra, Eid, Ganesh Chaturthi, etc. had great impact people's social lives. In rural areas,

---

19 The *purvaranga* precedes the performance of a *ranga* (play) and comprises activities like *jarjara sthapana, nandi patha, vishkambhaka*, etc.

20 Jarjara Dhvaja is a ritualistic stage prop.

Use of 'yavanika' in the play *Shakuntala*. Courtesy: Department of Theatre Arts, University of Hyderabad.

a temporary stage is made out of bamboo, mud and wooden planks in the village square for a few nights to present plays; the stage is dismantled soon after the event is over. Perhaps this practice of temporary theatre construction is a remnant of our ancient and medieval performance practices, of which there is no record except for a long-drawn legacy of tradition across the ages. Theatre, as a community ritual, has served the society for centuries. But unfortunately, except for a few, most theatre forms have neither been studied nor documented. The preceding discourse attempts to shed some light on the available performance spaces through the lens of precedence and tradition. Nonetheless, there may surely exist numerous other spaces and styles that yet remain unnoticed and deserve to be explored. Dedicated research and substantial effort may prove fruitful in bringing them to light.

References

i Kuritz, Paul. 1988. *The Making of Theatre History*. Englewood Cliffs, New Jersey: Prentice Hall. p.66.

ii Sharma, H.V. 2001. *Catura'sra Madhyama Natyamandapa*. New Delhi: National School of Drama. p. 41.

iii Varadapande, Manohar Laxman. 1987. *History of Indian Theatre*, Vol.1. New Delhi: Abhinav Publications. p. 11.

iv Beglar, J.D. 1882. *Report of Tours in the South-eastern Provinces in 1874–75 and 1875–76*. Calcutta: Office of the Superintendent of Government Printing. P. 39.

v Bhat, G.K. 1988. *Encyclopaedia of Indian Literature*, vol. 2, 'Drama (Sanskrit)'. Devraj to Jyoti, ed. Amaresh Datta. New Delhi: Sahitya Akademi. P. 1100.

vi Varadapande, Manohar Laxman. 1987. *History of Indian Theatre*, Vol.1. New Delhi: Abhinav Publications. p. 231.

vii Ibid. p. 231

viii Sharma, H.V. 2001. *Catura'sra Madhyama Natyamandapa*. New Delhi: National School of Drama. p. 38.

ix Appa Rao, P.S.R. 2001. *Special Aspects of Natya Shastra*. Translated by H.V. Sharma. New Delhi: National School of Drama. pp. 15–16.

x Ghosh, Manomohan. 1959. *The Natya Shastra: Ascribed to Bharata-Muni*, vol.1. Calcutta: The Royal Asiatic Society of Bengal. p. 20.

xi Ibid. p. 29.

xii Ibid. pp. 26–27.

xiii Appa Rao, P.S.R. 2001. *Special Aspects of Natya Shastra*. Translated by H.V. Sharma. New Delhi: National School of Drama. p. 26.

xiv Kuritz, Paul. 1988. *The Making of Theatre History*. Englewood Cliffs, New Jersey: Prentice Hall. p. 79.

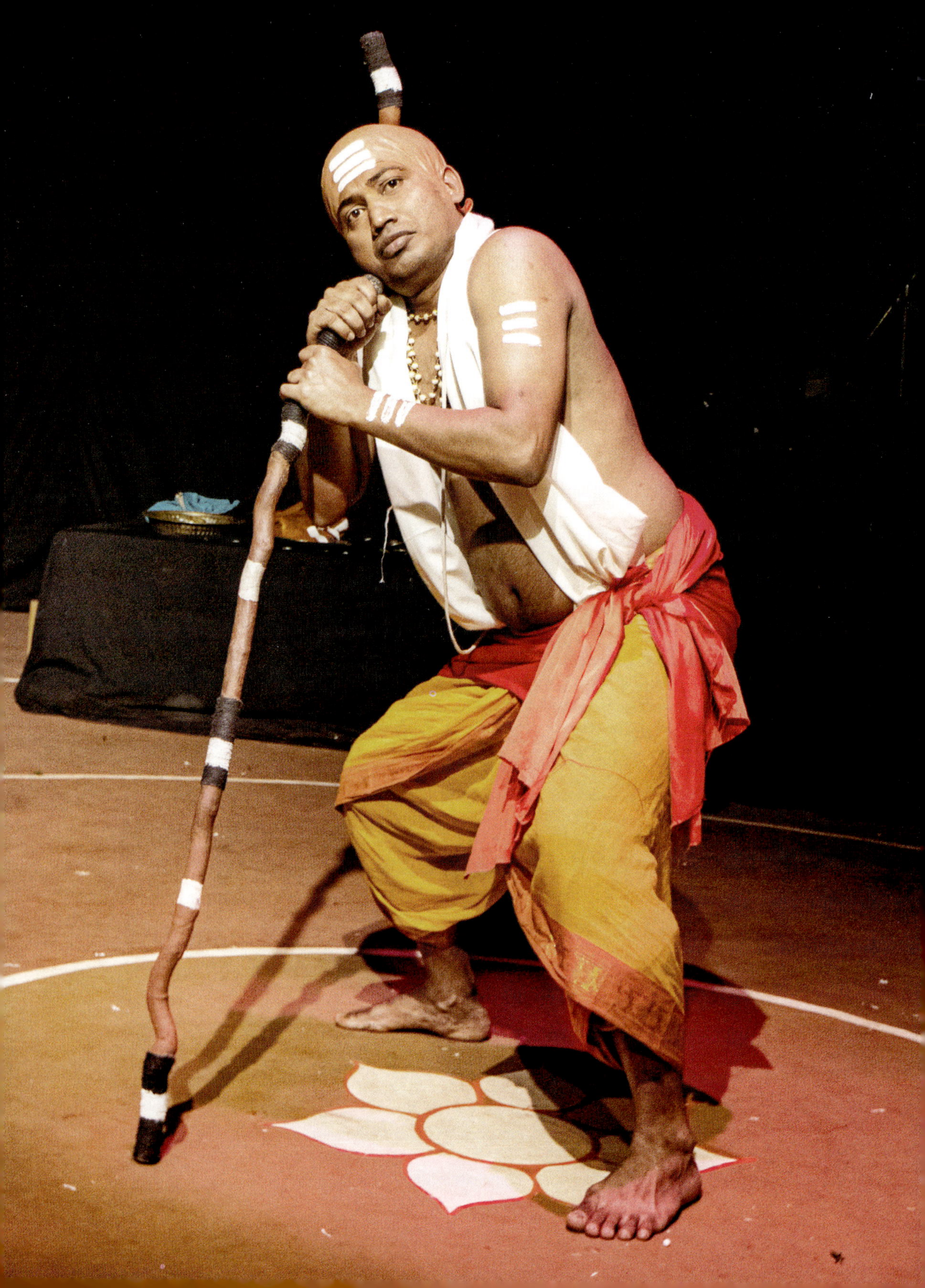

SPACE AND SCENOGRAPHY IN POPULAR INDIAN THEATRES

THE EMERGENCE OF FOLK THEATRE

Classical Indian theatre was in decline by the end of the 10th century. Buddhism, which had helped nurture Sanskrit theatre for many centuries, was on the verge of extinction in India at this time. Sanskrit language thus became confined to the royal courts and was only used for official uses. For the populace, languages found utterance in local dialects; the cultural milieu changed and so did theatre. In addition, multiple foreign invasions between the 11th and 13th centuries drastically altered the political and cultural landscape of India. Subsequently, between the 14th and the 17th century, regional theatres emerged as a significant social expression among the natives owing to the amalgamation of various religions—Hinduism, Islam and at a later stage, Christianity—and cultures—tribal, traditional, folk and semi-classical. During the reign of the Mughals, traditional theatre forms received due social recognition. Professor Sisir Kumar Das evaluates the decline of Sanskrit drama from a different perspective:

> The decline of the Sanskrit drama was mainly due to its inherent nature, its almost total identification with the aristocracy. Contrary to the general belief that the Sanskrit drama declined because of the Muslim rule, it began to lose power from the tenth century onwards when the

effect of the Muslim rule on the dramatic art was yet to be felt. Many Muslim rulers had shown great appreciation for Sanskrit. But there was hardly any popular base to sustain Sanskrit theatre.'[i]

During the 15th and 16th centuries, folk theatre emerged as a major community activity in India, expressed as it was in different languages and dialects. It became an articulation of localised culture—making theatre 'regional'. Though most of these regional theatres have changed in forms and colours over the course of time, they are still prevalent in various parts of the country today. A few folk theatre forms and the regions they are practised in are enlisted here for reference.

Folk and Traditional Theatre Forms	Region
Rasalila, Sumang Lila, Thang-ta	Manipur
Jatra, Pala, Daskathia, Prahallad Natakam, Mayurbhanj Chhau dance	Odisha
Jatra, Purulia Chhau	Bengal
Ankiya Nat, Ojhapali	Assam
Videshia	Bihar
Saraikela Chhau dance	Jharkhand
Nautanki, Ramlila	Uttar Pradesh
Bhavai, Akhyan	Gujarat
Khayal, Swang	Rajasthan
Bhangra	Punjab
Bhand Pather	Kashmir
Tamasha, Lavani, Dashavatar	Maharashtra
Therukoothu	Tamil Nadu
Burrakatha, Bomalatta (shadow puppetry)	Andhra Pradesh
Yakshagana	Karnataka
Theyyam, Krishnattam, Vellattam	Kerala

Apart from the above-mentioned forms, other innumerable folk theatres emerged out of the process of cultural integration and became quite popular among the masses. Emancipated from the principles of the *Natya*

Shastra, these performance cultures preferred native (*lokadharmi*) physical and vocal expressions for their presentations, which were conducted in any given improvised space. An ordinary space with an odd group of spectators interacting with the performers defines this theatre. Informal in nature, these folk and traditional theatre forms have nurtured our socio-cultural environment for hundreds of years. After the decline of Sanskrit theatre, regional theatre became a projection of the Indian identity.

Unfortunately, many regional theatre forms have now become extinct, not having been able to stay abreast of the changing value systems of the society. But those that survived underwent gradual transformation, adapting to and instilling contemporary sensitivities in their presentations. To keep pace with the times, these theatres also had to incorporate modern technologies into their presentations. The informal and improvised utilisation of space, which was once elementary in these regional forms, then paved the way for formal and elaborate spatial designs. The colour and texture of these articulations have also changed drastically. Nevertheless, these art forms remain quite popular among the common folk and serve the society even today. It would be difficult to analyse the performance practices of all these Indian forms in a single book, but a few theatre forms within reach are discussed below to understand the nature of these practices and their spatial conventions.

JATRA THEATRE OF BENGAL AND ODISHA

Jatra is a popular form of folk theatre practised in eastern India that has been traditionally performed in the states of West Bengal, Odisha, Assam, and Manipur for centuries. The connotation of 'Jatra' or 'Yatra' comes from the literal meaning of it— journey or procession—and the art is presumed to have emerged out of the Gaudiya Vaishnava Bhakti movement promoted by Sri Chaitanya Mahaprabhu during the 16th century. The movement started in Nabadwip in Bengal and later proliferated the north-eastern parts of India. Devotees of this tradition would sing, dance and celebrate ecstatically on their religious journeys while playing music on the *manjira* and the *mridangam*. This ritualistic practice of devotion perhaps gradually took the form of Jatra. There are mentions of Sri Chaitanya performing the role of Rukmini in the play *Rukmini Harana*, extracted from the episodes of *Krishna Lila*, in one of the earliest instances of a Jatra performance. Dhiren Das, a well-known exponent of Odia Jatra, has proposed an alternative origin of this theatrical form. Das maintains that the term Jatra is of Prakrit origin wherein the root word 'ja' means 'jata' or born, directly alluding to the unfolding of the story as depicted in the *Jataka Katha*. It is thus quite possible that Jatra bears a direct link with Buddhism, far preceding the Bhakti movement.

Irrespective of the provenance of Jatra, it became immensely popular in the rural areas of Odisha and Bengal, especially during the colonial period, and came to be seen as a major source of entertainment. Jatra troupes, with repertoires of mythological, historical and social plays, travel from one village to another round the year holding presentations and taking a hiatus during the monsoons, when the companies prepare fresh productions for the following year.

The popularity of Jatra depends solely on explosive dramatic action and histrionic, exaggerated dialogues. Loud music and comic gestures add to the flamboyance and dynamics of the performance. Jatra has been adopted as an effective and distinct medium of communication, with all its inherent characteristics, because of two main reasons:

- It communicates to a large gathering and hence allows loudness for audibility and understanding.
- Comic gestures and exaggerated actions, along with slapstick humour, are weaved into the narrative with the prime purpose of entertaining the masses, ensuring its survival.

In the early days, the conservative society did not allow women to perform on the Jatra stage, as a result of which all the characters were played by men. But with changing times and as a survival strategy, female actors were gradually inducted towards the last quarter of the 20th century. Like the Commedia dell'arte of Italy, stock characters feature in the repertoire of Jatra as well, such as the gatekeeper (*duari*), the entertainer (joker) and destiny (*niyati*). These generic characters are present in almost every presentation irrespective of the story. The show (*samaja*) used to open with song, music and dance, which was repeated between the scenes as the interlude to keep the audience entertained. This musical exposition, lasting for hours in a Jatra, was comparable to the ritualistic practice of 'purvaranga' of classical Indian drama. Even today, a Jatra performance typically starts late at night, is performed on an improvised stage assembled for the purpose and lasts for five to six hours. Musical instruments like the clarinet, harmonium and brass gongs that were commonly used in the olden days have now been replaced by electronic instruments.

Scenography of Jatra

Early stage design. A conventional Jatra theatre utilised a thrust stage comprising essentially of an open square area (*chabutra*) where the audience flanked three sides of the stage, leaving the rear part open for musicians to occupy during a performance. The stage used to be constructed with mud and clay, resembling a boxing ring, and was referred to as 'akhada' (wrestling yard) by the populace. A marquee (*shamiana*) was occasionally erected above the stage to protect the artists in case of adverse weather.

The size and structure of the Jatra stage, basically an improvised temporary construction, was contingent on the setting and the demands of each play. Nonetheless, an average stage would span 24 feet on each side with a height of 1.5 feet. A narrow path connecting the main stage to

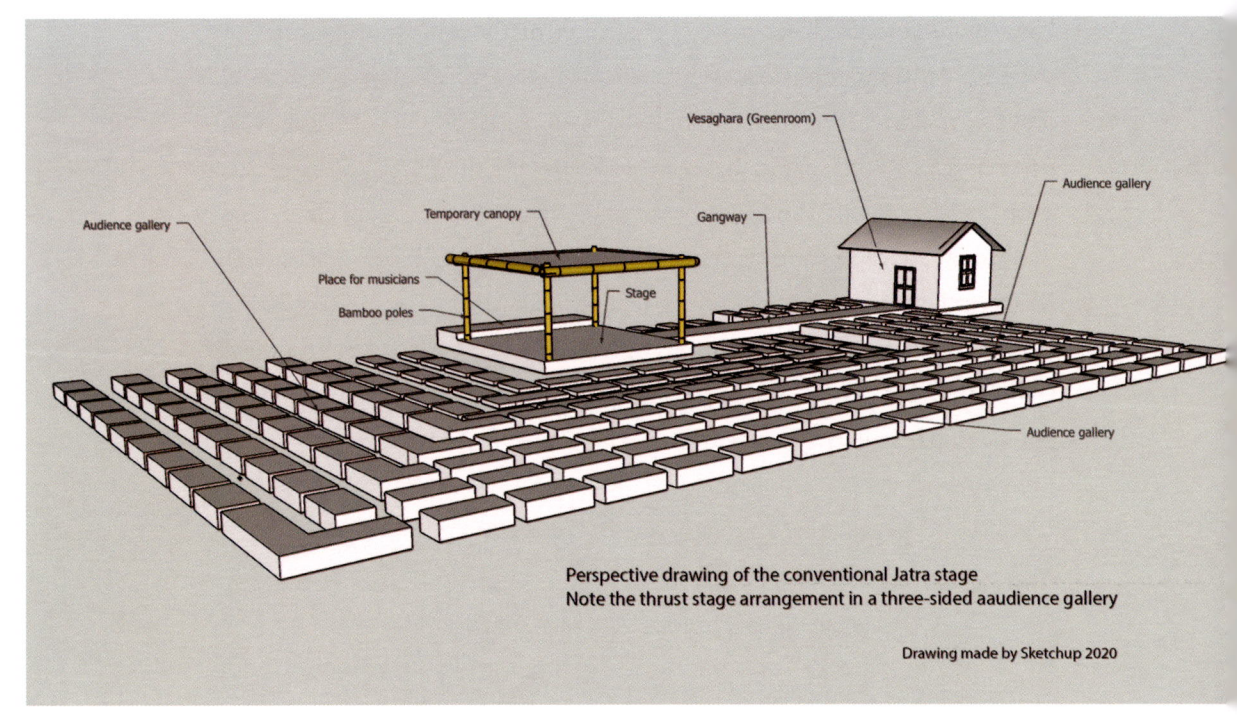

Perspective drawing of the conventional Jatra stage
Note the thrust stage arrangement in a three-sided aaudience gallery

Drawing made by Sketchup 2020

A sample drawing of the traditional Jatra Stage. Note the thrust stage with audience arrangement in three sides along with the gang way and the veshaghara.

the dressing room (*veshaghara*) was used to pass through the audience—a unique feature of Jatra theatre. This passage was used by performers for entering and exiting the stage proper from the veshaghara. It was also a common practice in Jatra performances to use the pathway as an extension of the stage proper, such that certain parts of a play may be performed there. For instance, while portraying the duel between Bhima and Duryodhana from the *Mahabharata*, the actors would take entry from the veshaghara while fighting, and continue to do so as they traversed the narrow gangway, flanked by the audience, to the main stage. This gangway was referred to as 'pushpa-patha' (flower-strewn path) and is comparable to the *hanamichi* of the kabuki theatre of Japan—a long corridor that passes through the audience to the main stage and serves the same purpose.

New stage design. Towards the beginning of the 1980s, in a quest for survival, a drastic transformation was brought out in the presentation of Jatra theatre. Due to the rapidly growing popularity of commercial cinemas and the television industry, Jatra audience began to dwindle. To adopt modern technologies and keep abreast of the changing times, the traditional concepts of 'performance' and 'space' had to be commoditised. Modern lighting and sound systems, multimedia projections, multi-layered spaces, redefined stories and new performance styles were gradually assimilated into presentations, generating renewed interest among the populace, particularly the youth.

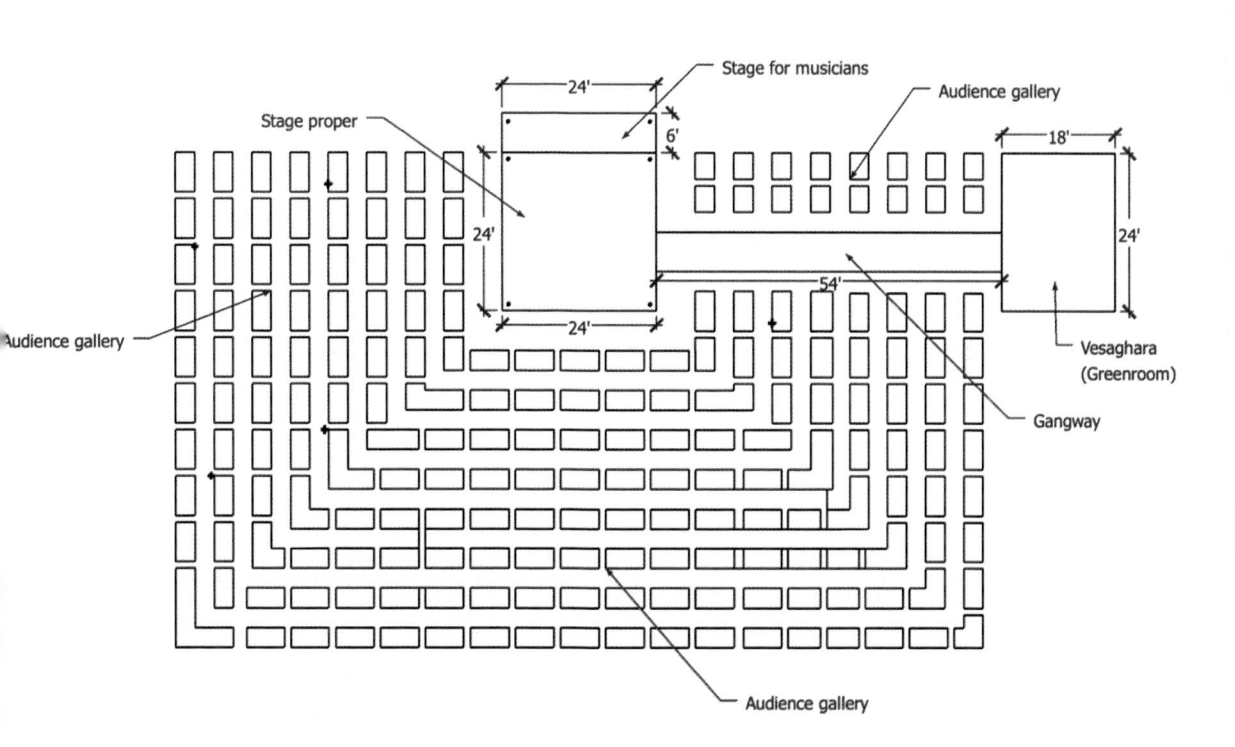

Ground plan of traditional Jatra mandapa (Stage)

Female actors were accommodated in variance with previous practices. Popular social dramas, influenced in part by mainstream cinema, replaced the age-old mythological, devotional and historical stories. Open-air performance spaces and improvised audience arrangements were reinstated by way of circus-like tents and makeshift auditoriums. State-of-the-art lighting and sound systems accorded novelty and glamour to the performance culture of Jatra. The old, arena-like stage was replaced by double- and triple-layered performance spaces that slowly became an inalienable feature of new-age Jatra presentations. In this complicated, multi-tiered space, the first level is commonly appropriated for the main performance, the second for flashback sequences and the third for stage effects and gimmicks. A white curtain covers the rear wall of the third stage, used for multimedia projections and special effects. The use of cycloramas has also become common in modern-day Jatra. Stage tricks and other such devices thus became central attractions in this popular genre of theatre, helping it regain popularity among the masses and bringing in handsome revenue for the troupes.

Stage Description. The main and the second stage are connected to the dressing room by means of long gangways on either side of the stage. Intervening these gangways, in the pit located subsequent to the second stage, sits the orchestra or the band comprising some 15 musicians and singers. Lighting and sound technicians place themselves in the pit behind the central stage. The gangways are used for the entry and exit of actors, as well as for portraying intimate scenes, cutscenes, etc. Opposing to the earlier convention of using the gangway as an extension of the stage, passing through the audience, the new one is placed towards the rear stage to join the veshaghara at the back. This new formation enables each character to take a certain amount of time for entry, allowing the audience to appreciate every individual's performance.

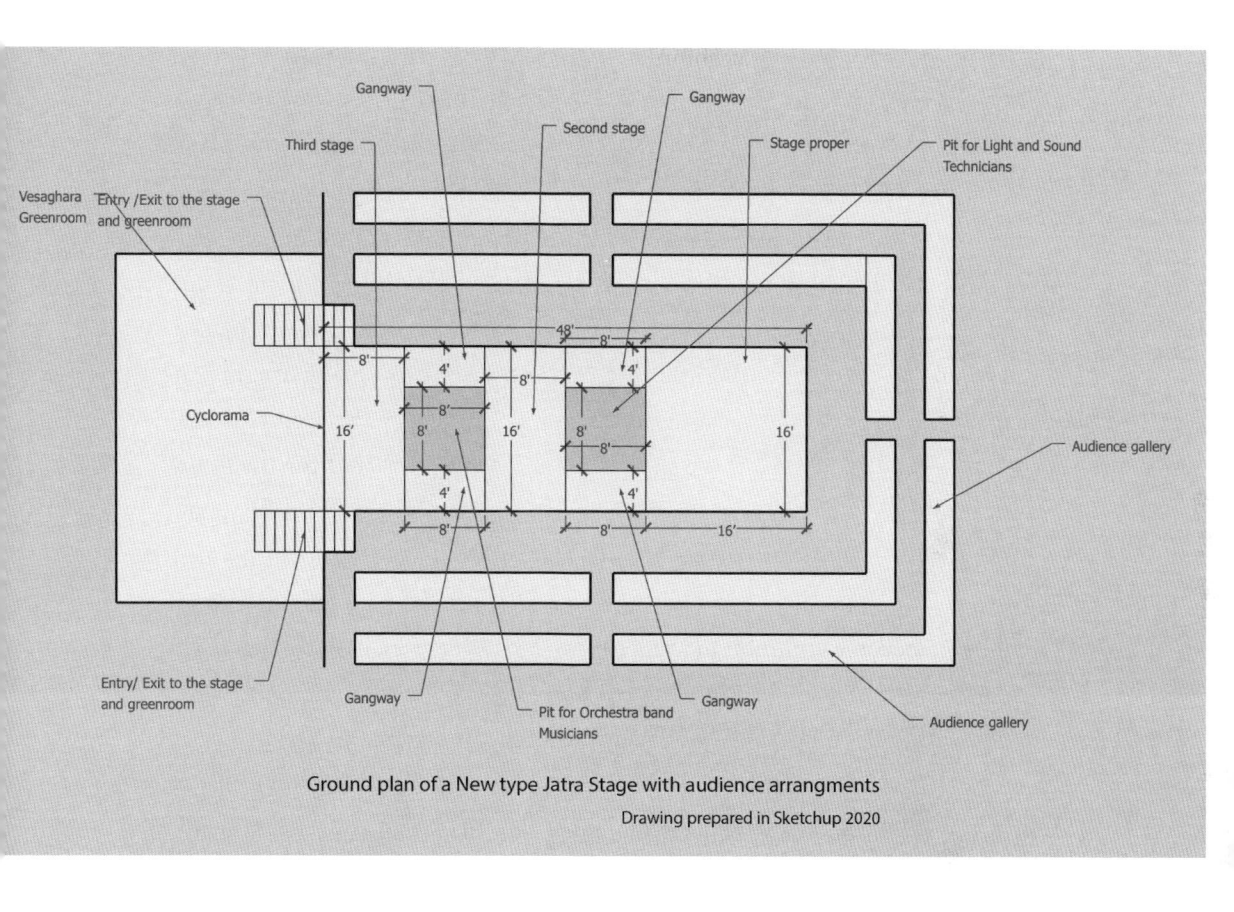

Ground plan of a New type Jatra Stage with audience arrangments
Drawing prepared in Sketchup 2020

Similar to the other theatre styles of the Orient, Jatra does not require elaborate stage props. Performances are rooted mainly in the text, music and dialogues, manifesting the only devices at the actors' disposal. In the earlier days, a single wooden chair, used as a stage prop, would be enough to represent all requisite visual expressions. As per the demands of the story, the chair would be used to represent a king's throne, a poor man's hut, a cot, a lover's bench, a tree, a hiding place, or even a weapon to fight with. But with the introduction of modern technologies in Jatra performance, scenography developed into an essential part of its presentation. For old stage design, the veshaghara, which used to be directly connected to the

Three-dimensional drawing of a new Jatra stage.

main stage by way of a gangway, had great significance. Any available space near the stage, such as a school, the village clubhouse, or even somebody's residence, was temporarily appropriated for the purpose, and the actors would make their entry and exit from there. Now in the new stage design, however, a temporary hutment is built behind the stage to serve as the green room. The practice of changing costumes for every scene is common in Jatra performances, and the veshaghara is consequently laden with wardrobes. Prof. John Russell Brown, who extensively studied Jatra in Odisha and West Bengal, further elucidates:

> Out of the Vesha Ghara—a tent with uneven earth floor, crowded with clothes-racks, make-up tables, and very busy people—the play's characters appear in a succession of new clothes, whether it is a

Photograph of a new Jatra stage (stage proper). Courtesy: Daitari Panda, Konark Opera, Odisha.

contemporary or historical drama. Careful choice was evident in each garment at Puri and every opportunity was taken to make a change. Reappearance in a new outfit was sometimes greeted with loud approval by the audience because it said so much and spoke so clearly of the latest change in the character's fortunes.[ii]

Jatra has been a source of entertainment for the rural populace of eastern India for centuries and continues to be so even today. Similarly, the mobile theatre of Assam, a variation of modern Jatra, is also a widespread medium of mass entertainment, travelling from village to village conducting performances round the year. Such professional companies adopt all available modern techniques and technologies to meet the expectations of the people and the times. Stories influenced by television serials and

Photograph of the artists doing makeup inside the veshaghara. Courtesy: Daitari Panda, Konark Opera, Odisha, 2013.

commercial cinema may also find a place in these theatres. However, the essence of Jatra will always remain rooted in the lifestyles and realities of the rural folk.

PALA: A NARRATIVE THEATRE OF ODISHA

Pala relates stories from the epics, as well as poetic renderings from medieval and post-medieval literature, accompanied by traditional and folk music. Like Jatra, it too grew out of the Vaishnava Bhakti movement in eastern India. Pala typically consists of six performers, who sing and narrate stories from the *Ramayana*, *Mahabharata*, etc. using dramatic improvisation. The main singer (gahana) sings, narrates and analyses verses with the help of his chief associate (siri-palia), while the remaining four serve as the chorus.

This form of theatre has been in practice in northern and central Odisha for the past 300 years.

Pala relies solely on the verses of well-known medieval Odia poets, such as 'Kavi Samrat' Upendra Bhanja, Abhimanyu Samanta Singhara, 'Kavisurjya' Baladeva Ratha, Gangadhar Meher, et al., for content. The epic poems of these bards are sung and analysed by the *gahana* as reference to the main story, with the help of the chorus singers (*palia*), who also play instruments like the brass cymbals (*jhanj*) and terracotta percussion instrument (*khol*). Pala performances have not yet been textualized, making it a completely improvised form of theatre. Though each performance has a fixed layout and progression, the basic content changes with the prevalent situation. The *gahana* and all his *palia*s, backed by a vast repertoire of verses from ancient and medieval literature, are adept enough to sing and thoroughly interpret the subject within a contemporary context. Unlike Jatra, Pala theatre does not call for a continuous flow of the characters. Rather, the singers themselves improvise and dramatise the scenes from time to time as the story unravels through narration. Even today, episodes from the *Ramayana* and the *Mahabharata* such as, 'Sita Vanavasa', 'Kichaka Vadha', 'Bilwa Mangala', 'Sati Anusuya', etc. are most affectionately and respectfully performed by the Pala singers and adorably accepted by the village folk.

Scenography of Pala

The presentation of Pala is not as complicated as Jatra. It can be presented anywhere—in a random open space, inside a hall, in a temple yard, or even in a private space like a courtyard. Pala requires a smaller set-up due to the fewer number of performers and spectators. The ideal stage, the 'Pala mandapa', used to be a square space, surrounded by spectators from all sides. Often slightly elevated with the help of clay and mud, if at all required, a canopy would sometimes be installed above the stage to protect the artistes from adverse weather conditions. The performance space may take the form of a 12-foot square area for comfortable presentation, but there are no prescribed rules for the same. Since spectators seat on all sides of the stage, the performers communicate with them by periodically circumambulating the stage, which quite naturally has become a characteristic feature of Pala.

Before the entry of the *gahana*, the *palia* would improvise on a theme parallel to the main plot to be performed. They sing, dance, make jokes and interact with the audience in a variety of ways. The *gahana* only takes entry when the audience is well settled. Like other Oriental theatre forms, this one too is based on the performers' ability to improvise the plot and narration. Stage props are hardly used in a pala performance, the only exceptions being the flywhisk (Chamara) and some local musical instruments like the *khol*, *jhanj* and *manjira*. The *gahana* wields the *chamara* in each presentation and uses it to convey a variety of effects while improvising on the scenes. For instance, this small hand prop may be used as a combat weapon while depicting the fight between Duryodhana and Bhima in the *Mahabharata* or may represent an oar in the sequence where Rama crosses a river while on exile in the *Ramayana*. Through multifarious movements of the *chamara*, the *gahana* can effectively establish various emotions in accordance with the narrative and situation.

Finally, the *gahana* blesses the audience by gently placing the *chamara* upon the heads of the people who pay offering as a ritualistic practice. The lyrical, wave-like movement of the *chamara* and the physical gestures of the singers, along with folk and traditional dance and music of the *manjira*, *jhanj* and *khol*, afford a unique experience to the viewers. A house near the stage or even an adjacent hut can be appropriated as the *veshaghara*, from where performers take entry to the stage. The performers then do not leave the stage for the entire duration of the presentation. At times, separate groups perform on a single night one after another, imbuing a spirit of healthy competition—this is popularly known as 'Badi-Pala'. The

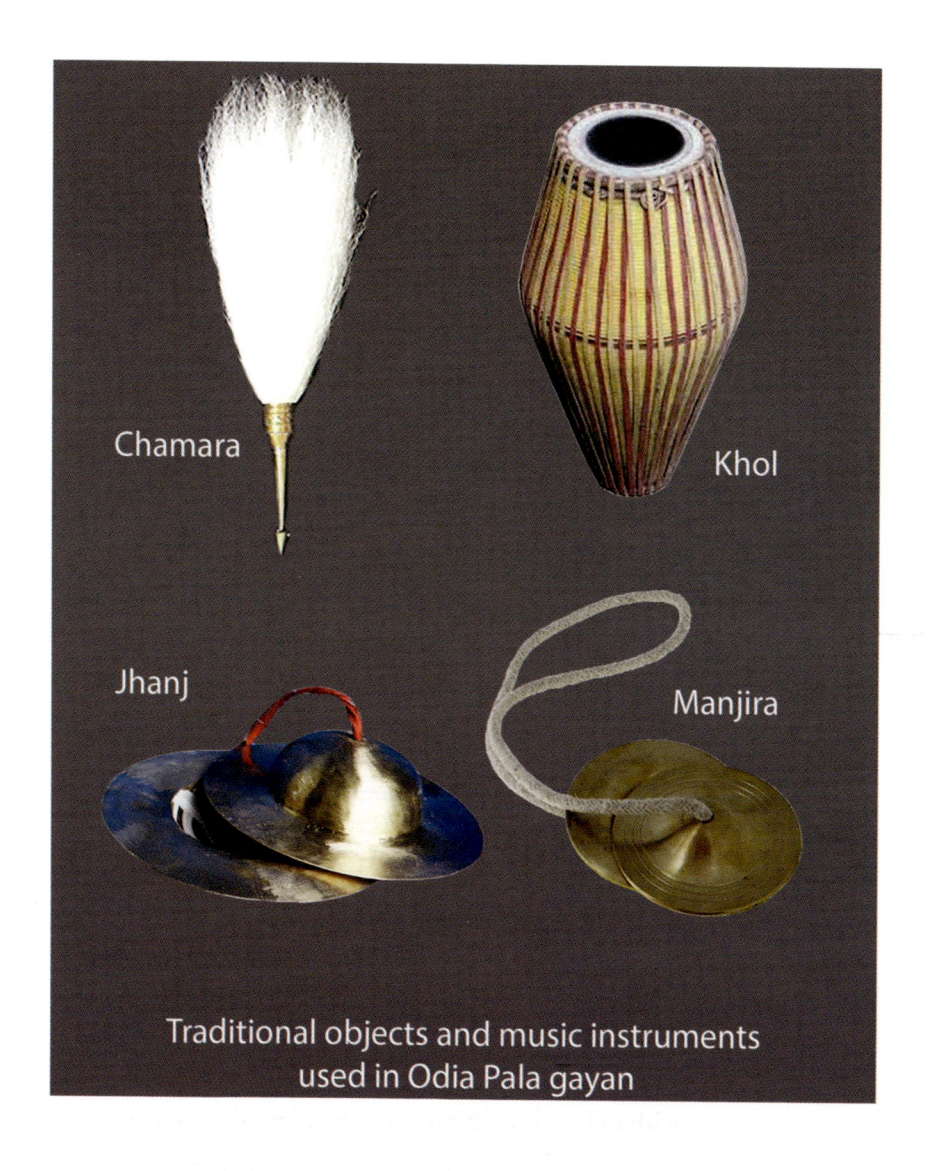

Traditional objects and music instruments used in Odia Pala gayan

contribution of Pala to society transcends mere entertainment. Going beyond that, it also helps educate and impart information to the masses by recounting folktales, social issues and seminal works of literature to the rural folk. Many medieval poems on morality and educational values are commonly recited by the performers of this art. This exposition

Ground plan of a traditional Pala stage

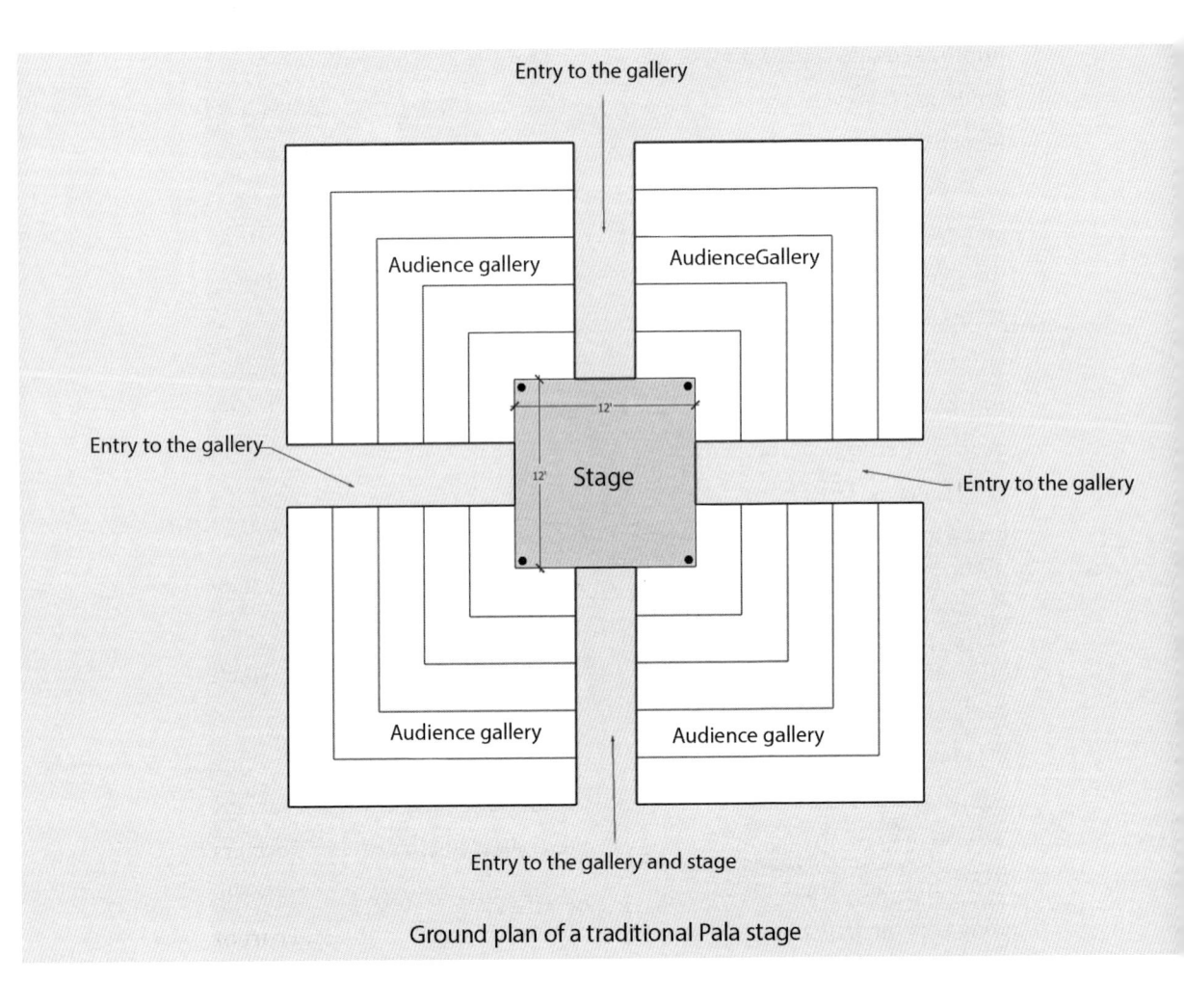

and exposure are perhaps the greatest contributions of Pala and other traditional forms of theatre to the world of culture.

RAMNAGAR KI RAMLILA: THE RAMLILA OF RAMNAGAR

Ramlila, a form of religious theatre dedicated to the retelling of the story of Lord Rama, is performed widely in India during the festival of Dussehra. This spectacular style of theatre is usually performed in an improvised open space temporarily created for the purpose, and comprises renderings of verses and cantos from the *Ramcharitmanas*. A number of painted sceneries are employed to portray the various locales of the play, which are changed in succession according to the scenes. Ramlila is generally presented for huge gatherings, who sometimes also participate in the performance. This ritualistic theatre is organised and celebrated with pomp and grandeur in various parts of India, particularly in the states of Uttar Pradesh, Delhi, Haryana, Himachal Pradesh, Uttarakhand, Bihar and Odisha. The celebration often continues for a number of days during the festive season. Nonetheless, the Ramlila of Ramnagar, popularly known as 'Ramnagar ki Ramlila', held in Varanasi, holds a distinct position in the performance history of the world.

The uniqueness of this festival lies in its style of presentation. The city of Ramnagar, situated on the eastern bank of the River Ganga, is converted into various locales depicted in the *Ramayana* for the performance, which continues for 31 days. The city palace, the sacred river, the roads and meadows, lakes and gardens, all are transformed into a huge stage for this unique presentation. The theatrical expanse of this ritualistic recital spreads over an area of 15 square kilometres, where the audience and performers move for each scene within this periphery—this progression is locally known as the Panchkoshi Yatra. The audience manifests an integral part of the performance by representing the collective of the citizens of Ayodhya, the kingdom of Rama. Ramnagar ki Ramlila is deemed to be the longest performance practice in the world by duration. Richard Schechner, author of the seminal *Performance Theory*, has conducted meticulous research on this age-old festival of Ramnagar and recounts his experience of this mythical observance:

> [...] Ramlila experience is a rich mix of texts: literary, dramatic, choreographic, ritual, religious, popular, musical, spatial, and temporal.

Photograph of a scene from Bharat milap, Ramalila of Ramnagar, Varanasi, India.
Courtesy: Vinay Rawal

The choreographic, spatial, and temporal texts concern me here. The crowds who attend the Ramlila join Rama on his journeys through the mythopoetic space of epic India. As they follow, they identify with Rama: Ramlila is not a theatre of make believe but of hyperreality.[iii]

The performance involves natural, environmental and artificial manifestations of the presentation. Participants explore natural habitats but also perform against artificial settings. Imparting clarity to the spatial composition of Ramnagar's Ramlila, Schechner further elucidates:

To the east is Sita's pleasure garden, 450 feet by 300 feet. In 1978 colorful birds were tethered to tree branches while a real deer grazed the grass next to one of papier-mâché (by 1988 the live deer was gone). A small, white Parvati temple completes the bucolic scene. On the west side of the road is King Janak's palace compound, 200 feet by 325 feet. Sita's garden is 'naturalistic,' while Janak's compound is pure theatrical convenience. The main structure is a moderate-sized temple where Sita sits. Three platforms of different heights fill out the environment. One is for Rama and Lakshman and their teacher, the sage Vishvamitra. Another is

Janak's royal residence where the wedding of Rama and Sita takes place. The third is for the *dhanushyajna*, the contest among princes testing who can lift Shiva's bow and win Sita's hand.[iv]

The Ramlila of Varanasi provides a metaphysical manifestation of myth in reality and vice versa. The entire setting becomes part of the stage, where reality and allegory merge to become one. Actors posit as deities and are worshipped by the local folk for a month. On the day Lord Rama is believed to have returned from exile to his palace, his wife Sita and brother Lakshman alongside; the locals decorate their houses with mango leaves and flowers and place oil lamps at their doorsteps to welcome him to the kingdom, recreating the ambience that is believed to have prevailed then in Ayodhya. The metamorphosis of Ramnagar into an environmental theatre, utilising the devices of reality, hyperreality and metaphor, makes this 185-year-old annual event a unique one in the performance culture of the world.

DHANU JATRA OF BARGARH, ODISHA

The Dhanu Jatra of Odisha, one of the largest open-air theatrical presentations in the world, is unique in many aespects. For instance, it constitutes the largest assembly of performers in a theatre space, with almost the entire population of Bargarh, a small town in the state of Odisha, and its nearby villages being cast. This ritualistic performance is enacted every year on the occasion of Makar Sankranti, during the month of Pausha (according to the Odia calendar), wherein the episode of 'Kansa-vadh', the killing of the demon Kansa, is enacted. In fact, it is an assemblage of several open-air theatres, the action taking place simultaneously at different locales. Consequently, the performers and spectators move from place to place as per the requirement of each scene. Nothing about the play in particular can be deemed unusual or extraordinary—Dhanu Jatra's uniqueness lies in its style of presentation and the wilful participation of the public, and that includes government servants, politicians, businessmen, as well as the common folk.

The play is comprised of three mythological episodes—Krishna-lila, Mathura Vijaya and Kansa-vadh. The age-old story of Lord Krishna vanquishing the tyrannical king Kansa of Mathura forms the central theme of Dhanu Jatra. According to the narrative, King Kansa, the maternal uncle of Lord Krishna, invites him and his brother Balarama to witness and participate in the festival of Dhanu Jatra being held in his

Still from the Dhanujatra festival at Baragarg, Odisha. Note the King Kansa is riding an elephant while traveling his kingdom, Mathura, during the festival. Courtesy: *The Indian Express*. Source: https://www.newindianexpress.com/states/odisha/2020/jan/10/kansas-kingdom-faces-elephant-loss-at-odishas-dhanu-yatra-2087554.html.

capital Mathura. However, Krishna pre-empts Kansa's evil designs behind the invitation and comes to Mathura to kill the tyrant, thus freeing his subjects from his perpetual oppression. The play thus comes to an end with Kansa's death. It is believed that the tradition of Dhanu Jatra began in 1948, just after Independence.

During this 11-day festival, Bargarh virtually transforms into the city of Mathura, the kingdom of Kansa, while the nearby Ambapalli village, located on the other side of the River Jeera, becomes Gopapura, the abode of Lord Krishna. The River Jeera, flowing between these two settlements, then becomes the River Yamuna during the performance. Vehicular traffic stands suspended inside Bargarh town for the entire period of the festival. The town administration and local apparatus are taken over by the tyrant king Kansa. Everyone in the town, irrespective of religion, caste, creed, gender or profession, becomes a subject of Kansa and abides by his rule. One can move freely inside the town but only on foot, while the king travels on a richly adorned elephant as the centre of attraction. This metaphysical exhibition continues for the duration of the festival. The play progresses as the king visits different parts of the town in the morning, and proceeds similarly till late at night, culminating in the 'ranga sabha', an improvised court for the king to pass judgement on his subjects. If the king finds someone guilty, the person is brought before him and fined on the spot, with the fine being doubled if the offender dares to argue. The money is collected with proper receipts and deposited in a public fund. Everyone is free to raise issues related to public interest in the 'ranga sabha'. The most interesting aspect of this performance lies in the cooperation of the local authorities and the public at large with the event. The extent of ecstasy prevalent among the people can be measured by the fact that King Kansa, riding an elephant, is escorted by the government police, who pose as the soldiers of the king during his morning peregrinations.

Scenography

The durbar hall of Kansa's *ranga sabha* is usually erected at a height of 8 to 10 feet inside the Dhanu Jatra field in Bargarh town. This royal court is lavishly decorated and equipped with proper lighting and sound systems. A few chairs are arranged below the stage for Kansa's courtiers—the government officers of Bargarh town. On the other side of the river, in Ambapalli village, Lord Krishna remains the centre of attraction. As the performance progresses, the birth of Krishna in prison, his childhood friendships with the cowherd boys of the village and his adolescent transgressions with the *gopangana* form the most spectacular sights. The story reaches its climax when Krishna, riding a beautifully decorated chariot with his brother Balarama, travels across the River Jeera and embarks on his final expedition to kill Kansa. Verses from the *Mathura Mangala*—a collection of poetry on this myth—are engraved on every wall of Ambapalli for the occasion, which is transformed into the mythical Gopapura during the festival.

The glorious cultural tradition of the region is showcased with full vigour during this ritualistic ceremony. It manifests distinctive Odia folk music and dramatic traditions like Champu and Chhanda. In the early days, actors used 'amitrakshar chhanda' in their impromptu dialogues and verses from the *Mathura Mangala*. Like other folk theatres of the country, Dhanu Jatra does not adhere to any formal text and relies rather on improvisation of an unpredicted context—a unique feature of this form of theatre.

People from far and wide come every year with great enthusiasm to participate in this ritual. Every household in the town brims with guests. This Jatra also provides an opportunity for commerce to the traders in and around the town. Men, women and children, dressed in the most colourful attire, roam about freely, adding lustre and gaiety to the atmosphere. Amusement parks, music concerts, medical camps, food stalls, etc. are temporarily installed in the town during the festival. The celebration is such that people belonging to different sects and religions enjoy this world-famous ritualistic theatre with equal gusto and fervour.

Dhanu Jatra is presented in perhaps the largest possible performance space, spanning up to 10 kilometres, with the entire town rejoicing and revelling in the festive atmosphere for 11 days. People eagerly await the arrival of King Kansa on his elephant and Lord Krishna on his horse-drawn chariot, forgetting the distinctions of caste, creed, class and colour; fostering a spirit of love and universal brotherhood.

PARSI THEATRE: CREATING TRADITION

Parsi theatre has been popular in India for more than a hundred years. Starting in the mid-19th century up until Independence, a number of Parsi theatre companies came up in the cities of Bombay and Calcutta and other towns like Lucknow, Varanasi, Kanpur, etc. These theatre companies were launched commercially by the Parsi diaspora in response to the emergence of English theatre houses in India. English theatre was introduced here by the British during the last decade of the 18th century and promptly grabbed the attention of the elite due to its unique presentation style. Ms Anita Singh, an Indian scholar and author, sheds some light on the practice of English theatre in India, particularly in the city of Calcutta:

> The early English settlers started a theatre for their own recreation and amusement, called the Play House (1753–56), in Lalbazar Street. This theatre was set up with the support of David Garrick (1719–79), a renowned London actor. However, it was destroyed during the siege of Calcutta in 1756 by Siraj-ud-Daulah (Nawab of Bengal 1733–57). Almost 19 years later, the New Play House or the Calcutta Theatre was built (1775–1808); it was called the New Play House to distinguish it from the 'old play house' of Lalbazar. […] For this theatre David Garrick sent a large number of painted scenes from London and an artist named Bernard Messink.[v]

It is well documented that the New Play House, at least to begin with, was staffed exclusively by the British and did not allow entry to Indians. Extravagant productions of the plays of William Shakespeare were presented in this theatre for the colonial elites. Plays such as *The Merchant of Venice*, *Richard III* and *Hamlet* were thus presented solely by English actors. After attaining much popularity in Calcutta, English theatre spread its wings in other British presidencies such as Bombay and Madras. Spectacular painted sceneries, assorted stage gimmicks and elaborate decorations were seen onstage as scenography gradually became an integral part of the performances. Theatre companies from Europe also periodically visited Calcutta, Bombay and Madras to perform in formal theatre houses or even in improvised spaces. The first theatre house in Bombay, the Grant Road Theatre, came up in 1844. In contrast to prevailing conventions, this theatre house was open to commoners and the general public as well.

Parsi theatre company called the Parsi Natak Mandali was established in Bombay in 1853, to produce plays in Urdu and Gujarati. Soon after, many new commercial theatres proliferated in Bombay and other parts of the country, such that by 1860, more than 20 theatre companies were operating in the city itself. These theatre companies would function as repertories, comprising a team of actors and actresses, stage technicians, scene painters and the director. It says a lot about the popularity of such theatres that the company owners managed to recover the money invested, along with a sizeable profit, just by selling tickets.

Scenography in the Parsi Theatre

The Parsi theatre incorporated three significant design aspects into its style of presentation—the use of painted sceneries, spectacular stage effects and elaborate costumes.

Performances were held in proscenium theatres with a grand curtain behind the arch separating the stage from the auditorium. This curtain was rolled up or parted to mark the opening of a play. Actors would perform in front of painted sceneries—each featuring a unique painted curtain. Parsi theatre thusly introduced efficient scene painters to Indian theatre who could create naturalistic visual effects on large canvases. The techniques of painted sceneries introduced by the British painters in India were skilfully adopted by these local artists. These sceneries manifested illusionistic reality, creating the apposite ambience for each performance. Magnificent paintings of palaces, streets, forests, courtyards, gardens, etc., along with appropriate costumes and make-up, became the primary attraction of Parsi theatre, succeeding in attracting large crowds. These painted sceneries were rolled up in sequence to reveal a new one for each scene, which became a unique feature of this style of presentation. The noted Indian scenographer Dr Nissar Allana thus states:

> Scene painters such as Anandrao and Baburao Mestry, Fatehlal, Damle, V.V. Divkar and P.S. Kale to name but a few, created unparalleled visual splendour, drawing inspiration from old monuments, temples and palaces, colonial architecture and Indian landscapes and cityscapes. Absorbing the techniques of western perspective painting, they used colour, line and stylization to create a new visual culture with an entirely urban sensibility.[vi]

Gradually, cut-scenes, extended scenes, net curtains and gauze curtains were introduced, adding further value to the scenography of Parsi plays. Painted cut-outs were also added as a design element, enabling actors to appear from and disappear behind them. In addition to the painted backdrop, painted wings were also placed on either side of the stage to create an illusion of depth and bestow a three-dimensional effect, placing the performers in the midst of the environment. For instance, if the painted backdrop exhibits the interior of a palace, the wings would be

A painted scenery of the jungle used in a play by Kolhapurkar Mandali in the year 1873. Painted by Mohan Rahul and P.S. Kale. The photograph is taken from the book *Painted Sceneries: Backdrops of the 19th Century Marathi Sangeet Natak*. Courtesy: Dr Nissar Allana.

painted as pillars to convert the entire stage into the palace. Sometimes, to establish the ambience of a jungle, the wings would be replaced with cut-outs of trees along with hanging foliage from the fly gallery. To add to the scenic visuals, cut-outs of trees were also placed on the stage, allowing the actors to interact with the set by hiding behind these trees or moving around them. The appearance and disappearance of actors, in full view of the audience, by using gauze and net curtains and double-gauze clothes created a sort of photographic illusion. Various special effects and illusions were realised using tricks and techniques following the conventions of medieval European drama. The spectacular disappearance of Sita into the earth, Hanuman flying across the sea to reach Lanka, the appearance of Lord Indra from behind the clouds, the flying entry of Vishnu on the back of Garuda, the killing of the demon Hiranyakashipu and other realistic effects like gunfire, rain, earthquakes, flowing rivers, etc. were the major spectacles of Parsi theatre.

Prof. M.N. Sharma, a scholar and theoretician of Telugu theatre, further elucidates:

> Audience were especially thrilled by spectacular scenes: Gods descending from heavens, demons descending into earth, beds flown into air, broken bridges fall into seas and so on. Such 'trick' scenes were the main attraction for the common people. In a play like *Inder Sabha* by Ananth, each angel came into Indra's court with great aplomb and flood of light to the wonderment of the audience.
>
> Usually there were 14 to 15 curtains that depicted different locales. The drop scene usually contained scenery painted on it. A street scene worked as a general scene. Several 'cut scenes' formed part of the general background, especially in the forest scenes. Big fighting scenes were advertised specially and drew crowds. The performance space was usually 60' (width) and 40' (depth) with an addition of 10' of wing space. Painted curtains dropped from pulleys, served as background to each scene.[vii]

During scene changes, to hold the attention of the audience, comic interludes were presented. The comic characters would create humour through songs and dialogue in front of a painted scenery—often a street scene—on the downstage while stagehands prepared the set for the next scene behind the curtain. Comic interludes were introduced as sceneries and sets had become increasingly intricate, taking longer to set up. The play used to resume with the blow of a whistle from the wings.

Influenced by the popularity of Parsi theatre, many commercial theatre companies started emerging in the smaller towns and cities. Improvising on the Parsi theatre, these companies preferred travelling from one place to another with all requisite paraphernalia to perform plays for the masses in local languages. The Gubbi Veeranna Nataka Company in Karnataka, the Annapurna A and B theatres and the Janta Rangmanch in Puri and Cuttack respectively in Odisha, the Maharashtra Natak Mandali in Bombay, the Surabhi Nataka Kala Sangam in Andhra Pradesh, etc. adopted the techniques of Parsi theatre and performed regularly for years, such that a few of them are still active.

> Parsi theatre had flourished under the influence of English theatre, supplanting it to become the most popular source of entertainment and remaining so for decades. It is accredited with introducing female actors to the modern Indian theatre. Apart from translating Shakespeare into various Indian languages—Urdu, Hindi, Marathi, and Gujarati—plays based on local folklore were also performed widely by these companies. Playwrights and actors such as Nawab Wajid Ali Shah (1822–1887), Agha Hashar Kashmiri (1879–1935), Radheshyam Kathavachak (1890–1963), Sohrab Modi (1897–1984), Master Fida Husain 'Narsi' (1899–1999), Prithviraj Kapoor (1906–1972), and many other exponents of Parsi theatre achieved great fame in their respective fields. Plays like *Rustam-o-Sohrab*, *Indra Sabha*, *Sultan Razia*, *Shahjahan*, *Laila-Majnu*, *Mashreeki Hoor*, etc. set the trend in Indian playwriting during the colonial period. However, slowly but steadily, newer mediums of entertainment detracted from the popularity of theatre. Most actors and playwrights of Parsi theatre migrated to Hindi cinema in the beginning of the 20th century. Moreover, many influential Indian theatre personalities such

as Bharatendu Harishchandra and Jaishankar Prasad rejected Parsi theatre outright, maintaining that it was not Indian theatre at its core. Consequently, the curtain fell on this 100-year-old legacy just after Independence. However, the influence of Parsi drama on Indian cinema was quite pronounced, especially between 1950 and 1970.[viii]

SURABHI THEATRE: ILLUSIONISTIC DRAMA LIVES ON

The Surabhi Nataka Mandali is a popular theatre company that has been actively engaged in the practice ever since it spread its roots in colonial India. The troupe is highly popular in both the rural and urban areas of the Andhra region. Regarded as the oldest surviving professional repertory of the country, Surabhi has travelled worldwide and been entertaining people for more than 135 years, wooing audiences with their spectacular productions and visual effects. Their first production of *Kichakvadha* (1885)—the killing of Kichaka—was performed by the family of one Vanarasa Govinda Rao, a Marathi Kshatriya belonging to the village of Surabhi in Cuddapah (now Kadapa) district of Andhra Pradesh.

The family of Govinda Rao had been in the profession of *Tholu bommalata* or shadow puppetry, and would travel from village to village holding performances, before eventually adopting theatre and forming the Surabhi Nataka Mandali. Today, the clan has branched out and segregated into several theatre groups, with each claiming to be the 'Surabhi Theatre'. Out of the many Surabhi groups, around five hold regular performances following the tricks and techniques of their ancestors. A few are based in permanent theatres while others travel round the year, performing in the region and nearby states. The most famous among these troupes is the Sri Venkateswara Natya Mandali, established in 1937 by Smt. Subhadramma with the help of her husband, Sri Rekandar China Venkata Rao. Now headed by Sri Nageswara Rao 'Babji', the company has been continuously presenting plays, both old and new, in Hyderabad since its inception.

Scenography in Surabhi

In its initial days, the Surabhi theatre presented only *padya natakam* (classical Telugu verse drama) but gradually adopted various stage techniques under the influence of Parsi theatre. The use of painted sceneries on a proscenium stage and spectacular stage gimmicks, etc. were incorporated into the repertoire and soon became synonymous with this commercial company. The Surabhi theatre companies usually perform in their own permanent theatres these days, but, while on tour, have to depend on temporary stage sets and constructions.

The Venkateswara Natya Mandali utilises an improvised proscenium stage with a rectangular space of 60 feet in length and 45 feet in width, including the wings and the backstage area. The height of the stage is around 3.5 feet while the proscenium opening is kept unusually low at

A scene from the play *Mayabazar*. Produced by: Sri Venkateshwar Natya Mandali, Surabhi, Hyderabad. Directed by: R. Nageshwar Rao (Surabhi-Babji). Courtesy: Babji, Surabhi, Hyderabad.

10 feet when compared to other theatres. The fly gallery, the space above the stage, is an important constituent of the Surabhi style of theatre. Having an approximate height of 20 feet, the fly gallery is used to store the myriad painted sceneries, different types of lights, curtain bars, pulleys, rows of microphones and other technical equipment similar to that of Parsi theatre. In a performance, each scene features a unique painted backdrop—a curtain is rolled down to the stage with the help of bamboo poles for a given scene and is rolled back up for storage in the fly gallery right after—to add to the visual grandeur of the presentation.

A *bhugruham* or stage pit with dimensions of 6 feet by 3 feet is an essential element of 'Surabhi drama'. This pit facilitates the presentation of gimmick scenes such as the appearance of demons or ghosts from hell, or the disappearance of Sita into Mother Earth. The portrayal of supernatural characters such as ghosts, gods, demons, various flying creatures, etc. is a regular practice in this theatre—a clear descendant of medieval European practices introduced in India by English theatre companies in the 18th century. To specify an instance of the use of *bhugruham*, Prof. M.N. Sharma narrates: 'It is from this pit devils or angels suddenly appear and disappear. Two important examples may be mentioned here: Bali Chakravarthy is crushed into the earth by Vamana when Bali goes down the pit. Similarly, the "Yagna Purusha" gives divine nectar to Dasaradha emerging out of this pit.'[ix] Similar to Parsi theatre, in Surabhi, the painted sceneries are skilfully crafted with realistic detailing, maintaining the principles of perspective, by the family painters. The wings and borders are also painted as extensions of the scenes, and to provide an additional dimension and depth to the stage. Sometimes cut-scenes and double-scenes are used to represent two different locales simultaneously (a concept already discussed in Parsi theatre). As many as 15 separate sceneries may be used in a play subject to the requirements of the script. Stage gimmicks such as fireworks, rain effects, the play of real animals and birds onstage, fighting tricks, flying objects and actors, the sudden appearance and disappearance of characters to and from the stage, the use of large stage props, etc. have ensured that Surabhi drama remains a distinctive source of entertainment among the masses even today.

The Surabhi theatre companies have produced innumerable spectacular plays over the years and are continuously engaged in entertaining audiences across the country. Some of the popular plays presented by the Venkateswara Natya Mandali that have been running for decades are *Sri Krishna Leelalu, Jai Pathala Bhairavi, Lavakusa, Maya Bazar, Veera Brahmam Gari Charitra*, etc.

Attempt at Mainstream Theatre

Initiatives have been taken in the recent past to introduce Surabhi to mainstream theatre. In 1996, B.V. Karanth, former director of the National School of Drama (NSD), tried to work with the Sri Venkateswara Natya Mandali in order to introduce contemporary sensibilities to Surabhi actors. With the support of NSD, Karanth directed D.L. Roy's *Bhishma* in 1995 to this end. He followed it up with productions of *Chandi Priya* (1997) and *Basti Devatha Yadamma* (1998), the latter a Telugu adaptation of Brecht's *The Good Woman of Setzuan*. Attempts were also made to incorporate modern stage techniques into these productions. The use of stage spectacles and painted sceneries as well as the melodramatic performance style were considerably toned down, employing instead symbolic three-dimensional designs and contemporary acting styles. However, these endeavours proved futile and impractical as neither the spectators nor the actors could accept such drastic changes. The performers as well as the patrons were so accustomed to the Surabhi style of presentation that these modern plays did little to fulfil their artistic appetite, and were eventually dropped from the repertoire. Sharing an unusual experience from the production of *Bhishma* with the company, Karanth narrates:

> Taking into consideration the talents, style and experience of the Surabhi troupe, I choose the play *Bhishma* by D. L Roy. A local scholar translated it into Telugu. The company at that time was camping in a village. I got the play rehearsed in the NSD style. Though the play and its language were good, the players didn't like it. It was difficult for a Company which had performed in an orthodox style for hundreds of years to change its style all at once.[x]

Surabhi continues to present its old productions in its own unique way with the same popularity it has always enjoyed.

BHRAMYAMAN RANGMANCHA: THE MOBILE THEATRE OF ASSAM

Bhramyaman Rangmancha is one of the most popular theatre forms of the North-east region and has been ubiquitous in the entertainment business for the last 50 years. Despite having a few similarities with the Jatra of Bengal and Odisha, Bhramyaman Rangmancha lays more emphasis on the use of modern technology, stage tricks and scenography. The shows are held in proscenium theatres created each time for the purpose. Unlike Parsi theatre and Surabhi drama, this mobile theatre of Assam never employed painted curtains as backdrops; rather, it incorporates three-dimensional set units such as platforms, flats, doors and windows, sofas and other furniture, and many other realistic stage props in its presentations. Plays based on historical and mythological stories are rarely found in the repertoire. Instead, nuanced family dramas and stories from popular cinema are preferred. Dramatic adaptations of movies such as *Jurassic Park*, *Anaconda*, *Sholay*, *Bandit Queen*, *Titanic*, etc. are regularly presented to thousands of spectators with much appreciation and success.

There exist more than 20 mobile theatre companies that hold regular performances in the towns and remote villages of Assam, ferrying with

A scene from a mobile theatre performance. Courtesy: Robijita Gogoi.

them all the paraphernalia of their craft including truckloads of stage equipment, generators, chairs and tent materials, etc. These groups, fully self-sufficient, assemble a temporary marquee in a large open space near a town or village for each presentation, where attendance usually varies from 2000 to 4000 people. The use of two separate proscenium stages is quite common in mobile theatres—such a set-up facilitates a quick change of scenes and the two can also be joined to form a single unit if a play so demands. Almost all of these mobile theatre companies travel with additional stage units; while a performance is in progress in one locality, an advance party sets up the stage at the next venue for the subsequent presentation.

A typical mobile theatre company consists of 75–150 personnel including professional artistes, technicians, stagehands, musicians, electricians and cook. These companies usually begin their tour towards the end of August, just after the monsoons, and hold presentations each night till mid-April the following year. The troupes return home at the onset of summer to prepare new productions for the coming season. Statistically speaking, each company performs at about 60 different venues in a year with three distinct productions in its repertoire. Thus, the average number of shows credited to a company per annum is around 180.

Scenography in Bhramyaman Rangamancha
Mobile theatre companies depend solely on audience response for their survival. As such, their performances are defined by the use of latest technologies in lighting, sound systems and multimedia devices, as well as costumes and props of the latest trend. The presence of actors from the regional film industry further adds to its popularity.

The mobile stage is a kind of proscenium structure with a height of about 5 feet and spanning almost 60 feet in length and breadth. The space is separated into two stages by a curtain in the middle, such that the stages can be operated one after another or even simultaneously depending on the requirements. Quite often, while one stage is being utilised for a performance, the other is prepared for the next scene. The visual axis of the audience thus changes for each scene with shifting of the lights from one stage to the other. Sets are usually elaborate and naturalistic, requiring a large performance area. Stage and sound effects, gimmicks and lighting serve as the centre of attraction, and are executed so convincingly that spectators are immersed into the world of fictitious reality. Skilled technicians rapidly change the set, leaving no time for the audience to ponder on the illusion.

In this age of technology, new media and captivating lighting effects make the technicians' work easier. Through spectacular visuals such as smoke, fire and water, as also lights that change colours, stroboscopic effects and the application of multimedia projections, mobile drama becomes alluring. Everything in the performance follows a rhythmic order, including the actors, music, lights, sets, props, supporting technologies and audio-visual mediums. Such theatrical spectacles create the impression of watching live three-dimensional cinema—perhaps the prime reason behind the wide acceptance and popularity of the mobile theatre of Assam.

The Experience of Watching Mobile Theatre

The surrealistic spectacle of the mobile theatre of Assam leaves spectators under a spell and forces them to frequent these presentations. I, too, have had a similar experience of watching a mobile play that left me spellbound. At Sivasagar in northern Assam in the year 2000, I had the chance to explore first hand this world of fantasy in the play *Anaconda*, where a life-sized Anaconda seemed to emerge from a deep river, grabbed a man from a moving steamer, dragged him into the water, swallowed him and vanished into the deep blue waters. A realistic boat-like object, blue waters with fast currents and a big snake were revealed in front of my eyes in a moment of shock and awe. This sense of wonder was further enhanced by other spectacles such as car crashes, burning houses and the like. When the show came to an end, I examined the stage to try and understand the techniques involved in effecting such gimmicks. Honestly, I was unable to trace much; just some wooden sets of a motor launch, a pile of polythene, some wooden cut-outs of houses, a wooden motorcar and a huge snake puppet. I could not figure out how they executed such spectacular illusions, and the troupe itself was obviously unwilling to reveal their stage tricks. I did notice a large cavity between the rear edge of the stage and the cyclorama. This space may have been used to manually manipulate polythene strips to create the impression of a flowing river and the huge snake. I could ascertain that the steamer was moved along the rear edge of the stage while water ripples were projected on the cyclorama. Nonetheless, I still can't fathom how the naturalistic effect of fire and burning houses was created. Certainly, the scenic visuals and stage craft techniques of mobile theatre is a complicated exercise.

Photograph of a mobile theatre camp. The temporary theatre construction in a tent-like arrangement at Shivsagar, Uppar Assam. Courtesy: Author's personal collection.

SCENOGRAPHY IN INDIAN FOLK CULTURES: A TRADITION OF COLOURS

India is a land of diverse socio-cultural expressions and multi-coloured lifestyles. The celebration of life is evident in its various endeavours and traditions. The country has been bestowed with innumerable natural bounties—mountains, rivers, seas, deserts, forests, etc. India is also the birthplace of a number of religions, sects and ideologies. It has witnessed the tyranny of foreign invaders from the inception of civilisation. Cross-cultural migrations and invading forces brought diversity to the erstwhile Indian society. Gradually, Sanskrit emerged as the predominant language that defined the socio-cultural ethos of the region and was considered divine.

Epics like the Vedas, Upanishads, Puranas and the *Ramayana* and *Mahabharata* were written and practised by the people of this land. Numerous rishis, yogis and sadhus took birth here and set the standard for a value-based lifestyle. Spiritualism, or the search for the supreme, came to be the ultimate truth for humanity. The fragrance of 'the truth of life' crossed the boundaries of this subcontinent and spread round the world. People from all parts of the globe assembled here to comprehend the philosophy and meaning of life. India, thus, emerged as the de facto cultural and philosophical centre of the world.

The influence of Indian philosophy and spiritualism leads its people to grasp life as *maya*, an illusion, and the fact that the 'eternal truth' can only be realised when one's soul meets the supreme. This belief became the primary motivation behind considering life as a blissful journey that is to be spent in search of the supreme soul, the result of which is the celebration of life—a celebration of this journey. Indian art and culture strongly manifest this belief. This ambience of celebration and festivity is synonymous with scenography in Indian folk and popular theatres. A performance is treated as 'ranga' (colour) and the performance space as 'rangmancha'—a place where all the colours of life are reflected.

Though Indian philosophy has determined the character of all performance cultures in the country, each of these forms is different from the other and complete in itself. The variety in India's performance traditions is articulated through its diversity of languages, customs, rituals, etc. In other words, Indian folk and traditional theatres are known for their varied colours and regional flavours. This diversity in popular art forms stems from the contrasting attitudes of the people—a direct extension of varying cultural ethos and differing social outlooks. Geography, ecology and the prevalent socio-cultural milieu of a region bestow the local performance arts with a unique character. The influence of political factors, though undeniable, remains secondary.

A popular folk adage thus states:

> 'The river decides the boundaries...
> The mountain decides the temperament...'

The above aphorism rightly implies that the social behaviour of people has invariably been influenced and moulded by the natural environment around them, which, in turn, has shaped the prevalent performance styles. From the vales of the North East to the Western Ghats, from the Himalayas in the north to the southern peninsula, India has been blessed with a long coastline, majestic mountain ranges, a multitude of rivers, vast deserts, dense forests, etc. These geographical features have played a vital role in shaping Indian life and art, so much so that each microsite contains a unique culture and language. Art forms that were begotten in the plains, developed with the changing lifestyles of the particular region and its vicinities, and the perennial influence of festivals, religions and urbanisation. Comparatively, fewer changes are marked in the arts that originated and evolved in the isolated mountain regions.

Art forms that developed in the plains and near rivers propagated freely and became part of mainstream Indian culture. The theatre culture of this region

Photograph of a mask maker with a tiger mask prepared for a play at Raghurajpur heritage art village, Puri, Odisha. Courtesy: Author's personal collection.

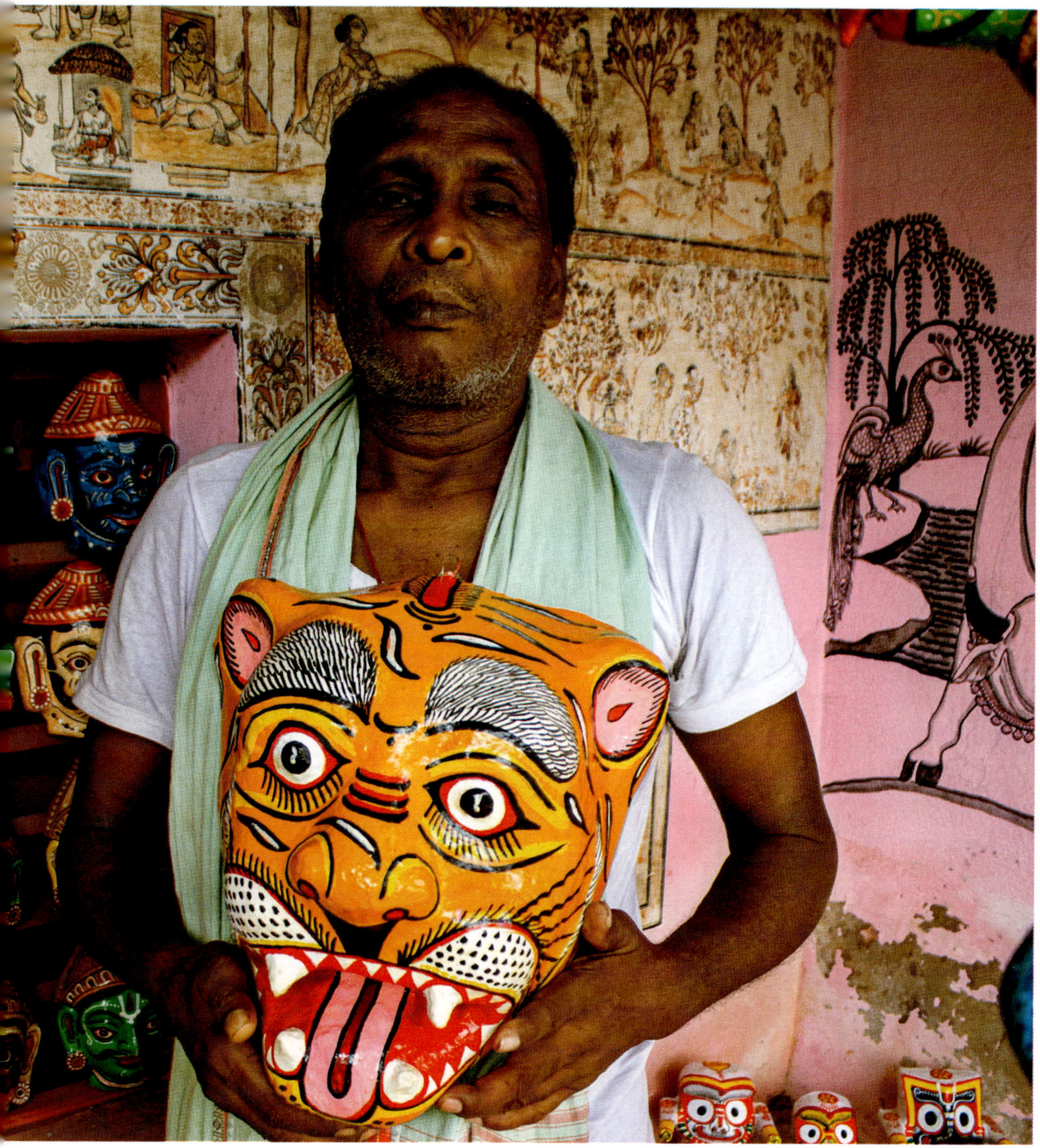

can thus be categorised as 'lokadharmi'—non-stylised people's theatre. For instance, the multifarious hues of village life are reflected in these forms and dictate their scenic visuals. Whether it is Ramlila or Krishnalila, *Nautanki* or *Khayal*, the celebratory mood created by music and songs generates the desired imagery and ambience. A few powerful visual elements developed in these indigenous folk theatres have been successfully adapted into the modern context of scenography. For example, the concept of object theatre[1] has been derived from folk puppet performances like Sandha Ladhai, Kachighodi, Kela-Keluni, Sakhi-Kundhei and Kathputli naach, wherein larger-than-life puppets are rallied for presentations in festivals such as Dussehra, Holi, Diwali and other celebrations. Sometimes handled by several persons, these large puppets are visible from long distances and easily attract viewers.

Nature itself sometimes contradicts the scenic visuals in art. We are able to examine a different dimension of picturesque beauty in the folk and traditional performing arts of the deserts. To our superficial observation, the desert may look monotonous—landscapes following a single rhythm with yellowish-brown colour tones. However, deeper study reveals another aspect of the land that is manifested in its various hues and forms. The folk arts and performance cultures of the people of the desert are particularly colourful and bright, perhaps in order to balance the monotony of nature. The magnificence of Kathputli naach, the puppet theatre of Rajasthan, lies in its use of a myriad colours and music. Similarly, other performance forms of the desert, such as Kalbelia, khayal and Dhola-Maru, are recognised for their splendidly colourful attires, delightful headgears and other accessories.

The performance style adopted by the people of the mountains is in complete contrast to that of the plains. Art forms fostered in the mountains are distinct and unique in themselves since they have developed in isolation.

---

[1] These performances mainly rely on large-sized puppets, masks and properties.

They are also ritualistic in nature. With the assimilation of supernatural characters like demons, ghosts and deities, local art forms represent the cultural ethos of the mountains. The use of large colourful stylised masks is a common practice of the people in the hills, with the masks of animals and birds commonly used by the central characters in presentations of these folk-tribal forms. For instance, in Purulia Chhau dance[2], one can observe the preponderance of supernatural characters in the form of gods and goddesses, demons, birds and animals in the performances. The mellifluous movements of the tribal performers complete the desired visual effect. Masks of animals and birds used in the presentation of Bhand Pather, a theatre form of the Kashmir valley, and the Cham Dance of Ladakh represent the raw and dynamic energy of nature. The natural chiaroscuro of the forests is reflected in art forms by way of the colours and the movement of lines in the design—choreography, costumes, makeup, masks, etc. Application of contrast colours with conical and triangular shapes is a common characteristic of tribal arts.

If one travels towards the Southern peninsula, one can observe a dramatic change in the socio-cultural milieu along with the changing geography and ecological conditions of the region. The visual aspects of the performing arts of South India are dominated by bright colours and wavy-circular lines. This repetitive circular rhythm is also traceable in their literary texts and performances. Long verses and poetic renderings of texts from the Indian epics, together with the wavy bodily movements of the performers and exaggerated costumes and makeup, create the scenic aesthetics of the local theatre forms. The ocean dominates the lives of the people in the southern peninsula and the same is reflected in the conception of their art forms. Tides and waves served as the primary sources of inspiration behind these art forms, making them highly stylised

---

2   Purulia Chhau is one of the three variants of Chhau dance practised in the border regions of the states of Bengal and Jharkhand. It is an amalgamation of folk and tribal theatre.

and manifesting the varied moods of nature typical of these coastal forms. These characteristics are apparent in the local performance art forms, such as Therukoothu, Yakshagana, Theyyam, and even in the classical dances such as Kathakali and Mohiniattam.

CONCLUSION

Indian theatre remains performance-oriented—visual imageries serve only as a symbolic representation of the text and human emotions. While classical Indian theatre avoids exaggeration and loudness in its presentation style, folk and traditional forms are defined by the use of music, a variety of stylistic elements, bright colours, bold lines and exaggerated movements. Utilising costumes, masks, makeup, headgear and other visual elements, rural art forms have been providing freshness and joy to the populace from time immemorial.

Unfortunately, the modern world is slowly but steadily moving away from this cultural milieu. Urbanisation and globalisation are bleaching us of our native colours, resulting in the loss and decay of a number of our folk and traditional art forms in the recent past. However, one should keep in mind that these native cultures are what make India unique. Folk theatre has helped expand the creative scope of artistes and designers through the ages, and should be fostered and preserved for this very reason.

References

i Das, Sisir Kumar. 2005. *A History of Indian Literature, 500-1399: From Courtly to the Popular.* New Delhi: Sahitya Akademi. p. 68.
ii Brown, John Russell. 2001. *New Sites for Shakespeare: Theatre, the Audience, and Asia.* London: Routledge. p. 20.
iii Schechner, Richard. 1995. *The Future of Ritual: Writings on Culture and Performance.* London: Routledge. p. 133.
iv ibid. p. 150.
v Singh, Anita, Matthew Isaac Cohen, Maki Isaka, Siyuan Liu. 2016. 'The beginning of spoken theatre in Asia'. *Routledge Handbook of Asian Theatre.* Oxford and New York: Routledge. p. 394.

vi   Allana, Nissar. 2008. *Painted Sceneries: Backdrops of the 19th Century Marathi Sangeet Natak.* New Delhi: Theatre and Television Associates. p. 10.

vii   Sarma, M. Nagabhushan. 2009. *The Surabhi Theatre of Andhra: A Living Legend.* Hyderabad: Ranga Sampada Publication. p. 12

viii Ibid. p. 166.

ix   Sarma, M. Nagabhushan. 2009. *The Surabhi Theatre of Andhra: A Living Legend.* Hyderabad: Ranga Sampada Publication. p. 166.

x   Karanth. B. V., Vaidehi. 2012. *Here, I cannot Stay; There, I cannot Go: Autobiography of B.V. Karanth as Told to Vaidehi.* New Delhi: National School of Drama. p. 346.

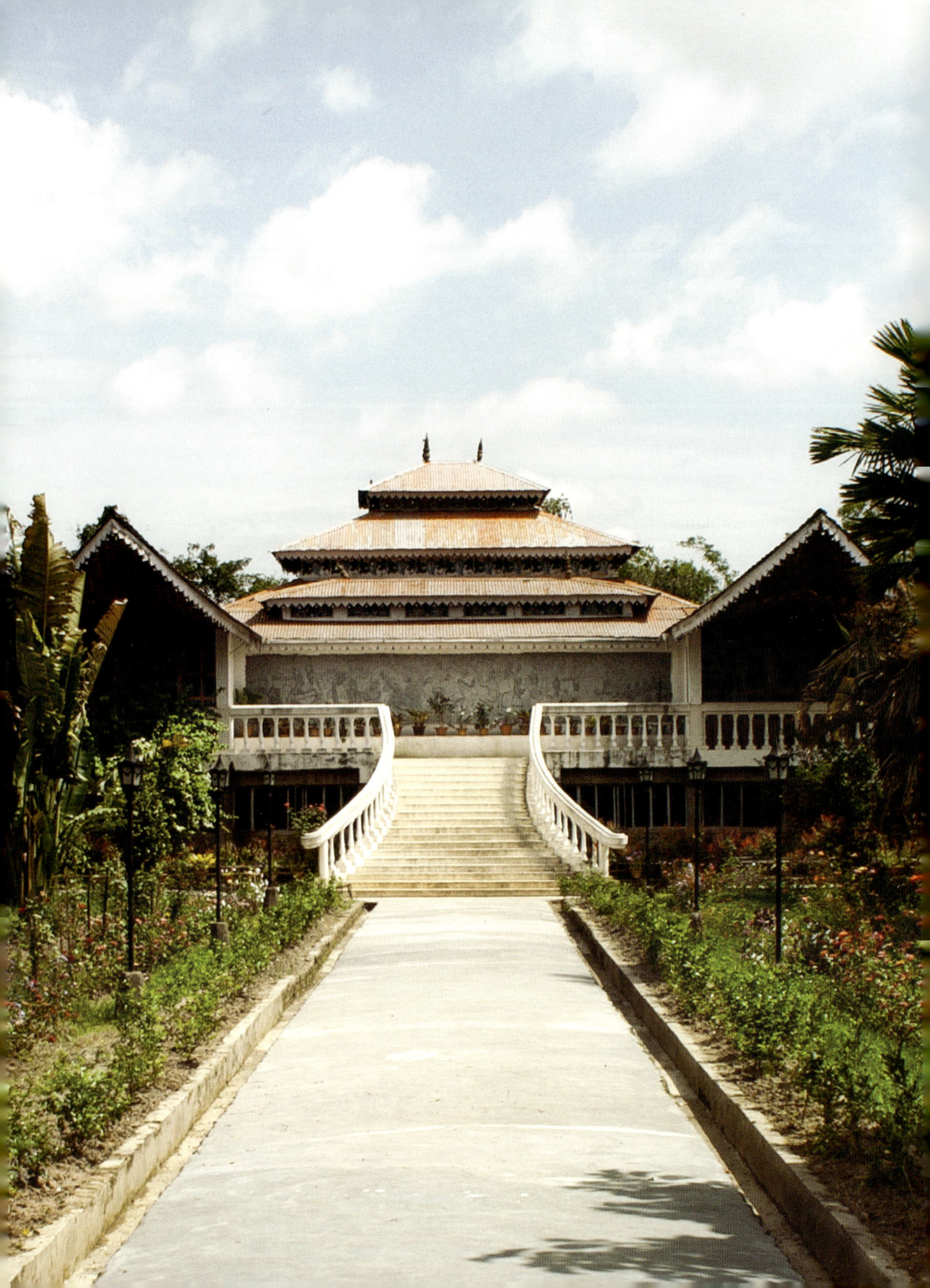

CONVENTIONS OF SPACE

THE DICHOTOMY OF SPACE

Manipulation of the available performance space has always been challenging for scenographers. Space functions as a launch pad for interpretative design and helps elevate the potential of a performance. It is regularly observed that an innovative design falls into disarray if the working space is not appropriate or functional. Spatial compositions, visual aesthetics, actors' engagement with the space and above all, the director's interpretation largely depend on the performance space—the acting space, wings, audience gallery and backstage area form the backbone of a successful presentation. Therefore, in order to create a proportionate design, scenographers usually collect the ground plan and layout design of the theatre where the performance is to be presented, before starting the design works for the play. As every performance space has its own identity, and is distinct from another, a design conceived for a particular space may not produce the same results in a different space with contrasting characteristic. For instance, the proscenium design may not be appropriate for an open-air theatre, or a play prepared for a thrust stage may not be suitable for an arena space. Scenographers are thus required to modify and rework the design plan separately for each performance space. While working on a play, scenographers try to blend the architectural nuances of the space with the presentation's design so as to create harmony. However, the performance space is a functional area that actors inhabit. Patrice Pavis hence argues:

> On one hand, stage space is determined by the type of stage design and its visualization by the director in his reading of the *dramatic space*. On the other hand, however, the stage designer and director have quite a bit of room for manoeuvre to shape it as they wish. This dialectics between determinism and freedom gives rise to the particular stage space used in performance, which is why it has often been noted that space mediates between dramatic vision and stage realization.[i]

It has already been discussed in the previous chapters that theatre is the oldest known communal activity and was being practised much before civilisation came into existence, for example, the hunting dance and primitive theatre, etc. These activities and rituals were performed in improvised spaces like the open area in front of caves, the dwelling space of tribes then, where folks would encircle the performance space to witness such activities. Even today, as a common practice, any improvised space used for local entertainment displays—snake-charming, magic shows, monkey dances, acrobatics, etc.—assumes a 'circular' form along the lines of primitive theatre. In a nutshell, these informal theatrical practices are likely to be improvised from time to time depending on the available space, audience and performers.

However, in the context of a conventional performance space, the possibility of improvisation is limited since the performers as well as the audience more or less adhere to the defined areas. The style of presentation is thus contingent upon the distance between the audience gallery and the performance area, as well as the size of the audience. As we are aware, the Greek and Roman theatres featured large open-air performance spaces with huge gatherings of spectators. As such, these presentations were exaggerated and highly stylised. Performers had to adopt theatrical devices such as masks, costumes, chorus and larger-than-life gestures, and use elevated stages to effectively interact with the audience. Incorporation of these theatrical devices meant that the Greek and Roman performance styles evolved into specific stylised art forms.

Conversely, Indian classical theatre could not adapt to a performance style suitable for presentation to a large audience in an open space. Plays were performed in enclosed spaces for specific audiences. Intimacy with the space and sensibility of the art determined the style of presentation, i.e. intricate, lyrical, symbolic or abstract with higher aesthetics. The motion of the actors, their gestures and postures—subtle, delicate and refined—thus elevated Indian theatre to the stature of fine art. In classical Indian theatre, the performance space would be transformed into various locales through stylised and ritualistic movements, commonly referred to as 'Parikramana' of the performers. With the help of a 'yavanika' (curtain), the space was made to change its identity in front of the audience. Contemporary scenography needs to realise this inherent ambiguity of space and its allegorical transformation during a presentation. The transformation of theatrical space in the Indian performance tradition can be comprehended through the following mythical tale. In *Shiv Purana* it is mentioned:

> When Siva and Parvati could not decide who between their sons should be married first, they called the boys together and told them that, as they loved them equally, they could not decide this problem. They suggested, however, that they had devised a noble plan to settle the matter. He who would make the full round of the earth first would also be the first to get married.
>
> Although Ganesh, like his brother, agreed to the condition, this competition was not to his liking. Because of his heavy size and the mouse as his mount, he was not likely to win the contest against Kartikeya who had a fine body and the peacock as his mount. While Kartikeya started

out immediately and began his travel round the world, Ganesha remained at home wondering what to do. At last, the solution occurred to him. He took the ceremonial bath and asked his parents to sit on their thrones while he worshipped them. On being reminded about the contest by his parents, Ganesh shrewdly answered that he has encircled the earth. On being asked how, he replied, taking recourse of the spiritual assertion, that parents formed the entire creation for the progeny. His going round the parents was tantamount to his encircling the entire earth. His parents found his argument quite convincing and arranged for his marriage to the two daughters of the Praja-pati Riddhi and Siddhi.[ii]

Ganesha, through the power of his imagination, transforms the physical space into a metaphoric one by placing Lord Siva at the centre. The above-mentioned story interprets 'space' from an entirely different perspective than usual by positing the following concepts:

i. Understanding of space in the Indian context markedly differs from that in the West.
ii. Time and space may be considered separately according to the needs of the situation.
iii. In the Indian context, greater emphasis is placed on metaphorical space than real space.
iv. 'Space' is an abstract phenomenon that can easily be transformed into any reality through symbolic gestures.

Theatrical space can only be realised after thoroughly understanding the intricacies of the above-mentioned perspective. A dramatic space is devised by the composition of actors and visual accoutrements along with the text or script. These are necessary to enable the appropriate interpretation of the spatial environment in a play.

Irrespective of its physical and metaphorical nature, the performance spaces, in general, can be categorised into two distinctive types: interior space and exterior space. Both the kinds have their own identity and purpose. Let us have a systematic understanding of two conventional theatre spaces: the interior performance space—proscenium theatre and the other space—open-air theatre.

CONCEPTION OF A FRAMED SPACE: THE PROSCENIUM THEATRE

The proscenium stage—an interior performance space, better known as the framed space—brings a sense of order to a performance and its visual aesthetics. With a formal distribution of space, and a balanced spatial order, the proscenium theatre has revolutionised world theatre. This kind of spatial arrangement in a proscenium was primarily developed in Europe in the beginning of the 17th century to entertain the royal guests. It garnered wide acceptance over time and was adopted across different cultures. Teatro Farnese is considered as the first proscenium theatre, designed by the famous Italian architect Giovanni Battista Aleotti (1546–1636) in 1618 in the province of Parma in Italy.

Towards the end of the 19th century, Richard Wagner[1] transformed theatre with the help of other stage designers and architects, namely Gottfried Semper, Wilhelm Neumann, Otto Bruckwald and Adolphe Appia. These visionaries built an opera house at Bayreuth[2], Germany, exclusively for the productions of Richard Wagner. This proscenium

---

1 Wilhelm Richard Wagner (1813–1883) was a German composer, conductor, theatre director and polemicist who is known primarily for his operas.

2 The Bayreuth Festspielhaus or Bayreuth Festival Theatre was built between 1872 and 1876 by the architect Otto Brückwald in accordance with Richard Wagner's specifications. The construction fulfils Wagner's primary demands—an effective structure without ornamentation, a lowered orchestra pit that remains concealed and an amphitheatre-like auditorium without box seats, balconies or a tent roof.

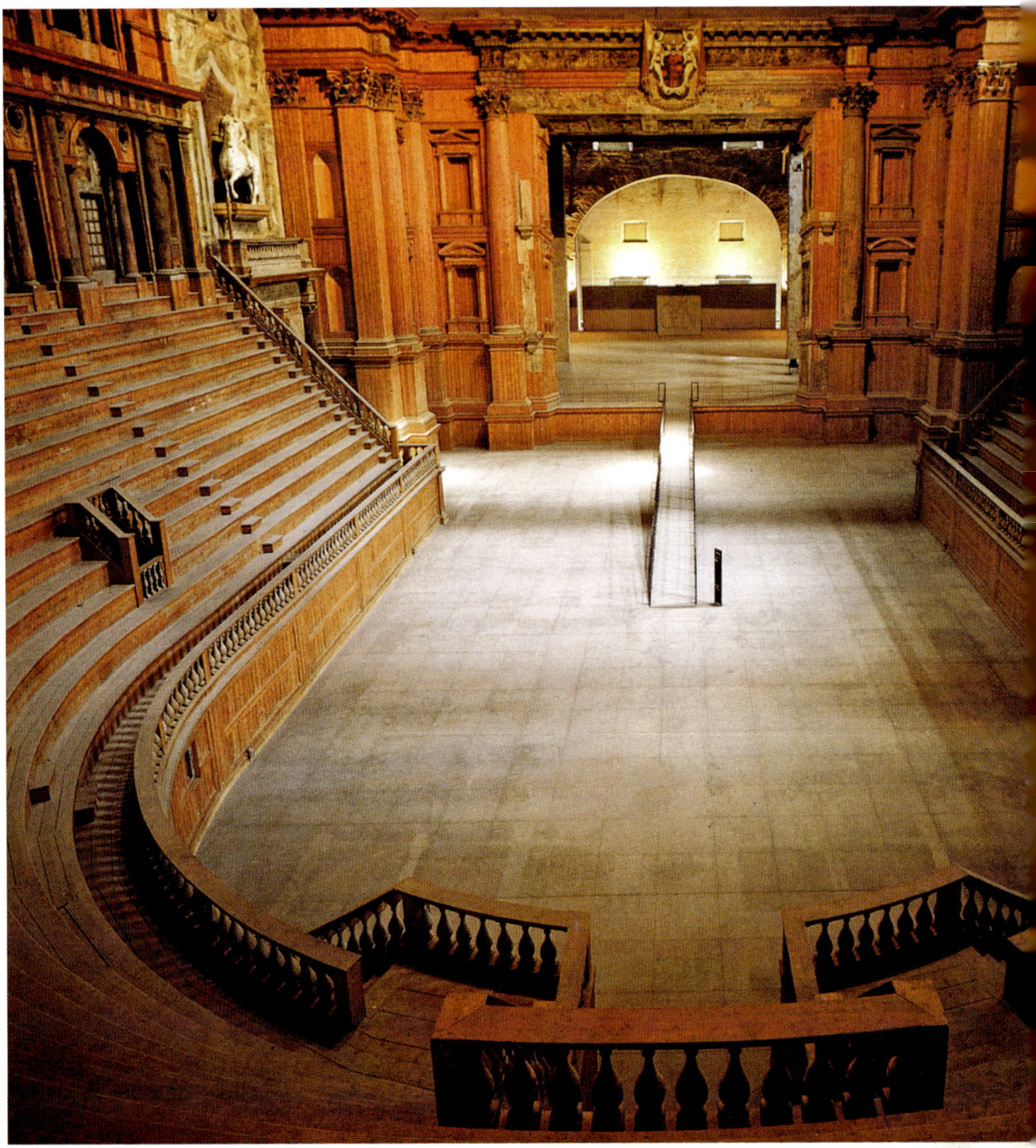

CONVENTIONS OF SPACE | 163

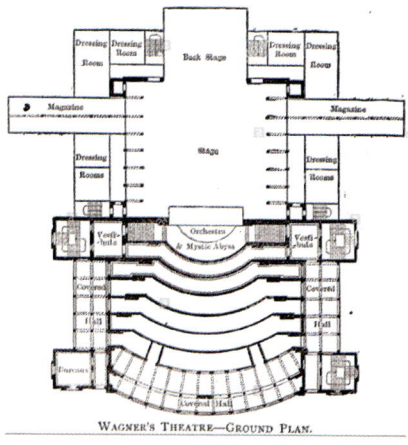

Left: Interior of Teatro Farnese at Parma, Italy. The theatre was designed by Giovanni Battista Aleotti in the year 1618. Source of the photograph: https://www.theatre-architecture.eu/en/db/?theatreId=376.

Top: Theatre The Bayreuth Festspielhaus in Germany. This opera house at the north of Bayreuth was built by the German music composer Richard Wagner in the year 1876.

Bottom: The interior of the theatre was constructed with wood and timber.
Source of the photographs: https://forum.cyclingnews.com/threads/race-design-thread.15517/page-296 https://www.theatre-architecture.eu/db.html?personId=844&theatreId=388.

theatre house differed from the Teatro Farnese of Italy, and the Theatre Royal at Covent Garden and Drury Lane in England. Wagner did away with the concept of box, pit and gallery that had dominated the auditorium since the beginning of the proscenium era. All the luxurious arrangements for comfortable seating were replaced with a racked auditorium featuring rows of seats. The balcony was pushed to the back of the last row.

To maintain the continuity of illusion from one scene to another, Wagner made the musicians sit in an orchestra pit underneath the stage apron. Earlier, musicians would perform in view of the audience gallery in front of the stage. Adolphe Appia, the renowned scenographer of the 20th century, began the trend of dimming the auditorium lights during performances, thus placing focus directly on the action. For the first time in the history of theatre, it became possible to envelop the audience in darkness to highlight the presentation. This new trend had a profound impact on the performance culture of the time as well as the audience, who became silent observers to the dramatic offering. For the duration of a play, spectators would forget the rest of the world and be immersed in the illusionistic reality depicted onstage, such that the depiction became a reality of life. According to Martin Banham, Wagner talked about a 'mystic chasm' [illusionistic gap] between the stage and auditorium, created by a double proscenium, by which the 'ideal' world of the stage was to be separated from the everyday world of the spectators. The goal was ... to create a communal experience that would unite the audience.[iii]

Gradually, towards the end of the 19th century, two-dimensional set materials—painted sceneries, gauze curtains and cut-scenes—were replaced with three-dimensional elements. Scenography became a vital component of presentations, bringing theatre closer to the real-life experience. Andre Antoine[3] of the Theatre Libre adopted naturalism as a means of theatrical

---

3   Andre Antoine (1858–1943) was the pioneer of naturalistic theatre and founder of the Theatre Libre, which became the model for the independent theatre movement in Europe and led to America's Little Theatre Movement.

A scene from the play *The Weavers*. The play was written by the German playwright Gerhart Hauptmaan. It was was designed and directed by Andre Antoin for the Teatro Libre at Paris in the year 1890. The production is an example of hyper-realism (Naturalism) that explores the three-dimensional stage space with a box set design.

Courtesy: Hakman digital archive.

Source: https://library.calvin.edu/hda/sites/default/files/imagecache/medium/cas788h.jpg.

expression and introduced box sets to the proscenium theatre. The box set represents a realistic living room with four walls—three exist physically while the fourth remains imaginary and open to the audience. This very thought of exploring three-dimensional design revolutionised the idea of theatre in the West.

Framed within the proscenium arch, the scenes in a play appeared like a series of well-composed paintings. Those paintings kept on moving continuously in a given time frame. Scenographers strived to form a world much closer to real life within this set-up. This approach for the performance, transiting in between illusion and reality, created an impression of make-believe which became the prime objective of realistic theatre in Europe. In the Moscow Art Theatre, Konstantin Stanislavsky[4] developed a technique of realistic acting that helped bring theatre closer to the human experiences and realities of life. Stanislavsky was able to achieve this by recreating the real world inside the proscenium theatre with the help of master designers such as Viktor Simov, Konstantin Korovin, Aleksandr Golovin and Mstislav Dobuzhinsky.

The proscenium theatre thus succeeded in codifying arbitrary space by developing the vocabulary for a specific type of presentation. Over time, new dimensions were added to stage design with the advent of technology, further leading to innovations and creative experiments. Visual aesthetics developed into a prime language of theatre, such that scenography emerged as a creative form of artistic expression. These developments only became possible due to the advent of a framed space. Posited as a limitation to creativity by many, the proscenium theatre gained popularity across the world in the 20th century and is still widely prevalent. Though a variety of performance spaces are available today, this conventional framed space is still preferred as the most convenient one for theatrical presentations.

Structure and Forms

The proscenium theatre is an architectural structure with specific arrangements for the audience as well as the presentation, wherein the two areas are clearly separated by an arch. The term 'proscenium' can be traced back to the 'proskenion' of ancient Greek theatre, where a raised platform was set up in front of the skene building for presentations. Like the frame of a painting, the proscenium arch outlines a performance,

---

4   Konstantin Stanislavsky (1863–1938) was a Russian actor and theatre director who codified realistic method of acting popularly known as 'Stanislavsky System'. He was the director of Moscow Art Theatre.

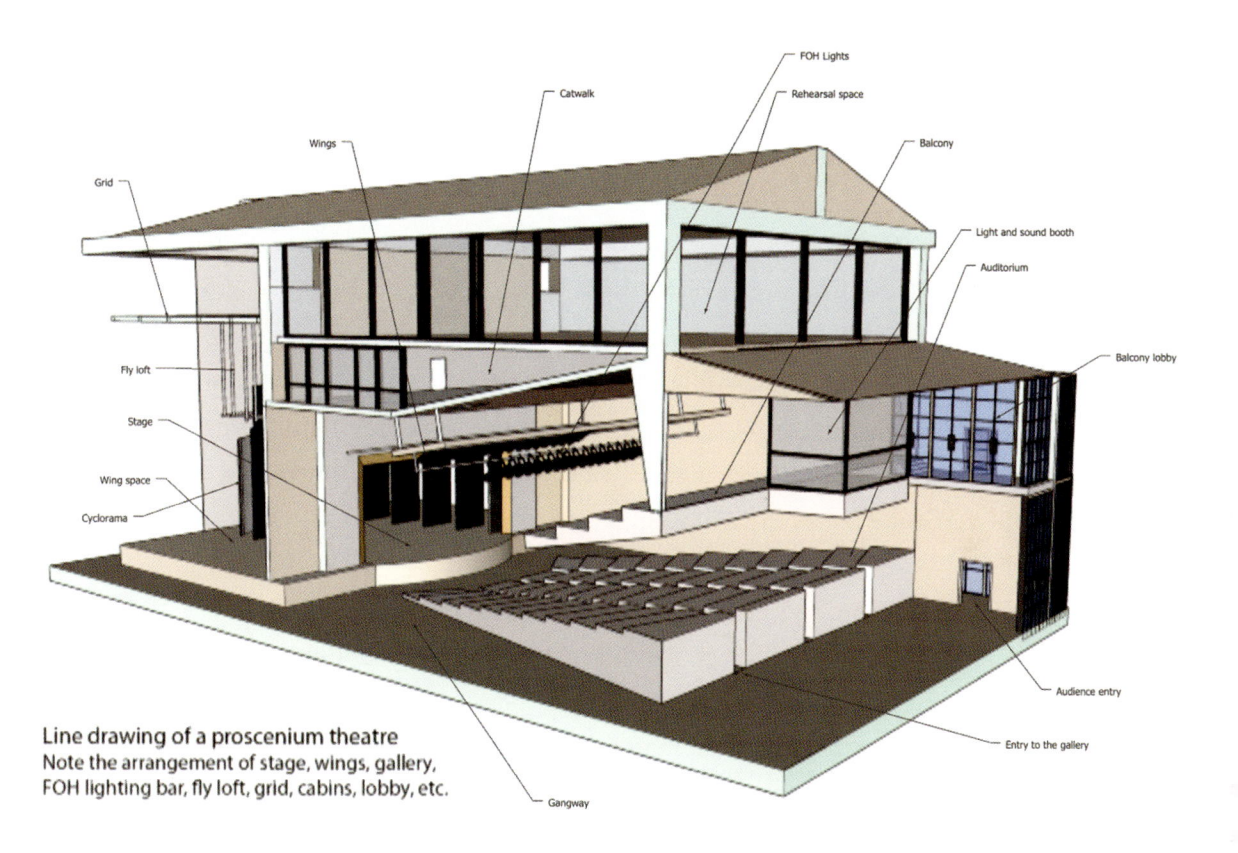

Line drawing of a proscenium theatre
Note the arrangement of stage, wings, gallery, FOH lighting bar, fly loft, grid, cabins, lobby, etc.

thus creating a 'framed space'. The audience looks through this frame, the proscenium arch, at a picturesque image of the performance while the other three sides remain covered with curtains and wings. The proscenium opening is also referred to as the fourth wall[5]—an invisible, imagined wall between the performers and spectators. This conceptual wall restricts actors from directly interacting with the audience and vice versa, which was a common practice during the period of Naturalism. A proscenium

---

5   The concept of the 'fourth wall' is usually attributed to the French philosopher and dramatist Denis Diderot (1713–1784). The term had also been initially used by playwright Moliere (1622–1673).

theatre is comprised of the stage and the auditorium. These two spaces face each other in an architectural building, forming a 'theatre', with the space for performers further segregated into 'onstage' and 'offstage'.

Onstage: The performance space, where the primary action takes place, is broadly categorised as onstage and opens to the audience gallery. Irrespective of the architectural design and other technical parameters of a theatre, the proscenium stage is invariably a rectangular space with an arch in the front and curtains at the back. The flanks of the performance space are arranged with wings and allow a frontal view to the audience.

Stage floor: The stage floor, better known as the acting area, remains in full view of the audience. Though the dimensions of proscenium theatres may greatly vary, the average proscenium stage floor usually spans approximately 40 feet in length and a little more in width or depth. The height of the stage floor also varies extensively from 3 feet to 4 feet, depending on the arrangement of the audience gallery. As for the material, a wooden floor is considered the most comfortable across the world. The floor usually features wooden dust, clay and sand for the base, with furnished planks of soft wood forming the upper layer. This method of flooring provides the requisite flexibility for jumping, leaning, lying, gliding, running or walking on the stage floor.

Stage Geography: The proscenium stage manifests some peculiar characteristics. Scenographers can explore these peculiarities through their knowledge and technical expertise to create a meaningful, interpretative design for each play. For the optimum utility of stage space, it is generally identified as three separate segments: down-stage (the area closest to the audience), centre-stage (the main performance area); and up-stage (the area

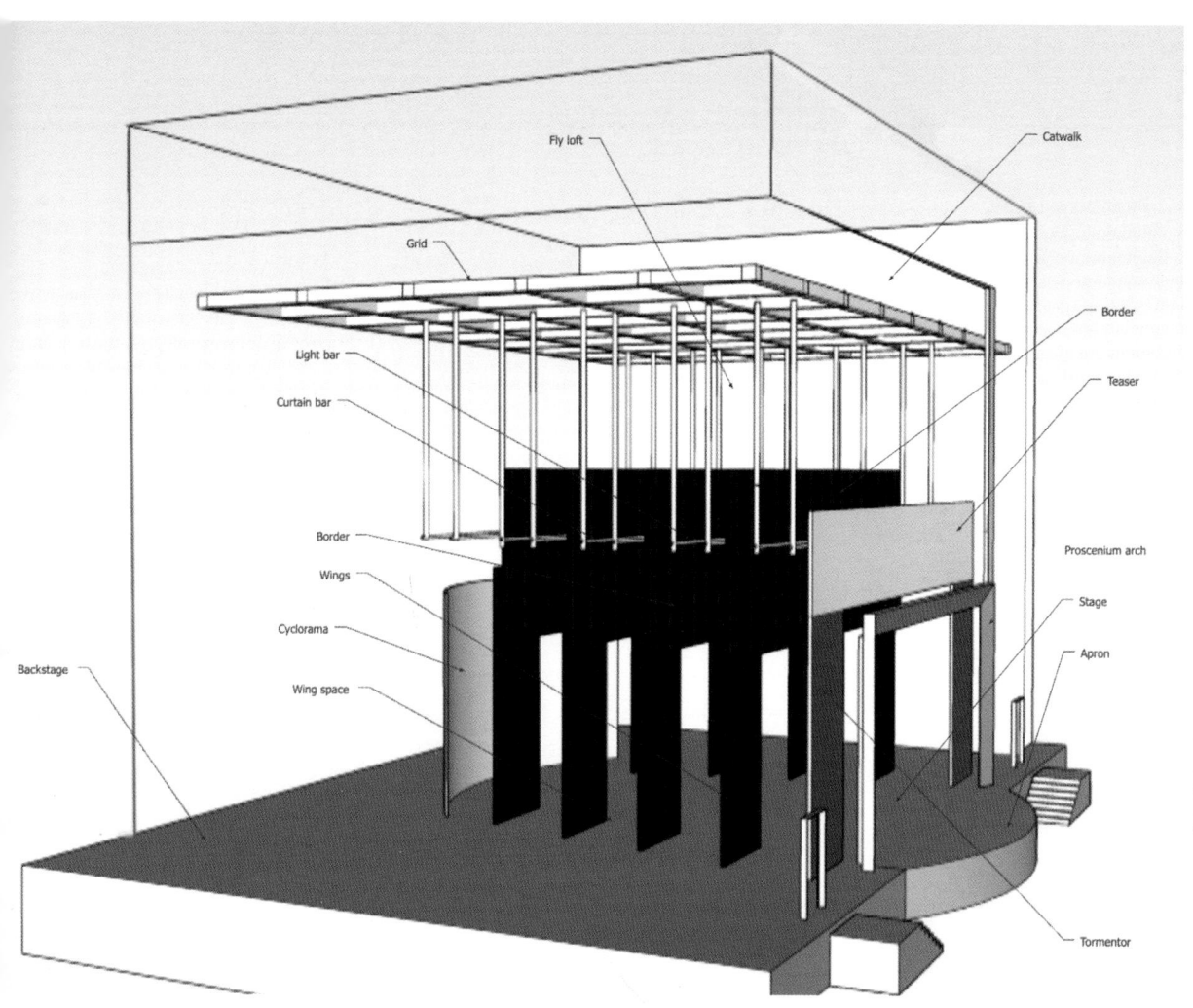

Description of the various components of the stage with specifications

near the cyclorama, used primarily for sceneries and stage effects). These three segments are further divided into the following nine sections for convenience: 1) stage-down-right (SDR); 2) stage-down-centre (SDC); 3) stage-down-left (SDL); 4) stage-centre-right (SCR); 5) stage-centre (SC); 6) stage-centre-left (SCL); 7) stage-up-right (SUR); 8) stage-up-centre (SUC); and 9) stage-up-left (SUL).

Stage Division

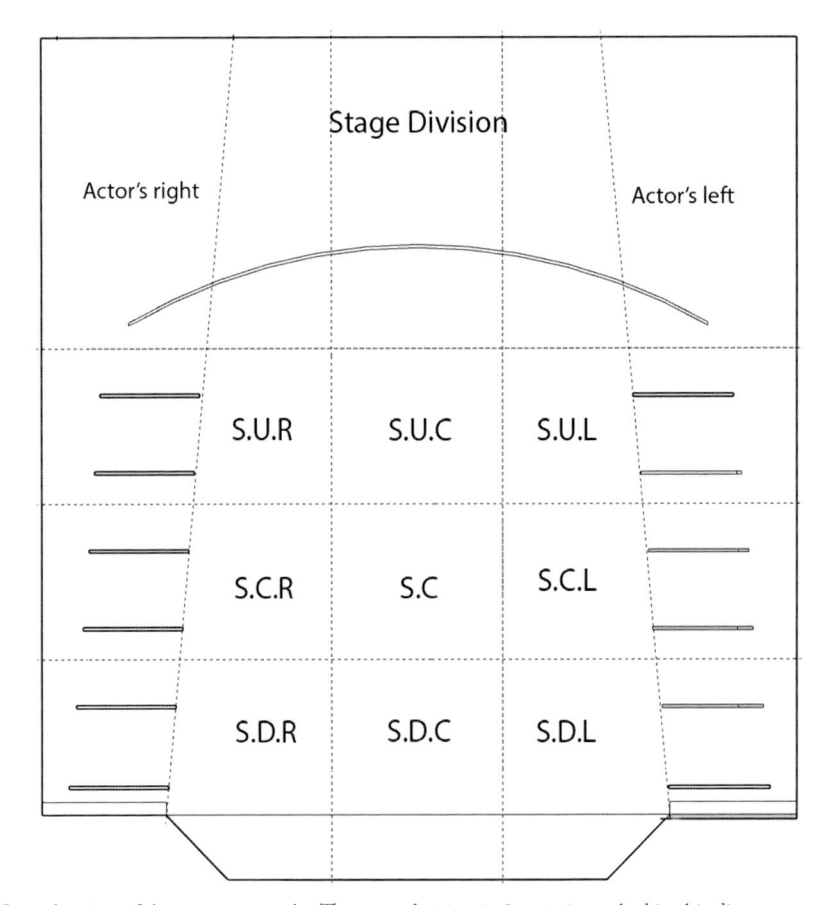

Line drawing of the stage geography. The stage division in 9 parts is marked in this diagram.

These sections are defined according to the perspective of the actors—when onstage and facing the audience gallery, the actors' right side is considered stage-right and their left marks stage-left. Conventionally, the stage-centre is the area best in focus. However, this convention may be challenged through the creative prowess of the scenographer and the director, who can bring any space into focus through their skills and imagination.

Proscenium Arch: This rectangular, frame-like structure separates the stage from the auditorium. The proscenium arch bestows a semblance of

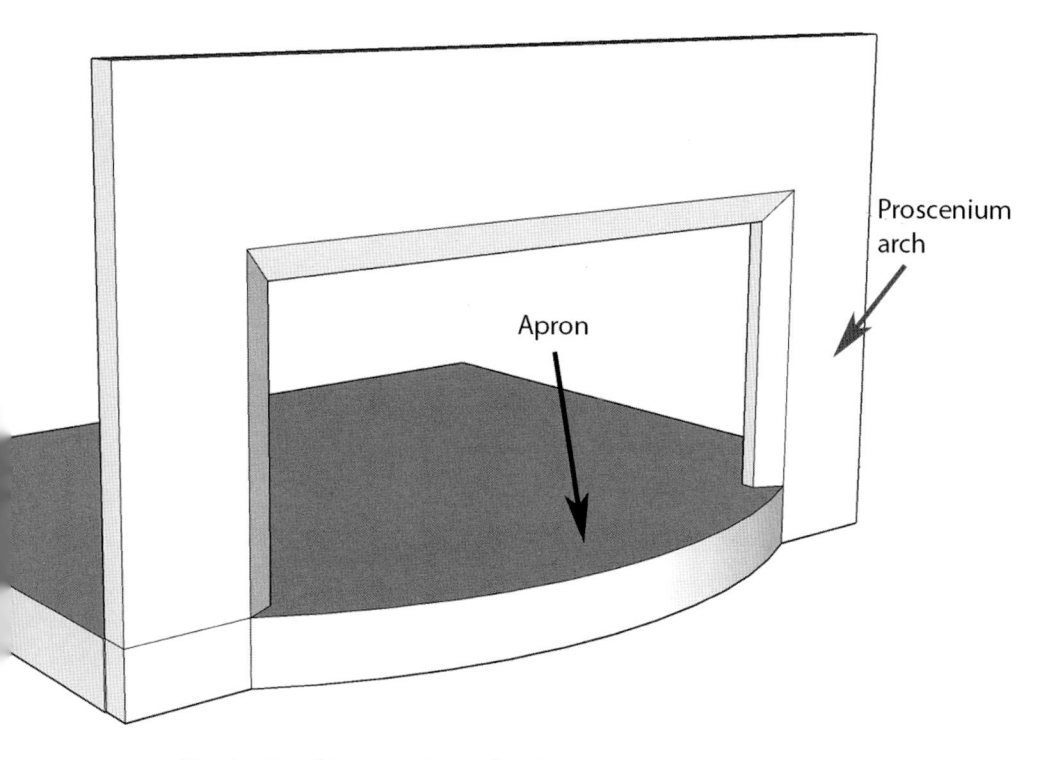

Line drawing of the proscenium arch and apron.

picturesque beauty and adds to the aesthetics of a presentation. Similar to a framed painting, it helps bring the performance into focus. The height of the proscenium arch is usually set at half the stage length to create a rectangular, framed expression.

Cyclorama: A cyclorama is a stretched white screen, attached to the curtain bar at the back of the acting area. Often concave in shape to create an illusion of depth, a cyclorama is used to produce lighting effects and depict exterior scenic elements like the sky, river, sea, or generic outdoor settings. The screen is usually illuminated by way of overhead cyclorama strips, such that effects like floating clouds, fire, water, rain and lightning can be projected on it to add to the grandeur of a production. However,

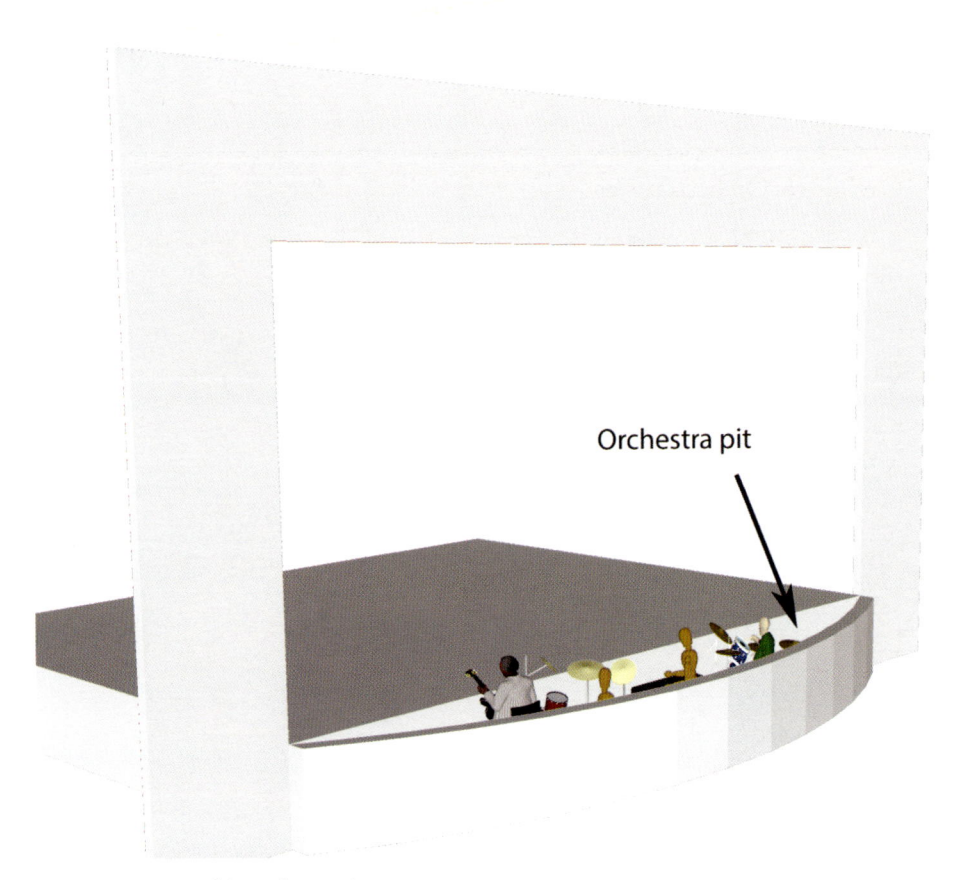

Line drawing of the orchestra pit.

in addition to the many possibilities, there also exist some adverse issues with the cyclorama. The screen's sharp white colour often diverts the attention of spectators if not used appropriately. It also tends to reflect stray lighting from the stage. As a result, scenographers occasionally avoid the white cyclorama if not in use, and replace it with a black curtain. Every proscenium theatre is thus equipped with a black curtain along with the cyclorama at the back.

Apron: The apron is an element of the stage floor that projects outwards from the proscenium line towards the auditorium, and may be used as part of the acting area. In some theatres, the apron extends further inside the auditorium to function as the main stage. (Ref. Thrust Stage)

Orchestra: Orchestra or orchestra pit, a derivative of ancient Greek theatre, was performed through chorus. In a proscenium theatre, the orchestra is the designated place for musicians—essentially a pit-like structure situated in front of the stage and below the eye level of the audience. Quite often, the wooden planks of the apron are removed to create this pit.

Trapdoor: A trapdoor is a conventional sliding or hinged door placed towards the up-stage of the acting area. This small opening allows actors to appear from and disappear beneath the stage. The entry of actors through the trapdoor was a common practice in medieval Elizabethan theatre in England. For example in Shakespeare's Globe supernatural characters such as ghosts and spirits used to appear from the trapdoor. This opening was also used to represent 'Hell' in medieval European dramas. However, with changing times, the trapdoor became obsolete and is now rarely used.

Wings: The term 'wings' collectively refers to the vertical black curtains present on either side of the stage to separate onstage from offstage, and are placed behind the proscenium arch in a definite spatial order. The primary purpose of the wings are to hide or mask actors, sets, props and all supplementary activities not meant for the audience. The vertical arrangement of the wings, along with the overhead borders, also enhances the aesthetics of a presentation by adding volume and dimension.

The working space near the wings is considered a vital part of the backstage, where actors usually wait for their turn to enter the stage. Sets and props are also shifted to this area between scenes during a show. As such, an ample amount of space is required between the wings, which usually spans from 6 to 8 feet, for the comfortable movement of actors and objects to and from the stage. The wings are generally kept black to avoid the undesirable reflection of lights during a presentation.

Tormentor and Teaser: Tormentors are narrow masking flats installed on both sides of the stage behind the proscenium arch. These black flats can be slid in and out of the stage to manage the size of the acting area. A teaser is a frilled curtain hung from the overhead bars in the fly gallery behind the grand curtain. With the help of these two components, the proscenium opening can be reshaped according to the needs of a performance. They also provide an inner frame to the stage proper, thus adding to the beauty of a presentation.

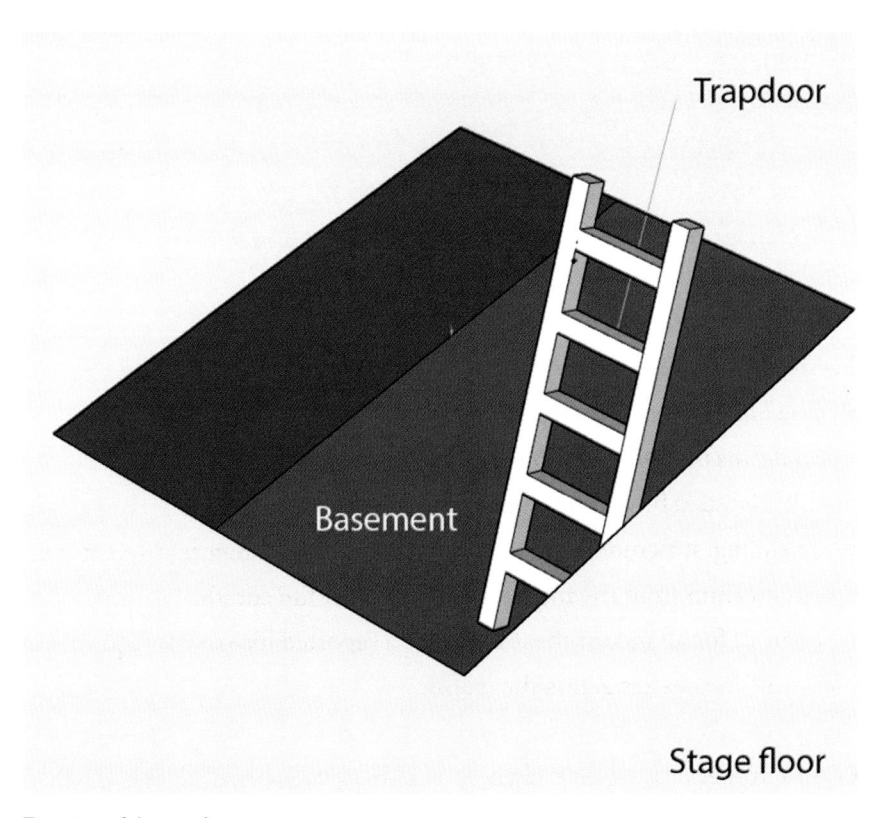

Drawing of the trapdoor.

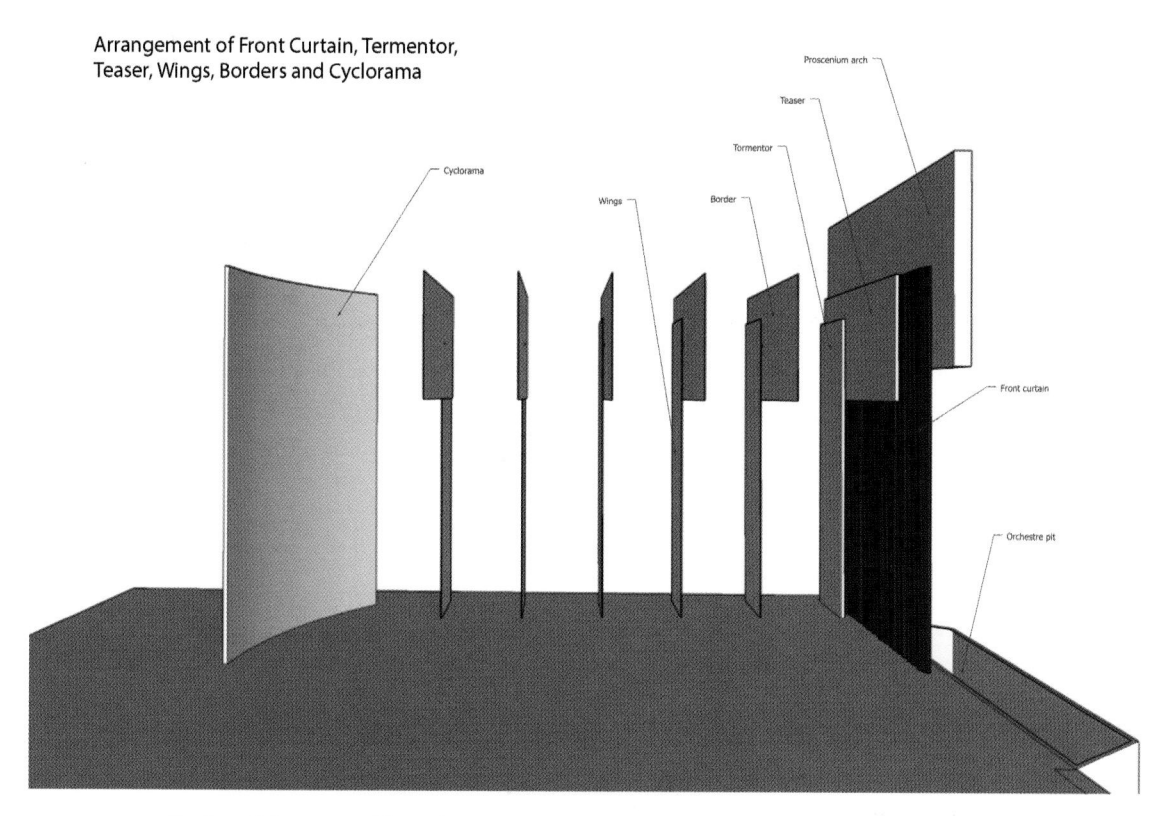

Arrangement of Front Curtain, Termentor, Teaser, Wings, Borders and Cyclorama

Section of the stage and its various components.

Fire curtains: Fire curtains are an important feature of the proscenium theatre, meant to separate the stage from the auditorium. These are basically massive sliding doors made of fire-resistant materials that are usually placed at both ends of the proscenium arch. In case a fire breaks out, these sliding structures are pulled along the proscenium line to separate the auditorium from the main stage. The use of fire curtains has long been mandatory for all indoor theatres due to a reported history of frequent fire breakouts in theatres across the world.

Grand drapery: The grand drapery is a decorative curtain made of velvet or muslin that hangs from the top just behind the proscenium arch.

Conventionally, this huge curtain is drawn up, or is parted to the sides behind the proscenium arch, to mark the beginning of a play. This curtain never comes down during a performance or in between scenes. When a play finishes, the grand drapery is rolled down or pulled in to mark the curtain call. However, this practice of rolling up and unrolling the grand drapery went out of fashion over the time and is hardly seen in contemporary theatres.

Borders: Borders are strip-like thick black curtains attached to the bars in the fly gallery. These borders serve the purpose of hiding the objects in the fly, such as lights, curtain bars, painted sceneries and other technical equipment.

Offstage: The success of a performance is contingent on the offstage or backstage. The offstage area should have adequate space to allow for the smooth execution of a performance. This space is always kept out of sight of the audience and is used exclusively by artists and technicians. Like the acting area, the offstage, too, comprises a number of components with specific functions.

Green room: The green room is placed behind or near the stage. It is the place where actors compose themselves and prepare for a show. The term 'green room' is attributed to the Elizabethan theatre culture prevalent in England during the 16th and 17th centuries. The chambers in the Globe were usually filled with plants and herbs to increase the moisture level in the room, which was considered essential to keep the actors' voice apt for dialogue delivery. Green rooms are normally painted in cool colours to sooth the eyes and provide a calming ambience.

Makeup room: The makeup room is generally attached to the green room. Makeup rooms are spacious chambers with large mirrors and plentiful illumination, so that actors can wear their makeup with ease and comfort.

Wardrobe: Wardrobe is the costume room of the theatre. Provisions are made in each theatre to keep costumes, props and masks in a systematic order inside designated cupboards or available racks. Generally, a separate section, equipped with sewing machines, is attached to the costume room for tailoring requirements. A well-disciplined and organised wardrobe and green room gives the impression of professionalism.

Wing space: This is the space adjacent to the wings, separated from the performance space by the wings and curtains. It is one of the most sensitive offstage areas in a proscenium theatre since actors wait here before their imminent entry to the stage. Often, stagehands are engaged in the wing space while waiting to change set pieces or to manipulate the appropriate curtains and sceneries in fadeout. These activities are carried out in the wing space with minimum illumination, accentuating the need for a capacious space.

Loading door: The ideal proscenium theatre is often equipped with a loading door at the back of the structure, through which sets and props are brought to the stage. As a result, this opening is kept wide enough to allow a smooth movement of stage materials such as sets, props, costumes, lights, etc. In some cases, it is even possible for a lorry carrying stage equipment to directly access the stage proper through this loading door. Conversely, in some theatres, large freight elevators are installed to carry the requisite equipment to the stage.

Storage shades: Storage shades are used to safely stash set pieces and props before and after a performance. Materials like platforms, flats, steps, pillars, shelves, etc. can be conveniently stored in these shades.

Control rooms: The light-and-sound control rooms are usually placed at the back of the auditorium, facing straight to the stage. It is advisable to keep these rooms in front of the stage since the light and sound operators need to be able to watch the performance to appropriately control the consoles during a show. These control (light and sound) rooms should ideally be separately constructed.

Fly gallery: Standing on the stage floor in a proscenium theatre, if we look up, we will see a large storage space directly above the stage. This overhead space is called the fly gallery or fly loft, and is used to store hanging curtains, bars, sceneries, lighting equipment, microphones, projectors, etc. These components can be lowered to the stage or lifted up by way of ropes and pulleys, and placed in the fly gallery, with the help of 'counterweights' operated from pin-rails. The fly gallery should be spacious enough to accommodate all the requisite technical equipment. It is not considered a good practice to push painted curtains or sceneries to the wing space, or roll them up behind the borders, since they are quite valuable and may develop cracks at the folds. These precious curtains are thus best lifted up into the fly gallery with the help of counterweights and safely stored there. The height of the fly gallery is usually kept more than the proscenium height to facilitate the storage of all such materials.

Grid: The grid is an iron framework placed between the fly gallery and the roof of the theatre. Pulleys, ropes, bars and other kinds of weights and counterweights are attached to this grid.

Catwalk: This is a cramped and narrow platform, fixed above the grid that enables technicians to fix and adjust lights, curtains and other stage equipment. Theatres round the world have witnessed many mishaps

CONVENTIONS OF SPACE | 179

Flyloft or Fly gallery

Drawing of the fly gallery (fly loft) of the proscenium theatre.

related to people or equipment falling from the catwalk; so proper care must be taken for the safety of the technical crews. It is thus always advisable to hook to a nearby bar, essentially wear a fall arrest, while working on the catwalk.

Counterweight system: The counterweight system is generally attached to one of the sidewalls of a theatre in the backstage. With the help of this device, one can lower or lift the bars, loaded with lights or curtains, inside the theatre. The rows of thick ropes and heavy steel weights used in this system are thus apparent on the sidewalls of any given proscenium theatre. These ropes are attached to the bars in the fly by way of pulleys

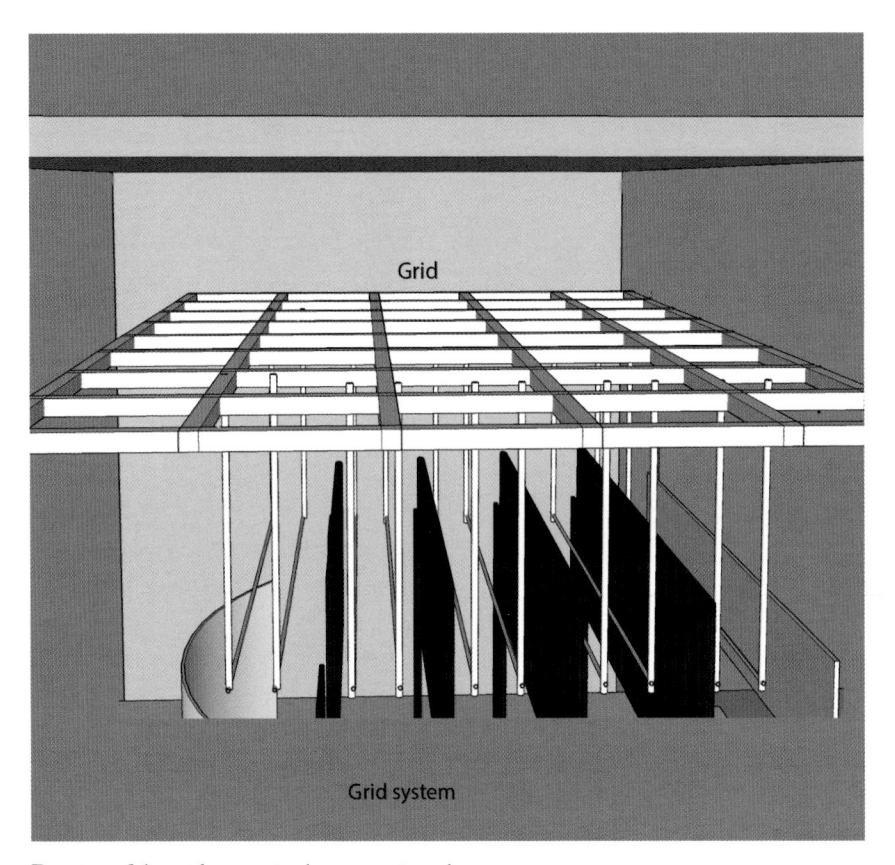

Drawing of the grid system in the proscenium theatre.

with appropriate counterweights on this end. When a particular rope is pulled down or released, the loaded curtain or light bar attached to the rope moves up or down accordingly. Sometimes, the system becomes fatal if it loses balance—an improper counterweight may result in the sudden collapse of the bars onto the stage. As such, one should have proper understanding of this device before trying to operate the system.

Sightline: A presentation would be of little value if it does not afford the audience a proper view of the performance. The wings, borders, and sometimes even the chairs in the audience gallery are arranged and

Drawing of the catwalk.

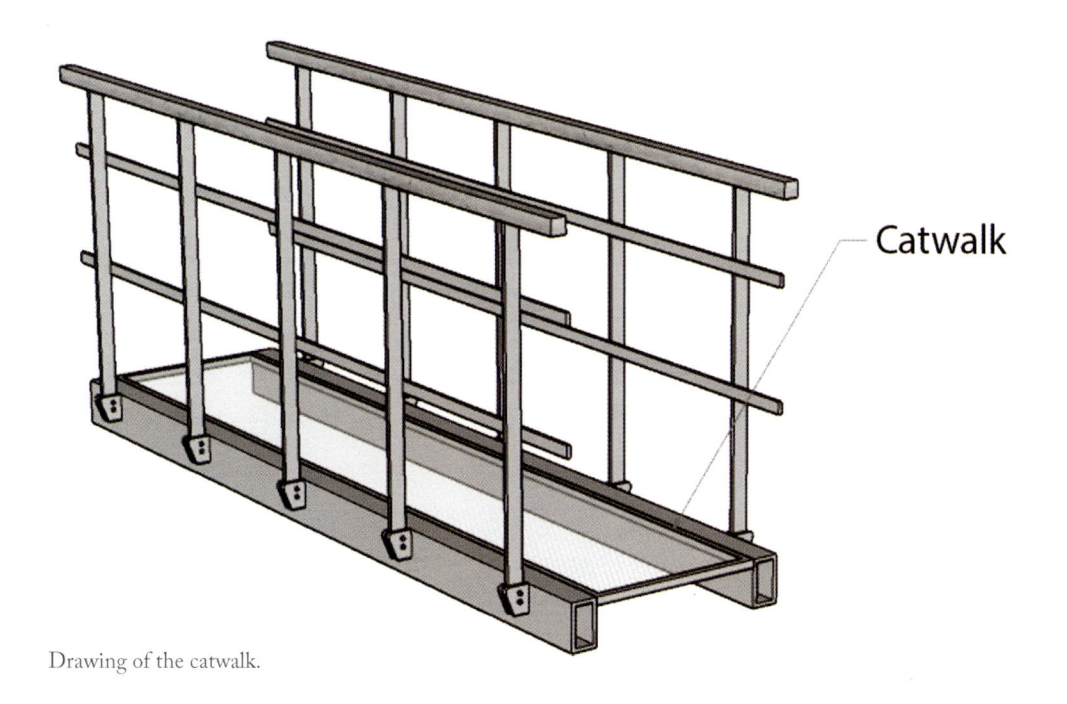

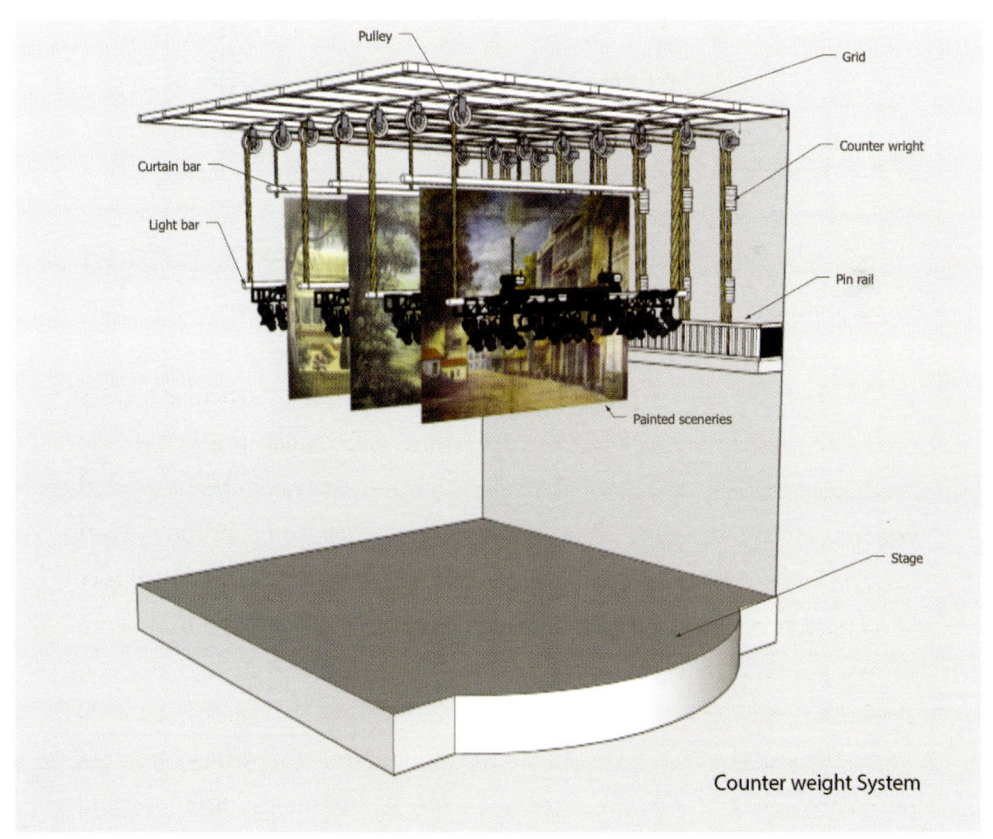

Three-dimensional drawing of the counterweight system and arrangement of curtain and light bars in a proscenium theatre.

rearranged for proper exposition of the scenes. This act of manipulating the wings and borders is called 'fixing the sightline', essentially the field of vision, from the perspective of the audience, who watch the performance within the limits of this imaginary line. In a proscenium theatre, where space is segregated into onstage and offstage, the sightline plays a crucial role, so that each member of the audience is privy to every visual in a play. For instance, when sitting in the front row of an auditorium, one might not be able to see the stage floor. Such issues can be conceptually resolved with a basic understanding of the sightline, which applies in both the horizontal as well as the vertical plane in a proscenium theatre.

Horizontal sightline. The principle of horizontal sightline can be understood by fixing the field of vision of the audience between the extreme ends of the first row of the auditorium. If the spectators sitting on either end of the first row are able to clearly watch a performance, the rest of the audience will also be able to do so. In the following image, the line of vision of spectator A is restricted on either side by the proscenium walls, i.e. points a and b, such that spectator A would be unable to see beyond these points. However, the spectator can see the entire stage along their line of vision, through the arches up to the cyclorama, and also see the wing space on stage-left. To restrict this visibility, the wings are arranged one after another on stage-left. At the same time, it must be ensured that the line of vision of spectator B, seated on the right end of the gallery, is not restricted by the wings. In this way, wings are arranged on both stage-left and stage-right in a definite succession. The scenes in a play may thus be planned and executed only after appropriately fixing the positions of the wings in the above manner.

Vertical sightline. The vertical field of vision can be identified from the perspective of the spectators sitting in the middle of the first and last

CONVENTIONS OF SPACE | 183

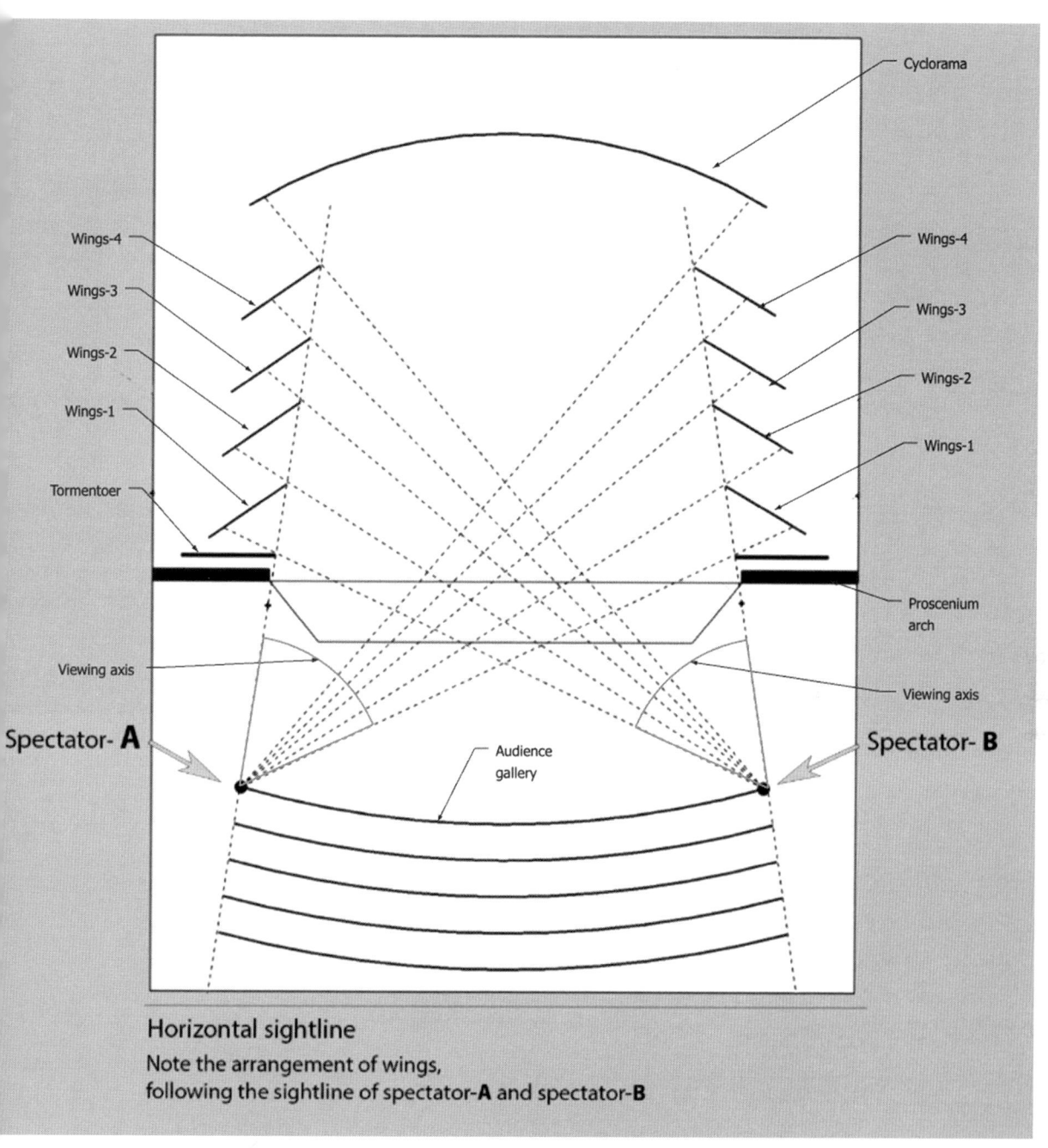

Horizontal sightline
Note the arrangement of wings,
following the sightline of spectator-**A** and spectator-**B**

Line drawing of the horizontal sightline and the arrangement of wings.

rows of the auditorium. It is often observed that a presentation in the up-stage area is not properly visible to the audience in the balcony due to the improper arrangement of borders and curtains in the fly gallery. In the adjoining illustration, the spectator A in the first row sees everything in the fly loft if the borders are not fixed along his visual axis. Similarly, if the borders or curtains come within the vertical visual field of the

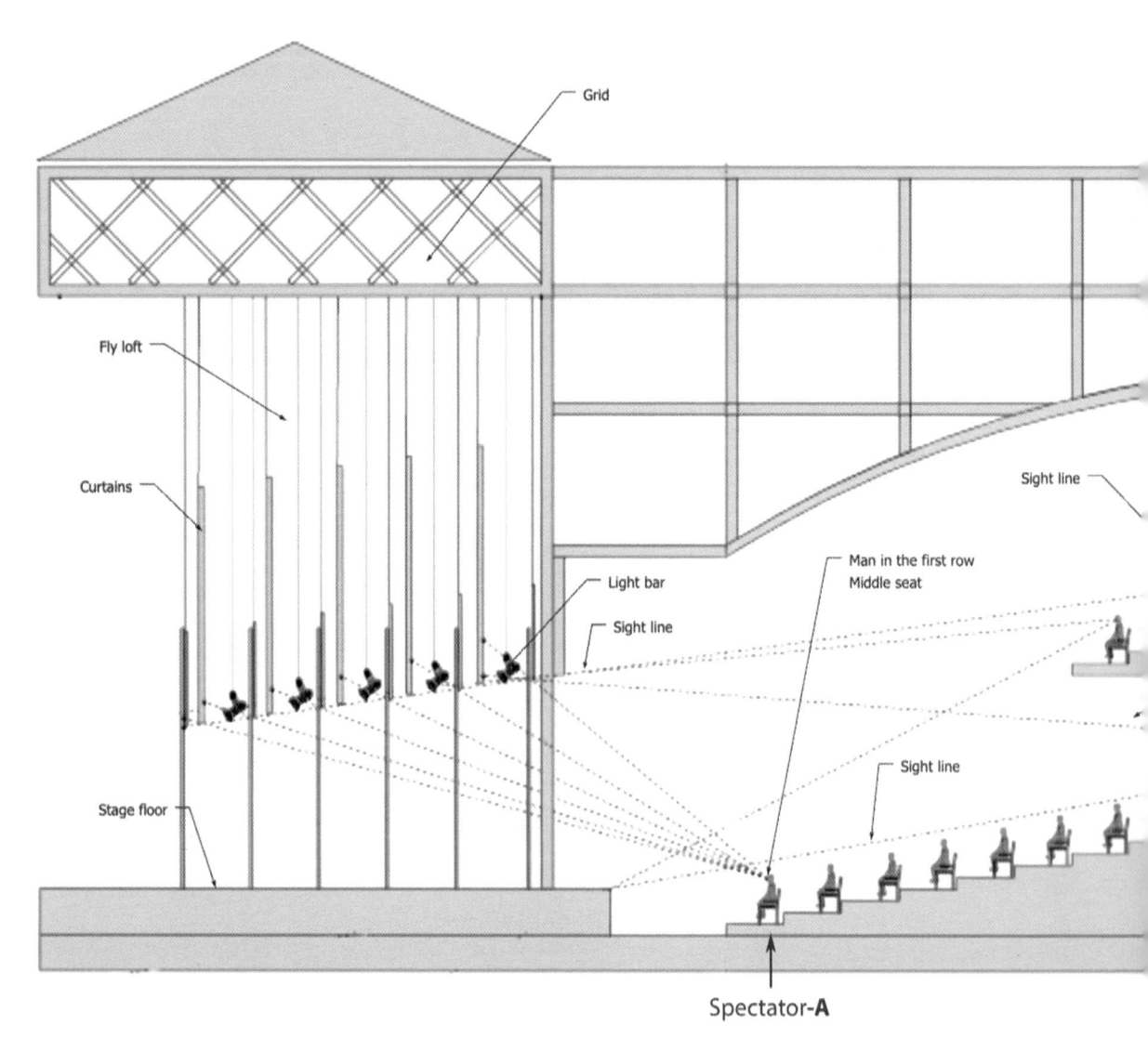

Line drawing of the vertical sightline and arrangement of borders, light bars, etc.

spectator B, watching the play from the last row of the balcony, he may not be able to see some parts of a presentation. These issues can easily be resolved by aptly arranging the borders and curtains in the fly gallery.

Audience gallery: The audience gallery is commonly referred to as the auditorium. In the initial days of the proscenium theatre, the audience gallery used to be horseshoe-shaped. Eventually, a staircase-like arrangement was adopted, wherein successive rows of seats were elevated by 6 to 9 inches as one moved towards the back of the auditorium, to provide the best possible visual comfort to the audience. The height of the performance area was also reduced to a level approximately 4 feet from the ground. The auditorium must also be designed so as to have proper acoustics for clear audibility.

Gangway: The gangway is the passage or carpeted area in an auditorium. Large auditoriums may feature more than one gangway, with each spacious enough to lead the audience into the gallery. The entry and exit doors of an auditorium are generally kept to the sides in order to avoid disruptions during a performance—external illumination and late entrants to the gallery, if allowed through doors facing the stage, may distract the performers. Therefore, any doors at the back of the gallery usually remain closed during a performance.

A proscenium theatre is similar to a factory with a regulatory mechanism, per se. Everyone discharges their duties independently but also in collaboration with the others. Actors, directors, scenographers, designers, technical crews, et al. coordinate with each

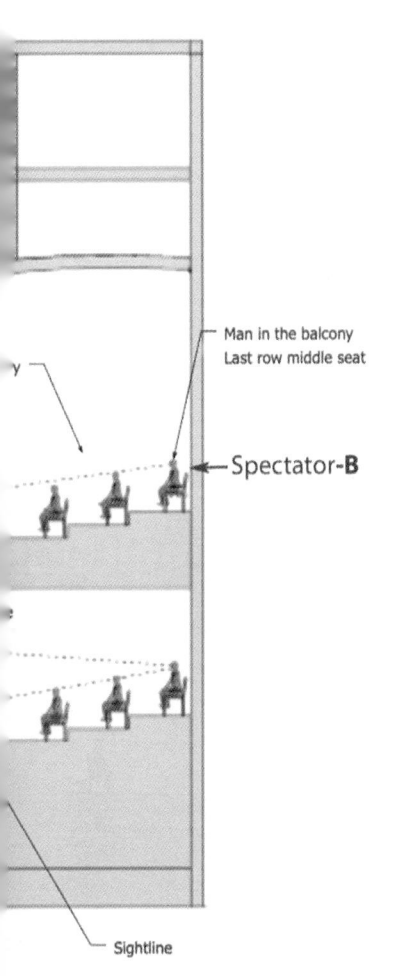

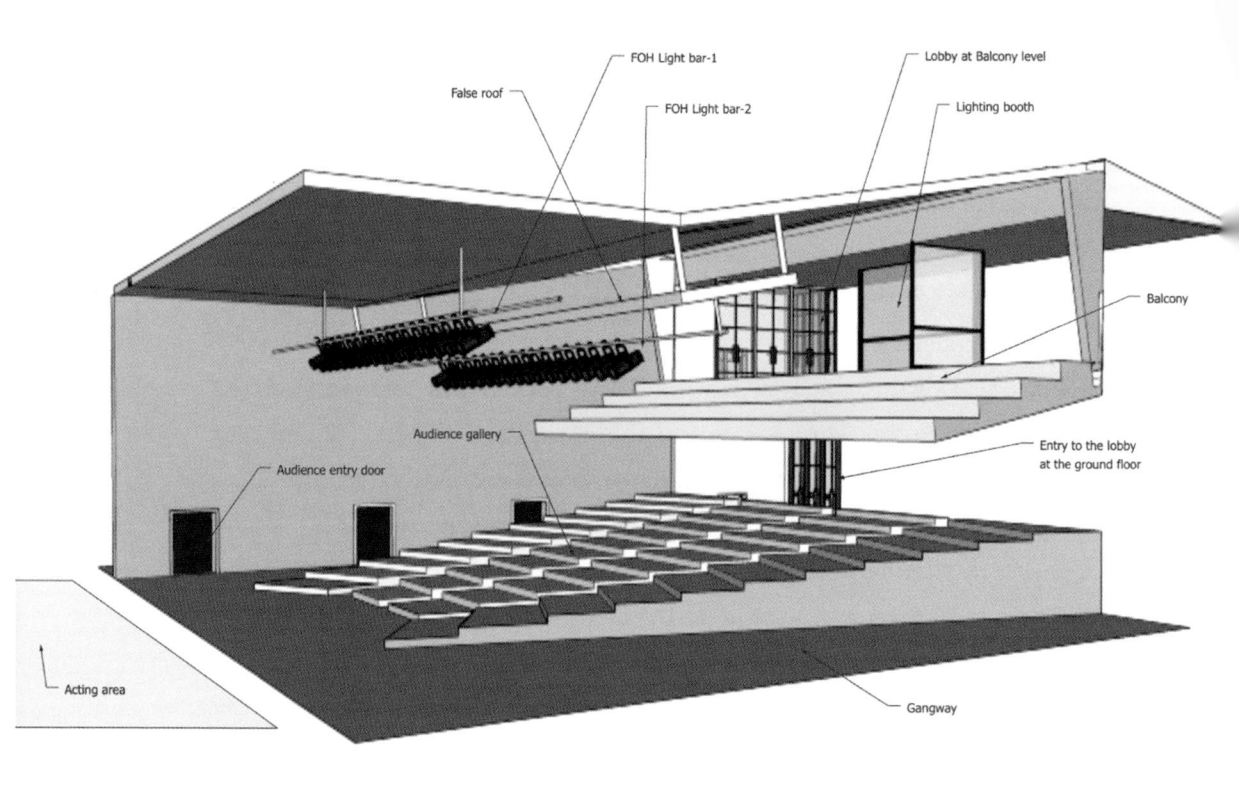

Three-dimensional drawing of auditorium. Note the arrangement of FOH light bars, audience gallery, balcony and lighting booth, etc.

other to make a presentation successful.

THE OPEN-AIR PERFORMANCE SPACE

The open-air performance space is the most ancient theatre space, continuing from the prehistoric period till today, passing through various transformations. This space, in the form of the 'primitive theatre', came in to practice for the ritualistic community activities among the tribes before civilisation came into existence. The open-air performance used to take place in the ancient Greek, Roman and the medieval European theatre, and are still continuing across the world with modifications in patches. Irrespective of its diversified forms, open-air theatre performance provides a similar kind of ambience in each of its performances. While many of the existing open-air theatres are large enough to accommodate a huge number of viewers, a few of them are more intimate with limited numbers of audience.

Most of the times, open-air performance space, quite suitable for a specific genre of plays, fascinates the scenographers. An open-air theatre can be a thrust, arena or a proscenium, but its characteristic features are different. In this theatre space, the performance is exposed to an openness which may divert the attention of the viewers from the major actions of the play. But with the help of careful acting along with lights, costumes, sets, etc., the attention of the audience can be focused. Performance in an open-air theatre needs little exaggeration, in all respects, due to large gatherings or the openness of the space, though this notion may not always be true. In an open-air performance, the direct effect of the lights gets absorbed by the surrounding atmosphere. Therefore, a lighting designer usually increases the amount of lighting equipment or the intensity to achieve desired effects. Even, at times, the performers express with exaggerated oral and physical gestures for communication. Often it becomes a challenge for the artistes to present realistic detail in an open-air performance unless it is an intimate open theatre.

Natya Shastra Rejects Open-air Performance: A Reason

Though open air performance is a common practice in Indian traditional and folk theatres, it was not so in the classical theatre. The ancient treatise of theatre, the *Natya Shastra*, has restricted open-air performance in its practices, except in the genesis of theatre with the mythical presentation of *Amritamanthanam*[6]. According to the treaties, this early play was performed in an open air theatre at the Kailash Parvat in the Himalayas,

---

6   Also known as 'Samudra-Manthan', a 'samavakar' in three acts dealing in the myth of churning of the ocean. This play is said to be the first ever play performed by the disciples of Bharata in open-air. Reference has been found in the *Natya Shastra* but no script is available for study.

the abode of lord Shiva, which was interrupted by the demons in the middle of the show that led to the stopping of the play in between. Except this there is no references of open-air performance in *Natya Shastra*.

Indian classical theatre restricts open-air performances due to the following probable reasons:

i. The climatic conditions
ii. The aesthetics of the performance
iii. The presentation for selective audience

Classical Indian theatre, known for its higher aesthetic values, metaphoric and symbolic gestures, has included ritualistic activities in its presentation at temple premises or at similar kinds of places. Unlike the Greek theatre, the Indian classical theatre was not an occasional practice; rather was developed as a regular performance culture approved by the society. Even the plays in ancient times were performed at different times of the day according to its related rasa. Apart from that, Indian classical performances were not meant for a large gathering as we commonly observe in the ancient Greek and Roman theatres. Indian classical theatre, with the help of delicate facial expressions and hand gestures, is elevated to the level of spiritual invocations in the domain of fine arts. The audience, through the performance, goes through a blissful experience, where a singular hand gesture or an eye-expression holds a specific importance. Intimacy and immediacy are the essential factors in the presentation of Indian drama to realise its aesthetics. Indian classical plays are also categorised into various types according to its structure: Nataka, Prakarana, Anka, Prahasana, etc.—each having a definite predominant emotion. Each play is meant for a specific group of audience who can appreciate these sentiments. Therefore, audience in Indian classical theatre is also called 'Rasika', which makes them distinct from the very beginning. These are perhaps the most probable reasons for which open-air performance practice could not be developed as a culture in Indian classical theatre.

Contrary to the above observations, the folkloric tradition in India gives importance to the open-air performance. Since folk performances are an outcome of common human activities, it is preferred to grow in the crowd which requires a space without restriction and distinction so as to express itself fully. Since folk performances are closely related to ceremonial activities, such as harvest festivals and rituals, open-air theatres are found suitable for these kinds of activities.

A few open-air theatres in India like Meghdoot and Bahirang have significantly contributed to the contemporary theatre practices.

The Meghdoot Open-air Theatre in Delhi

The Meghdoot, a modest open-air theatre complex at the Mandi House, is situated right at the heart of Delhi. It was conceived by Ebrahim Alkazi, the grand master of modern Indian Theatre, for the National School of Drama Repertory Company in the mid-1960s. This theatre was built to accommodate approximately 250 audience. In the beginning, this rectangular stage, without any proscenium arch, was an earthen elevated area. The unique feature of Meghdoot is the presence of a gigantic peepal tree at the up-centre of the stage which also serves as a backdrop to all the performances. The branches spread over the stage to form a natural canopy. This not only adds to the ambience of the performance, but also to the blissful experience of a breezy evening under the stars. At the downright of the stage, an artificial Mughal architectural structure was erected to serve as wings as well as for the entry and exit of the actors. Musicians occasionally placed themselves atop this 7-feet-high construction during the show. The other side of the stage was equipped with makeshift bamboo structures to serve as wings. The backstage behind the peepal tree was also

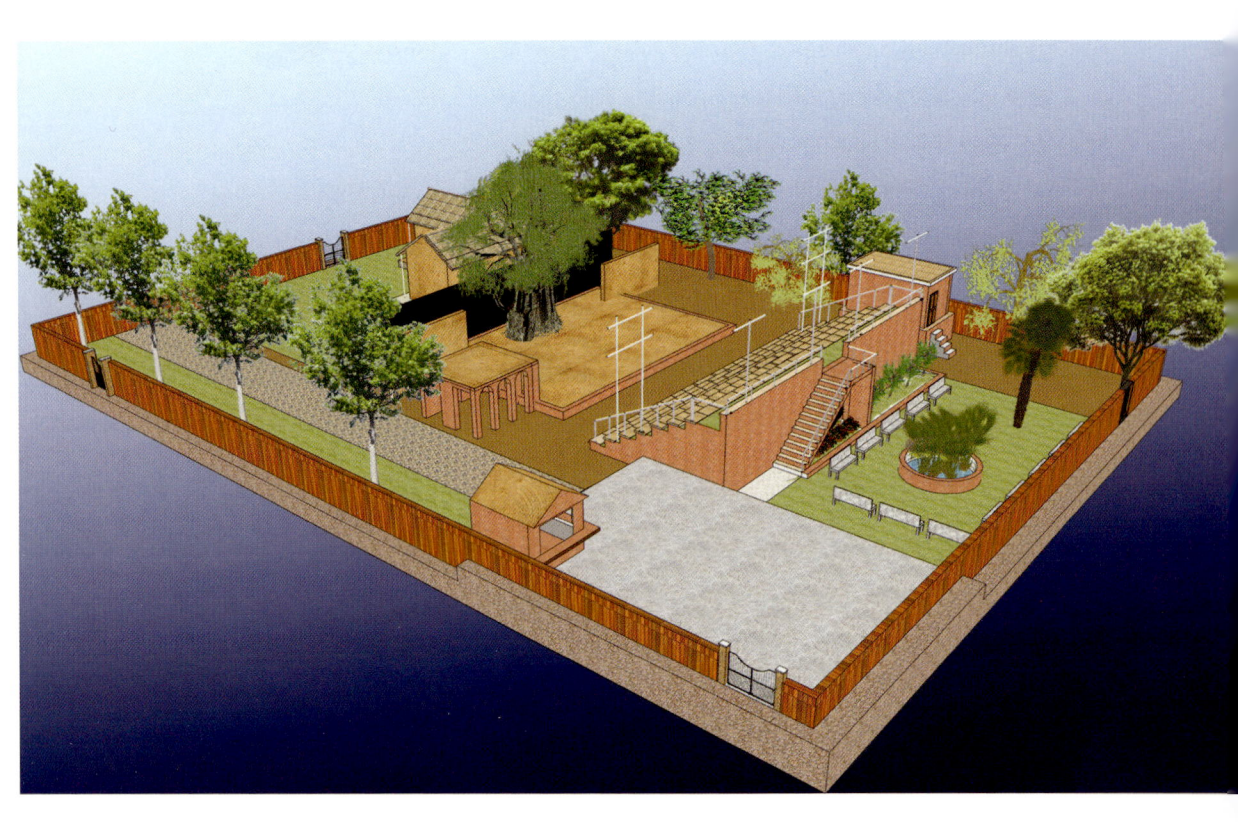

Three-dimensional model of Meghdoot open-air theatre complex. The theatre was built by Ebrahim Alkazi for the National School of Drama Repertory Company in the mid 1960s. The theatre has changed its shape in the course of time. The drawing is prepared out of memory of the author.

separated from the main acting area by a bamboo wall. However, the stage has been replaced with a concrete structure and the artificial architecture of the right wings were demolished after the Central Sangeet Natak Akademi took over the space from the National School of Drama while the audience gallery retains its original form. Still, the gigantic peepal tree stands tall on the up-centre to speak of the glorious history of this theatre space.

This theatre also provides ample opportunity for creative lighting design. Finding a suitable angle for fixing lights never becomes a problem in this space. The tree branches above the stage function as the grid where the lights can be easily installed. E. Alkazi had meticulously designed this performance space underneath the tree to bring it into focus amidst the surrounding structures. There were makeup and costume sheds and a small carpentry workshop attached to the backstage which is no more. These thatched hutments behind the stage were purposefully designed to create an impression of a rustic ambience in the midst of the city. The audience usually sit on mats or cushions on the staircase-like arrangements which rises one and half feet upwards. The yard behind the audience gallery is a small garden replete with sculptures, where the viewers gather for the show. The theatre complex is a harmonious blend of architecture and nature that co-exist in a perfect sync.

Many reputed directors, actors and scenographers have creatively explored this intimate open-air theatre for numerous repertory productions of the National School of Drama. *King Lear* (1964), *Mukhyamantri* (1978), *Barnam Vana* (1979)—an adaptation of the *Macbeth*, *Uncle Vanya* (1979), *Mr Puntila and His Man Matti* (1979), *Chote Shayad Bade Shayad* (1980), *Mena Gurjari* (1980), *Sayan Bhaye Kotwal* (1980), *Begam ki Takia* (1980), *Antarang* (1980), *Bury the Dead* (1982), *Mahabhoj* (1982), *Cherry ka Bageecha*—an adaptation of *The Cherry Orchard* (1983), *Kabhi Na Choden Khet* (1984), *Yamgatha* (1990), *Karmawali* (1990) and many more memorable productions of the National School of Drama repertory have added to the credit of this open-air intimate theatre space.

The Bahirang Muktakashi Manch

The name 'Bahirang', derived from two Sanskrit terms—'Bahir' meaning 'outer' and 'Ranga' meaning 'theatre'—is conceived as an an open-air platform. Situated on the bank of the 'Bada Talaab'—the huge lake at the foot of the Shyamla hills—this elegant amphitheatre was designed by Charles Mark Correa, a noted Indian architect. This theatre is an integral part of the Bharat Bhavan Rangamandal, Bhopal, built in the year 1982, which holds a special attraction for the people all over the world. The performance area is a kind of a thrust stage, almost like a miniature of the Greco-Roman theatre, surrounded by a semi-circular audience gallery with a seating capacity of around 400, just above the water level. The stage floor is an earthen structure while the auditorium is built with the famous pink stone slabs of Jaipur. The stage up-right leads to the green room and the left side slopes down to the lake. Each row in the gallery rises 1 foot 6 inches up to the back to form the lobby where the audience takes entry to the gallery. The presence of the lake provides an ethereal ambience to all the productions. The gradual appearance of the actors from down below

CONVENTIONS OF SPACE | 193

the lake at the back of the stage creates an illusion of a psychological distance. Watching a performance on a summer evening would definitely add to the pleasant experience of the viewers.

Many memorable productions of Rangmandal, such as, *Malavikagnimitram* (1982), *Gara ki Gaadi* (1982), *Do Kashtion ka Sawar* (1982), *Ghashiram Kotwal* (1983), *Hayavadana* (1984), *Banjh Ghati* (1985), *The Trojan Women* (1986), etc. were presented here with great applaud.

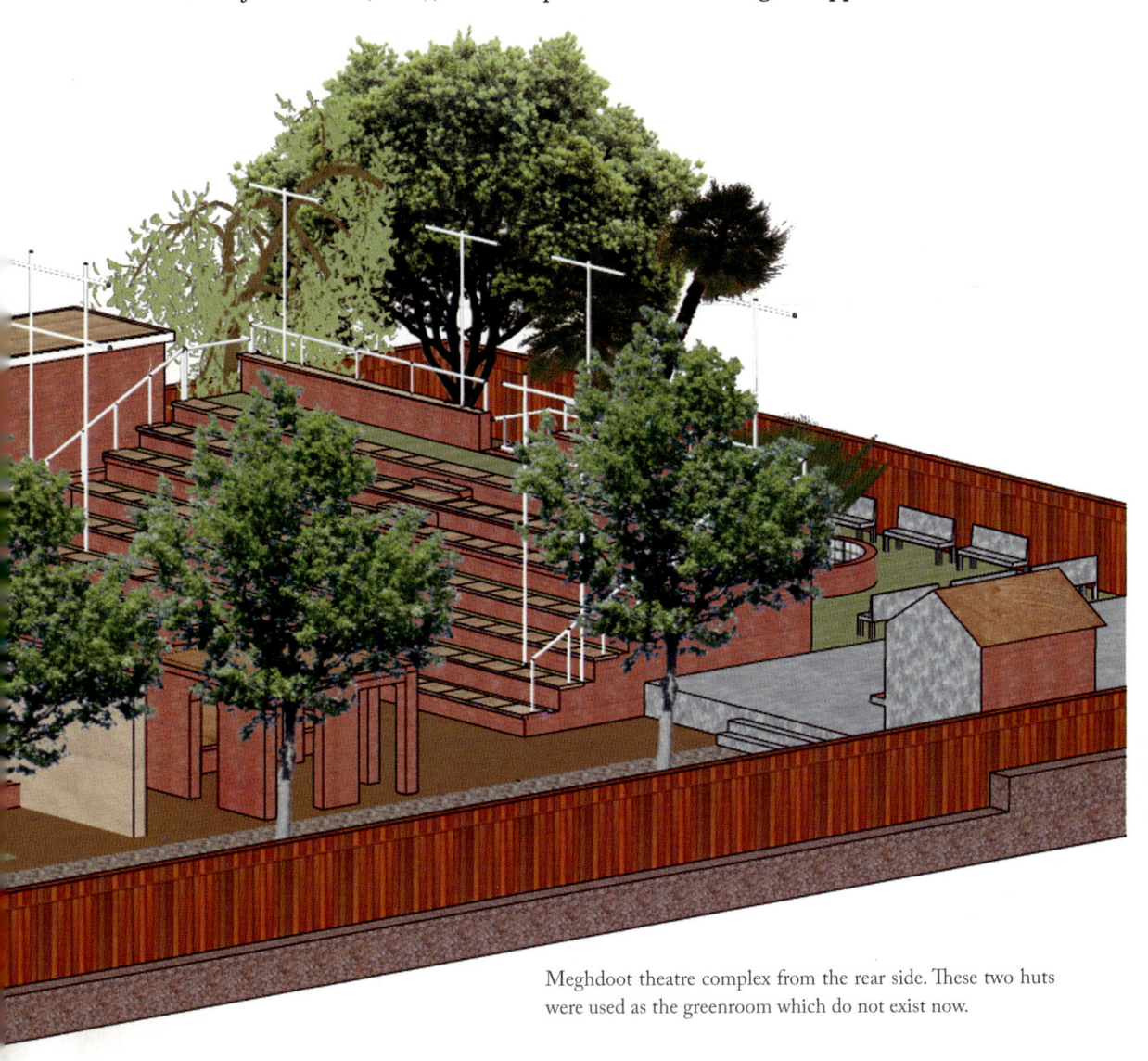

Meghdoot theatre complex from the rear side. These two huts were used as the greenroom which do not exist now.

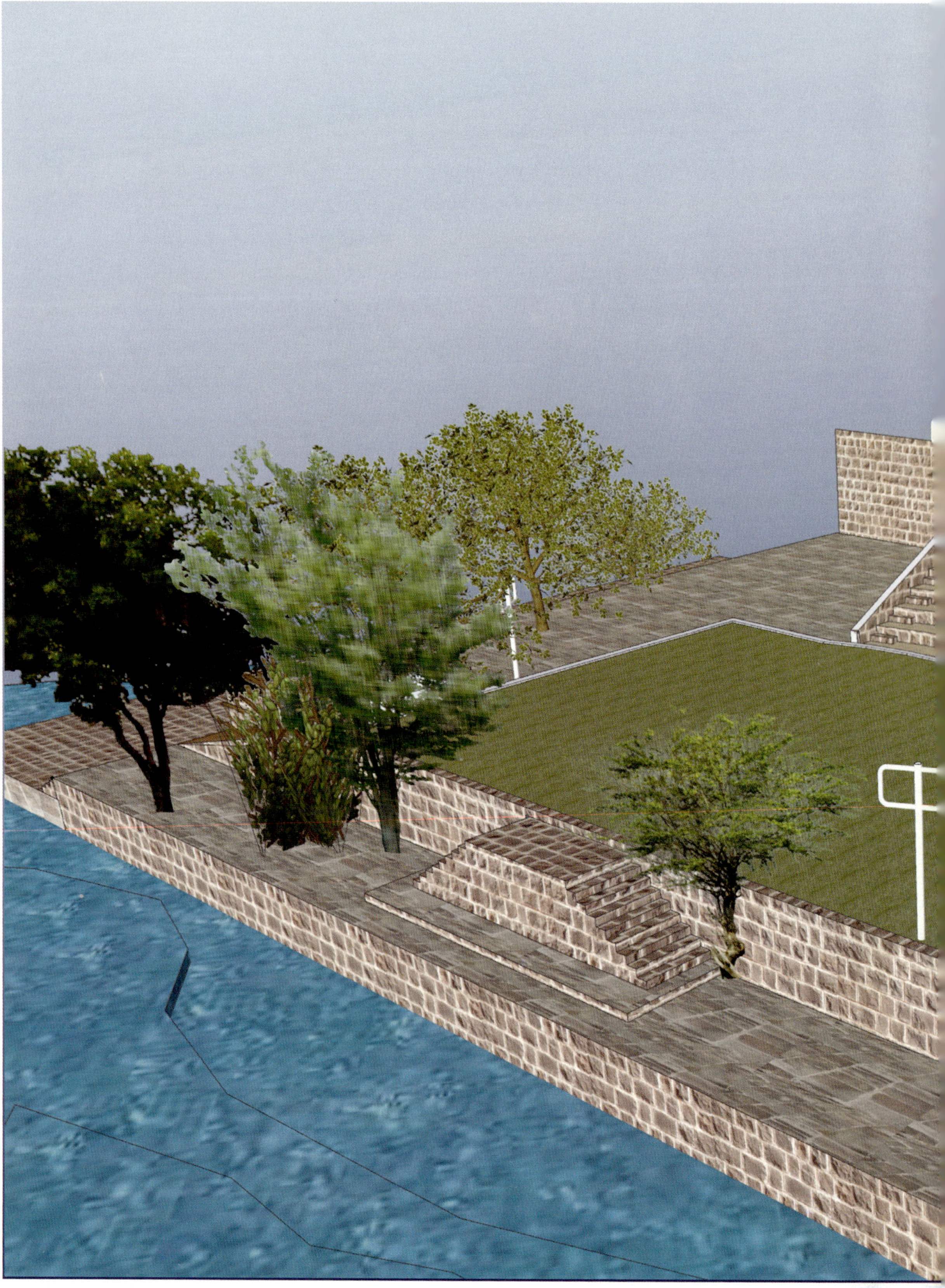

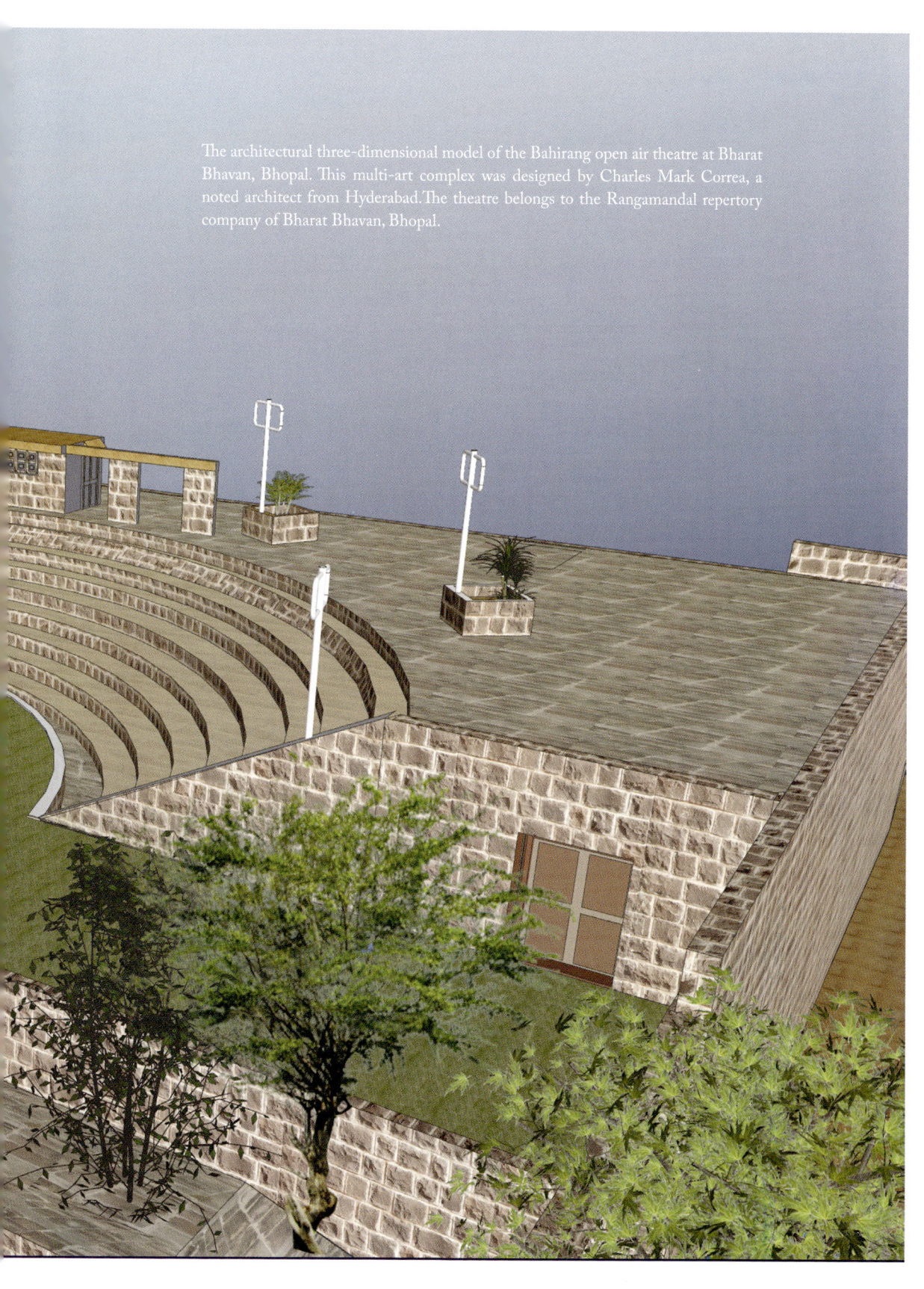

The architectural three-dimensional model of the Bahirang open air theatre at Bharat Bhavan, Bhopal. This multi-art complex was designed by Charles Mark Correa, a noted architect from Hyderabad. The theatre belongs to the Rangamandal repertory company of Bharat Bhavan, Bhopal.

CONCLUSION

In the history of performance, there has been a constant artistic urge to come closer to the audience, involving them actively to make them realise the relevant issues dealt in the play in a more direct way. However, the formal proscenium and the large open-air restrict the possibilities of creating intimacy with the audience. This may happen due to these following reasons:

i. The remarkable distance between the gallery and the stage restricts the audience from interactive participation.
ii. The conceptual imaginary wall or the fourth wall, a major characteristic feature of the proscenium theatre, does not allow the direct involvement of the audience in a presentation. The audience has to peep through the imaginary yet persistent 'fourth wall' to watch the play.
iii. In the proscenium or open-air theatre, a performer does not find means to involve the audience in the dramatic situations. The audience only watch, enjoy and appreciate the performance from a definite distance. Therefore, active participation is not possible in these performance spaces.

Over the years, theatre has been developed as the most powerful communicative medium and a major political tool. The Primitive theatre, the Greek theatre, the Roman theatre, the Indian Classical theatre, the Folk traditions, the Commedia dell'arte, the noh and kabuki theatre and all other kinds of performance cultures of the world have served mankind across time. But a proscenium theatre, in order to bring beauty and grandeur to the production, can to some extent limit the power of communication. Even though performing on the apron in front of the proscenium arch is an attempt to come closer to the audience by challenging the concept of 'fourth wall' of the proscenium theatre, it could not fully solve the purpose of total participation of the audience in the presentation.

It has already been discussed in the previous chapters how the audience enjoys the traditional or folk performances from all possible angles. There is no restriction in terms of a direct involvement of the audience in these plays. The audience associate with the characters, share their feelings and consider the characters' emotions as their own. In folk and ritualistic theatres, the audience become a vital part of the presentation which is not possible in this framed space for which alternative theatre spaces and their practices become essential.

References
i   Pavis, Patrice. 1998. *Dictionary of the Theatre: Terms, Concepts and Analysis*. Toronto: University of Toronto Press. p. 360.
ii Chaturvedi, B.K. 2004. *Shiv-puran*. New Delhi: Diamond Pocket. pp. 55–56.
iii Banham, Martin and Sarah Stanton. 1996. *Cambridge Paperback Guide to Theatre*. Cambridge: Cambridge University Press. p. 1209.

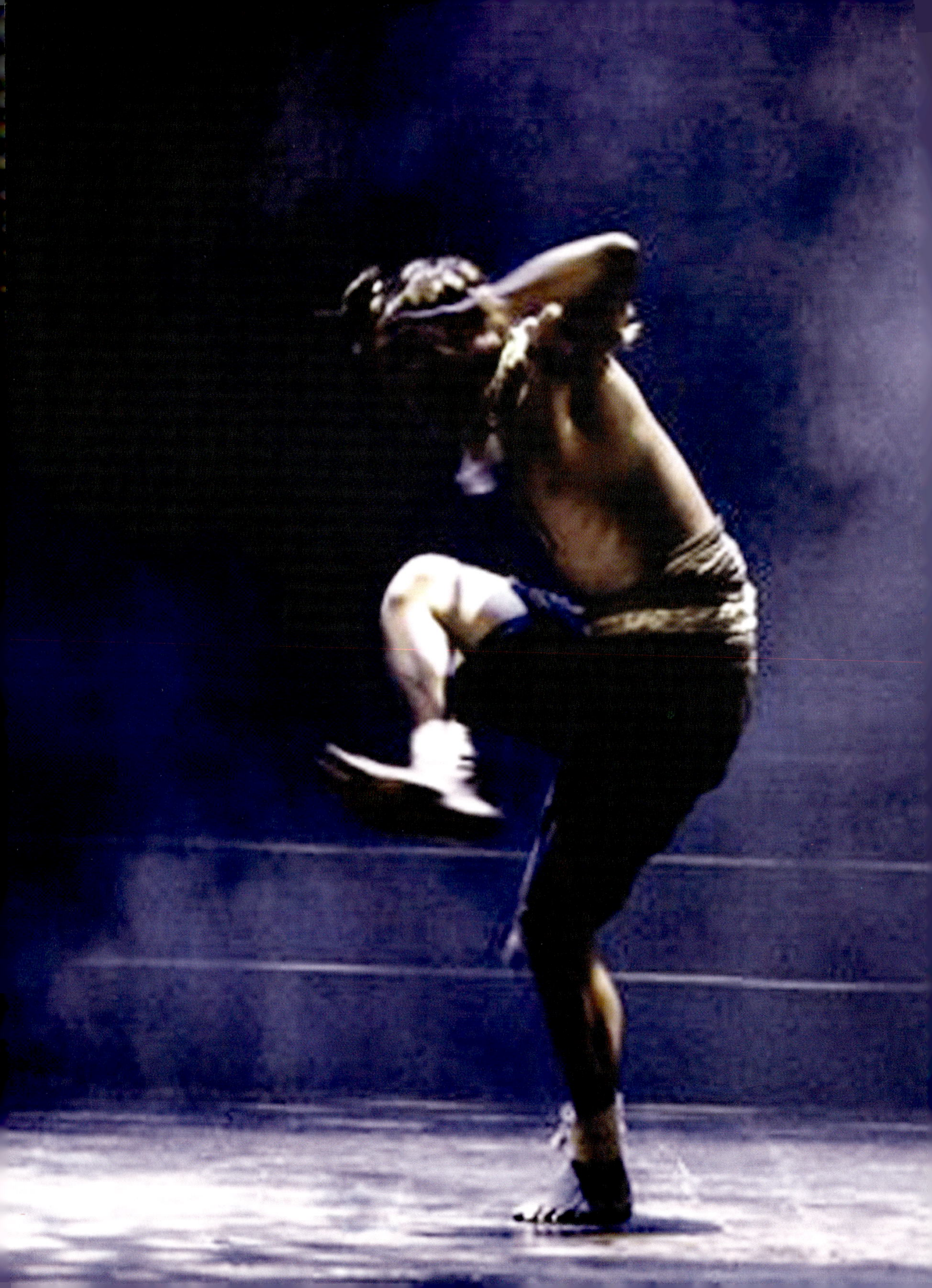

ALTERNATIVE PERFORMANCE SPACES

Right from the early days of theatre, a quest for new spaces continues to explore new potentiality for performances. Scenographers across the globe have been constantly trying to break away with the convention of 'space' for an alternative practice which would wipe out the distinct line between the performers and the spectators. This concept of togetherness in theatre can be easily noticed in folk and traditional theatres—the best examples of community-based activities. The involvement of audience in these performances is deep enough to achieve a live communion, a direct connection.

In the context of alternative theatre practices, Jerzy Grotowski opines, 'It cannot exist without the actor–spectator relationship of perceptual, direct, "live" communion. This is an ancient theatrical truth, of course, but when rigorously tested in practice it undermines most of our usual ideas about theatre.'[i] This was the primary concept behind his practising alternative theatre, which rejects the major theatrical conventions and disciplines: text, scenography, lighting, architecture, design and even acting. For Peter Brook, theatre is an engagement between an actor and audience in an empty space. He writes, 'A man walks across this empty space whilst someone else is watching him, and this is all that is needed for an act of theatre to be engaged.'[ii]

The above statements endorse the fact that space must have an intense potential for meaningful interactions between the actors and the spectators. But this intensity of relationship varies extensively in different performance spaces. The experience of watching a play in a huge Greek theatre would be different from viewing it in a proscenium theatre, just as the experience of an arena performance would certainly be different from that of a found space. The style of presentation in the Greek, Roman and medieval liturgical dramas has paved the way for a synthetic kind of theatre inside a proscenium for a class of audience, which gradually gained popularity across the world. The audience in a proscenium theatre used to watch the play from a definite distance. Yet, within this framework of performance, there was a lurking desire from the performers' part to diminish that distance, come closer to the audience and share common thoughts and feelings. The craving to draw the audience into the performance resulted in an active participation of the viewers and made theatre an interpersonal activity. Therefore, conceptual performances and alternative theatre spaces gained momentum in the contemporary times. The changing values of human life has changed the outlook of the society and thus subsequently the outlook of the theatre or performance art in general over the years.

The urge for a parallel narrative to the mainstream theatre practice, the need for an alternative theatre space, gained momentum in India during the second half of the 20th century possibly due to the following reasons:

i.   The growing economy and industrialisation
ii. Decentralisation of the social structure
iii. Searching for newer mode of expressions in life

The exploration of space is an ongoing creative urge, which continues to reflect in different cultures time and again. Let us discuss a few alternative performance spaces and their practices.

THRUST STAGE

Unlike a proscenium theatre, performance in a thrust stage occurs on the extended platform that protrudes into the auditorium by crossing the proscenium arch. The main performance area is surrounded by the audience on three sides which allows a greater intimacy between the performers and the audience. While the actors perform amidst the audience, the area behind the proscenium arch is used only for the entry and exit of the actors. The urge to come closer to the audience, by breaking away with the 'fourth wall' convention of the proscenium, brought this kind of theatre into practice.

The thrust stage is the oldest kind of performance space in the history of theatre which was redefined during modern times. It first appeared

Perspective drawing of a thrust theatre with a projected stage.
Note the performance area is penetrated into the auditorium, pushing the audience to three sides.

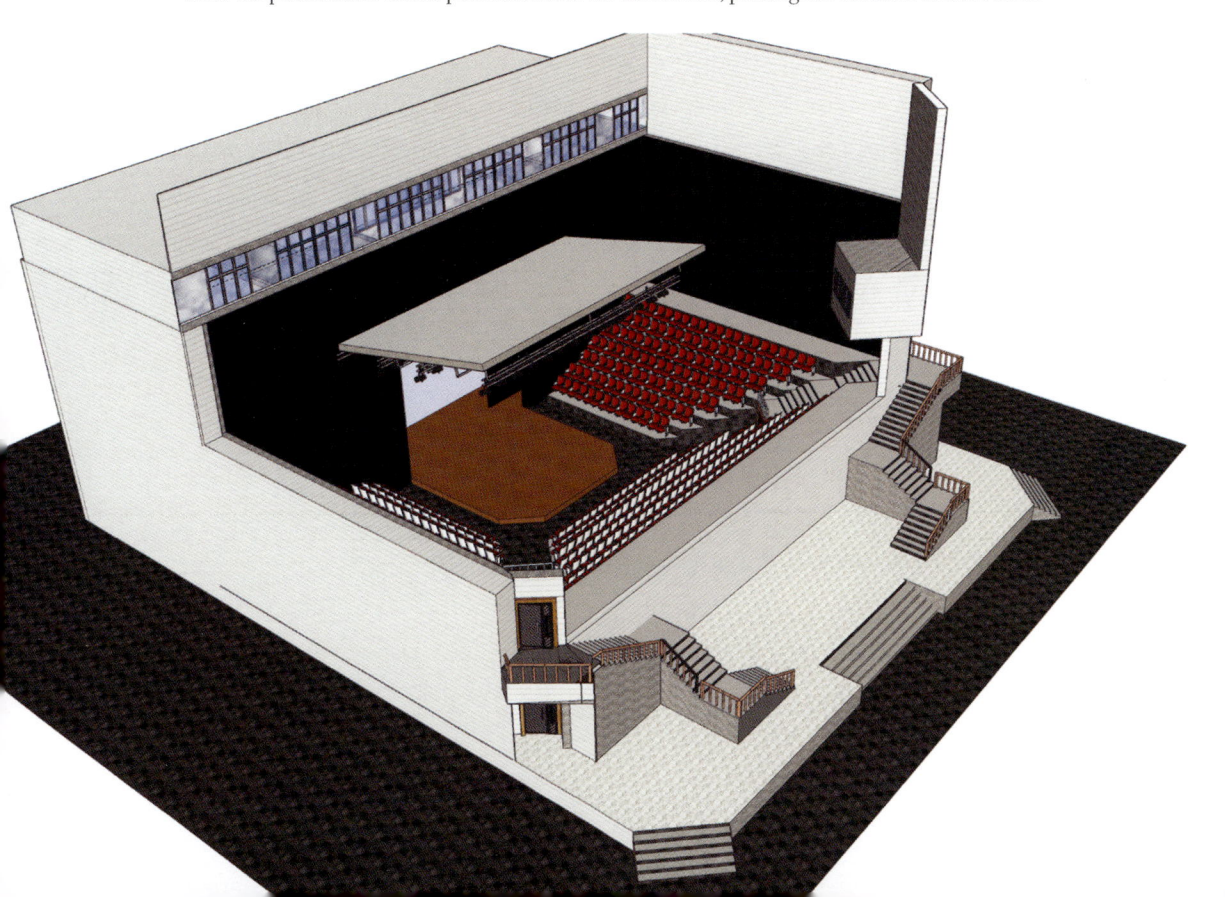

in ancient Greek theatres and continued through the pageant wagon presentations in the medieval Europe, also found its place in the famous Globe Theatre in London. The Globe Theatre stage is a thrust performance space that is extended into the auditorium in the yard. During the time of Shakespeare, the lower-class audience watched the plays standing on all three sides in the yard.

Since the idea behind this kind of space is to develop greater intimacy between the performers and the audience, contemporary thrust theatres across the world discard the practice of a large audience by accommodating comparatively lesser number of viewers. Like the proscenium, thrust theatre also provides two major functional areas: stage and auditorium, but their characteristic features are somehow different from the proscenium theatre.

THE PERFORMANCE SPACE OF THRUST STAGE

The performance area in a thrust stage is an extension of the apron of the proscenium theatre. It seems, as if the apron is pushed into the audience gallery, thus creating a three-side vision for the audience. Due to this sitting arrangement, the performance differs extensively from the proscenium theatre. Since the major dramatic actions take place on the downstage, the upstage area remains passive, leaving it open for the entry and exit of the actors, creating minor scenes and fixing of sets. The concept of the fourth wall cannot be applied for a thrust performance. Thus, conventional styles of acting methods are not encouraged in a thrust stage.

The thrust stage remains a challenge for the scenographers every time they plan to design a play in this space. Since performance in a thrust stage is visualised from three different sides, the visual perspective from a single point of view is not possible. Any kind of vertical arrangement on the stage might obstruct major stage actions and create blind spots for the audience. For example, if we fix a flat on

This is a wrong arrangement of set units in a thrust stage, since any voluminous object would obstruct the vision of the audience. As we can identify in image-A, the audience sitting on the right of the auditorium is deprived of watching the scene properly. This is due to the placement of the flats in the middle (ref. Image-B)

Image-A

Note this drawing carefully. The audience sitting towards the extreme right of the auditorium cannot watch the action comfortably, because of the flat that stands in between.

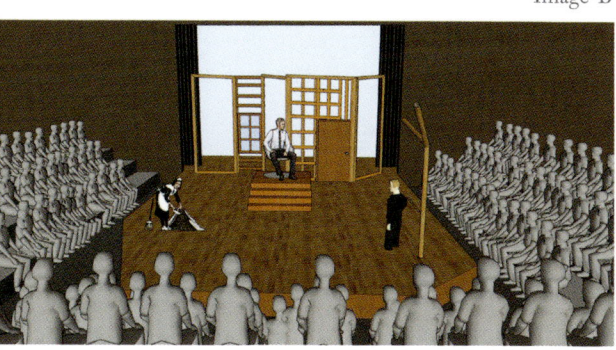

Image-B

This is the right arrangement of placing the set units in a thrust stage, (Image-C) and any stage with multiple visual angles. In this design the flats are replaced with structural set units which is a cleaver idea for designing a play in a thrust stage.

Image-C

Illustrative drawings of wrong and right design and the placement of objects on a thrust stage.

the left side of the stage, the audience watching from the right cannot see the actions beyond that flat. That is why large sets are usually avoided in a thrust stage design. The implementation of realistic box set in a thrust stage is not possible, instead the scenographers depend more on suggestive, skeletal or structural designs for the plays. Lighting for such cases also remains a challenge for the scenographers. Fixing the angles for cross lights are nearly impossible in this kind of theatre because the light rays may hit the viewers' eyes in such a way that they cannot comfortably watch the performance. The same kind of issue persists in the fixing of the backlights. These problems can be avoided with careful execution of stage lights. High-angle lighting is the best option for a thrust stage. There is also a chance of over-exposing the stage floor while watching the play from a high-rising gallery. But that can be reduced with the application of dark colours on the sets and props.

THRUST STAGES IN INDIA

Though performance on thrust stage is not a very common practice in India, a few technically equipped thrust theatres are still available for us. These theatres are primarily run by the private and autonomous organisations or academic institutions. The Prithvi Theatre in Bombay, the Antarang theatre at Bharat Bhavan, Bhopal, the Thrust Theatre at Bhartendu Natya Akademi (BNA), Lucknow, and the Ranga Shankara Theatre in Bangalore are some of the well-known thrust theatres in India. These theatres, equipped with modern amenities, provide opportunities for alternative practices, thus contributing towards the progressive theatre movement in India.

The Prithvi Theatre

The famous Prithvi Theatre in Mumbai is one of the remarkable intimate thrust theatres, established in the year 1978 in the cherished memory of the legendary actor Sri Prithviraj Kapoor. Prior to the establishment of this theatre, it was a traveling company, run by Prithviraj Kapoor from 1944–60. But he had a dream to have a permanent theatre house in Mumbai which could not be actualised during his lifetime. After the demise of the stalwart, his son Sashi Kapoor and his wife Jennifer Kendal, a famous actress, constructed a theatre at Juhu in Mumbai and named it 'Prithvi theatre'. This moderate theatre was designed by the well-known Indian architect, Ved Segan, with a seating capacity of about 200 audience. The stage, projecting into the gallery, is raised 9 inch above the ground, with 20 feet and 26 feet in length and breadth respectively. The audience sit in a racked gallery which covers the three sides of the stage while the entry and exit of the actors are pushed towards the upstage area behind the proscenium arch. The entire auditorium, including the stage, is painted black for the enhancement of the performance. A few illustrative drawings of the Prithvi Theatre are provided below for reference.

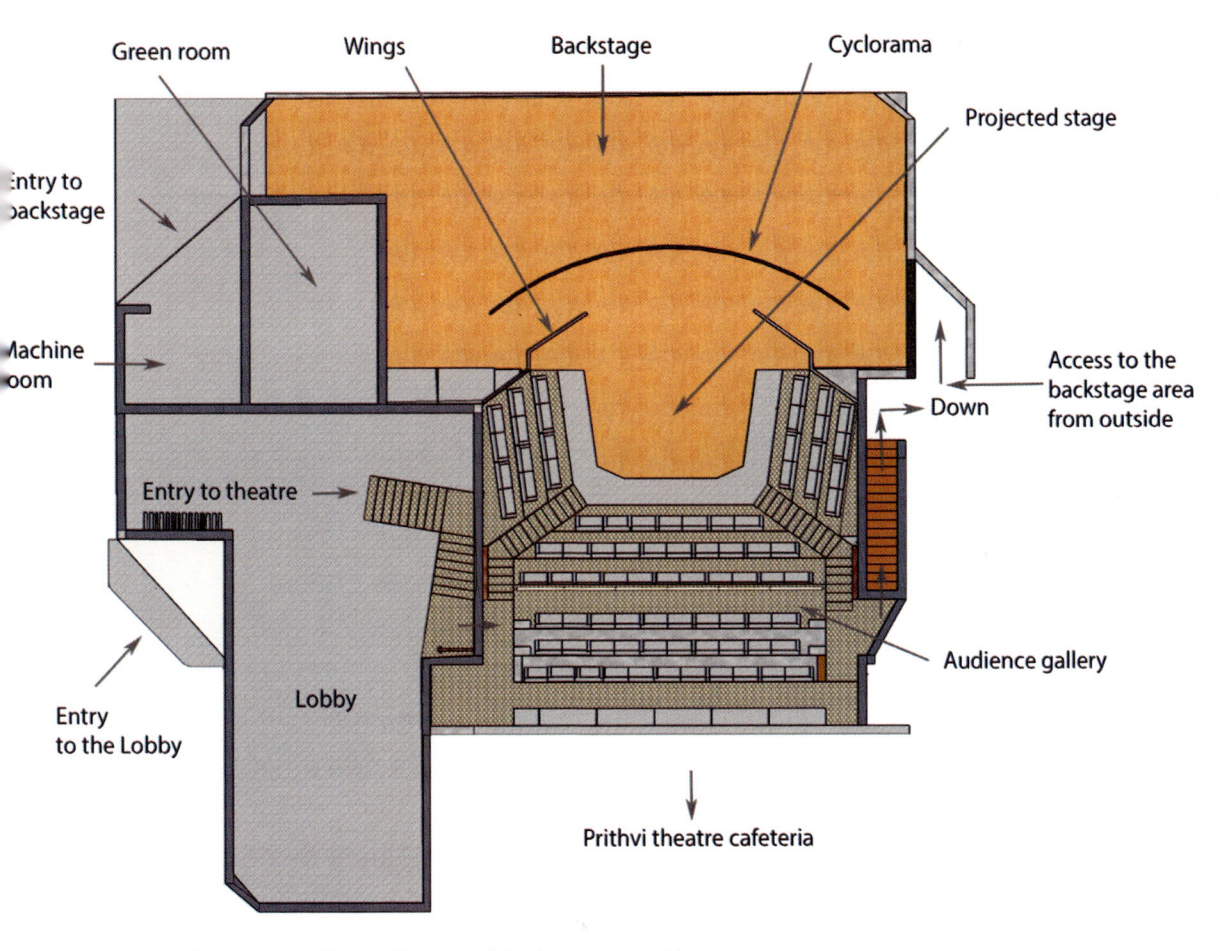

Ground plan of Prithvi Theatre at Mumbai (not in scale).

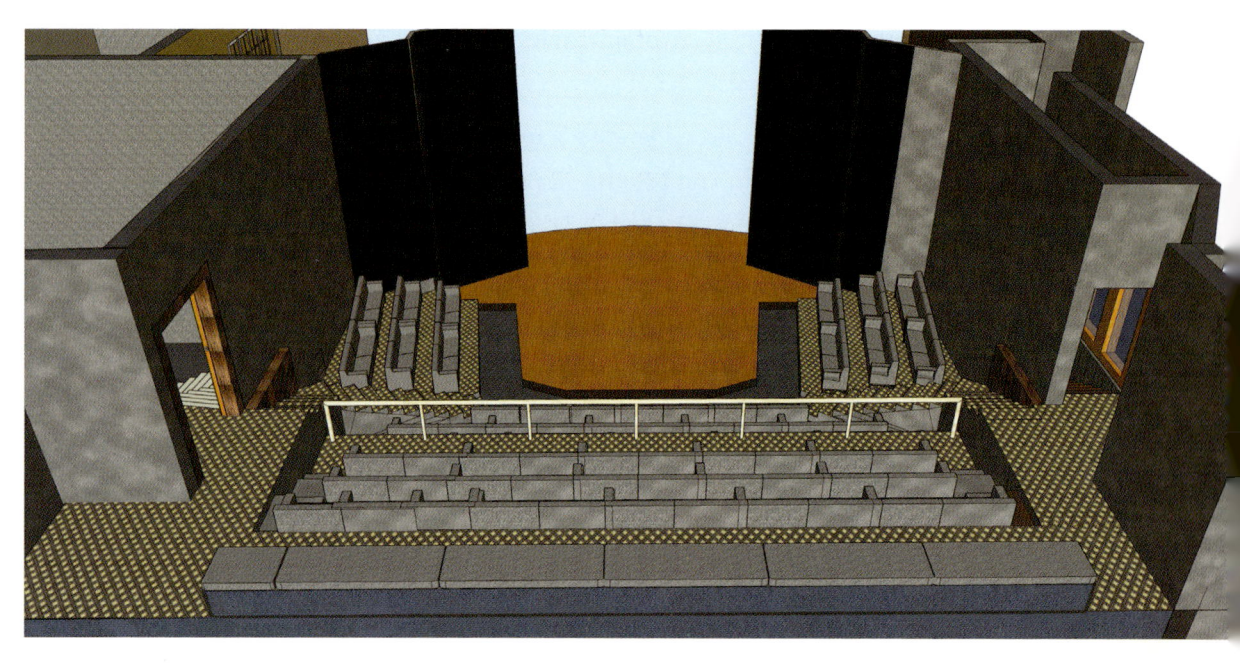

High-angle perspective drawing of the Prithvi Theatre.

The Antarang Theatre

The Antarang theatre at Bharat Bhavan, Bhopal, was built for the Rangamandal Repertory Company in 1982. This intimate theatre used to function exclusively for repertory productions in the beginning years. The theatre was the brainchild of B.V. Karanth, the founder director of the Rangamandal. The Antarang, being an integral wing of the famous Bharat Bhavan multi-art complex, was designed by Charles Mark Correa, one of the finest architects of India in the year 1981–82. Antarang indoor theatre has a projected stage with wooden square floor measuring 36 feet in length and breadth. The performance area—the stage floor—instead of rising above the ground, forms a pit-like structure that goes 1 foot below the ground level. The actors usually take entry and exit to the stage from the stage up-left and-right passages. The green room is connected to the stage left. The acoustic system of the theatre is good enough for the sound to reach every corner without the use of microphones. The audience gallery is raised upward in a staircase-like arrangement, which covers the three sides of the stage in seven rows. The audience enter the gallery from the back of the auditorium. Instead of chairs in the gallery, the theatre provides cushions for the audience to sit on the floor to watch the performance. The only limitation of the stage is its height, which is 13 feet from floor level. This low height of the theatre does not allow to fabricate high-rising sets and elaborate vertical designs. Also, getting a desired lighting angle from the ceiling often becomes difficult due to the low height of the roof.

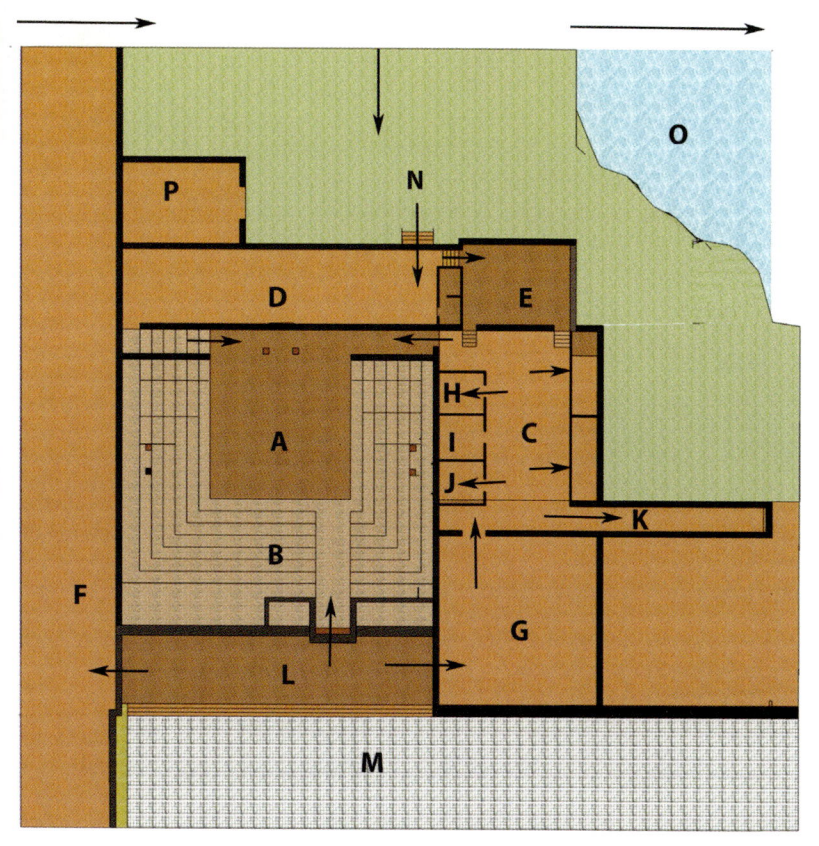

A- Stage
B- Three-sided Audience gallery
C- Backstage
D- Carpentry section
E- Abhirang intimate theatre
F- Roopankar Art gallery
G- Rangadarshani Theatre exhibition hall
H, I & J- Makeup rooms
K- Corridor towards Bahirang open air theatre
L- Foyer
M- Yard
N- Loading door
O- Lake
P- AC Plant

Ground plan of the Antaranga indoor theatre at Bharat Bhavan, Bhopal (Not in scale).

Isometric projection of the Antaranga indoor theatre. Note the wooden floor and the three-sided stage along with the backstage area.

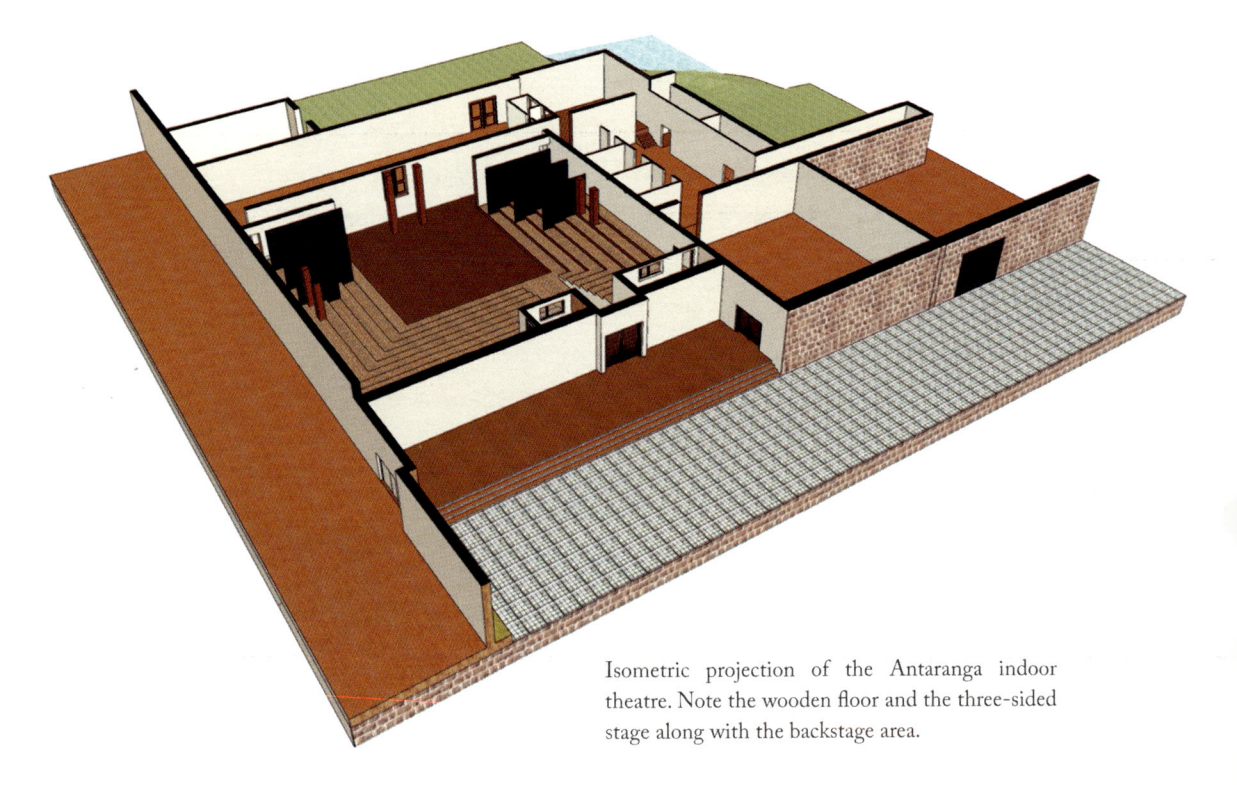

The Thrust Theatre at BNA

The thrust theatre of the Bhartendu Natya Academy, Lucknow, provides ample opportunities for its students to carry on experimental theatre activities at the academic level. It has a well-structured formal stage with approximately 250 chairs in the audience gallery covering all the three sides. The actors can take entry from both sides of the wings behind the proscenium arch. This theatre is equipped with a well-designed proscenium arch with wings, borders and a proper white cyclorama. Apart from the entry and exit through the wings, there are also provisions for the actors to take entry through the audience gallery on both corners of the downstage. However, the stage floor seems overexposed from the audience gallery because of their high-rising staircase arrangement.

The Arena Stage

The performance in an arena stage takes place amidst the audience surrounding all the sides. In this kind of performance space, there is no possibility for the actors to mask or hide since there is no scope for employing any wings or curtains. The stage is exposed to all four sides in a square or circular form like a circus ring. Sometimes, one can interact with improvised arena arrangements in street theatres or roadside entertainment programs.

Photograph of the auditorium of the thrust theatre at Bharatendu Natya academy, Lucknow. Courtesy: Author's personal collection.

In an arena stage, while the actors communicate with a group of audience at one side, the rest of the audience, sitting on the other sides, are usually left deprived of their actions. Therefore, for a constant communication with the viewers, the performers keep on moving frequently from one spot to another during the performance, which is one of the vital characteristics of the arena performance—continuous mobility. Unlike thrust, the domination of a specific stage space is not possible in arena stage; instead it gives equal importance to all the stage spaces. Elaborate set materials are usually avoided in this kind of space since they block the audience vision. Instead, it would be a good choice to employ minimum stage props and structural design for an arena performance.

According to Parker and Smith:

> The visual elements have to be confined to small low units or open pieces that can be seen through. Design detail becomes more important because of the intimacy of the theatre and the lack of larger elements of scenery in the composition. This type of staging is intentionally simple, depending upon a suggestion of scenery to set the scene and stimulate the audience imagination to fill the rest.[iii]

Though using an arena stage was not a regular practice in colonial India, it was quite common in the folk and traditional theatres (Ref. Pala stage). In recent times, a few Indian theatre practitioners are shifting their focus from the conventions of proscenium theatre to the arena space, since it provides plenty of possibilities for experiments and interpretations. But unfortunately, India does not have enough well-equipped arena theatres for regular performances, which sometimes leads to improvising the space for performance. Badal Sircar (1925–2011), the celebrated Indian playwright and practitioner, is regarded as the pioneer of the

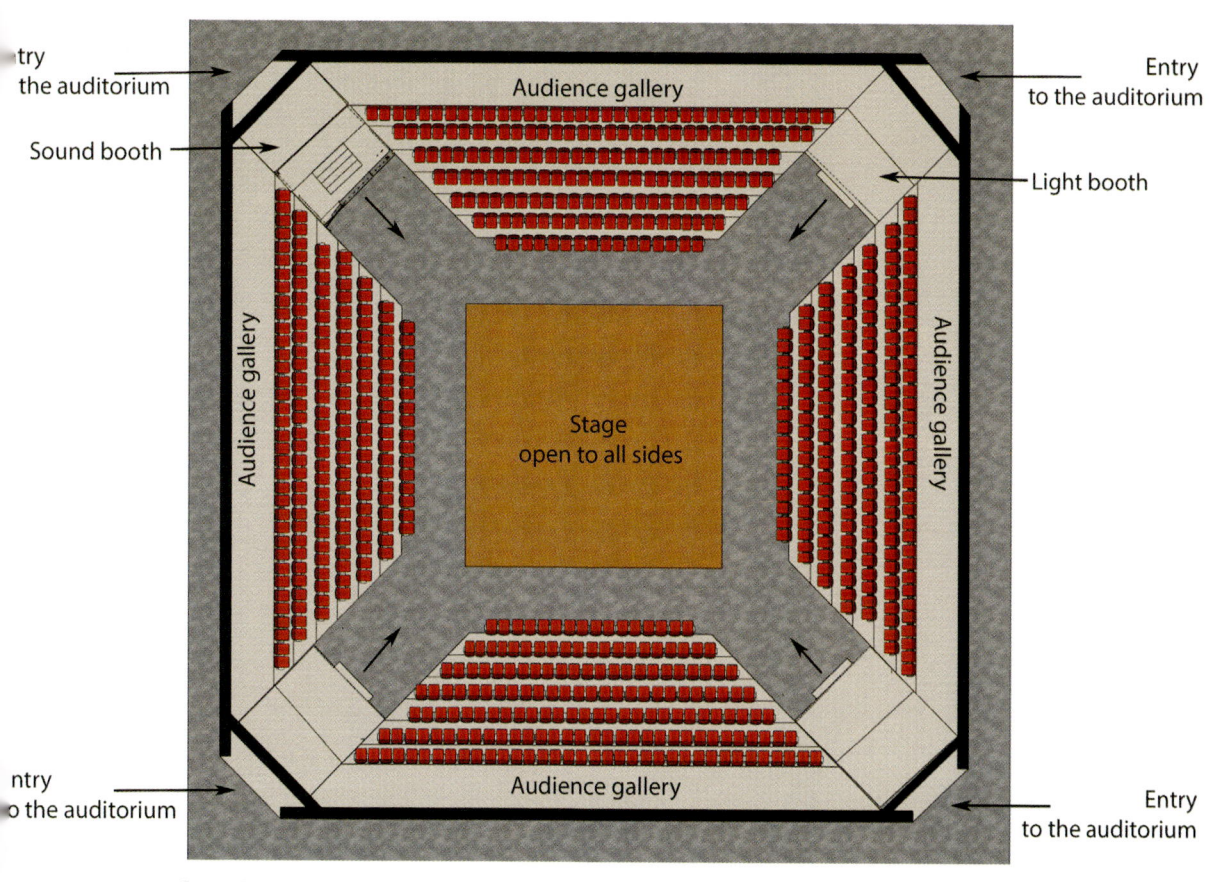

Ground plan of an arena stage (not in scale).

arena performances in India. Keeping this kind of space as the prime element of his theatre expression, he wrote plays such as, *Evam Indrajit* (1963), *Baki Itihash* (1965), *Paglaghoda* (1967), *Julus* (1972), *Bhoma* (1974), *Basi Khabar* (1979), etc. The significance of space and its visual expressions remains fundamental for this genre of theatre. Scenographers find the means to explore this space, using minimum set elements, to communicate with the spectators by triggering their imaginations in the maximum possible ways.

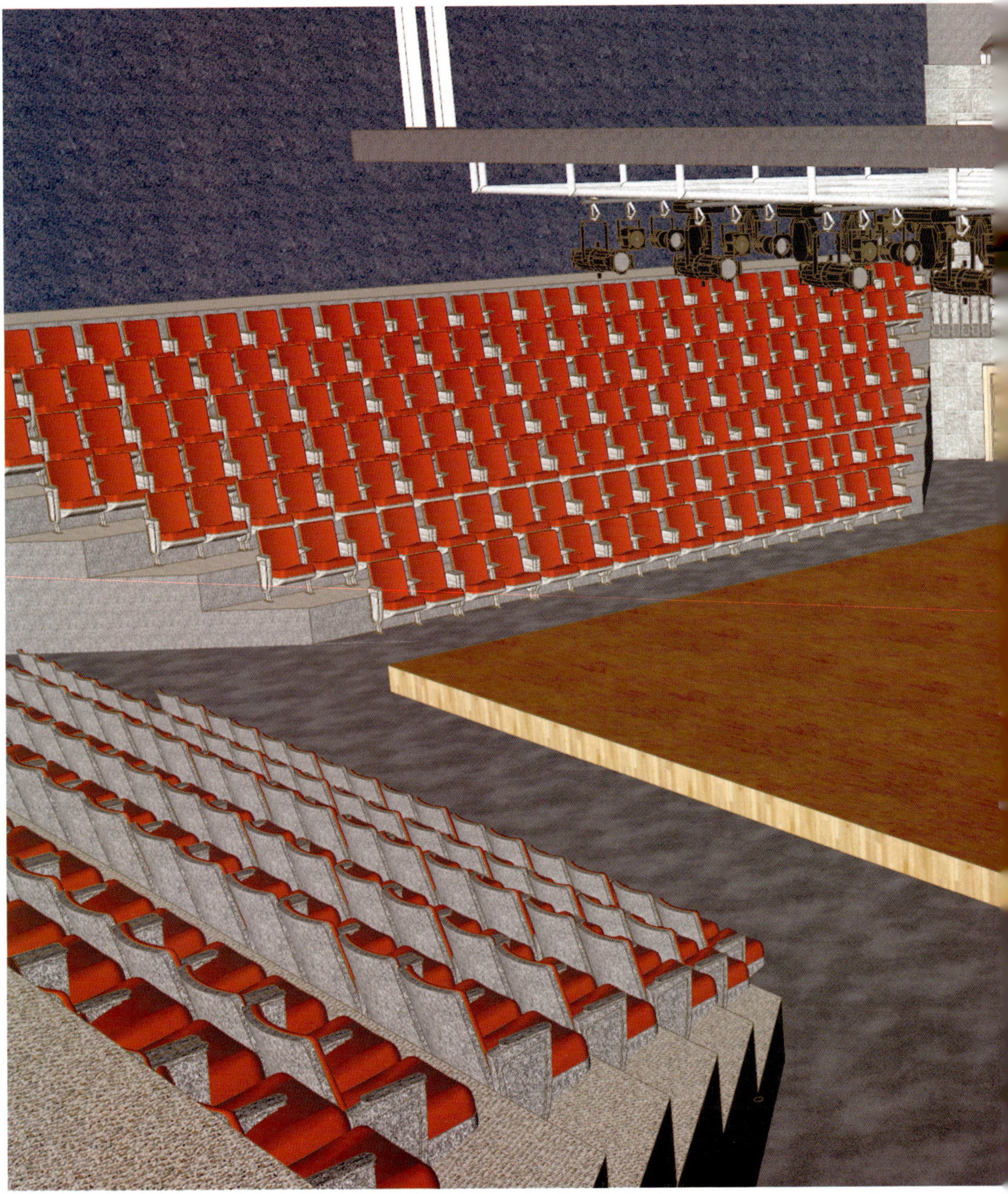

Interior of an arena theatre. Note the arrangement of audience gallery, entry and exit point of the actors, light grid and the four-sided square stage in the middle.

THE TRAVERSE STAGE

In the exploration of space for creative design with a possibility of a different impact on the audience, traverse stage came into being. Though the use of traverse stage is not so common in theatre like that of modelling and catwalk, it still provides a suitable platform for new experimentations.

Like a thrust stage, a traverse stage is also a projected performance area that passes through the audience by dividing the spectator's space equally into two halves. In its true form, it is a raised platform with no back wall behind the actors. This stage is also called as 'alley stage' and is popularly used for catwalk. Often there exists two separate areas on both end of the theatre, separated from the backstage through a divider or a curtain. These areas are used for the entry and exit of the actors and also for erecting set units, if at all essential. Since it becomes impossible to create any kind of set in a traverse stage that would block the audience vision, these two areas at the extreme ends of the stage offer opportunity for employing symbolic and functional design, and often are taken into use for this purpose.

Creating lighting effect on this stage is a challenge for the light designer, since lighting the stage from one side would cast shadow on the other side of the actors. Also, there are good chances of the light rays to hit the audience eye on both the sides if they are not executed carefully. High-angle lighting is the best possible option for a traverse design.

Performance in a traverse stage provides different experiences for the viewers as well as the performers. Since in this theatre the sitting position of the audience is front-to-front and the performance is held in the middle, audience have two different visual perspectives, resulting in different experiences. At the same time, the actors must be careful enough to provide optimum aural and visual experiences to the viewers in both the sides.

The most effective part of a traverse stage is the entry and exit of the actors on the stage from either of the entry points. They stay in the

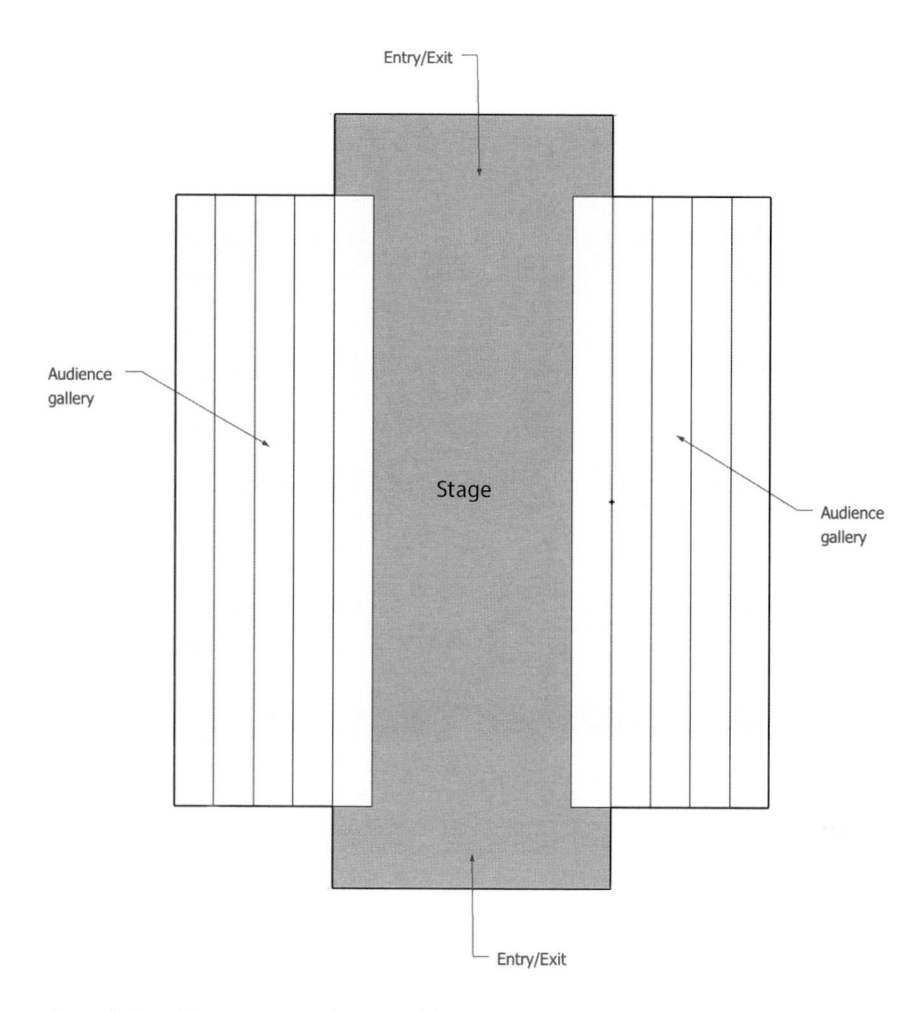

Ground plan of a traverse stage (not in scale).

full view of the audience during this time, thus projecting the entry and exit with meaning and conviction. There is also an adverse effect in a traverse performance—to build the dramatic tension. In a confrontation scene, the actors' profile image is strongly projected to the viewers which may prove less effective, looking into the dramatic situation. But concurrently, performance in a traverse stage is more participatory than any conventional presentation.

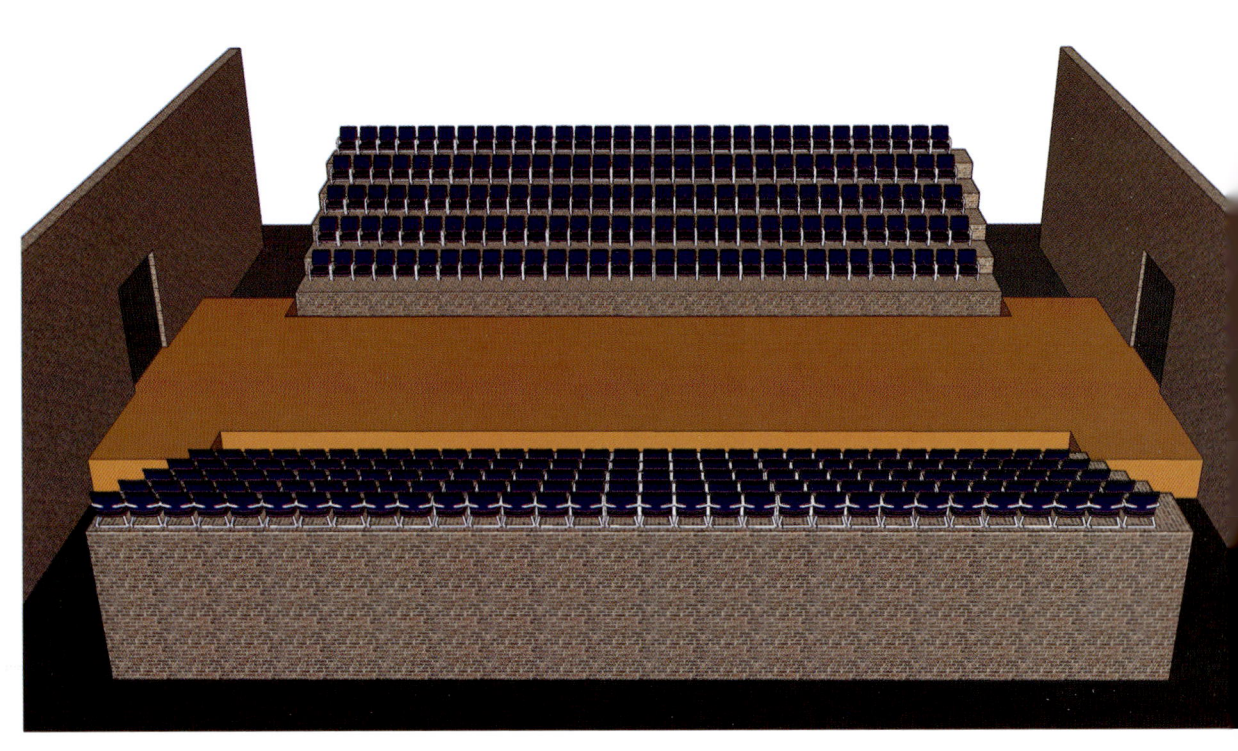

Perspective drawing of a traverse stage. Note the two-sided arrangement of the audience, the stage and the entry and exit doors for the actors and the audience.

Unfortunately, in India we do not have any traverse stage. Therefore, the scenographers usually improvise the space at the time of requirement. Often an existing proscenium stage is converted into a traverse stage by creating space for the audience to sit on both sides while the performance is held in the middle. Once at Banaras, I faced a similar challenge of converting a proscenium stage into a traverse one at Nagari Natak Mandali in the year 2005. The experience of transforming a proscenium theatre into a traverse stage has been elucidated later in this book.

THE FOUND SPACE

Sometimes, certain spaces with dramatic potential are improvised for theatre presentations. Though primarily these spaces are not meant for any sort of theatre activities, creative improvisation can transform them into performance spaces. The informal environment and unpredictable nature of a space like this quite often stimulates the imagination of the scenographers to adapt it for performance. But there must be a perfect blend of interpretation and imagination to juxtapose the existing environment with the dramatic visuals. A found space can be visualised anywhere—a community hall, a public lawn, a classroom, a street corner or even an old ruined monument. After thorough investigation and exploration, the scenographers can bring a found space with an extraordinary potential into the reality of a performance space through the power of their visual aesthetics. Due to an informal nature of a found space, its performance may differ from that of a conventional space such as proscenium or thrust, etc. To integrate this space into a performance design, the scenographers usually avoid their pre-conceived design ideas for the play. They try to develop the design after a thorough investigation of the space through many interactions so as to interweave the rhythm of the space into design. Through this process a harmonious bond between the space and the production is developed. To avoid the contradiction of the style of presentation between the 'space' and the 'design', the scenographers try to find complementarity through the potential energy of the space and then allow their instinct and intellect to flow with the inner rhythm of the space and design. Once the space is finalised and rehearsal begins, the scenic elements are gradually added to the space, thus contributing to an interesting and innovative creative interaction.

Modern Indian theatre design has revolutionised the exploration of space in many ways and opened avenues for new experiments. The scenographers have found ample opportunities in 'found spaces' resulting in a few remarkable productions in the recent past. This has created deep impressions in the chronicles of theatre design in India. The production of *Andha Yug* at Feroz Shah Kotla ground, Delhi, in the year 1963, and its revival production at the ruins of Purana Qila following kabuki style of presentation along with the presentation of *Tughlaq* in the year 1974 and the production of *Skandagupta* (1985) at the Ater Fort at Bhind, Madhya Pradesh, are a few examples of exploring the potential strength of the 'found space' that brought alternative spatial practices into Indian theatre.

The objective of exploring the potential strength of a 'found space' is to create an aura closer to the real-life experience, a real incident than that of a fiction, a direct association to the human belief.

THE FLEXIBLE THEATRE SPACE

The nature of a theatre space is often decided by the style of the play. For example, a play designed for a proscenium theatre may not be presented suitably in an arena or thrust stage without significant modifications. Under these circumstances, the play needs restructuring according to its shift from one kind of space to another. Such re-modifications quite often result in chaotic situations that may affect the production to a larger degree. Keeping these technical issues in mind, the flexible space was brought into practice. This kind of space can be altered, reshaped and modified depending on the demands of the production design. Scenographers have explored possibilities in this kind of space in many ways. However, spaces like this usually have folding audience gallery and stage elements that can be instantly assembled according to the necessity of the production. A flexible space can be converted into any space such as, proscenium, thrust, traverse or arena, and is suitable for the experimental theatre. Many innovative productions have been presented worldwide in this kind of space. A flexible theatre space is more intimate than any of the proscenium and thrust stage; it accommodates fewer audience for close interactions.

But unfortunately, the practice of flexible space is not common in India. Yet some of the important Indian theatre productions have

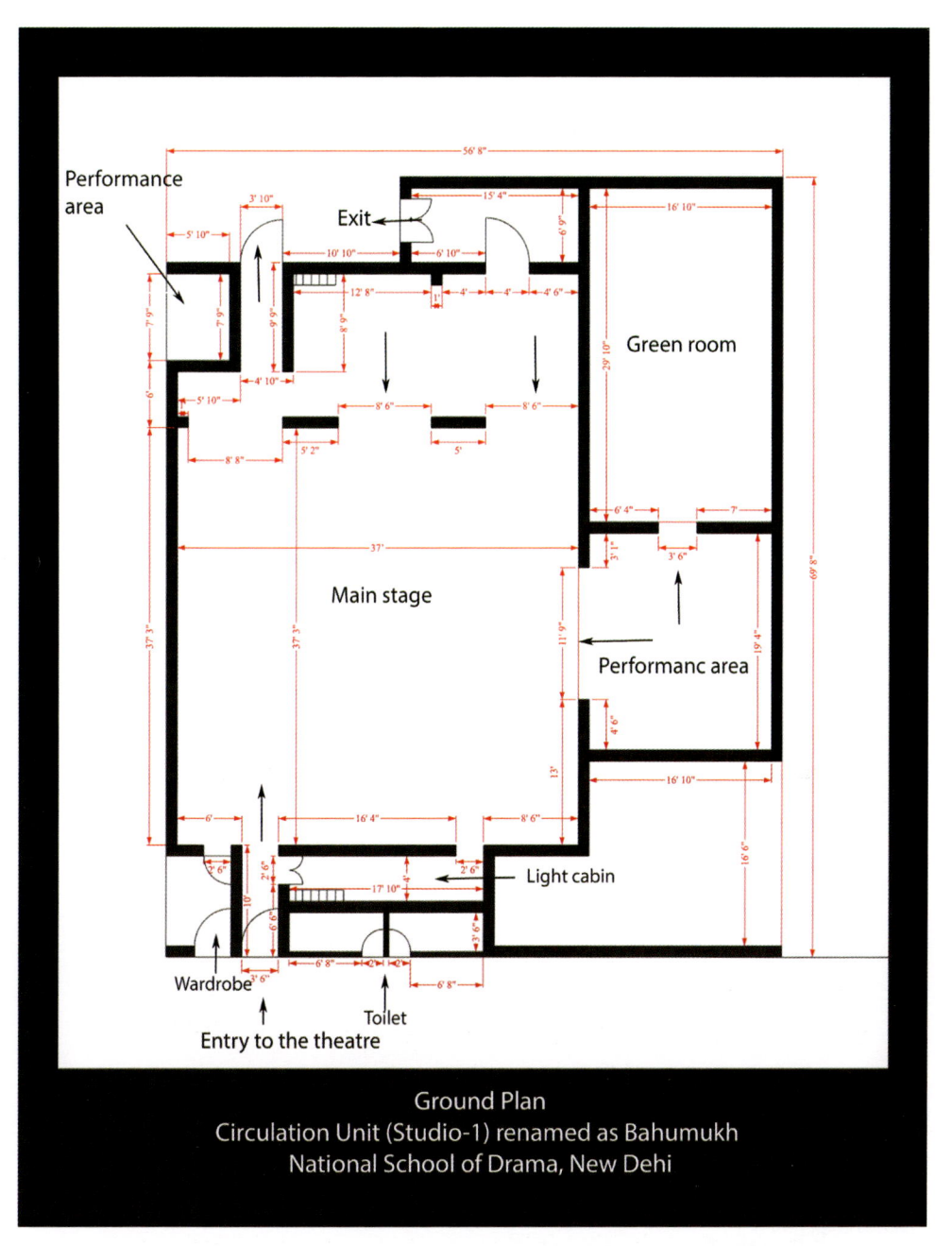

ALTERNATIVE PERFORMANCE SPACES | 219

Ground Plan
Circulation Unit (Studio-1) renamed as Bahumukh
National School of Drama, New Dehi

Ground Plan of the Bahumukh theatre with measurement. The plan is prepared by Sauti Chakravarti, the noted Indian lighting designer. Courtesy: Rajesh Kumar Singh.

been successfully presented in a few available flexible performance spaces and it remains a preferred choice for contemporary Indian scenographers. Out of a few, the Circulation Unit of the National School of Drama—a studio theatre which was recently renamed as 'Bahumukh' —is one of the most discussed flexible theatre spaces, explored in diverse ways by many noted directors and scenographers across the world. There is also another flexible space, called Experimental Theatre at National Council for Performing Arts (NCPA) in Mumbai, successfully contributing to the Indian theatre. With a capacity of 300 movable seats, this space is equipped with modular seating and staging units. It offers an ideal platform to promote alternative spatial practices.

A few illustrative diagrams of the Bahumukh theatre space is provided here for detailed study of the space.

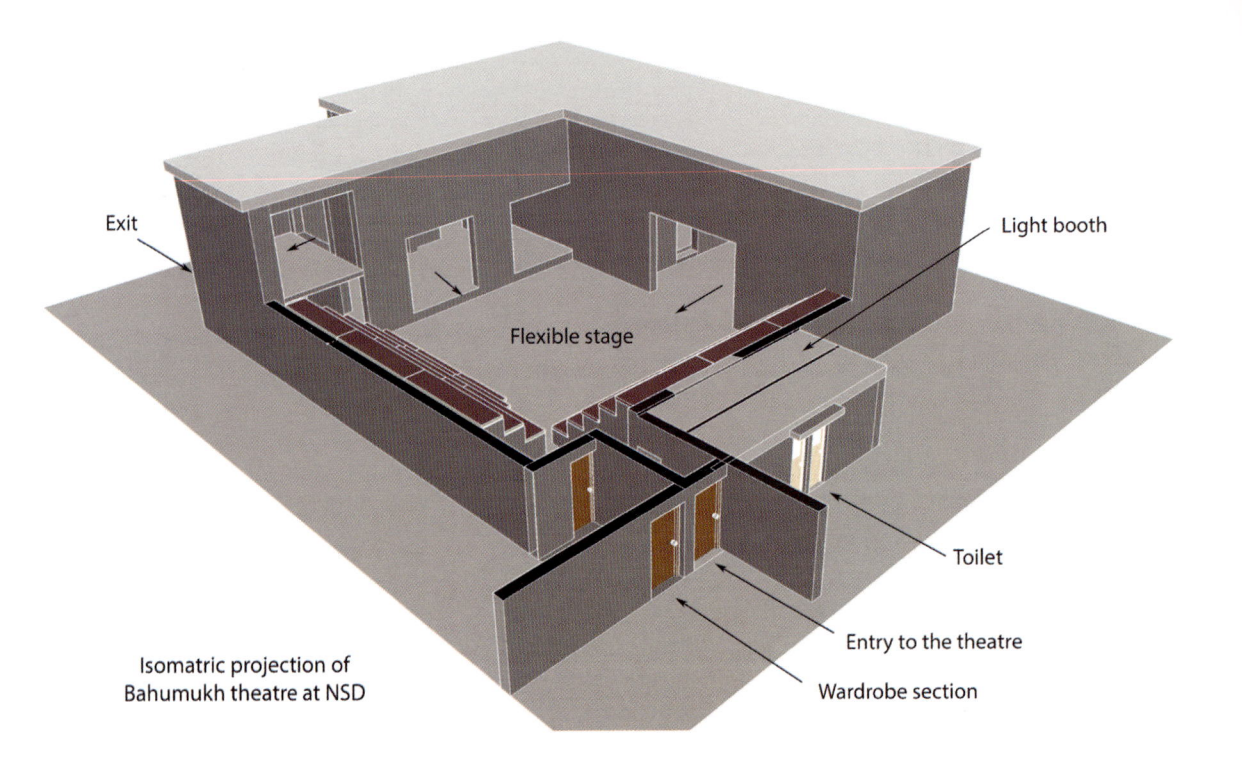

Isomatric projection of Bahumukh theatre at NSD

Drawing of an imaginary performance at the Bahumukh theatre. The drawing is to provide a demonstrative view of the presentation.

THE ENVIRONMENTAL THEATRE

The Environmental theatre wipes out the gap between the performers and the spectators by providing a common space for both viewers and performers. For, an environmental theatre does not demand any specific performance area and designated audience gallery. In this way it differs from other kinds of theatres in the world. This theatre brings new spatial practices by exploring all possibilities to treat the actors and spectators as a single entity. Unlike proscenium, thrust and arena, environmental theatre does not segregate the actors from the spectators, and discards the distinct line between the performers and the viewers, bringing them to a single platform. It breaks the earlier notion of watching a play, setting another belief of indistinguishable identity where the audience behave as active participants while watching a performance.

Paul Kuritz argues:

> Environmental theatre encourages give and take throughout a globally organised space in which the areas occupied by the audience are a kind of island or continent in the midst of the audience. The audience does not sit in regularly arranged rows; there is one whole space rather than two opposing spaces. The environmental use of space is fundamentally collaborative; the action flows in many directions sustained only by the cooperation of performers and spectators.[iv]

The exploration of the space in an environmental performance emerges out of the production process. Action, text and space evolve through group collaborations. According to Richard Schechner's principles, the following factors are essential for an environmental theatre:

i. For each production, the whole space (both the actors and spectators) is to be designed.
ii. The design takes into account the space-senses and space-fields.
iii. Every part of the space in the environmental design should be functional.
iv. The performers and spectators are included in all phases of the performance (planning and making).

My personal experience of watching a production of *Cherry Ka Bagicha*, a Hindi adaptation of Anton Chekov's *The Cherry Orchard*, with an environmental setup can be discussed here. The play was directed by

Still from the play *Cherry ka Bagicha* (1983), an adaptation of Anton Chekhov's *The Cherry Orchard*. Venue of the performance: Meghdoot Open air theatre, Rabindra Bhawan, New Delhi. Courtesy: Dr Nissar Allana.

Richard Schechner for the National School of Drama repertory company in 1983. As I remember, the Meghdoot Open-air Complex of the National School of Drama in Delhi was transformed into an environment, suitable for the play, designed by the noted Indian scenographer Dr Nissar Allana. The stage and its surroundings together formed the performance space. In the set, the central character of the play, Mrs Ranevskaya's house was placed towards the rear left of the stage proper, which was extended up to the nearby areas at the backyard where the natural environment including trees and bushes became a part of the design. The backyard with real trees represented the cherry orchard. The reception scene of the play was performed in the coffee lawn at the entrance of the Meghdoot theatre complex in which the audience were involved with the performers as a part of the scene. As the play opened, Richard Schechner entered into the space addressing the spectators to feel free to find a place to sit, stand, move and even participate in the production, wherever required. Since the common Indian theatregoers were not familiar with this kind of presentation before, the performance brought a new sensation, making the production a memorable one.

Contemporary Indian theatre was not exposed to this spatial exploration before the histrionic presentation of *Cherry Ka Bagicha*. This became a unique experience for those who witnessed and participated in this production. Indian scenography also entered into a new realm of experiment with this environmental production. Richard Schechner's concept of the environmental theatre, sufficed with Nissar Allana's design, opened avenues for alternative spatial practices in Indian theatre.

THE SITE-SPECIFIC PERFORMANCE

The site-specific performance is a kind of radical activity that explores the collective energy of the audience in the performance which is devised and presented in a specific place, charged by the inner rhythm and psychology of the text, idea and space. This practice of alternative theatre emerged out of the revolutionary artistic milieu in the late 1960s in the West and gained momentum worldwide in the beginning of the 21st century. It is perhaps the most ambitious and avant-garde theatre practice conceived in the current times. Like the environmental theatre, the site-specific performance also involves three major factors: space, performance and the spectators.

In a site-specific performance, the actor's physical and internal expressions pulsate and reverberate in tune with the vibration of the space. The performance can be conceived anywhere: inside a park, a museum, a building or an arena. Sometimes, even multiple spaces for different scenes can be taken into account with the spectators moving along with the actors in different scenes during a performance. Thus, it has also broken the barrier of conventional spectatorship by putting the audience into a simulation, playing with the spatiotemporal dynamics.

One of the prime objectives of the site-specific performance is to expand the range and dimension of a natural space to make it conducive for a theatrical presentation. The performance is often conditioned to a particular space and its environment where it is devised. Therefore, the performance cannot be shifted to a different local under any circumstances. Still debate persists whether a site-specific performance can be presented in another space, other than the space where it is devised. But the statement of Richard Serra, 'To remove the work is to destroy the work'[v], questions its repetitive performances in venues other than its original devised space. If the work is shifted to another venue, the art might lose its original bond with the space and becomes irrelevant.

The sight-specific performance is the outcome of the progressive fine arts movement called minimalism[1], which came into practice in the late 1960s in North America. It was a strong reaction against the formalism[2]

---

1   Minimalism describes movements in various forms of art and design, especially visual art and music, where the work is set out to expose the essence, essentials or identity of a subject through eliminating all non-essential forms, features or concepts. As a specific movement in the arts it is identified with developments in post-World War II Western art, most strongly with American visual arts in the 1960s and early 1970s. Prominent artists associated with this movement include Ad Reinhardt, Tony Smith, Donald Judd, John McCracken, Agnes Martin, Dan Flavin, Robert Morris, Larry Bell, Anne Truitt and Frank Stella. Minimalism is often interpreted as a reaction against abstract expressionism and a bridge to postminimal art practices. Source: https://en.wikipedia.org/wiki/Minimalism_(visual_arts).

2   In art history, formalism is the study of art by analysing and comparing form and style. It also includes the way objects are made and their purely visual or material aspects. In painting, formalism emphasises compositional elements such as colour, line, shape, textures and other perceptual aspects rather than content, meaning or the historical and social context. Source: https://en.wikipedia.org/wiki/Formalism_(art).

to bring out the minimum requirements of art to the public domains—markets, streets, squares, etc. from the sophisticated art galleries. The artists used the local surroundings to create their piece of art, installed within that particular site. Theatre presentation in a site-specific condition is the extension of this radical art movement initiated by Richard Serra.

Celebrated directors and scenographers such as Peter Brook, Ariane Mnouchkine, Deborah Warner, Janet Cardiff, Prof. Pamela Howard, Prof. Jene Collins, as well as a few progressive theatre organisations of the West like the Grid Iron, the Wrights & Sites and the Bread & Butter Theatre

Still photograph of Richard Serra's sculpture—*Junction/Cycle* (2011). Medium: Waterproof steel. Size: 62ft. x 56ft. x 14ft. + (height). These site-specific monumental sculptures of Richard Serra, one of the pre-eminent sculptors of the 20th century, emphasise on alter viewers' perceptions of space and proportion. It's all about centralising the space in different ways and to realise how people move in relation to space. A series of sculptures with the same idea are exhibited at the Gagosian Art Gallery, NYC, USA.

Source: https://www.artsy.net/artwork/richard-serra-cycle.

Still from the play *Clown and Clouds* (2011). Directed by: Dr Abhilash Pillai. Scenography: Rajesh Kumar Singh. This was a theatre-circus project, undertaken by the National School of Drama, New Delhi. Courtesy: National School of Drama and Rajesh Kumar Singh.

Company, etc. have pioneered the site-specific performances as a platform of alternative theatre practice. Though this practice is not so common in India, few scenographers and directors have tried their hands in this new experiment with conviction and success. Indian directors and scenographers such as, Anuradha Kapur, Abhilash Pillai and Deepan Sivaraman have done some remarkable works in this specific area. Anuradha Kapur's production of *Ghosts* (2017) with the theatre students of University of Hyderabad, Abhilash Pillai's presentation of Arundhati Ray's novel, *God*

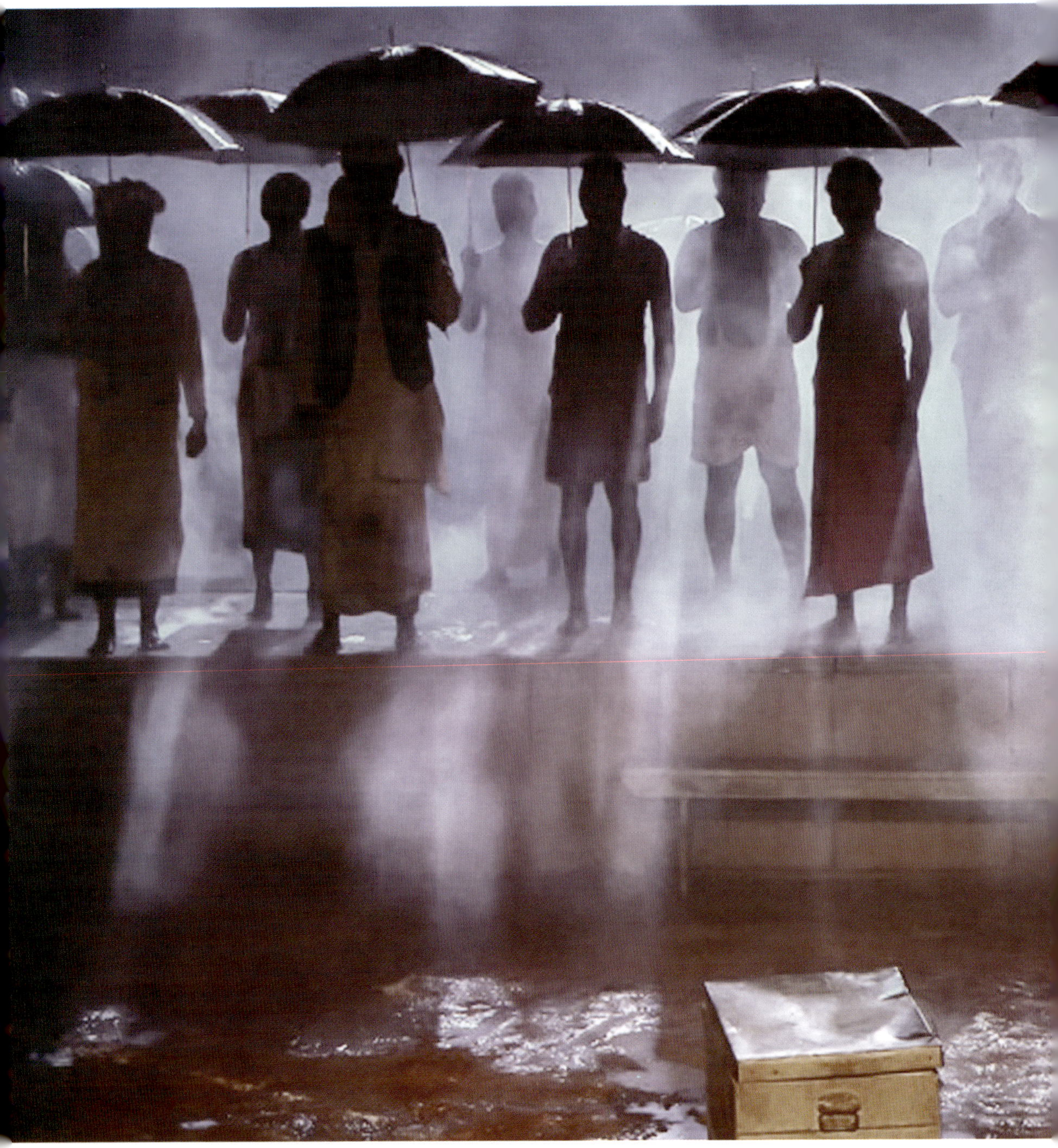

of Small Things (2000) and *Clowns and Clouds* (2011) at Kozhikode, Deepan Shivaraman's *The Legends of Khasak* (2013) in a remote village of Kerala, Bansi Kaul's *Gadhon ka Mela* (1996) at the hills of Bhim Baitka, Madhya Pradesh, and Satyabrata Rout's site-specific presentation of *Rashomon* (2005) in a forest near Faridabad are a few experiments done in this regard in Indian theatre.

THE INTERACTIVE PERFORMANCE SPACE

Indian theatre witnessed a great deal of innovative works that have been undertaken in the beginning of the 21st century. Exploration of unusual spaces, new performances and the changing mindset of the spectators marked a departure from the old conventions which were practised after Independence. Scenographers tried to expand the horizon of 'space' with the interactions of new medium of expressions. To add to this radical change, digital medium of communication came into practice in a live medium like theatre. Alternative practices of

Still from the play *The legends of Khasak* (2013). Based on the famous Malayali novel *Khasakkinte Ithihasam* by O.V. vijayan. One entire village was converted into the performance landscape for this unique presentation. Scenography and Direction: Dr Deepan Sivaraman. Photography: The *Indian Express*. Courtesy: *The Indian Express* and Deepan Sivaraman.

scenography crept into all the interdisciplinary areas of performing arts. The experience of space became synonymous to the modern-day performance culture and intrinsic to the further alternative practices.

In India, this new wave of theatre practice has broadly based on two distinctive mediums: live and digital, merging with each other at the same time and space. Visual imageries, multimedia projections, video mapping and other digital devices formed the syllable of cutting-edge scenography. The metaphor of the visuals through digital images, synchronising with the text, emerged as a new style of performance.

In some of the recent Indian productions, such as *The Antigone Project* (2003), *The Spinal Cord* (2009), *Sex, Morality and Censorship* (2010), *Water-Station* (2011), *Lady Macbeth Revisited* (2013), *The Manganiyar Seduction* (2009), the quest for interactive space is clearly visible.

Looking back to the West, Polish director Jerzy Grotowski is the first to succeed in finding a different theatre expression in alternative spaces. The passion for practicing theatre in new interactive spaces grew momentum during the second half of the 20th century in the West. While practicing environmental theatre, the American author-director Richard Schechner traced its origin in the performance of the Ramlila of Banaras[3] in India and developed the concept of the 'Performance Theory'. Richard Schechner rejects the conventional practices and brought innovative concept of inviting the viewers to the performance. In this concept, the performer–spectator dynamics is subjected to a certain role reversal, that offers different spatial perspectives to both the performers and the spectators. It also provides an opportunity for the spectators to behave as active partakers of the dramatic happenings which is not possible in a conventional theatre; in a conventional performance the audience is allowed to watch the play as passive observers.

---

3   Ref. chapter: 3: According to Richard Schechner, the Ramlila of Ramnagar, Banaras, popularly known as 'Ramnagar ki Ramlila', is a kind of environmental theatre practice.

The union of spectators and the performers forms the interactive space. Practitioners and academics across the world are engaged in searching for a new theatre genre through rituals, festivals, social or community-based activities, popular entertainments and folk and traditional performance cultures. Jerzy Grotowski, through his concept of 'Poor Theatre'[4], employed his dramaturgical skill to freely mould the text and carve a space where his 'rituals' take place. Eugenio Barba, a disciple of Grotowski, tries to explore the potential of the spaces in his long and painstaking experimental work based on the concept of the 'Third Theatre'[5] in collaboration with a group of promising actors at the Odin Theatre in Denmark. Augusto Boal, the Brazilian director and activist, focusing on a particular ideology, continued working for an oppressed society till his end. This led him to develop a kind of interactive theatre, the 'Theatre of the oppressed' which he discovered through 'the Forum theatre and the Invisible theatre'[6].

---

4   'Poor Theatre' is a concept, developed by Jerzy Grotowski, a celebrated theatre philosopher of Poland. He has explained its concept in his seminal book *Towards a Poor Theatre*.

5   Third Theatre deals with a social commitment which reflects in his (Eugenio Barba) plays every time. Third Theatre was formed by imbibing ideas from the traditional and folk theatre with the amalgamation of urban theatre. At the same time, it had an identity of its own. It creates awareness among the common people on many social issues. There is no concrete characterisation in the plays based on third theatre concept. The actors play many characters and events according to the situation. Even the audience can take part in the live performances. Further, there is freedom of movement and no restriction of space. In this theatre, the body language of the performers becomes important than their facial expressions. In India, Badal Sircar has greatly contributed towards the concept of Third Theatre and has written a book on the same name.

6   Invisible theatre is a form of theatrical performance that is enacted in a place where people would not normally expect to see, for example; in the street or in a shopping centre. The performers attempt to disguise the fact that it is a performance from those who observe and who may choose to participate in it by encouraging the spectators to view it as a real event. The Brazilian theatre practitioner Augusto Boal along with Panagiotis Assimakopoulos developed the form during their stay in Argentina in 1970s as part of 'Theatre of the Oppressed' which focused on oppression and social issues. Boal developed his concept as 'Forum theatre'.

Indian theatre practitioner Badal Sircar also pioneered a new practicing method, popularly known as the 'Psycho-physical theatre'[7], influenced by Grotowski in the mid-1960s. In the recent years, initiatives have also been taken among the school children to bring awareness on socio-political issues by using theatre as a powerful tool of interactive education. In Barry John's 'Theatre-in-Education' (TIE) (1989)[8] programme , the students are frequently encouraged to nurture the ideas taken from their textbooks to understand the subject with more clarity through theatrical means. In fact, Dorothy Heathcote and Gavin Bolton's book *Drama for Learning* (1995) precisely talks about this idea. In order to practice, a group of professional 'actor-teachers' guide the students for discussions through a series of interactive theatrical sessions. This method of learning through theatre inspires the young minds not only to understand the prescribed texts, but also to experience life, which leads to a complete education through the experience of theatre.

CONCLUSION

Attempts have been made over the years to break away with the fourth wall of the formal proscenium theatre to come closer to the audience to share a common platform for interaction. That is why alternative theatre spaces exist along with the formalistic theatres. Quite often, the formal proscenium theatre has also been remodelled to create an

---

7   Psycho-physical theatre is a concept developed by Badal Sircar in which the physical gestures and body movement is majorly guided by the psychology of the actors.

8   'Theatre in Education' is an interactive process that applies theatre technique and practices to help aid the education, practised mainly in the school level. In the process of using theatre as a tool for educational activities, a group of adult 'actor-teachers' perform for the children by deriving topics from school curriculum through direct participation of the students by using the technic of 'role play', 'hot-seating', 'forum theatre', etc. Theatre-In-Education (TIE), as a repertory company, was established by the National School of Drama, India, in the year 1989 under the directorship of Barry John (A British-born Indian theatre director).

opportunity for the audience to involve themselves as active members of the performance.

Practitioners around the world have tried in many ways to break away with the proscenium arch. Scenographers have found new prospects in alternative theatre spaces and interdisciplinary theatre activities. Even contemporary Indian scenography is not only confined to theatre practice and research, but also has expanded its wings to other applied and allied art forms. To redefine the idea of 'theatre for all', Indian scenographers have broken away with the convention of individual idealism of theatre by entering into the realm of interdisciplinary activities. The impression of spatial practices and scenography can easily be experienced in the disciplines of paintings, dance and installation arts, etc. The practice of these new performances is growing and being widely accepted and adopted by the new generation of theatre practitioners in India. The dynamics of paintings, sculptures, installation art, digital media and many other new visual expressions are slowly being redefined in the context of theatre practices to offer an alternative experience to the viewers.

References

i   Grotowski, Jerzy. 2015. *Towards a Poor Theatre*. London: Bloomsbury Methuen Drama. pp. 19.
ii Brook, Peter. 1996. *The Empty Space*. New York: Touchstone Book Publication. p. 7.
iii Parker, Wilford O. and Harvey K. Smith. 1979. *Scene Design and Stage Lighting*. New York: Holt, Rinehart and Winston. p. 41.
iv Kuritz, Paul. 1988. *The Making of Theatre History*. Englewood Cliffs, NJ: Prentice-Hall. p. 391.
v   'Richard Serra'. *Wikipedia.* https://en.wikipedia.org/wiki/Richard_Serra.

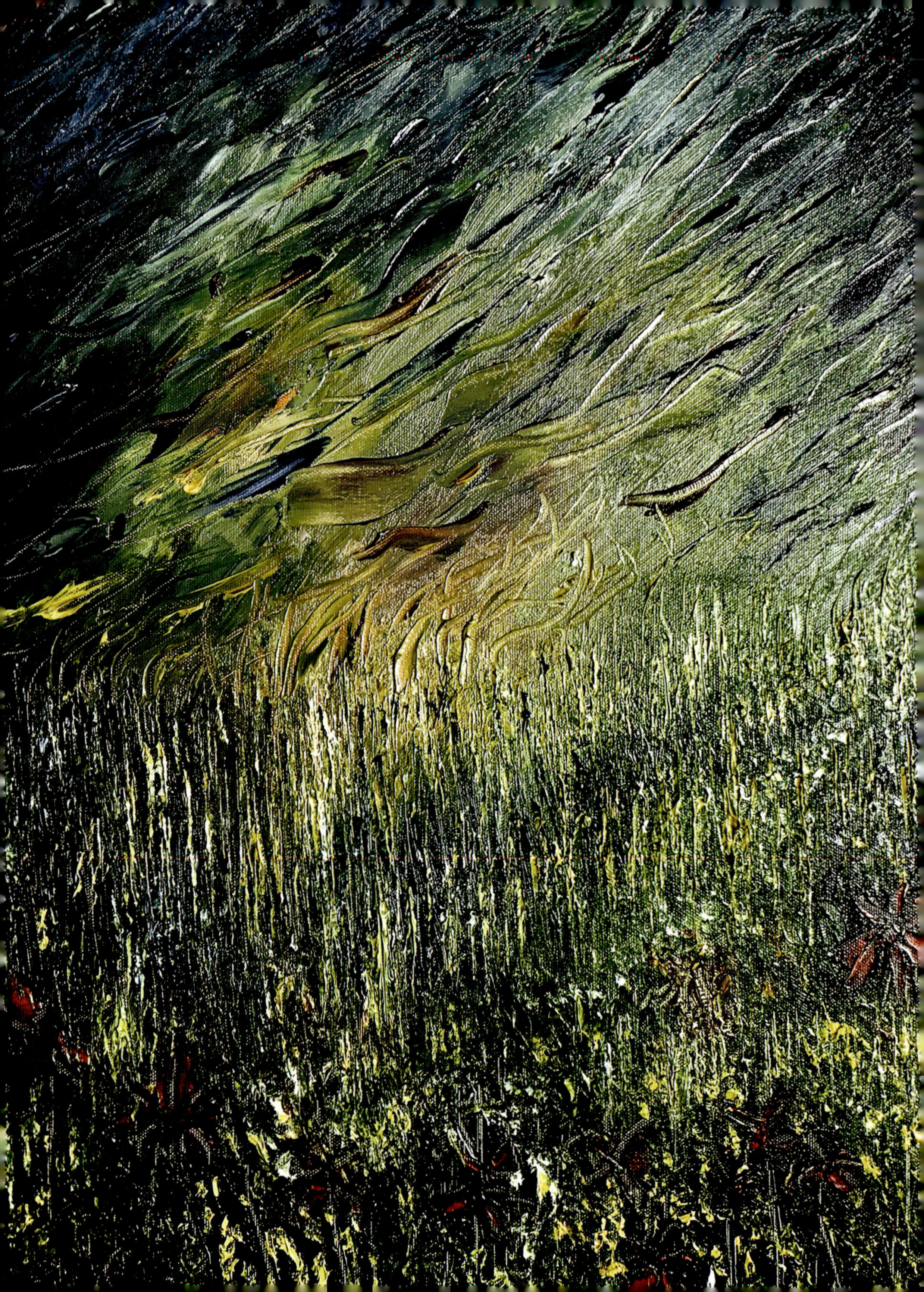

MULTIPLICITY OF ART: Perception, Interpretation, Aesthetics

COMPREHENSION OF HUMAN FEELINGS

Art enriches the quality of human life, stimulates our senses and makes us aware of our own self. It is an extension of our thoughts, feelings, desires, emotions and instincts. It is personal and at the same time, universal. The expression of our intimate feelings that cannot be released through any other means is expressed through art. The natural environment we live and the ordinary lives we lead serve as the impulse behind the creation of art. Art reinvents and re-interprets life in many ways and in many forms. Yet, it is important to see the fine line separating 'art' from the 'life'; life is not art, but it inspires us to create art, and art, in turn, becomes a derivative of life and not life itself.

Therefore, art becomes the manifestation of the purest forms of human emotions and lies where 'N'ature and 'L'ife intersect. The urge to give an expression to the perfection of nature is what motivates the musician to compose, inspires the painter to paint and a poet to create magic by using the same lexicon that is appropriated for our everyday utterances. This transformation is possible through the power and delicacy of life's dynamism and vigour. Because of this, it is possible for the artist to create his own notion of existence. Just like life, art can never be repeated or rewound.

In the process of creation, an artist explores the 'self'. In composing a new life in the form of art, an artist never imitates life, rather they put forward their own 'interpretation' of life into the creation. Thus, art becomes a metaphor of life.

The world of creativity is based solely on two factors—sensibility and skill. An artist, influenced by their sensibility and aided by the power of execution, becomes the master of the creation. Sensibility is related to intellect and emotions, while skill or craft can be developed through arduous practice of the medium; sensibility is linked to the mind while execution is associated with physical activities. Skill is pure craft and the craftsmen, with the help of their sensibilities and perceptions, can transform craft into art.

PERCEPTION

Most of us know the parable of the blind men and the elephant. A group of blind men once encountered an elephant and decided to touch and feel the animal since they could not see it. One among them, after holding the leg of the elephant, declared that the elephant resembled a pillar. Another, on touching the animal's ears, said it was like a husking basket. Similarly, he who touched its trunk, or its belly, talked of it differently. The question arises, how could the same elephant seem different to every individual, and whose experience was real and authentic? The crux of the argument lies in 'perception', the way one looks at an object or situation.

We tend to look at the world from our individual point of view, akin to these blind men. Every time we interact with life, each one of us has a different story to tell. Since all of us have had different experiences; our perception also varies. Like the blind men and the elephant, a single object or situation appears different to different people. In the same way, a work of art is appreciated and analysed in various ways by individuals. The appreciation or criticism always remains subjective—it is how the work

Horse. Medium: Oil on canvas. Artist: M.F. Hussain. Courtesy: Wikimedia Commons.

of art is interpreted. The value of art solely depends on its interpretation and analysis which are developed and nurtured by our socio-political and cultural backdrops.

But is art irrespective of all the circumstances around? Is art independent of an individual's perspective at the time of its birth? We all have heard the old adage, 'Beauty lies in the eyes of the beholder.' Only an artist's eye can catch the glimpse of the beauty of nature, hidden in each atom and molecule. A nondescript piece of rock or a wood log might be seen but ignored by many, as it may appear ordinary to the common people. But for a sculptor, the story is different. He perceives a hidden form in it, notices the divine dance of nature inside the piece of stone and carves the object to bring forth the perceived image out of it. All the creative works of art bear the testimony of this subjectivity that express the human feelings—joy, sorrow, sufferings, etc. For example, in the works of Vincent Van Gogh, the pain and sufferings of the common labour-class people is passionately expressed; his world famous paintings like, *The Potato Eaters*, *The Sorrow* and *The Starry Night*, etc. speak loudly of the emotional outcry of the artist for the struggles of the labour-class people, which may not be significant for many. We can sense the power of perception in the creations of all great artists, irrespective of their forms of expression. For example in M.F. Hussain's 'Horses' and J. Swaminathan's 'Bird' series, a sense of power and freedom is always perceived and felt.

THE COMPONENT OF PERCEPTION

When we say, we 'like' something, it means that the particular object possesses certain power to draw our attention and we are able to associate with that object at a personal level. Such a feeling can often lead the observer down the memory lane to some past experience, which might proceed further to an altered state of mind. The forms, lines, colours and textures of an object, or the memory of certain events in one's life, have

Untitled from 'Bird, Tree and Mountain Series' (1983). Artist: Jagdish Swaminathan. Dimensions: 82.2 cm x 106.7 cm. Courtesy: Wikimedia Commons.

the power to make an observer undergo an emotional journey. Similarly, the suppressed feelings of an artist are stimulated through the interactions of an object which can be vented through the medium of art. However, without a rational and logical approach, the creation would be meaningless; a work without interpretation, an art without thought is gruesome—like an emotion without a truth.

While designing a play, the scenographers must understand the language of visual art, its principles of compositions, the interrelationships of various forms and their symbolic representations. These factors facilitate the ambience and set the mood of a performance. They hold the interest of the spectators and contribute towards the meaning of the performance.

Human life is always guided by the environment we live in. Landscape, desert, sea, forest, mystic morning, moonlit night, ruins of monuments, ceremonies, rituals and countless factors of nature as well as life have direct impact upon our emotions. The scenographers, being visual artists, bring all these emotional stimulants into their works through various elements of design and put them in designated spaces in relation to their subjects, i.e. the actors and the play.

The concept of employing design into theatre through various elements and to create the mood and ambience out of their potentials was realised primarily by Adolphe Appia and Gordon Craig in the beginning of the 20th century. Their approach to scenography changed the face of modern theatre. Exploration of the dimensions of space, rhythmic movements of the forms, visual compositions through lines and colours, use of textures to create mood and the distribution of space to bring the actors into focus have thus become the synonym of contemporary scenography.

MULTIPLICITY OF ART

Encyclopædia Britannica online defines arts as 'modes of expression that use skill or imagination in the creation of aesthetic objects, environments, or experiences that can be shared with others.' The noted author *of Foundations of Art and Design*, Alan Pipes believes: 'The word *art* derives from Sanskrit and means, "making" or "creating something". It might have been derived originally from the Sanskrit term "Rtih", meaning "human behaviour".'[i]

However, 'art' is defined through various means. Out of its numerous forms and expressions, a few can only be elevated to the level of fine arts. The creation that captures the finest nuances of life and truly reverberates with the inner rhythm of mankind can be termed as 'fine art'; it should form a conduit between the mind and the universe. Music, painting, sculpture, literature, dance and theatre are a few of numerous art forms considered of the stature of fine arts. While some of these expressions stand independently, others are interdisciplinary and hybrid, expressed through each other's mutual energy, such as theatre and dance, etc. Architecture and design are termed as 'applied arts' since the skills and crafts of diverse visual faculties are exercised to develop these mediums. One basic characteristic of the applied art form is that, while fine arts serve as an intellectual stimulation for the viewers, applied art is related to functional behaviour. Design, which may include graphic design, fashion design, ceramics and pottery, interior design, architecture and photography. manifest the principles of fine arts but is very much functional. Scenography, as one out of many visual designs, follows similar principle.

Irrespective of the multiplicity of art and its various distinctions, it can broadly be categorised into two branches: visual and auditory. Some forms of art stimulate us through their physical attributes and presence while others are experienced through the medium of sound and voice. Visual art is physical and occupies space whereas the other one, being abstract, passes with the flow of time. There also exists another form of art, expressed through both the dimensions of space and time. They can be broadly categorised into three distinctive art forms:

- Spatial art: Pertaining to space
- Temporal art: Pertaining to time
- Spatio-temporal art: Pertaining to both time and space

SPATIAL ART

An art that occupies certain space and is typically experienced through vision, an art that is independent of time but remains bound by a given space is regarded as spatial art. Such art, though regulated by certain dynamics of space, surpasses the boundary of one and thus remains virtually everlasting. Sculpture, painting and architecture are the best-known forms of spatial art. A painting, sculpture or a piece of architecture remains in a defined space for as long as they can exist, an aspect suitably illustrated by the fact that the great masters' works still exist and can be appreciated irrespective of the time of their creation.

TEMPORAL ART

Temporal art exists in the dimension of time. Therefore, it comprises a marked beginning and a definite end. After culmination, the art remains only in our collective memory and consciousness. Music, recitation or any art related to sound, for that matter, can come under the category of temporal art, since all of these have a particular finishing point to which they gradually approach with the forward movement of time. One can argue that music and other similar arts can be captured through technical means to be listened innumerable times at any point of time. But one must know that listening to a particular recording is not the form of art which we are discussing in this context, rather it is the technology of capturing art beyond the temporal frame that is detrimental in terms of the ideal fundamentals of art that says art cannot be repeated again. Unlike paintings and sculptures, we can only listen to a live music within a definite time frame but not at any moment of our choice. Temporal art manifests the following characteristics:

- The structure primarily is expressed through time.
- The creation and presentation of the art is simultaneous.

SPATIO-TEMPORAL ART

Art that is expressed in a certain space and within the bounds of time is called spatio-temporal art. Spatio-temporal arts are apprehended through performances, such as, theatre, dance and all other similar genres.

A meticulous space and a designated time are the required mediums for this art to be created; it takes birth, flourishes and perishes within a definite time span in that space itself. Spatio-temporal art can only be experienced while it is being created, akin to temporal art forms but with the added constituent of a meticulous space. As the performance is a continuous progression towards the end point, the ever-changing immediate past is spontaneously wiped out for which the present has to be recreated each time.

Theatre and dance, deemed as the metaphors of life, can only be visible during an unambiguous span of time. It is both visible and audible at the same time and is considered the most poetic of all the other forms of art. The *Natya Shastra* recognises theatre art as 'drishya-kavyam'(visual poetry) by describing it as the most pleasing and sublime creation. It imbibes elements from various forms of art. It is like an ocean where all art streams meet. For example, the three-dimensional compositions in theatre are inherited from sculpture; all the visual aesthetics and picturesque backdrops, including scenic design, costume, properties, masks and make-up, etc. are the derivatives of painting; text and sound are the finest forms of sound and music, and the gestures, postures and gaits are borrowed from dance.

OBJECTIVES OF ART

Irrespective of different genres, art is created for a purpose. It takes birth at the extreme emotional state of the artist and makes the society aware of its existence. It makes us conscious of ourselves and speaks of the current times. The collective consciousness of the society of every period is reflected in its arts. A chronological study of the art and literature can distinctly portray the socio-political development in human history. The social life, style, human behaviour and temperament of the people, is reflected all the times in artistic creations, through its diverse forms. Therefore, art

Still from the play *Andher Nagari Chaupat Raja* (1881). Playwright: Bharatendu Harishchandra. Direction: B.V. Karanth (1979).
Courtesy: National School of Drama, New Delhi.

can be contemplated as the collective history of the mankind. A piece of art sometimes can change the perception of the society. The aesthetics of art can be codified through the following objectives, such as, (i) social consciousness (ii) metaphor of life (iii) selectivity (iv) aesthetics (v) interpretation.

Social Consciousness
Art brings awareness in the society. The concept of art, the sole expression of the artist, helps explore new ideas and understanding among the

masses. There are numerous examples of mass awareness through art expressions. The realistic style of paintings of Indian women by Raja Ravi Varma inspires to change the perception of our society for women during the colonial period. Plays such as *Neel Darpan*, *Andher Nagari*, *Nabanna* and *Ghashiram Kotwal*, etc. succeeded in arousing social consciousness among the people time to time.

For over a century, *Neel Darpan* enjoys the reputation of a fundamental text, which speaks of human tragedies and sufferings through the farmers at Champaran—a small province in the Indian state of Bihar. The play depicts Indian liberalism against British rulers. *Neel Darpan* serves as a commentary on the British imposition of the Dramatic Performances Act (DPA) in India. *Andher Nagri*, a 19th-century comic satire, depicts the misrule of an idiotic king whose kingdom is in a mess—a parallel to our modern-day politics. Similarly, Bijon Bhattacharya's *Nabanna* also raises a voice for the victims of the great Bengal Famine in 1943 and Vijay Tendulkar's *Ghashiram Kotwal* exposes the hypocrisies and corruption of the statesmen of the Maratha regime and the Brahmins of Pune during its time.

There are also numerous examples of spreading mass awareness through art organisations, such as, Indian People's Theatre Association (IPTA), Jana Natya Manch, Jana Sanskriti, etc.

All the above examples show that art indeed has the strength to change society. Picasso's most celebrated 20th-century painting *Guernica* perhaps captures the relationship between societal change and art most succinctly. It was created as a reaction to the horrors and destruction of war. It depicts the terrifying effects of the bombardment by the Nazis on Guernica and Spain during the Spanish Civil War. Picasso painted this masterpiece to express the meaningless carnage during the wars. *Guernica* epitomises the tragedies of war and becomes a perpetual embodiment of humanity and a plea for peace.

Still from the play *Ghashiram Kotwal* (1972). Playwright: Vijay Tendulkar. Scenography and direction: Satyabrata Rout (2018).

Courtesy: Department of Theatre Arts, S.N. School, University of Hyderabad.

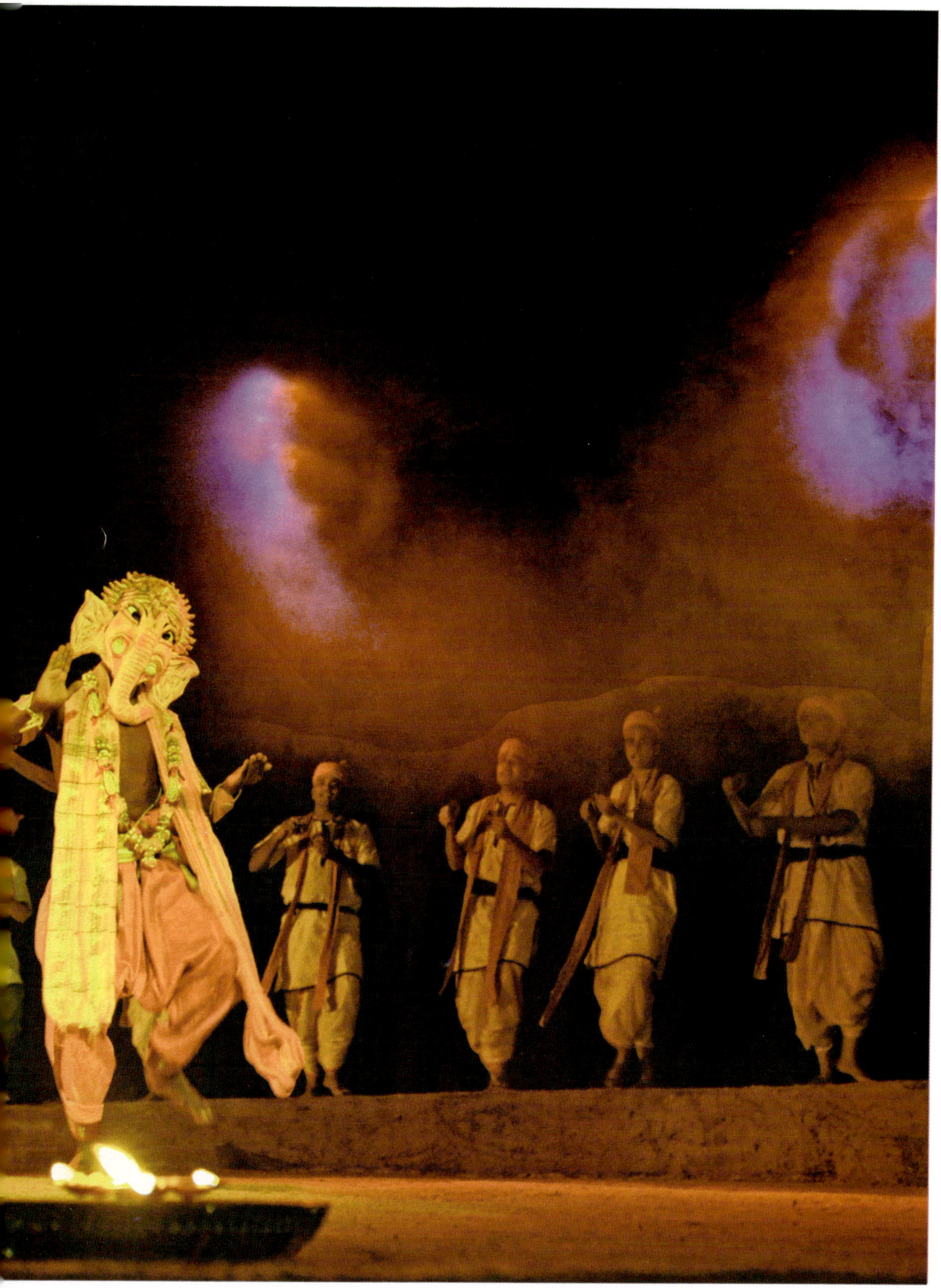

Guernica (1937). Medium: Oil on canvas. Artist: Pablo Picasso. Dimensions: 339.3 cm x 776.6 cm. Location: Museo Reina Sofia, Madrid, Spain. Courtesy: Wikimedia Commons.

Metaphor of Life

Art mirrors human behaviour through the artist's perceptive lens. Art is not even the photography of life; it is the symbolic representation of human existence and its voice. Art never imitates life as it is, but portrays the reality of it. It is not a perception of life as seen through our naked eyes but becomes a metaphor of collective livelihood.

The characters of a play, the subject of a painting, the idea behind a piece of music or gestures of a dance performance, are all inspired from the reality of life that forms a part of the artist's personality—a personality that impregnates universal expressions that can never be confined to a single individual's perception. It has to transcend the ordinaries and the mere facts into something that is a finer truth.

Now, let us analyse how a metaphor works in the realm of arts through a few examples from plays, sculptures and paintings. The suffering of Mallika in *Ashad ka Ek Din*, the miserable life of Savitri in *Aadhe Adhure*, Hayavadana's search for completeness in the play *Hayavadana* or the implicit ambition of Macbeth, the repentance of King Oedipus—all of these cannot be confined to an individual artist's limited territory of understanding and experience. They transcend into the realm of a limitless universal human experience and condition. Michelangelo's sculpture *Pieta* (1448–49) universalises the profound grief of mother Mary as the pain of universal motherhood, while in *Mona Lisa* (1503–06), Leonardo Da Vinci has perceived the enigmatic smile of the most beautiful woman in the world. Van Gogh has seen the shadow of the sorrow in all womanhood through a woman's suffering in his masterpiece *The* Sorrow (1882). Therefore, the language of art is universal, and it is articulated through symbols and metaphors.

Pieta (The Pity) 1498–99
Artist: Michelangelo
Medium: Marble
Subject: Jesus and mother Mary
Dimensions: 174 cm x 195 cm
Location: St. Peter's Basilica, Vatican City
Courtesy: Wikimedia Commons.

The Sorrow (1882). Artist: Vincent Van Gogh. Medium: Lithograph.
Dimensions: 44 cm x 27 cm. Van Gogh considered it to be one of his most effective portraits.
Courtesy: Wikimedia Commons.

Selectivity

Life and art may appear identical to the common eyes, but there is a big difference between these two. The subjects from ordinary life are interpreted in the expression of art. Real life contains everything, no matter how incidental or irrelevant it may be, but in art, each and every sequence, object, or element, even the smallest of gestures, is meticulously selected by the artist to give meaning to the form in its entirety.

An artist, a designer or an actor, while recreating life either on canvas or on the stage, subjects the work of art to a rigorous 'selection process' in order to create a pulsating and authentic work of art. Ordinary objects from life must undergo a process of many transformations and refinements in order to be deemed as relevant and to be interpreted in the context of the present society and time; and thus, art always remains relevant. To interpret art, the artist selects a few essential elements out of many that resonates the meaning. With the help of these selected elements, there develops an idiom or a vocabulary of expressions, which becomes an integral part of the creation. This intensive process of selection helps us understand the importance of art in society. A painting or a play with vague, random or aimless ideas brings nothing productive to the spectators, but an intense selection of conceptual elements within a work of art succeeds in providing meaning, conveying the artist's carefully formulated ideas.

In scenography, the process of selecting elements from various sources becomes even more complex. Scenography, as an artistic expression, includes performers as well as design. Therefore, it has to be imagined and realised from the point of view of the performance. Applied art does not have the freedom of independent expressions; it has to be comprehended through practice and functionality. Particularly for theatre presentation, each element of design becomes important. The scenographers usually confront a number of tricky issues every time they conceive design ideas within a given space.

A few relevant questions that usually crop up while designing a play are specified below:

i. Why is this design?
ii. What purpose would it serve?
iii. What would be its significance in the given space?
iv. How would the space help the actors?
v. Would the design contribute to the interpretation of the play?
vi. How relevant is it in the context of society?
vii. How many objects would be used to execute this design?
viii. Would it bring any psychological atmosphere into the play?
ix. What would be the relationships between the design elements and the actors?
x. In what way would it represent the play?
xi. Do the colours, textures and flow of the lines complement the nature of the production or contradict it?

All these issues orient a scenographer to opt for the appropriate elements, while conceiving the design or exploring a space. It is also essential to survey the potential of the design elements to reinforce the symbolic and metaphorical meaning of the work. Sometimes a scene can be communicated with the help of minimum design elements. Often a particular atmosphere and effect is achieved with a least amount of design units. In this circumstance, a scenographer may cleverly avoid implying additional set elements which may prove unnecessary. They must realise that the stage design is not about adding surplus elements, no matter how attractive they appear. On the contrary, it must be functional in projecting the surrounding, the actors and the actions. Therefore, if the desired result is achieved with less design elements, it is needless to clutter the space with ideas and objects. It becomes the responsibility of the scenographers to develop an atmosphere through the spatial design that must enhance the whole experience of the production, and every single inch of the space has to be explored by the actors. In a theatrical presentation, the representation of 'time' may vary from a few minutes to many years, but one visualises it within the performance time. The most essential elements of life are to be portrayed within this stipulated time by rejecting unwanted events.

Aesthetics

The word 'aesthetics' is derived from the Greek word 'Aisthetokos', which means a sense of perception, responsible for appreciating or rejecting an object. This sense differs for every individual. Aesthetics stands as the foundation of all the creation of arts. It is the study of beauty. The German philosopher Immanuel Kant named it 'Enjoyment'. He analyses aesthetics as an enjoyment that results in pleasure, which stems from our sensory stimulation by engaging our capacities of reflective contemplation. In another interpretation, Bharata, the author of the *Natya Shastra*, has termed it as, 'Anand'—a state of bliss. According to him, watching a piece of art would lead the viewers to a state of blissfulness, where a union of happiness (*Ananda*) and bliss (*Paramananda*) takes place, resulting in the birth of *rasa*. According to Indian theory, aesthetics is the point of spiritual enjoyment.

Aesthetics can be judged by two factors, i.e. emotion and intellect; they work simultaneously at any given point of time. Interpretation and value of art always depends on its aesthetics and taste. While aesthetics is the philosophical notion of beauty, taste is the result of awareness, education and cultural value. An artistic creation is appreciated or criticised on the basis of these two prime factors. Aesthetics and good taste depend upon the temperament of the audience. For example, a folk performance can be appreciated within a rural proximity, but it may not get that much applaud, warmth and intensity within an urban environment which may seem crude. People in the cities have developed different tastes, different from those of the rural folks. Aesthetic sensibilities depend upon the taste and temperament of the person who is experiencing it. But there is also a universal aspect to the experience of aesthetics, that caters our collective taste. Arts, pregnant with this universal appeal, are appreciated globally as 'classic arts'.

Aesthetics in Design

We have discussed earlier that the art of scenography is not an independent entity. It has to be perceived through the context of the performance. A well-articulated design facilitates the intensity of the production. It supports the idea, plots and actions. The aesthetics of a scenic design can be apprehended through its formation of lines, application of colours and textures and finally, the adopted forms in which it needs to be moulded. While judging the aesthetics of a production in the light of scenography, the following factors cannot be overlooked. They not only bring exquisiteness to the production but also add meaning to the interpretation of the play. The following points need to be taken care of while designing a play:

i. The visual elements in the space must be proportionally arranged.
ii. The colours and texture of the design must follow in pursuance of the inner rhythm of the production.
iii. Monotony of space is to be broken to create stimulation and impulse for the visual compositions.
iv. Sufficient and proportionate negative space[1] in the design is necessary to avoid clumsiness of space and project the actors effectively.
v. The objects, elements, props and other components of the design must have higher aesthetic value.

---

1 Negative space is the space around the main subject in the composition. For more details please refer to chapter 10.

vi. There must be harmony and coherence between the elements of design and the actors.
vii. Design idea must be expressed through the idiom of symbol and metaphor.

The exploration of the space to convey various meanings, constantly adds to the aesthetics of the production. Transformation of a performance space into a dramatic space involves higher sensibility and intellectual pursuance of the scenographer. While a well-proportionate design with proper distribution of space brings pleasing effect into the production, a picturesque composition is always appreciated with gratifications. Out of many, one important concern of a production is to provide aesthetic enjoyment to the viewers. Irrespective of the interpretation and thematic value, the play must be presented with beauty and elegance. The productions of Kavalam Narayana Panicker and Ratan Thiyam can be referred to in this context. Even the most grotesque image of the production has to be portrayed with utmost artistry so as to be appreciated by the spectators.

Interpretation
The transformation of subjective individual ideas into universal concepts is the fundamental phenomenon of art. Therefore, there could be multiple meanings for a single piece of art. This is the universality of art that allows different audiences to grasp different meanings out of the same work. This justification of the meaning is termed as 'interpretation'. Arguably, there might be a number of interpretations for a single piece of art and each one stands valid and convincing with truthful justifications. The aesthetic theory of interpreting art with various meanings is called 'pluralism', where no true or false interpretation is applied to art. Art cannot be measured as wrong or right, it can only be treated as relevant or irrelevant.

Still from the play *Shakuntalam* (1982). Playwright: Kalidasa. Director: K.N. Panikkar. Presented by: Sopanam Theatre Group, Thiruvananthapuram. Courtesy: Wikimedia Commons.

A theatre performance has to undergo many layers of interpretations for its final presentation. At the end of the day, it is the spectators who interpret through their individual perceptions. During the course of this multi-layered journey, a theatre performance passes through many stages of transformation:

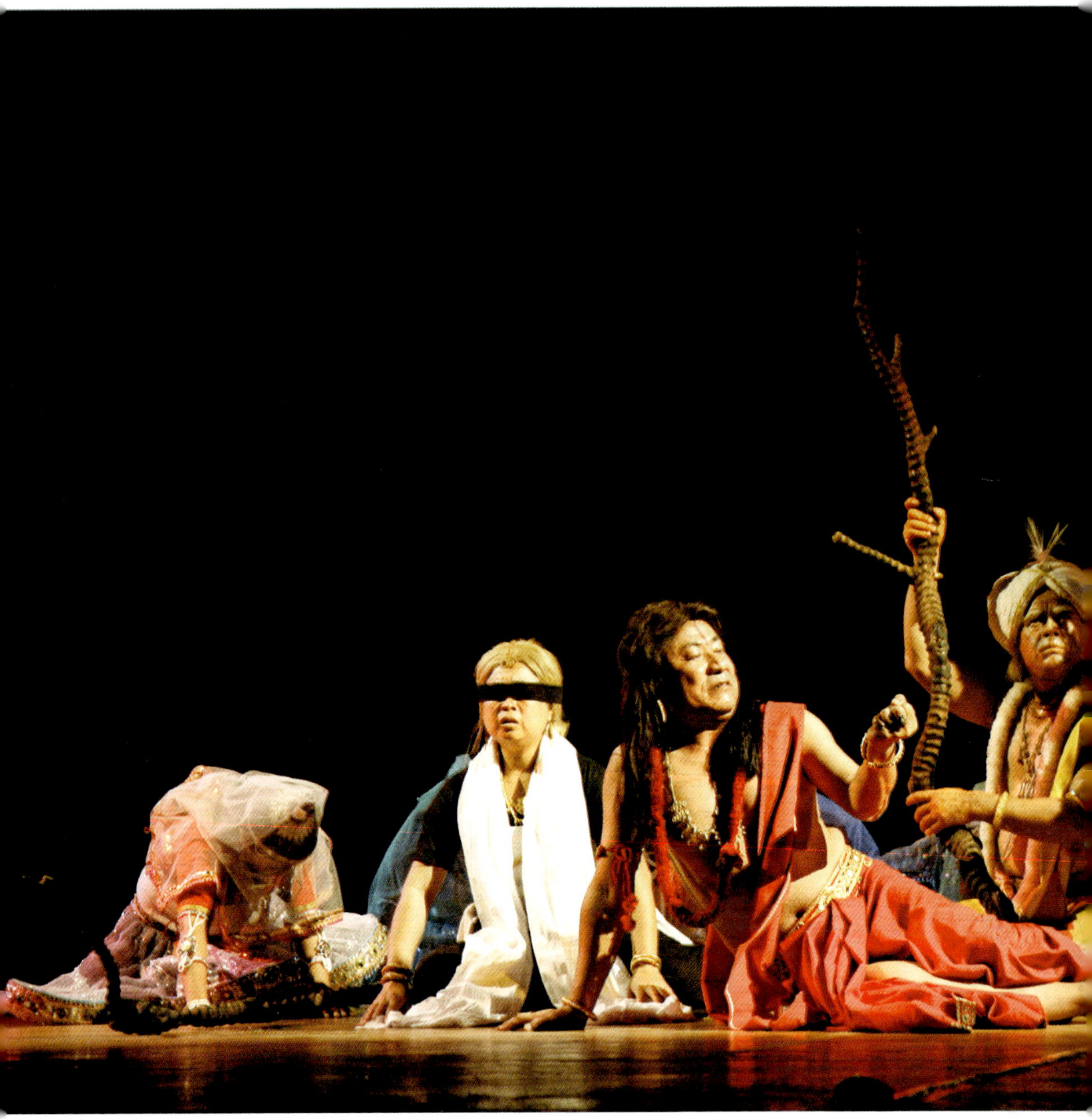

i. An idea is transformed into text with the playwright's interpretation.
ii. A director interprets the same text to find relevance for the contemporary society for which the play is being made.
iii. The director's concept is re-interpreted by a group of actors during rehearsal process.
iv. The technical aspect of the production is visualised and redefined by the scenographer and other designers.
v. Finally, in the form of a performance, the play passes through multiple interpretations and is critically evaluated by the audience.

This pluralistic approach of theatre arts, with manifold interpretations and reinterpretations, keeps this form alive for centuries. A play written thousands of years ago can even be treated as contemporary and modern because of its social relevance in the light of today's context. For example, Kalidasa's *Abhijnanasakuntalam*, written about 1600 years ago, has been interpreted and re-interpreted several times in various ways by different authors, directors, scenographers and actors. If one of its presentations interprets the play as the

Still from the play *Urubhangam*. Design and direction: Ratan Thiyam Presented by: The Chorus Repertory Theatre. Courtesy: Chorus Repertory, Imphal.

passionate love story of Dushyant and Shakuntala, another interpretation can read it as the betrayal and domination of the kingship on the weaker sections of the society. Similarly, Bhartendu Harischandra's *Andher Nagri*, a play written in the last quarter of 19th century, was initially interpreted as a political satire against the British rule. It has been modified and reinterpreted from different angles by the directors in different times. It has also been re-visualised to illustrate the current political situations of the country. Bertolt Brecht's *The Caucasian Chalk Circle*, *Three Penny Opera* or Shakespeare's classic texts have received multiple interpretations by various scholars, directors and actors all over the world. The scenographer creates an environment in the space for the play by defining the director's interpretation with the help of design elements. Interpretation is a relative term, which changes meaning with the changing times of the society, so that art form continues to acquire new meaning as time passes on, for centuries without end.

CONCLUSION

Sometimes we are unable to understand the meaning of art because we cannot connect ourselves to its language. To understand the language of art and to associate our thoughts with the meaning, we have to understand the socio-political and cultural perspective behind that creation. A particular kind of art is created aiming at a definite group of people who would understand and appreciate it. This is the social nature of art, which decides its language and prepares the ground for communication. The ability of understanding the language of art purely depends on the audience who receives it. That is the reason why multiple interpretations come out of a single creative work. Still, a particular creative work carries a definite message, which can be universally understood in a wider perspective. To talk about the language of art, Moshe Barasch, the 20th-century Israeli art historian argues:

The ability of art to convey a distinct message to the spectator is based on the audiences' familiarity with an accumulated, though ever-growing and evolving, body of crystallized figures and visual formulae. These figures and formulae were invented to say something definite and specific, and they fulfilled this task for many centuries. In other words, we understand art—this is particularly manifest in the case of a work created in the past, but it is valid also for one that is contemporary—because we have a cultural memory, because we remember expressions in both words and images.[ii]

To analyse the relevance of art, we can plunge into some of our past memories. Everyone must have interacted with the kind of performances, which were developed in ancient times, like 'Kathakali' and 'Koodiyattam'. These performances have passed the test of time and are still being performed, garnering a lot of appreciation. They still remain relevant because we understand their language—visual and aural. Because we have a continuity of cultural memory, we understand the sign language of these art forms. Without that, it becomes difficult to associate and interpret the presentation. Sometimes, it has been observed that an intricate design or abstract arrangement of space becomes a hindrance to understand at the beginning. But as the story unfolds, the dramatic action adds meaning to that abstraction and helps us in understanding the language of those visuals, which seemed obscure just a few moments ago.

References
[i] https://www.etymonline.com/word/art.
[ii] Barasch, Moshe. 1997. *The Language of Art: Studies in Interpretation*. New York: New York University Press. p. 6.

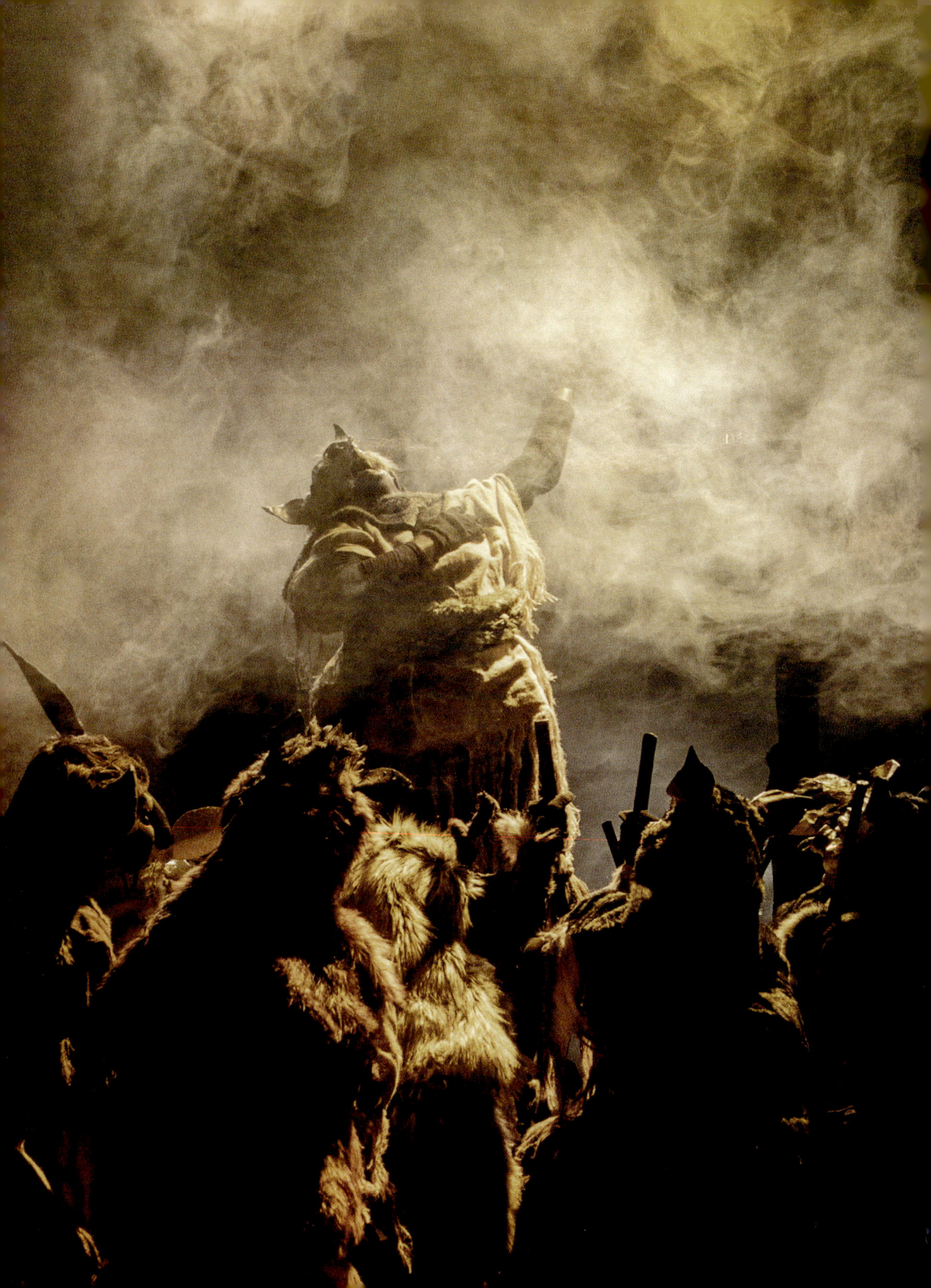

UNDERSTANDING SCENOGRAPHY: Exploring Ideas

How does a scenographer perceive his design idea?—How is his journey of creativity?—How nature plays a key role in creating this art?

Having discussed the above-mentioned aspects in the previous chapter, we will now move onto analysing the process through which the scenographers conceive the design ideas from texts or concepts, provided by the directors. Before formulating an idea, the artist must recognise that scenography cannot be envisaged in seclusion, and that its concept depends on an array of factors including text, the vision of the director and the actors and the overall functionality of the performance. Quite often scenographers visualise compositions according to their own perceptions of life and that of art. In this process, both the characters and the conceptual framework are reinterpreted in correspondence to their subjective emotional and intellectual understanding. The scenographers explore varied approaches and techniques for creating a new visual language which is to be written on a three-dimensional stage space. The space developed by the scenographers is often symbolic that metamorphoses the text into visual compositions. It often revitalises the entire production by the tool of optical phantasm.

It has been observed that the idea of designing a play germinates, sprouts and grows along with the production process to such a degree that the idea often becomes the foundation of the performance. Interestingly, the design idea triggers the imagination of an artist for spatial compositions which is realised through the 'performance text' combining the actors, space and the audience. The creation of a dramatic space with the help of artistic imagination, its functional behaviour through a series of interactions of the actors and the final participation of the spectators who interpret the play through their subjective experiences come under the domain of scenography. Parker and Smith (1974) observe:

> The design idea is aimed at stimulating an intellectual or emotional response in the audience. The control of the design elements may be broad and sensational to arouse primitive emotions, or they may be subtle and refined to stimulate an intellectual response. Good design is a result of logical yet imaginative thinking and intuitive feeling expressed through an idea or central theme.[i]

As mentioned earlier, unlike other singular art forms, scenography cannot be conceived in isolation. It has to be evolved and evaluated through practice and can only be comprehended by the parameters of presentation. It cannot dissociate itself independently from the play for interpretation. It requires a text or an idea for flourishing, without which it is impossible for the scenographer to actuate a space for portraying the realities of life. The psychological atmosphere created through the design helps the audience to explore layers of dramatic components—conflict, tension, suspense, actions, motif and finally the aesthetics of the production. They stimulate the dramatic factors and that is the major contribution of scenography in theatre. Robert Edmond Jones (1887–1954) argues:

> The designer must strive to achieve in his setting what I can only call a

high potential. The walls, the furniture, the properties, are only the facts of a setting, only the outline. The truth is in everything but these objects, in the space they enclose, in the intense vibration they create. They are fused into a kind of embodied impulse.[ii]

Different forms of art stipulate different rules, so does scenography. Each new production poses new challenges for the scenographers. For many, the idea clicks while reading the play, while for others it is an internal journey of their own selves. Sometimes, the scenographers perceive and develop their ideas by interacting with the performance spaces prior to the rehearsal process. Alternatively, the scenographers explore the ideas with the help of a group of actors during practice. Often, an unprecedented behaviour of the space, which often occurs accidentally through the interaction between the actor and the space, helps evoke an idea to take shape in the scenographer's mind. For some, this creative accident inspires a scenographer to such an extent that it becomes the take-off point to start their journey into the world of imagination. Out of numerous means of germinating design ideas to trigger at the dramatic imagination, here are certain approaches:

Out of numerous means of germinating design ideas to trigger the dramatic imagination, the approaches such as, reading and interpreting the text, understanding the dramatic conflict, realising the characters' interpersonal relationships, defining the locations of the scenes, researching and presenting the design idea, and finally selecting the performance space to execute the final design, hold significance. Let's discuss them in greater detail:

SECTION I

READING THE TEXT

The text (script) is the fundamental source of a play production. The text, which is a convolution of words defining writer's perception, is enlivened in a play through performance. And thus, theatre, as the popular saying goes, is born twice: first by the playwright and second by the actors through the performance. In Sanskrit, it is termed as 'Dvija' which means, 'he who takes birth twice'. In this creative journey of nurturing an idea, the metamorphosis of the text (into performance) holds an immense significance. The task of interpreting a script and visualising it as a live performance is endowed exclusively on the scenographers. Through their endeavours the audience enters a performance for an active visual experience of the text.

There are varied methods of interpreting the text into visuals that Indian scenographers have experimented with. Most of the artists usually keep a sketchbook and a pencil while reading a play. I have seen many noted Indian scenographers such as Professor Robin Das and Professor Bansi Kaul invigorating the ideas of a text into sketches simultaneously while reading. Quite often, Professor Das would be seen scribbling random sketches, working on haphazard lines and forms, in an entirely absent state of mind while reading the text. These untidy lines would finally become the source of his scenography. He often finds it difficult to control the flow of thoughts leading to a propagation of numerous images, juxtaposed while reading the text and later, while working on its functionalities. Also a few other scenographers such as Dr Nissar Allana and Sri Bapi Bose would go through the text multiple times before developing their ideas, meticulously executing them through sketches, drawings and finally developing the models before transposing those to the stage space.

Often the first reading of the text may not help the scenographers to end up with the final idea, but it certainly provides basic understanding of the play, in general, along with the characters' psychology, mood and atmosphere. Also, scenography takes an upper hand when the production is dependent on the collaboration of various sources or is devised without any well-structured text and is based on an idea only. An intense discussion with the director to understand their perspective and approach towards the production can also help to visualise the design.

However, while designing, the scenographers should be aware of the possibilities of falling into the trap of preoccupations. Therefore, they should liberate themselves from the preconceived notions that often create hindrance in imagining new concepts. A text must trigger the insight of the scenographer. Analytical reading helps in understanding the intention and interpretation of the playwright and leads the scenographers to plunge into the world of 'subtext'. In this mysterious world the psychological atmosphere of the play lies hidden in dormant states underneath the text and in between the words and lines. These subtexts are capable enough to break the hegemony of words to be expressed through images, visible or invisible, in the hands of a competent scenographer.

Reading the text can make the scenographers clear about the various prevalent conflicts, essential to develop the idea of the design. One can interact with different types of conflicts in different situations in the text. A few major conflicts that we generally come across while reading the plays are mentioned below:

External conflict: It arises between the characters; for example, the conflict between Kalidas and Vilom in *Ashad ka Ek Din*, or that of Mahendra Nath and Savitri in *Aadhe Adhure*.

Internal conflict: It is an encounter of the character's inner and outer self; for example, the dilemma of Devadutta for Padmini that leads to cutting of Devadutta's head in the temple of Kali, as narrated in the play, *Hayavadana*.

Situational conflict: It is created through the dramatic action of the play. For example, the dramatic events in the play *A Midsummer Night's Dream* leads to create irony and humour.

Environmental conflict: It is the conflict between time and space. This kind of conflict usually remains hidden in the plot. For example, *Abhijnanasakuntalam*, a 5th-century Indian classical play written by Kalidasa, bears the testimony of a harmonious bond between man and nature. The environment consisting of forest, trees, creepers, animals and birds form the major component of its atmosphere along with the dramatic plot. The temperament of various characters like Dushyant, Shakuntala, Anasuya, Priyamvada, Kanva are time and again established and guided by these visual components of the play. The untimely blooming of the jasmine vine, the attack of the bumble bee on Shakuntala, attracted by the fragrance of her body, the shrivelling of the trees and creepers at the time of Shakuntala's departure for her husband's palace and the weeping deer who holds Shakuntala back with utmost compassion at the time of her departure are a few examples among many environmental conflicts of the play. There are also many different visual components of such conflict in all the plays which need expositions by the scenographers as well as the directors.

It is not necessary to translate the playwright's vision and interpretation every time. Scenographers can reinterpret the play through their subjective intellectual and emotional understanding by keeping the design relevant with the current times. But before doing so, they should be very clear about the writer's objectives and motivations behind the writings. A text can be realistic, abstract, mythological, folkloric, melodramatic, musical, fantastic or absurd according to the political, social or psychological background it passes through. Also, the background of the characters, their social circumstances, economic conditions, political situations and their interpersonal relationships play an internal role in building up the narrative. Therefore, the scenographers must have a clear understanding of these factors before jumping into the design works. All these points would help in the research process during the post-reading session.

Types of Plays
There are different types of plays that require specific attentions. A good understanding of the text will help the scenographers discover varied layers of emotional and technical outlines for structuring the design. Every text is unique in terms of their sound, rhythm, pace, texture and style of writings. While some follow a definite rhythmic pattern, others do not. Some are poetic and musical, like Dharmavir Bharati's *Andha Yug*, while others are psychological, such as Badal Sircar's *Pagla Ghoda* and Girish Karnad's *Nagamandala*, etc. By depicting the absurdity of mankind, the meaning of some plays exists within the broken lines of their texts as we found in Samuel Beckett's *Waiting for Godot* and Ionesco's *Rhinoceros*. Most significantly, the sound pattern of the texts varies from one another, so do their visuals.

A scenographer must figure out and try to sense the colours of different texts while reading the play. By drawing a parallel between the sound of the text and the colours of the visual compositions, one can create wonders. Professor Pamela Howard observes: 'This sense of sound is very near to the sense of colour, and later when I am composing the images it will lead me to a choice of colour keys in the major and minor that visually mirror the music of the words.'[iii]

In any Sanskrit play, one can identify the embodiment of visual images hidden underneath the texts, enriched with varied textures and colours. We can quote a few lines from any Sanskrit play in order to observe its visual imageries, expressed through the text only. We can take an excerpt from *Urubhangam*, written in 2nd century BC by Mahakavi Bhāsa for discussion.

(Entry of three soldiers)

Soldier-1: This is the place of death and life. A noble sacrifice…
A great yagna…paving the bridge from earth to heaven.
Soldier-2: Yes, yes, you are right! The hipbones of elephants immobile,
Make new life in the nests of vultures,
Chariots lie empty…With no one to ride…
Gone are the heroes to the heaven… None alive, none alive!
They are busy with Yudha-karma,
Their duty overriding the foreseeing of death.
Soldier-3: Not only this! You see here.
Once the pillar of victory stood aloft,
Now fallen making new structure.
With the distorted bodies of the dead!
Now, not even a whisper comes from those courageous lips
That once hosted roaring voices.
Silence struggling against the sounds of vultures
Seemingly chanting mantras for their sacred meals of flesh.'[1]

In the above-mentioned text, the colours, textures and the ambience of the battlefield of Kurukshetra inspire the scenographers to perceive its visual design. Similarly, in another contemporary play, *Ashad ka Ek Din*, the scenographers can visualise the picturesque beauty of the Himalayan valley and its lush green colours against the dark grey clouds at the

---
1. Original Sanskrit play by: Mahakavi Bhasa. Hindi Translation by: Bharat Bhushan Agrawal. Hindi to English translation by: Stephe Jones and Satyabrata Rout

outset of the monsoon in their imagination. These imaginary visuals take shape in the scenographers' mind to formulate the design of the play. Scenographers can take help of various visual art expressions to realise the idea. Intense reading of the text would dig out the hidden images and meaning underlying the phrases.

Before designing a play, a scenographer should be aware of the genre of it—a classic, periodical, contemporary, mythological, melodramatic, musical and so on.

The Classical Plays

The term 'classical' is referred to the exemplary ancient art forms that have a strong cultural significance beyond the barrier of time, inspiring the generations. Classical plays, literature and art are rooted to a definite vocabulary of expressions. The regulations for the performance of a classical play are tabulated in the classical texts that are passed onto the world for further adoption. For example, Indian Sanskrit plays, globally popular as classical plays, are codified through Bharat's *Natya Shastra*. Similarly, Aristotle's *Poetics* establishes the rules for the presentation of Greek tragedies. Noh theatre of Japan follows the Zeami's theory of Aesthetics.

In India, the term 'classical' is known as 'shastriya', which means knowledge based on principles. The relevance of classical plays is not restricted to a particular era or geography as it remains relevant and significant to the world across ages. Some of Indian classical plays are, Bhāsa's *Urubhangam* and *Karnabharam*, Kalidas's *Abhijnanasakuntalam* and *Malavikagnimitram*, Sudraka's *Mrcchakatika* and Vishakhadutta's *Mudrarakshasa*, etc. These plays follow the principles of 'natyam'— performance prescribed in the *Natya Shastra*.

The Classic Plays

The term 'classic' is often misinterpreted as 'classical'. But it has altogether a different meaning. A piece of literature, art and architecture whose thematic significance remains relevant for every age is regarded as classic. A play that stands out across time for its form, content and interpretation and is relatable to the socio-political issues is called a classic play. Some examples of classic plays are *Othello, Macbeth, Waiting for Godot, A Doll's house, Andha Yug, Ashad ka Ek Din, Hayavadana,* etc. The commonality between these plays is that they deal with basic human nature such as jealousy, greed, revenge, ambition, lust, sacrifice, suspicion, love and hatred and therefore, are timeless and relevant for every generation.

Classical plays are based on codified principles, whereas classic play does not have any principle of presentations. For example, Indian Sanskrit plays are based on *Natya Shastra* principles whereas a classic play like *Othello* or *King Lear* or *Andha Yug* do not follow any presentation criteria. But the theme of a classic play must be universal and relevant for all the ages.

The Periodical Plays

The periodical plays are restricted to a definite time frame and are always guided by historical evidences. They can be contemporary or classic in nature, but their plots are borrowed from real incidents with authentic social value. Construction of scenic visuals in a periodical play needs thorough research. The visual objects used in periodical plays must have a resemblance and a direct connection, a reference to the contemporaneity and historicity of the matters. An in-depth understanding of the social lifestyle, custom and architecture of the period are essential to design a periodical play. Scenographers can take the help of reference books and can explore museums for understanding the time period in reference. Plays such as Jaysankar Prasad's *Chandragupt* and *Skandgupt*, D.L. Roy's *Shahjahan,* Jagdish

Ch. Mathur's *Konark*, Girish Karnad's *Tughlaq*, etc. are a few examples of Indian periodical plays.

The Contemporary Plays
Contemporary plays are based on the concurrent times and deal with the topical issues. They can be expressed through historical facts, myth and legends, imaginary ideas and current socio-political issues. They can be tragedy, comedy or satire. These plays can be realistic or non-realistic in approach, but they become almost obsolete with the changing values of the society.

While presenting an art or literature that is written to fulfil the taste of the time and the demand of the society, an artist has to draw a significant link between the play and the current time to make it relevant. The term 'contemporary' lives upon the contemporary preferences of the society that goes out of fashion once the trend is changed. Contemporary presentations also remain significant with the need of time and die their natural death thereafter.

A prominent example of rise and fall of a particular style of theatre in India is the Parsi theatre. Plays written for this theatre were presented during the mid-19th century and had run with houseful shows for almost 100 years. Today, it has completely vanished from the Indian theatre scenario, except in the academic curriculum. It was the need of the time that made Parsi theatre one of the significant entertainment industries of the colonial India for which hundreds of plays were written. But with the advancement of society and the changing values of our lifestyle, this theatre was pushed behind time, so were its plays. However, if any contemporary art survives and remains relevant across the times, it is regarded as 'classic'. Contemporary plays can be of any genre. They can be classic, musical, periodical, mythological, etc.

A few post-Independence contemporary Indian plays and their playwrights are enlisted below:

Contemporary Indian Plays	Language	Playwright
Andha Yug	Hindi	Dharmavir Bharati
Ghashram Kotwal, Khamosh Adalat Jari Hai, Sakharam Binder-	Marathi	Vijay Tendulkar
Tughlaq, Hayavadana, Weeding Album	Kannada	Girish Karnad
Aadhe Adhure, Ashad ka Ek Din-	Hindi	Mohan Rakesh
Agra Bazar, Charan Das Choor	Urdu/ Chattishgadi	Habib Tanvir
Charpai, Azayab Ghar	Hindi	Rameshwar Prem
Surya ki Antim Kiran se Pahli Kiran Tak, Shakuntala ki Anguthi	Hindi	Surendra Varma
Evam Indrajit, Pagla Ghoda, Baki Itihash	Bengali	Badal Sircar
Thirty Days in September, Dance Like a Man	English	Mahesh Dattani
Court Martial, Sabse Udash Kavita	Hindi	Swadesh Dipak
Hanush, Madhavi	Hindi	Bhisham Sahani
Konark	Hindi	Jagadish Ch. Mathur
Virashat, Yugant	Marathi	Mahesh Elkunchwar
Mahanirvan, Begum Barve	Marathi	Satish Alekar
Nandan Kathai, Aurangzeb	Tamil	Indira ParthaSarathy
The mother Supreme, Siri Sampige	Kannada	Chandrasekhar Kambar
Aranya Fasal, Katha Ghoda	Odiya	Manoranjan Das
Koipen Ek Phooluu Nam Bolo (Kisi Ek Phool Ka Naam Lo)	Gujrati	Madhu Rai
Ek Aur Dronacharya, Are! Mayavi Sarover, Poster	Hindi	Dr Shankar Shesh

The Mythological Plays

Mythological plays are based on accepted mythological stories and are expressed through mystical and supernatural characters. Stylised by nature, these plays can be presented with the help of music, dance and other interdisciplinary artistry. The presentation of these plays can be folkloric or imaginative. Mythological stories emerged in the ancient past before the beginning of the recorded history. Multiple interpretations can be derived from mythological tales as it employs multiple symbols.

Scenographers, while working on myth, can adopt all means of expressions into their designs. The cultural ethnicity of the region is always reflected in mythological presentations. In India, plays based on the *Ramayana* and *Mahabharata* or the folkloric tales are regarded as mythological plays. After Independence, a good number of mythological stories and folkloric tales were revisited and adapted into contemporary theatre. Plays such as, *Andha Yug (1954), Yayati (1960), Suno Janmejaya (1960), Ek Aur Dronacharya (1971), Chakravyuha (1984), Jhimiti Khela (1988), Karna katha (2008), Eklavya Uvaach (2011),* etc. have created landmarks in the history of modern Indian theatre.[2]

The Melodrama

The word 'melodrama' is usually referred to the act of intense emotions involving larger-than-life gestures and loud music. This type of literary work sensitises the audience through its loud emotions. It was a common

---

2. *Andha Yug* was written by Dharmavir Bharati in the year 1954. The play is based on the last day war of the *Mahabharata*.
   Yayati (1960) is a Kannada play written by Girish Karnad. The play is based on an episode of the *Mahabharata*.
   Suno Janmejaya was written originally in Kannada language as *Kelu Janmejaya* in 1950s by the famous scholar and playwright Adya Rangacharya.
   Ek Aur Dronacharya, a play by Shankar Shesh, was written in the year 1971 with a contemporary approach based on the story of Dronacharya in the *Mahabharata*.
   Chakravyuha (1984), a Manipuri play, was written and directed by Ratan Thiyam. The play narrates the death of Abhimanyu through illicit means by the seven warriors in the battlefield of the Mahabharat.
   Jhimiti Khela (1988) is an Odia play, written and directed by Satyabrata Rout. The play draws elements from the Adiparva of the *Mahabharata*.
   Karna Katha (2008) is an adaptation of the famous Marathi novel *Mrityunjay*, written by Sivaji Savant. The novel was dramatised into Hindi and directed by Satyabrata Rout.
   Eklavya Uvaach (2011) draws elements from a peripheral story in the *Mahabharata*. It is written originally in Hindi by Kuldeep Kunal and is adapted into Kannada by K.D. Ramayah as *Matte Eklavya*. The play was directed by Satyabrata Rout for which he received the META award-2013 as the best director. The play also has travelled to Colombia to participate in the International Theatre Festival at Bogota in 2011.

practice in 18th and 19th century European theatre and opera where plays were presented with exaggeration accompanied by orchestral music and songs. While composing a melodramatic text, the playwright gives specific emphasis to the plot, characters and incidents entertaining the audience through high drama. However, melodrama often lacks delicacy.

The trend of practising melodrama in India is very common in the folk and traditional theatres. We can witness the presentation of this sort in the Jatra, Nautanki and Ramalila, etc. Even in Hindi movies and in soap operas, we can find elements of melodrama that mesmerise the common mass. Scenographers can resourcefully explore the melodramatic magnificence and loudness into their design with contemporary sensibility by upholding the aesthetics and delicacy of the production through their skills. Parsi plays were considered melodramatic in nature, for example, *Indar Sabha (1853)*, *Khubsurat Bala (1910)*, *Veer Abhimanyu (1916)*, *Rustam-O- Sohrab (1929)*, etc.[3]

The Musical Plays

In this genre, music holds an upper hand, so much so, that even the text is often rendered with rhythm and musical notes. The delicacy and lyrical quality involved in the production can be extended to the design and expressed through elements such as lines, colours and textures. The flow of the rhythm and music can mirror the design. Opera is a good example of musical drama, for example, Sheela Bhatia's [4] famous Punjabi opera *Heer*

---

3. *Inder Sabha* was written by Agha Hasan Amanat.
   Khubsurat Bala and *Rustam-O- Sohrab* were written by Agha Hashar Kashmiri.
   Veer Abhimanyu was written by Radheshyam Kathavachak.

4. Sheela Bhatia (1916–2008) was a famous Punjabi director and playwright. Born in Sialkot, Pakistan, she settled in Delhi after partition in 1948. She was a professor of acting at the National School of Drama, during the time of its inception in 1958. Sheela Bhatia was the founder director of Delhi Art Theatre, one of the earliest repertories of independent India. She has written and directed more than 50 plays in Punjabi, Urdu and Hindi. She has been awarded with Padmashree for her contribution to the modern Indian theatre.

Ranjha (1957), *Chand Badla Da* (1975), *Dard Aayega Dabe Paon* (1979) and *Omar Khayyam* (1990) in Urdu. Habib Tanvir's famous play *Agra Bazar* (1954), Jabbar Patel's Marathi production of *Ghashiram Kotwal* (1972) and B.V. Karanth's Kannada presentation of *Sattavara Naralu* (1974), *Jokumara Swami* (1972), *Hayavadana* (1971) *and Gokula Nirgamana* (1993) are a few examples of musical plays in post-Independence Indian theatre.

SECTION II

RESEARCH

Each play, irrespective of its genre, speaks of the cultural history of mankind. The value system of a society and its politico-economic status gets reflected time and again in the form of a play. Thus, any play can be relevant for the society with ever-changing interpretations in accordance to the value systems for all times to come. For creating a link between the play and society, scenographers excavate related references into their design. Professor Pamela Howards observes:

> The visual artist deals in extracting the essence from actuality, and presenting it with clarity on the canvas. The viewer's memory and recognition is activated, seeing through the selective eye of the artist, clothing, objects, or colours, that reawaken forgotten memories and provoke the joy of recognition. The spectator is connected to the subject when a scenographer has been able to choose an object which expresses more than its physical reality.[iv]

Let us take examples from two classical plays—*Abhijnanasakuntalam* and *Mrcchakatika*—written around 1600 years ago. They narrate the social customs like the duty and morality, ecological bonding of nature and man and above all, the life under the despotism of the power profoundly.

Precisely, while *Abhijnanasakuntalam* demonstrates a life lived under the popularly accepted social conduct, derived from the value systems of ancient Indian society such as, human rights, respect, dignity, sacrifice, patriotism, rationality, equality, democracy and harmonious living between man and nature, *Mrcchakatika* projects the encounter between tenderness, love and sacrifice with revenge, jealousy and power. All intertwined together give rise to a social history, which needs an intense observation to be transcribed into images on stage. More specifically, a scenographer has to dwell into sociological, cultural, political, historical, philosophical, economical and anthropological references that are involved in the writing of the texts in all times. The artist has to take detailed notes on the social behaviour, human relationships, architectural artistry of the related time and everything that needs to be visually presented in the play.

India has undergone many transformations since Independence—the social, economic, political, cultural and religious dynamics have been reformed, restructured and redefined on the basis of various knowledge sets acquired over the years. The education system has also changed drastically across decades.

Life today has been radically changed with the advent of globalisation in the last decade of the 20th century. Indian rural village, which to Gandhi is a metaphor of the entire nation, has undergone many transformations after Independence till today. Urbanisation, globalisation and digitalisation have changed Indian society significantly. With that, our life and values have also been restructured, leading to new demands. Indian literature and theatre have recorded this socio-cultural history of transformation of the nation in details. In any of the contemporary plays written in the post-Independence time, one can extract these social dilemmas through various characters, plots and actions that stand as question mark in the annals of a developing nation.

In the plays written during the post-Independence period such as, *Ashad Ka Ek Din, Aadhe Adhure, Ghashiram Kotwal, Tughlaq, Shakharam Binder, Kamla, Evam Indrajit, Baki Itihash, Andha Yug, Hanush, Charpai, Mahanirvan, Virashat, Aranya Fasal, etc.* one can find a struggle for social justice and existence as the demand of the time. If *Ashad ka Ek Din* deals with the confrontation between an ambitious city life and a peaceful village dwelling, questioning the significance of urbanisation in the 1950s and 1960s India, *Aadhe Adhure* narrates the rising demands of ambitions of an urban lifestyle. There exists in the play a constant conflict between the pursuits and dreams of the modern urban era and the core Indian value system, where the protagonist, Savitri is forced to compromise with many social demands such as family, office, unwanted relationships, in order to fulfil all the needs to lead a comfortable life in the society only to finally confront her own self.

In the play *Tughlaq* (1964), Girish Karnad narrates a situation where great ideas are shattered due to poor execution. He emphasises on the conspiracy, selfish motivations, impractical ideas, nasty politics, ego and inferiority complex that drew the curtain of a great empire. Karnard, by placing the play in the backdrop of India's medieval history, tries to draw a parallel to the Nehru's vision of new India that began with ambitious idealism and ended up in disillusionment.

The scenographers need to revisit these notions for myriad interpretations in accordance with the contemporary society and politics. The scenographers' responsibility lies in constructing an appropriate atmosphere through which the viewers can cast a brief look into the current realities and introspect for better existence. For establishing the relevant contexts from history that are crucial in the contemporary times, scenographers work on a larger perspective. They work on each minute scene and draw a social picture which needs to be reflected time and again in each of the visual compositions of the play.

Scenographers work on specific units by extracting clues from the text. Since visual images usually lie hidden underneath the text, those need excavation. Therefore, scenographers need to tune their eyes and mind to disclose those unseen images, the apparently invisible traces of the text. The playwrights also need to create challenges for the scenographers to involve creatively in search of those invisible traces in order to develop a visual narrative, parallel to the verbal text. But ironically, most of the playwrights have a tendency of over-depicting the visuals in their texts. Quite often, they elaborately describe the visual narrations before the scene starts. They also intervene in the stagecraft by describing specific locales of the scenes and stage business such as, handling of the props, placing the objects or even detecting the colours and textures of the furniture, walls, doors, etc. The rise and fall of the curtains in between the scenes and acts are often meticulously worked out by the playwrights. For example, in *Ashad ka Ek Din*, the playwright has provided long narrative descriptions with detailed visual effects before the scene starts. He portrays:

> Light thunder and rain are heard before and for a few moments after the curtain rises. Then they gradually fade out.
>
> The curtain rises slowly.
>
> The room is ordinary. The walls are of wood, caulked with soft clay along the lower sections. Swastikas are dawn with red dye at intervals on the walls. The front door opens onto the darkened veranda on either side of the door are niches in which extinguished lamps are kept. The door at the left leads into another room. With the door open the corner of a bedstead is visible. The planks of the door are also caulked with clay. A conch shell and a lotus are drawn on it with red chalk. Occasionally, flashes of lightning are seen in the large window on the right.
>
> […] By the window is a wooden seat with a tiger skin spread on it. There are two chairs near the hearth. Ambika is sitting on one of

these chairs winnowing paddy into a basket. Looking towards the window she takes a deep breath and then resumes her work. The front door opens and Mallika enters shivering in her wet clothes. Ambika continues working without looking up. Mallika hesitates momentarily, then comes over to Ambika[v]

By portraying such detailed descriptions, unintentionally the playwrights condition the scenographers' visual sensibility, leaving a relatively less scope for further imagination. Moreover, it is the scenographer who develops stage visuals, not the writer. The real clues for the visual design remain underneath the speeches and not in the superfluous indicators mentioned by the playwrights. The scenographers can effectively extract the visual hints from the dialogues of the characters. But an illustrative, superficial and unimaginative representation of those stage descriptions narrated by the playwrights may not contribute towards an innovative interpretation.

Conducting a research on the contemporary history would save the scenographer from falling into the trap of illustrative visuals narrated by the playwrights. To begin with, scenographers depend on various sources such as reference books, archives, museums, architectures, art galleries and internet. They can also rely upon past memories for creating the historical essence. Detailed observation of life is the most effective research process for the visual artists which can be incorporated to the creative process at any time. Each single movement and activity of nature and life holds significance for visual compositions, for the most ordinary endeavour of life can become a take-up point for a design idea of a play.

Finally, the scenographers pass on their research to other members of the group—the director, actors, managers and the technical crew who further share their views and carry those ideas into their respective works. The scenographers usually prepare sketches, collect photographs of their observations about the costumes, props, sets, masks and makeup, etc. and

Preparatory drawing and research work for the play *The Ballad of the Cosmo Café (2019)*. Concept, scenography and direction: Professor Pamela Howard. Presented by: Royal Central School of Speech and Drama, University of London. Courtesy: Prof. Pamela Howard and Martin Gannon (UK).

exhibit them on the walls of the rehearsal space adding something new every day. This idea of converting the rehearsal space to a dynamic and live museum acts as a reference for the performers and the directors. The walls of the rehearsal spaces, filled up with the photographs, sketches, drawings, sample textiles, under-processed masks, props, etc. provide a constant emotional link between the actors and the characters. Scenographers can also create a specific area in the rehearsal room, equipped with white chart papers, sketch pens, colour pencils, colours and brushes to motivate the actors to draw random sketches related to their respective characters. This would enable the actors to discover new dimensions in their characterisations. A preparatory pen drawing made by Professor Pamela Howard for the play *The Ballad of the Cosmo Café* which she designed and directed for the Royal School of Speech and Drama, University of London in the year 2019, is displayed here for understanding.

During the 'Vincent Project'[5], the design team did an innovative job helping in devising a unique presentation. The team collected minute reference materials related to the life and work of the great master Vincent Van Gogh. We explored the internet, library, journals, collected newspaper reviews and several anonymous sources of information. The team satisfactorily collected intrinsic details on the life of the Dutch painter. Gagan Deep, the designer of this project, collected lots of photographs related to the painter's life and photocopied

---

5. 'Vincent Project' was funded by the Ministry of Culture, Govt. of India, to be undertaken at Hyderabad in the year 2014–15. This was a research-based project that ended up with a devised production *Tumhara Vincen*t, which was performed by the actors of Rangakalpa theatre group, Hyderabad. The play was written, designed and directed by Satyabrata Rout. Twenty-five actors and a few designers across the country worked in this project for a few months till the final presentation in Hyderabad and Delhi. They still continue to perform this play. The play was a product of 'Visual Theatre'—a concept which has been undertaken by Prof. Rout in India.

them, along with many sketches, paintings, letters of Van Gogh which he had written to his brother Theo, thus gathering authentic information on the costumes of the characters of the play.

Our collection also included a series of works of the French impressionists such as, Paul Cezanne, Paul Gauguin, George Seurat, Edgar Degas, Claude Monet, Edouard Manet, August Renoir, etc. All the four walls of the Gurbax Singh Hall (G.B. Hall) at the University of Hyderabad were filled up with these research materials where the project was conducted. Interestingly and of course coincidentally, the actor[6] who was portraying Van Gogh had a liking for sketching and paintings. Throughout the process, he utilised his leisure hours drawing a number of sketches related to the rehearsal process and blocking compositions and pasting them along with the other research works in the designated space. The entire atmosphere of our working space rejuvenated into that of a thriving art gallery, bringing new energy and dynamism to the production in each moment during the rehearsal.

But there is also a side effect of this. Though the creative instinct of a scenographer always wants to discover something new, overdoing the research often hampers the production and limits the creative energy of the performing artists, therefore constricting the space for a meaningful exploration of the enquiries. Moreover, by doing this, a scenographer can fall into the trap of exhibiting all the conclusive details of scenography, limiting the imagination of the artists and the crew involved. In this respect, the process becomes the center of attraction relegating the primary functionaries of the play to a secondary position.

Quite often, executing the research through illustrative means may lead to an academic coursework production. If a play does not reach to the

---

6 Md. Sahidur Rahman, an actor from National School of Drama performed the character of Vincent. Mr. Sahid is a wonderful actor with an inclination for research works.

spectators in a meaningful way, it becomes a bad presentation regardless of the amount of research and inputs invested in it. One must be aware of these issues while processing a research-based play. A play needs to evolve and should be designed with the help of the research, but it should not become the slave of the study. Research is only a medium to channelise the thoughts into action upon which a play can take shape. Often during the research, insignificant objects such as, an ordinary photograph, any common object or even a relevant newspaper column can form valuable documents of reminiscence through which scenographers can draw design elements for the production.

SECTION III

PRESENTING THE DESIGN IDEA

Frequent reading and analysis of the text opens some insight of the visual artist, but it must be registered from the beginning of the process. A scenographer must not forget to take notes of the interpretations, style of presentation and thematic intricacies of the play while reading the text. The characters' interactions with sets, props, costumes, etc. and the spatial relationship between the two must not be overlooked. Appropriate locales, props and objects as per the demand of the scenes need to be identified by sieving through numerous visual ideas. But before finalising the design, scenographers must work on the feasibility of the entry, exit, area of interest in the space (refer to Chapter-10), characters' interactions with the design, spatial arrangements of the visual units and finally the style of the design presentation. A meeting with the director becomes essential at this point of time where many new ideas can come up and new style of presentations can be formulated.

Scenographers usually assemble ideas in a definite framework. They find their methods to give shape to the expression, which in other words, termed as the 'style of presentation'. A theatre presentation involves various styles such as the style of writing, style of acting, style of production and style of the visuals that includes set, lights, costume, props, mask, etc. All these components may have different modes of expression, but they work in coalition with each other for conveying focused meaning. A scenographer needs to prepare a harmonious visual atmosphere out of the written text with the help of a group of actors. This physical embodiment of the text may or may not follow the literary style of writings, but it must identify itself with the essence of the text.

We can cite quite a few major Indian productions where the scenography and performance design differ extensively from the text yet implying similar connotations. Here are a few examples. Girish Karnad's *Tughlaq* is written with a realistic approach backing it with an authentic Indian history. But different directors and scenographers have tried this play with varied styles. Ebrahim Alkazi[7] has visualised this play by keeping 'naturalism' as the style of presentation. His histrionic production of *Tughlaq* (1974) at the backdrop of Purana Qila, Delhi, still remains afresh in audience's memory. Another noted Indian theatre director, Prasanna[8] presented the same play (1982) for the National School of Drama repertory company through symbolic and suggestive design in a proscenium set-up.

---

7. Ebrahim Alkazi (1925–2020) was a legendary Indian theatre director and is regarded as the father of contemporary Indian theatre. He studied theatre at Royal Academy of Dramatic Arts (RADA), London, in 1950s and became the founder director of the National School of Drama in New Delhi. He has been conferred with numerous national and international awards and honours including Sangeet Natak Akademi award and Padma Vibhushan by the Government of India.

8. Prasanna (1951–) is a noted Indian theatre director from Karnataka. He is one of the pioneers of modern Kannada theatre. He graduated from the National School of Drama (NSD) in 1976 and founded Samudaya, a theatre group, with an ideology in 1970s where he continued his practices. He is also a social activist who fights for human rights following Gandhian philosophy. He is conferred with Sangeet Natak kademi award and B. V Karanth Samman for his contribution to Indian theatre.

Still from the play *Tughlaq (1982)*. Original Kannada play by: Girish Karnad. Urdu translation: Surekha Sikri and K.K. Nayyar. Design and direction: Prasanna. Presented by: The National School of Drama Repertory Company, New Delhi. Courtesy: National School of Drama, New Delhi and *Ranga Yatra* magazine.

Similarly, the stylised and lyrical text of the classical play *Mrcchkatika* has been explored through a structural design in an obscure space designed by the noted Indian scenographer Robin Das (1998) which extensively differs from that of Habib Tanvir's *Matigadi* (1959), another adaptation of the same play. There are numerous examples of presentations where the design and performance differ extensively from the style of the original play text, yet pulsating with the emotional journey of the characters and interpretation of the author.

Some scenographers even try to adopt different rhythmic compositions, contrasting to the textual rhythm of the play, to develop their space. Yet they maintain the harmony of the productions. Through innovative approaches, they succeed in conveying a different perspective and a new take altogether. While exploring an idea, scenographers quite often evolve their personal style of expressions which get reflected in their creative process time and again. Like a painter, a scenographer also creates a signature, their own style of presentation. However, scenography should not be a literal translation of the text but a representation of the subtext that builds the psychological atmosphere of the play. It is more about the motif and the traces a text leaves behind, hidden.

Parker and Smith argue:

> Scene design, as a visual art, can reinforce and heighten literary and acting styles. Strangely enough, it can on occasion be a contrast to the acting style without breaking the unity of the production. The designer has always felt that stylized scenery does not necessarily call for stylized acting [...] The reverse, however, is not true. If the acting is stylized, the scenery must be, too. The important thing is that the audience will accept any degree of departure from the real in scenery as long as it is consistent and in good taste.[vii]

Since there is no definite method of evolving a style of presentation, the scenographers set their personal approaches while expressing the design ideas. We can however identify some broad outlines to classify a few methods. In a general sense, a design that tries to imitate life and is expressed through its physical embodiment on the stage, is termed as 'representational' design. But the work that does not imitate the outer physical form of life and is explored through the interplay of colours, lines and textures is called 'non-representational' style of design. In this style of presentation, the visual compositions liberate themselves from the framework of the physical reality and breath in the world of abstraction to achieve desired visuals. There is also another approach of expression which involves theatricality and stylisation in its presentation. Termed as 'presentational' style, it is executed through various theatrical means including physical expressions, gestures, theatrical masks or stylised makeup and indicative design, etc.

Representational Style
When life is imitated on stage reflecting the natural behaviour of the people, events and environment, it can be termed as the representational style of presentation. This style tries to create an illusion of reality. According to Moises Kaufman: 'In representational theatre the artists strive to create a visual and performance reality on stage that tricks the audience into accepting the idea that what they are seeing is real, [...] The audience becomes a passive viewer of the experience that is happening to the characters in the drama.'[vii]

For the viewers, representational style of theatre is believed to replicate the real-life events as they are, thus cautiously substituting reality with illusion. Scenographers in a representational style of design need to emphasise upon the physical shape, size, proportion, mass and texture of the visuals in order to create the impression as real. Realism and naturalism are the main sources of creating the representational style of design which are expressed through various methods. To garner more clarity about representing life on stage, we must understand the significant cause that forces the artists to perceive their arts in the framework of realism across history.

Aspects of Realism
'Realism', as a movement, emerged in Europe in response to the thoughts and ideologies of philosophers like Auguste Comte, Charles Darwin and

Karl Marx in the mid-19th century. Auguste Comte (1798–1857), often regarded as the 'father of Sociology', developed a theory called 'Positivism'. Comte's idea of the 'cause-and-effect system' of nature is analysed through observations followed by *The Origin of Species* by Charles Darwin in 1859. These two great ideas in 19th century enthralled the world by spreading logical awareness and reformations of chronological developments of life and the evolution of it. At that point of time, on the other hand, emerged the new political philosophy of Karl Marx that argued against capitalism by favouring equality, and as usually became revolutionary.

These ideologies modified the perception of the world and helped develop modernism in art. This changing perception also gave rise to a new form of expression that got reflected in art, craft and literature of the western world. Realism is a product of this belief, that primarily is based upon the principle of 'objective truth'—a belief that redefines 'truth':

i. Truth resides in the materials that can only be perceived through our five senses.
ii. Truth can be verified through scientific methods.
iii. Human problems are the major crisis of the world and that is the greatest truth of life.

Realism in Theatre
During 1850s, the theatre of the West began expressing realistic ideas in its productions. Though initially it faced criticism, eventually the concept of realism grew into a prominent artistic expression and was accepted widely. In the beginning of the 20th century, almost the entire Western theatre witnessed a change in its language of art through realistic expressions. These art expressions were symbolic and metaphorical in nature with a well-plotted story and the development and journey of the characters. Within the framework of interpretative set design, these expressions follow

Still from the original production of *The Cherry Orchard (1904)*. Direction: Constantin Stanislavsky. Presented by: Moscow Art Theatre (MAT). Courtesy: https://library.calvin.edu/hda/node/2123.

the logic of space and time and became a distinctive art form graduating from the popular practice of naturalism.

During the second half of the 19th century in Europe, most of the playwrights tried to adopt realism in their writings and presentations. Henrik Ibsen's *A Doll's House* (1879), Leo Tolstoy's *Power of Darkness* (1886), Anton Chekhov's *The Seagull* (1896) and *The Cherry Orchard* (1904) and Maxim Gorky's *The Lower Depths* (1902) unleashed a trend of realistic theatre in Europe. The 1879 production of *A Doll's House* at Copenhagen, directed by the noted theatre director Hans Peter Holst, dominantly adopted naturalism as its style of presentation, contrary to the production of *The Seagull*, *The Lower Depths* and *The Cherry Orchard*

Still from the premier show of the play *A Doll's House* (21 December 1879). Written by: Henrik Ibsen. Directed by: Hans Peter Holst. Presented by: Royal Theatre Copenhagen, Denmark. Courtesy: https://library.calvin.edu/hda/node/2123.

directed by Konstantin Stanislavsky for Moscow Art Theatre, which were entirely based on realistic framework. These productions followed the technique of 'method acting' pioneered and propagated by Stanislavsky in the beginning of 20th century. A few selective photographs from the above-mentioned plays are displayed here for reference.

Set design in realistic theatre no longer remained confined to decorations and appreciations, a common practice of the 18th-and 19th-century European theatre. It became a complete integration of the performance with logical derivations. Eventually, realism became the language of the 20th century modern theatre and drew worldwide attention from the elite audience.

Realism can be expressed in many ways and through many means. It can be articulated through photographic realism, where one can experience mirror image of the reality. Or it can also be expressed through symbols and suggestions. Often the scenes can be communicated through outlines and structures. But with all these types of expressions, representational style of design and its presentation follows the rationale of time and space which remains linear throughout.

Non-representational and Abstract Style
Ideas, irrespective of the framework of space and time and not drawn from the experience of physical reality, are often considered as non-representational or non-objective style. When an element, visual or oral, does not pass through our common worldly experiences, it can be termed as non-representational or abstract, for that matter. We generally judge and differentiate any perceived image or sound according to our life's experiences. But there are many images and sounds in nature that do not fall under the interactions and experiences of human realisation. For general understanding, they do not represent the reality but significantly contributes to a larger truth, thus becoming abstract or non-representational to our perception.

When we come across images of non-representational entity, we usually try to locate their representations through our imaginations. But ironically, our imagination also is guided by our physical perceptions and sensibilities. These non-representational art forms take shape in our psyche by challenging our worldly interactions and thus, they seem abstract to us. Since they do not belong to the common human perceptions, they are always open to subjective interpretations.

Abstraction, as a concept, remains from the beginning of the human life. For example, none of us has any physical experiences of ghosts or fairies, gods or demons in real life. But if one is asked to create an image of

Photograph of the painting *Number 1, 1950 (Lavender Mist)*. Medium: Oil, enamel and aluminium on canvas. Dimension: 87 x 118 in. Artist: Jackson Pollock (1912–1956), National Gallery of Art, Washington DC. Courtesy: Author's personal collection.

a demon or fairy those will be conceived according to the collective popular belief and imagination. While for the demon, they may be visualised with some prototypes like large and sharp teeth, long horns and round-bulging eyes in order to express its wilderness, for a fairy, feathers and wings are to be imagined. In this exercise, anyone can compare a demon with a wild beast or a fairy with a flying creature and create an image parallel to the worldly observations. We generally visualise images through our personal experiences of life as lived in different dimensions of space and time, irrespective of reality and abstraction. In such a case, we usually combine multiple experiences derived from different non-linear life sources for constructing an image which we never experience at one point of time.

It is a general notion that an abstract art or design is the child of an artist's active imagination that has no direct connection to the reality. It is partly true since in abstraction, 'reality' is reduced to something fine and minimal only to be expressed through lines, colours and texture. Therefore, it cannot directly be associated with worldly experiences. In abstract art, the basic elements of art and design are usually taken into consideration through the application of minimum lines and colours

Left: *Otobo Mask (1916)*. Material: Wood. Height: 18.5 in. Courtesy: Indiana University Museum, Bloomington; Raymond and Laura Wielgus Collection.
Note: African masks such as this hippopotamus mask (Otobo Mask), etc. had a profound influence on the European painters such to develop the concept and technique of Cubism.

Right: *Ma Jolie* (painting, 1911–12). Artist: Pablo Picasso (1881–1973). Medium: oil on canvas, Dimension: 39.3/8 x 25.3/4 in. Courtesy: Museum of Modern Art (MOMA), New York. (photographed by the author).

that underestimate the superfluous realistic details. One might have interacted with the abstract or non-representational art forms of the rock or cave paintings or in the tribal or folk arts. Alan Pipes argues: 'Abstract art is not new. The earliest cave paintings depicted animals reduced to their basic forms, most likely drawn from memory and often inspired by the shapes in rocks, they were drawn on. The African tribal masks that inspired and excited Picasso and kick-started Cubism seem strange and abstract to Western eyes.'[viii]

For developing visual images for a non-representational style of design, scenographers mainly depend on the dynamism of lines, colours and textures that capture emotions through their movements. A non-representational theatre design can only be understood in a larger context, depending on the actors' interactions with the space and other spatial objects. Abstraction in art or design advocates for a complex human existence searching for a deeper meaning, which can only be experienced through human feelings, often without comprehending the literary meaning of the work. These art forms are the outcome of the socio–political and cultural behaviour of the human community. In the history of art and design, abstract art is manifested through various idealistic styles such as, expressionism, cubism, fauvism, abstract expressionism and postmodernism, etc. These expressions portray human consciousness in different phases of time, influenced by the political philosophy of the world.

Non-representational art and design is neither expressed by a literal translation of the form nor does it adopt the realistic logic of being identifiable by mundane observations through shape, size, proportion and form. The rationale of time and space is also not conventionally followed in this art expression. Often it becomes insignificant to draw literal meaning of the visual images of an abstract design out of common observable phenomenon. The human feelings generated out of the interactions with art become more significant and transform art into a metaphor.

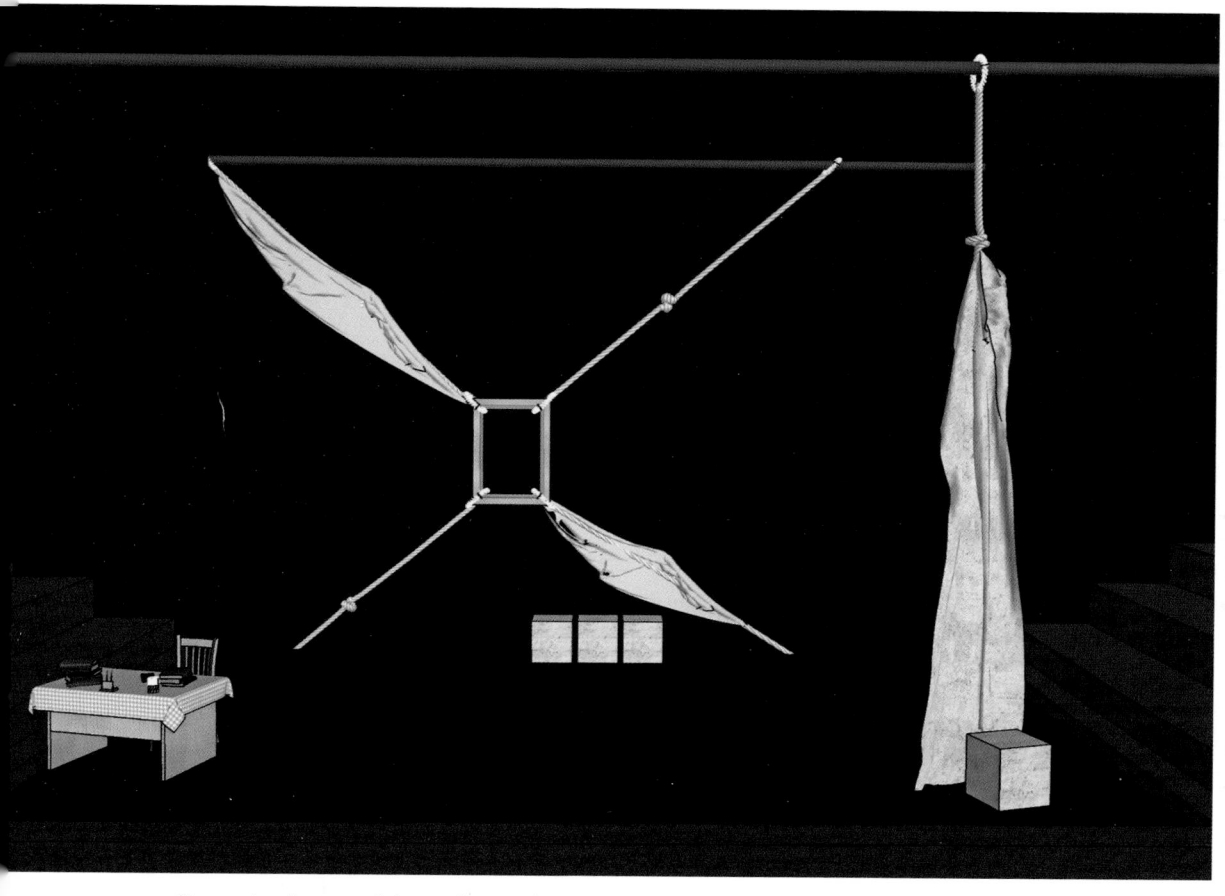

Perspective drawing of the set design of the play *Evam Indrajit*.
(Drawing made by the author)

While directing *Evam Indrajit*[9] for Avartan theatre, Hyderabad, in the year 2010, I tried to assimilate the interpretations and the emotional wavelength of the production through a non-representational design. The design idea was conceived through a juxtaposition of some bold and striking white lines against a black background on the stage space. A bold

---

9   *Evam Indrajit* is the most discussed play written by Badal Sircar in Bengali in the year 1963. It was first presented by Shatabdi, a theatre group established by Badal Sircar himself in Kolkata.

and vertical white stroke on the down-left of the stage was moving upwards against a few diagonal white lines at the up-stage crossing the entire performance space. Both the white striking lines were counterbalancing each other through their arrangements. A rectangular frame was hung at the mid of the rear stage with the help of these diagonal lines, suspended in the mid-air.

It is not essential to adhere to a definite, one-dimensional meaning while working on a non-representational design. The work can define itself by creating its own meaning through interactions with the actors during the performance. The spatial design of *Evam Indrajit* neither conveys any particular meaning nor does it represent any tangible object separately. Its dynamism gets revealed along with the context of the play during the performance and consequently, the visual compositions are interpreted as the action surmounts further. Now, let us delve deep into a few interpretations of the stage (space) craft of *Evam Indrajit* in patches: the vertical line created out of white muslin cloth becomes the symbol of the social conventions that stand as a towering image, which Indrajit wants to break away with. The diagonal line that crosses one end of the stage to the other may symbolise the struggle of the protagonist against the social order. In between these lines, lies the suspended rectangular frame, a gateway to the outer world. The counteraction of two strong and opposite forces (symbolised by the vertical and the diagonal) creates dramatic tension and conflict, which was the demand of the presentation. This non-representational design for the play brings an emotional feeling of human struggle and existence in the midst of various counter forces and indicates for a life that is suspended in the mid-air with uncertainty.

Non-representational art is always open for subjective interpretations. The above analysis of the spatial design of *Evam Indrajit* is my personal viewpoint and the example mentioned here is only to make the reader understand a non-representational scenic idea.

Presentational Style

In the context of performing arts, presentational style of design emphasises on the theatricality of the presentation by making the spectators conscious of their role as the audience in a theatrical performance. This style of art and design is 'non-realistic' by nature and follows the principles of stylisation. The presentation takes help of all possible theatrical devices such as stylised gestures, sound and dialogues, music, rhythm, elaborate and decorative costumes, masks and makeup, painted sceneries, lighting. Unlike a realistic design, the presentational style usually shares a common locale without any formal or specific characteristic of the space, therefore making the design suggestive, symbolic, abstract and flexible enough to be blended into different environments in different scenes. Thus, sometimes, presentational and non-representational arts share a common space. This style gives more emphasis on psychological atmosphere than creating any specific ambience of the performance. In this genre, the actors can perform multiple characters by shifting from one role to another without much external changes. Kaufman adds, 'The audience is challenged to keep up with what is developing on stage as the story is told.'[ix] In this design, the spectators try to create their own understanding by adding to the actions of the scenes from moment to moment, thus participating actively in the production.

We can find a number of illustrations of presentational style through a few performances across the globe. Bertolt Brecht's plays are good examples of the presentational style of performance where the audience is put to the task of investigating the play while watching. To remind the audience of the pseudo-reality of a theatre piece but not real-life event, Brecht used many theatrical devices onto the stage. Exposition of lighting sources to the audience, use of large and stylised masks, performing multiple roles on stage, use of narrative speeches, songs and music in between the dramatic actions and sudden burst of anticlimaxes were being employed into the performance. The concept of 'alienation'[10] is employed into the presentation to refrain the audience from the emotional flow of the story. Brecht's initiation of 'Epic Theatre'[11], with numerous scenes and locales, does not permit any scenographer to adopt realistic means of expression into the presentation, thus assenting upon any kind of formalistic or suggestive design.

In the Indian Classical theatre, 'natyadharmi' style of presentation is considered as presentational style. The abstract hand gestures (hastamudra),

---

10   Alienation Effect: Brecht had adopted a different method with the help of theatrical devices and technical elements in to the productions. This device he called: *A-Effect* or *Alienation effect*. To keep the audience, alienated from the emotional involvement of the play as well as the actors, Brecht adopted music and narration in between the scenes. For that he structured his plays episodically with small scenes and inserted music in between, sung by the same actors who came out of their characters purposefully to involve in singing and narrating. The representation of the character from a third person's point of view alienates the actors from direct involvement and thus, they refrain from identifying themselves with the characters. The application of masks, puppets, projection of multimedia, harsh and bright lights irrespective of the mood of the situation creates ample scope for alienation. Brecht always insisted on antithesis. For Brecht's theatre, one has to go through theatrical contradiction in the play in order to create alienation effect. Situation and action may contradict each other; a tragedy can be portrayed in a humorous manner, a comical situation can also be played in a satirical approach. According to Brecht, it is not necessary to create the music of same mood in a tragic song where the lyrics create the meaning; it can be a contrast to the lyrics and situation also. The same method can also be adapted in scenic visuals, lighting and costume design in a Brecht's play. This contradiction of idea would certainly restrict the viewers to identify themselves with the characters.

11   Epic Theatre: The functional relationship between stage and public, text and performance, producer and actor, remained almost unchanged. Epic theatre takes as its starting point the attempt to introduce fundamental change into these relationships. For its public, the stage is no longer 'the planks which signify the world' (in other words a magic circle), but a convenient public exhibition area. For its stage, the public is no longer a collection of hypnotised text subjects, but an assembly of interested persons whose demands it must satisfy. For its text, the performance is no longer a brilliant interpretation, but a rigorous control. For its performance, the text is no longer a basis of that performance, but a grid on which, in the form of new formulation, the gains of that performance are marked. For its actor, the producer no longer gives him instructions about effects, but these for comment. For its producer, the actor is no longer a mime who must embody a role, but a functionary who has to make an inventory of it'. (Walter, Benjamin. *Understanding Brecht*. London: Verso, 1998.)

Perspective drawing of the set design of the play *Animal Farm* (Drawing made by the author).

rhythmic movement of the body, rendering of text and music, and finally the portrayal of—character (patra) make Indian classical theatre stylised. Portraying the presentational style, classical Indian theatre never imitates 'life' in its rendering, rather depicts it through poetic imageries by engaging all the aforementioned theatrical means. For a Sanskrit drama, an empty performance space fulfils all the necessary requirements of presentation where the audience becomes an integral part of the spatial design (Refer to Chapter 3). Traditional and folk-based performances across the globe also adopt this style of presentation. Noh theatre of Japan, Beijing Opera of China, Indonesia's Ramalila and shadow puppet theatre, Indian folk theatres, Italian Commedia dell'arte, etc. are a few examples of the presentational style of performances practised across the globe.

Two of my productions, *Animal Farm* and *Tumhara Vincent*, demonstrate some examples of presentational style in their performance design. George Orwell's *Animal Farm* was adapted into Hindi and was presented by the students of Sriram Centre for Performing Arts, New Delhi in the year 2005. In the performance design and scenography, we never tried to create a world of fantasy by adopting the common animal gestures and their natural behaviour which could be an easy option for the play, rather we tried to crack the inner conflict and politics in the light of contemporary society using the animals as a metaphor. We used an empty space with minimal stage props leaving a large open space for the actors to perform and interact with the audience. This formalistic spatial design along with the actors' portrayal of different characters through indicative and suggestive gestures prevented the audience from gliding into the real animal world, rather the performance generated irony leading to humour and satire quite often. Throughout the play all the actors were holding two bamboo sticks in order to suggest the forelimbs of animals. These sticks, quite large in numbers, actually formed the major element of scenography through various creative means, adding visual images to the production. Often these were used as weapons to fight among each other, clubbed together to form the outline of farmhouse, entrance gate, barricade, horse stable and numerous images. All these were acquired just by a little permutation and combination of the entire arrangement.

The actors themselves created various rhythmic sounds by hitting those sticks on the stage floor in different ways, helping in creating a particular music, suitable for the play. These visual effects were enhanced by the use of stylised and structural masks, worn by the actors. We never attempted to cover the actors' whole face through realistic animal head masks, rather we incorporated symbolism to designing those masks as well

Still from the play *Animal Farm (2019)*. Adapted from George Orwell's novel in the same name. Hindi adaptation: Satyabrata Rout. Kannada version: C. Basavalingaiah. Presented by: Students of National School of Drama, Bengaluru Centre. Courtesy: The National School of Drama, Bengaluru.

as costumes to portray them as metaphor, linking with the current Indian political scenario. Those structural masks created out of thermocol carving, aluminium wires and canes, were twisted and moulded just to form the outline, thus creating an impression of the animals through which the actors' unmasked faces were clearly visible. The design brought both the actors and the characters together at one time and place, thus breaking away with the fundamental principles of representational style. Quite often in the play the performers narrated the story, unmasked, a style borrowed from Brecht's theatre. The audience witnessed a play equipped with all the theatrical devices with full awareness.

In 2015 I undertook a project that was culminated with the presentation of a play *Tumhara Vincent*. The project strengthened my search for a new kind of theatre expression that confirms the potential of presentational style. This was a devised production based on the path-breaking works of the great master, Vincent Van Gogh. Creating a suitable spatial arrangement and psychological atmosphere that could interact with the spectators parallel to the play was a challenge for me as the scenographer and director of the play. Moreover, the devised text and the process of play making did not create any scope to present the play through any representational means. My fundamental approach was not to recreate the life of Van Gogh on stage, but to portray his agony, pain, humiliations, frustration, weirdness, madness and eccentricities through his works. I was frantically searching for an idiom concurring to the painter's reckless and passionate lifestyle, trying to develop a design that could articulate the flamboyant raw energy and aggression of the painter along with the provision of an interactive space for the performers. For me, designing Van Gogh could be anything but stationary. I was searching for a dynamic design that must narrate his restless journey in various places—London, Amsterdam, Borinage, Brussels, Hague, Neunen, Paris, Arles—till his final journey to Auvers where the painter committed suicide.

In the initial days of the rehearsal, I slipped into pictorial realism by fruitlessly trying to imitate the painter's life and his relationships with others in order to develop a representational style of the performance design. With the help of a group of trained actors, initially I started reconstructing the world of Van Gogh through realism which I borrowed by watching a few movies. However, my approach for the production did

Drawings of the spatial design for the play *Tumhara Vincent (2015)*
Scenography: Satyabrata Rout
Note: These drawings are a few out of many illustrations prepared by the scenographer for various scenes of the play.
Top: Beginning Scene 'Wheatfield and the Crows';
Bottom: Night Café at Hague
Top (facing page): The Landscape at Arles
Bottom (facing page): The Coalmines at Borinage

not work, since this method did not go along with my text, texture of the characters and design, which I realised within a few days of the rehearsal. Every moment, my working method collides in between the actors and characters, text and its delivery, space and action, ideas and execution, etc. which was frustrating for a scenographer and director. Finally, this approach of presentation was discarded and withdrawn through a mutual understanding with the actors and my technical team. The multiple sets, duplicate flex paintings, realistic approach for characterisations and all fabricated wooden platforms, doors, windows, which we have already made for the sets, were withdrawn by creating space for simple structural design that led towards a presentational style. Finally in the performance, scenography helped elevate the production through a unique visual appeal and added another feather to the development of visual theatre in India.

We tried to create an appropriate atmosphere suitable for the performance in the play. A structural and theatrical design took shape out of mundane objects through multiple improvisations. A bunch of plastic conduit pipes, paper-made larger-than-life sunflowers, a few structural frames, etc. were taken into use to create our structural and indicative design. To create an impression of coal *terril* (slag heap) in a scene located at Borinage coalmine in the play, we hung a large black drapery from the grid, hooked with threads at different heights, spreading over the entire stage floor. This created a vague impression of the *terril* and the coal mines. Our purpose was not to establish a representation of coal mines but to portray the gloomy and dark atmosphere and the miserable life of the miners with bold and striking blackness. His dark, striking and bold lines are continuously reflected in almost all the works of Van Gogh throughout his life. The flexibility of the black drapery from the ceiling occasionally tried to break the illusion of the coal heaps because of the flexibility of the cloth. This ambiguity, supported by imaginative and abstract stage props, developed multiple imaginary visuals in the audience psyche in different situations of the play. Many indicative and suggestive visual images were created through improvisations with the props. Out of many imageries, waving a few black and white cloths to create thick black smoke, oozing out from the mines, water flooding out inside the caves and using plastic conduit pipes to create the impression

Stills from the play *Tumhara Vincent* (2015). Courtesy: Author's personal Collection.

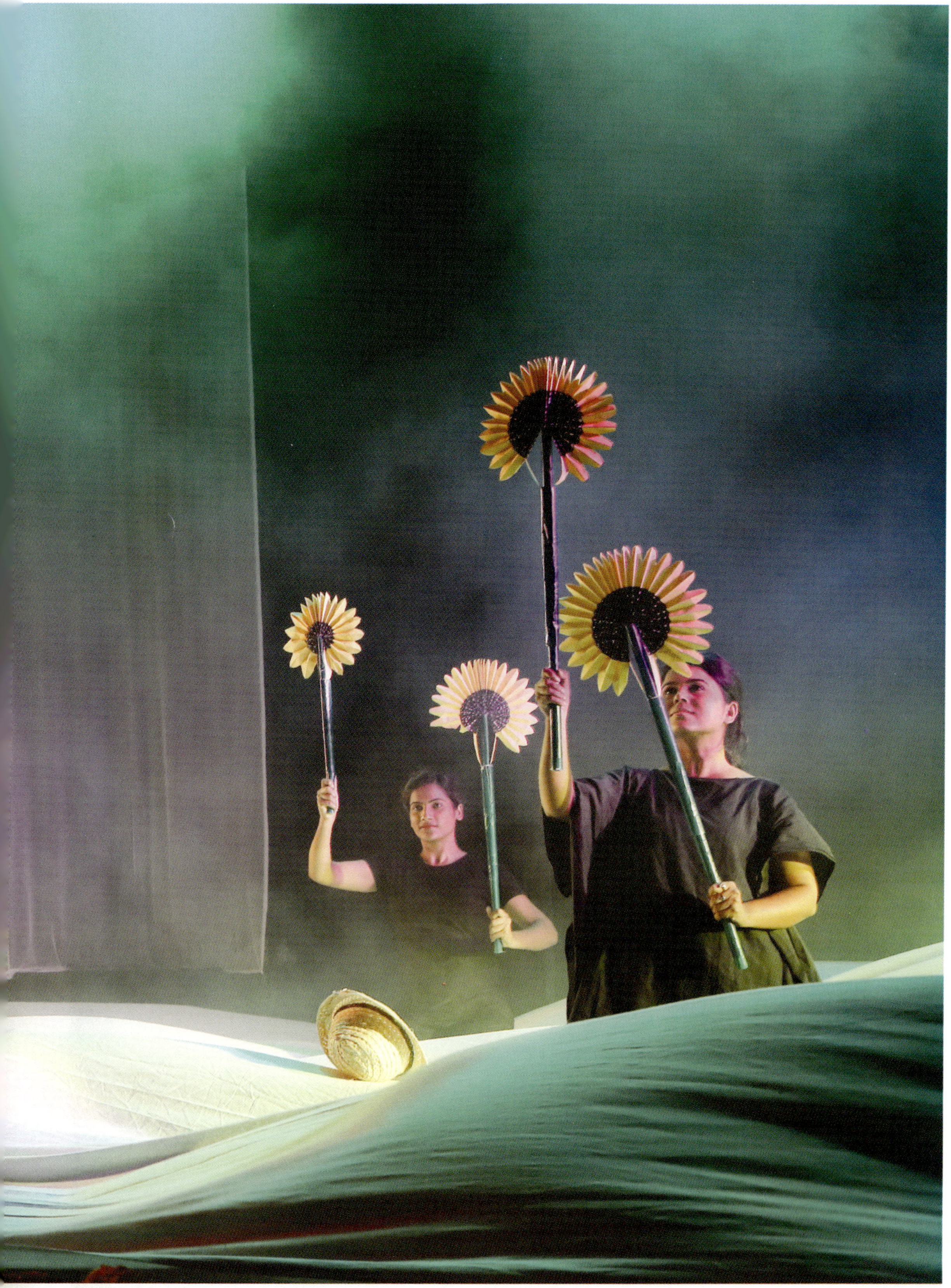

of windows, doors, painting frames and canvases were a few out of numerous images that added to the innovations. Also, many abstract visuals were created to express the internal feelings and motifs of the characters. Using the actors themselves as the subject of the paintings, fixed inside those frames and to make them live by coming out of the frames, only to go back again to their previous positions to become a still image was accepted by the spectators with much appreciations. The visuals of endless sunflower field, meadows and landscape, streams, the starry night, the sketch of the *Sorrow* and many great works of Van Gogh formed the most dynamic factors of the design developed structurally out of improvisations. They all combined together to bringing out inexplicable atmosphere to the production that no representational style could have offered. Simultaneously, they also provided an experience of watching a 'theatrical performance' as a major component of presentational style.

The possibilities of new experimentation in the presentational style of design are immense, but those explorations depend on the scenographer's imagination. In a country like India, where there is always scarcity of finance, presentational style can serve as a powerful and economical tool of creation. A creative design with the help of few stage and hand props, masks and costumes can also add dynamism to the performance which may not be possible in any other style of presentations.

Theatre is a make-believe medium. Anything presented truthfully with conviction is respectably accepted by the audience. Quite often the viewers try to connect the missing links of the design in their psyche to complete the visuals that are left deliberately by the scenographers to keep the spectators actively engaged in the production. Through this approach we can involve the audience energy to the performance. The visuals that are perceived in the psyche of the viewers are always open to subjective interpretations. In this way, scenographers widen the window for mutual dialogues between the performance and the spectators.

Scenographers can also set their own rules and lead the audience in getting the pulse of the performance through various theatrical means. The viewers may not connect themselves with the dramatic space and actions in the beginning but repeated interactions with the actors, space and design would train the viewers' eyes to connect with the performance.

SECTION- IV

TYPES OF DESIGN

There are various means and methods to express design ideas and visual images. They can be pictorial or realistic, symbolic or suggestive, fragmental, structural or skeletal, surrealistic or abstract. It is observed that stylised design does not necessarily implement stylised acting; the reverse however, is not true. It means, stylisation in design is a common approach adopted by the scenographers around the world.

Now, let us understand various types of stage design and their functions.

Pictorial or Realistic Design

Realism is a 19th-century phenomenon in the world of art in the West. And design of this kind is just an extension of that on stage. In this style, art is expressed as a mirror image of life. Since this kind of design tries to portray the real-life events or elements on the stage without any modification, it is identified as 'pictorial' or 'objective' realism. In this approach, the truth is constructed in such a manner that it offers the viewers a sense of credibility. For example, if the scene of a play is set in a drawing room, the common usable objects such as, sofa, table, chair, television, walls, doors, windows, etc. become the integral part of the spatial design which makes the locale identifiable and therefore seems real for the audience. Quite often, realistic design is articulated through various symbols and suggestions assimilated through daily objects with an artistic approach. In these circumstances, the design no longer follows the principles of pictorial realism, though remains in the perimeter of representational style.

Pam Morris provides a clear understanding of imitation and representation:

> Closely associated with this meaning are the two terms 'mimesis' and 'verisimilitude' that often crop up in discussions of realism as an art form. Mimesis is a term that derives from classical Greek drama where it referred to the actors' direct imitation of words and actions. This is perhaps the most exact form of correspondence or fidelity between representation and actuality. As it developed as a critical term, the meaning of mimesis has gradually widened to encompass the general idea of close artistic imitation of social reality, […] 'Verisimilitude' is defined as 'the appearance of being true or real; likeness or resemblance to truth, reality or fact'.[x]

The above statement strengthens the fact that realism is mainly based on imitation and always corresponds with the 'real'. So, a realistic design must resemble the space and time of the actual event, represented through the designer's artistic skill and imaginative power.

Modern Indian theatre has also encountered realism in its style of presentation. It emerged as a challenge to the spectacular melodramatic presentations of the 19th-century Parsi theatres, folkloric theatres and company theatres. It was incorporated as a major mode of expression in the post-Independence Indian theatre and was highly appreciated by the elite Indians of 1950s and 60s. Modern Indian playwrights adopted realism in their writings. Some of the significant realistic plays written at the dawn of Independence such as Girish Karnad's *Tughlaq*, Mohan Rakesh's *Aadhe Adhure* and *Ashad ka Ek Din*, Vijay Tendulkar's *Khamosh Adalat Jari hai*, Jaywant Dalvi's *Sandhya Chhaya*, Manu Bhandari's *Mahabhoj*, Mahesh Elkunchwar's *Virasat*, etc. used to receive immense appreciations by the audience.

During the period of pictorial realism in theatre in the 1950s, a few integral parts of the props of Parsi theatre like painted sceneries, cut scenes, etc. were replaced by box sets and three-dimensional stage props in the proscenium theatre. Drawing room sets adorn with sofa, bed, balcony, walls, doors, windows and a moon on the cyclorama were common stage decors of the theatre of the time. The Indian designers in the mid-20th century left no stone unturned to bring the reality of life and nature into the stage space in order to show a mirror image of life. This illusion of reality was borrowed from Western theatre as a spectacle in the Indian theatre practices. However, realism in theatre did not survive for a longer period in India, though its presence is still felt in many theatre performances across the country.

Symbolic or Suggestive Design
This approach for the design emphasises more on the symbolic representations of the objects through indicative and suggestive means, contrary to the detailed realistic design work as we have discussed above. We have also argued about the 'selectivity in art' in the previous chapter. Careful selection of minimum necessary design elements and their meaningful spatial arrangements would enhance the artistic exuberance of a design. For example, to create a scene of a railway station on stage, one has to recall the objects immediately related to the station and its activities such as people, stalls, ticket counters, announcement boards, benches, dustbins, vendors, architectural design of the railway station, trains and a lot more. Out of all these, only a few are enough to suffice the idea of a railway station in the audience's mind. The ambience of a railway station can be well established with bare minimum elements, supported by sound effects of the station; railway lines, trains, platforms and any other larger objects are often unnecessary to build an atmosphere. Therefore, suggestive design depends upon a few essential stage elements that can resonate the space and action, by avoiding the details.

Still from the play *The Lower Depths (2015)*. Playwright: Maxim Gorky (1968–1936). Lighting design: Souti Chakraborty. Costume: Tanmay Gupta. Design and direction: Aniruddha Khutwad; photography: S. Thyagrajan. Presented by: the students of NSD. Courtesy: National School of Drama, Delhi.

Sometimes in a suggestive design, the scenographer develops only a portion of the set unit, therefore constructing only a pseudo-reality of the atmosphere leaving the rest of the space obscure. The cohesion of the filled-up and the vacant space becomes decipherable only during the performance through the interaction of actors with the space. Often in a suggestive design, the participation of the audience becomes pivotal in digging out the meaning of the play. In this context, a major portion of the design becomes clear to the viewers through their constant interaction

Perspective drawing of the play *Mrigtrishna*. (Drawing made by the author).

with the dramatic actions. In a suggestive design, the desired truth can be achieved with selective application of the props and sets. The design does not necessarily follow the rigidity of realism by creating a mirror image of dramatic happenings but it must indicate the situation through the interaction of the actors. For example, to create a drawing room scene, it is not essential to drag all the usable and unusable elements of our mundane life onto the stage space. It is even not at all essential to create a complete picture of a natural environment with the help of levels, walls, doors, windows and many such things. These clusters would only occupy our creative space and block our imagination significantly. Instead, we can establish a drawing room with the help of a few essential objects, depending on the demand of the scene. Rest of the things can be imagined by the viewers through the actors' performance ability.

The actors for a suggestive design usually follow the principles of realism. Often the actors mime a few objects and props without their presence. These indicative actions may not be accepted in pictorial realistic format.

Unlike pictorial design, suggestive spatial arrangements never dominate the performance space and the dramatic actions; rather this design projects the actors by pushing itself into background, thus reinforcing the acting.

Still from the play *Mrigtrishna (2011)*. Playwright: Anupam Kumar. Scenography and direction: Satyabrata Rout. Presented by: Students of Bharatendu Natya Academy, Lucknow. Courtesy: BNA, Lucknow.

Scenographers can also juxtapose two-dimensional painted sceneries and wash colour techniques etc. along with the three-dimensional set elements to establish a suggestion of the dramatic locales. For example, to establish the magnificence of a palace, the scenographer can create a few three-dimensional realistic arches and pillars to provide a realistic feel, while the rest of the details can be visualised through painted sceneries as an extension of the palace. Plays with multiple locales can easily be presented through suggestive design.

Let's argue upon a suggestive design, developed for the play *Mrigtrishna*. This periodical play was written by Anupam Kumar[12], which was designed and directed by me for Bharatendu Natya Academy, Lucknow, in the year 2010. With references from ancient India, this play was written within a realistic framework with multiple scenes and various locales. But we took the liberty to present the play following the principles of suggestive realism in design as well as in actions and characterisations. We created our space with the help of few set units such as a palace gate, few risers and steps, a half pillar and a suggestive wall with periodical motifs. Most of the acting area was intentionally kept empty for the actors. The arch, the pillars and the wall were created with realistic details whereas rest of the units, roads, marketplace, the interior of the palace, the cosmetic chamber of the court lady, etc. were suggested. Attempts were made to create an ambience of ancient India adopting Buddhist arts and architecture into the design, sets, costumes, props, jewelleries, hairstyle, etc. thus creating a replica of the contemporary reality.

---

12 Anupam Kumar is a contemporary Indian playwright, who writes in Hindi language. He has written a number of plays such as *Mrigtrishna, Brihannala, Charvaka, etc.* Most of his plays have been directed by Professor Ram Gopal Bajaj for the National School of Drama, New Delhi.

Fragmental set design of the play *Einstein: The Story Till 1905*. Text, design and direction: Prof. Mohan Maharshi. Presented by: NSD Repertory, New Delhi. Courtesy: Dr Anjala Maharishi and NSD.

Fragmental Design

With a little difference from the suggestive design, this kind of work deals with the essential elements of a set and other visuals. This design is presented through pieces of visual units by breaking a pictorial design; thus it is termed as 'fragmental'. The scenographers, while creating a fragmental design, delete a major segment of the visuals such a way that it brings a sense of aesthetics to the work through their artistic exuberance. The set units have to be arranged on the stage floor synchronising with the space and the actors. Much like suggestive design, this kind of work leaves scope for the audience to imagine many unseen visuals, thus helping the viewers for active participation. This fragmental set design was made for the play *Einstein: The Story Till 1905*, written, designed and directed by Professor

Structural design of the play *Adding Machine*. (Drawing made by the author).

Mohan Maharishi for the National School of Drama Repertory Company in the year 1994. Professor Maharishi, who was also the scenographer of this play, tried to create an ambience by employing few fragments of the flats with doors and windows along with chairs and stools. To interpret the design in the context of Einstein, a few geometrical shapes were employed into the design such as semi-circular wall, cylindrical pillar, circular moon, rectangular flats with doors and window frames, etc.

Structural or Skeletal Design
In a few circumstances, structural or skeletal design is adopted into scenography by using the outline structures of the design elements. This reduces the volume and mass of the set units. Structural or skeletal design widens the possibilities of presenting a play in diverse performance

Still from the play *Adding Machine* (2018). Design and direction: Satyabrata Rout. Courtesy: BNA, Lucknow.

spaces like arena, thrust and traverse with minimum alterations. In this kind of design, the geometrical arrangement of lines, curves and angles becomes more important, thus demanding thorough control over the visual sensibility. A little displacement of the geometrical order breaks the spatial balance and disturbs the viewers psychologically. Since this kind of design is structural in nature, the audience can watch the play from all possible sides without any physical hindrance. But there is a chance of over-exposition of the visuals in this skeletal design also. Quite often the application of lines and colours diverts the attention of the viewers due to their over-expositions. The scenographers, in this situation, try to maintain the visual aesthetics by carefully manipulating and managing the lines and colours of the design elements.

Surrealistic Design

Surrealism is a particular condition or state where an idea or a thought process, blended with a certain element of fantasy, hits deep in the collective 'subconscious' of mankind. In a way surrealism certainly has surpassed the realism and rest in a state beyond our conscious physical perception. Initially it began as an artistic and literary movement in Europe after the First World War in the early 1920s. The movement was primarily dedicated to express the dreams. A juxtaposition of reality and dream, this art liberates from the conscious control of human logic by expressing itself in the world of fantasy and is reflected in our subconscious. Apart from its application in fine arts and literature, it has also been extensively explored in the area of various designs, architectures and performing arts.

In a surrealistic design, the artists allow formulation of ideas by digging into their unconscious mind to find inspirations for creativity to express those psychoanalytical ideas of the unconscious desire, which even they are not completely aware of. In this genre, the personal viewpoint of an artist is liberally applied to bring out an alien philosophy of life to the creative work. Andre Breton, who is regarded as the initiator of this movement, defines surrealism in his *Surrealist Manifestos* as a 'pure state of mind that allows someone to express thoughts freely without the encumbrance of rational thoughts and societal rules'.[11]

We all must have strange interactions with surrealism in our regular life. While looking into the cloudy sky we might have visualised strange images taking shape and melting again into the moving clouds. These images that resemble various shapes and forms, are the physical manifestations of something beyond our conscious mind. Similarly, a weathered lonely tree in a full moon night may resemble a ghost or some weird figure through the power of our imaginations that sprouts in our subconscious. Dreams are the finest examples of surrealism, where time and space juxtaposed in various layers, disconnected. The effect of surrealism can be achieved in stage design through multi-layered dream-like imageries that project the inner mind. Scenographers can bring surreal effects into their designs through the use of unusual stage elements and properties, strange colour schemes, weird masks and makeup, and hazy lighting effects. The curious interplay of lines, colours and shapes in the design can effectively produce surrealistic effect on stage.

Though the concept of surrealism in art was developed in the West, a few Indian playwrights, directors and scenographers have effectively adapted this style into their works. Playwrights such as Girish Karnad, Chandrasekhar Kambar, Badal Sircar and a few more have tried to weave elements of surrealism into their writings. In the plays such as Karnad's *Hayavadana* and *Nagamandala*, Kambar's *Aks Tamasha*, Sircar's *Pagla Ghoda*, one can trace the elements of surrealism that forms the core of the writings, thus allowing the scenographers and directors to manifest these plays accordingly.

In this circumstance, we can cite one of Ratan Thiyam's productions where surrealism forms the central nerve of the performance design. Being one of the pioneers of 'visual theatre' in India, Thiyam structured the Manipuri version of Ibsen's *When We Dead Awaken* (2009) through surrealistic imageries. To intertwin surrealism in the design, Thiyam depended heavily on the works of Salvador Dali. 'Time' being a major element of design in this play, the director–scenographer Thiyam explored the multifarious potential of Dali's famous painting *The Persistence of Memory* (1931) in a three-dimensional performance space through which he tried to project the human memories that melt continuously in the annals of time, a major interpretation of the play. There were quite a few surrealistic images interweaved into the scenography of this play. A floating boat in a lotus lake with flying fish and underwater birds, dancing statues, moving puppet girls, grotesque animal masks, larger-than-life-sized gramophone and many such dreamy images were imagined and manifested,

Persistence of Memory (1931). Medium: Oil on Canvas. Dimension: 9.5 x 13 in. Museum of Modern Art, NY. Courtesy: Wikimedia Commons.

Still from the play *When We Dead Awaken* (2008).
Design and direction: Ratan Thiyam
Courtesy: Chorus Repertory, Imphal.

representing the subconscious mind of the characters in the play.

Let's discuss another play *August Ka Khwab*[13], a 2017 National School of Drama production, designed and directed by me. This Hindi adaptation of August Strindberg's *A Dream Play* (1901) creates ample scope for a scenographer to imagine beyond the sphere of realism that targets at a much complicated subconscious mind, hidden underneath in the labyrinth of human brain in dream-like situations. This idea instigated me to create a world of surrealistic visuals to portray the harsh reality of life which was also moulded into the play and characterisations.

August ka Khwab poses an interesting philosophy on human existence in this earthly world and

---

13 *August ka Khwab* is an Indian adaptation of Swedish playwright August Strindberg's *A Dream Play*. This expressionistic play was restructured in Hindi by Kuldeep Kunal. It was designed and directed by Professor Satyabrata Rout for the National School of Drama. Surrealism forms the foundation of the performance design of this play. This production adds another feather to the concept of 'visual theatre' after the pioneering presentation of *Tumhara Vincent* (2015).

Still from the play *When We Dead Awaken (2008)*. Courtesy: Chorus Repertory, Imphal.

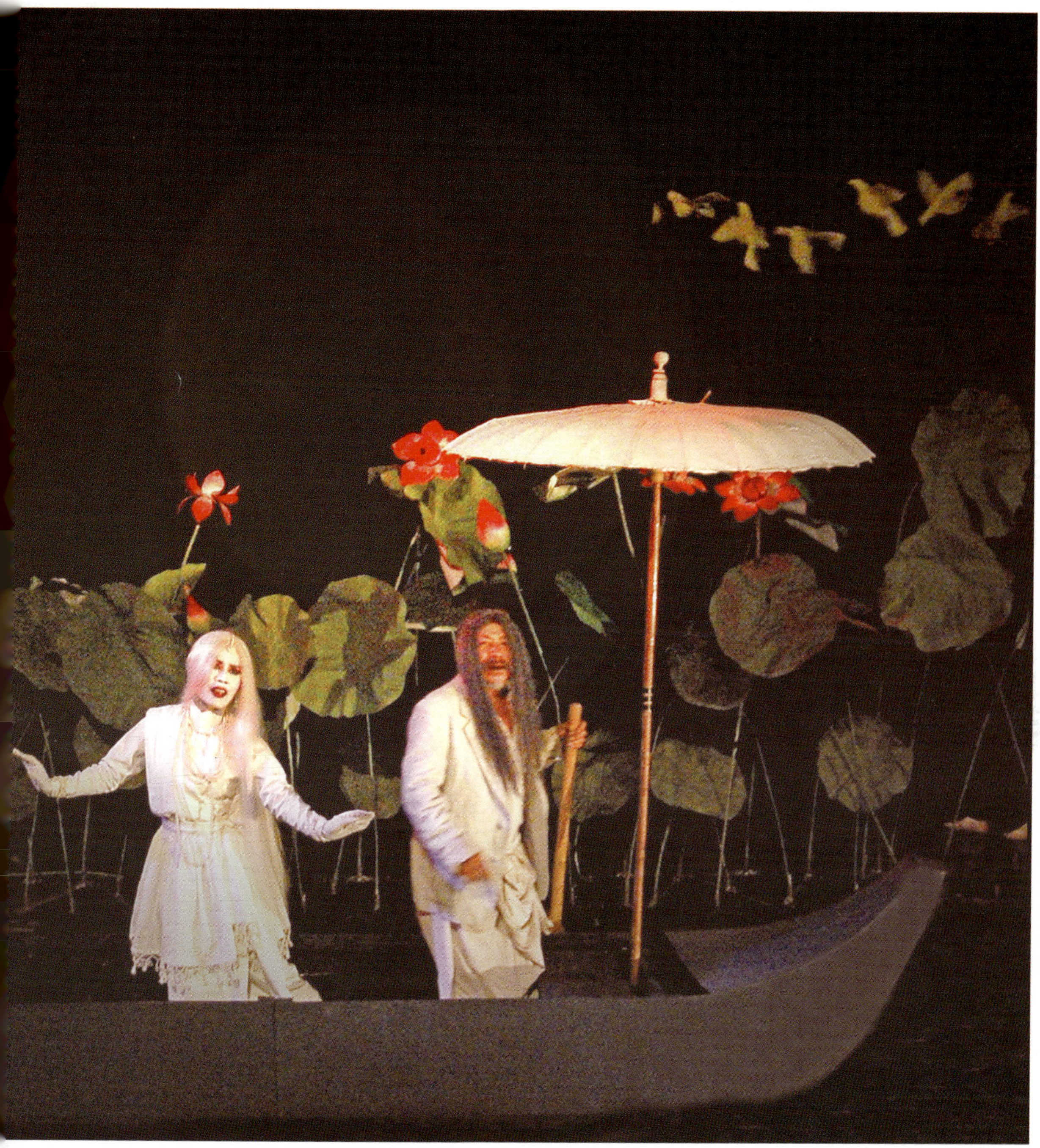

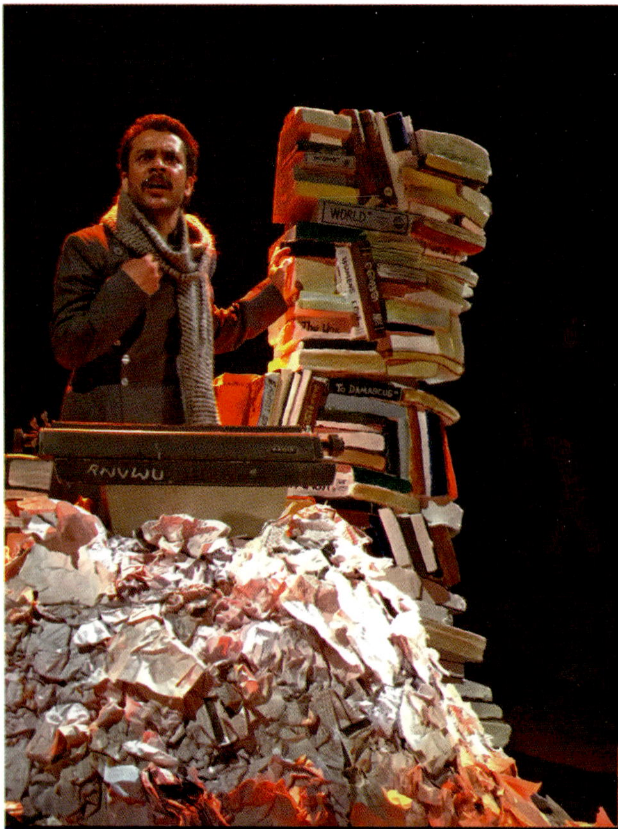
WORLD
TO DAMASCUS

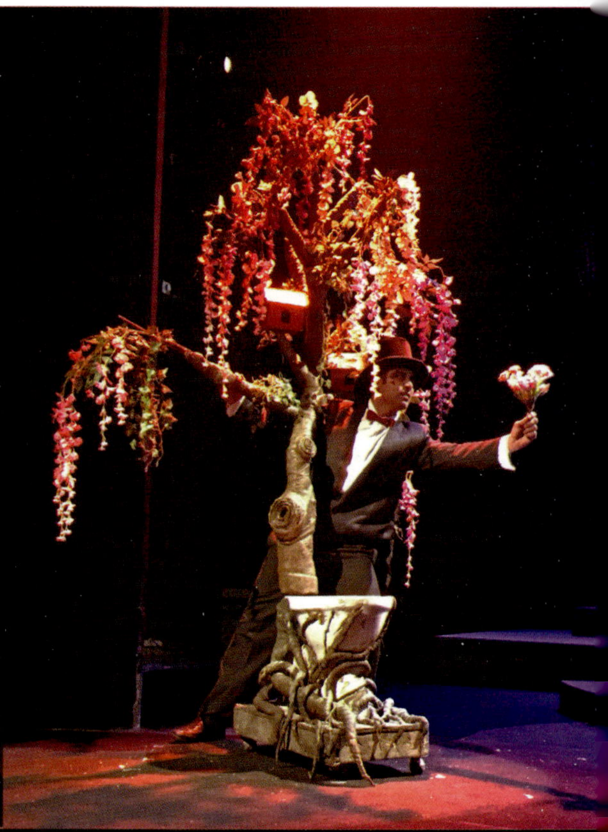

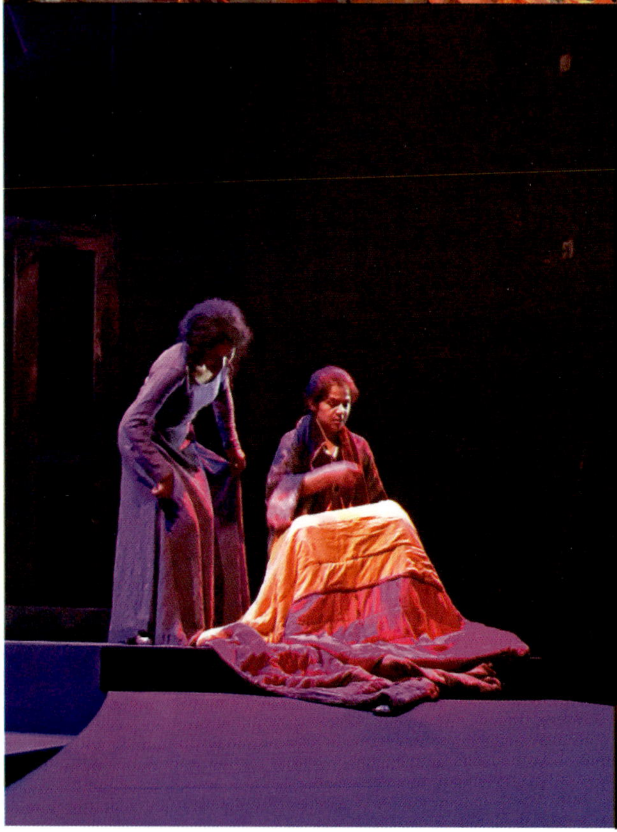

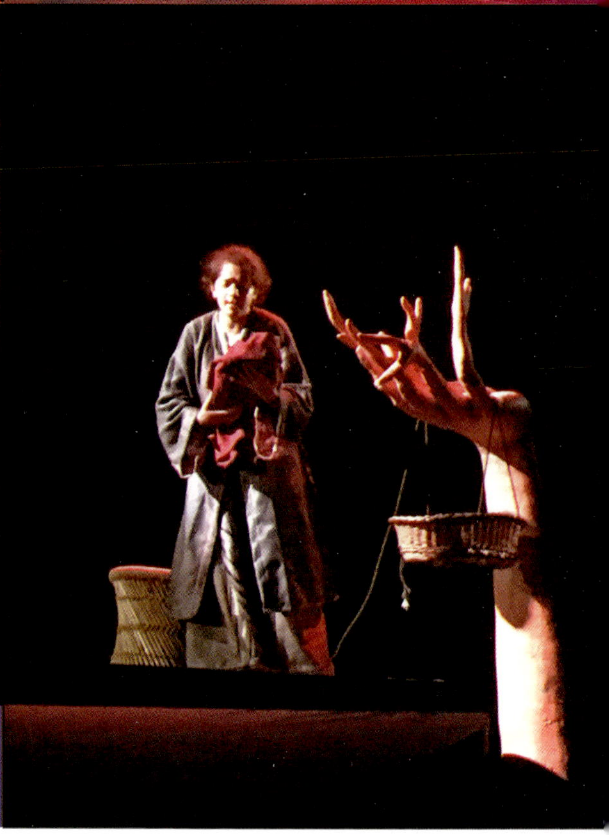

tries to blend the worldly affairs with the divine forces. This alchemic phenomenon, a perfect metaphor and symbol of human life, is intricately weaved into the production design. This makes the scenography of this play an assemblage of collected dreams that forms a journey from 'unconscious' to 'super-conscious' through many layers of subconsciousness. The play oscillates in between illusion and reality, conscious and subconscious, life and death, focusing on various dream images through an entirely surrealistic and expressionistic approach. Scenography of this play explores many images borrowed from paintings, sculptures and other visual arrays. Norwegian painter Edvard Munch's famous painting *The Scream* (1893) was vaguely painted on the wall and the door of the sets, while in the design of the props, masks, costumes and other visuals, influence of surrealistic painters such as Dali and Max Ernst were felt.

Let us have a brief look at the characteristic features of a surrealistic design:

i. Dream-like atmosphere
ii. Transparent and hazy design
iii. Irrational and non-linear behaviour of time, space and action
iv. Bewildering movement of lines, textures and forms
v. Application of strange colour schemes
vi. Para-psychological atmosphere of space and design with similar behaviours of the characters

Facing page: Still from the play *August ka Khwab* (2017). Scenography and direction: Satyabrata Rout. Presented by: National School of Drama, New Delhi. Courtesy: Author's personal collection.

SECTION-V

SELECTION OF SPACE

Scenographers, through their sense of design, create visuals apt for the play that generate mood and environment of the production. After thorough reading of the text and several meetings with the director and other crew members, the scenographers put their ideas on papers in the form of sketches, drawings and models. They work out various functionalities of the design—scene changes, entry-exit of the characters, distribution of the space—for creating different locales. These arrangements help develop coherent relationships between the set units and the actors and create a unique harmonious bond through the actors' interactions with the space and design objects. After working on these technicalities, the scenographers roughly finalise a working design for the play, which would undergo alterations or modifications during the rehearsal process. But the most important factor is the selection of a performance space where the final execution of the design would take place. The scenographers start searching the space much before the finalisation of the design idea. A space can be anywhere—conventional or unconventional. It can be a newly discovered space or something more intimate as a drawing room, a classroom or a community centre. But irrespective of the space, they are subject to further improvisation according to the demand of the script.

We have already discussed about the potential of the different performance spaces in the previous chapters. The space is to be identified much before the performance and even before the rehearsal starts, so that the scenographers can develop their design accordingly for the rehearsals. If possible and affordable, the scenographers prefer to work in the original space from the day one of the practice, since the space often inspires to develop their design. It must be kept in mind that a design developed for a particular kind of space may not be effectively executed in another kind of space. For example, a proscenium design may not go along with an arena stage, an open-air design may not be suitable for a thrust space; they need modifications as every space is different with different demands. The scenographers usually adopt the possibilities and the potential of the particular space, into their design in order to integrate its architectural and environmental characteristics into the performance design. Like every space has its own character, every play has its own specific demand of the space. It has been observed that, a well-designed production sometimes loses intensity and focus due to poor selection of the space.

A play with lesser number of actors with a more compact design prepared for intimate theatre usually loses its power of communication in a larger performance space and vice versa. As a general rule, while solo performances need intimate space for presentation, plays with multiple locales and characters need larger space for the obvious reasons.

Another important concern for the scenographers is the backstage and the wing space area where the actors keep themselves ready for immediate entry and exit. I have seen many good plays suffer due to lack of wing spaces in the theatre. The momentum and dynamics that an actor carries forth onto the stage from its immediate backstage is not possible in a clogged wing space, thus affecting the intensity of the performance. The layout plans of the theatre help understand the dimension of acting area, backstage, wing space, light and sound facilities, audience arrangements, entry and exit doors, etc. With a suitable selection of space, the scenographers start working from the beginning of the process. From day one of the rehearsal they contribute with innovative ideas, add, modify and alter the design and finally achieve the desired scenographic experience through the coherence of the space and actors. Through this method, an interactive performance is charged with the mutual energy of the space, actors and audience during the show.

Exploring the Design

Scenographers often exercise their emotional, rational and aesthetic senses to create balanced compositions in the space. For that they cash upon their academic and practice-based knowledge to manifest an environment that can be realised through dramatic actions. While executing the design idea on the stage space, scenographers focus on some essential factors of design.

i. The design must bring out the performers and the dramatic content into focus, irrespective of its style and form.
ii. A few specific areas in the space are created to develop an interest and emotional understanding for the performers. This is to share their personal emotions and intimacy with that space.
iii. The design must help create balance between the space and the dramatic actions, and provoke the spectators to connect with the events of the play.

But irrespective of many brilliant ideas, scenographers must keep in mind that actors are the prime components of a presentation. Scenography is to enhance the level of the performances. It ought to throb with the pulsation of the play by creating suitable ambience.

Often, a wonderful design spoils the show by diverting all the attentions of the audience towards it. This happens due to over-domination of colours, lines, textures and forms in the design. Even an effective spatial design can unreasonably draw attentions of the audience, if it is not properly reciprocated by the actors. For a successful performance, a harmonious and balanced space is essential that must stay tuned with the performers. To achieve a regulated and actor-friendly design, scenographers distribute the stage space and arrange the design units in order to reinforce the performers and the dramatic actions of the play.

Distribution of the Stage Space

The most vital component of design is the distribution of space in order to decide the flow of the dramatic action. While allocating the space into various locales, the scenographers technically create the layout of different visual units. Meaningful placement of these visual units in the space helps bring the dramatic actions into focus and highlights the contents and the characters. The visual compositions created out of the placement of these set units need to be reciprocated each other through proper balance to convey the director's interpretations. A well-composed space always contributes to the success of the production. Now let's note the spatial compositions of the play *Ashad ka Ek Din* as an example of the above arguments.

Ashad ka Ek Din is regarded as the first modern Indian play in the postcolonial time. The play is set in a small thatched house in a mountainous village where people live in utter poverty but peacefully. As the story moves, the peaceful atmosphere of the rural vicinity turns tense and the situation worsens with each passing day. Though it is a three-act play spread in the time span of more than ten years, the playwright, Mohan Rakesh has synchronised the entire text in a single locale in one set condition.

The major visual-units of the play as depicted by the playwright are—

i. Kitchen
ii. Veranda with a door to enter the room.
iii. A small window through which lightning flashes occasionally.
iv. An entrance.
v. A weathered tree.

Among the stage properties are some earthen pitchers, household goods, palm leaf manuscripts, a charpai (cot), old mats and cushions, etc.

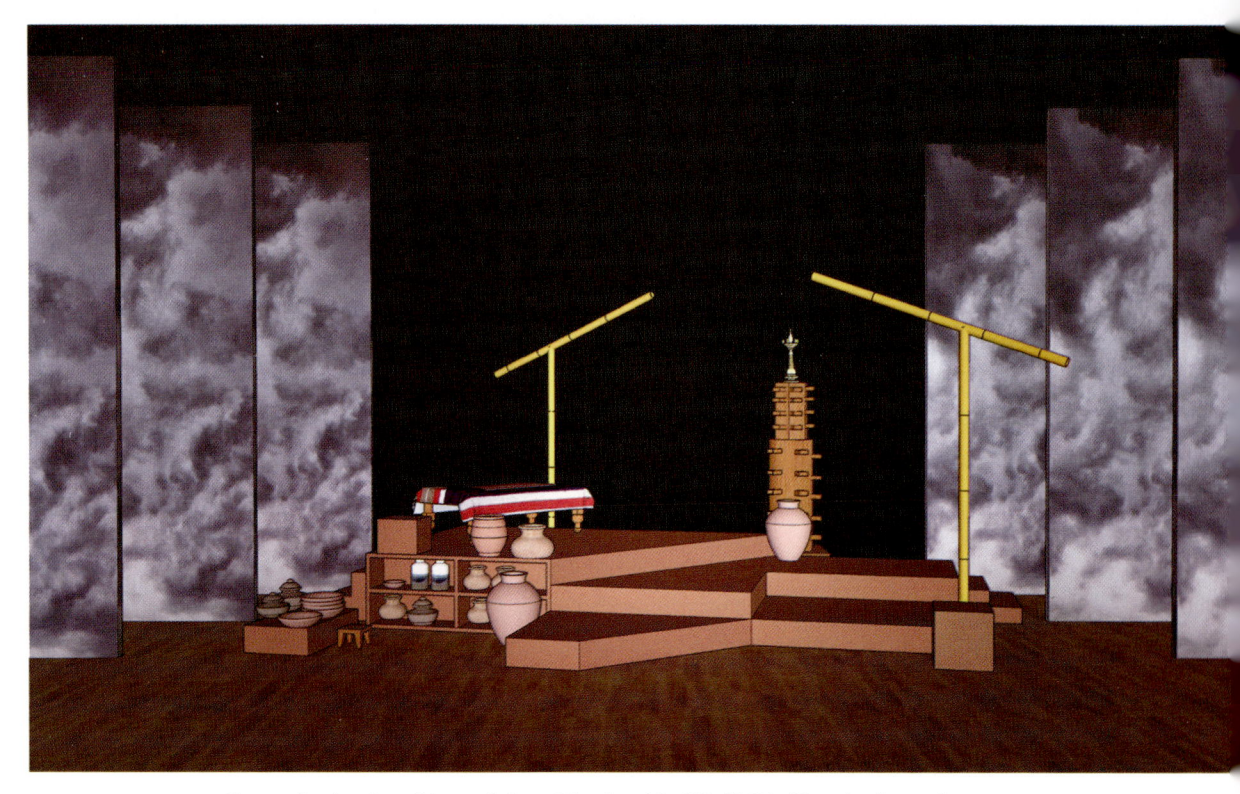

Perspective drawing of the set design of the play *Ashad Ka Ek Din*. Note the diagonal arrangement of the set units.

While designing this play, the scenographer should incorporate all these units to create a harmonious interaction with the actors. Though the play is written by following the principles of pictorial realism, it is the scenographer, who can take the artistic freedom to explore several ideas of design that can range from pictorial, suggestive to structural and fragmental within the framework of the text. In one of the productions of *Ashad Ka Ek Din*, the scenographer-director Bapi Bose explored possibilities in the spatial design by creating a structural framework in the stage space in which the horizontal and diagonal lines of the design that includes the platforms, staircases and the vertical bamboo pillars, create the dramatic tension through their interplay in the design. Bose designed and directed this play for the Circle Theatre Company, Delhi, in 2016.

The analysis of the text revels the conflict of the play in three distinctive layers. The major conflict is created out of the inter-personal relationships of the characters. It can be recognised through the dramatic actions and amidst the incidents of the play. The conflict between time and desire remains the major psychological conflict of this play. And then there is, on another plane, 'the conflict between the self and the dramatic situations', which the scenographers must showcase by creating a few 'area of interest'[14] in the design where the actors can confront themselves in isolations, for example near and underneath the vertical bamboo structure in the set design at stage left.

From the Memory Lane: An Experience of Finding a Space
In the year 1982, Ranjit Kapoor was invited to direct a play with us when I was in second year at the National School of Drama (NSD). He had a planned to do Irvin Shaw's anti-war play *Bury the Dead* (1936) with us. The director initially intended to present the play in a proscenium theatre. We were excited to work with a creative director like Ranjit Kapoor, who had already enthralled the Delhi audience with his NSD diploma production of *Woyzeck*[15] in 1976. But somehow, we were not thrilled with his plan to do this play in a proscenium theatre. We wanted to explore new forms which would challenge the ongoing conventional theatre practices and to enrich our personal experience as student. Then Professor Robin Das stepped into the scenario. He was deputed by the School authority to guide us in design on our request. By that time, Robin had proved himself as an avant-garde theatre practitioner in Delhi. As an intellectual he was searching for new and innovative concepts in his practices. He agreed to our demand for experimenting on new design, rejecting the conventions of proscenium. Under his guidance and without the knowledge of our director,

---

14 Detailed description of Area of interest is given in chapter 10.

15 *Woyzeck* was written by the German playwright, Georg Buchner in 1836, but could not be completed till his death in 1837. The play was finished posthumously by a few authors and was published in 1876.

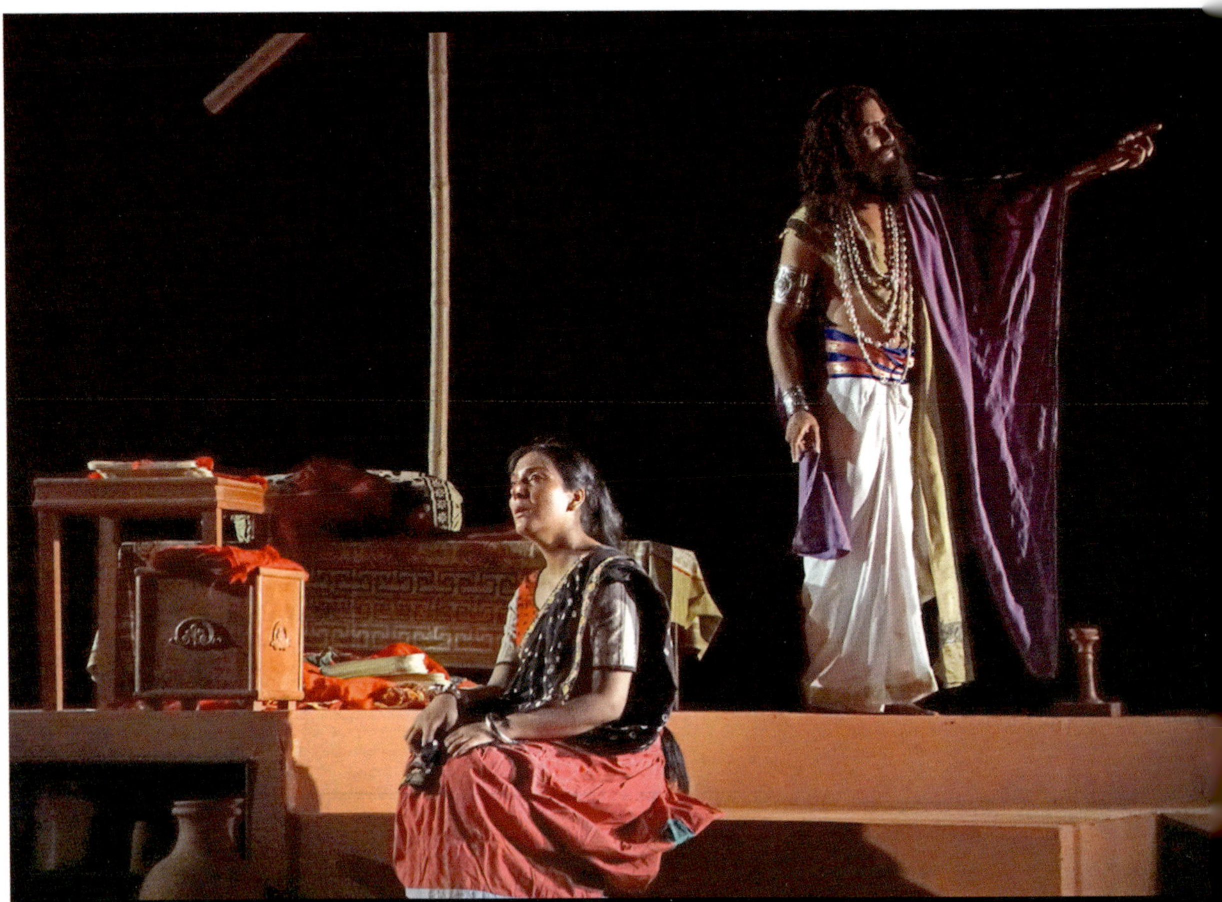

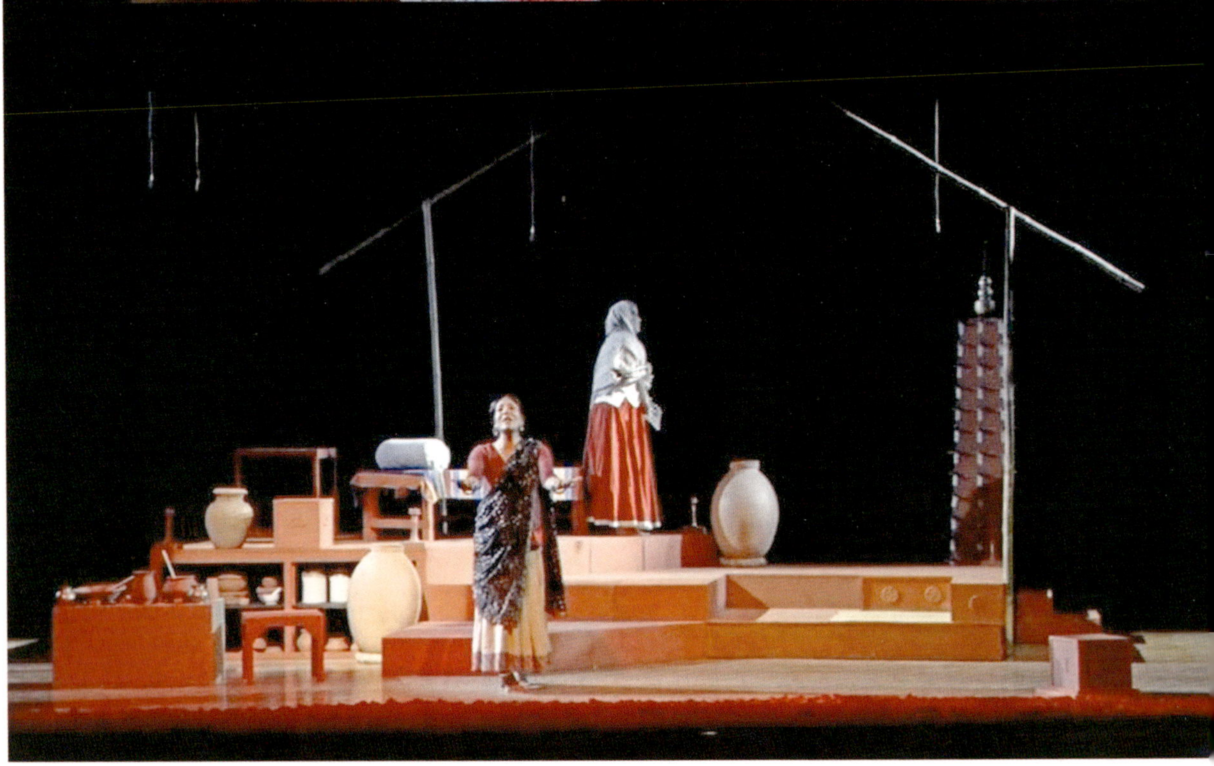

we started searching an alternate performance space around the drama school, which we located at Meghdoot open air theatre behind Rabindra Bhawan complex. Working in unusual spaces other than proscenium was a challenging factor to the conventions of theatre practices in those days. Initially the idea of presenting the play in open space was unacceptable to the director as he had a proclivity for proscenium style. After repeated meetings and endless convincing, he reluctantly agreed upon our proposal.

The practice was in full swing in the Meghdoot open air theatre. Every day after rehearsal, we the design students, used to spend quite some time in the complex with Robin Das, exploring many new possibilities of presenting the play. Every day new design elements were added to the space as per the demand of the text. Yet we were not satisfied with the approach of the director as he was moulding the play again in the proscenium style even after shifting to an intimate open-air theatre space under a huge peepul tree. We got frustrated again.

One night, after the rehearsal was over and the director left the venue, a few of us stayed back with Robin Das to discuss certain issues related to our production process, which was our usual practice. While arguing upon certain things, Robin Das jumped into a lower pit area behind the peepul tree and vanished in the darkness. After a while, we heard him calling us from behind the bushes at the backyard of the theatre complex. Reaching there we discovered Robin Das standing on a low-height mound surrounded by trees and thorny bushes right behind the stage in the backside. We discovered a pit nearby and curiously out of fun we started improvising a scene from the play where a few dead soldiers are waiting to be buried in the pit. It was a stimulating moment, a moment that broke all the boundaries and opened the gateway of our imagination. After a thorough inspection of the space, we

FACING PAGE: Stills from the play *Ashad Ka Ek Din (2016)*. Playwright: Mohan Rakesh (1925-1972) Indian. Scenography and direction: Bapi Bose. Presented by: 'The Circle Theatre Company' (CTC), Delhi. Courtesy: The Circle Theatre Company.

decided to perform *Bury the Dead* in that found space in any circumstances; Robin Das took the responsibility to convince the director.

The next few nights we quietly explored the space, distributed locales and created apt atmosphere suitable for our production design. Without the knowledge of our director, we worked on the entry and exits of the actors, seating arrangements, etc. Robin Das drew a few sketches while we engaged ourselves to create a war-field around the mound and the pit with much excitement. On a tree branch, nearby the mound we fashioned an improvised hammock by collecting ropes and bamboos from the surroundings. This would be the resting place for the tired soldiers in the war field. A few sandbags and debris were collected from here and there, and were thrown in the space to create the required ambience. Finally, we fixed some iron hedges found in a junkyard to mark the line of control. Our new space was ready for the rehearsal.

Finally, with much argument, Professor Das succeeded in convincing the director. He pleaded for this new experimentation that would help the students in their learning process. Though initially sceptical, the director eventually agreed upon this challenging condition and restructured the play in that found space. Finally, we had an interactive space waiting to be explored jointly by a group of enthusiastic young practitioners and the audience, who at the outset of the show were confusingly searching for a suitable place to sit and watch the play. Delhi theatre was not fully exposed to this kind of experiment in the beginning of 1980s; thus, the experience was more exciting.

CONCLUSION

As I have observed and experienced in my designing career, a slight diagonal arrangement of visual units on the stage floor, helps felicitate the interactions in between the actors and the space with full intensity. Also, diagonal entry of the characters on stage can enhance curiosity by adding dynamics of the dramatic movements. Application of diagonal forces through lines and colours would highlight the conflicts, thus emphasising the dramatic tension.

Scenographers should try to create multiple interactive spaces through the arrangement of stage props which can be integrated into the actions meaningfully. While placing these props on the stage space such as, a sofa, a table, chairs, a cupboard, etc., the scenographers should select only the significant objects that are barely necessary for the scene. A small symbolic prop or an object in the space holds greater metaphoric significance than a bunch of clustered props and objects. Through meaningful interaction with the actors those props come alive and are activated to develop visual dialogues with the spectators.

Quite often, a small portion of the stage space, a piece of furniture or a fraction of the design forms the entire world that is arrested in the psyche of the actors and the spectators. For example, in the production of *Aadhe Adhure* by Amal Alana for the NSD Repertory Company in the year 1976, the scenographer Dr Nissar Alana incorporated a few fragments of set units and minimum hand props functioning as certain symbols of a fragmental design—mismatched furniture, a portion of a textured wall, scattered newspapers, cut-outs from magazines which were pasted randomly on the wall, leftover teacups on the centre-table and unusual sitting arrangements of the audience, suggesting a house full of tension at the Rabindra Bhawan studio theatre, Delhi. These fractional and small set units would grab the viewers' attention and arrest their mind towards a dilapidated house where the stage visuals gradually develop unspoken dialogues with the audience. In the beginning of the play, with the entry of a tired and unaffected Savitri (performed by Surekha Shikri) from the office and her eventual interactions with those stage objects, and the gradual emergence of other characters such as Mahendra Nath (performed by Manohar Singh), Binni (performed by Uttara Baokar), Kinni (performed by Anila Singh) and Ashok (performed by K. K. Raina) would activate the space and make it alive for an active interaction with the spectators.

But sometimes overemphasised set may spoil the show by drawing unnecessary attentions of the audience, thus disrupting the major actions. This is perilous for the play and must be taken care of by the scenographers.

Still from *Chakkar Chalaye Ghanchakkar* (Adaptation of Shakespeare's *Comedy of Errors*). Scenography and direction: Salim Arif, Group: Essay PPL, Mumbai. Presented by: Adyaam, Mumbai, 2016. Courtesy: Adyaam, Mumbai.

References

i   Parker, Wilford O. and Harvey K. Smith. 1979. *Scene Design and Stage Lighting*. New York: Holt Rinehart and Winston Inc. p. 71.

ii Jones, Robert Edmond. 2004. *The Dramatic Imagination*. New York: Routledge. E-book. p. 21.

iii Howard, Pamela. 2009. *What is Scenography?* London, New York: Routledge. p. 34.

iv Howard-Reguindin, Pamela F. 2009. *What is cenography?*. Florence: Taylor and Francis. p. 63.

v   Kambar, Chandrasekhar. 2000. *Modern Indian Plays. Vol-1, One Day in Ashadha*. New Delhi: National School of Drama. p. 167.

vi Parker, Wilford O., and Harvey K. Smith. 1979. *Scene Design and Stage Lighting*. New York: Holt Rinehart and Winston Inc. p. 80.

vii Kaufman, Moises. *Presentational Theatre and Representational Theatre*. https://www.laguardia.edu/laramie/presentational-theater.htm.

viii Pipes, Alan. 2008. *Foundations of Art and Design*. London: Laurence King Publishing Limited. p. 50.

ix Kaufman, Moises. *Presentational Theatre and Representational Theatre*. https://www.laguardia.edu/laramie/presentational-theater.htm

x   Morris, Pam. 2003. *Realism*. London: Routledge. p. 5.

xi Breton, Andre. *The Surrealist Manifesto*. https://study.com/academy/lesson/what-is-surrealism-definition-art-characteristics.html.

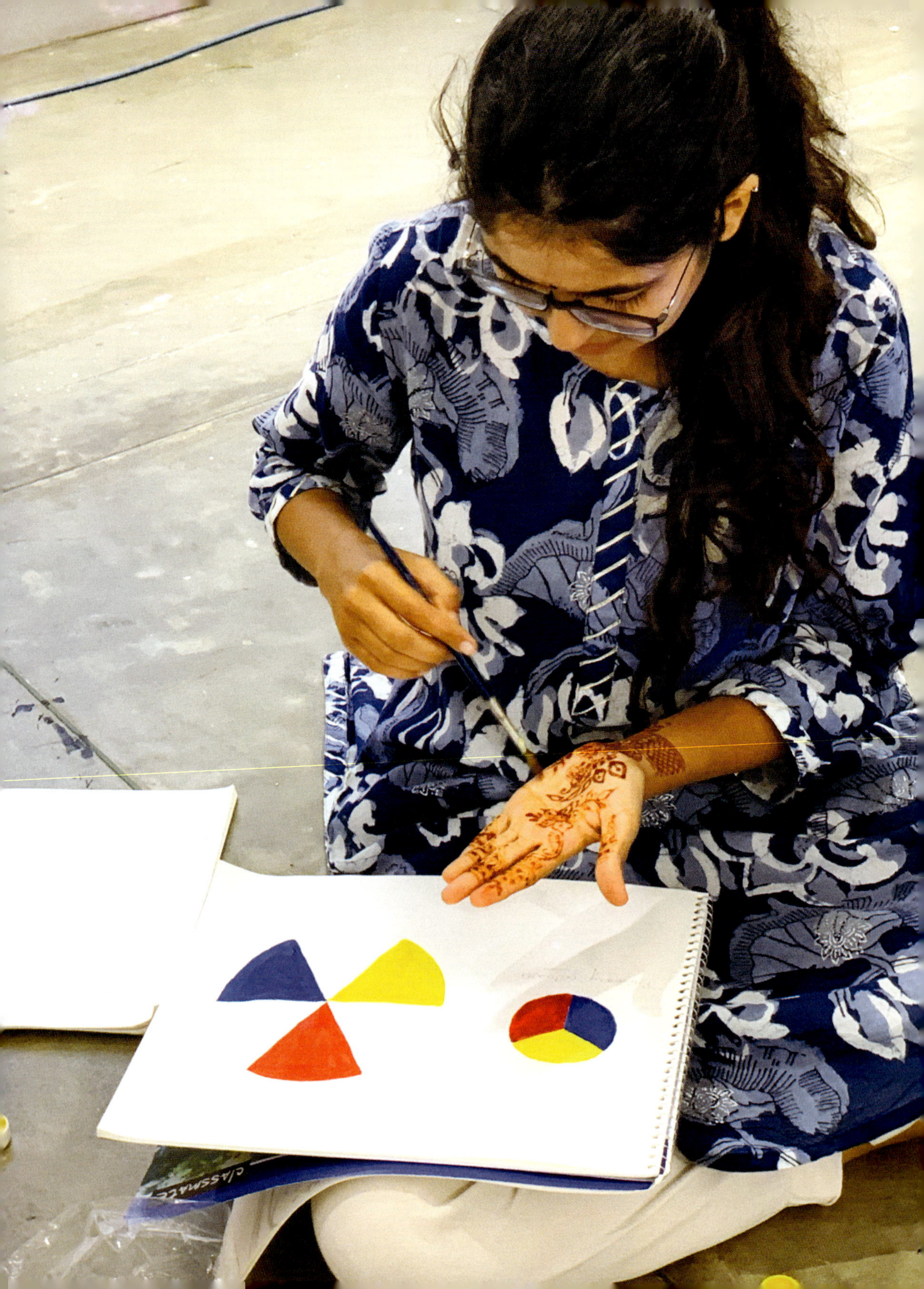
classmate

REPRESENTING DESIGN IDEAS: Paper Works

SCENOGRAPHER'S STORYBOARD

There is a general misconception about the habit of maintaining a storyboard in theatre. To many, storyboard is only essential in filmmaking and has nothing to do with play productions. However, it has been substantiated over the years that eminent scenographers of the world such as Adolphe Appia, Casper Nehar, Karl Von Appen, Pamela Howards and Peter Cook used to prepare detailed layouts of their scenographic ideas along with a series of sketches before initiating a production. In India as well, scenographers like Bansi Kaul, Robin Das, Bapi Bose and Satyabrata Rout, etc. prepare their preliminary visual actions, narrated through a series of sketches.

Scenography is the visual narration of a story, retold through a series of images: linking one with the other. It takes the audience to a creative journey which is unique and exciting. This voyage induces the audience to flow along with the story emotionally, intellectually and spiritually to re-live and interpret the narrative.

Telling story through visuals has been a common practice of human race right from the dawn of a conscious human civilisation. The prehistoric remains like ancient cave paintings narrate these stories through a series of

Scene-1

House of Mr and Mrs Zero

The design would alter according to the sequences in different scenes by keeping the basic structure same.

Scene-2

Office of Mr Zero.

Mr Zero and Ms Daisy are seen working.
Ms Daisy is thinking of Mr Zero while working.
Mr Zero at the same time is thinking of his next-door neighbour Ms Judy whom he loves.
Judy is visible behind a net curtain on the stage centre.

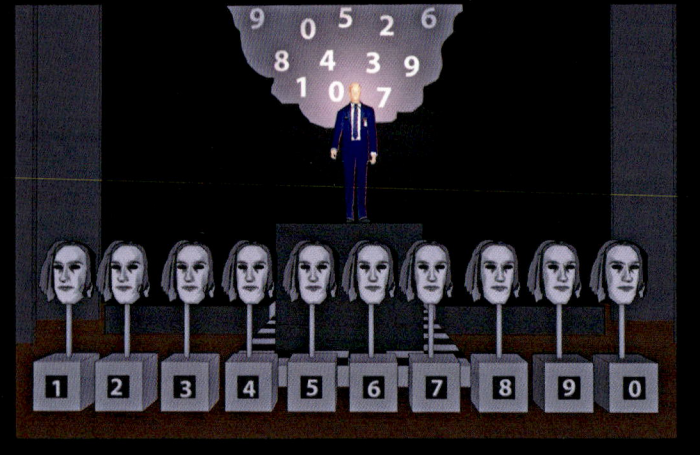

Scene-3

The Trial Scene

Mr Zero is tried for murdering his boss in the office.
He is found guilty by the jury and ordered for capital punishment.
The jury is represented by white-faced masks.

Scene-4

Prison

Mr. Zero is imprisoned and is kept for public viewing before the punishment.

Scene-5

The Crematorium

Mr Zero is hanged and cremated.
After death he meets Judi whom he loved.
Judy has killed herself by getting the news
of Mr Zero's death.

Scene-6

The Elysian Fields

Mr Zero is brought to a
heaven like place (the Elysian fields).

There he meets Ms Daisy,
who also killed herself after Mr Zero's
hanging.
They sing love song.

Scene-7

The Human Factory

The mind of Mr Zero is updated and
repaired in the factory in order to
send him back to the earth to work
with complecated machinery.

Storyboard presentation. Production design of the play *The Adding Machine*. Playwright: Elmer Rice. Scenography and direction: Satyabrata Rout. Presented by: Bharatendu Natya Academy, Lucknow (2018). Note the change in set units in different scenes of the play.

inscriptions depicting animal hunting, expeditions, invasions, community rituals, etc. Storytelling through images and illustrations is also an old practice of few Indian communities who used to travel, singing and narrating fables with the help of drawings and sketches from the *Jatak* tales, *Panchatantra* and from other local mythical stories. Scenographers, being visual storytellers, can adopt all the elements of storytelling that complement their visuals.

A play is a journey of the characters from one state of life to another, overlapped in various layers, events, actions, thoughts, relationships and locales. This journey unfolds and is tendered to the viewers by the performance through emotions, interactions and interpretations. A scenographer collects the essential data and information for the play in detail and confers them on the stage through motley of scenes and locales, therefore building an atmosphere befitting the text. The scenes can be conjoined with each other or can be diversified in different spaces and times.

Occasionally, altering the colours and textures of the design in different scenes in plays with single locale, a scenographer can produce diversity in the overall atmosphere. For example, in plays like *Khamosh Adalat Jari Hai*, *Aadhe Adhure*, *Ashad ka Ek Din*, *The Lower Depths*, where there is only one locale throughout the play, the monotony is broken through change of lights in various actions. Colours and textures can be valuable tools for portraying fresh and supplemental timeframe in the same space. Similarly, many a time, scenes are remoulded with the alteration of a few props and furniture for showing a different time and space. In other cases, scenographers do not employ any considerable modifications with the change in scenes and allow the audience to imagine those changes and alterations following the action of the play. A scenographer exhausts every possible creative mean to sustain the visual movement of the play. For smooth mutation between the action and the scenes, scenographers take the help of storyboard that depicts the visual journey of the play. The visual artists are seen doing a series of chronological sketching and drawings or taking rough notes during the rehearsal for manifesting the design idea in the production. With the help of sketches and drawings, scenographers can express the design idea more convincingly, which serves as the basic material for the storyboard. A detailed drawing of the design idea for the storyboard showing chronological development of dramatic visuals for the play *Adding Machine* has been depicted earlier for further understanding.

A well-adapted storyboard marks entry, exit, spatial distribution of set units, arrangement of props and furniture and many technical aspects for effortless and smooth operation of stage visuals during the performance. When the scenography is at developing state, a production meeting between the scenographer and the director along with the producer and the technical crew is absolutely essential. This is to discuss the design for appropriate implementation.

The meeting is also important for calculating the financial expenses involved in the production according to the storyboard and the scenography. In India, many creative and innovative design ideas cannot be realised just because of the financial constraints. Post-Independence Indian theatre was never developed commercially like the cinema or the television. It has experienced so much of ignorance that theatre in India stands solely on the shoulder of a collective human spirit. In a condition where financing a theatre is a distant dream, the scenographer should always keep an alternative idea ready without compromising on creativity. It is also observed that a low-cost creative and conceptual design invariably inspires the director and the actors to help boost up their creative impulse towards an innovative production.

REPRESENTATION OF IDEAS

Most scenographers express their design ideas through sketches and thumbnail drawings. Those are then converted into scale drawings and then to a three-dimensional model before being executed on the stage floor. These artists follow a sequential order to carry their ideas onto the stage. Many scenographers also work in a unique way by collecting day-to-day ordinary materials including scraps, papers, wires, tubes or anything suitable for the expression and transforming them into an improvised model, sketching it and modifying the entire conception repeatedly by re-modelling. The final scale drawings are sent to the workshop for construction.

As discussed earlier, creativity does not follow any specific rule and can be expressed through multiple processes. Similarly, a design idea has myriad ways of presentation. For example, a three-dimensional model can be created through pencilling a number of sketches and converting the final one into three-dimensional form. A model can also be achieved with the help of technical drawings made by the scenographer. By looking into the viability of the design through many improvised three-dimensional trial models or by exploring the design elements and props with the actors during the rehearsal, the final set model can also be prepared. Irrespective of the different means of representation, scenographers develop their language through images, which is realised through sketches, drawings and models for which they must acquire the fundamental skill of drawing and sketching.

SKETCHING THE DESIGN

It is the initial stage of representing a design idea on paper, an activity that continues throughout the production process. Sketching is an essential tool for the scenographers through which they elaborate and express design ideas and begin to actualise those. Colours and shades can also be used in the sketch works to create ambience which in no other means can be achieved at this stage. Scenographers often make multiple-coloured sketches, displaying different lighting effects in different situations.

Constant work on sketches would bring new ideas and possibilities to the design, for which the scenographers invest a lot of time doing sketches in the initial phase.

Thumbnail sketches are drawn in large numbers portraying actions, scenes and props to communicate the scenographer's idea with clarity. This also contributes in visualising the representations and fluidity of the stage space as deciphered by the scenographer. During the initial stage of exploring design idea, the scenographers usually avoid making three-dimensional models out of vaguely prepared sketches. But they ought to go through a preliminary painstaking process of making a series of sketches exploring ideas until something innovative is achieved. Finally, the initial storyboard with all the technical drawings and a three-dimensional model can be opened up for the audience through an exhibition before the show. This act of presenting the design ideas would season the audience towards the process of performance-making.

The sketch, however, is not the final design but a rough outline of the concept which should not be judged only through its beauty primarily, but through its functionality. A design can only be realised with its final execution on the stage floor along with the actors' exploration of the space. The dimension of design units cannot be calculated only through a sketch work, since sketch is only an instant reaction of the design idea, an improvised expression of the visual artist for creating a suitable space for a play. It is only the take-up point that provides a first-hand atmosphere but not the absolute one. To mould the design idea workable and to bring it into actuality, the scenographers prepare scale drawings with dimensions that are used by the technical crews (i.e. stage technologists, fabricators, moulders, carpenters, lighting designers) and the director for composing the scenes. These are absolutely essential in the bildungsroman of a theatre.

A few Sketches from the Storyboard prepared for the play *Charlotte: A Tri-Coloured Play with Music*

Character drawings
Medium:
Water colour
Collage and pen.
Toronto 2015

drawings made by Pamela Howards

(Continued from the previous drawings)

Storyboard presentation and Costume design for the play *Charlotte: A Tri-Coloured Play with Music*

Scenography and direction: Prof. Pamela Howard (U.K)

Toronto 2015

Scene-2
The Funeral of Charlotte's Mother.
A Three-dimensional staging of the 'split-scene'
Gouache painting
Acrylic and Collage
Toronto 2015

Drawings of the costume and set design; For the play *Charlotte: A Tri-Coloured Play with Music* (A Theaturtle work-in-progress production based on Charlotte Salomon's artwork *Life? Or Theatre?*). The play was presented at Luminato Festival, Toronto, in 2017 and the drawings were presented at the World Stage Design Scenofest in Taipei City in 2017. Courtesy: Prof. Pamela Howard and Martin Gannon (UK).

SCALE DRAWING

It is the graphic representation of the design with accurate measurement that helps in adapting the ground reality and constructing the sets without fallacy. To prepare the scale drawing, scenographers have to learn skills of drawing and drafting. They also have good command on scale conversions that follows certain rules to prepare the technical drawings. In drafting, while some designers prefer to work through conventional methods of working with paper, pencils and drafting tools, a few adopt the modern digital technology such as computer-aided design and drafting system (CADD). There are many software applications available to prepare the drawings through computer which can also be tried out by the scenographers. But a scenographer must acquire a sound knowledge on both the methods—hand practicing and computer programming.

SCALE CONVERSION

The process of proportionately converting the original measurement of an object to an appropriate and workable size is called scale conversion. When a drawing is described as 'to scale', it means that each element in that drawing is in the same proportion, related to the real one. The relationship between the dimensions of the drawing and the dimension of the real object is known as 'ratio'. To know the real size of the object, one can multiply the measurements of the drawing with the ratio. The ratio must be measured in reciprocal units, such as, 1in = 1ft or 1cm = 1m., etc. To understand the scale conversion, one can undertake some practical exercises. Now let us measure the dimension of a tennis court—a rectangular field having four facets—two lengths and two breadth. The drawing below represents this rectangular field with a measurement of 78 ft and 36 ft in length and breadth respectively. Let us convert this measurement into a proportionate scale drawing on paper. One important thing to be noted here is that the conversion should

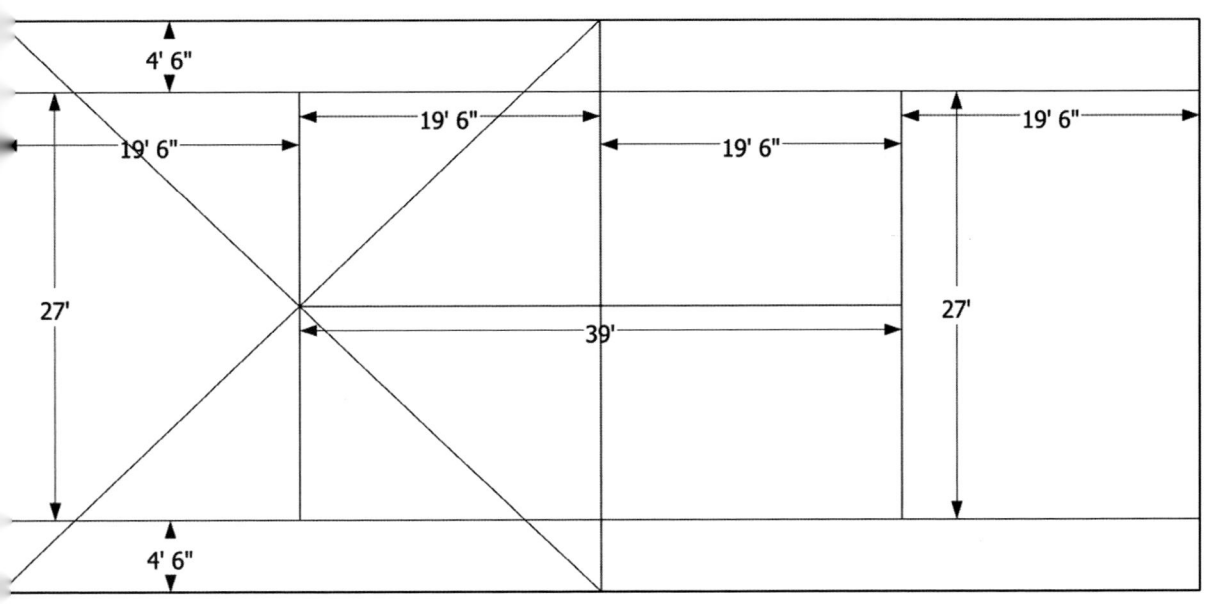

Scale Conversion of a Tennis Court
Scale: 1/4 in. = 1ft.

always be made according to the size of the drawing paper. A conversion that does not fit in the drawing paper would not be workable. Now, let's keep the equation as, ¼ in = 1ft, which means ¼ in measurement in the drawing is equal to 1ft of the actual tennis yard. Accordingly, the conversion on paper would be: 19 ½ in x 9 in.

The scale drawings usually follow the unit of scale in metric (meter and centimetre) or imperial units (foot and inch). These technical drawings make an artisan's job way easier converting the measurements with accuracy. Let's do a few basic scale drawings such as, ground plan, front elevation and side elevation of a few sets and performance spaces to practically understand the subject.

GROUND PLAN

It is also called the floorplan of the design in a scale unit. In ground plan, a section of design with the cutting plane is placed at such a level that it shows the horizontal view of the design. This two-dimensional scale drawing is expressed through the measurements of length and width, computing the 'height' to zero. It helps the scenographers to fix the design units accurately on the stage floor. It also provides accurate information of the stage dimensions and the arrangement of set and props on the stage. With the help of a ground plan, a director can work on the stage blocking and manage the actors on the stage space in the rehearsal. With the help of a ground plan, the lighting designer can prepare the lighting layout plan, while the sound designers work on the sound areas. The scenographers usually prepare the ground plan of stage design on a layout drawing of the stage proper in order to exactly place the set units on the stage floor. The layout plan of the stage floor can be collected from the theatre administration. Working on a ground plan, while placing the set units in their respective places, the scenographers need to take care of these following issues:

- Arrangement of the wings on stage must coincide with the entry and exit of the actors, marked in the performance space. This would enable for comfortable access of the actors to their respective locales on stage.
- Adequate space must be left between the cyclorama and the rear edge of the set. This arrangement would create depth of field in the design. Occasionally, this space is also used to place stand lights and projectors that help creating stage effects on the cyclorama. This space is always kept away from the audience's vision. There should be enough space behind the sets for the preparation of the actors and for the backstage activities.

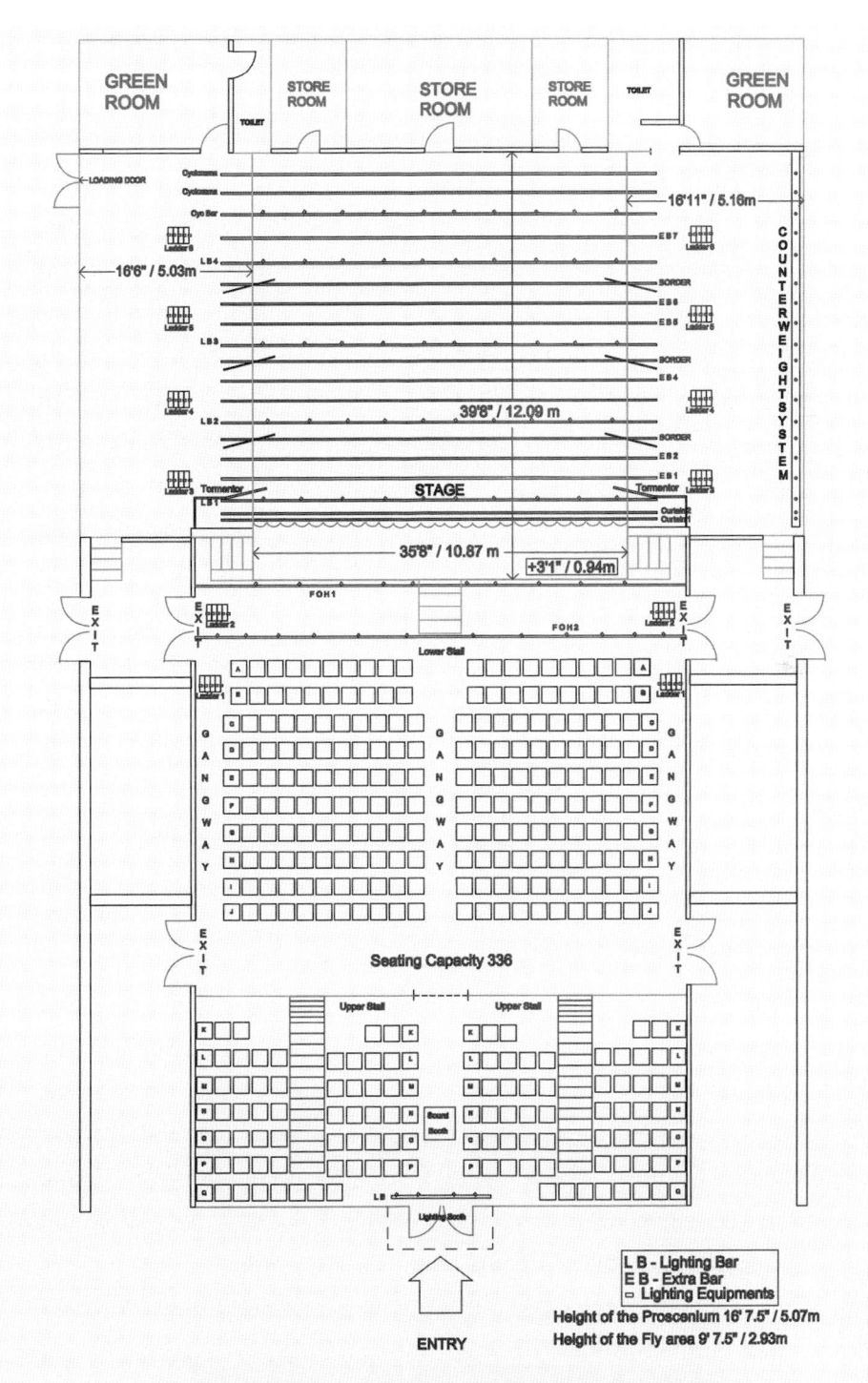

ABHIMANCH AUDITORIUM
(GROUND PLAN)

Ground Plan of Abhimanch Theatre at the National School of Drama, New Delhi. Plan prepared by: Sauti Chakraborty. Courtesy: NSD and Sauti Chakraborty.

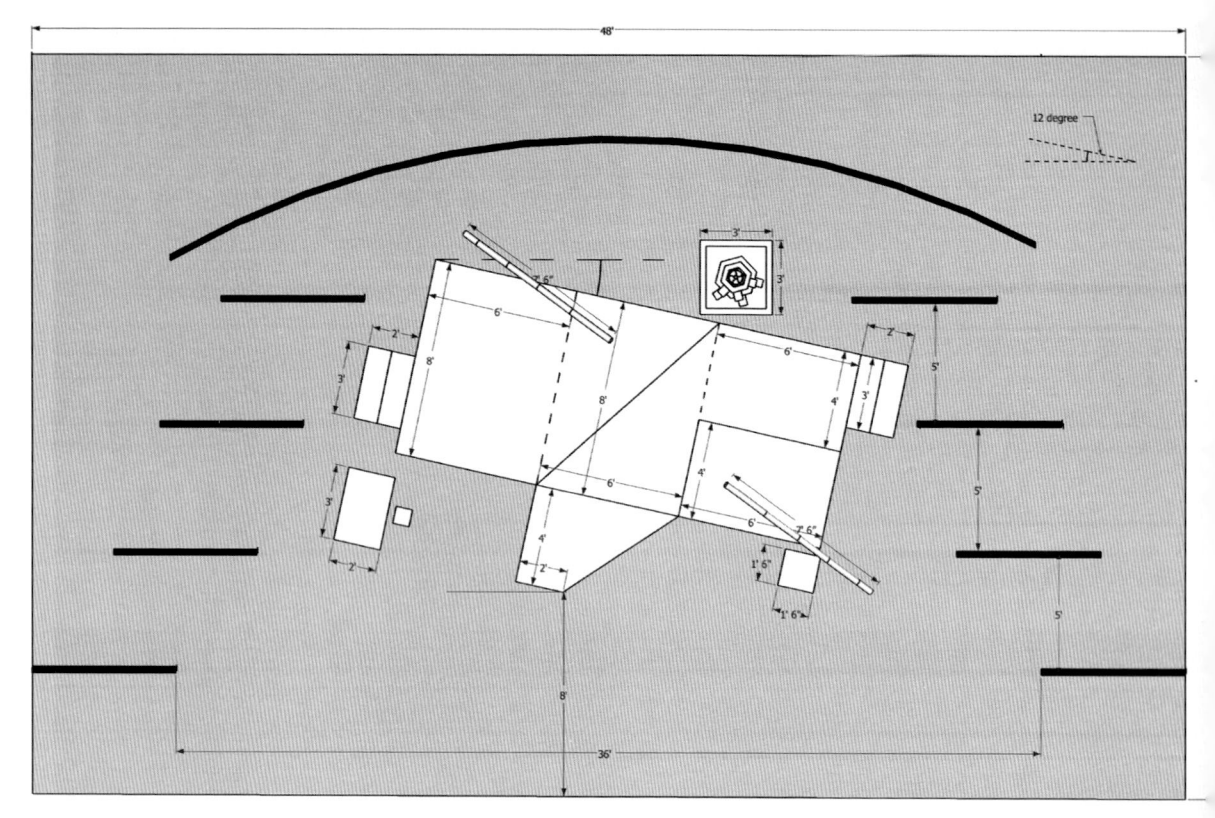

Designed by- Bapi Bose
Presented by Circle Theatre Company, New Delhi

Ground Plan
Set design of Ashad Ka Ek Din
Scale- 1in. = 2ft.

- The viewing distance between the audience and the sets must always be taken into consideration while designing a play. There is a chance of low proclivity between the performers and the audience if the viewing distance is more. On the other hand, closer proximity of the set to the audience makes the performance loud. Therefore, an aesthetic distance between the performers on stage and the viewers in the gallery must be maintained. The set should not be far away from or too near to the viewers. As a general rule, the set units are placed in the centre stage area, leaving the down stage bare for the actors' movements.
- The sight line and visual axis of the set must be carefully followed while preparing the ground plan. This must be perfectly executed on

the stage floor and all the set units must be kept in between the visual axis. This would enable all the audience for proper viewing and care must be taken while preparing the ground plan of a set.

Floorplans of various designs from different productions are illustrated below for reference.

FRONT ELEVATION

Front elevation is a two-dimensional drawing that portrays the flat facial view of the design. It provides a detailed description of the vertical

Ground plan of the set design of *August Ka Khwab*. Adapted from August Strindberg's *A Dream Play*. Scenography and direction: Satyabrata Rout. Courtesy: NSD.

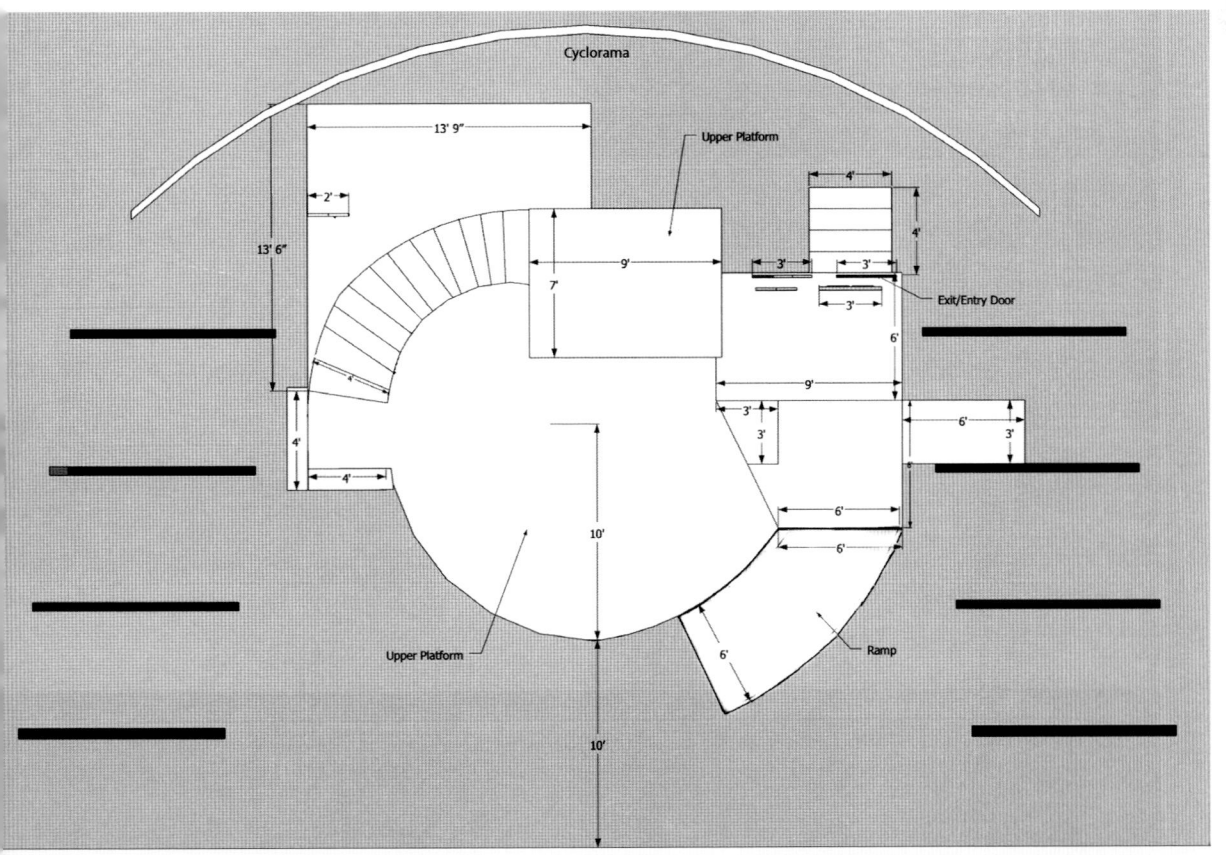

National School of Drama 3rd Year Presentation-2017

Ground Plan of the Play *August Ka Khwab*
Scale 1in. = 2 ft.

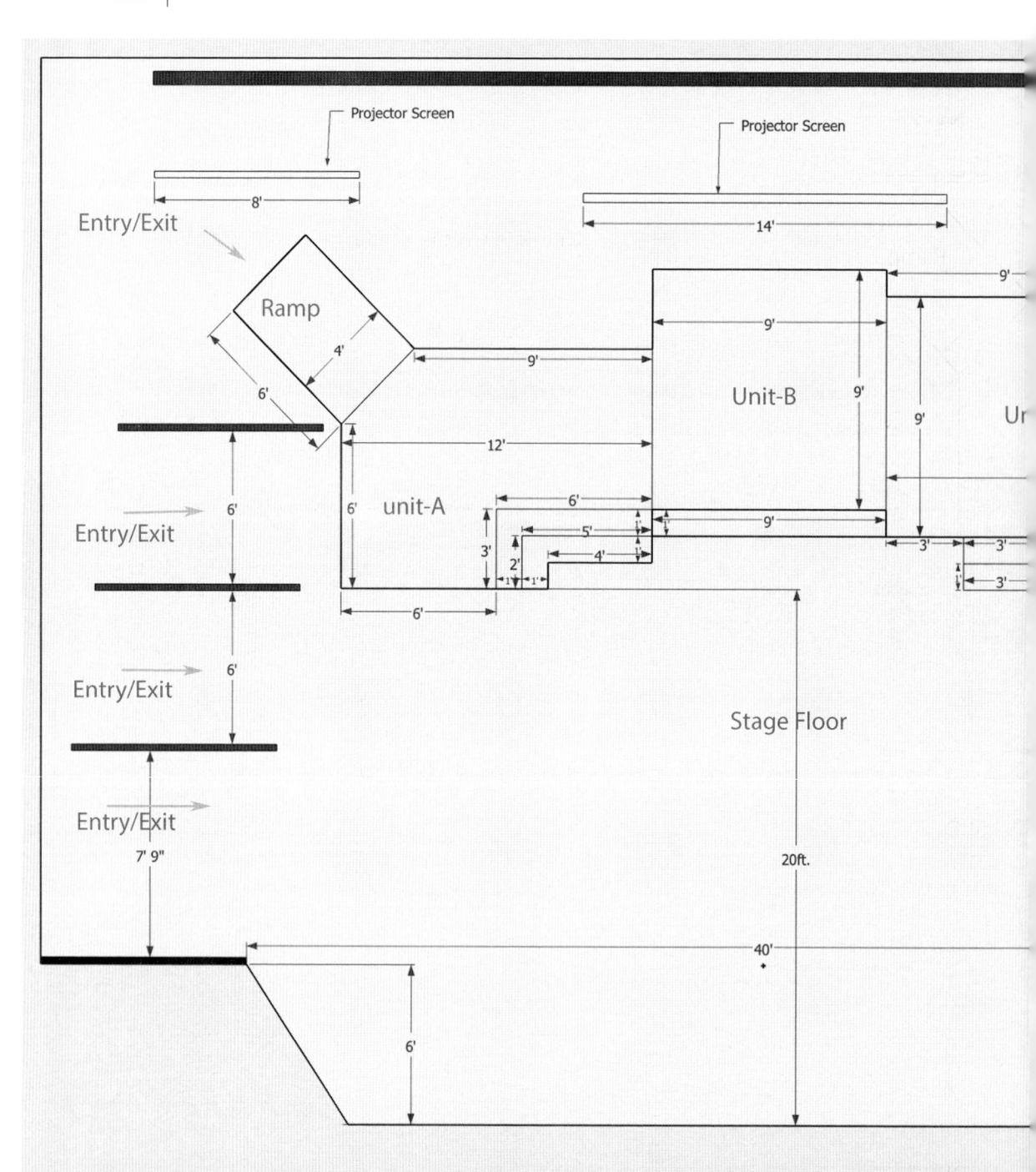

Presented by Rangakalpa Theatre, Hyderabad
Designed by Satyabrata Rout

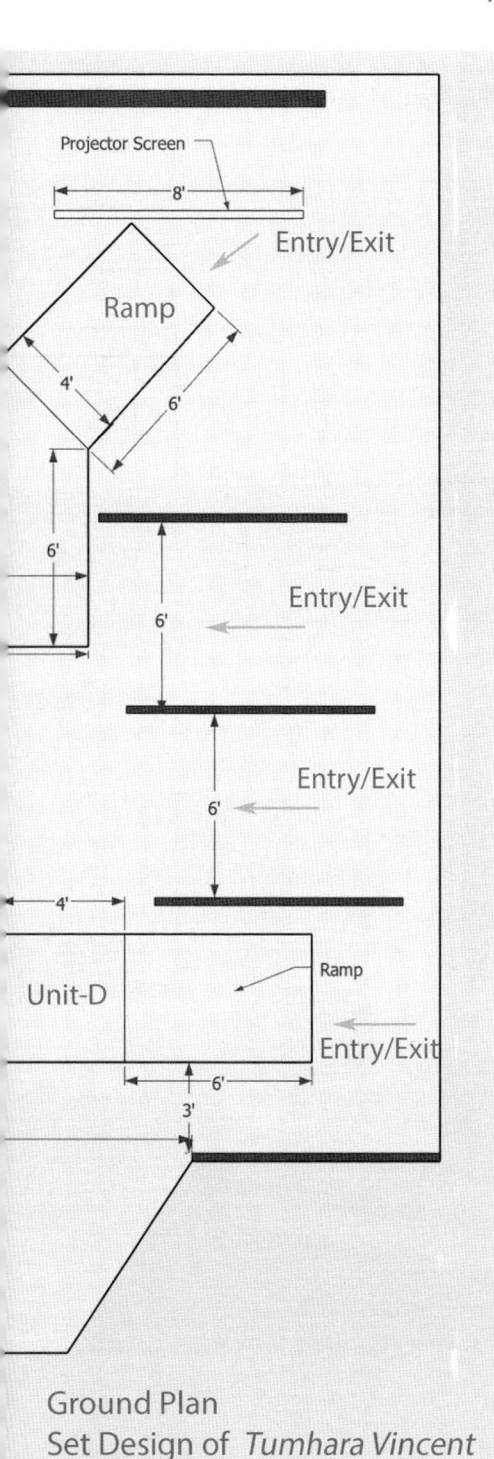

placement of set and props, etc. on stage from the frontal view by bringing all the visible objects through a linear arrangement. In front-elevation drawing, length and height of the object is taken into account, in which the width or depth is considered as zero. For example, if a set has three walls with door, window, staircase and a bookshelf, the front elevation drawing would bring them into one plane discarding the depth and view of the stage space. The drawings here would give a clear idea of the real arrangement of elements such as door, window and staircase in a three-dimensional space and their position in two-dimensional front-elevation drawing.

SIDE ELEVATION

Side elevation follows the same principle of front elevation but is visualised from the side periphery of the design. It is a two-dimensional scale drawing in which the measurement of the width and the height are taken into consideration without reflecting the length of the object. This drawing is also known as the 'cross section'. The drawing in below demonstrates the cross section of a few props such as a table, chair, staircase, pillar and a few platforms, etc.

Ground Plan
Set Design of *Tumhara Vincent*
Scale: 1in. = 2 ft.

Perspective drawing of a realistic box set. Note the three sides of the set is covered by walls; the fourth side is opened for viewing.

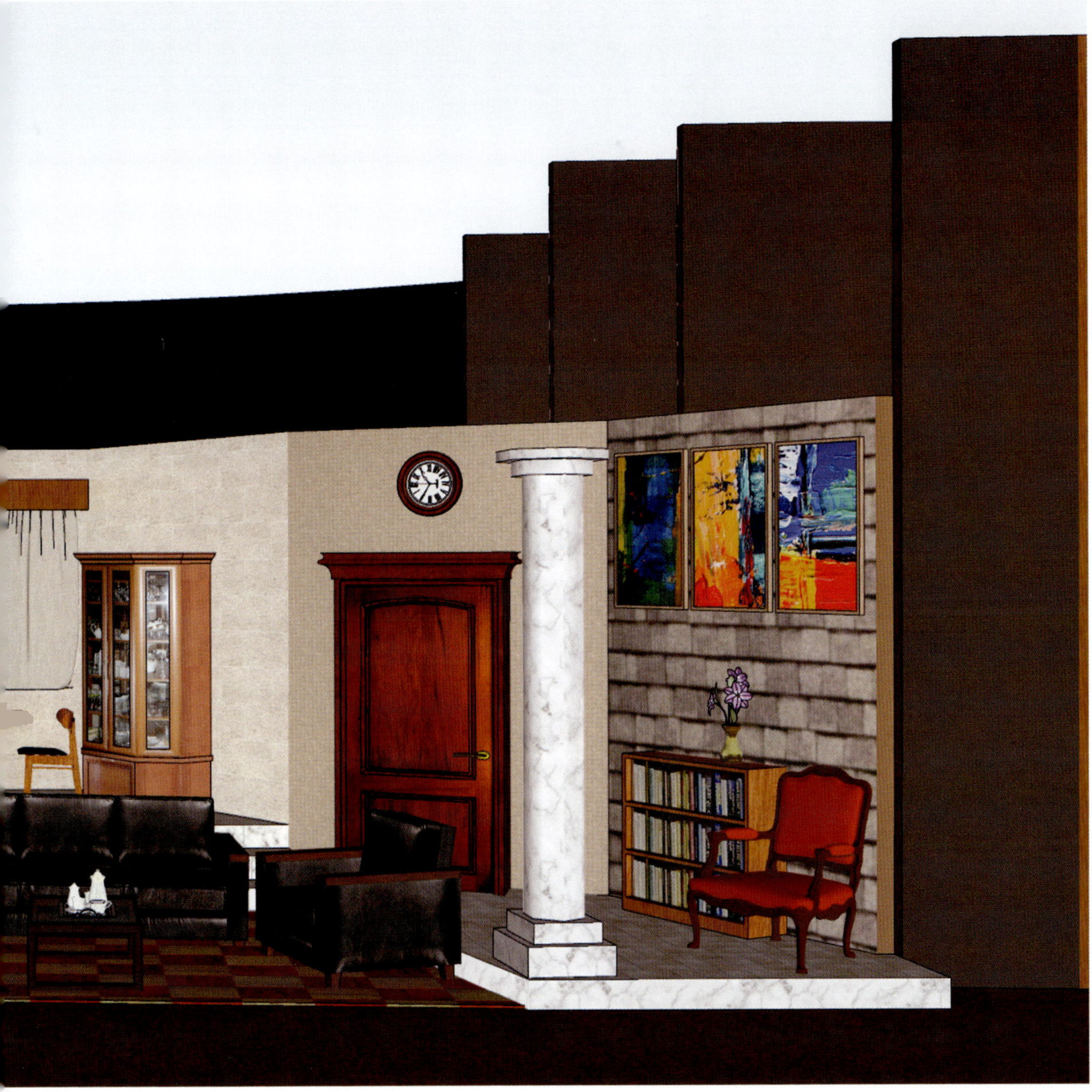

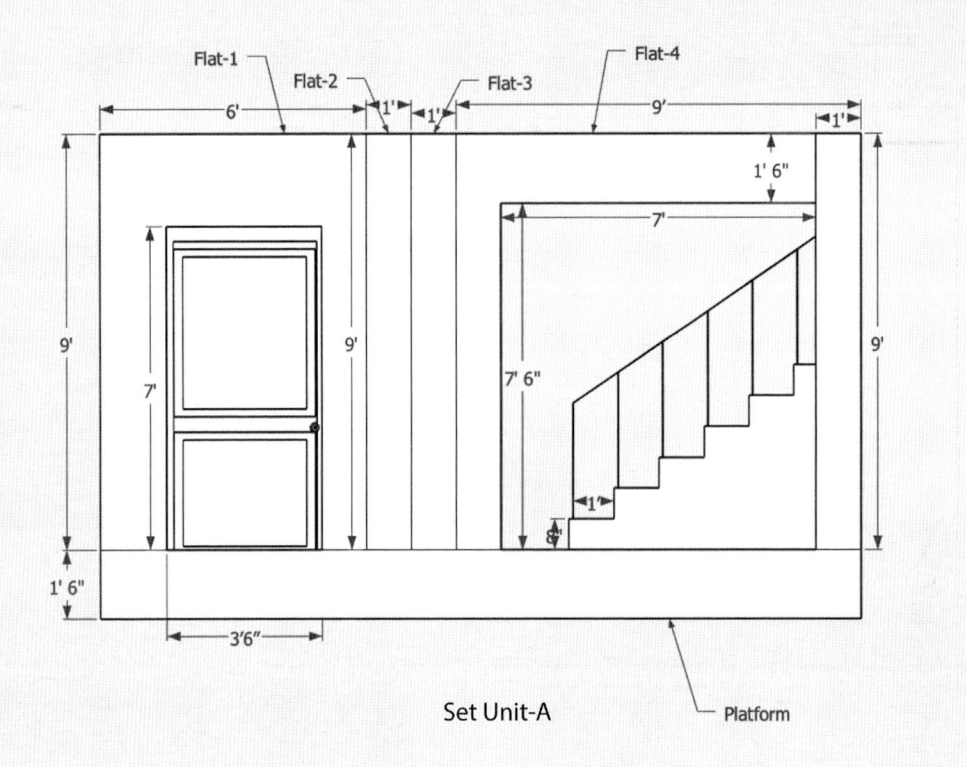

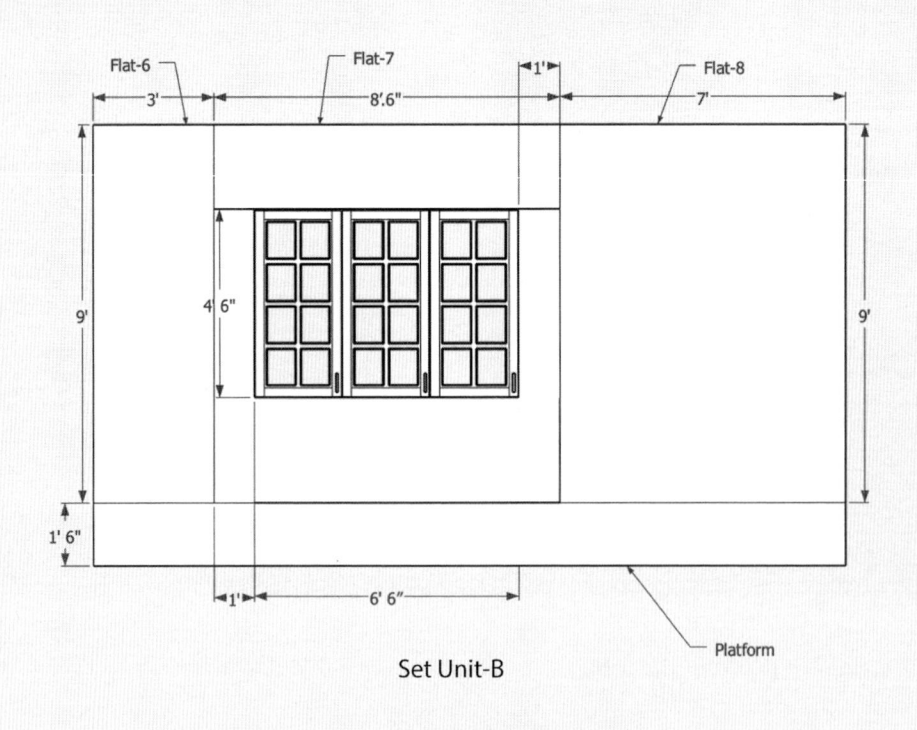

Front Elevation of the Realistic Set
Scale: 1in. = 1ft.

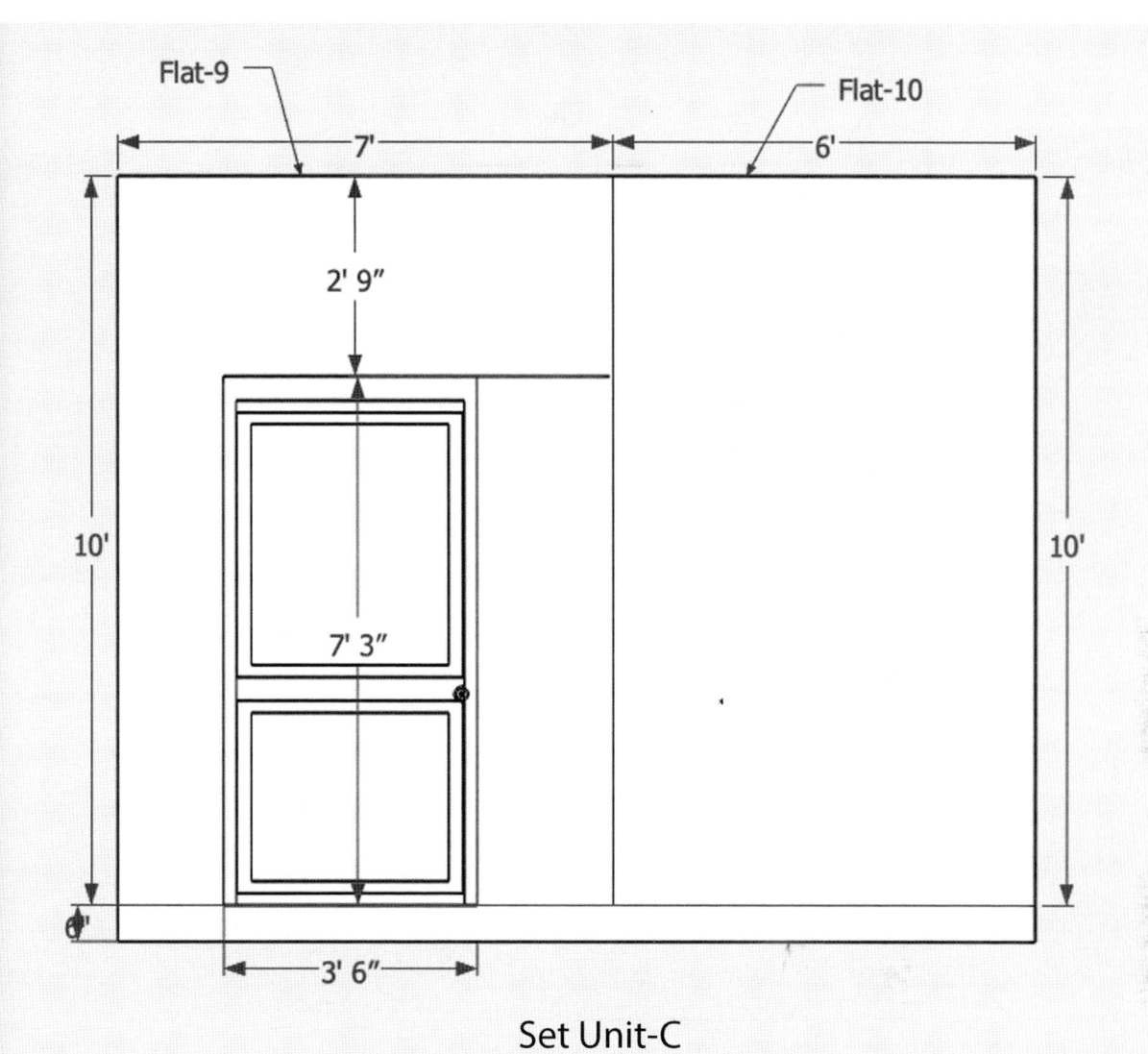

Set Unit-C

Front Elevation of the Realistic Set
Scale: 1in = 1ft.

DRAFTING TOOLS

A student of scenography must learn to draw and draft accurately with drafting tools. These tools make the work easier and faster.

Some commonly used drafting equipment are precisely described below:

- **Drawing Board:** It is a flat wooden board with smooth surface with a rectangular plane of 90° on each angle. The drawing paper is fixed and flattened above its surface with the help of drawing pins. Often the board is attached to a table to form a unit for smooth drawing work. They are also available separately and can be kept anywhere conveniently. While using a T-square to draw straight and parallel lines on paper using a drawing board, the edge of the board must serve as a guide for drawing horizontal base lines on paper.
- **T- Square:** This T-shaped tool is used for drawing straight and horizontal lines on the drawing paper. The head of the T-square is always anchored to the left side of the drawing table or board. It glides on the paper and make straight lines, parallel lines and horizontal lines, etc.
- **Pencil:** Pencils are the most important drafting tools available in many shades. They are hard, medium and soft depending upon their quality and usage. (example: H— Hard, HB—Medium and B—Soft) While H grade is used for drafting, HB pencils are used for marking and lettering and B grade pencils are used in free-hand sketching and shadings.
- **Drawing Paper:** It is a white ivory sheet especially designed for drawings and artwork. A low-grade white sheet is also available for rough works. Those are called chart papers. A minute observation reveals two different textures on both the surfaces of the drawing sheet. While one surface is smooth, the other is slightly rough. They have different purposes—the former for drawing and drafting and the latter for sketches.

Drawing-A

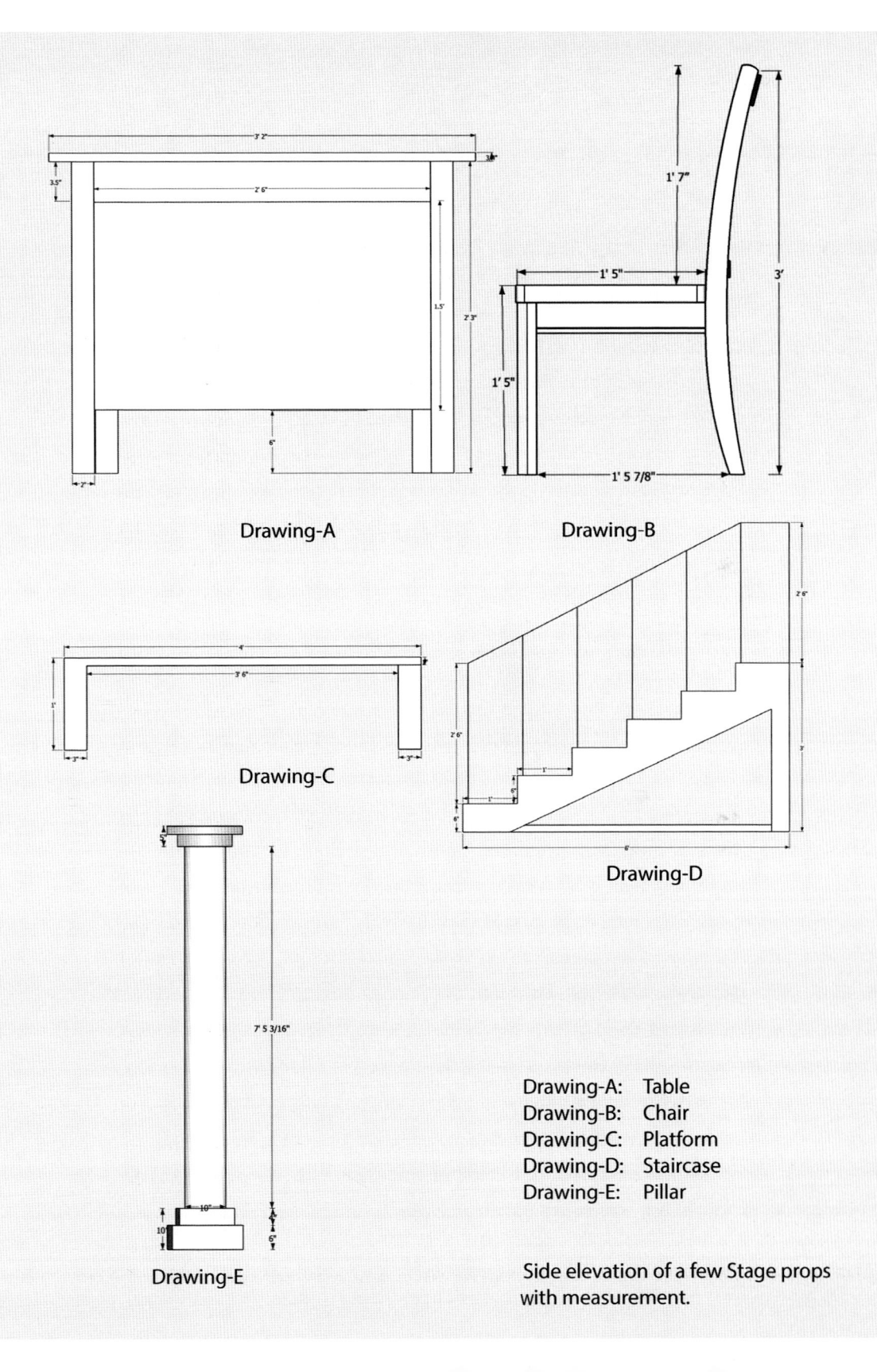

Drawing-B

Drawing-C

Drawing-D

Drawing-E

Drawing-A: Table
Drawing-B: Chair
Drawing-C: Platform
Drawing-D: Staircase
Drawing-E: Pillar

Side elevation of a few Stage props with measurement.

- **Scale:** It is available in various lengths such as 6 inches, 12 inches and 24 inches and even more. They are made of wood, plastic, steel, etc. But for the drafting work, transparent plastic scales are more useful since they make the underneath lines visible.
- **Sets-Square:** It is a set of two geometrical equipment in the form of triangles, having '90°, 45°, and 45°' and '60°, 30°, and 30°' respectively. They are simultaneously used to draw vertical and perpendicular lines; one forms the base upon which the other glides. The sets-square is also used to draw parallel lines.
- **Rounder and compass:** These are small but very useful equipment in drafting. They are used to make circle and measure the distance between two points.
- **Eraser:** This handy tool should not be crudely used on the drawing paper since hard rubbing may damage the drawing.

The drawings must be neatly presented to ensure accuracy and proficiency. The scenographers must follow certain discipline for ensuring clean and clear drawing. The drawing table must be neatly arranged before starting the work, since a clean table ensures a neat drawing. One must be careful of his own hand that holds the pencil, since there are possibilities of rubbing the drawings by the hand. Draftsmen usually place a white paper sheet or tissue paper above the work to avoid contact of the hand and the drawings. Dark pencils such as 2B and 4B should not be used for drawing works. 2H and HB shades are always suitable for drafting. While working on a drawing, the pencils must be kept sharp to ensure even lines. A sharpener or a cutter blade should always be kept along with. In no case, pencil shades are applied to the drawing which would spoil the work. For all the drawing works—ground plan, elevation drawings and perspective drawings—there must be one common conversion of scale unit, either in inches or in centimetre scale with a common ratio. For example, if we use the conversion ratio such as 1in =1ft, it must be reflected in each of the drawings—ground plan, elevations, etc. Proper handling of pencils ensures good drawings. There must be enough lights from all angles around the drawing table. One must avoid to sit against the light while working on the drawing table. It would create shadow on the table which may create error in the work. One should never fold or roll one's drawings, rather it is better to keep them flat inside a large folder for final presentation to the production team.

STAGE SYMBOLS

Stage symbols are the global codes of convention, used to make the design works easier. While preparing the drawings one should use these symbols for technical communication. Symbols make the scenographers' job easy and trouble free. It helps the entire technical team to understand the artist's intention and demand. While in travel, often it becomes difficult to carry large set-units along with the productions. In this situation, drawings and stage symbols solve the problems. With the help of technical drawings with stage symbols and measurements, the sets can be fabricated and executed anywhere across the globe with accuracy. A list of stage symbols is enlisted.

SYMBOLS OF LINES

There are symbols for various lines, used in the drawings to show different characteristics.

Visible lines are generally used to draw the outlines of the design units in the drawing. Imaginary lines are invisible yet exists for the performers and technical crew, such as proscenium arch line, curtain lines, sightlines, etc. Central line is also an imaginary line that divides any space into two equal halves such as stage central line, etc. Thick line symbolises any solid construction on the stage such as a wall.

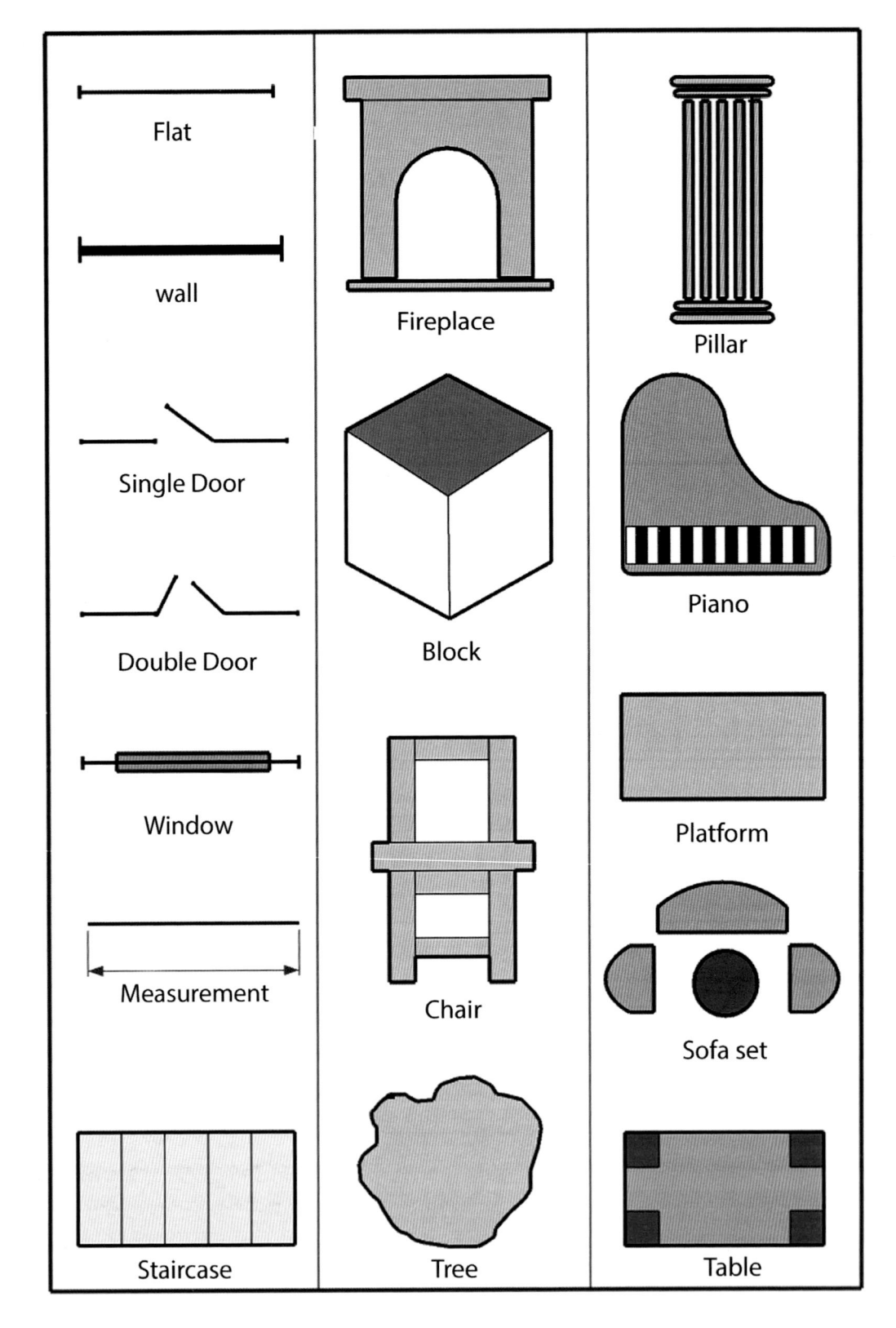

Flat	Fireplace	Pillar
wall	Block	Piano
Single Door		Platform
Double Door		
Window	Chair	Sofa set
Measurement		
Staircase	Tree	Table

Stage Symbols

Visible Line
– – – – – – – – – – – – – – – Imaginary Line
–·–·–·–·–·–·–·–·–·–·–·–·–·– Centre Line
▬▬▬▬▬▬▬▬▬▬▬▬▬▬ Line for Thick Wall

Symbols of different tyle of Lines

PRACTICAL ISSUES

Scale drawings make the fabrication, management and execution of the set and stage props easy. In many professional theatres in Europe and America, there are set shops with trained carpenters, moulders, painters, craftsmen and fabricators. These trained artisans create three-dimensional real-size set units with the help of these two-dimensional working drawings with utmost proficiency. These experts also execute those units on the stage floor with great perfection. Unfortunately, in India, theatre design and scenography has not been practised as a serious profession till today. Therefore, this creative skill has suffered a major setback due to the lack of attention and proficiency. There is hardly any set manufacturing shop in India, except a few carpentry workshops attached to some professional theatre institutions and repertories. But in the remote corner of the country, with a significant numbers of theatre activities, this technical awareness among the practitioners is a far cry. Consequently, a scenographer in Indian theatre is bound to depend on untrained hands. In some situations, even the scenographers try to fabricate the set units by themselves resulting in an unprofessional, amateurish presentation.

Scenography, a creative art with technical pursuance, must be practised through systematic and scientific methods. An untrained artisan cannot comprehend those drawings and an amateurish fabrication of the design would certainly make a scenographer frustrated. Even, improvising new ideas directly on the stage floor also create confusion among the actors as well as technical crews. For these reasons, technical training in theatre is essential over and again in India. Reading and understanding the language of visuals should be an integral part of the performance design which is of immense importance. A few practical factors that we always come across at the time of the execution of a design on the stage floor are mentioned below:

- The length, width and height of the set-units should be proportionate to the stage floor or else it would look dissonant and may lead to a disastrous presentation.
- Flats, platforms, furniture and stage props should be handled carefully because of their fragile nature.

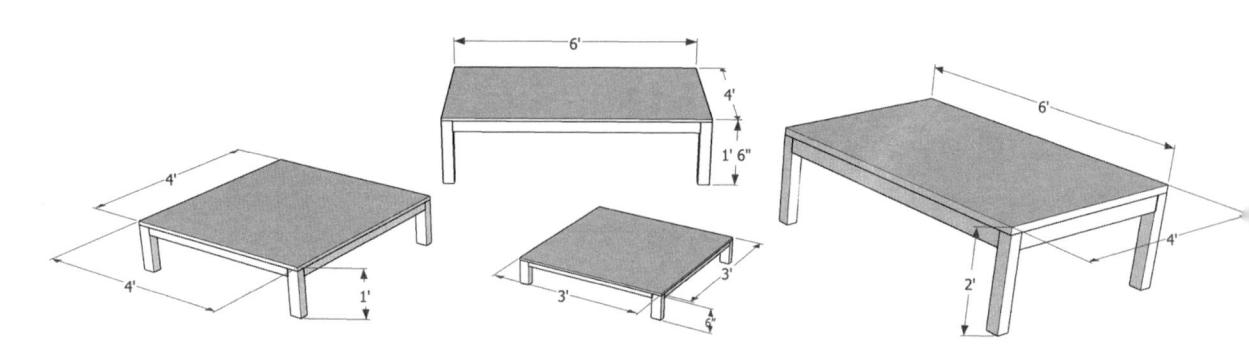

Platforms with Standard Measurements

Flats with standard dimensions

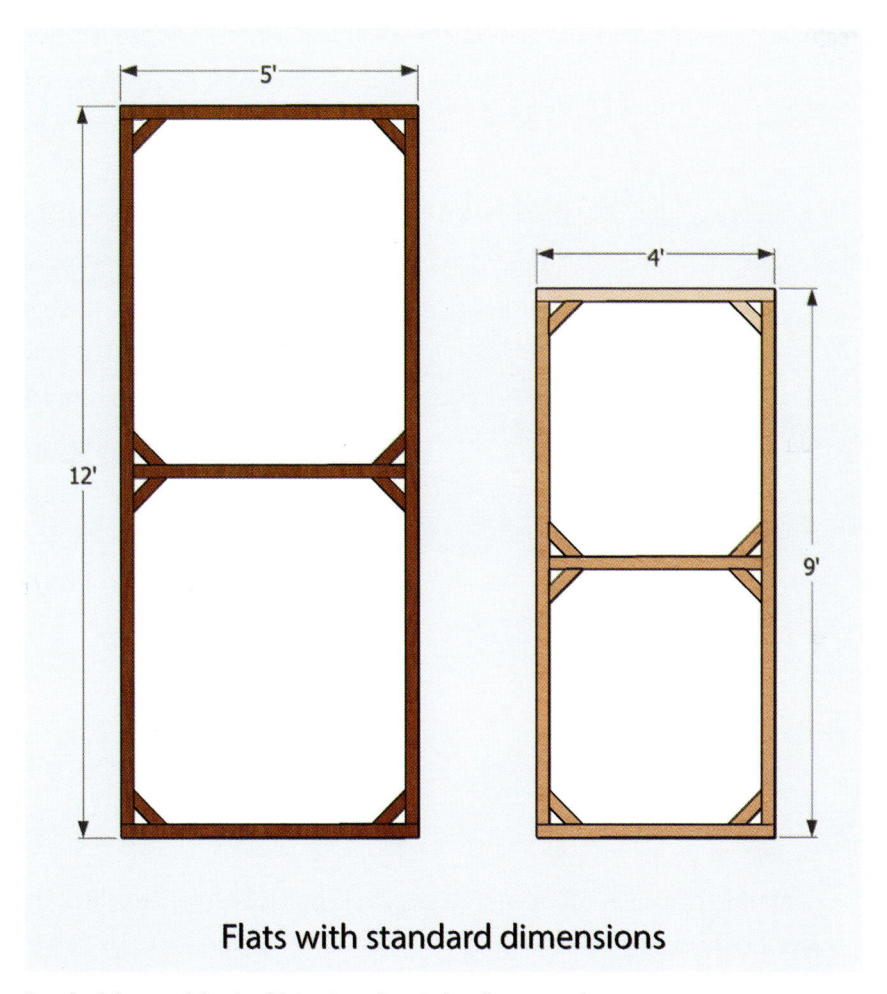

Standard flats used for the fabrication of vertical walls, etc. on the stage.

- The commonly used platforms for creating levels on the stage are usually prefabricated and are available on rent from any tent house in India. These platforms usually come with a standard size of 6 ft x 3 ft or 6 ft x 4 ft or 3 ft x 3 ft and 4 ft x 4 ft. The legs of these platforms are available separately and can be fixed with the platforms at the time of set constructions. The average size of these legs are 6 in, 1 ft, 1.5 ft, 2 ft, 2.5 ft, etc. A scenographer should keep these size

| SCENOGRAPHY

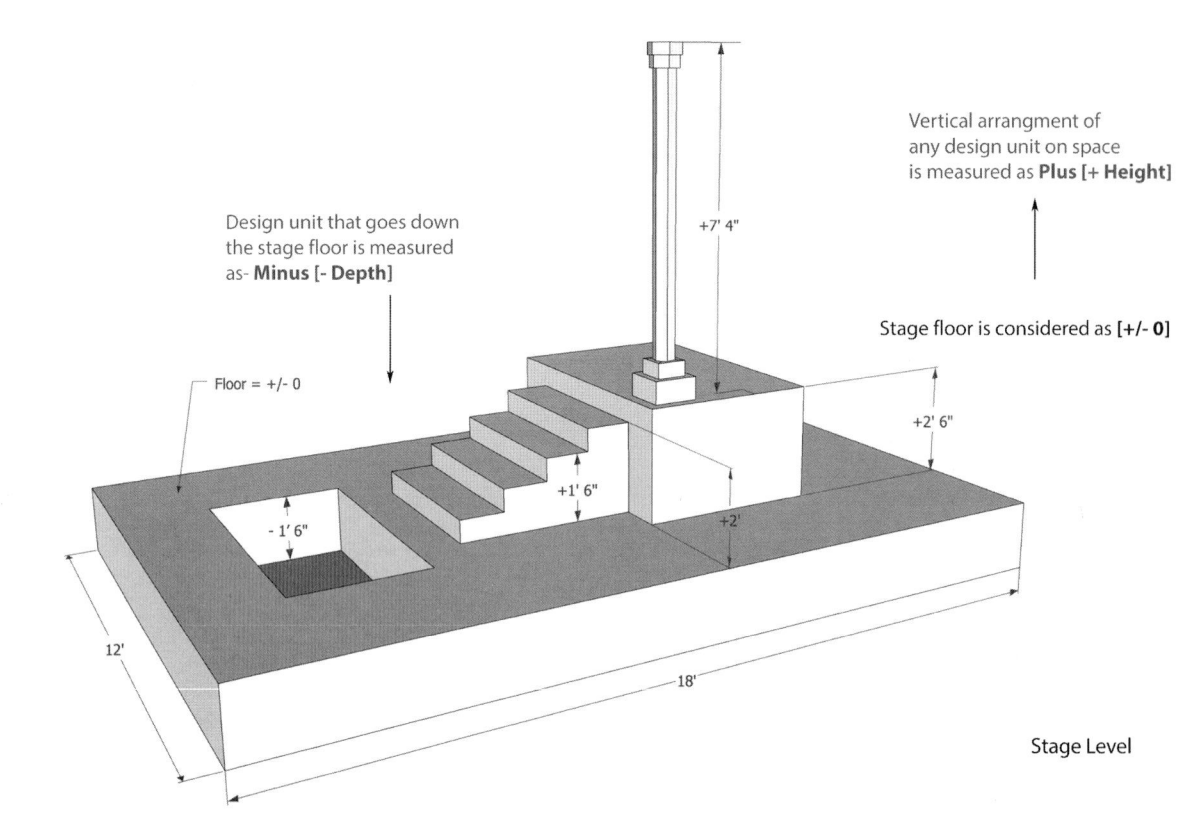

Technical drawing to demonstrate levels in Plus and Minus.

and dimensions in mind while designing the sets so as to reciprocate with these sizes. For creating the levels with a different size other than these, we have to fabricate new platforms which may involve a good amount of money, often unaffordable in Indian theatre scenario. Therefore, it is important to develop a design keeping these common measurements in mind.

- The size of a commonly available flat for making the set should be of 12 ft x 5 ft or 9 ft x 4 ft. so that it can be carried easily by one person during set fabrication.
- Anything that is raised above the stage floor is measured in 'Plus' (+) unit and that goes below the stage floor level is measured in

'Minus' (-) unit. For example, if the height of a pillar is 2 ft, it is to be mentioned as +2 ft and if there is a pit having 1 ft deep, it must be mentioned as -1 ft. The stage floor is considered as zero level which is to be marked as +/- 0 ft. The best example of 'Minus' (-) level is the 'trapdoor' of any theatre.

SET MODEL

This is a means of presenting the set design in a three-dimensional form. This presentational model is prepared with the help of all the drawings such as ground plan, front elevation and side elevation. The scale model is the accurate miniature version of the original set with proportion. The scenographers must follow the same scale unit which they use for the scaled drawings. The model carries each set units and the sceneries in proportion with the original sets so as to give a correct picture and feel of the design. It also provides an opportunity for the director and other members such as actors, stage manager, technical director, light and costume designers to understand the virtual space prior to the production. The scenographer can practically also verify the visual axis, sightline, scene changing and the impact of the set colours, etc. through the help of a model. Finally, the model helps the technical crew to execute the actual set on the floor with accuracy.

MODEL MAKING

A model can be constructed through various materials, such as, plywood, cardboard, mount board or straw board, etc. The model can also be made out of clay or Plaster of Paris. The base of the model should be strong enough to steadily hold the entire work on it. After preparing a proportionate base for the model, the ground plan of the set needs to be marked on it. Accordingly, the height is given to the plan to form a three-dimensional model.

List of model-making materials:

i. Plywood, cardboard or mounting board, etc.
ii. Scissors for cutting paper and fabric, etc.
iii. A heavy paper-cutter with retractable blade for cutting cardboard, mounting board, etc.
iv. A small cutter with narrow-size blade for delicate cutting.
v. A steel straight-edged scale to guide the blade while cutting the board or paper. Plastic or wooden scale should be avoided.
vi. Glue or adhesive to paste the cardboard and paper.
vii. A fine-toothed hacksaw blade for cutting plywood or any hard material.
viii. A few other materials like thermocol, cloths, gunny-cloths, canvas, wooden sticks, etc.
ix. ½ in, 1 in and 2 in flat brushes, few round brushes and poster colours of all shades are required for colouring the model.
x. A pair of hand gloves can be worn to save the hands from getting injured by the blades.

CONCLUSION

Designing a space for the performance is like a dream coming true for an aspiring scenographer. Sometimes the visuals start playing hide and seek with the visual artists while staring at an empty space constantly. This triggers at the imagination of the artist to envision the design idea. Till date no theory has been developed for pushing a visual artist to imagine the space for a play: it comes through impulse and is achieved through years of practice. It is the sensible and creative mind that helps sprouting of those ideas. Though Indian theatre as a whole has not fully exposed to this creative medium, but in the recent times many international scholars have turned their attentions towards the precious and ethnic

Three-dimensional model of the play *A Caucasian Chalk Circle*. Playwright: Bertolt Brecht. Design concept and model prepared by: Rajesh Singh under the supervision of Peter Cook at NSD 2005. Courtesy: NSD.

performance cultures of India. Therefore, new ideas and techniques are gradually creeping into the medium. Consequently, a considerable amount of experiments has been undertaken in the field of performance design and scenography in India following the West. But new experimentations in the area of scenography is required through an Indian perspective which have not been significantly explored yet.

This creative medium has been overlooked in India with a plea that scenography is a highly technical medium that involves a good amount

Set model of *Ashad Ka Ek Din*. Prepared by: Students of the Scenic Design Workshop-2019. Organised by: Jawahar Kala Kendra, Jaipur. Courtesy: Jawahar Kala Kendra and Ms Babita Madan.

of money which is unaffordable in Indian theatre practices. But this notion is completely false. The younger generation of practitioners must wake up to this highly creative and exciting subject with positive attitude. It is true that a significant number of Indian practitioners work under immense financial constraints. They work in many adverse conditions where payment to the artists is a daydream; most often the artists spend money from their own pockets to keep good theatre sustainable. Even in other parts of the globe, the scenario is not of much hope. Under these circumstances, we must explore an alternative scenography by identifying materials from our own grassroot theatres—folk, traditional and popular cultures. In India, scenography must be developed and explored through alternative ideas, challenging the privileged practices influenced by the West. Young Indian scenographers must be motivated for low-cost design and should be encouraged to develop projects collecting materials from our common ordinary life. This would lead to the exploration of an alternative but creative design for theatre, accessible to all the practitioners, parallel to the theatre design that grows with extravagant expenses, so that the future scenographers would be able to deal with both the conditions.

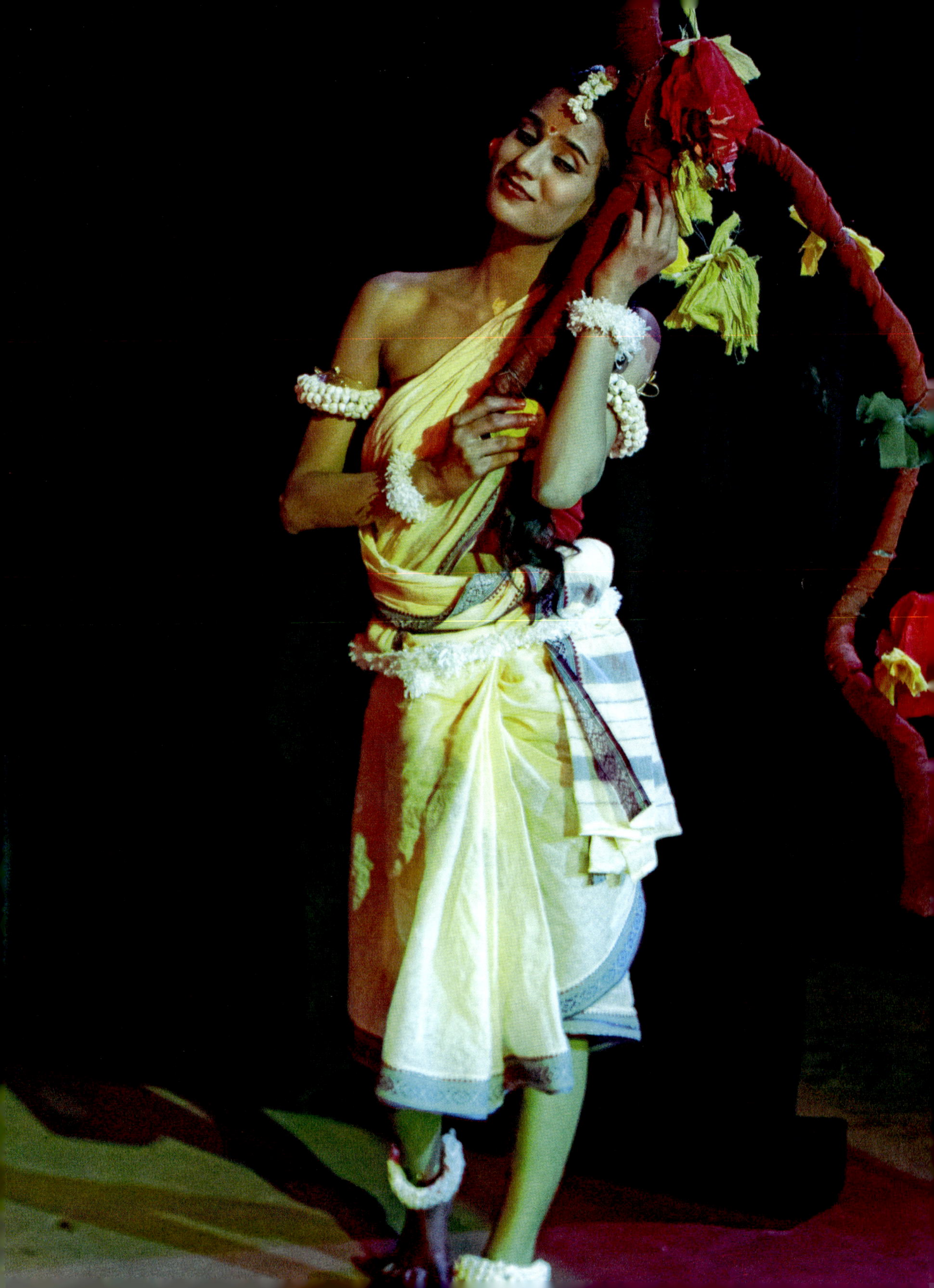

ELEMENTS OF DESIGN

9

NATURE'S ARTISANS

There is an omnipresence of intricate patterns in our natural surroundings. A small and tiny weaverbird knits its nest by weaving leaves and sticks evenly, following a line of pattern of every individual element. Similarly, honeybee collects nectar from the flowers and gather them in the honeycomb which is yet another architectural wonder of hexagonal wax cells. The spider weaves intricate webs with the help of its legs and fangs. The silkworm makes oval-shaped cocoon. The termites construct high-rising earthen dwellings. One cannot stop appreciating the natural artistry these little creatures are gifted with. These tiny artisans make their dwellings adaptable suiting their natural habitat and thus, replicate an intricate pattern of a bigger canvas in the creations of their own.

It is the basic instinct for creation that has always fascinated mankind throughout the ages. In the monolithic period, the primitive man lived in the soothing lap of nature inside the rocks and caves. They observed the natural mechanism of insects, birds and animals and gradually developed the skill to create. They understood nature's law and explored it for their benefit. And thus, the first seed of civilisation was sowed.

And once that was done, mankind became the master of the creations. They started building enormous and detailed architectural wonders, invented gigantic boats and ships and sailed to conquer the world. Even today, globally, artisans make bamboo or straw handicrafts; weave fabrics and cloths by intertwining the knots and knitting like a weaverbird's nest. The first instinct of an artisan lies in learning the natural pattern and imbibing it in their own work.

Over centuries humans have developed their mind from creating a simple knot to the magnificent design of palaces, bridges, ships and rockets; from the rock paintings and crude art forms to sophisticated artistry. The civilisation has already witnessed quite a few art revolutions like Naturalism, Realism, Impressionism, Surrealism, Cubism, Fauvism, Abstract expressionism and Radicalism, etc. It is through their hands that humans transform and transcribe their imaginations into reality. Their handicrafts, with all artistic exuberance, have shaped the visual wonders.

'These hand-crafted objects pulsate with the heartbeat of human creativity and move with the life-breath of human imagination'.[i] Humans became the master of skills and techniques that evolve through the understanding of the mystery of design. Artists train their eyes for perceiving the magnificent creations of the nature. This is a long and painstaking process that demands commitment, concentration and practice since no great art is born without pain.

THE PHENOMENA OF NATURE

Life is full of events. Celebrations, festivals, ceremonies and rituals make it colourful. Humans celebrate special occasions through many visual patterns that express feeling, of faith and happiness. Every individual has a sense of design, depending on their taste and temperament. However, irrespective of the individual sense of appreciating visuals, there is a common sense of understanding the medium of art whose sensibility is almost similar for every human being. This fundamental sensibility for art appreciation is burrowed into our creations which is also a reflection of nature on human subconscious.

Nature follows its own path in making this biosphere. Its ever-changing moods continue affecting human life significantly. These changes in the contours of natural world occur due to the interplay of various lines, colours and forms that create vivid expressions in different situations of life. The striking zigzag lines of lightning in a dark cloudy sky make one terrified, while the vast lush green valley revs up one's excitement of joy. An artist draws certain conclusions through their constant observation of these natural contours. Natural phenomena have motivated all forms of visual arts including painting, sculpture, scenography, costume, graphic design and photography.

Human beings observed the systematic order that constitute the natural world. These orders of nature are interpreted in the visual medium that form its vocabulary and become the language of art. In every creation of art and design, the physical presence of these natural phenomena are always tactile and felt by the senses. They are the syllables of art and design, captured through lines, colours, textures, shapes and forms, value, space, volume and dimensions, etc. Visual artists observe the natural phenomenon to realise the mystic interplay of these features that forms the splendours of art and design.

SECTION - I

THE MAGICAL LINES

Line is the most primitive medium of artistic expression. A close observation would reveal the rhythmic flow of lines in visible and invisible form that follow certain order and pattern in various conditions. This flow of line, tangible or intangible, is felt throughout. In art and design, the usage of lines acts as distinguishing guide between different forms, shapes and patterns. The American painter Marry Rathbun argues in a different way: 'Line is an abstraction; there are boundaries but no actual lines in nature. Objects merely come to an end and other objects begin, but the painter represents this fact by a line.'[ii] The formation of a line and its multifarious definition have fascinated mankind throughout the ages. The Greek mathematician Euclid (4th C. BCE) had defined line as a 'breadth-less length', which 'lies equally with respect to the points on itself'.[iii] Line comprises of 'single dimension'—the length that joins two distinct points. In an artistic creation, a line joins two definite points, therefore forming boundary and outline of a shape both physically and conceptually. In joining one point with the other, the artist adds a certain movement to the form, which is responsible for its visual expression. In the process of viewing that expression, a viewer passes through multiple emotional experiences that are realised through various movements of the lines.

The arrangement of lines in different ways can be traced in the ancient rock arts, spread over the world. The earliest pictorial images of animals and human beings, expressed through line drawings, are traced in the ancient cave paintings of France, Spain, Africa and India. These art expressions are created out of simple straight and curved lines, coloured with black charcoals, red ochre, etc. In most of the folk and tribal art forms, lines create wonder through its smart application—for example, Warli and Madhubani paintings. These tribal and folk creations formulate an interesting pattern in stirring Indian arts.

'Line' works as a metaphor in a dramatic composition which has numerous connotations in theatre. Here, they are expressed as bodyline, storyline, proscenium-arch-line, straight line, curve line, diagonal line, line

FACING PAGE: (above) Warli Paintings, Maharashtra; (below) Madhubani Painting, Bihar

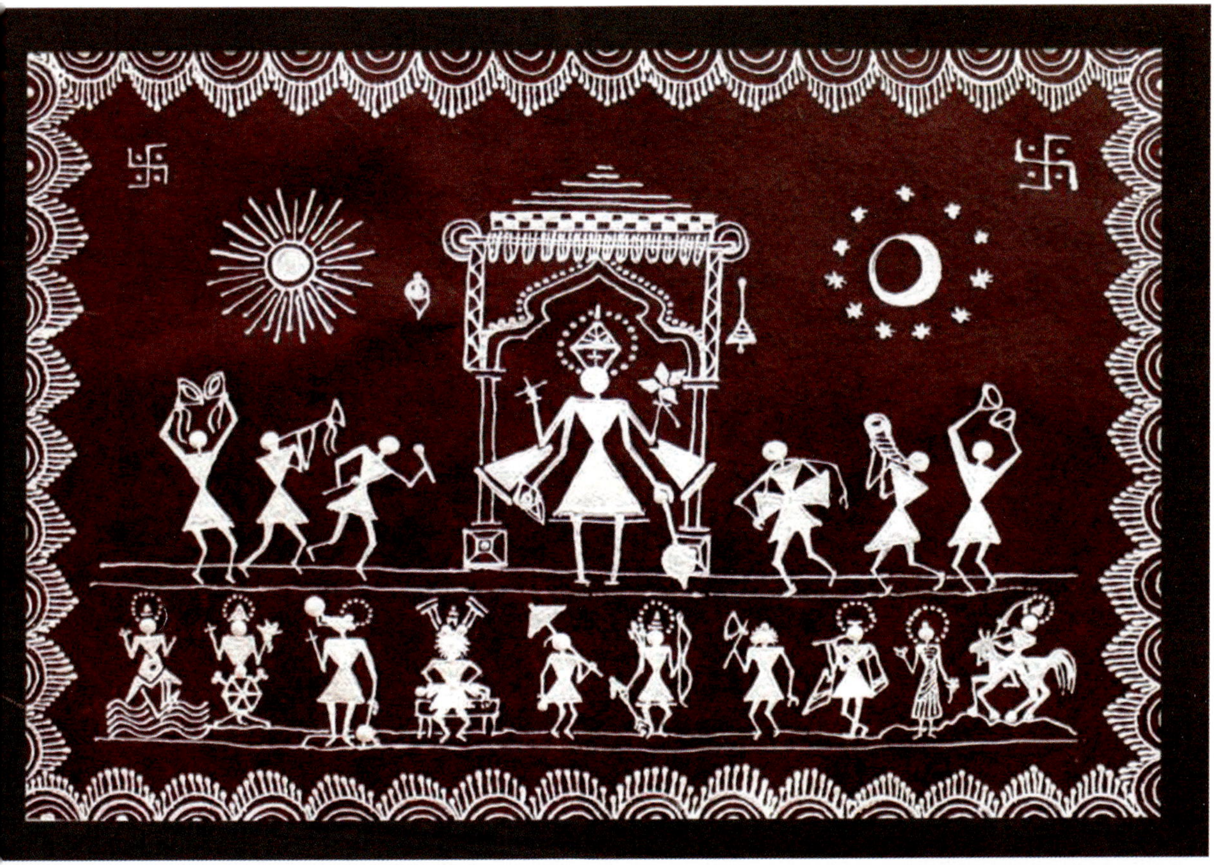

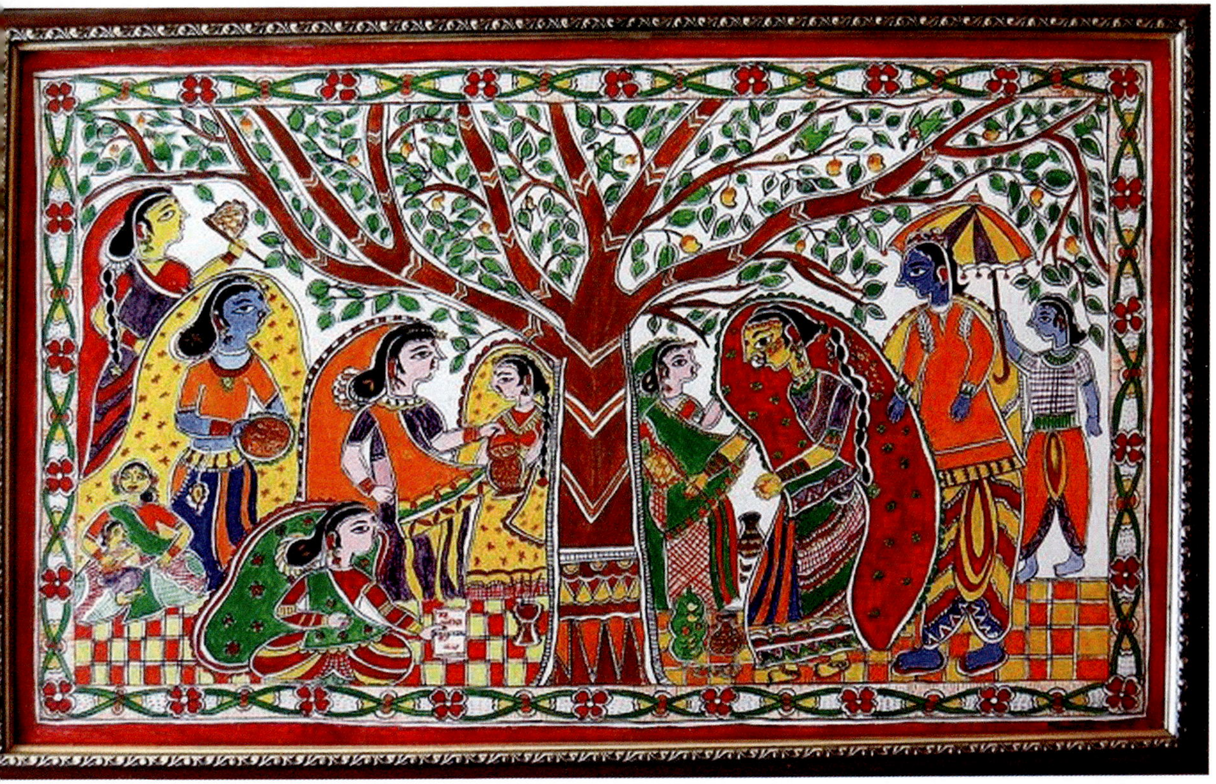

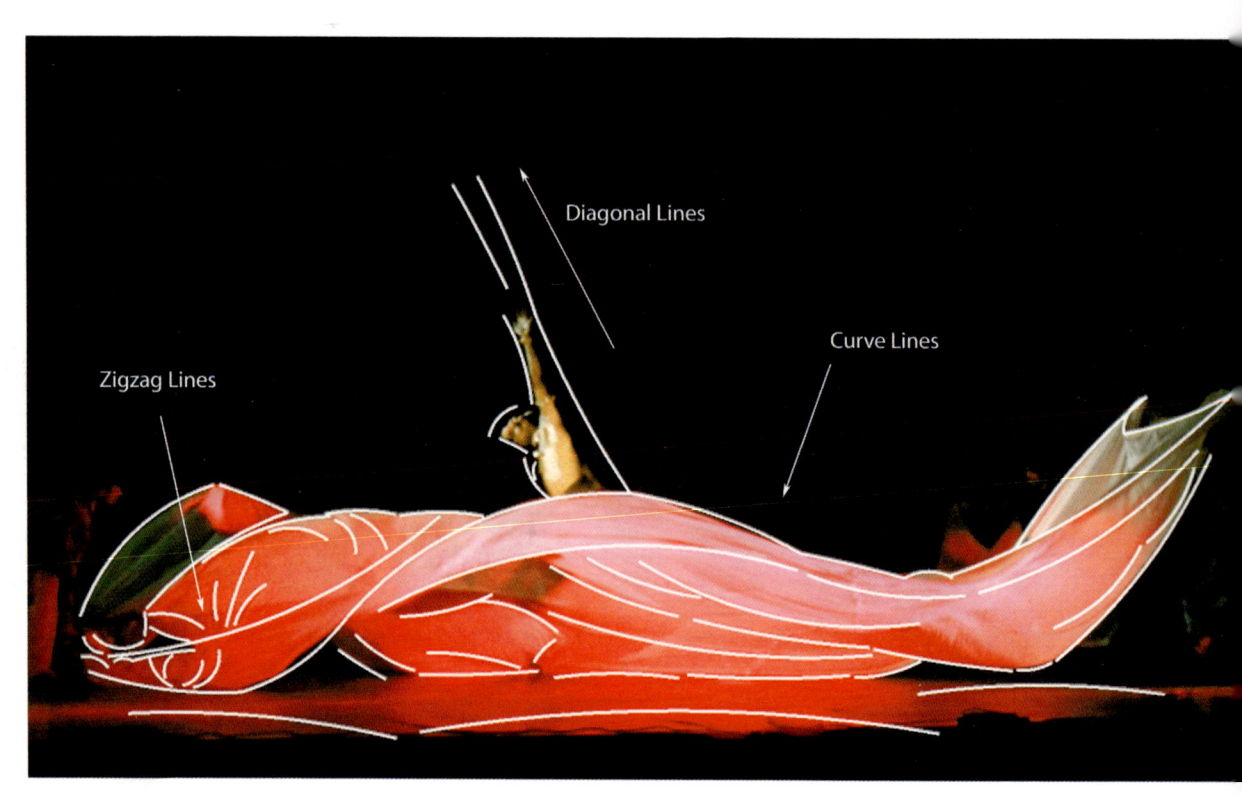

Demonstration of 'Movement of lines'. Still from the play *Matte Eklavya* (2013). Playwright: Kuldeep Kunal. Scenography and direction: Satyabrata Rout. Presented by: Adima, Kolar goldfield, Karnataka. Courtesy: Author's personal collection.

of action, visible line, invisible line, imaginary line, sightline, etc. Theatre performance always involves certain kinds of movements, either in physical or psychological form, that keep the audience engaged with the flow of the action. These movements, responsible for the dramatic development of the plot, are comprehended through the movement of lines whose miracle is felt through the interplay of actors, sets, costumes, makeup, props, masks, lights, etc. It is present within each action, conflict and tension during a performance. An actor, during a performance, creates various types of lines through the movements such as, straight, zigzag, diagonal, linear, nonlinear, etc., depending on the character. These lines, though not tangible, exist in the space along with the action, invisible yet playing a pivotal role in establishing moods and atmosphere, like nature's varied rhythms.

Line is the universal language of the art expressions and carries emotional graph of the visual arts. While wavy and curved lines provide comfort with pleasing effect, strong, broken and zigzag lines express annoyance and aggression, depending on their uses. A vibrant diagonal line, rough textural line or line created through a dry brush stroke, can speak universally without further explanations. One can sense the pain, agony and struggle for liberation in the works of Van Gogh, expressed through his rough, crude and wavy textural brush strokes. His passion, madness and struggle for new creations formed a whirlpool of movements through his dynamic brush strokes. (Example: *The Starry Nights*, *The Cyprus Tree* or the *Sunflower* series, etc.). Similarly, delicacy and beauty find extreme expressions in the classic works of Leonardo Da Vinci, Raphael and Michelangelo. The scenographers and directors across the world have also explored the potential of lines through their productions.

CLASSIFICATION OF LINES

Broadly, lines can be classified as straight and curved. Combination of these lines gives rise to wavy, fuzzy and zigzag patterns. Horizontal, vertical, diagonal or curvilinear movements of lines generate emotions, therefore creating diverse moods. Even a singular gesture of a simple line becomes responsible for an emotional expression that can be identified through its performance in creating the art. The art critic and author, Alan Pipes observes: 'A single straight line is one of the most abstract of elements, but it is capable of conveying all kinds of moods and emotions—anger, calm, fear, grace, excitement—when its attributes of size, shape, proportion, direction and density are varied.'[iv]

Accordingly, while a straight line is capable of expressing a sense of confidence, curved lines are lyrical and poetic in nature. While, a straight line pleads for affirmation, a curved line is however cannier, blending beauty with aesthetics. While the pattern of curvilinear lines is found in Indian dance, Indian miniature paintings and ancient temple architecture, the ancient Western arts and architecture are expressed through straight and linear movements of lines. Different attributions of lines send different messages to the human brain.

Line drawing, demonstrating 'horizontal lines'.

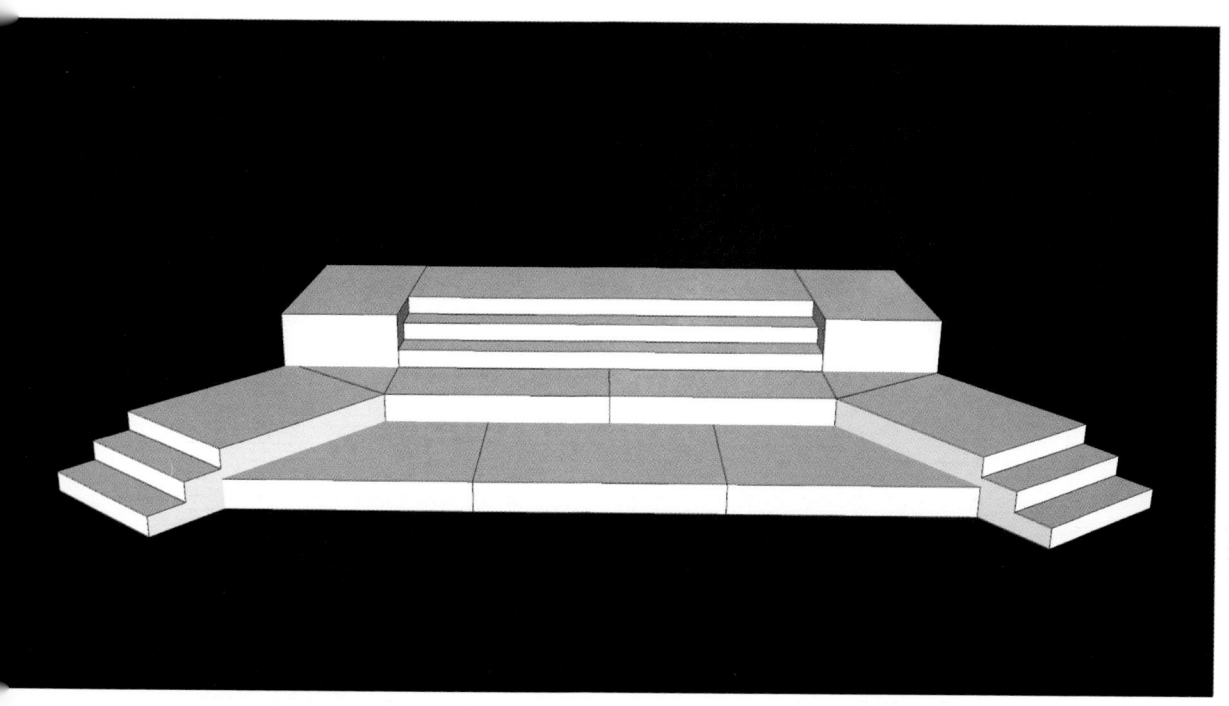

Demonstration of horizontal line on making the stage floor; with the help of platforms and steps.

HORIZONTAL LINE

Horizontal line always remains parallel to the ground and moves horizontally. It expresses the feeling of peace, tranquillity, satisfaction, vastness, expansion, repose, etc. Horizontal line exists in the outline of natural landscapes. In theatre, it felt its presence in the arrangement of levels, steps, platforms, and all those stay parallel to the stage floor. Psychologically, horizontal line reduces the height. We all must be aware of the works of Adolphe Appia, the noted scenographer of 20th century. The presence of horizontal lines makes his visuals poetic. The magnificent immensity of the atmosphere in his design becomes possible due to the interplay of horizontal lines with the vertical arrangements of pillars, walls and arches. The rhythmic horizontal lines create discipline and order in his brilliant designs.

Adolphe Appia's design for *Orpheus Hellerau* in 1913. Appia made a series of drawings as a part of Eurythmics, a concept developed by Jaques Dalcroze. Courtesy: Wikimedia Commons.

VERTICAL LINE

This line in design heightens the situation and denotes potential for an action. It exists in all the objects that move upward from the ground such as, pillars, towers, skyscrapers, trees, forts, etc. Vertical line stands for ego, vanity, royalty, status and loneliness. One can sense its psychological manifestations in the plays like *Oedipus Rex*, *Macbeth*, *Tughlaq*, *Hamlet*, etc. The scenographers, for such plays, create spaces to position the protagonists on an elevated plane compared to other characters of the play. This is to project their superiority as a demand of the dramatic action. As

Line drawing, demonstrating 'vertical lines'.

a usual phenomenon, at the end of these plays, falling of the lead character from the raised heights gives rise to dramatic tension, thus leading to the tragedy. Vertical line has tremendous contribution in theatre. It has a practical aspect too. Composing the main characters on a higher level drags immediate attention of the viewers towards them, thus sufficing vertical symbols—ego, status, etc. We have already discussed about the magnificent presentation of *Tughlaq*, directed by Ebrahim Alkazi for the National School of Drama Repertory Company in 1974. Alkazi had created an atmosphere of 14th-century Delhi Sultanate by manipulating the magnificent ruins of the Old Fort in Delhi. To design this play at the ruins of the Old Fort, he gave height to the stage by engaging multiple levels of platforms against the existing gigantic arches of the fort. The horizontal lines, formed by the arrangements of the steps and levels against the vertical and glorious arches, created a unique composition of a periodical text. In this particular space-design, the scenographer had purposefully balanced those horizontal lines against the vertical stage units to achieve a balanced visual composition. The potential of vertical lines in a design can be well explored in periodical plays or plays with characters that have psychological values.

DIAGONAL LINE

This is the most dramatic line, found in nature as well as in the domain of art and design. This line seems to be in constant movement, and thus always remains active. It brings force, energy, excitement and dynamism to the characters as well as to the visual design of a play. It also highlights the emotional graph of the conflict and tension. Diagonal line has the ability

Line drawing, demonstrating 'diagonal lines'.

A scene from the play *Tughlaq* (1974). Directed by: E. Alkazi. Note: An existing space at the famous Old Fort, Delhi, was explored for this play. Courtesy: *The Hindu*.

to create suspense and bring tension into the situation, thus generating interest and curiosity of the viewers.

Two diagonal forces, physical or conceptual, colliding each other, heighten the energy graph of the performance, which gets transformed into a dramatic tension. For example, the transposition of day and night in

Scene from the play *Baji*. Playwright: Rameshwar Prem. Scenography and direction: Satyabrata Rout. The play was prepared by the student participants of NSD workshop at Bhopal, 1998. Courtesy: Author's personal collection.

the play *Nagamandala* and the encounter of mind and body in *Hayavadana* create dramatic tension in the play. A scenographer, through a creative application of diagonal lines, can enhance the tension of these plays and also interpret the space accordingly. While designing and directing Rameswar Prem's *Baji* (1997), a play based on Indian freedom struggle and martyrdom, I attempted to establish the impact of revolution through the application of many diagonal forces, which I developed through the actors' physicality, set and hand props and through diagonal lighting effects. The visual compositions in this play narrates the juvenile spirit of Indian youths who fought against the mighty British imperialism during the nationalist movement.

We can also feel the impact of lines that create tension in the visual compositions of the play *Tumhara Vincent*. In one visual composition, vertical canvas frames were broken into scattered diagonal compositions to develop high tension and conflict within the painter and the scene. The scene depicts a raged Vincent tries to throw Christine's (a street woman) new-born baby out of these frames after a furious quarrel with her. The sudden meltdown of the compositions from their vertical arrangements to the diagonal ones, brings excitement among the audience, thus boosting up the dramatic tension of the incident.

ZIGZAG LINE

These lines form irregular movements. They are used to create a planned disorder in the compositions. The occurrence of zigzag lines can be felt in nature in situations like earthquake, tornado or cyclone, that shatter everything into ground. To establish a composition of anger, madness, indecisiveness and violence, etc. this line can be taken into consideration. While creating a similar atmosphere for a play, the scenographer can creatively use these lines for the visuals. The play *Andha Yug* can be a good example of exploring zigzag lines in its design. The effect of devastation,

Line drawing, demonstrating 'zigzag lines'.

ELEMENTS OF DESIGN | 395

Still from the play *Andha Yug* (1984). Design and direction: Ratan Thiyam. Presented by: Chorus Repertory Theatre, Imphal. Courtesy: Chorus Repertory.

horror of war and madness can be well established through the application of zigzag lines in this play. Ratan Thiyam's 1984 production of *Andha Yug* for Chorus Repertory Theatre, Imphal, justifies the above statement where the protagonist, Ashwathama, tries to kill everyone out of rage and madness.

CURVED LINE
Curved line is lyrical, poetic and sensuous by its nature. Sometimes curved line is also associated with mischief and cunningness; for example, the

← Curve pattern

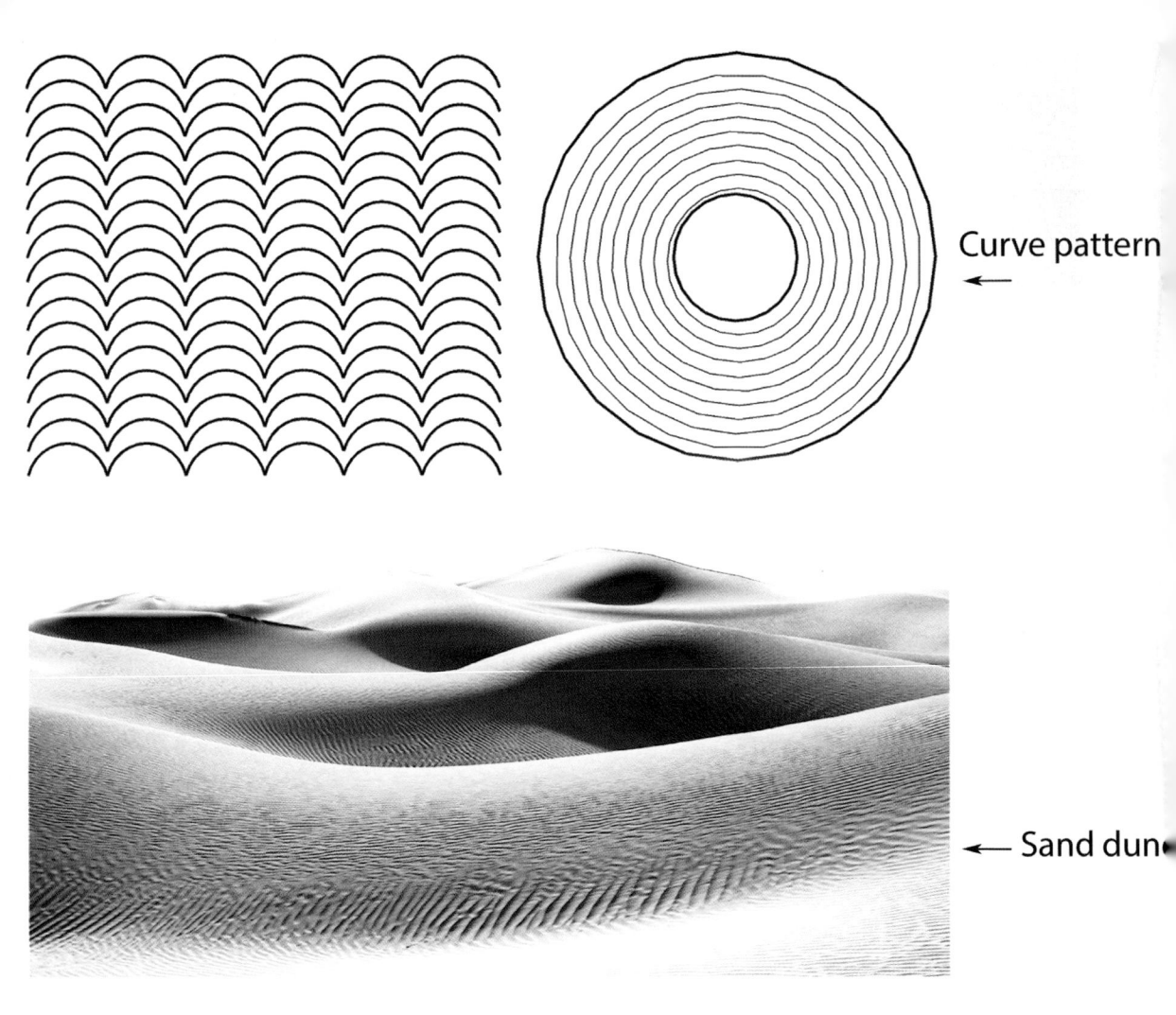

← Sand dune

usage in the presentation of the characters of Krishna and Shakuni in the *Mahabharata*. Curved lines can be traced easily in Indian classical arts, such as, theatre, dance or miniature paintings. Often the playwright also weaves the plot through various curved lines to create complexity and humour into the situation; first creating a mesh out of the interplay of many curves and then realigning them in order, for example Shakespeare's *A Midsummer Night's Dream*. Indian classical plays explore curve lines in its writing structure to establish aesthetics and beauty into the presentation, for example *Abhijnanasakuntalam*, *Mrcchakatika*, etc. A photograph from

Still from the play *More Naina Rang Chadhe* (2009). Presented by: Bharatendu Natya Academy, Lukhnow. Courtesy: Author's personal collection.

the play *More Naina Rang Chadhe*, an adaptation of *A Midsummer Night's Dream*, is displayed here to demonstrate the application of curve lines in to the production design.

APPLICATION OF LINES IN DESIGN

A play consists of a series of dramatic sequences, interweaving through different layers within the plot. This intrinsic arrangements of the story line always hold interest of the viewers. A scenographer, being the visual writer of the performance, structures the design by interlacing different lines and shapes to create the visual compositions to develop an interesting interaction with the spectators. For an evocative design, all kinds of lines have their roles to play. In this role-playing some lines become obligatory and some remain compensetory.

Lines are the elementary units for any of the visual art forms. However, these should not counteract with the dramatic actions; rather enhance those actions through their potential strengths. These lines interact with the context and help project the visual compositions with meaningful interpretations.

SECTION - II

WONDERS OF THE COLOURS

Colours: A Way of Life

Colours psychologically balance our mental order and influence our day-to-day activities. We constantly perceive colours from our environs and are connected with its vibrations. Our natural world is surrounded by the electromagnetic waves, and colour is a part of that wave. When sunlight falls upon any object, it absorbs rest of the colours by reflecting a particular hue according to its physical property. When these light rays are reflected in our eyes, we perceive those in the form of colours, as reflected from that particular object.

We perceive colours in nature as red, blue, green or yellow, etc. A minute observation reveals that a single colour has numerous shades. One may be more or less dark or bright than the other one. There may be hundreds of green shades that differ from one another; while red colour has different hues, so do yellow, blue and orange have. Green colours have different shades like grass-green, sea-green, olive-green, sap-green, almond-green, parrot-green, and the list continues, so as red, blue and yellow. These shades are called 'colour hues' or 'colour bands'. They are like the musical notes that form a visual composition. Often, we perceive all the colours in

Illustrative diagram of chromatic colours.

one composition and sometimes it could be a single colour hue. The very moment we open our eyes, we perceive the world through colours and that is continued eternally. The perception of colours has entered into our nerves and become our way of life. Thus, colour becomes an integral part of our livelihood.

Chromatic Colours

Chromatic colours are more than one colour in a single composition with varied degrees and intensity. Some colours transmit high energy while others disperse low, depending on their scientific properties. Psychologically, we may have liking and disliking for a certain colour or colours which again depend on our way of living.

Left: Illustrative diagram of monochromatic colours
Right: Illustrative diagram of achromatic colours

Monochromatic Colours

Monochromatic colours comprise of the hues of a single colour. These colours often seem monotonous, as there is no variation of colour shades in it. But it can be creatively used in art and design that can change its connotation to an interesting pattern. The dynamism in this composition is subtle and delicate due to the absence of vibrant colours with contrast. But a visual artist can create diversity within this colour composition and can break the monotony of design.

Achromatic Colours

Achromatic colours are a band of hues without any saturation, such as, black and white. Black is the total absence of colours whereas white is formed by the prismatic confluence of all the colours. A mixture of white and black creates a number of grey shades. These grey shades though stimulate our vision to certain extent, no physical stimulus is generated in black colour since it absorbs all the colour spectrums from the nature and reflects nothing. Similarly, white comprises of all the hues of nature. Therefore scientifically, black and white are not considered as colours. But this concept does not apply to art and design. In the world of art and design, often black is considered as more reactive than white. Symbolically, black stands for protest and negativity and white for positivity and peace. However, these two colours are important for visual artists. They also have strong symbolic assertion in society and define the meanings in different cultures.

The Colour of the Stage
Black is a preferred colour for theatre. A small and intimate theatre is often called the 'black box'. The wings, borders, curtains are generally kept black. Sometimes, even the walls, ceilings, doors and windows of a theatre are painted black. This is due to the non-reflective nature of black and it absorbs lights. Therefore, on stage, a prop or a set unit that is painted black, allows the performers to remain in focus by making itself passive. On the contrary, white reflects light and creates an illusion of depth. White cyclorama at the back of the stage is used to create an effect of outdoor. White reflects all the colours in their true forms without any distortion.

Nature produces two distinctive categories of colours—one through lights and another through pigments. They are called 'additive' and 'subtractive' colours. They are of different characters in perception and behaviours.

Additive Colours
This is referred to the colours created through lights. They are perceived through sunrays and other natural and artificial sources. Red, green and blue (R-G-B) are the primary colours in this category. All the other visible

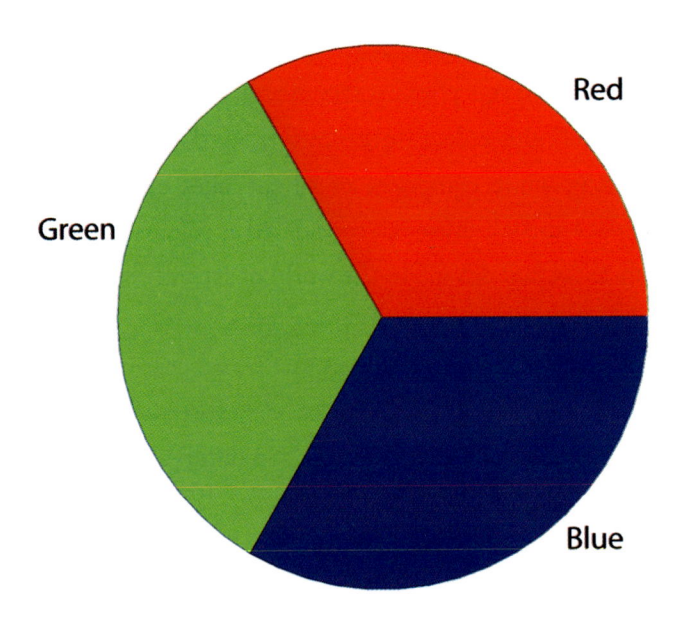

Illustrative diagram of additive colours.

colours of the light are the combination of these three primary colours. For example, a ray of red when mixed with blue, produces magenta colour in lights. Similarly, when blue and green lights are mixed together, they produce cyan colour. Yellow is created by the combination of green with red light rays. When all these colours are mixed together, they give rise to white. We can dissociate the white rays and separate them into various colours and create the effect of rainbow—*V...I...B...G...Y...O...R*— Violet, Indigo, Blue, Green, Yellow, Orange and Red through a prism. All the colours in our solar system are the combination of these seven colour hues. We follow this colour scheme in lighting design where RGB colour scheme is used.

Subtractive Colours
When a white incident ray of light falls upon an object, all its colours are absorbed by that object except its true colour, which is transmitted

to our eyes through the reflected rays. Then only we perceive that object in its colours. Since all the colour hues of white light are dissociated and subtracted by that object except its original one, it is termed as subtractive colours. These colours exist in nature in the form of dye, paint, ink, natural colorants or pigments, etc. If we mix all the subtractive colours it would turn black. The physical properties of these colours are different from the additive colours in many ways. These colours can be touched, felt and used for all our mundane purposes. The primary colours in the subtractive colour scheme are red, yellow and blue (R-Y-B). These are pure forms of colours from which another subtraction is not possible anymore. The rest of the colours in the world are obtained by adding two primary colours with each other proportionately. The set of colours achieved through this addition are categorised in two distinct sections such as, 'secondary' and 'tertiary' colours. While the secondary colours are achieved by mixing two primary colours of equal quantity, tertiary colours are created by adding one primary colour with its nearby secondary colour equally. Colours such as, orange, green and violet are the secondary colours and yellow-green, blue-green, blue-violet, red-violet, red-orange and yellow-orange fall under the

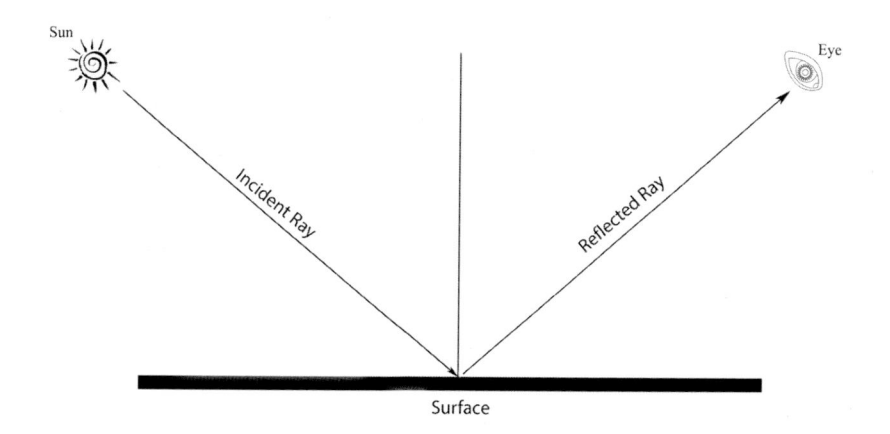

Illustrative drawing of 'reflection of light rays'

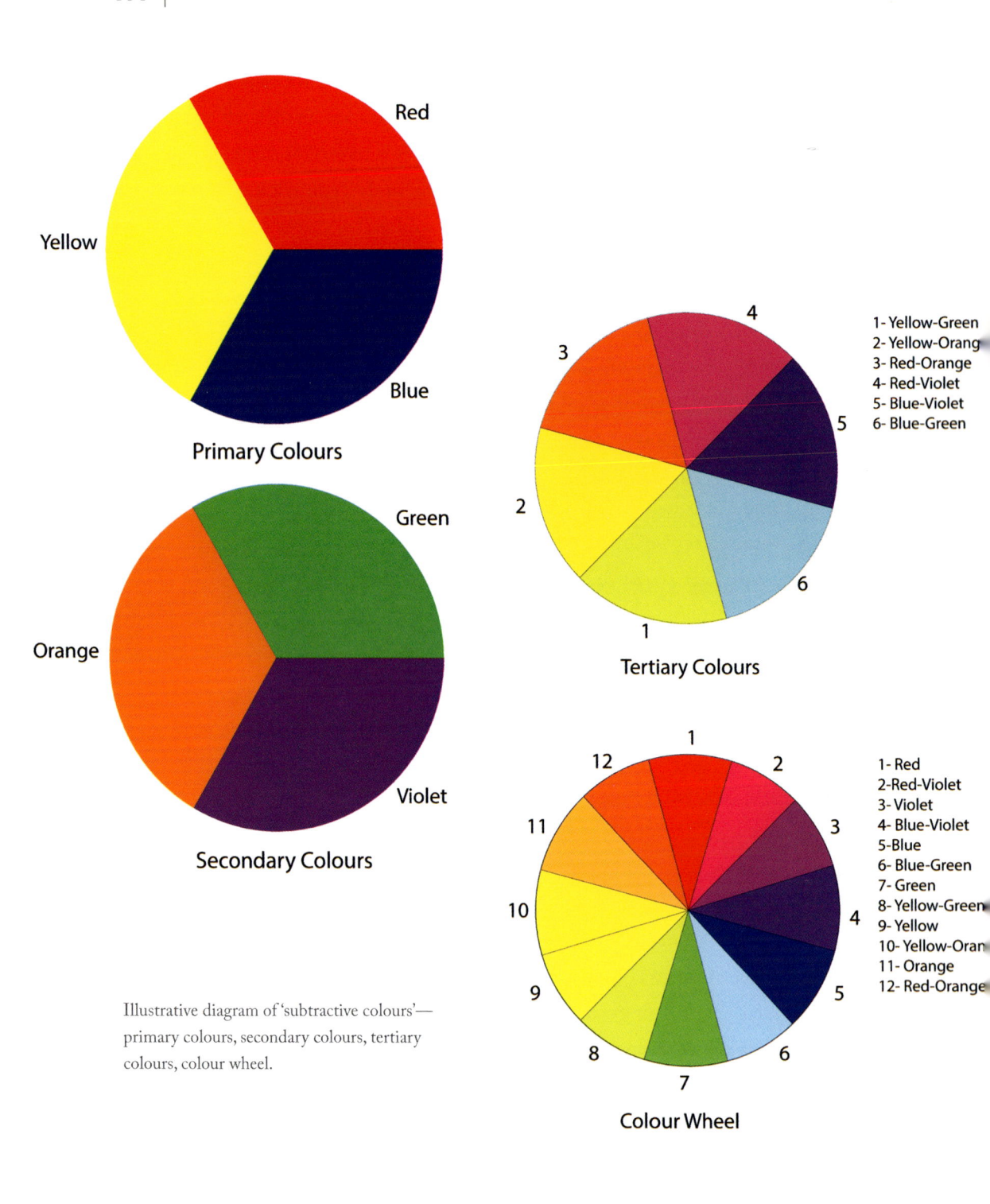

Illustrative diagram of 'subtractive colours'—primary colours, secondary colours, tertiary colours, colour wheel.

category of tertiary colour scheme. In all we have only 12 colours—three primary, three secondary and six tertiary colours. The rest of the perceived colours in the nature are the tints and shades of these 12 colours, and they are countless in numbers.

Colour Divisions

Colours are like characters of a play. While some colours keep close relationships with other colours, a few are in a bitter relationship with each other. Certain colours help boosting up other hues by remaining passive, while many drop others' identity by dominating them. A few particular colours generate higher energy compared to others that produce relatively lower energy, thus making them a little dull and gloomy. We can understand the colour energy by drawing a line in the middle of a colour wheel, intersecting yellow and violet that would divide the circle in two equal halves. Part A, consisting of the red and the yellow hues, generates more intensity compared to Part B, comprising the hues of blue. These are called warm and cool colours respectively, decided by their energy.

Warm Colours

These colour hues generate high energy, thus producing more intensity. They are brighter and warmer in nature, thus capturing viewers' attention without delay. These hues dominate the world of colours because of their high intensity, brightness and energy. While preparing a colour scheme by using both warm and cool colours for the visual design in theatre set, costume and props, etc., the scenographers take extra care to avoid domination of warm colour over the cools. Application of large quantity of warm colours in a single composition would make other colours passive, thus resulting in a disproportionate composition. On the contrary, a small quantity of warm colours can easily balance a larger quantity of cool colours such as blue, violet and green, etc. Creative and imaginative

Warm Colours

Red-Violet
Red
Red-Orange
Orange
Yellow-Orange
Yellow

Violet
Blue-Violet
Blue
Blue-Green
Green
Yellow-Green

Cool Colours

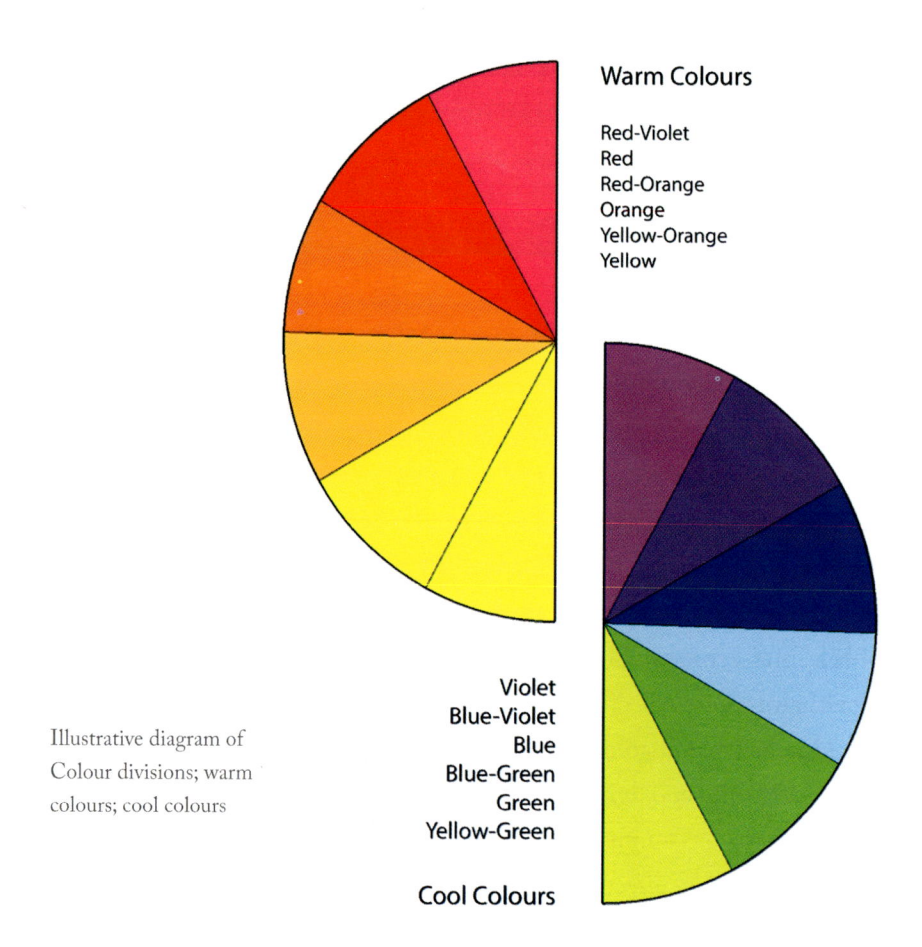

Illustrative diagram of Colour divisions; warm colours; cool colours

application of warm colours against cool colours often create spectacular wonders. For example, a girl wearing a blue or violet dress with a red scarf round her neck or brilliant blooming reddish orange flowers with lots of leaves around, would catch immediate attention of the viewers. The morning and evening hue can magnetise our eyes because of their brilliant and majestic combination of warm reddish orange with a vast cool background of blue sky.

An aesthetic exploration of the beauty and majesty of warm colours brings energy and vigour into the visual compositions of the performance. In most of the Ratan Thiyam's productions, we can observe the magnificent, creative application of warm colours, particularly red and orange, purposefully dominate the dramatic compositions. With the dominating power of these warm colours, in Thiyam's productions, they remain balanced with the other colour schemes which create an aestheticism in his productions.

Cool Colours
These colour hues are cool and passive in nature and radiate low intensity. They prefer to remain in the background to serve as a complementary support to the warm colours. The major cool colours are blue and so are its components, such as, violet, blue-violet, blue-green, green and yellow-green. The amalgamation of these colours provides soothing effects to the viewers' eyes. In theatre, a cyclorama with blue colours create illusion of depth and dimension, generating pleasing effects on stage. Combination of blue and green would create an atmosphere of exterior locale such as forest, garden, etc.

Blue and green colours can be used in colouring the sets, props and also in costumes and light design as a complementary support to the warm colours used in costumes and makeup. Tints of magenta and blue lights can create magical effects on stage.

Colour Compositions
Combination of multiple colours in visual compositions can add to the interpretation of design in theatre. It is like a piece of music where each shade of colours represents a singular musical note. Placing one grade of colour against other creates a visual composition in which one hue exists in relationship with the others. Similarly, every visual artist has their own colour schemes that dominate their compositions. Some artists use both the grades of warm and cool colours—placing one against the others, while a few work on singular-colour scheme. As a whole, every artist uses more than one colour shade in their creation. Before planning a colour scheme for

theatre design, the scenographer must develop a systematic understanding for various colour shades, their properties, nature, behaviour, psychology and inter-relationships in order to bring out the best in them. There are certain grades of colours that look different when placed against other shades. Many colours look brighter when placed against certain categories of colours, while others look dull.

The visual artists must understand the nuances of colour psychology before proceeding to apply them in their compositions. Watching a colour-wheel through various shades is a creative journey for an artist. Though all the colour shades belong to a 'three-colour-family' (red, blue and yellow), their psychological behaviour is different from one another. While some colour hues of two different families share common characteristics, others show rigidity and stand out independently. For example, 'yellow-green' belongs to the family of yellow and blue, but this shade is always nearer to yellow than to blue. Similarly, red-orange or vermillion is the combination of red and orange but its inclination for red is astonishing. However, artists are always free to create their own composition by choosing different colour shades depending on the subjective interpretation of that composition. Let us understand some common natural colour compositions and try to imply them into our creative medium. Colour compositions are otherwise known as colour harmony.

Analogous Colours
Analogous colours are three or more hues of colours located adjacent to each other in a colour wheel. They generate soothing effect in compositions and provide harmonious colour journey without any jolt because of their smooth movement. These shades share almost equal scientific and psychological property for which they behave similarly. Though this kind of colour combination seems closure to monochromatic colour-scheme, somehow it is different and more active. Since monochromatic colours

are the shades and tints of a single colour, analogous colours are the combination of two nearby colour family. They are:

i. yellow-orange, orange, red-orange
ii. red-violet, violet, blue-violet
iii. blue-green, green, yellow-green

Complementary Colours

This colour combination is created when two opposite colours of the colour wheel come together. They intrinsically produce vibrant colour effects and radiate high energy due to their contrasting characteristics. Their physical properties are also very different from each other. Therefore, they produce almost equal impact when used in equal quantity, thus keeping their individual identities intact to the bare eyes. Two complementary colours often balance each other and appear brighter when placed side by side. They are the combination of (i) red and green, (ii) yellow and violet (iii) blue and orange and so on. Two complementary colours are mixed to produce dark grey tones—red mixed with green produces warm brown, yellow mixed with violet produces warm grey, blue and orange produce a cool brown. When all of them are mixed together they generate black.

These colours, complimenting each other, thus miraculously balance the nature. From the colourful gardens to the dreaded deserts or from the golden morning hue to the ink-black night, these colours harmoniously complement each other to portray nature's varied moods. Even, a small red rose is distinguished amongst others because of the surrounded green leaves that work as contrast. This composition of nature provides a harmonious balance to the red rose and makes it stand out against green. Similarly, yellow is projected against violet, orange against blue, etc. The rays of the setting sun turn into warm amber against the cool blue sky, complementing each other in creating a miraculous effect during the sunset.

Split-complementary Colours

Split-complementary is another group of colours where instead of two, a total number of three hues of colours are used. But the only condition in this composition is that out of all the three colours one must be a primary colour—either red, blue or yellow. The rest of the two colours are the adjacent colours of the complementary one. With the help of these two hues the primary one forms an excellent colour combination. In situations, where complementary colour looks extremely contrasting to the other one, split-complementary can be a better replacement. This colour combination is extensively used in costume and property design. When multiple colours are applied to a single costume or to a particular prop, split-complementary forms a better choice. A designer can create homogeneous colour composition for design by applying this split-complementary composition. A few examples of this scheme are: (i) red, blue-green and yellow-green, (ii) blue, yellow-orange and red-orange, (iii) yellow, red-violet and blue-violet. Nature is full of this colour scheme. It spreads its hues abundantly in all the flora and fauna. Nothing is deprived of nature's colour scheme. All it needs is a pair of sharp eyes to realise the nature's gift for humanity.

Triadic Colours

Triadic colours are the unit of three equidistant colours of the colour-wheel, forming a pinnacle of equilateral triangle. These colours, being an exact contrast to each other, produce higher energy and hence appear colourful, balanced and harmonious. Some of the triadic colours are: (i) yellow, blue and red, (ii) yellow-green, blue-violet and red-orange, (iii) green, violet and orange, (iv) blue-green, yellow-orange and red-violet, etc. These colour compositions are a guide for the selection of colours in art and design. However, they are the basics to help in widening the imagination. There are thousands of colour combinations in nature

ELEMENTS OF DESIGN | 411

Analogous Colours

A.

B.

C.

A. yellow-orange, orange, red-orange
B. red-violet, violet, blue-violet
C. blue-green, green, yellow-green

Complementary Colours

A.

B.

C.

A. red and green,
B. yellow and violet
C. blue and orange

Illustrative diagram of colour compositions—Analogous colour scheme; Complementary colour scheme; Split-complementary colour scheme; Triadic colour scheme.

Split-Complementary Colours

A. red, blue-green yellow-green

B. blue, yellow-orange red-orange

C. yellow, red-violet blue-violet

Triadic Colours

A. yellow, blue, red

B. yellow-green, blue-violet, red-orange

C. green, violet, orange

D) blue-green, yellow-orange, red-violet

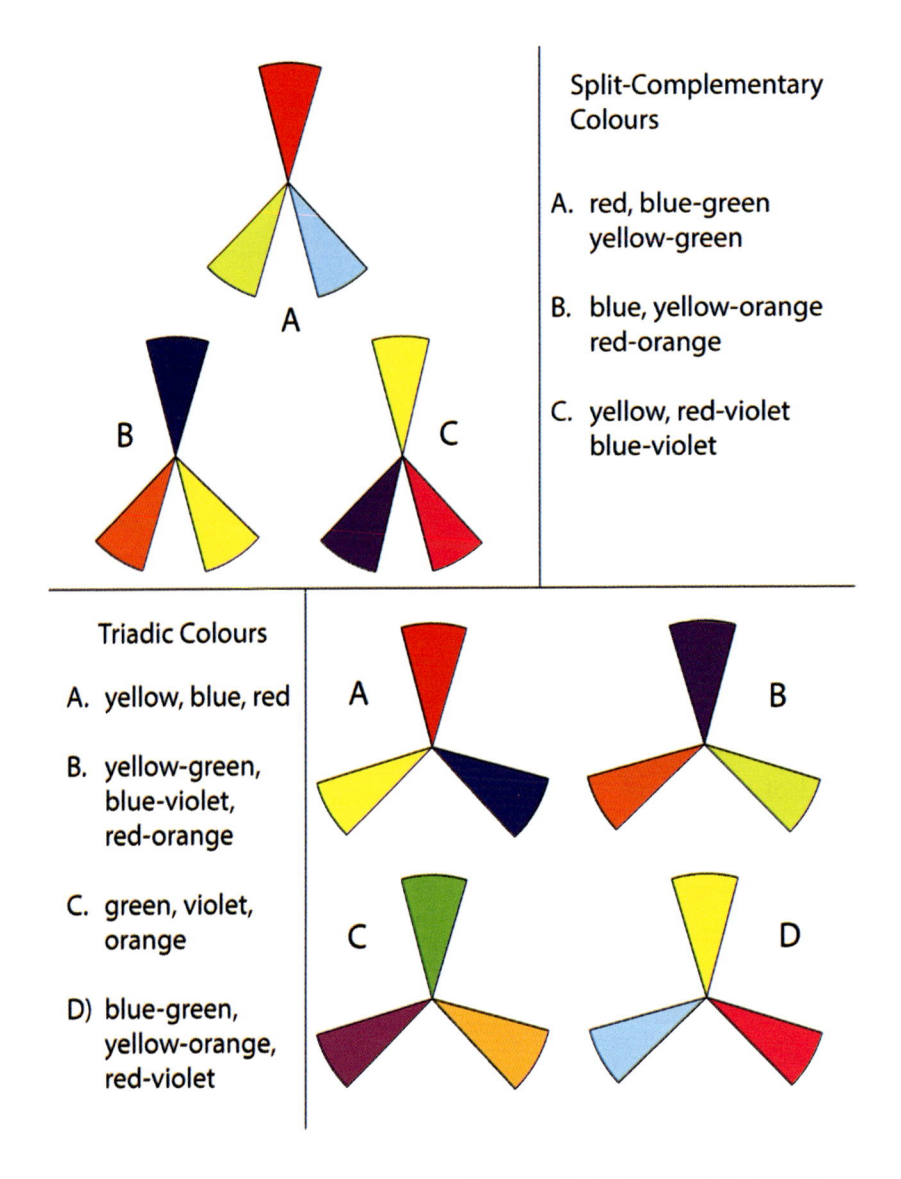

which appear different with the gradation of shades and lights. These natural compositions coexist to contribute to nature's equilibrium. A scenographer, being a creative visual artist, must develop an intense and intimate relationship with the nature to realise its mystery and to refine their colour sensibility.

Tints and Shades

These are the common terms applied to colour scheme. We all know that colour has upward and downward journey. In the process of its upward journey, it moves towards white and in backward journey, it moves towards black. With white it becomes lighter, which we call 'tint', and with black it produces 'shades'; both are of the same colour hue.

Colour Psychology

Every individual has a personal liking and disliking for certain colours and that personal choice of colours is reflected in their works time and again. But irrespective of personal preferences, a scenographer has to develop an understanding towards the psychological behaviour of all the colours and their impact on human mind. We have already discussed at the beginning of this chapter about the colours that come to us through the reflected light rays. These rays take a while, may be a millionth of a second, to be perceived through our eyes. Every colour hue has its own speed of movement—some move faster, some take more time. Bright colours such as yellow and red move faster in comparison to the colours like mauve, blue, etc. The speed of the movement of colours from the object to our eyes are measured through its wavelength and frequency. This nature of colours influences human psychology significantly across the times. That is why colours stimulate our feelings, thus affecting our psychological behaviour. Now, let us study different colours and their psychological comportments.

Legendary Red

Red is the most brilliant and vibrant colour that draws attention of the viewers quickly, therefore standing out amongst other colours. It can be visible from a longer distance due to its higher frequency and is therefore regarded as the most sensitive colour. Emotionally

RED

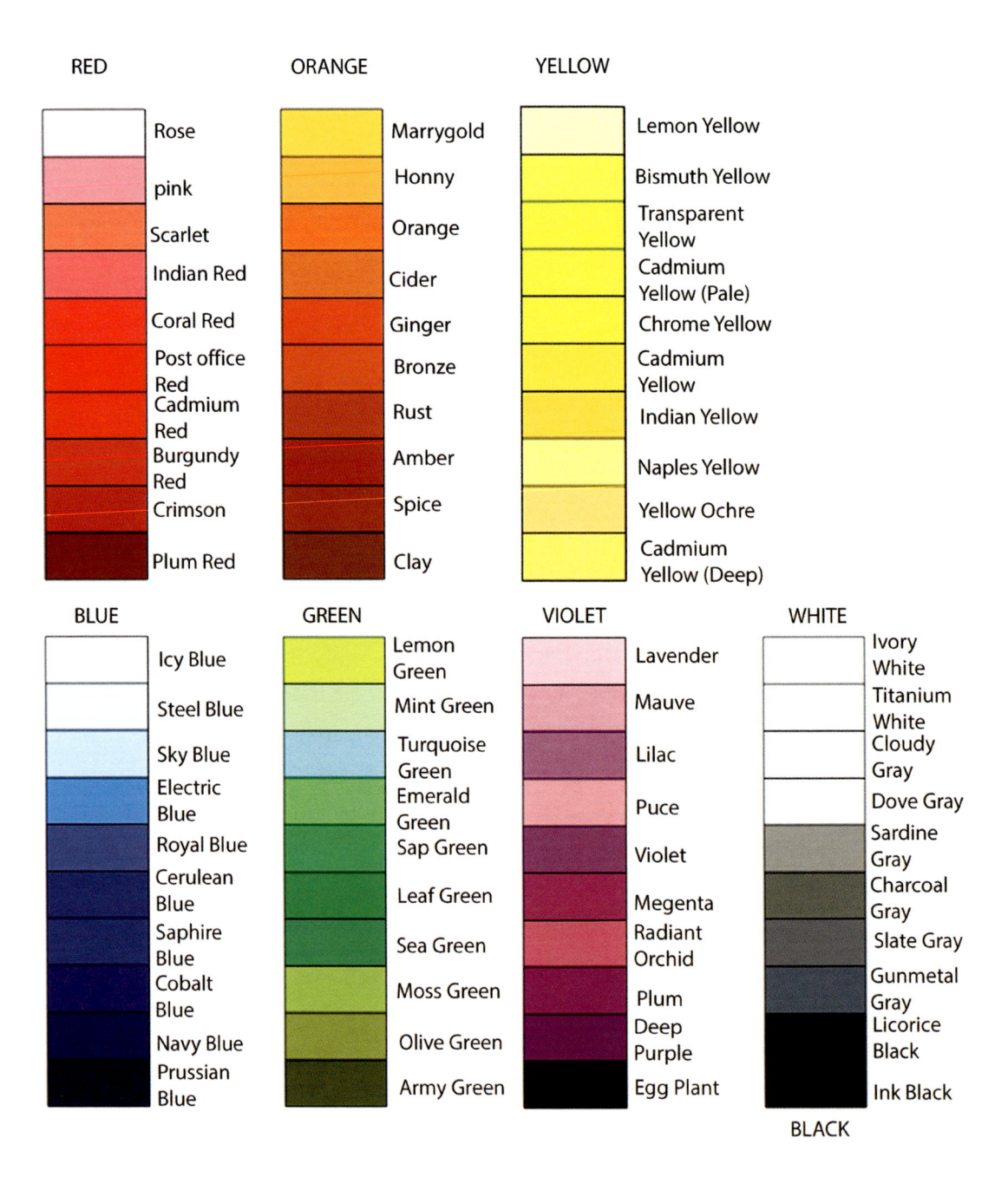

- Rose
- pink
- Scarlet
- Indian Red
- Coral Red
- Post office Red
- Cadmium Red
- Burgundy Red
- Crimson
- Plum Red

ORANGE

- Marrygold
- Honny
- Orange
- Cider
- Ginger
- Bronze
- Rust
- Amber
- Spice
- Clay

YELLOW

- Lemon Yellow
- Bismuth Yellow
- Transparent Yellow
- Cadmium Yellow (Pale)
- Chrome Yellow
- Cadmium Yellow
- Indian Yellow
- Naples Yellow
- Yellow Ochre
- Cadmium Yellow (Deep)

BLUE

- Icy Blue
- Steel Blue
- Sky Blue
- Electric Blue
- Royal Blue
- Cerulean Blue
- Saphire Blue
- Cobalt Blue
- Navy Blue
- Prussian Blue

GREEN

- Lemon Green
- Mint Green
- Turquoise Green
- Emerald Green
- Sap Green
- Leaf Green
- Sea Green
- Moss Green
- Olive Green
- Army Green

VIOLET

- Lavender
- Mauve
- Lilac
- Puce
- Violet
- Megenta
- Radiant Orchid
- Plum
- Deep Purple
- Egg Plant

WHITE

- Ivory White
- Titanium White
- Cloudy Gray
- Dove Gray
- Sardine Gray
- Charcoal Gray
- Slate Gray
- Gunmetal Gray
- Licorice Black
- Ink Black

BLACK

Shades and Tints of Different Colours

intense, red stimulates our heartbeat and invokes excitement within us, sometimes leading to rage. For its brilliance and dynamism, red becomes the symbol of power, arrogance, dignity and strength. Globally across varied cultures, red has different connotations. While in Japan and China, red is associated with heroism and courage, in India it is the symbol of productivity, fortune and divine power. In Central Africa, red is associated with tragedy. It is the most frequently used colour in national flags of the world. Red colour was the symbol of communism and socialism during the Russian Revolution. In theatre, red is directly associated with royalty, arrogance, egoism and violence. Creating a scene of such nature, the scenographers carefully use bright red colours into their design, particularly in lights and costumes. For set design red colour is minimised due to its dominating power. Red colour may divert the attention of the viewers from the production to itself through constant interactions in the play. Eventually, red is avoided for colouring any vertical objects in the space that remain static for a longer period. On the contrary, it is gladly used in costumes, lights and props. In Indian theatre, Ratan Thiyam has explored the potential of red in a few of his productions such as, *Ritusamhara, Antigone* and *Andha Yug*, etc. In *Karnakatha* and *Ekalavya*, I have used red as the prime colour of the lighting design.

Vibrant Yellow
Yellow symbolises joy, enlightenment, warmth, happiness and comfort. It is the brightest colour found in the nature. Yellow has many shades, such as, Cadmium-Yellow, Lemon-Yellow, Chrome-Yellow, Raw-Sienna, Yellow-Ochre, etc. In India yellow is associated with royalty, joy and purity. In the Hindu tradition, sacred yellow threads and clothes are worn during festivals and rituals. But in art and design, over-application of yellow in the background may divert attention

from the main content. Being a colour of folk and rituals, yellow has a significance in Indian traditional and classical plays. Indian scenographer Bansi Kaul prefers yellow and its analogous colours in designing costumes. And it is evident in a few of his productions such as *Khel Guru Ka, Tukke pe Tukka, etc.*

Cool Blue
Three-fourth of the entire universe comprises of blue and its analogous colours. Blue offers pleasing effects to our eyes and is associated with vastness, softness and love. Blue is considered as one of the coolest colours in the nature. Two important Indian mythological characters, Rama and Krishna are of blue colours. While Rama stands for victory and respect, Krishna is the symbol of love and tenderness. In theatre, the shades of blue are used to project tranquillity and vastness in atmosphere.

Natural Green
It is the colour of nature. Forests, mountains, landscapes are perceived in different shades of green. Most often, green is balanced with other warm colours such as yellow and orange. Green is the symbol of fertility and tranquillity. The combination of green with its complimentary red forms a nice composition.

Flamboyant Orange
Orange radiates higher energy, thus is visually more dominating than other colours. Created by red and yellow, it shares common quality with its parental hues. Orange represents energy and warmth but is less aggressive than red. It has inherited cheerful nature from yellow and stimulates the emotions profoundly. This colour is also very much present in the natural surroundings, found in the shedding leaves during spring and summer. Yellowish brown indicates the change in

season, thus influencing human moods profoundly. It is a transitory colour between hot summer and chilly winter. Orange-brown colour and its shades have been extensively used in the world of arts during the Renaissance. In India, orange is an auspicious colour and has a strong connection with our culture. Like yellow, this colour is also used extensively in our folk and traditional theatre performances in the rendition of several characters such as Kathakali, Theyyam, etc.

Imaginative Violet
Violet is the colour of mystery and dream. Its temperament is gracious, spiritual and luxurious. The colour is associated with royalty. Violet is regarded as the colour of imagination. Application of large amount of violet in design indicates the departure from reality to the world of imagination and fantasy. Violate colour on stage creates dreamy atmosphere leading the dramatic situation towards surrealism to some extent.

Loving Pink
Apart from the primary, secondary and tertiary colours, there are countless shades and tints, prepared out of the combinations of the 12 colours of the colour-wheel. For example, rose and pink tones can be achieved by mixing white and red. This tint of colour is related to warmth, love and beauty. Pink is a soft colour, which is more appealing than red. Pink colour can be used to reduce depression and anger. But its use in theatre is rare, particularly in painting the sets and props.

Earthly Brown
This is the shade of earth. It symbolises simplicity. It is a mixture of orange and black, thus belongs to the family of warm colours. Often brown colour is associated with depression. Like orange, brown is a

transitory colour, which always points towards a new environment. Brown is used extensively in theatre because of its non-reflective properties. It is also a preferred colour of the scenographers. The stage floor, steps, platforms, etc. are generally painted with dark brown colour because of its passiveness. Major brown shades used in art and design are—Turkey umber, burnt umber, vandyke brown, raw umber, golden brown and burnt sienna, etc. Sometimes brown is classified as the colour of the 'tragedy'.

Colour: A Form of Visual Music
Starting from darker shades to lighter tints, colour eternally adds astounding effects to our visuals. Have we ever observed how magically the colour of the sun changes at every passing moment of time? Long before the morning, it spreads a band of golden hue, mixing with pink and violet before it appears in the horizon. Then gradually its colours transform from amber to vermillion, finally to become white. Similarly, at the fall of evening, the white band of hue again transforms into purple and pink and finally turns violet just before it disappears in the horizon. Similarly, new foliage in nature shed their colours through a series of transformations— from orange-brown to dark green to pale yellow and finally to dull brown.

Kalidasa has immortalised nature's magical effect through his verses in *Ritusamhara*, *Kumarasambhavam* and *Meghadutam* He had keenly observed the change in nature through the changing seasons that starts from summer to monsoon then autumn, winter and finally to spring and its influence on human nature. He had noticed the changing hues of the great Himalayas with the reflection of the golden rays of the morning sun that transforms the silver-white snow-capped mountains into a melting golden river. His poetic representations of *Kumarasambhavam* becomes an epitome of nature's mystic magnificence. In *Meghadutam*, the poet transcribes how the monsoon affects human mood, and how nature transforms from a dull-brown earth to a lush-green valley. Kalidasa has painted the colours of nature in the form of words in the truest sense.

A single colour even sometimes revels the mystery of the nature. One perceives the sky, the mountain, the ocean and the river all as blue yet ironically, not a single shade of blue is identical; they differ in shades, so as yellow, green, red and other colours. It starts with the darker shade and moves towards lighter tint. It blends with other colours and produces a different shade, just like a musical composition with multiple notes.

Apart from the seven primary notes in music, there are many other soft (*komal*) and hard (*tibra*) notes. In between these notes, there also exist numbers of sub notes (*shruti*) which are essential in creating a musical piece. Similarly, Colour marks its journey through different shades and tints to create a composition. Like the chords of a harmonium or piano, it creates visual notation. This musical harmony of colours is reflected in all forms of visual arts, including Indian miniature paintings. These paintings are like music, expressed through colours. In Indian Ragamala paintings, the musical compositions are painted on canvases depicting the varied moods of nature.

Colour Perception

The perception of object in nature depends on two basic factors—form and colour, which is visualised as a unit. This section is aimed at analysing the perception of colours as a total composition. When we talk about the colour composition, we intend for more than one colour hue which comprises of tints and shades. Through the harmonious arrangements, these tints and shades reciprocate each other through a relationship. According to colour theory, a few colour tones look brighter and stay focused when placed against certain other colours. Similarly, a colourful visual composition of a play that stands against a dark background may lose intensity against lighter background. Therefore most of the scenographers in the world prefer using black curtain at the back of the stage instead of white cyclorama, until essential. A visual artist needs to understand the interplay of colours within themselves in creating a composition with aestheticism.

Colour vs. Shape and Size

This is an optical illusion but can be effectively explored in visual design—sets, costumes, masks, etc. When two objects of same colour but diffrent size are kept together, the smaller one looks darker than the larger one. This happens due to their varied sizes and shapes that the large one is exposed to more amount of light because of its large area. For example, there are three objects of same colour but different size and shape. The larger one would seem to be brighter than the smaller one. Therefore it always becomes confusing for the costume designers to match a sample with the original fabrics.

Interplay of Shades

When two different shades of the same colour are placed against each other, the lighter tint looks darker and the darker shade appears brighter. For example, a pink rose seems pale and gloomy against a purple background, a set of furniture painted with raw sienna looks darker against a background of burnt sienna and vice versa. While working with different shades of similar colours, scenographers carefully explore the possibilities of achieving the desired expressions through the process of permutation and combination.

Larger Colour Space Affects the Smaller Ones

In a colour composition, a small object is brought into focus against a larger space of its contrast colour. For example, a small patch of light yellow looks way brighter against a dark background of a contrasting colour, whereas the same yellow patch may look defused and pale against a lighter background. In fig.C, a yellow patch is placed against a dark background. Since the dark background occupies a larger space than the patch of yellow in the

A- Colour vs. Shape   B- Interplay of Shades
C- Larger vs, Smaller Colour Space D- Outlines and Borders

Illustrative diagram of colour perceptions

centre, it brings yellow into focus. But in the other figure (below image) the same yellow circle looks dull and defused against a lighter background since both the colours belong to the same family. While preparing a colour scheme for the visual design, the scenographer must keep an watching eye to the colour combinations so as to create a dramatic effect on stage.

Outline and Borders

A framed painting or any bounded object seems to be focused and projected. Similarly, a performance inside a proscenium theatre stands out with all its richness. This is due to the bold and strong outline of the frames that restricts our vision within the periphery and guide us to look into the subject inside the frame. Similarly, colour plays a crucial role in creating the boundary. One must be cautious in selecting the colours for the outline or the edges of any costume, prop or set, since lighter outline may spread its colour to the adjacent areas, thus reducing the strength of the main object. On the contrary, a dark frame or outline focuses on the main subject by controlling the colour of the subject from spreading into its surrounding atmosphere.

Scenographer's Colour Scheme

Every individual artist may have their personal likings and resentments for certain category of colours which they never apply into their creation. But a scenographer has a lot of limitations and adjustments in selecting the colours for the design. While a painter is free to select any colour according to their subjective preferences, a scenographer may not. Theatre is a composite form of art where all the visual expressions are interconnected and projected with the support of mutual energy. In these circumstances, the scenographer is bound to depend on other visual expressions to conceive the design. The concept and exploration of a design are also significantly dependent on other factors including director's vision, colour of lights, colour and pattern of the costumes, makeup, props, etc. Therefore, scenography is a functional form of art that is restricted to many related issues. Scenographers need to collaborate with all the technical faculties of performance in order to bring coherence into their visuals. Often over-application of colours in design draws unnecessary attention of the viewers. A colourful design may appear wondrous at the first appearence, but with gradual unfolding of the scenes, it may appear awful due to the higher intensity of colours, and it may spoil the show. Even occasionally a normal colour scheme seems brighter than usual when it comes in contact with the stage lights. Before preparing a suitable colour scheme for a design, the scenographer must be careful enough of its application.

Set Painting
The stage is a platform whose sole purpose is to project the actors as the central figure. In any circumstances, the stage should not be highlighted undermining the performers. The vivacity should never overshadow the vitality of a performance. Design works as a launch pad for actors by adding dynamics to the production. Accordingly, the colour schemes for the sets are to be decided, avoiding overexposition of the stage space. Therefore, the horizontal set units such as, platforms, steps, ramps, floors, etc. are usually painted with darker shades, often with the shades of brown. The vertical arrangements on the other hand, (pillars, doors, windows, arches, walls, etc.) can be painted with slight bright shades. Care must be taken to tone down the vertical painted objects in comparison to costumes and props, so that a contrast between the background and the characters can be well established.

For set painting, scenographers usually prefer colours such as, burnt sienna, raw sienna, burnt amber, vendek brown, ash grey, steel gray and sometimes jet black. Bright shades are commonly avoided in set painting since they reflect the stage lights that strike the audience's eye. In no circumstances, oil-based colours are used in set painting. When exposed to the stage lights, objects painted with oil-based colours create dazzling effect

A- Different size of Brushes

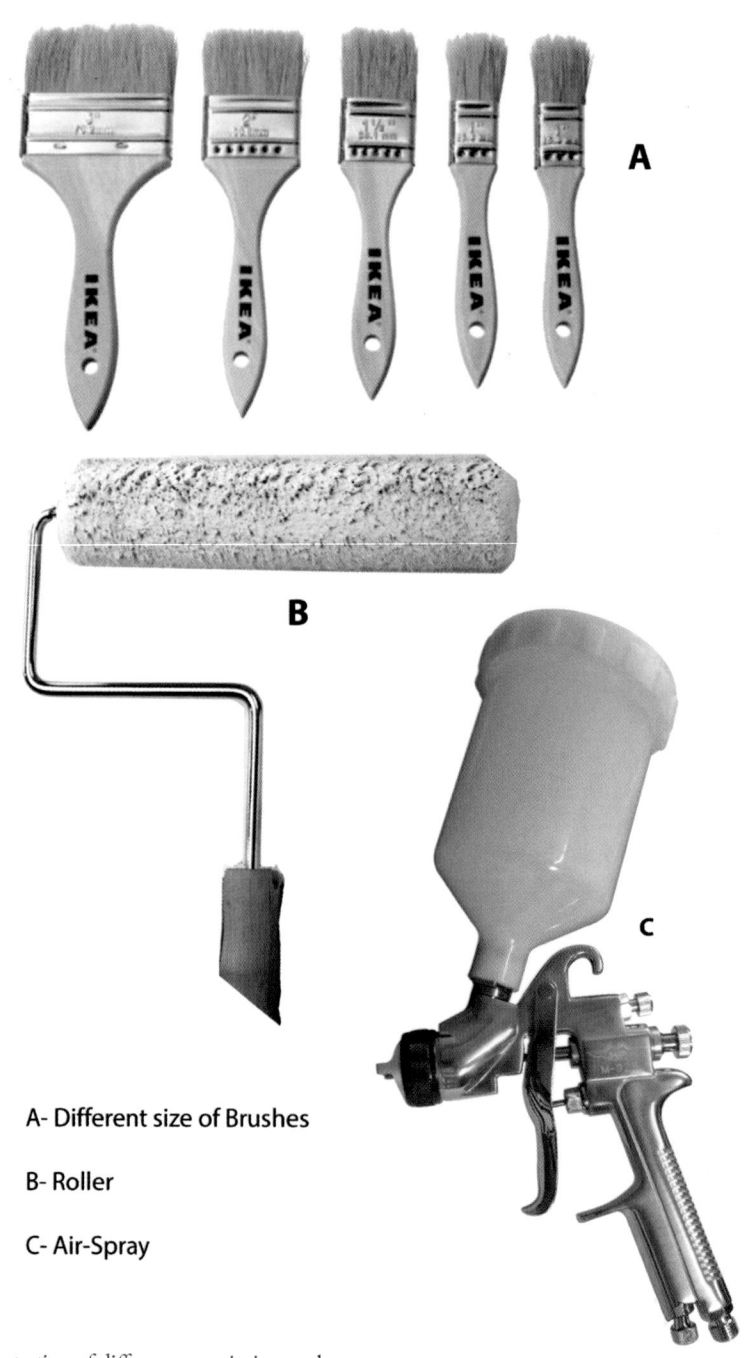

B- Roller

C- Air-Spray

Illustration of different set painting tools.

that reflects in the eyes of the viewers, thus disturbing the performance. Water-based colours, such as emoltion paints, distemper and stains of different shades can be effectively used for the stage painting. These paints are easily soluble in water and dry fast. Before painting the set, the stage designer must consult the costume and light designers to discuss about the colour schemes of the play.

A set can be painted with the help of brush, spray, roll, etc. A smooth surface with even colour gradations can be achieved through brush painting for which 4' and 6' brushes are used. However, it takes a lot of time to paint the entire surface area through brushes, especially for larger sets. In this condition, one can take the help of air-brush-spray which is the easiest and fastest way to paint a set. In air-brush-spray system, painting is done with the help of an air compressor and a spray gun. While high-compressed air passes through a small nozzle of the spray gun filled with paints, it evenly sprays the colours on the surface through air pressure. A scene painter can create variety of colour effects through the help of a spray gun. Textural effects, tonal effects and effects of different colour shades can be achieved through this process. The scene painting can also be done through a roller brush. This process creates smooth texural effects on the surface of the set. Sponge rollers are available with different sizes in any paint or hardware shop.

Care must be taken to join the flats with each other to achieve the finishing. The gap between the joints in the flats and platforms can be patched up with paper tapes or scroll tapes. The surface area can be plastered with a layer of wall putty which needs to be rubbed with sandpaper before the paint work begins. The wall putty, as a base coat, would enhance the richness of colours and make the surface smooth and even. Before painting the sets, the scenographer must check a sample of colours under the original stage lights in order to find the right colour tones.

SECTION - III

FEELING THROUGH SEEING: THE TEXTURE

If we slowly glide our hand over a few objects such as, a piece of glass, a marble, a pebble, a brick, a piece of paper, a lump of bread, etc., we would feel different sensations for different objects, because of their surface qualities. The material out of which a piece of glass is made is invariably different from a piece of stone. Similarly, the feel of a sponge piece is different from that of wood and clay. In nature different objects stimulate our feelings in different ways which are directly associated with our sensory experiences. This is due to their different textures which in art, represents the inner connotation of the subject.

Life is a journey that passes through various stages of experiences. When these experiences are moulded into the form of arts, they bring different feelings through colours, lines, dimensions and characterisations. These feelings enhance our sensory pleasure, thus invoking our interest in viewing them. In a play, texture hits the collective vision and experience and is more related to the human feelings than the tactile experience itself. The emotional graph of the dramatic situations becomes the key to experience the texture of a play. It is the scenographer who discovers them in the visual imageries that coincide with the characters' living experiences. A dramatic text is not a collection of words; they are the human feelings in the form of letters which needs to be expressed through images with appropriate textures.

Classification of the Texture

By representing the symbolic milieu of life, texture contributes to the interpretation of the play. They can broadly be classified as: smooth and 'rough'. Rough texture portrays harshness, cruelty, torture, hardship and tragedy while soft texture stands for softness, delicacy, love and the brighter

ELEMENTS OF DESIGN | 427

Hard Texture

Soft Texture

Visual presentation of different textures.

aspects of life. Different art mediums have their own interpretations and dimensions for understanding the texture. For example, while in textile it can be touched and felt, in paintings, texture is a visual illusion which cannot be touched but felt through our sensory organs. Theatre, being a combination of both art forms, provides an experience of touch (by the actors) and feel (by the viewers).

The selection of materials to create textural effect in design depends on the scenographer's sensibility. However, the visual artist must develop an understanding of materials and its potential possibilities to bring the desired textural effect into design. To create a sensation of various texture the visual artist can depend on a few materials such as, plaster of Paris, sponge, papier-mâché, wood, bark, fibreglass, latex rubber, tat and gunny cloths, etc. Adoption of these materials in theatre design, and their creative execution in sets add a different metaphorical and emotional layer to the meaning of the play. With the help of lighting effects, these materials with different textures make the design lively and enhance the mood. There are other kinds of materials that provide a feeling of softness. Application of these materials such as velvet cloth, glass or fine fabrics, tiles, sun-mica, plywood, plastic sheets, etc. bring lighter moods, and thus generate a feeling of happiness. A scenographer should explore the materials through research and market survey to bring out the best possible result out of them.

Psychologically, while a smooth surface provides an experience of calmness, resulting in a quiet and peaceful environment, a rough texture allows our eyes to move, thus becoming more active. Stage lighting, being an integral part of scenography, plays a crucial role to enhance the texture, thus heightening the psychological atmosphere of the play. For example, cross lighting on rough texture can deepen the feelings of the characters on stage and brings a sense of compassion and mood into the dramatic situation. On the contrary, the same texture can become dreary and flat with front lighting. Cross lights create light and shade effects and facilitate

Still from the play *Ashad Ka Ek Din* (2016). Design and direction: Robin Das. Presented by: National School of Drama. Courtesy: NSD, Sauti Chakraborty. Note: Appropriate mood and atmosphere of the scene is created through sharp cross lights.

the meaning when it falls on a rough-textured object, whereas front light diminishes its value. Occasionally, coloured lights complement the textures. Scenographers must examine their visuals with proper stage lighting before giving the final touch to their creation. Brush strokes and spray paint can also bring desired texture into the design. Smooth texture can be achieved by applying fine and bright colours on the surface area evenly. For example, a drawing room set painted with light colours by a paint-roller generates pleasing effect. One can try with dry brush and spray paints to bring tragic mood by creating rough textures on the set surface.

SECTION - IV

THE MYSTERY OF SHAPE AND FORM

Nature never repeats its creation. Every form is different. Everything is unique in the nature. Even two leaves of the same tree are not identical; they are different in structure and their outlines are also different.

We can start a survey from our immediate surroundings. Let's examine our own study room. This place must have books, table, chairs, laptop, wall clock, wall hangings, paperweight, pen and stand, files, etc. Let's check their shapes. They are rectangular, squarish, triangular, curvilinear and sometimes irregular in structure. These shapes are the enclosed area formed through the outline of the objects. Alan Pipes argues, 'A shape is an enclosed area that is identifiably distinct from its background and other shapes. It can be bounded by an actual outline or by a difference in texture, colour, or value surrounding a visually perceived edge, even when the edge is so blurred that the shape is amorphous.'[v] Shape is a two-dimensional structure and it can be perceived as symmetrical or asymmetrical figures. They are geometrical, natural or abstract entity having different applications in art and design.

Symmetrical Shape

Any configuration that produces mirror image of its other half, if divided equally, is called a symmetrical shape, for example our body structure. Most ancient and medieval architectures of the world have symmetrical structures that look elegant, gorgeous and beautiful. Symmetrical designs bring harmony to the presentation. It seems organised, thus generating a feeling of order and discipline. This kind of structure always looks pleasant to the eyes and is enriched with sublime beauty. However, with all its beauty, a symmetrical object is less intensive. In theatre, symmetrical design may not be elevated up to the dramatic tension and conflict of the action. But its innovative and creative exploration would be able to project the tension with aesthetics. For example, the symmetrical set design of *Aurangzeb* (2006) always brings aesthetic pleasure to the audience and simultaneously portrays the political tragedy of the protagonist Aurangzeb. The play was directed by Prof. K.S. Rajendran and designed by Indian scenographer Prof. H.V. Sharma. There are many such examples of plays where symmetrical design brings beauty as well as conflict to the productions, but it needs a skilled hand to be explored with innovation. There are many types of symmetrical shapes, such as, bilateral, rotational, translational, etc.

Bilateral Symmetry

It is the most popular kind of symmetrical shape, used in the design and architecture, where one half of the shape mirrors the other half by balancing each other. This kind of shape seems complete in itself, thus projecting its beauty. But in theatre design it provides less opportunity for the performers to interplay with its space. Therefore, for a bilaterally symmetrical design, the scenographers often create some specific area to break its symmetry within the framework. This specific area serves as 'area of interest' for close interactions of the performers and space during the course of the action. To counterbalance a symmetrical design, directors often create interesting asymmetrical compositions in the space that breaks the monotony of the design.

Rotational Symmetry

Rotational symmetry in design and architecture creates a sense of psychological and rhythmic movements. This kind of design usually brings the centre into focus and evokes a poetic experience into the artwork. Rotational-shaped is found in Indian tantric arts, temple architectures and Indian classical performances. Indian 'Alpana', a traditional motif design, is an appropriate example of rotational symmetry. Rotational symmetry in

Still from the play *Aurangzeb*. Design: Prof. H.V Sharma, Direction: K.S Rajendran. Presented by: New Delhi Theatre Workshop. Courtesy: K.S. Rajendran.

design has been explored to some extent in contemporary Indian theatre, particularly during the Theatre of Roots movement.

Similarity Symmetry

This kind of symmetry in design is created when the design elements change their scales but retain the symmetrical shape. By breaking the monotony of its own shape, this design captures the attentions of the viewers. A few examples of similarity symmetry in architecture and design are the Sydney Opera House in Australia and the Lotus Temple in Delhi.

ELEMENTS OF DESIGN | 433

Line drawing demonstrating bilaterally symmetrical design.

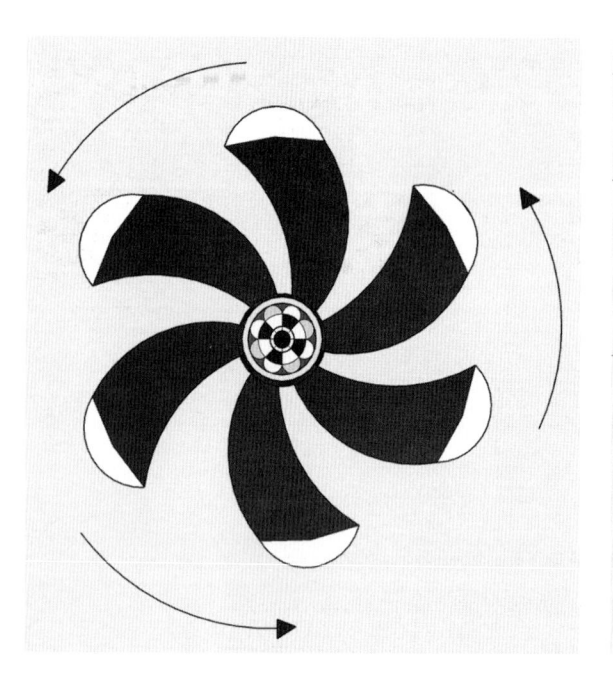

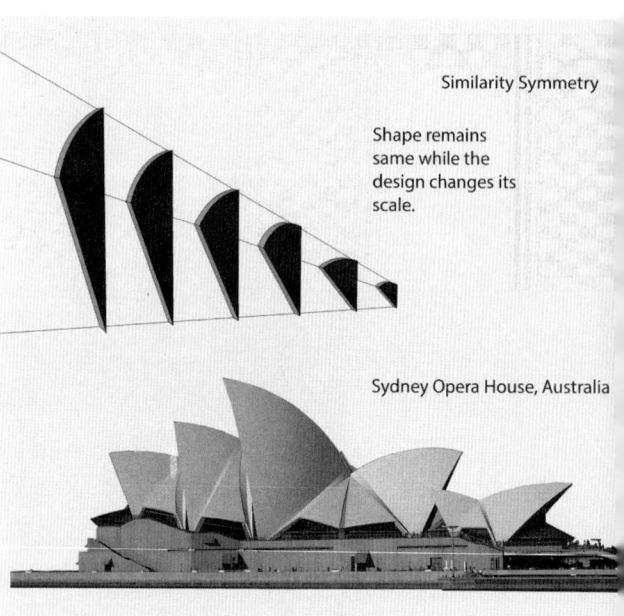

Left: Line drawing, demonstrating rotational symmetry.
Right: Line drawing, demonstrating similarity symmetry. Note: Displaying a photograph of the Sydney Opera House, New South wales, Australia, in order to represent similarity symmetry in its architectural design.

Translational Symmetry

Popularly known as 'space-group-symmetry' in architecture and design, this kind of shape often creates monotony because of its repetition. However, it brings a sense of discipline into design. Creative application of this type of shape into scenography may appear interesting to the audience. In theatre design this shape has been used in many ways, for example, arrangement of multiple arches, pillars and doors, etc. in designing the space for performance.

Asymmetrical Shapes

Asymmetrical shapes are irregular and are mostly found in the natural objects. They make interesting compositions in scenography by

Translational Symmetry — Repetition of the design elements

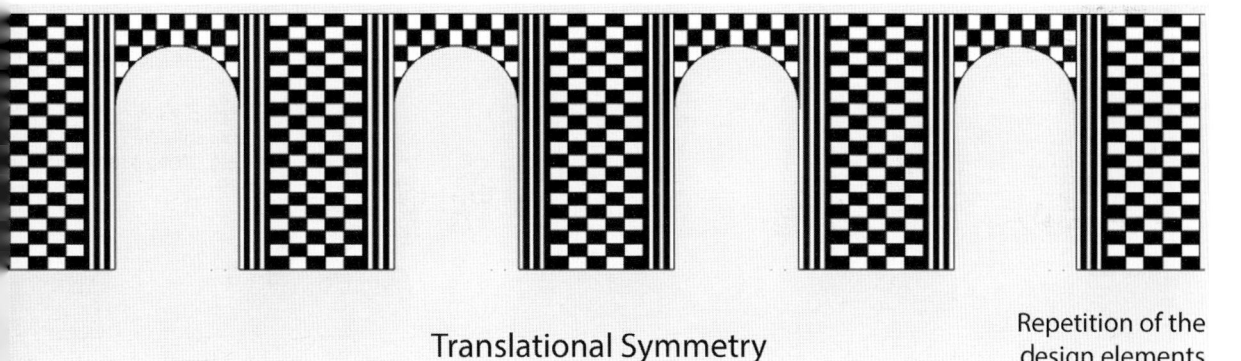

Line drawing, demonstrating translational symmetry.

creating opportunities for the actors to interact with the design. Often asymmetrical design is balanced within its own components. It can also take the support of actors during the performance to distribute the visual weight (ref. Chapter 10) within the entire space all the times. Unlike other spatial art, theatre design keeps on changing with the compositions of actors in the play, shifting the focus from one composition to the other every time. It is like a series of live paintings that keeps moving every time during a performance. An asymmetrical design opens avenues and opportunities for creative compositions of the actors in relationship with the entire space. Often asymmetrical design in theatre brings new challenge for the scenographers by evoking innovative ideas in the work.

Geometrical Shape
Geometrical shapes are mostly regular and mechanical, defined by mathematical formulas. We can recognise these shapes in the forms of square, circle and triangle, etc. Some other shapes like octagon, hexagon, star, sphere and cone are obtained by combining these three basic shapes. These shapes have been explored in numerous ways in the context of design and scenography. Before applying them into design, the visual artists must be

Example of Asymmetrical Design. Still from the play *Iphigenia at Aulis* (2010). Playwright: Euripides; scenography and direction: Satyabrata Rout; presented by: Department of Theatre Arts, S.N. School of Arts and Communication. University of Hyderabad. Courtesy: Dept. of Theatre Arts.

aware of their physical and philosophical concept, dated back to prehistoric times. From the cave-dwelling days till the modern times, mankind has observed the nature as well as its various shapes. The sun, the moon, rivers, mountains, trees and landscapes have profound impact upon human beings and have inspired to draw and paint. Human observation has resulted in discovering these shapes in art and design which have influenced human wisdom for thousands of years. These shapes are geometrical and scientific, yet they bear philosophical connotation with deeper meaning. Let us try to understand their structures and the meanings behind.

Circle

This is the most regular and organised entity rediscovered in geometry. The point that is equidistant to the periphery of the circle is called the 'centre'. The line that passes through the centre and touches the periphery at both the ends is known as the 'diameter' of the circle. Half of the diameter from the centre of the circle to the periphery is called the 'radius'. The outer rim of the circle is the 'perimeter' or the circumference. In geometry, they are symbolised as: C= circumference, D= diameter, R= radius. The mathematical formula to calculate a circle is: C=2 π r (π =22/7). For example, if the radius of a circle is 3 feet, its circumference (C) would be: 2 X 22/7 X 3 = 44/7 X 3=132/7=18.85 feet. The angle of a circle always remains 360°. The concept of wheel came from the circle that becomes the symbol of movement.

The connotation of a circle went much beyond the realm of its physical structure and formulated an essential part of philosophy and art. It stands for the iconic representation of time, which is constant since the materialisation of the universe. In India, a circle is called 'Chakra' or 'Mandala', an essential 'yantra'—a geometrical diagram for meditation used in tantric Buddhism and also in Hinduism. Circle creates an impression of an unending and constant movement which represents the relentless encircling of life around its epicentre, without any beginning or end. In Indian philosophy, this is called 'Jivana-chakra'—the cycle of life. According to this philosophy, the journey of life moves in a circle that tends to converge into the centre in order to merge with the cosmic energy or 'Garbha-dhatu', situated at the epicentre.

Triangle

According to Euclidean geometry, a triangle is a two-dimensional shape, formed by three lines joining each other in three angles. These angles may be similar or dissimilar, depending on the length of the lines. All the three angles of a triangle are summed up to form 180°. Triangles are of various

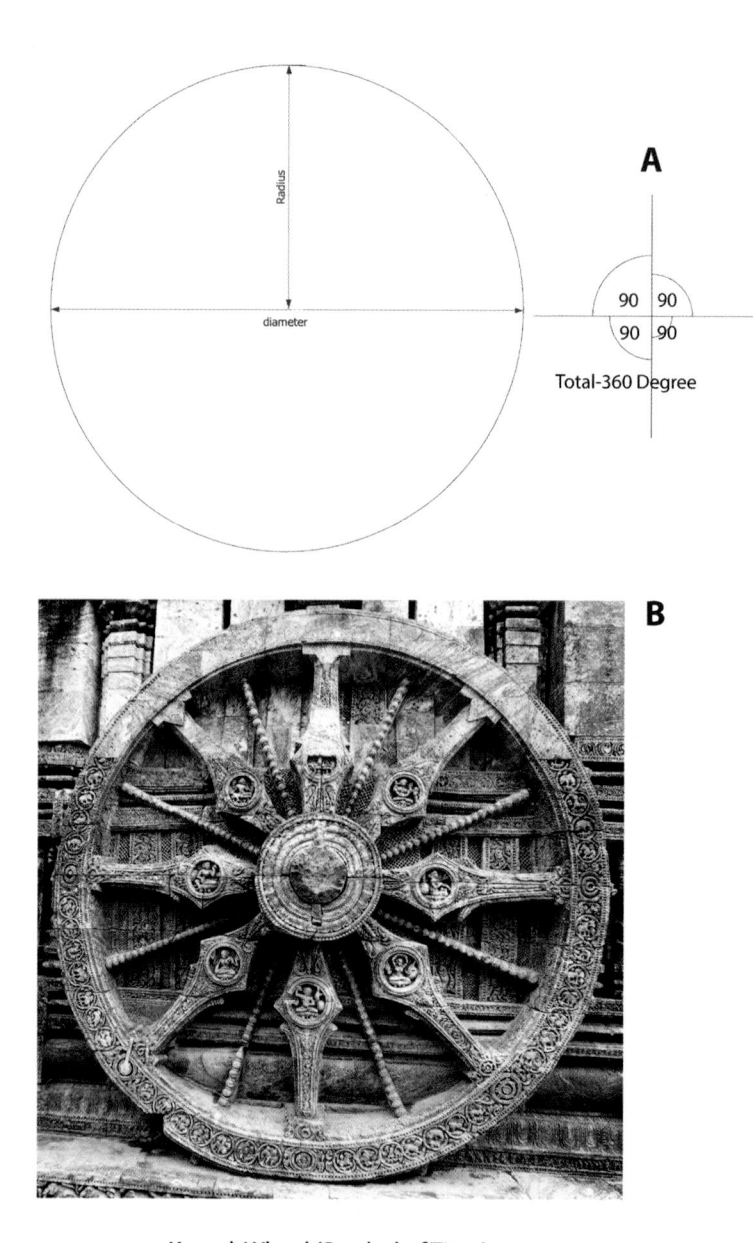

Konark Wheel (Symbol of Time)

Line drawing, demonstrating 'circle'.
Note: Displaying a photograph of the famous Konark Wheel of the Sun temple of Odisha in order to demonstrate the use of circular design as a symbol of movement and time.

shapes such as, right-angled triangle, equilateral triangle, isosceles triangle. In a right-angled triangle , the base angle is 90º while other two angles sum up to 90º, thus completing 180°. The longest arm of a right-angled triangle is called hypotenuse, while the other two arms are called legs. If the legs of the right-angled triangle are 3 feet and 4 feet respectively, the hypotenuse will be 5 feet. An equilateral triangle has three legs equal in measurement, thus forming equal degree of angles i.e. 60° each angle. An isosceles triangle can be formed by two equivalents and one uneven leg. Since its side legs are equal, its opposite angles are also equal.

The shape of a triangle can be easily observed in our natural sphere. It is one of the important constituents of the natural make-up and has been abrasively enthused into different geological functionaries such as, mountains, trees, rocks, sea waves, sand dunes, etc. Humans have intelligently adopted this shape in the creative process with mathematical infusion and have created wonders of the world including the majestic pyramid. Textile designs, folk arts and tribal paintings also employ this triangular shape significantly into its pattern. One can trace them in the detailed configurations of Warli paintings of Maharashtra, Jhoti Chita wall design of Odisha, tribal paintings of Jhabua, a district in Madhya Pradesh, and in many other cultures. Numerous examples of its espousal include the costumes and headgear of Theyyam dance of Kerala, border design of Bengali kota saris and many other intricate handicraft art works.

The philosophy of the triangle possesses as much value as in science and as in arts. It becomes the receiver of the cosmic energy and power when one triangle represents male (*Purusha*) and the other inverted triangle represents the nature (*Prakriti*). The former is the symbol of fire and the latter, the water. Assimilating together, they form the concept of productivity, a great ritualistic symbol of Hinduism. The base of a triangle is wider and firmer than its pointed tip which generates tremendous energy, for example the great pyramids.

1 & 2. Warli paintings of Maharashtra
3. Applique work of Pipli, Odisha
4. Wall design of Madhya Pradesh
5. Himalayan Art
6. Jhoti-chita Design, Odisha

Application of Triangles in Indian Art and Design

Square and Rectangle

These geometrical structures have four arms with equal angles of 90º, combining to sum up 360º in total. The area inside the square is measured by the multiplication of two arms, which we call as square feet, square yard, square meter, etc. In a square, all the arms are of equal length whereas in a rectangle only the opposite arms are equal. The origin of these shapes can be dated back to the ancient history when humans would cut a piece of land to construct his first dwelling in the plain. The vast plain land at the foothills or near by a river would be converted into human settlements. The dwellings bounded by four walls usually divide the space into two distinctive areas through the enclosures—outer and inner. The space inside the boundary becomes special for him and the outer one remains generic which has significantly contributed to the rituals and performances. A close look at an empty performance space indicates every component of the space as equal, with no particular emphasis on any specific area. But placing a chair or a block or any small object in this empty space would immediately divide the space into two parts: specific and generic. The space in and around the placed object would draw immediate attention of the viewers making it specific, while the space away from that object would remain insignificant. Similarly, while constructing a house by separating it from the rest of the area through boundary, the dwellers of the house feel secured. With the development of civilisation, the square or rectangle shapes were adopted for architectural constructions and design whose trace can be found in the archaeological sites of Mohenjo-daro and Harappa civilisations. The layout design or the ground plan of these ancient cities are still prominent even in ruins. The exploration of angular lines, squares, rectangles and triangles can be easily perceptible in the pre-classical and ancient architectures and arts of the world.

The use of square and rectangular shapes is very common in theatre design. Commonly used stage objects such as, platforms, levels, flats,

Aerial view of the excavation site of Mahenjo-daro in the province of Sindh, Pakistan.
Note: Exploration of rectangular and square shapes in the architectural constructions of the city, around 5000 years ago. Courtesy: Wikimedia Commons.

doors, windows, pillars, steps, blocks, etc. are either rectangular or square in shape.

Abstract Shape
Though recognisable, these shapes never resemble any real object in nature. Abstract art, however, can symbolically represent any object in art and design. It is a dominant artistic tool in theatre. Abstraction is an expression of human imaginations that stimulate feelings without resembling to any

natural form. These shapes can also be regular, irregular, geometrical, organic or combination of all these. They become the symbols of visual grammar and art expressions. We have already discussed about abstraction in Chapter 7.

Form

Form gives meaning to the shape and occupies a definite space. It is three-dimensional in its structure and is usually found in the natural, geometrical, regular or irregular shapes. Because of its dimensions—length, breadth and height—it has a definite volume. The common natural objects such as, stones, trees, houses, glass, paper weight, table, chair, television, computer, mobile, books, platforms, flats, steps, ramps, pillars, props, mask and anything that exists in its physical form are always voluminous. They are of rectangular, squarish, triangular, hexagonal, octagonal, conical or abstract in shapes. We recognise them by their individual names.

Forms are the physical dimensions of an element which can be touched and felt by giving a tactile experience. But there are some objects that appear three-dimensional by creating a sense of volume which actually is a fallacy, such as, paintings and photographs. They are in reality two-dimensional elements whereas the third dimension—depth—is created through the application of different shades of colours and lines. Thus, the form, which we see in a painting, photograph or other illusionistic mediums are not the real one. That is why unlike sculpture, a painting does not require any three-dimensional space to be expressed. Eventually the three-dimensional set design provides ample scopes for actors to interact with the space and facilitates the dramatic actions. Forms can be classified as: representational, presentational and non-representational or abstract.

SECTION - V

VALUE

Value is the significance of an object. It creates volume and projects the object with dimensions in the space. The measure of lights from brightness to darkness on an object is the projected value of that object for which it looks three-dimensional. In the absence of light there is darkness, and nothing is visible. Only through a ray of light source, either natural or artificial, things are visible to us. The quality of light on an object decides its value. For example, if an apple is kept under a light source, its gradation of lights would diminish gradually from brightness to darkness through various grades of lights which becomes responsible to create a three-dimensional perception of the apple. But the same object would seem flat (without any volume) in the absence of appropriate light. The value of the objects depends on their use in art and design. Alan pipes comments: 'Artists and designers employ light and dark for many reasons: to depict the time of day; to enhance the three-dimensionality of a scene; to direct the viewer's attention to the important areas of the picture; to create emphasis or add meaning to a subject; or to establish a mood.'[vi] Value can be achieved through many ways, through lines, colours, textures and the placement of the objects in the space, etc.

Value of Colours

Colour controls the value of an object, which is essential to create visual compositions. The colour intensity of the object decides its significance in the compositions and creates an opportunity to be perceived accordingly. For example, an object painted in dull brown colour would possess less value against a yellow-painted object, while the same brown would be projected well against the black background. When we move from brighter to darker shades, the value of the colours diminishes. Broadly, there are three grades

A- Three-dimensional effect is created through balanced lighting.
B- Apple is losing value due to flat lighting.

Illustrative drawing displaying the value of lights upon objects.

of colour values according to their utility which can be achieved through their application on the object and the subsequent lighting effects on it.

Transitional Colour Value
This grade of colour brings smooth and pleasing effect into the subject. This value can be achieved through a smooth blend of colours from lighter to darker shades without any abrupt changes in between; for example, the gradual blending of yellowish white light of the day with the blue-green to bring out night effects on stage or creating a smooth visual composition with the help of a three-dimensional lighting effect: source light, key lights and fill-in lights. The gradation of colours from dark to light creates an illusion of depth.

Abrupt Value
An abrupt change of colours and lights on an object often brings striking effects on the visual perceptions and creates curiosity within the forms. While a round object such as a dome or a round pillar generates transitional

446 | SCENOGRAPHY

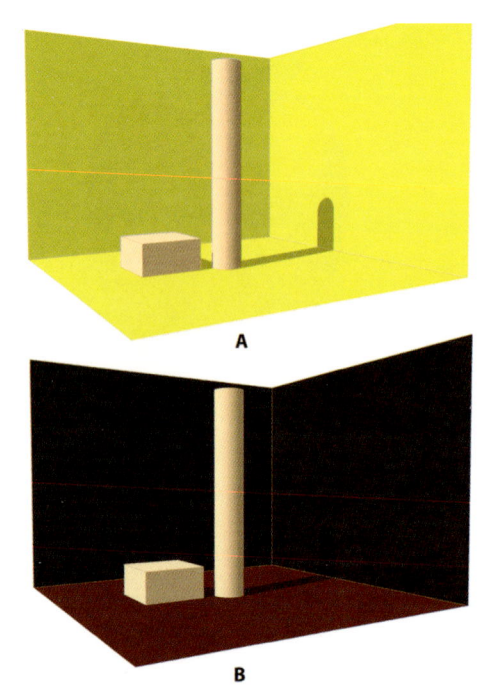

Illustrative drawing displaying the value of colours.

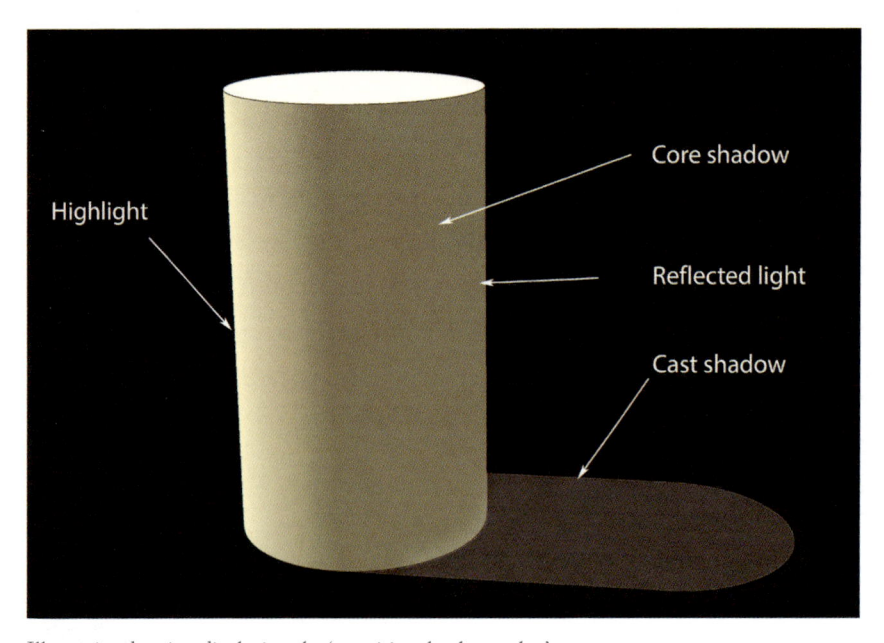

Illustrative drawing displaying the 'transitional colour value'.

value, a rectangular object such as a block, square pillar, steps and platforms brings sharp light and colour effects by creating abrupt value. This value generates dramatic effects in the presentation.

Broken Value

This colour value creates textural effects in design and becomes responsible for a dramatic ambience in the production.

Colour contrast is also an important phenomenon to create value in the compositions. It brings the brighter objects into focus, thus arresting immediate attentions. The darker shades or the objects with less colour value while serving as the atmosphere, compensate the obligatory images with higher degree of colour value, thus creating interpretations of the

Illustrative drawing displaying 'abrupt value of colours and shapes'.

compositions. The dramatic colour contrast is clearly visible in the works of the 17th century Dutch painter Rembrandt. In his paintings the colour values gradually increase from darkness to light where the central image is drawn. This sharp contrast of lights brings dramatic effects to this composition (facing page). In a performance design also, the colour value is decided according to the interpretations of the scenes; different values have different impacts upon the dramatic moods. But in general conditions, bright colours bring joy and happiness while dark reflects gloom, decay and despair. One colour hue, when stands against the other, emphasises the latter and vice versa. The photograph from the play *More Naina Rang Chadhe* (page 450) can clearly advocate for this statement. In

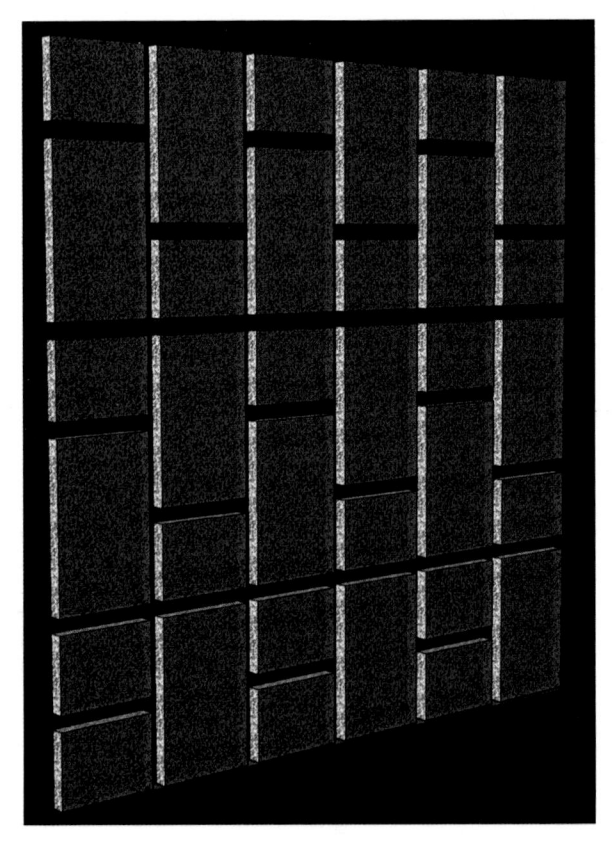

Illustrative drawing, displaying 'Broken value'

ELEMENTS OF DESIGN | 449

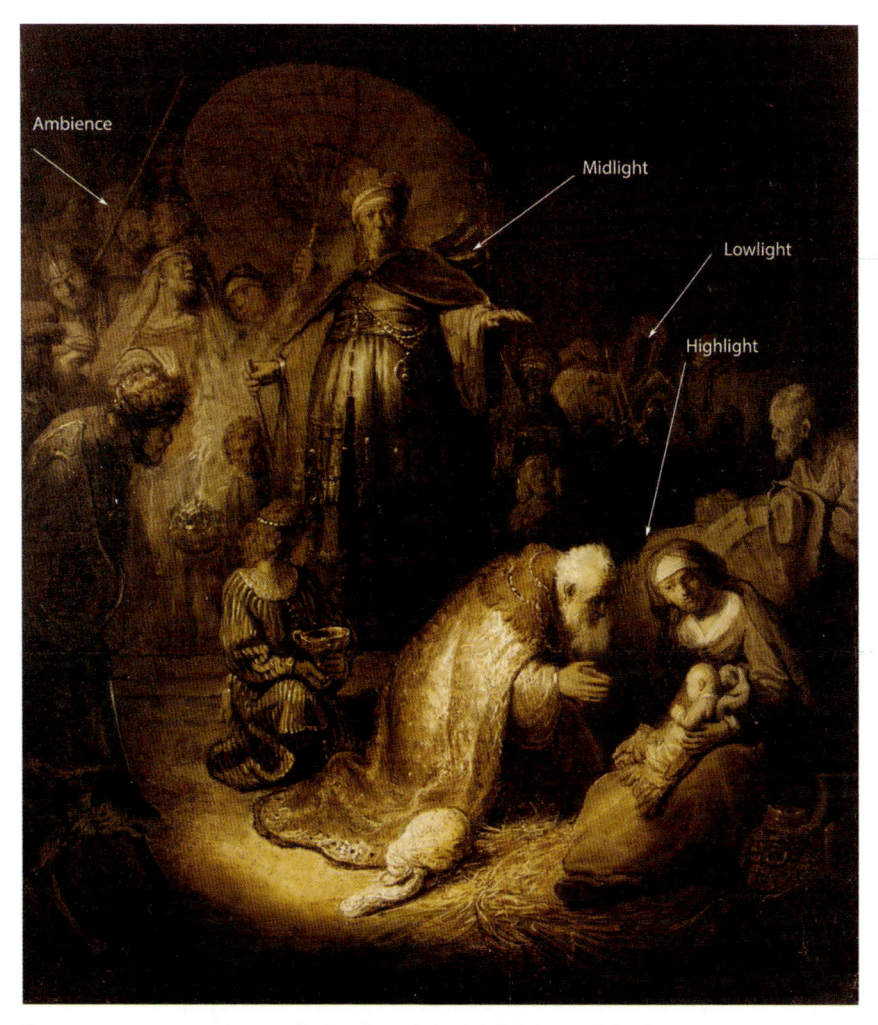

Painting: *Adoration of the Magi* by Rembrandt (1632). Medium: Oil on canvas.
Note: The painting demonstrates the control of lights to make the highlighted area focused whereas the mid-light area compensates the visual composition, while the low-light area forms the ambience of the composition, thus narrating the story with meaning.

this composition, Titania, the fairy queen is sleeping on a swing made of red satin cloths in a mystic environment created through spatial design, lights and smoke effects. The fairy queen in this dreamy atmosphere wears an off-white costume that gets highlighted predominantly against

Still from the play *More Naina Rang Chadhe*. Note: The photograph is displayed in order to demonstrate the gradation of light value from brightness to the darkness. Courtesy: Author's personal collection.

the darker background. The red-coloured swing gradually loses its value upwards, blending with the darkness, projecting the character at the down centre. Usually, an object gains higher value at the downstage than the upstage since that object is nearer to the audience than an object placed on upstage.

Value of Lines
Lines enhance the value of a space by producing the desired meanings. Various forms of lines like horizontal, diagonal, vertical, curve, zigzag, etc. are explored to create value in design. To project the value of a particular object, the scenographers often add elements of different line structures at the background of that object. For example, to project the value of an actor standing on a staircase, scenographers place vertical pillars or arches at the back against the staircase. Through this design arrangement, the verticality of the arch and pillars at the back with low intensity of light projects the staircase horizontally. An actor standing on it with a long shadow of him created through high-angle back light against the low lit arches and pillars at the back would certainly create dramatic tension by adding to the value of the composition. Architecture and design utilise these lines significantly for creating the desired effect.

Theatre, as a visual medium, deals with a three-dimensional space, where all design elements—horizontal, vertical or diagonal—co-exist on various levels and planes. The platforms, steps, ramps are usually fixed horizontally while the flats, pillars and arches are placed vertically in a theatre space. A scenographer creates composition in the space by orchestrating these elements to meet the need of the play. By doing so, the scenographer manipulates with the visual strength and the value of the stage elements that keep on interchanging between themselves. It is observed that, sometimes a small object dominates the entire visuals by psychologically pushing back a large object. This happens due to the

Illustrative drawing to represent the value of lines in a composition.

domination of the small object, powered by the value of colours or lines and texture, etc. In this way, the energy of the performance space is channelised and distributed properly to maintain the interrelationships of the visual units. A visual design, through the interplay of the values of its units and its components, can be meaningfully expressed with zest.

SECTION - VI

THREE-DIMENSIONAL SPACE

Performance space is a three-dimensional working space with length, with and height, thus creating a definite volume. All the elements of theatre, including the actors and the design, are bound to interplay through lines, colours and forms in this three-dimensional space. Performance space is like a block of wood, which is chiseled every time by the scenographers for creating visual compositions with each new production. Theatre is a live medium, an occurrence, a ritual that is performed between the actors and spectators in a designated space. It has imbibed elements from different art faculties to be manifested but it differs from other art forms in a way that theatre is realised only through the parameter of time and space. All the concepts and ideas pertaining to performance is to be comprehended in a given space within the framework of a stipulated time.

A space comes alive and articulates along with the performers during the presentation. It gets meaning only through interactions with the performers and plays its visuals when lit up with lights. A living space becomes responsible in establishing the mood and atmosphere for the play through the interplay of its visual elements like sets, props, masks, costumes, lights, etc. only during that stipulated time of the performance. Beyond that particular time frame, it is nothing but a 'dead space'. To find the difference between a 'living' and a 'dead space' we have to visit a theatre. Before the performance, when all the elements of the stage—set, lights and props—are yet to be exposed to the viewers, and just before the entry of the audience when there is no stage lights glowing on any actor, a visit to the space is always very dull. At this moment all the elements lying on the stage floor are like wood logs, a bunch of nonresponsive objects. We may not draw any sense out of their existence, identity, functions, purpose and expressions; they are still in the ovary. The space seems to be disconnected, almost alien and mysterious and thus, it is a 'dead space'. However, with the ringing of the third bell and dimming of lights in the auditorium, with the first beam of stage light on the actors in the space, it rises up to a living entity. The space then interacts with the performers and creates various meanings by transmitting the spatial energy to the performance. With the changing colours and intensity of stage lights, the objects lying like wood logs a moment before, rise up to establish a visual dialogue with the actors as well as with the audience, who gradually starts recognising those alien objects through their involvements.

Theatre, every time, is expressed through integrity, and that makes it different from other forms of art expressions. A painter, a sculptor or an architect can keep themselves aloof from their art once it is done and opened for public viewing which theatre artists cannot. Their responsibility grows more during the performance than the process. They are subject to the audience's disposal. They have to incarnate the characters of the play and interact with the space. Since it is a presentation of a continuous development during the performance, the actors have to cover the length and breadth of the stage, climb up and down the staircase, take entry and exit for many times in various ways. In every evening, they have to portray life and interact with the space in front of the audience.

Interactive Space

Theatre space has been explored with diverse ways across the world. In classical Indian performance, it is an intimate and empty space that metamorphoses into various locales supported by the stylised performance of the actors. In ancient Greek theatre, it is a huge open air space that remains unaltered potraying one location throughout. In medieval Europe, a performance space was defined through illustrations, paintings and sceneries, though there could not be any interactions of these painted sceneries with the performers and the space remained unresponsive. These two-dimensional painted sceneries could only display its illusionistic reality but not the reality in the truest sense. Actors in medieval times could only perform in front of the stage without interacting with the multiple dimensions of the space.

Over the course of time, these two-dimensional painted sceneries paved the way for three-dimensional design. Levels, platforms, steps, pillars, flats, doors, windows and all three-dimensional furniture such as, table, chair, bed, sofa, shelves, etc. were taken into theatre space in the begining of the 20th century. With the entry of these three-dimensional objects into the theatre space the performance space became functional and interactive. The performers in this space could comfortably establish contextual relationships with these objects. In this cohesion the space rises up to articulate with its inmates as an active member of the performance. A statement of Adolphe Appia can justify our arguments:

> As a consequence of this new relationship, the dramatic text will be able more precisely to determine the role of the actor, and this in turn will allow the actor to determine the spatial arrangement of the setting. This, consequently, will increase the already existing antagonism between the three-dimensional and painted scenery, because by its very nature the latter must always be in conflict with the actor and work to his disadvantage. This conflict between the representative potential of scene painting and the more dynamic forces of the theatre will eventually diminish the importance of painted settings. Lighting, once liberated for the most part from the task of simply illuminating painted flats, will recover its proper independent role, and will begin to serve actor actively…[vii]

Since the space has a volume and dimension and is used through its length, breadth and height, and since the actors only can reciprocate this space, involve it in the action and develop a relationship with it, theatre space is regarded as an interactive space. In this three-dimensional space, the actor can come through a real door, hold it and use it in the performance and can sit on a chair and lean on the table as a part of the action. He can climb the steps up to a balcony where the scene takes place. He can even sit under an arch and stand against its pillar, hold it and can look through a window for someone to come. The three-dimensional space changed the conotation of 20th-century theatre significantly. The space can involve in a dialogue with the audience and behave as a supporting character along with the actors and can be a major component of dramatic interpretation.

CONCLUSION

A creative artist stands firm in his medium through the power of imagination. However, imagination needs a ground to be flourished. For an artist, nature is the prime source of formulating ideas. Through this chapter we have attempted to examine the syllables of design that have been brought into practice through a careful observation of nature. Their application into theatre design formulates the language for visual compositions. We have also tried to conceptualise various expressions of design elements such as, line, colour, texture, shape and form, value, space and dimension. An understanding of these syllables would certainly orient young scenographers towards the methods of spatial design in theatre.

Writing a stage space needs total integration of all design elements in view of their interrelationships. However, they never work in isolations; they are expressed in totality. For example, a form needs lines to be composed, colours to establish mood and emotion, textures to speak out the feelings and finally a space to be expressed with all its dynamism. But, too much of juxtaposition of design elements in the space would lead to a complicated design. Overexposure of elements in a single production also spoils the work, failing to establish a dialogue with the audience and stands apart from the context of the performance. On the contrary, a creative design with minimum exploration of elements enhances the level of the production and interprets the performance convincingly. In the former case, the design could not live up to the expectation of the performance and could not express the concept due to unimaginative application of various elements, defocused. This kind of spatial design cannot establish coherence among themselves and is left out of context. In the latter case, it vibrates with the language of the production and articulates the text visually. It should be the responsibility of the scenographers to find consequential solutions to design the space through these various elements and make the performance a memorable experience.

References

i   Dehejja, Harsha Venilal. 2010. *Akriti to Sanskriti: The Journey of Indian Forms*. New Delhi: Niyogi Books. p. 14.
ii Rathbun, Mary Chalmers. 1949. *Layman's Guide to Modern Art*. New York: Oxford University Press. p. 35.
iii "Line (geometry)." *Wikipedia*, Wikimedia Foundation, 29 Oct. 2020, https://en.wikipedia.org/wiki/Line_(geometry).
iv Pipes, Alan. 2008. *Foundations of Art and Design*. London: Laurence King Publishing Ltd. p. 18.
v   Ibid. p. 43.
vi Ibid. p. 127.
vii Beacham, Richard C. 1993. *Adolphe Appia: Texts on Theatre*. NY, London: Routledge Inc. p. 35.

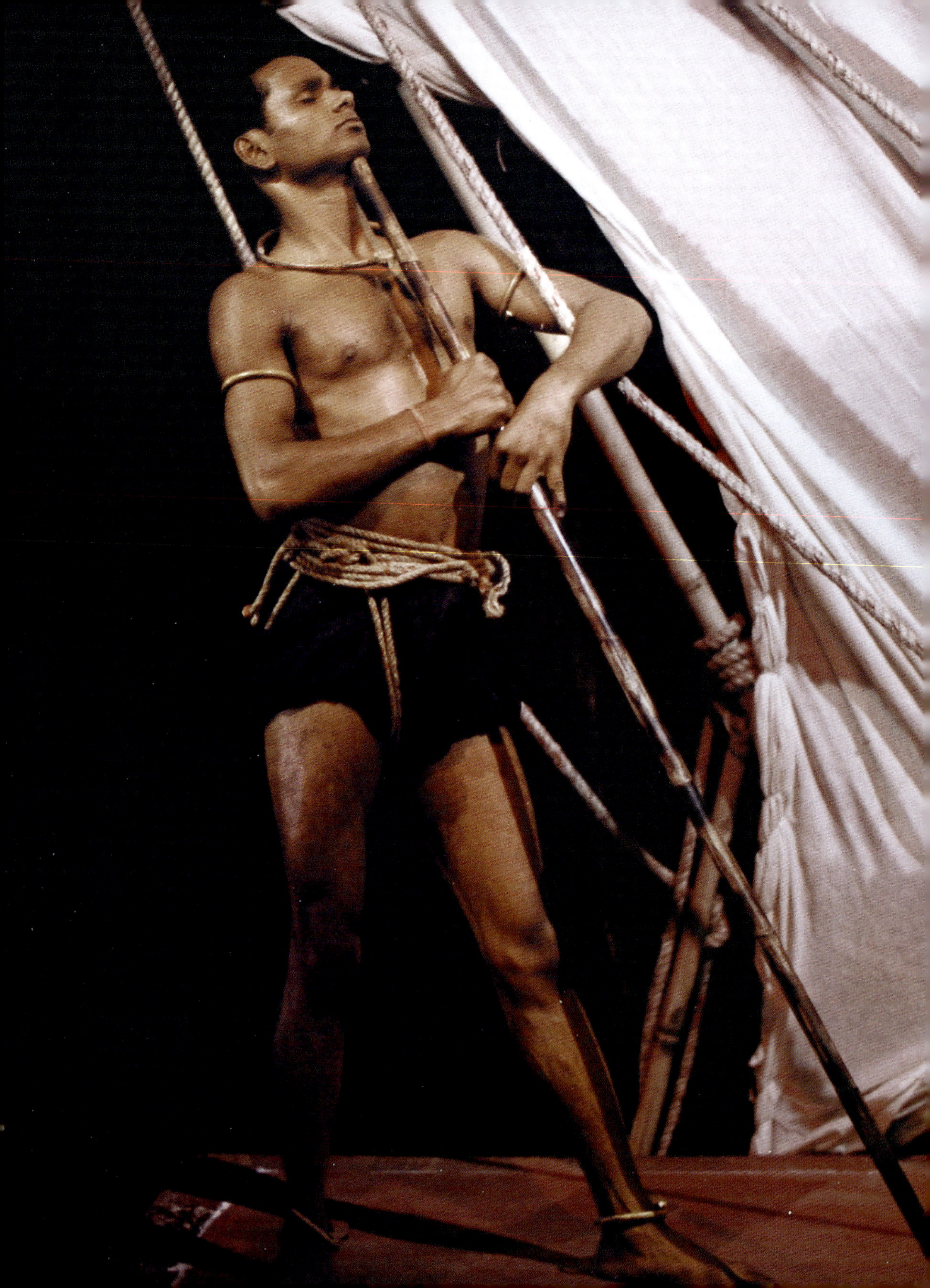

PRINCIPLES OF DESIGN 10

SPATIAL COMPOSITION

Composition creates meaning for art and design. It organises the design elements and helps establishing the desired relationships in between the objects and interprets the form. Thus composition, as a term, is pregnant in itself, which can only be achieved through the interplay of more than one object or element in a given space. Like a piece of music that needs minimum two notes to be expressed, visual composition also requires more than one object to be expressed. We can only compose a table with a chair, a tree with its branches, a painting against a wall. Similarly, on stage, an actor can compose himself along with a few props, or even with a single object such as, by keeping a cigarette in hand, or sitting on a block, etc. However, a single image can also compose individually with the help of its various components in which all its elements arrange themselves with each other in relationships to the entirety within their spatial entity. We can understand this statement through the illustration of *David* by Michelangelo (1501–04). This is a unique example of single image composition in which each part of the body—the hands, legs, palms, feet, torso, muscles, head—are placed in such a relationship among themselves that it creates a poetry in a piece of stone.

Irrespective of different genres of art, the principles of composition are same for all. The only difference is, while a musical composition is measured through time, a visual composition is measured through space. The orchestration of space brings order into the design and establishes a relationship among various elements. In theatre, only with the interactions of actors, the stage objects get meaning and articulate the visuals. Professor Pamela Howard argues:

> Objects and elements do not speak by themselves. They must be placed in a relationship to the space, and to each other, in order to have an eloquence and meaning. Then they talk to each other across the empty space. The way the image is placed transforms actuality into art. In a stage composition, the object is much more than its literal self. It becomes an emblem for the hidden world of the play, something that lies behind but supports the player's words. Its power and appropriateness will carry significance beyond what it appears to be, as well as a satisfying sense of beauty and authority.[i]

The prime objective of compositions in scenography is to create visual images that hold interest of the spectators and to provide interpretative meaning for the play. A comparative study of paintings and can bring new perspective to the meaning of visual compositions.

David (1501–1504). Medium: Marble stone. Artist: Michelangelo. Place of display: Galleria dell'Accademia, Florence, Italy. Courtesy: Wikimedia Commons.

While visiting an art gallery, we keep on moving from one painting to the other, hanging on the walls. But watching a theatre is different. Here the viewer sits at one place (though there are a few exceptions) and the images keep on moving one after the other in a defined space. These images keep on changing their compositions through the reciprocity of lines, colours, textures, mass, volume and space.

The master artist of Indian theatre, Ratan Thiyam, has conceptualised this reciprocity through a method to create his visual compositions. He coined it as, 'Paint and Erase' method. For him, the visual compositions in theatre are like series of paintings, which continuously keep on erasing on the stage one after the other, giving rise to new compositions. A theatre consists of numerous visual images like a series of paintings. While these moving visuals are wiped out on the stage one after the other, they are transported to the spectators' psyche where they permanently are engraved as persistent memory and judged through subjective experiences. They reside in the collective psyche of the audience forever. The concept of 'Paint and Erase' method can only be apprehended through watching his productions, such as, *Chakravyuha* (1984), *Andha Yug* (1984), *When We Dead Awaken* (2008), *The King of the Dark Chamber* (2010) and *Macbeth* (2016), etc.

Often the lived experience creeps into the creations. We can draw a stark resemblance of these experiences being imitated onto the creations of the scenographers with examples. In the scenographic ventures of Bansi Kaul, the terrain and staircase-like landscapes are intelligently and artistically blended into the design elements according to the arrangement of lines and colours in his spatial compositions. Rhythmic pattern of lines and bright primary colours on the stage have their importance in Kaul's visual sensibility. They easily emerge out of his personal association and live experiences with the northern Himalayan valley of Kashmir, his nostalgic childhood memories. Application of geometrical shapes, contrasting

Set design for the play *Zindegi aur Zonk*. Design and direction: Bansi Kaul. Courtesy: Rang Vidushak, Bhopal.

colours and striking yet repetitive rhythmic patterns of lines form his visual compositions. Similarly, in another observation, the intricate lines, sketchy compositions and unprecedented approach for the space is the way of theatre design of Professor Robin Das, which make his visuals complexly interesting. His dramatic expressions are the outcome of his keen observation of human nature at the rural vicinity, particularly people living in the low-hill areas. The multifarious, suspicious, cynical and complex yet innocent characteristics of these countryside people subconsciously creep into his spatial design time and again which forms his personal approach for design and scenography. Though apparently unfinished, haphazard, broken, complicated and random, the works of Das are actually dynamic, expressive, interpretative and often challenging for the actors.

Nature and Art
Any living and non-living entity in nature narrates its story in silence by creating appropriate atmosphere around it. This narrative, when told through visuals, needs to be manifested through space, lines, colours, shape and form. Creative art, being the interpretation and comprehension of these natural phenomena, needs a careful survey of nature before its application in the medium. The natural surrounding and its various factors are always responsible to shape art, in which human life is interpreted. All the elements of nature are fastened harmoniously with each other to exist in coherence. In this coexistence, while some elements push themselves to the background to remain passive by creating space for others to be expressed with meaning, the opposite is also possible. Some elements interestingly coexist and are expressed contextually, powered by their mutual energy. This is the beauty of our natural environment where every element has its role to play. In this order of unified existence, objects are managed according to their significance. In this coexistence, when an object changes its shape, colour, form and space, others are to be modified accordingly in order to maintain the harmony. This is the law of nature and is indiscriminately applied to all the existing beings.

In art and design, these natural phenomena are creatively interpreted through individual artistic sensibility. Therefore, their ethics may vary from person to person, whose expressions depend solely on the artist's singular perception. In theatre, scenography is always determined through various factors, such as, space, costumes, lights, sets, masks, make-up and finally, the actors who interact with these components. Therefore, an interpretative and conceptual design created through these elements, becomes necessary for a relevant presentation which can only be achieved by incorporating certain phenomenon derived from nature. These are called the principles of composition, essential for creating a harmonious and interpretative relationships among all the elements. Some of the commonly observed principles, applied into art and design are:

- Balance
- Proportion
- Emphasis
- Contrast
- Domination
- Area of Interest
- Isolation
- Strangeness
- Rhythm
- Unity
- Energy

BALANCE

Designing a play is a highly creative process. It involves tremendous making and unmaking of ideas until finally executed. During the process of conceiving a design, new ideas often challenge the scenographers. In the process of developing visuals, the elements of art and design undergo numerous transformations before they are finally executed in a stage space. This procedure is common for all arts, as a nascent creation grows critically and aesthetically with the artist, each moment adding new edges to the work. Out of many factors responsible for evoking aesthetics to the visual compositions, stage balance is perhaps the most pivotal. By balancing a composition in the stage space, scenographers not only create stability but also make their visuals meaningful and interpretative. Eventually, all the visual elements in the three-dimensional space are evenly distributed on either side of the stage space, making the centre point of the stage as visual axis. In this distribution of design elements on space, the 'visual weight' is evenly dispensed, forming a visual equilibrium targeting for our physical and psychological sense of stability.

Visual Weight

Visual weight is the measure of the force of an object on space that attracts our eyes through the elements of colours, lines, texture, mass, volume and shape. The visual weight solely depends on the power and intensity of the object that arrests our eyes instantly. In fig. A in the next page, a pillar on down-right is effectively balanced by an ancient temple on stage-centre-left, though the temple is much bigger and massive in size in comparison to the pillar. Similarly, in fig B, a single hexagonal shape in red and green is balanced by a cluster of shapes on the other side of these axis in a two-dimensional space due to the power of its visual intensity. In both the contexts the objects have nothing to do with their gravitational or the physical weight as we generally know. Through this principle, a tiny object can also effectively balance a larger object on the other side of the visual axis, depending on its power of attraction, expression and intensity. Like an old-fashioned scale, where a heavyweight object nearer to the fulcrum is balanced by the weight of the scale from pivot, a small object can balance the entire space, projected through its colour, texture and shape.

An empty performance space is always considered neutral and is visually balanced by its emptiness. Entry of an actor on one corner of the stage space makes it visually intense like one-sided weight of a fulcrum. Eventually, this particular space becomes heavier and draw our attention, thus making the entire space imbalanced psychologically. To compensate the heaviness of that specific area, a large visual unit (object or actor) is required at the other end to balance the visual weight of the space. In

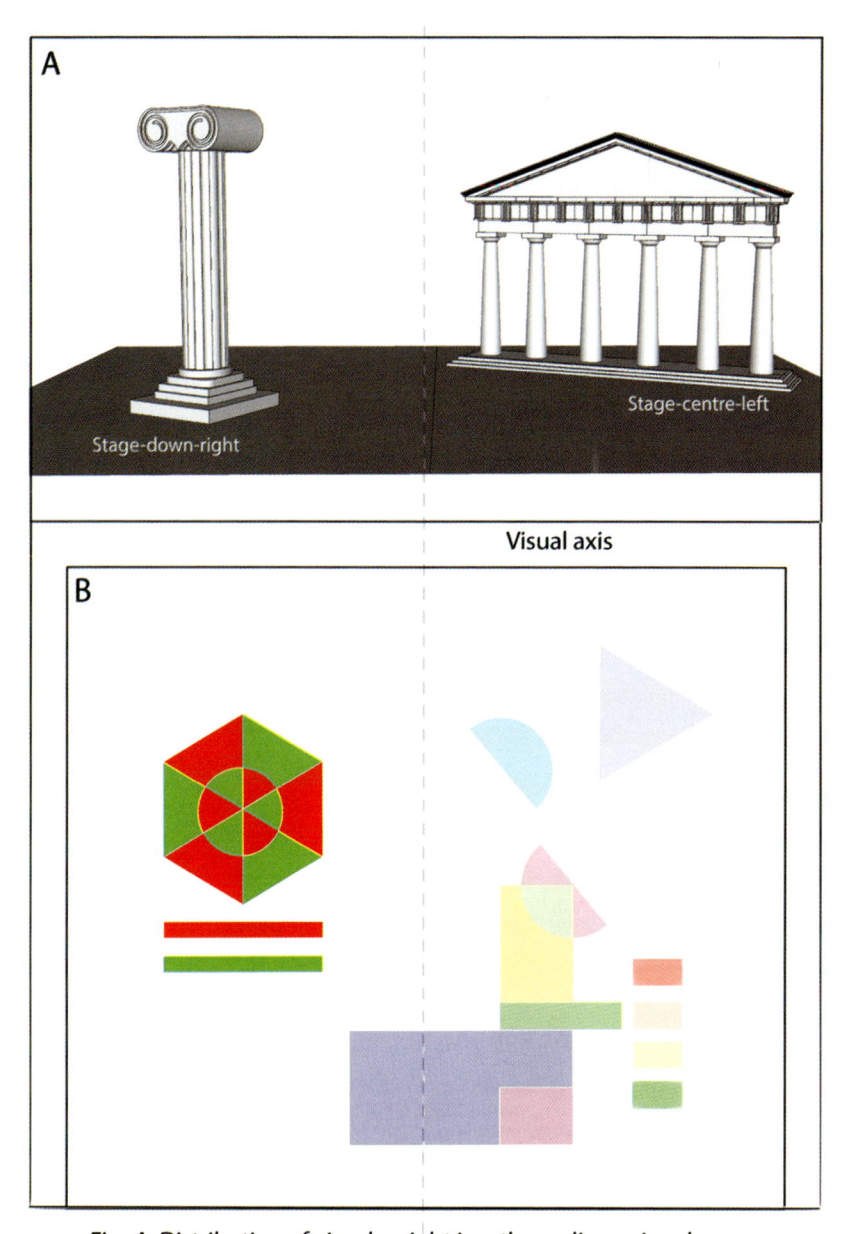

Fig- A: Distribution of visual weight in a three-dimensional space
Fig- B: Distribution of visual weight in a two-dimensional space

Still from the play *Tumhara Vincent*. Playwright, scenography and direction: Satyabrata Rout. Actor in the photograph: Md. Sahidur Rahman. Photography: Thyagrajan. Courtesy: Rangakalpa, Hyderabad.

the photograph above, a large visual unit (landscape with sunflowers) is incorporated towards the stage centre and stage left in order to balance a single character (Van Gogh) on the down right. Visual weight is always judged through human eyes. This is the primary principle of composition that brings equilibrium and aesthetics to the visuals. In theatre, the actors continuously balance the space while interacting with the design elements. Sometimes, visually imbalanced space creates tension and disturbs our visual stability, but it can be creatively explored to project dramatic conflict whenever required.

Balancing a Three-dimensional Space

For our own convenience we can equally divide the performance space into two halves through an imaginary centreline from the audience's point of view. Since the visual axis of different performance spaces differ depending on the audience arrangements in the gallery, the centreline also varies. A space is always dead and empty until it is interacted by an actor or any object. With a single prop or an actor in the empty space, a sudden physical change happens in that emptiness. A portion of the space where the object or actor is placed, gets awakened into action. Accordingly, that particular space is charged, supported by the actor's or the object's spatial energy. The intensity of the space solely depends on the dimensions and the proportion of the object, props or the status of the character in relationship with the stage space. But the entire space may not be warmed up and activated by a single actor or a prop placed at one corner of the stage and may not keep the visual weight balanced as discussed above. It may seem to be inclined towards the area where that object or actor is positioned. To make the space visually balanced, another actor(s) or object(s) can be proportionately placed at the other side of the axis.

While balancing the composition in the space with actors and design, scenographers should consciously watch the visual impact of the stage space and the actor, because an actor or a stage unit composed on the downstage would produce more intensity than the objects placed on the upstage. When an object moves away from the audience view, it loses visual energy and intensity, yet depending on its size, shape and colour. Therefore, a proportionately smaller object on the downstage may reasonably balance a large object on the upstage and the opposite is also viable.

The importance of the actors in balancing the space must not be overlooked; they formulate the major components of the visuals. It is often observed that an outwardly imbalanced space gets balanced with the actors' meaningful interactions with the spatial objects. Unlike other

A

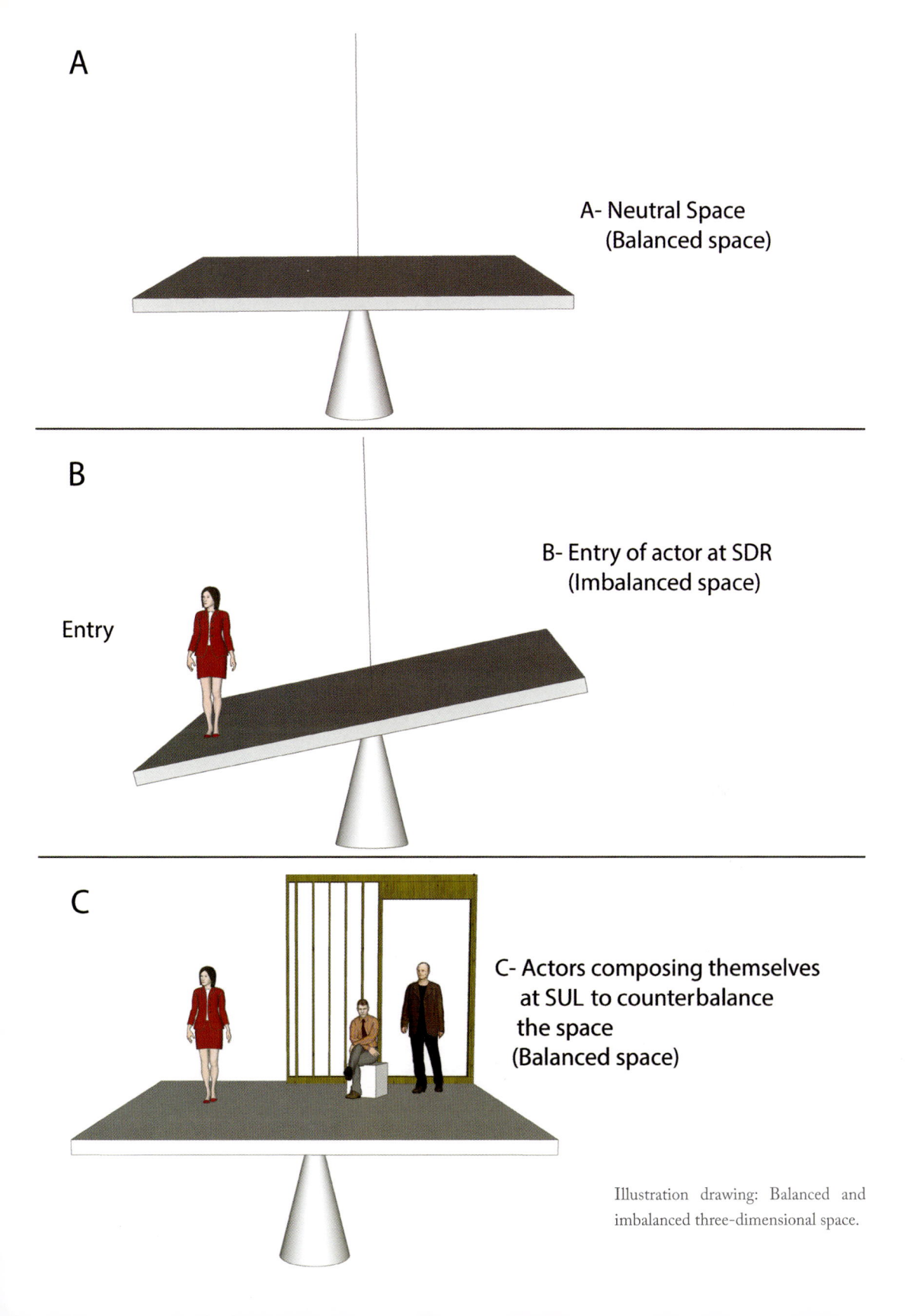

A- Neutral Space
(Balanced space)

B

Entry

B- Entry of actor at SDR
(Imbalanced space)

C

C- Actors composing themselves
at SUL to counterbalance
the space
(Balanced space)

Illustration drawing: Balanced and imbalanced three-dimensional space.

470 | SCENOGRAPHY

A - Two-dimensional space (Balanced)

B - Application of lines and colours at one corner of the canvas (Imbalanced)

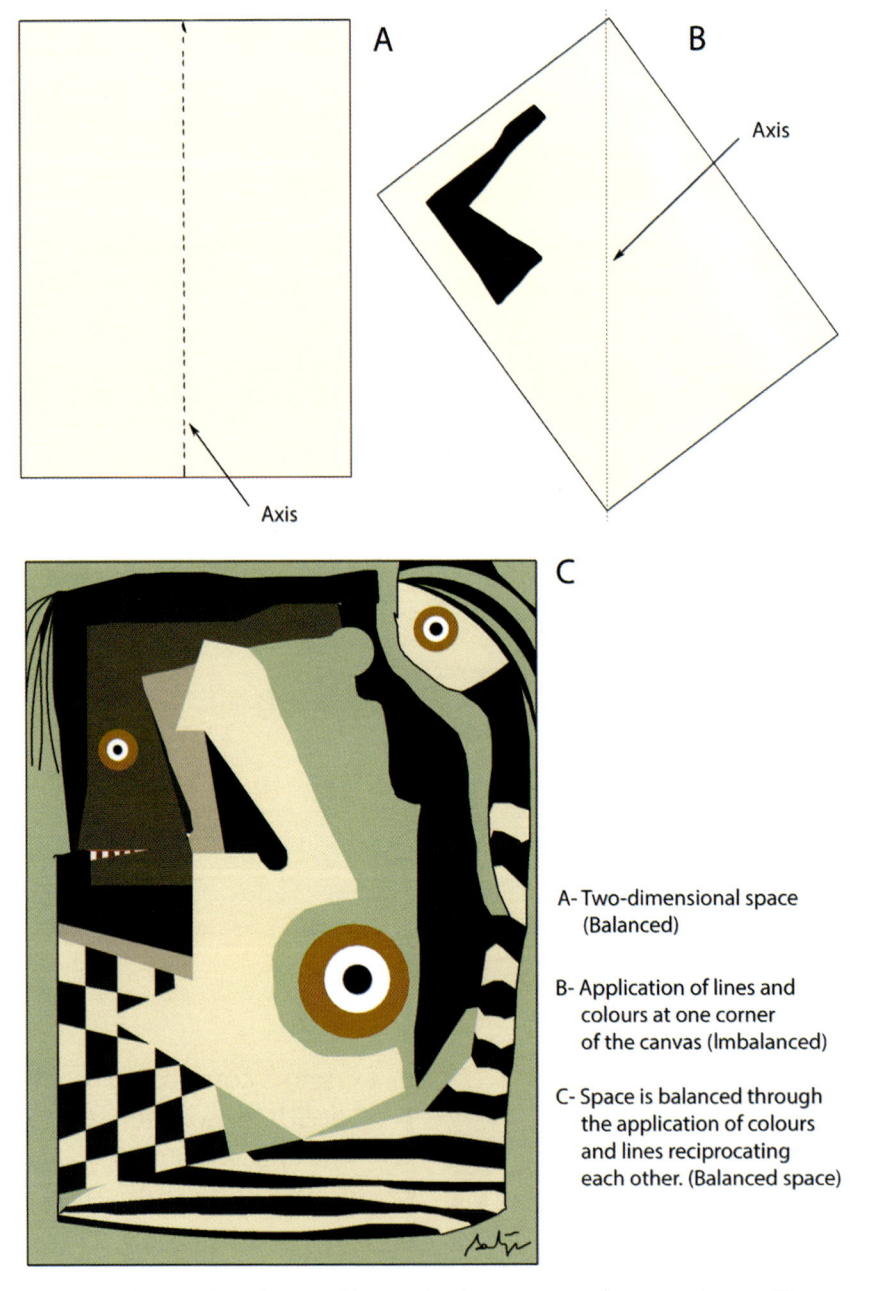

C - Space is balanced through the application of colours and lines reciprocating each other. (Balanced space)

Illustration drawing: Distribution of lines and colours in a two-dimensional space. (Drawing made by the author).

forms of art, scenography cannot rely on an absolutely balanced space, but a provocative and interactive space in which the actors can live in, feel its warmth and play with each other's mutual energy.

Balancing a Two-dimensional Space
There is a potential difference between a two-dimensional and a three-dimensional space. For a painter or a graphic artist, a piece of paper or a stretched canvas is synonymous to 'performance space'. A blank white paper works as an empty and neutral space without any visual expression. A brush or a pencil stroke can evoke the space and bring it into action. The first slash of colour or a pencil line activates the two-dimensional space—paper, canvas, etc. At the same time, it makes the space unsteady because of the visual weight that shifts towards that space, created through lines or colours. The artists usually balance their works and activate the entire space by adding colours or lines reciprocally. Alan Pipes mentions: 'Balance in a design aims to distribute the visual weight of the elements so that they appear to be in equilibrium'.[ii]

Distributing space and balancing the compositions for a spatial design can be achieved in many ways through the reciprocal arrangements of its visual units. Like shape demands shapes, colour also demands colours for a balanced composition. The photographs on the next page would throw some lights on compositions that are balanced through colours. In this spatial design the scenic visuals create appropriate ambience for the play by combining warm and cool colours together. Trapped in the splendour of beauty generated by the analogous colour combinations in costumes and lights, the spatial compositions of the play set a perfect romantic mood, appropriate to the characters of the play.

Stage balance can be measured as symmetrical, asymmetrical and radial which can also divide the space vertically, horizontally and diagonally depending on the arrangements of design units.

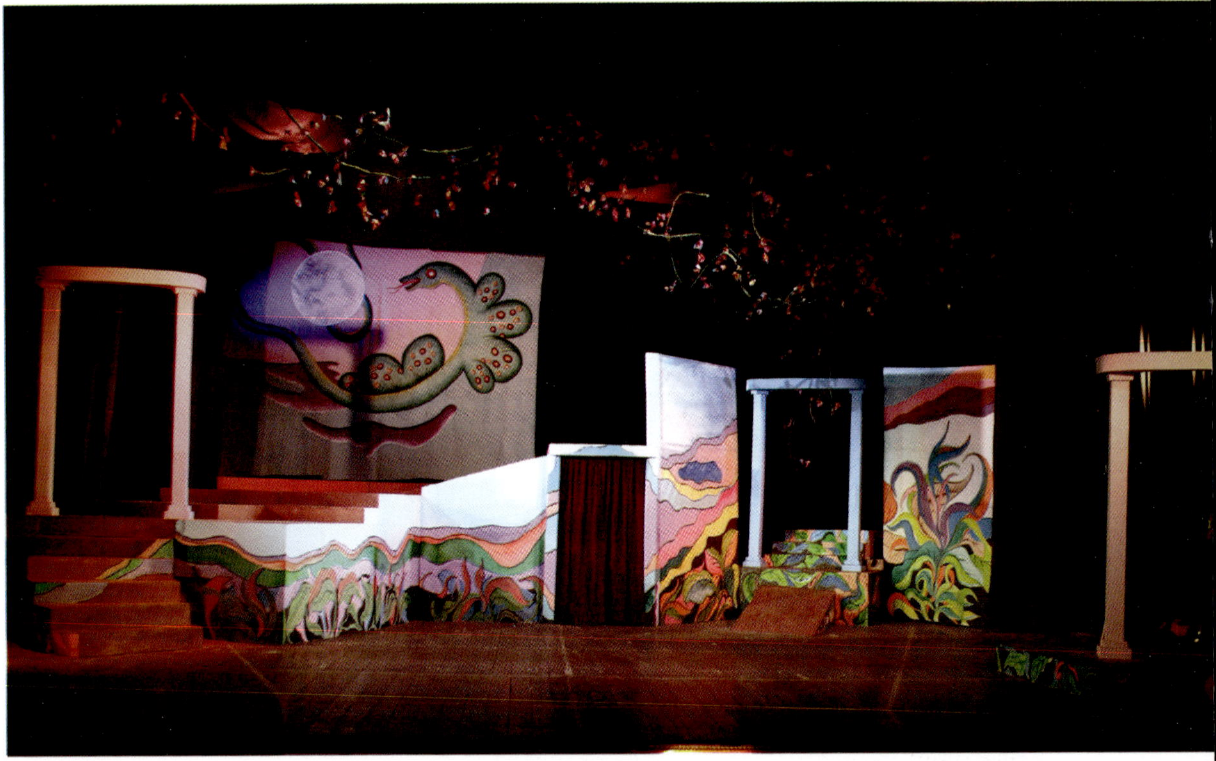

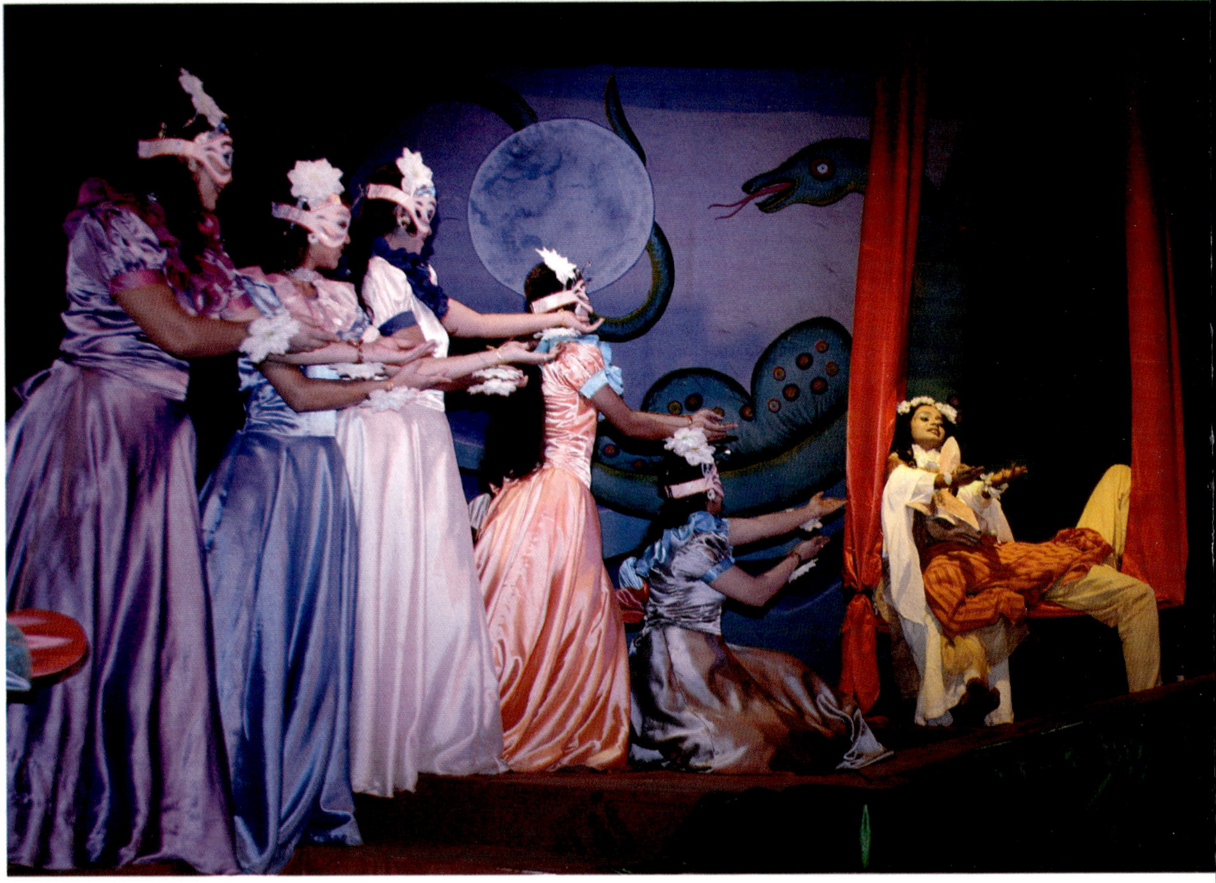

Symmetrical Balance

When one side of the axis becomes the mirror image of the other, it is called bilaterally symmetrical balance. Symmetrical balance can be understood by the illustration of *The Vitruvian Man* (1487) by Leonardo Da Vinci. The drawing is based on the ideal human-proportions in which symmetry was described by the ancient Roman architect Vitruvius in the first century BC. The drawing symbolises the symmetrical balance of human body and its extension in the universe as a whole. Vitruvius insisted on the classical ideas of beauty, which lies in symmetry and is achieved through the higher sensibility of art and aesthetics.

However, symmetrical balance in scenography, though pleases our eyes and mind, often creates monotony and fails to activate the space. Bilaterally symmetrical design tries to emphasise the centre, making the rest of the performance space insignificant. Reciprocating each side, bilaterally symmetrical composition generally forms stagnancy in the space. It seems complete in itself, leaving less opportunity for the actors to interact. But the purpose of scenography is to provide opportunity for the actors to interact in a unified space. A bilaterally symmetrical space often fails to interplay with the dramatic actions and decline to integrate with the performance. It may not provoke for reactive, articulate and interesting space design. On the contrary, symmetrical balanced space brings stability and enrich the production with grandeur and beauty. However, creative application of symmetrical design would transform the space into the dynamic theatrical expression.

FACING PAGE: Stills from the play *More Naina Rang Chadhe*. Courtesy: Bharatendu Natya Academy, Lucknow.

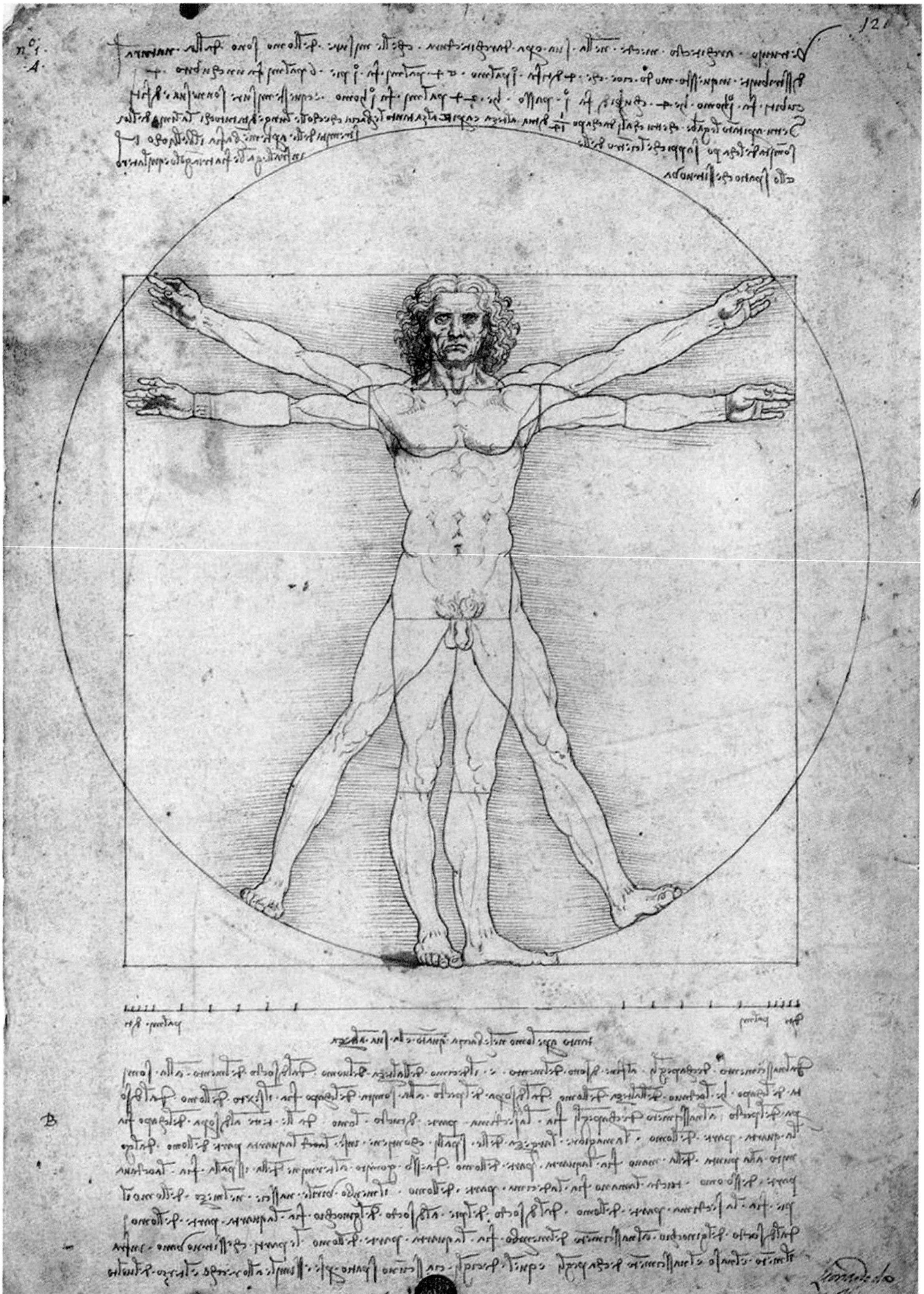
121

Asymmetrical Balance
This is an informal kind of balance which is not expressed through regular identical images in the composition. Asymmetrically balanced design is always active and dynamic because of the multiple ways of organising elements and objects in the space. This kind of design balances the compositions in such a way that all the visual units of the composition reciprocate with each other around the axis, focusing the desired one in every action. The attention of the viewers is guided towards the focused area through the interaction of various stage elements during a performance. This type of composition is more dynamic than a symmetrical one and helps building the dramatic tension wherever required. But every time, it depends on the arrangement of various design units in the space and their relationships with the actors. However, diagonal forces in design is more provocative than a horizontal or vertical one. It is more intense and dynamic.

The scenography of *More Naina Rang Chadhe* is a perfect example of asymmetrical balance. This design (ref. to the figure on the next page) comprises of four major visual units of various heights and levels, balanced by each other's visual weights. The force generated from all the design units was directing towards the down left centre, thus charging the space as focused area where most of the major actions take place. Powered by the spatial energy from all the design units those were diagonally conserved around that space to emphasise the action. The space that projects the dramatic action, can be achieved anywhere in the space through the arrangements of the design elements and objects in an asymmetrical composition. Another example of asymmetrical design that balances the space by focusing the stage down centre is the scenography of *Iphigenia*

FACING PAGE: *Vitruvian Man* (1487). Artist: Leonardo Da Vinci. Location: Galleria dell'Accademia, Venice, Italy. Courtesy: Wikimedia Commons.

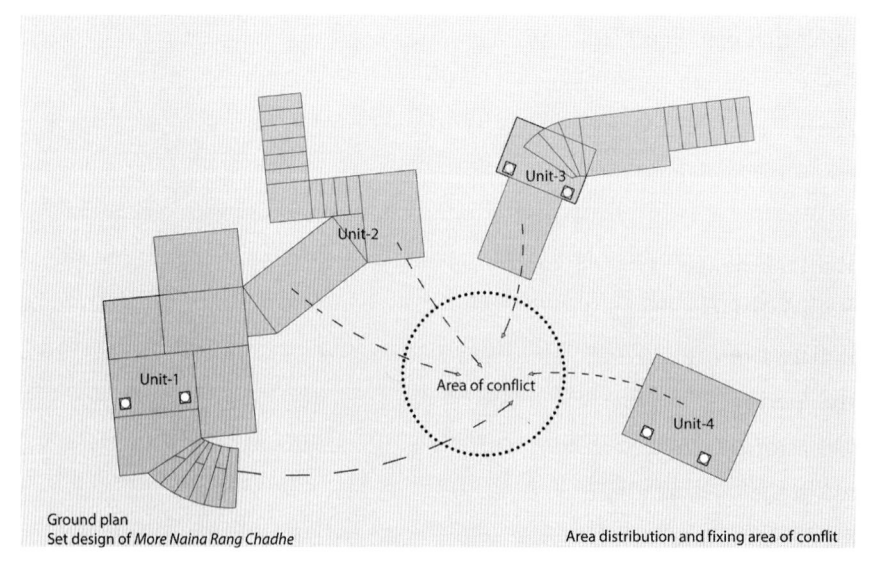

Ground plan of *More Naina Rang Chadhe*.

in Aulis (see page 436). In this spatial composition, various design units were placed through vertical, diagonal and horizontal planes to create visual balance between the space and the performers. The space creates opportunity for the actors to be balanced by the energy generated through these units. For example, an actor standing on the staircase is balanced by other spatial units, such as, flags on the vertical up-right position, puppet-chorus on the horizontal level against the wall, and the sail of the boat, placed in a slightly diagonal position at the back.

There are many means to create asymmetrical balance in a design. As already discussed, a small but visually powerful object that produces high energy can easily balance a larger object or area, depending on its shape, size, colours and arrangement in the space. We can experience the dynamics of asymmetrical balance from our own surroundings. A sharp look at our own living room can reveal how interestingly our usable objects develop their relationships with each other, providing enough focused space for our use. The common household goods are arranged in such a sense of unity and order that one object seems to be an extension of the other. A well-designed living room represents proper array of asymmetrical balance and proportion. Asymmetrical balance creates dramatic effect and brings dynamism into the composition, which has influenced the visual artists across the times.

Radial Balance

Radial balance is another form of symmetry in which the elements radiate from the centre point to the edge. These elements travel towards the periphery of the composition in straight or curved movements. Occasionally, they create spiral movements, encircling the centre as we can see in the seeds of a sunflower. Therefore, radial balance in a design is often expressed through curve lines.

Passionflower is also an apt example of radial balance. The energy from the centre of the flower radiates like a centrifugal force to its fringe through its spike-like petals, radiating energy to the outer. On the contrary, in a sunflower, the energy is focused to the centre through its spiral arrangement of seeds. In a radial design, the curve movements of its lines and colours tend to converge towards or diverse out of the centre by projecting the central image. It is not necessary for the central image to signify the centre of the space; it can be composed anywhere within the space. The study of Van Gogh's *Starry Night* (1889) would provide a lot of hints to understand the radial balance in a composition.

The composition of radial symmetry in design is common in Indian dance, theatre, architecture and visual arts. Ancient Indian philosophy has always depicted life as a cycle. It moves in a spiral pattern, tries to converge towards the centre. Indian philosophy has a profound impact on Indian arts, literature and architecture as well as classical dance and theatre where the gestures, postures and movements are radially balanced with the space. Radial balance in design has always dominated our traditional patterns and shapes. Rangoli (floral design), a sacred radial pattern originating in

Indian floral design (Alpana).

the Indian subcontinent, is another good example of radial composition. In scenography, a radial design can facilitate the actors' energy and enrich its aesthetics.

While balancing a space for theatre, it must be clear in the mind that scenography is not just scattering the required objects in a space and then balancing them according to some academic theory. It is more natural, spontaneous, that stems from the scenographer's higher sensitivity for visuals and must be placed in order. It is very crucial to unify the elements in respect of the context and interpretation, thus creating a relationship among the elements.

PROPORTION

Proportion sets appropriate relations among all the components of a composition by placing them in affiliation to each other. In theatre design, it not only establishes rational relationships among the visual units, but more significantly, it helps establish sensible connections with the actors who eventually use the space as their personal environment and interact with the spatial objects during a performance.

Proportion universally is interplayed in between more than one element in design. Like a human structure, which is anatomically proportionate, in design all the elements are to be placed in their correct proportions in order to compliment and sync with each other. Now let us find some examples from our ordinary life, where this toying with space is prevalent. While in a film, objects on screen seem larger, in a TV or laptop screen, the same objects and space get proportionately diminished—they look like miniatures, almost a microcosmic representation of the giant screen. In all these cases, the viewing experience remains proportionate to the actual size of the space, actors or objects, etc. We create our own environment in right proportions for comfortable living, where each object is in correct ratio to our dimensions. If we measure the dimension of our house, we would find the height of our ceiling is approximately 10 feet. Similarly, the height and width of the door of our living room in general is 6 feet and 3 feet respectively. An ordinary chair is 1.5 feet high while the height of a writing table is 2.5 feet.

The same concept is also applicable to art and design, with a different connotation. In realistic art, proportion is perceived in relation to the reality of life, but in a non-realistic and stylised form, it is contextual. Proportion in these circumstances is decided through the narrative, status, background, personality, visual symbols, metaphors and at last but not the least, the visual aesthetics. In Indian art, Ravana with ten heads or Ganesha with a large elephant head and a tiny mouse as his vehicle appears proportionate

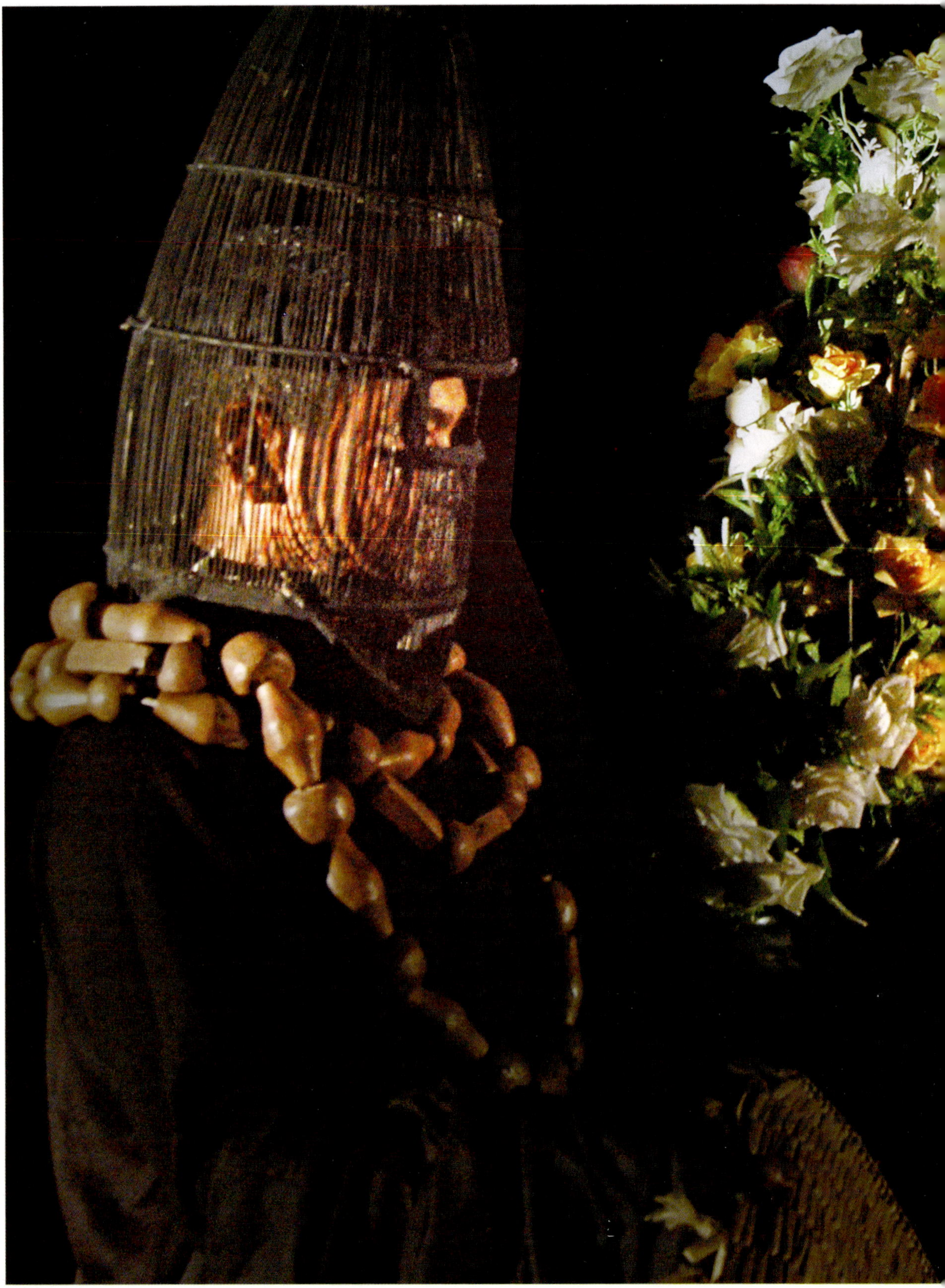

Still from the play *Macbeth*. Adaptation into Manipuri: Ratan Thiyam. Design and direction: Ratan Thiyam. Courtesy: Chorus Repertory Theatre, Imphal.

to our cultural perception; proportion here is contextual. In art and design, the aesthetics and the style of presentation decide the nature of proportion. The photograph of the play *Macbeth* affirms the statement. Macbeth, the Scottish general, is being greeted by Lady Macbeth with a bucket of flower which per se is disproportionate through a realistic vision because of its larger than life dimension. But contextually the bucket represents Macbeth's overwhelming ambition and lust for power, thus contextually proportionate in this sequence of the play.

Proportion, as a principle of design, largely depends on the arrangement of the visual units in the space. In scenography, stage proportion is decided by keeping the actors as the prime factor of performance. All the spatial arrangements must have a proportionate and harmonious relationship with the actors. In a theatre presentation, there are basically three types of spatial arrangements that work. They are—object-to-object relationship, object-to-space relationship and actor–object–space relationship.

Object-to-Object Relationship

The exploration of a space and the selection of stage objects is the call of the scenographers. All these objects share a common space—the stage. The harmony of sharing the energy among these stage elements depends on their size, colours, textures and usage in a particular context. Their relationships are established by the fusion of their spatial energy.

In a stage space, objects coexist within a definite synchrony whose degree of intensity vary contextually. For creating a living room on stage, we commonly engage stage props and set units such as, sofa, bed, chair and table, television, showcase, dining set, doors and windows, staircase, lamp shades, etc. These stage objects share common energy and exist in relationship with each other. However, some objects share intimate relationships than others. For instance, a table has a direct association with a chair because both are expressed jointly. Similarly, a bed is associated with

PRINCIPLES OF DESIGN | 483

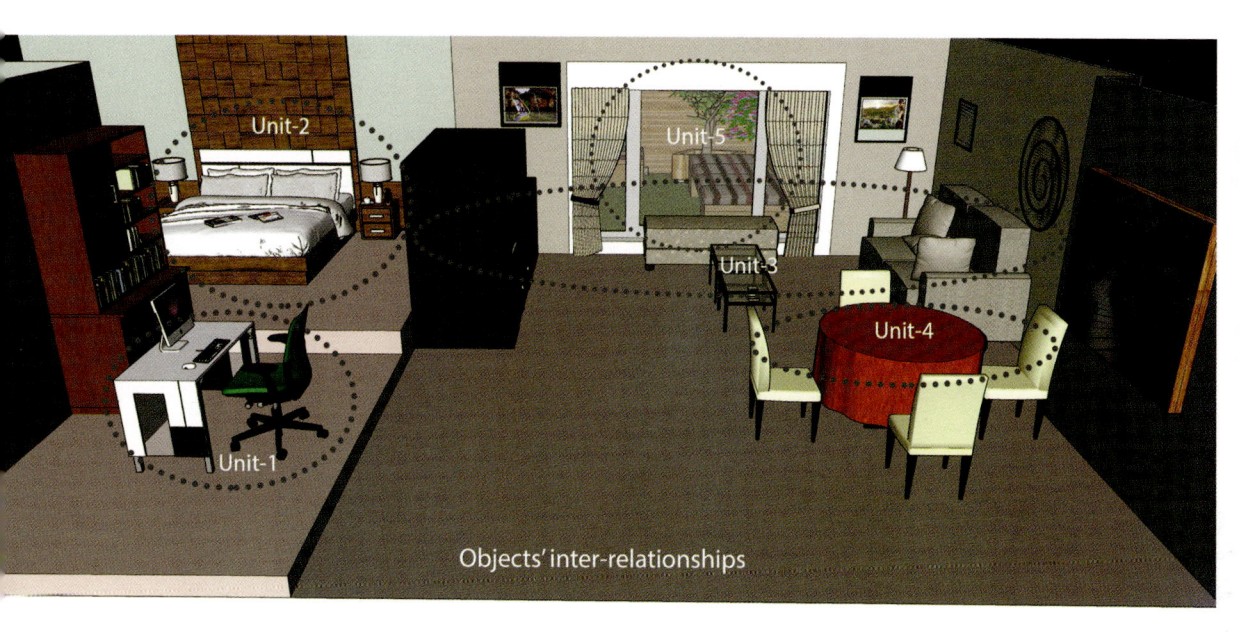

Unit-1: Study area -- Table, chair, computer and bookself
Unit-2: Bedroom area -- Bed, lamps, corner table and wall decor
Unit-3: Livinroom area -- Sofa set, floor lamp, wall hangings, painting, central table, cabinate with television
Unit-4: dyning table and chairs, painting
Unit-5: Outdoor unit- Lawn, garden bench, tree

Illustrative drawing demonstrating the relationships between the objects and props in a defined space.

a lampshade and a corner unit, or a sofa which is normally used for sitting and watching a television, and so on. But again, these relationships are completely contextual, depending on their uses in the play.

Object-to-Space Relationships

Anything perceived in its physical form occupies space and exists with commitment to that particular space. This is the law of nature as well as art and design. In theatre, we come across the terms like wing space, breathing space, negative and positive space, virtual space, dead space, living space, neutral space, empty space, etc. These spaces share reciprocal relationships with the objects and actors. The significance of the objects or actors depends on their exploration and distribution of the space. For example, a chair near the door at down stage creates a different meaning from a chair placed against a table at the centre stage. Similarly, different gestures of two individuals with the same object at the same space depict different meanings. For example, a stranger and a family member knocking at the same door have different connotations. Arrangement of objects in a space always remains challenging for the scenographers. While composing the visual elements in a space with their finer spatial relationships, the scenographers try to build a narrative around them that interprets the space. In a visual composition, the scenographers often create some strangeness in between the space and the objects that bring theatricality into the situation. But an unimaginative arrangement of objects in the space seizes to narrate the story and remains isolated from the rest of the spatial units and eventually stops releasing the energy. This occurs due to unfeasible relationships among the objects and the space. This issue can be rectified by recomposing and rearranging those spatial units proportionately with each other.

In a dramatic composition, each design unit has its own role to play in which it pulsates with the vibration of the space like a character of the play. Quite often, a considerable amount of 'negative space' (space around the objects, or actors) helps identifying that object and projects it properly. As a general rule, to bring an object or actor into focus, the negative space around that object or actor must be larger than the 'positive space' (space occupied by the object or actor) of that particular object or actor. On the other hand, if the objects are to be displayed in groups or the actors are composed as chorus, the negative space between individual objects or actors should be less than the positive space of the single unit. The drawing (facing page) clarifies the statement. In fig. A, there is a group of figures standing in rows by sharing a common space. Their identity in the space are equal and unified and are well projected due to the equal amount

A

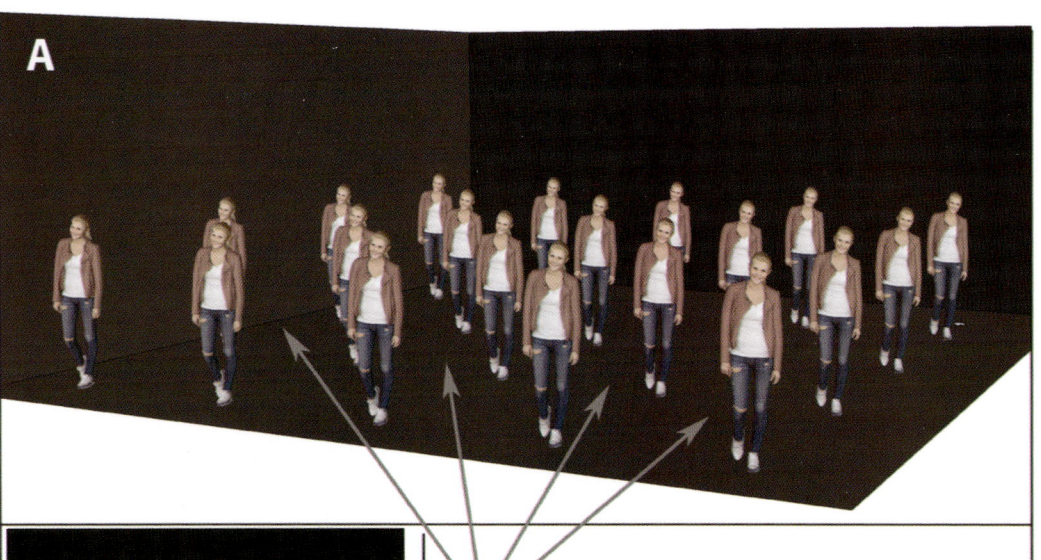

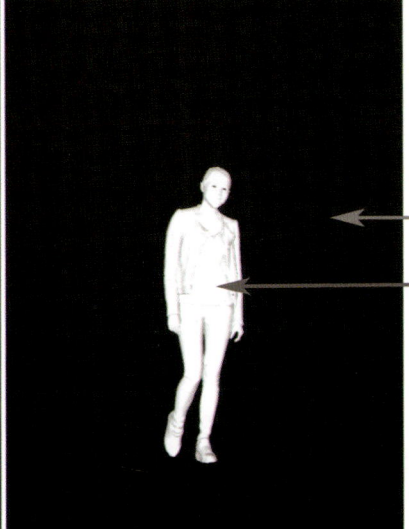

Equal negative space around the figures to project them as a group.

Negative space

Positive space

Apt negative space around the man on the level to be focused in the composition in relationship with the space.

B

Chair at the door

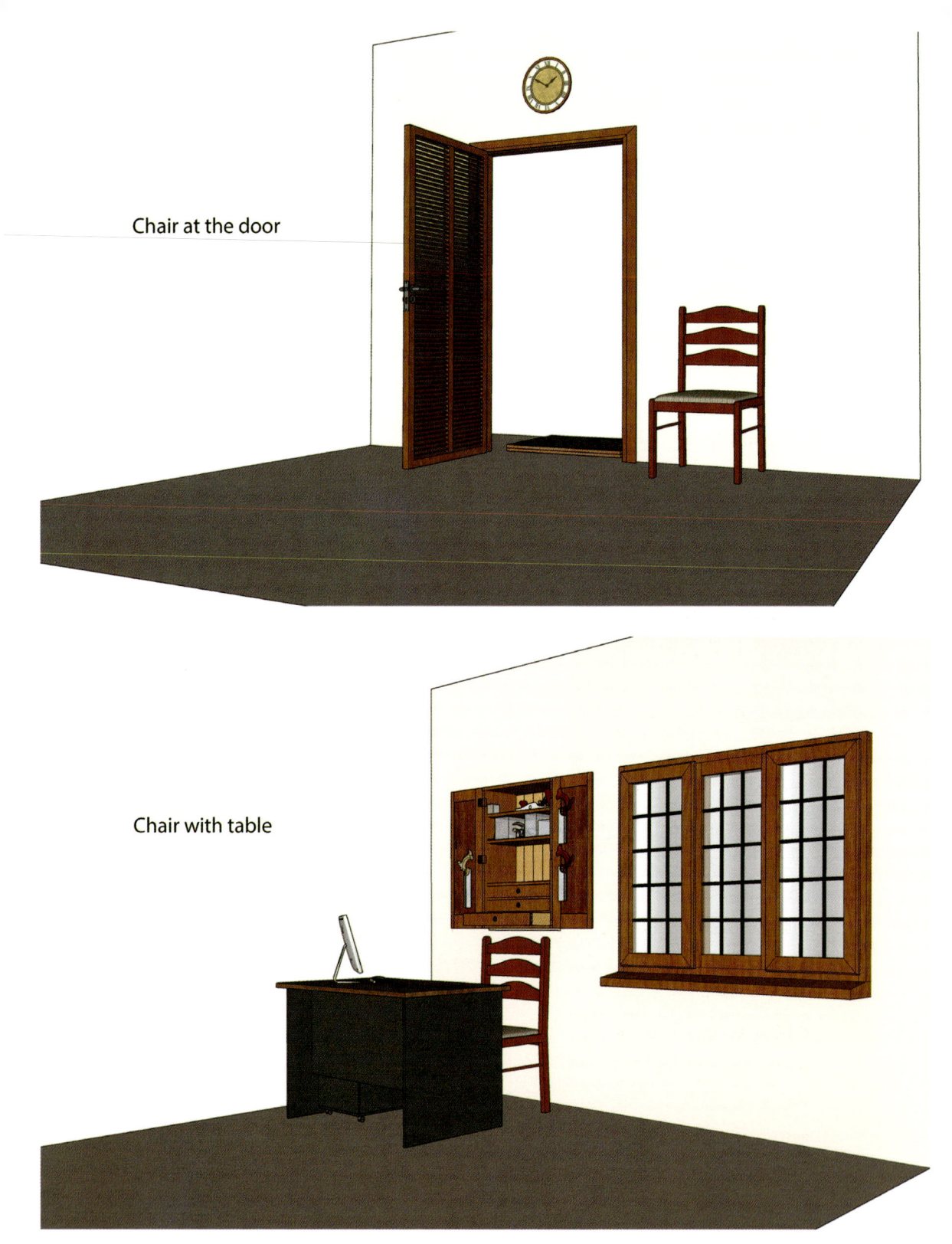

Chair with table

Illustration drawing, demonstrating object-to-space relationship.

of 'negative space' around them. And we can clearly see that this space occupies more area than the 'positive space' of individual figures.

On the other hand, in fig. B, there are two types of human figures. The figure standing in the higher level is a single unit with lots of 'negative space' around. The surrounding 'negative space' enhances the figure and projects it. On the contrary, the figures standing in the lower level, have less space in between them, thus losing their individual identities to form a group. The scenographers are to maintain proportionate spatial relationships among objects in the space to bring meaning to their design. If the objects fail to establish interpretative relationships with each other due to the inappropriate distribution of space, they can't communicate effectively, as we can mark them in fig. C. In this composition the negative space around the man standing on a higher level is too large to develop the relationship, thus losing communication. The individual identity of the objects in the space invariably depends on their spatial arrangements.

Actor–Object–Space Relationships
This is perhaps the most significant bond related to proportion in theatre design and scenography. The actors' individual interactions with the space and the related objects form this relationship. In this collaboration, all the elements of design breath to their fullest, creating contextual associations with the performers. Scenographers try to create an atmosphere for the play by the fusion of all the energies radiated from the space, objects and actors. However, a certain amount of 'negative space' around the units or objects is essential to channelise their radiant energy in the space during the performance. This 'negative space' is also necessary to maintain balanced relationships between the actors and the objects. Sometimes a well-designed play fails to express itself due to weak performances of the actors who would not able to evoke the space to articulate with full energy. Therefore, the space seems disproportionate and appears loud. Eventually,

there must be a balance between the space and the performance for a successful production.

A play portrays the socio-political, cultural and psychological picture of the society through various characters. To project them in a performance, 'negative space' in between the objects and the characters is essential that interprets the social and psychological status of the objects and characters in that space. The illustration (on the right side) depicts a classroom situation in which the space is distributed in two segments. Area-A is occupied by the teacher and Area-B by the students. 'A' is an elevated area with table, chair, blackboard, projector screen and the teacher. The character and her personality in this area is projected, empowered by the spatial energy of the objects around. On the other hand, 'B' is a larger area, occupied by a group of students, a cluster of benches and desks, books, etc. Though Area-B is larger than Area-A with a group of students, the entire classroom is balanced by the visual weights of both the units. Rather, the teacher is in focus more than the students due to the amount of 'negative space' around her. Moreover, she is supported by the radial energy of different objects in that space. However, the amount of 'negative space' is decided by the method of teaching and the strength of the students in the classroom.

The concept of 'actor–object–space relationship' is also applicable in designing a play. The physical distance from one object to other often depends on the energy and status of the character who use those objects. It is important to understand that different objects radiate different intensity of energy in the space. To illustrate, the massive pillars used in the set design of *King Oedipus* would certainly not radiate the same intensity of energy as that of the doorframe of *Aadhe Adhure*. In the former case, the intensity of the spatial energy, radiated from the pillar at the king Oedipus's palace, is way higher than that of Savitri's house door in *Aadhe Adhure*. The character, leaning against the pillar, would certainly be elevated and focused by its spatial energy in *King Oedipus*, which may not

PRINCIPLES OF DESIGN | 489

Illustrative drawing, demonstrating object–space–actor relationship.

be possible with the doorframe of *Aadhe Adhure*; the demand of space is different in this situation. The radiant energy of the space, actor and object must coincide with the emotional graph of the text to transmit the feelings of the characters. Disproportionate coalition of objects, characters and space may contradict each other and fail to build a reciprocal relationship. Right environment, both psychological and physical, in a right situation is essential to establish a relevant dialogue in between the space and the spectators. Only a competent actor would be able to translate those visual dialogues of the space and transfer its vibrant energy to the audience with truth and conviction.

EMPHASIS

We all are fond of watching street shows, clowning, snake charming, juggleries, cockfighting, magic shows, etc. We gather at any improvised space where these performances usually take place—in a street corner, in the market square or inside any open field at the outskirts. These entertainers keep on moving round the year and always present their shows in makeshift arrangements. While pushing ourselves forward in between the crowds to peep at the performance or standing in an improvised circle, toiling to occupy a seat, our eyes focus at the place where these activities are performed. We also have similar experiences of watching plays inside the auditorium. Before the play starts, the audience gallery would fill up with noise and buzz which gradually fades away to silence with the house light going dim and the curtain rolling up. All the eyes in the gallery are drawn towards the actors who just take entry and then follow the actions of the play.

This arresting of our eyes for the visuals in all these cases are due to the power of the performance that orient our focus towards it. This is called 'emphasis' that helps generate interest for an object or a situation. It projects an object, a situation or an actor to be focused in a composition and guides the viewers for a particular point of interest to communicate the ideas. In a complex composition, there are many design elements that need to be arranged according to their values. Scenographers often develop a parallel narrative in the space by distinguishing the roles of those design elements. Through systematic visual compositions, they engage the spectators in finding meaning within an array of techniques. In different contexts and actions, a particular space, object or actor is brought to focus through 'centre of interest'.

Developing 'centre of interest' in design is one of the most creative crafts. Occasionally it is noticed that, a section of the space fails to interact with the dramatic situations, seems drab and becomes monotonous. Often the space does not develop rapport with the actors, in spite of their brilliant performances. This happens due to the indifferent nature of the space; this needs evoking. In this critical situation, the scenographer creates 'centre of interest' by evoking the space through placing a few props, or re-arranging the lines, colours and texture of that particular section to draw attention of the audience. Often, 'centre of interest' can be achieved by evoking imaginary visuals instead of actual ones in the spectators' psyche. Unlike paintings and sculptures, in scenography this travels through various compositions within the space along with the dramatic actions. When a character, a prop or a specific action shifts from one place to another, it may continue to remain in focus or gives way to another one in the composition with the help of the spatial energy of the design units. 'Centre of interest' can be creatively channelised through the actors' performance dynamics with the help of the design elements. Shifting of interest from one composition to another creates visual movement that makes the space active and alive.

In the photograph of the play *When We Dead Awaken* (2009), we can identify a few circular rings around the performer that divide the space into two segments—'inner space' (space inside the rings) and 'outer space' (space outside the rings). While the outer space acts as a general area, the space inside the rings becomes specific. Powered by the spatial energy of those rings, the characters in the inner space remain focused. We can also see the performer's hand inside the ring which draws our immediate attention towards it. This is again because of the spatial energy created by the ring. As the play moves further, different masked and unmasked faces appear inside these rings that emphasise the action, thanks to the power of the space that is created by these simple stage objects. Stage lighting also significantly contributes to emphasise a composition. By controlling the intensity, the images can be brought into focus.

Scenography relies a lot on the presentation of the visual images for its composition. In this assemblage, a few elements, including the actors, play obligatory roles, while the rest remain compensatory. But these

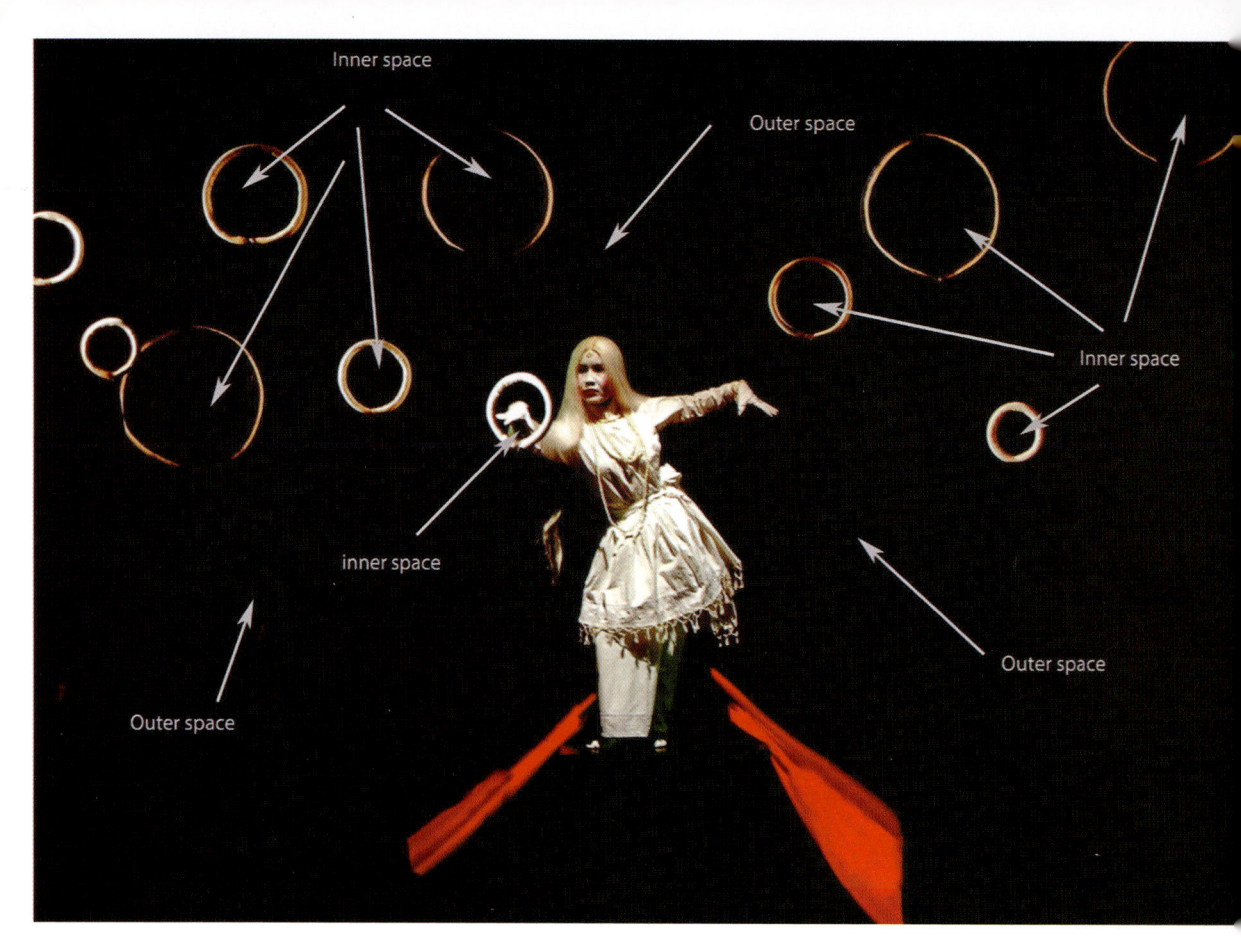

Still from the play *When We Dead Awaken*. Adaptation, design and direction: Ratan Thiyam. Courtesy: Chorus Repertory Theatre, Imphal.

compensatory images become responsible in creating the ambience for the composition. In a visual composition, ambience is equally important as the focused action, since the ambience, by supporting the dramatic action, tells a parallel story. Here, a scene from the play *Matte Eklavya* (2013), depicts the importance of ambience in a composition. The characters in masks and the supernatural images at the back within a low intensity of lights provide an apt surreal environment against the protagonist at the centre stage, focused. The interplay of dramatic lights with the space evokes a cinematic presentation, highlighting the intense dialogue between the character and the space. This dramatic composition generates tension and initiates the conflict by conveying interpretative meaning to its viewers.

Still from the play *Matte Eklavya*. Playwright: Kuldeep Kunal. Scenography and direction: Satyabrata Rout. Courtesy: Adima Kala Tanda, Kolar, Karnataka.

'Emphasis' in a theatre composition somehow differs from that of the other related visual arts. Despite its close association with paintings, sculptures and graphic design, the theatre art is expressed invariably through a distinctive temporal dimension. The emphasis in painting can be achieved permanently through the value of the subject by the interplay of lines, colours, texture and forms. The composition in a painting falls within a given frame is static, persistent and space bound. It is absolute and complete in itself. But theatre is a dynamic art medium that captures a slot of time to freeze another slot(s) of a different time frame. It gets its complete meaning only with the performers penetrating into the space, interacting with the elements of design, supported by a group of viewers who watch them performing. In this interaction, the space vibrates with the impulse of both the performers and the spectators. This vibration always is kinetic and dynamic but remains time bound.

Unlike paintings or sculptures, the dramatic compositions are ought to shift their focus from one centre of interest to another, moving with the dramatic actions. In this process, the scenographer has to create more than one 'centre of interest' to emphasise various compositions. Instead of creating a well-balanced design, which seems absolute and complete by itself, a scenographer should go for an environment that builds the dramatic tension and brings the action into focus. In a dramatic presentation there are many visual compositions, created out of multiple actions, situations, characters, and locals, etc. In this context, emphasis needs to shift its focus from one image to the other, creating space for the principal image(s). This principal or obligatory image is always reciprocal in scenographic compositions.

Centre of interest has the power to draw quick attentions of the audience. But a well-emphasised design never keeps rest of its elements out of sight by focusing the obligatory image(s). Rather it builds an atmosphere through its compensatory elements through which the desired object or character stands out, supported by the compensatory elements or characters. In emphasising a particular object in the composition, the subtext behind the action and situation plays a vital role. The scenographers must have an in-depth study of the psychological aspects of the characters and situations before creating emphasis in a composition. Emphasis in scenography can be created in many ways, which will be discussed in detail here.

CONTRAST

A flock of white herons flying in a cloudy sky draws our immediate attention. A blooming red rose arrests our vision amongst other bunch of flowers in a garden. The eyes of a dark-complexioned man seem more expressive than that of a fair one. These phenomena occur due to the colour contrast, which makes an object stand out against its background. Universally, bright objects placed against dark background arrest the vision, thanks to the intensity and gradations of colours and dimensions of the objects. The reduced value of the background, darker than the obligatory image, results in the powerful projection of that image. An evocative composition, by carrying all its components with different gradations and values of colours, textures and lines, brings out a contextual significance to the visuals.

Occasionally, with higher gradation of contrast between the complementary and the obligatory image, the composition may lose meaning. This happens due to the disconnected relationship between both the elements, thus isolating the obligatory image from its context. A scenographer's responsibility is to know the value of the object in relationship with the actor and space in a composition. Apart from colours, contrast can be achieved through lines, textures, shapes and forms. In a visual composition, an object can stand out against another object(s) of different line structures. For example, vertical objects stand out among horizontal objects, straight line can be projected against curve and zigzag lines, etc. Similarly, a fine-textured object catches immediate attention against a rough-textured object, a bold image is projected more prominently against weaker images.

The works of the great masters always teach us the value of contrast in compositions. The paintings made by the Dutch painter Rembrandt (1606–1669) bemused us through its dramatic application of contrast colour values and controlled brush strokes. In his painting *The Storm on The Sea of Galilee* (see page 497) the artist creates emphasis towards the centre left of the painting (marked in a circle) by projecting the horror and turbulence of the sea along with the sufferings of the people inside the boat. Rembrandt purposefully applied two major design elements to

Illustrative drawing displaying contrast through colours.

PRINCIPLES OF DESIGN | 497

The Storm on the Sea of Galilee (1633). Artist: Rembrandt Van Rijn. Medium: Oil on canvas. Dimensions: 160 cm x 128 cm (62.99 in x 50.39 in). Location: Stolen in 1990 from Isabella Stewart Garner Museum, Boston, USA. Courtesy: Wikimedia Commons.

evoke the composition—lines and colours. He deliberately projects the subject through bright colours against a dark and cloudy sky. Moreover, the boat and the sea waves are placed diagonally antagonising the horizontal patterns of the clouds in the sky. Rembrandt intentionally distributes

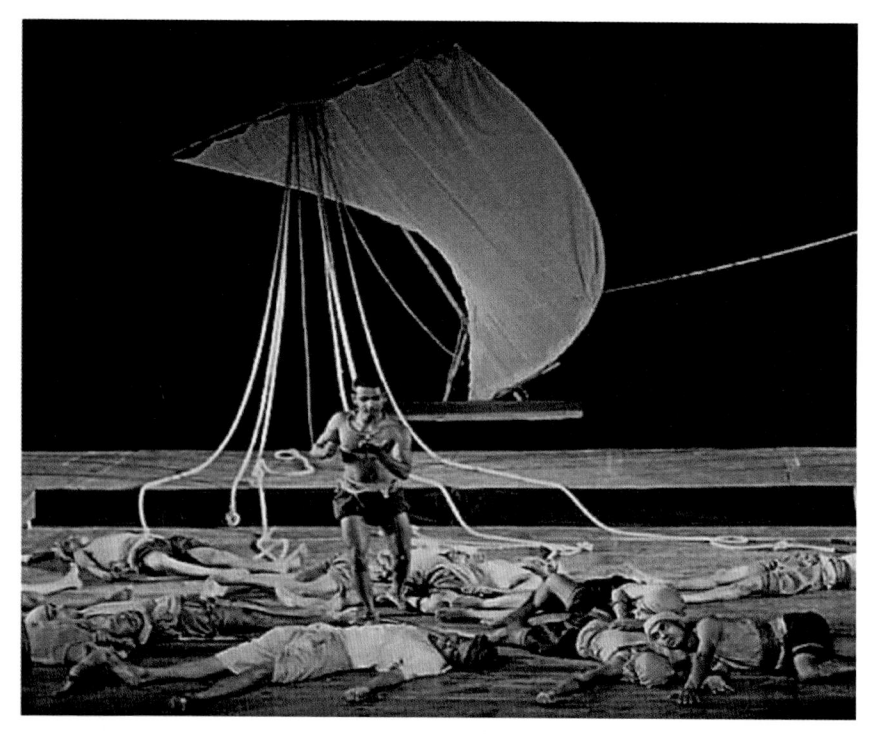

Still from the play *Baji* (1998). Playwright: Rameshwar Prem. Scenography and direction: Satyabrata Rout. Presented by: NSD workshop students at Bhopal. Courtesy: The National School of Drama, New Delhi.

various gradations of colours harmoniously to make the central image of the miracle of Lord Jesus stand out in the midst of the whole composition against many complementary images.

A similar kind of contrast through lines is marked in the theatrical presentation of the play *Baji* (1997), written by Rameshwar Prem. The play is set at the backdrop of Indian national movement, in which a group of villagers stands affirm at the bullets of the British tyranny and become martyrs. In this particular composition, when all are dead, the protagonist of the play Baji Rout, a young boatman boy, rises out of the urns of martyrdom and becomes the universal symbol of revolution. The central scene depicts the sail of the boat unmoved and intact though some of its ropes have been torn out, symbolising the massacre. In the midst of the dead, Baji Rout stands out vertically as the hotspot of interest against the diagonal lines of the sail and ropes of the boat and the horizontally placed dead bodies. The emphasis on the vertical force—the boatman emerging out of the horizontal plane in the stage centre against a diagonal background—is a perfect example of contrast created through the application of lines.

DOMINATION

Often a large image draws attention when placed against smaller images. This is due to the energy generated from the large object that reduces the value of other compensatory images. Like 'contrast', in domination, the central image needs to maintain harmonious and reciprocal relationships with other compensatory elements for meaningful interpretation of the visuals. The image from the temple of Konark (see next page) narrates a story through a human figure, probably a king who is riding an elephant and is placed at a higher level in the centre. This image is supported by a cluster of smaller images including a giraffe opposite to the elephant. The background is adorned by a decorated Indian ashoka tree. The composition is framed by adorable stone slabs with panel motifs below. Analysis of this composition reveals domination as the major factor of composition. The central image, the king at the higher level, arrests the vision towards it due to its large size and position. This also reduces the energy of the peripheral images and dominates the composition. We can find a contextual relationship between the obligatory and compensatory images that help narrating a story.

In a performance, where the visuals interact with each other through compensatory and obligatory images, the subordinate elements become responsible for projecting the central image or the character. These images also emphasise the 'centre of interest' in the space by interacting among themselves or being isolated from the central image, thus projecting the

Murals on the walls of the Sun Temple of Konark, Puri, Odisha (13th century). Creator: Narasimhadev: I. Courtesy: Archaeological Survey of India.

image fully. The photograph (facing page) narrates the story without any verbatim since the visual text dominates the dramatic action. This is a scene of disrobing Draupadi from the play *Karna katha* based on the episode of the *Mahabharata*. The central character Draupadi, in this situation, stands tall at the down-centre of the stage, dominating the composition by her vertical stance. At the time of offering of clothes (*Vastra-dana*) by lord Krishna, Draupadi extends her hands, stands still where a long strip

PRINCIPLES OF DESIGN | 501

Still from the play *Karna Katha* (2008). Adapted from the Marathi novel: *Mrityunjay*. Author: Sivaji Sawant. Adaptation, scenography and direction: Satyabrata Rout. Presented by: Triveni Sahaya Smruti Sansthan, Allahabad. Courtesy: Author's personal collection.

of yellow cloth extends from one end to the other on the down stage. While Draupadi, stands on a higher level at the centre, invoking the Lord Krishna, the other characters of the play, such as, Bhishma, Duryodhan and Sakuni look at her from a distance, nervous and spellbound by the miracles of Krishna. The vigour and energy of the central image dominates the composition, while the other characters are positioned apparently in a lower level against that tall and high image, thus adding to the narrative. The wavy and diagonal movement of the cloth, crossing across the entire stage, makes this composition a perfect example of 'emphasis through domination'. The negative space around the image is also appropriately responsible to project the image.

A perfect visual composition should be like a musical orchestra where each note finds its place according to their use. Fundamentally, there should not be more than one dominating image in one composition in a given time and space, otherwise it may lose its focus by contradicting each other, thus leading to confusion. If several components get equal importance at the same point of time, they would try to dominate each other, and fail to tell the story. However, a creative scenographer may experiment on multiple dominations in a single composition through the power of artistic skill, since new challenges are always welcomed.

AREA OF INTEREST

Quite often, the scenographers create a few interesting spaces in the design. When an actor moves there, he draws the attention of the viewers immediately. With an actor, the area gets charged and becomes prominent out of the entire generic spaces; it stands apart from the rest. The character is focused and projected, powered by the spatial energy of that particular unit.

In scenography this is called 'area of interest', which can be achieved by arranging relevant objects near and around that space to underline the dramatic effect. In this situation the scenographers must know that it is not the space that comes into focus by the beautiful arrangements of props, but the arrangement of the space that provokes the action.

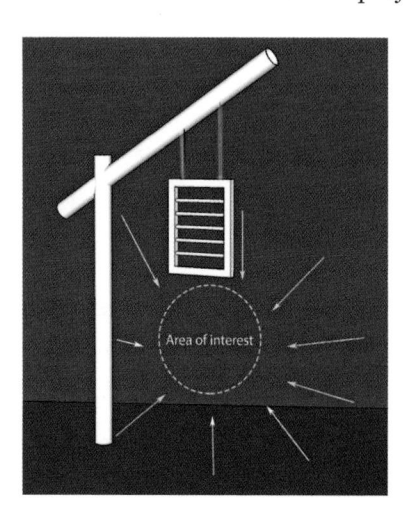

PRINCIPLES OF DESIGN | 503

A

Energy diverted   Energy diverted

B

Area of interest

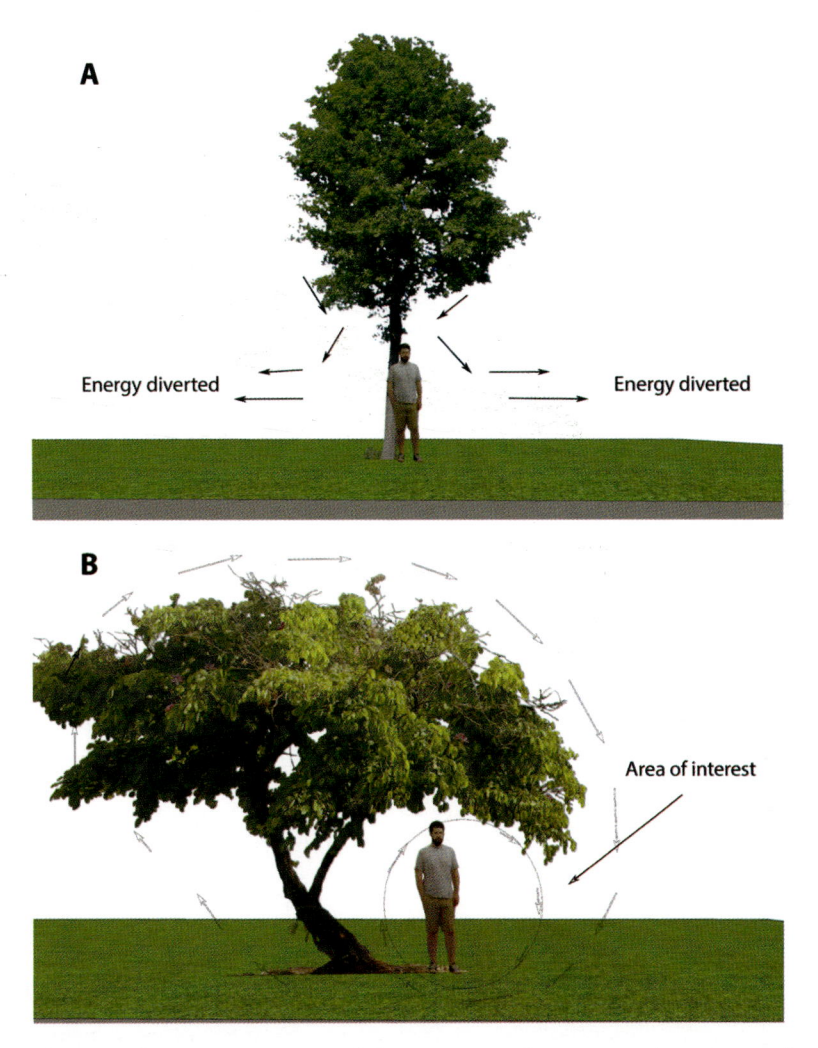

Illustrative drawing comparing two different position of trees creating 'area of interest'.

Let us understand with demonstration. In this figure, we can see two images of trees with a man standing underneath. They apparently look similar with difference which may not be realised by a spectator but that little difference means a lot for a scenographer. Tree 'A', a centrally balanced composition, would draw the viewer's attention towards it, quickly and

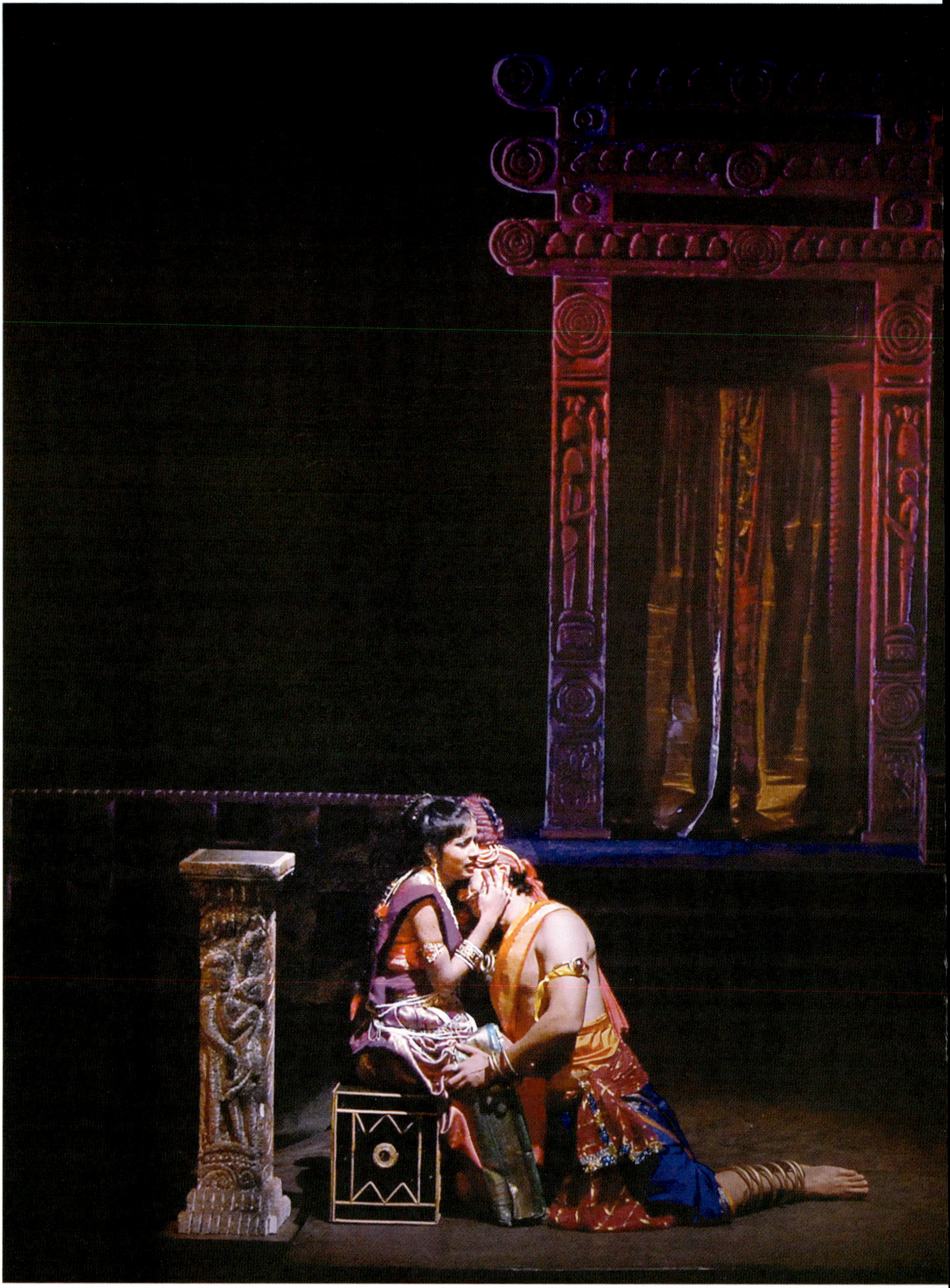

Still from the play *Mrigtrishna*. Playwright: Anupam Kumar. Scenography and direction: Satyabrata Rout. Presented by: Students of Bharatendu Natya Academy (BNA), Lucknow
Courtesy: BNA.

independently through its power of domination. This centrally composed tree is absolute in itself and may not create any dramatic space around it that would allow the man to be focused. This tree can only orient the viewer's mind for making the surrounding area passive. On the contrary, Tree 'B' creates 'area of interest' through the arrangement of its branches. As we can see, the right branch of the tree bends a little downward, creating an interesting area underneath. Through this arrangement, the tree helps creating an interactive space (marked in circle) instantly by projecting the man standing underneath. In this composition the bending tree branch creates 'area of interest', focusing on the man in the space. It is not necessary to fill that space with design elements; the space charged by its nearby spatial arrangement can effectively project anyone who interacts with that space.

In scenography, 'area of interest' develops a kind of psychological curiosity only when someone interacts with that particular space. The actors can establish their characters with the help of the spatial energy, generated through its arrangements. Often the actors find this space intimate to connect with their self, and thus use its energy to enhance their action most favourably in 'swagat'—talking to the self. Often, with the help of the stage units such as, a window, door frame, a pillar, a tree, a hanging curtain or drapery, a chair and a table, a dressing mirror and countless stage props, an actor can meaningfully project their character and interpret the composition. The composition in one of the scenes of the play *Mrigtrishna* is an appropriate example to understand 'area of interest'. In this image (previous page) the action takes place on the down right of the stage against a half pillar. The area on the right of the pillar is focused, supported by the spatial energy of that stage unit. The arch and other stage units from a distance also help in projecting the space, thus highlighting the action. The same intensity in emphasising this composition may not be possible in any other segment of the space.

ISOLATION

When an object or an actor in a composition is projected separately, being isolated from other elements, it captures immediate attention of the viewers. When isolated from all other spatial units, the element creates space around it which is known as negative space. This negative space holds responsible to bring out that object into focus. Eventually, the amount of negative space is decided depending upon the importance of that isolated object in that particular composition and the amount of intensity that isolated image radiates.

The logic of spatial order creates identity and entity in a composition; or else the composition seems chaotic, overlapping each other that leads to confusion. There are many examples of good design having lost its splendour and visual appeal because of overlapping arrangements. Creating breathing space in between the visual units is one of the primary functions of isolation in art, design and architecture. We must have observed many monumental and archaeological heritage are slowly getting crammed and congested during these days due to increasing population. These man-made marvels need themselves to be isolated leaving a good amount of negative space for visual perspective with aesthetics.

Scenographers, by isolating the major object from the rest of the images, make the composition communicative. By doing so they create ample negative space around the central image.

STRANGENESS

Anything that looks different in structure, style and nature from the rest of the elements, catches immediate attention. Often it becomes difficult to identify an object or an actor when they are placed as a group since group is a collective expression. In this condition everyone exists in togetherness. In that togetherness if someone behaves differently, the 'centre of interest' shifts from collective expression to individual one.

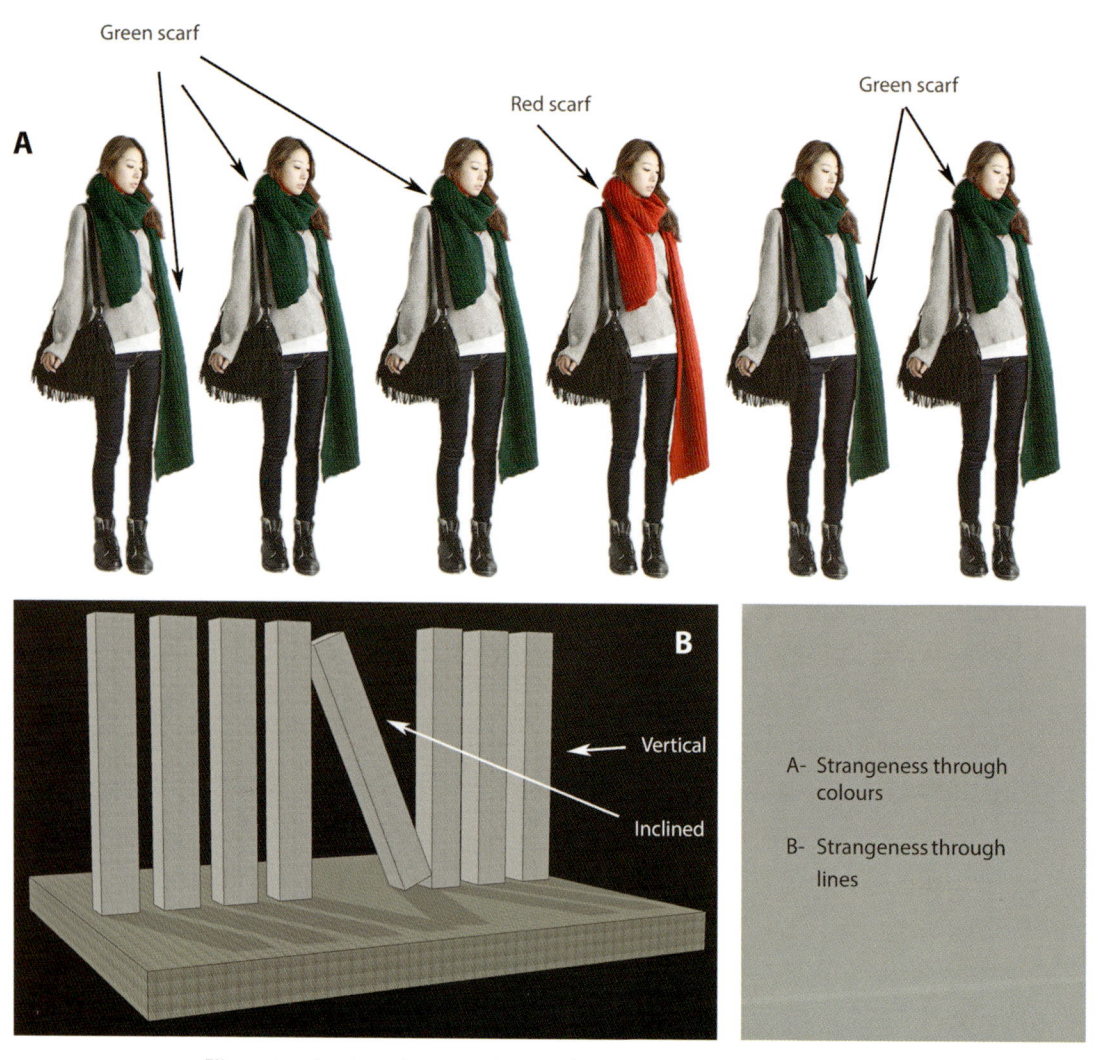

Illustrative drawings demonstrating emphasis created by the strange behaviour of elements through colours and lines.

In theatre, scenographers can direct the attention of the viewer for an object which they intend to project through the change of colours, lines, textures and forms from the rest of the images. This may disrupt the style of presentation, but this disruption in the composition can be creatively explored through scenographer's imaginative skill.

Let us have a look at this figure. In drawing A, the girl wearing a red scarf, catches our eyes instantly, making all the other girls passive those wearing dark green scarfs, while in drawing B, focus is centralised to an inclined object that stands out against other vertical images due to its unusual behaviour, an example of strangeness created through lines. Strangeness in design can be meaningfully implemented in scenic compositions as well as in costumes, props, masks and actors.

RHYTHM

When space is measured by the flow of the lines, colours and textures, thus allowing our vision to follow a regular path along with their arrangements, it can be termed as 'visual rhythm'. While the rhythm of sound is received through the ears, rhythm of space is perceived through the eyes.

The presence of rhythm creates predictability and order in a composition. It is the tempo of lines, colours and forms, which can be achieved through repetitive arrangements of visual elements that invites our eyes to jump rapidly or glide smoothly from one element to another. This nature of reappearance and recurrence, as a principle of design, becomes the fundamental characteristics of 'visual rhythm'. Reappearance of objects more than twice at regular intervals in a spatial design, creates a sense of order in the visuals. This continuation of sequential order creates rhythm in the composition.

Rhythm in Life and Nature

Our life is always guided by natural rhythm that brings discipline to our day-to-day activities and stops us being chaotic. Even the entire universe including stars, planets, sun and moon, etc. follow a single rhythmic pattern to stay in balance with each other. And this rhythm itself makes human life a microcosm of the bigger palette of nature. In Indian philosophy, this cyclic order of nature is called 'Avartan'—the rhythmic life cycle.

One can realise the formation of various visual rhythms in the changing moods of the natural environments through different phenomena. Rhythmic flow of space expands everywhere—in patterns on sands, in the hilly structures of mountain ranges, in landscapes, sea waves, in the rippling water, in the breezing air. Even in natural calamities like cyclones and earthquake and in the endless natural occurrences, there exists a pattern of rhythm.

Every rhythmic pattern has its own characteristic. When a visual movement follows regular path, it generates consistent effect. But this regular order of the movement can create tension if it abruptly breaks its flow in between. Our natural environment has significantly influenced our life and controlled all our expressions. Environment has a direct access to our cultures. Human vocabularies, gestures and behaviours are directly guided by the natural rhythm of the particular region he belongs to. The reflection of the local rhythms finds its place in the regional music, dance, paintings, attires, customs, rituals, ceremonies and the community life. For example, the rhythmic patterns of the sand dunes not only influenced the attires of the native people of the deserts of Rajasthan, but also gets reflected in its native music, dance and performances. Similarly, the staircase-like mountain ranges of the lower Himalayan region have a deep influence on the art and cultures of the Pahadi—mountainous people. An in-depth study of life and culture revels that the north-eastern tradition of India is heavily guided by the dense forests and the hills of the region and the south Indian art and culture is the extension of the rhythmic expressions of endless sea, flowing rivers and valleys.

Rhythmic Space in Scenography

Parker and Smith argue:

> The conscious inner relation and rhythm is present in a stage composition in many ways. It may appear in the quiet dignity of a formal arrangement or in the vigorous movement of a dynamic composition. It may be expressed in the rhythmic flow of the harmonious forms or in a nervous, staccato-like organization of shapes.[iii]

In a spatial composition, horizontal rhythmic lines create the impression of wideness and stability and a vertical division of space tenders the feeling of formality. The diagonally arranged space appears more dynamic than the rest and the curvilinear rhythmic movement of the lines, colours and shapes adds grace and elegance to the composition. In theatre arts, diverse spatial rhythms bring different moods and ambience to the performance, responsible for breaking the monotony of the space in scenography. An alert and conscientious scenographer can sense the demand of space for the performance.

The rhythm in a spatial composition essentially depends on the distance in between the elements, their placements and relationships, heights and widths, etc. For example, a bold and straight line in the space creates force in the movement whereas a curved line seems to be lyrical and stylised. A performance space should assimilate all these rhythms and express them meaningfully. A performance space has various expressions—atmospheric, symbolic, graceful, tense, exciting, poetic, intricate, or abstract. Different

Illustrative drawing; demonstrating visual rhythms through the arrangements of staircase, arches, levels, etc. (Drawing made by the author).

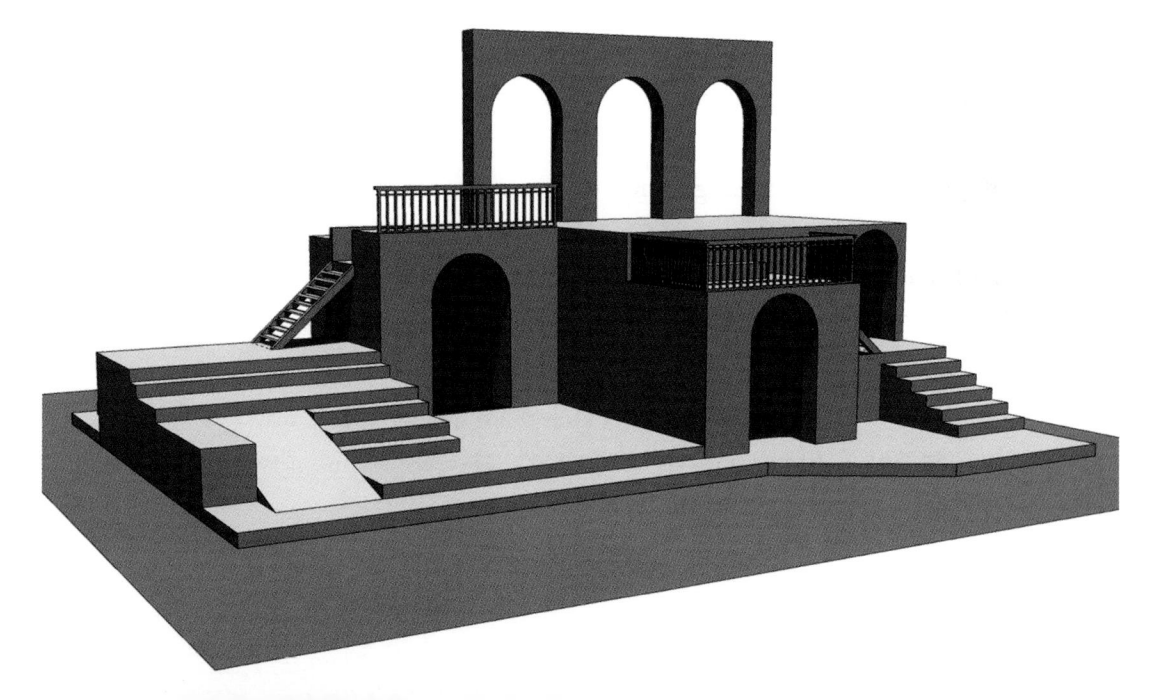

design units in the space are also expressed through various tempo and speed, different from each other. For example, the rhythm of a staircase differs from a ramp and the rhythm of a platform is different from a flat or a frame. The rhythm of a vertical unit differs from the horizontal one.

The scenographers employ different rhythmic objects into their design in order to break the monotony of space. While designing a space, the scenographers generally follow the rhythms of the scenes which they imbibed through the text, dialogue delivery, actors' movements, music, etc. Though sometimes they approach it in the other way round, where the performance is moulded into the rhythm of the space. However, scenographers must go through the dimensions of the space and its architectural rhythm before designing that space for a performance. This would bring coherence into their design ventures.

Adolphe Appia and the Rhythmic Space
The importance of rhythmic space was not realised in scenography until the Swiss designer, Adolphe Appia (1862–1928), introduced it into theatre during the first decade of the 20th century. Appia believed that the performance space gets its strength by the combination of the fluid and curved movements of the actors and the vertical and horizontal rhythmic lines of the design in the space. To achieve this contradiction, Appia employed large-size blocks and platforms, staircases, vertical pillars and ramps in the stage to create a unified space derived out of the situations of the play and conveyed by the actors. With the help of lights, he tried to create a sense of music in the space. In the year 1906, Appia along with Jacques-Dalcroze (1865–1950), a teacher of harmony at the Geneva Conservatory of Music, started developing a new concept by combining music, space and performers, initially developed by Dalcroze for his music classes. Appia began to understand the potential of this system and tried to explore it for an advanced theatrical reform. It was coined as

'Eurythmics'—the translation and transmission of music into the space through the actor's physicality. Initially invented by Jaques-Dalcroze, Eurythmics is a scientific method of exploring the inherent instinct of rhythmic sense of the human body in order to acquire the knowledge of music through a perfect coordination of body and mind created for a new artistic expression.

Appia had a plan to diminish the gap between the performers and the audience. As he observed, traditional theatre makes its audience passive by pushing them to semi-darkness, thus making them dull. He voiced against this convention by saying: 'Eurythmics will overthrow this passivity! Musical rhythm will enter all of us, to say: you yourself are the work of art.'[iv]

While working with Dalcroze, Appia developed a series of drawings that were meant to be the settings for the performance of the Gesture Songs (1906) at the Hellerau Institute as a part of the concept of Eurythmics. Appia had expressed feelings for his own experience of creating those drawings after attending one session of Jaques-Dalcroze at the Geneva conservatory in May 1916. He wrote:

> The result troubled me greatly, and I made a decision: I took up paper and pencil and designed two or three spaces for rhythmic movements every day with feverish determination. Once I had around 20 of them, I sent them to Jaques-Dalcroze… He was greatly enthused when he saw my drawings, and I was convinced that, both for his sake and for mine, I had brought to realisation something convincing. The Raumstil (spatial style) for bodily movements had been found.[v]

UNITY

Unity is one of the essential principles of design that summarises all the elements with coherence and harmony. The purpose of unity is to

1, 5 & 7. A series of drawings made by Appia as a part of *eurhythmics*. (1909-10)
2 & 3. Set design for *Tristan and Isoled* (1923)
4. Set design for *Orpheus* (1913)
6. Set design for *Parsifal* (1896)

Works of Adolph Appia and his rhythmic space.

(Source: https://emilylynch09326138.wordpress.com/2016/11/01/a-revolution-in-stage-design-drawings-and-productions-of-adolphe-appia/).

make design elements work together to develop communication with the performers and spectators as well. In a unified composition, each component contributes metaphorically to the interpretation of the design. Unity fastens the composition and creates a meaning. Through unified composition, the scenographers become able to connect the space with the emotional chord of the viewers and guide the spectators for a journey of varied experiences in theatre. All these factors are possible only when the entire visual composition is able to articulate harmoniously. Unity, as a principle of art and design, brings all the visual elements together with right proportion and creates a sense of completeness through harmony, variation and repetition. Unity helps develop the style of design for a scenographer.

ENERGY

Energy brings grace and elegance for the creation. The movement of lines, colours and textures of the forms in the space decides the energy of the performance. As we know, the visual elements on the stage symbolise many imaginary and invisible images that are articulated in the spectators' mind. The potential of the existing lines, textures and colours of these visuals are transformed into kinetic forms of energy that are able to target at the emotional state of mind of the viewers with the help of the actors.

In this chapter, we have already discussed, how the flow of energy from an object influences the nearby space. A performance space can only be activated with the amalgamation of various intensity of energy from different spatial arrangements and is transmitted to the spectators in the emotional form. However, the intensity of the spatial energy from the stage to the audience gallery always depends on the arrangement of the lines, colours, textures, shape and their position in the space and finally the interactions of the actors in the space. It is observed that a large and dominating object on stage generates higher intensity of energy. The energy produced by regular objects tend to move around that object, making the nearby area more active than the entire space. This type of energy distribution of the design elements can be experienced in a framed space like a proscenium theatre or in a box set where the energy of the performance is encapsulated more within the performance space than to transmit it in the gallery. On the contrary, zigzag, irregular and diagonal objects transmit their energy to a wider space, thus engulfing the audience gallery . However, these observations are always subjective, depending on the way of the viewers' perception. Principle of energy distribution in the space is an essential factor for scenography.

CONCLUSION

In this chapter we have understood the principles of compositions and their influence on the space and design. We learnt to create dynamic spaces for theatre performances and tried to realise the basic nature of compositions, discovered the mystery of spatial orders. We gathered adequate knowledge on how the focus is shifted from one point to the other in a composition. We also recognised the role of nature in creating orders in design.

However, even after all these observations and developing working methods to realise those observations, there is no absolute rule in manifesting art and design. It eternally depends on circumstances and the context in which we work. For a scenographer, every moment is the moment of discovery and every new day brings newer opportunities for novel ideas. Therefore, a space can only be apprehended through sensibility and not through any technical measure. The principles of compositions are only the basic tools that connect our worldly observations with the artistic imagination. In this context this chapter would certainly help us to recognise the scientific analysis of dramatic compositions, but the final artistic creation would depend on our deeper understanding of the space. Sensibility and deeper understanding of the space can only be achieved through a conscientious process of observation, understanding, analysis and realisation of life and nature.

The visual artist has an eye for the sensitive vision. They visualise the world in an entirely different perspective. A single line, a stroke of colour or a shape and anything differently visible in this world, would definitely strike at the sensitive nerves of the visual artists. Often it profoundly disturbs them, if it is not employed harmoniously and coherently in relationships with the surrounding space, which is beyond the realisation of a common man. A little flaw in creating balance, harmony, rhythm and emphasis into a composition may create disorder, thus affecting the production profoundly. A common theatregoer may not realise these technical disorders but nonetheless, it certainly creates a sense of incoherence in him. A flawed artistic space creates contradiction with the dramatic actions since the conflict between the space and actors ends up bringing out a poor production. The success of the performance majorly depends on its spatial arrangements and proper distribution of design elements in the space and therefore, cannot be overlooked.

References

i   Howard-Reguindin, Pamela F. 2009. *What is Scenography?*. London, New York, Florence: Toylor and Francis, 2nd Edition. p. 93.

ii   Pipes, Alan. 2008. *Foundation of Art and Design*. United Kingdom: Laurence King Publishing Ltd. p.192.

iii   Parker, Wilford O., and Harvey K. Smith. 1979. *Scene Design and Stage Lighting*. New York, USA: Holt, Rinehart and Winston. p. 64.

iv   Appia, Adolphe. 1911. *Die rhythmische Gymnastik und das Theatre*. In: Der Rhythmus. p.129

v   Appia, Adolphe, cited in Edmund Stadler, 'Jaques-Dalcroze et Adolphe Appia,' in: Emile Jaques-Dalcroze. p. 418.

*(Source: Adolphe Appia and the Eurhythmic Promise of Hellerau by Ross Anderson)

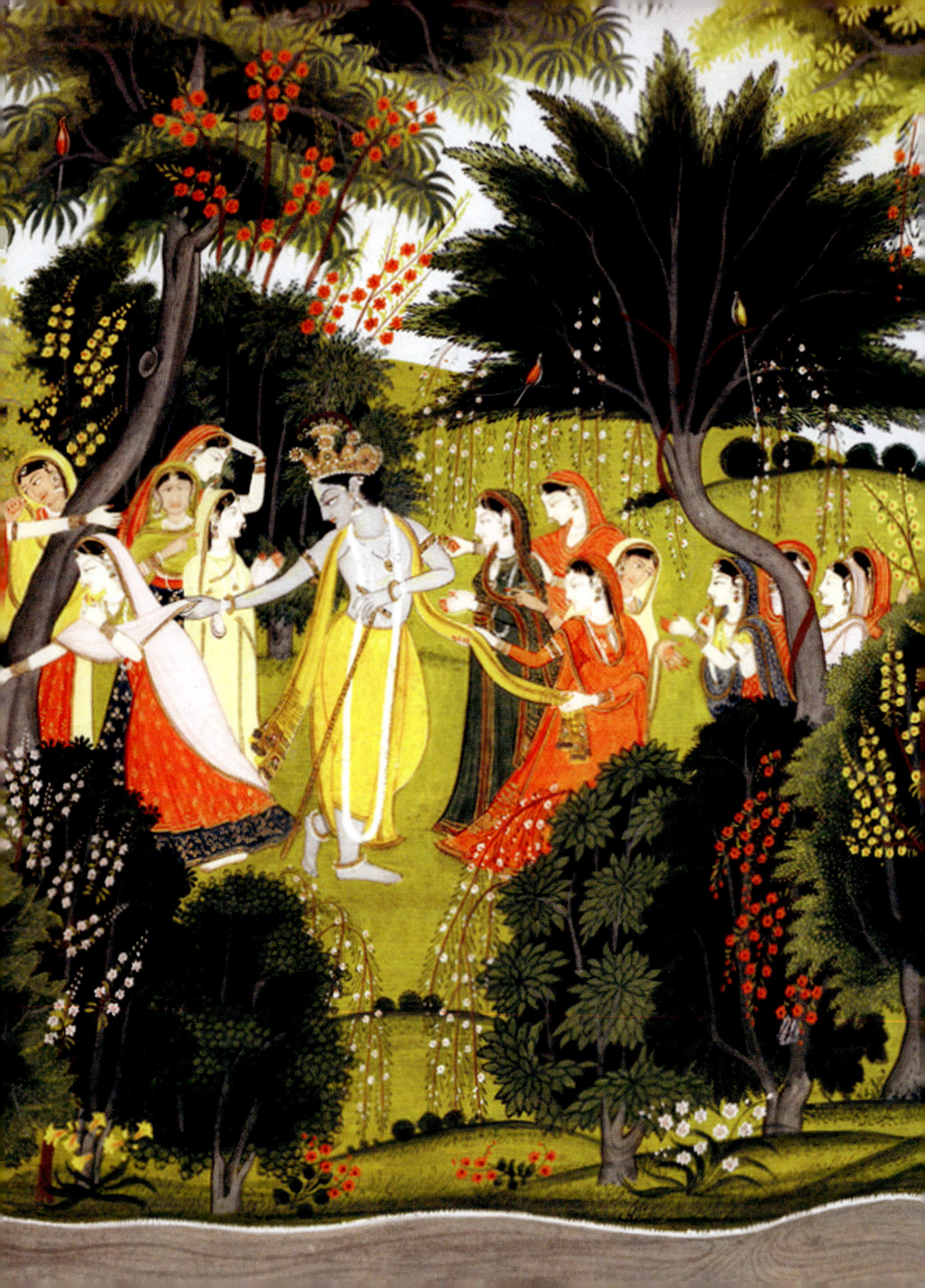

SCENOGRAPHIC DRAMATURGY: THE SPACE GAME

HIDDEN TEXT

Reading a play and watching a performance are two different things. In the act of reading, we go through a writer's text, which allows us to conjure events, situations and characters up in our imagination through the author's written words. However, when the same text gets visualised on a stage and performed, the spectator comes across a trajectory of life experiences shared by the collective input of writer, director, scenographer, performers and co-spectators. The artists also share their own experiences and exclusive interpretation of the play. The personal life experience of the scenographer can possibly creep into the setting up of the sceneries, thereby contributing to the visual narration of the play. These personal experiences of the various artists involved in creating the performance are usually evoked by the content of the written text, and these experiences emerge from the collective subconscious, further colouring the creative enterprise at hand. This can be termed as the 'hidden text,' a text that arises from the human experiences. Such a hidden text cannot be transcribed but finds expression through the strings of inner emotions that stirs in the spectators.

Through several instances, we have elaborately discussed the diverse working methods of the scenographers. Most of them write their own narrative, in the space, parallel to the verbal text. These visual narratives are the manifestation of their personal interactions of life that finds place along with the play in the theatre space.

The interaction between life experiences and art is possible through a creative process irrespective of its genre. Artists connect their encounters with life to the artworks they create and craft a parallel text along with it. The art form is created with the combination of both these texts, involving the artist's conviction and interpretations. Many of us have confronted the vast and endless landscapes of the Kashmir valley through the narrative of Bansi Kaul, which worked as the hidden text in all of his creations. For him, the hidden text of his art rests in his childhood memories. But how does this hidden text emerge and take the centre stage? What is its source? A detailed study reveals that the hidden text rests somewhere beneath the surface of the play and emerges during the time of exploration. It might be hidden beneath the words and lay as an embryo in the dramatic pauses, actors' silences and in between the transitions of the scenes. But it is suddenly exposed and visible through an interaction of the artist's multi-layered relationship with life and nature which predisposed the artist to recognise this hidden text, underneath. The artist then writes this text out of his personal observations, imagination and his understanding of life. The prime responsibility of a scenographer is not just to provide illustrative locales or build a magnificent set for a play but to discover and unearth those hidden texts lying between hundreds of layers beneath the text and to bring them out to form the scenographic dramaturgy of the play.

With the scratching of the text and plunging into its depth, a whole new world of experiences suddenly appears, ready to tell us another story parallel to the apparent central narrative of the play. Quite often the scenographers tend to overlook this parallel narrative and try to construct the visuals through the dramaturgy they have formed separately. By doing this, they end up with a misrepresentation. Their created visuals in the space fail to develop coherence with the play since they are based only on the surface layer of the text. The scenic visuals that are formed out of the preconceived notions of the scenographers are always harmful to the production. These spatial arrangements fail to fuse with the performance, and stand separately. The colours, textures, rhythms and movements of the scenography cannot be moulded with the production through this superficial process; it has to undergo a process of rigorous interactions to create an interdependence between the written text, performance and the stage design. Without this, it only projects the scenographer's individuality and nothing more. This kind of a hollow experiment keeps the involvement and participation of the audience miles away from the play, keeping the production almost esoteric to them.

The scenographic dramaturgy, created in conjunction with the hidden text of the play, is an enhanced extension of the mother text; without its presence, a meaningful presentation is not possible. Peter Brook writes his experience of *Titus Andronicus* production[1]. He explains:

> That's where people so often misunderstand what the work of directing is. They think, in a way, that it's like being an interior decorator who can make something of any room, given enough money and enough things to put into it. It's not so. In *Titus Andronicus*, the whole work was to take the hints and the hidden strands of the play and wring the most from them, take what was embryonic perhaps, and bring it out. But if it isn't there to begin with it can't be done. You can give me a police thriller and say, 'Do it like *Titus Andronicus*,' and of course I can't, because what's not there, what isn't latent, can't be found.[i]

---

1 *Titus Andronicus* is an early comedy of Shakespeare, directed by Peter Brook for The Royal Shakespeare Theatre Company, Stratford-upon-Avon, England in the year 1955. The play was performed at Shakespeare Memorial Theatre with Laurence Olivier in the title role.

The mother text provides sufficient indications to the hidden texts. Sometimes, the sound of the text also offers material for scenographic dramaturgy. By following the sound pattern, a scenographer can often successfully dig out the hidden texts into light and convert them into visual experiences. Therefore, it becomes necessary for the scenographers to listen to the play frequently. They should allow their ears to react to the pitch, volume and timber of the sound and music. By listening to the sound quality of a text, the scenographer can create a whole world of visual images following the aural rhythms. Ironically, each play contains a different sound quality and different aural rhythm. For example, the sound in the plays of Mohan Rakesh is different from that of Girish Karnad's and the sound of a Sanskrit drama is in no way even close to that of any Western play. This diversity and exclusivity of sound becomes a source for the scenographic dramaturgy.

THE FINAL TRUTH

Peter Brook, in the preface of his book *The Shifting Point: Forty Years of Theatrical Exploration, 1946–87*, writes: 'I have never believed in a single truth. Neither my own, nor those of others. I believe all schools, all theories can be useful in some place, at some time. But I have discovered that one can only live by a passionate, and absolute, identification with a point of view.'

According to Brook, 'there is no absolute truth in art'. The visuals we create today and the interpretations we draw now would change for tomorrow's audience. Another time would bring different politics, diverse ideas, new vision and different challenges with newer interpretations for the same text and the same play; there lies the universalisation of art. And thus 'our viewpoint shifts'. Theatre rests in time; the 'present moment' is more important than anything related to performativity. If it traverses across the time, better; if it doesn't, even then doesn't matter.

A scenographer should allow for flexibility in time and space without worrying about the final result. Every repeated performance should leave scope for rectification and amendments. Often it is observed that the actors become reluctant to accept any change and alteration to a used setup of spatial design. A little change disturbs them physically and psychologically, leading to catastrophes, in some extreme conditions. A practitioner must have observed, in some conditions, the actors forget their lines or get nervous, leading to their quitting the stage, if some of their props are missed or forgotten to carry along. The same can also happen with a little change in the sets. This occurs due to the actor's familiarity with a particular object or atmosphere, whose absence makes him conscious and brings him out of the character. In these circumstances, it is the duty of the actor to inspect the space every evening before the performance and arrange and inspect his own props or any portable stage materials required at a particular scene. It is also an acute problem in Indian theatre, particularly in the amateur set-up, that the actor at the time of his entry gets panicked for not finding his hand props at the place he has kept before the show starts. But one should be warned for this attitude in theatre. In no case, any props, masks, costumes laying in the wing space are to be replaced or removed during the show which may lead to disaster in a well-going production. If the director or scenographer wants to change something at the last moment, it must be notified to the actors immediately and a quick rehearsal is necessary with that change. The scenographer and the director need to re-evaluate a production several times before the final presentation. Some even make last-minute changes in order to improve the overall production, but it should be well informed to the entire team who use it on stage. The German director, Fritz Bennewitz[2], used to conduct a run-through of his

---

2   Member of Berliner Ensemble and close associate of Bertolt Brecht. He was a regular visitor to India during 1970s and 1980s till his death in 1995 at his home town Weimar, Germany.

plays just few hours before the show starts, with multiple rectifications, which he would note down during the previous night's performance. His actors performed every evening with new changes and sometimes with new interpretations. The Indian scenographer-director Robin Das seems to be in search of something innovative every time he starts a new production. While designing or directing, he tries out various ideas, interpretations and styles. His rehearsal process is a true laboratory of narratives where multiple truths are tested.

A true artist is engaged in the search of truth through modifications, rectifications and amendments and the process continues eternally. Occasionally, the visuals and the compositions of a play are left unfinished and flexible for interpretation and are suffused with a fragility—this inspires the spectators to explore their subjective truths within them. In such experiments, the process remains more provocative than the final performance. Some performances too occasionally remain unfinished and open-ended to give way to the radical idea for a single 'truth' is like a mirage, an illusion. The journey into the world of theatre itself is like an expedition into a mystic land and that is the only truth one can ever hope to state with any finality, because that journey is the only constant, not the destination.

BIRTH OF A DESIGNER

The process of creation never takes permission from the artist to be explored, neither does it flourish within any given time frame. It is sudden and self-sufficient. It geminates at the core of our subconscious, takes birth and blooms on its own; the artist becomes a medium of this creation. Like divine intervention, it sparks and illuminates the artist at any moment in time, whether awake or in dreams. Meaningful art cannot be measured in the span of time; it is evaluated through social milieus. It comes unannounced and takes birth within a fraction of a second. This is the universal truth of art, which can be applied to all its forms including direction and scenography.

The birth of the design marks the birth of the designer. Often an accidental idea that comes to mind all of a sudden may seem futile; yet out of that unplanned moment, when you are least expecting it, the most fruitful art may flicker. It creeps to your brain silently when the mind is in a state of rest without any tension. Right in that moment a designer is born to explore the inexhaustible world of visuals. In this process of creation, nothing goes to waste. Everything that is in our conscious or subconscious mind comes to work in the creation. An idea that comes at the speed of lightning changes our total perception, style and interpretation of the work and almost saves our creation from a gruesome end. A boring and clichéd concept thus unexpectedly appears exciting and changes our entire perception. This is possible only when we keep our mind, ears and eyes open and build a conducive and creative atmosphere around us, so that new inspiring ideas could flood our imagination.

Working in the area of scenography and direction for almost forty years, I have come across such countless stimulating moments when I was least expecting them and these creative accidents have been my most fulfilling experiences—both as a person and as a creative artist.

CREATIVE ACCIDENTS

Many directors and scenographers work hard to develop the style of presentation for the play much before the production process is sufficiently explored. They develop certain forms and then try to mould the play accordingly within that framework. The actors often feel suffocated within that frame and struggle to breath fresh air and try adjusting themselves in the form. Despite a pre-conceived set-up, imposed by the director and the scenographer, during the rehearsal, the 'actor–space encounter' evokes opportunity for an actor-friendly production process. But unfortunately, many a time this opportunity is not recognised by the directors and scenographers who overlook any unknown factors that counteract their pre-conceived ideas about the performance design. They are more comfortable with their cliché ideas, detrimental to any unknown element to develop. But the presence of this element is palpable throughout the process. The directors and the scenographers are so indulged in their rigid ideas that they are not able to perceive any new situation from a different viewpoint. And then, one fine day, miraculously, this overpowering intensity of the 'unknown' forces its way in the imaginations of some creative directors or scenographers and suddenly overthrows all the preoccupied notions with which they were struggling for a long time. This sudden emergence of a new wisdom, born out of the fusion of the space, actors and text, breaks away all the earlier monotony with the permeation of new meaning and style for the presentation. For me this is a 'creative accident', which quite often gives new life to a banal production.

While directing *More Naina Rang Chadhe* (Indian adaptation of *A Midsummer Night's Dream*) with the students of Bharatendu Natya Academy, Lucknow, I met a series of creative accidents that influenced the production design and interpretation to a larger extent. Initially, I was working on the melodramatic Shakespearian style of the text for this play. In one rehearsal, two of the actors, playing the character of Lysander and Demetrius, got injured during a sword fight. From then, I insisted on doing the act from a safer distance without touching each other in the fifth scene. To my utter curiosity, one day during leisure hour, I found these actors engaged in a mock fight with the help of pre-recorded funny music. I watched them hiding to find them jumping, hopping, merrymaking with lots of fun following the music. Suddenly, the idea of creating 'irony' in the space flashed in my mind. I decided to treat the play in a caricaturist style which I found was devised by the actors, rejecting my Shakespearian melodramatic presentation. With a little effort, the entire play was transformed into a 'parody of love song' with fun and clowning gestures. Once the play was redesigned and liberated from the previously practised and prejudiced thoughts, it turned into a playground for the actors. Interestingly, I found my actors, who were previously suffocated under the pre-decided style, were enjoying their characters in this new exploration of space and action. An exciting style was thus born out of the fusion of Shakespeare's text, narrative traditions and the actors' improvisations. There are countless examples of such creative accidents during the production process that transforms the play into a unique, exciting and out-of-the-ordinary exercises. Unfortunately, most of the Indian directors and designers are not letting them exposed to this practicing method, resisting new challenges. Pre-occupied and pre-determined ideas resist the artist's adaptability. The process of creation is essentially a discovery; a journey from the 'known to the unknown' and for that flexibility, spontaneity and openness to change, is paramount. There are countless paths that lead us to 'unknown' and we must actively seek them. For me, creative art is like entering into the world of mystery where we open our eyes to the world of the unknown like a newborn baby. Once we allow the inspiration for the new venture to shine in, thousands of doors would open in our subconsciousness, leading us to divinity.

ADOPTING A SPACE

Performance space is like oxygen for a scenographer who is continuously on a perpetual hunt for new spaces. Selection of the right space makes the scenographer's job easier. Often the space pre-empts the scenic visuals and helps the production to flourish. Despite the dominance of the proscenium theatre in India, most of the contemporary scenographers prefer alternative spaces for their experiments. In the past few decades, some memorable site-specific performances succeeded in writing the history of space-making in Indian theatres. Besides Alkazi's production of

Andha Yug at Purana Quila in 1974, Bansi Kaul's spatial arrangement for his play *Gadhon ka Mela* (1993) at Bhimbetka rock shelter near Bhopal, Robin Das' design for *Skandagupta* (1986), by altering a dilapidated courtyard at the ruins of a 17th-century Ater ka Qila at Bhind, a district in Madhya Pradesh, Abhilash Pillai's *The Clown and Clouds, The Circus-Theatre Project* (2011) for the National School of Drama, devised at the Kozhikode sea beach in Kerala inside a circus tent, the environmental design of *Rashomon* (2004) conceptualised by me inside a semi-forest location near Faridabad and Deepan Sivaraman's scenography for *The Legend of Kashak* (2016), where an entire village was transformed in to a performance space at Thrissur—all of these, mark the departure from the black box to nonconventional interactive spaces. The scenographers have creatively attempted to merge the potential of the space with the performance, thus providing an alternative visual experience to the spectators.

These experiments with space, though plentily found in our traditional and folk theatres, have been thoughtfully revisited with new elucidations in the recent times. One similar experiment of space was the production of *Romeo and Juliet* and *The Security Guard* (2011) devised jointly by Professor Jane Collins and Deepan Sivaraman for the Department of Theatre, University of Hyderabad, India. This devised production, based on Shakespeare's text, portrays an unconventional, site-specific performance. In the presentation, the dramatic plot was segregated into various locales identified in and around the S. N. School campus at the University. Collins and Sivaraman composed the scenes in the backyard, corridor, classrooms, toilet, a semi-constructed hall, and in the central yard of the school, etc. Interestingly, these scenes were exposed to the viewers without any specific distinction of stage and gallery. The audience were free to watch the play from any possible angle—standing, walking, peeping—moving along with the scenes in different locales.

An improvised character, 'security guard', was introduced to guide the audience to viewing the play in respective locations. The purpose of this exercise was to involve the audience in the performance and to offer them an active experience of the happenings. This audience participation and the fluidity of the performance are absent in the conventional performance cultures.

In occasions, a few scenographers and directors find difficult to visualise their play without any suitable space from the very beginning of the process. For them, the space is the prime source of creation. Some of these visualisers cannot even imagine a production without the original space from day one of the rehearsal. For them, their art flourishes by drawing energy from the combined sources—the space and the actors. A similar experience occurred to me while making *Iphigenia*[3]. I was searching for a suitable space that brings an appropriate atmosphere for the play. Simultaneously, it should provide an intimate ambience for the actors as well as the audience. I was not in favour of any proscenium that never contributes in performance-making. I was looking for a space that would provoke me to design my production through its spatial energy and motivation, and therefore an alternative space became essential to conceive this play. Along with my students, I searched desperately to find a provocative space around the university campus. Interestingly, University of Hyderabad has some dramatic spaces in its forest and rocky environment. Till then, I could not identify any apt space due to many practical issues. Our rehearsal process was getting delayed as a consequence. Finally, we came across an abandoned spot behind our own department. We investigated the space and found an interesting corner, facing nearby dense bushy green belt of foliage. We decided to settle

---

3   *Iphigenia* is an edited Hindi version of Euripides' ancient Greek drama *Iphigenia in Aulis* written in the 5th-century BC. I directed this play for the Department of Theatre Arts, University of Hyderabad, in the year 2010.

in that space to make *Iphigenia*. Eventually that dilapidated rocky area, with gravel and bushes, was restructured according to the need of the play. We shaped it to form a round arena, resembling a small-scale Greek orchestra with a semi-circular audience gallery, yet intimate. Adjacent to the rear stage space stands our department building and there was a belt of wild bushes behind the audience gallery. This arrangement provided a pertinent atmosphere of intimacy I was searching for. Once we had our space settled, we made it our home for a month, and finally presented the show that received much appreciation.

A SPACE TRANSFORMED

Architecture and the performing space are always set in a context. Every performance space has its own stories to tell. The stage floor, the wing-space, the green room and the auditorium have many untold stories of their being and becoming. Describing the history of space, Professor Pamela Howard writes:

'To understand this, it is important to research and understand the history of the space. What secret do these walls tell? For stones speak, and space holds memories. In this way the dramaturgy of the space is created.'[ii]

Each architectural construction of the space holds a character, that affects directly the performance. Presenting a play in various spaces provides different experiences both for the spectators and the performers. During a winter break in 2005, Dinesh Khanna, a leading director and teacher at NSD, was conducting a theatre workshop with Nagari Natak Mandali at Banaras. Khanna was supposed to direct *Hamlet* with the workshop students in which I was engaged to do the scenography. Nagari Natak Mandali is the oldest theatre company of the holy city of Banaras with an old proscenium theatre. This theatre has a long performance history. In the production meeting, Khanna shared his idea of presenting the play in arena or traverse stage. But to find an alternative spatial arrangement in that crowded city was a daydream. But Khanna was insisting upon a traverse stage and started the rehearsal accordingly.

Listening to a reading session sitting in the audience gallery of the theatre in the initial days, an idea flashed in my mind. 'Why can't we construct a traverse stage with two-sided audience on the stage space?'… I thought of myself looking at the space. In front of my eyes a space flooded with audience sitting on both sides of the acting area with the performance in the middle mesmerised me with its endless possibilities. I immediately shared my ideas with Khanna who gladly agreed upon my concept. From that very moment, I forgot my previous design of *Hamlet* and engaged in creating a performance space on proscenium stage. My initial encounter with the space was the existing architectural construction of the old theatre building. The audience gallery was also a major hindrance that attracted my vision unnecessarily. My first job was to separate the performance space from the gallery through a partition which we did with a thick black cloth in between these two spaces. That was the beginning of the transformation. A traverse stage for a hundred audience facing each other on both side of the stage was constructed. A permanent concrete beam of the building architecture which came in between the stage space was moulded into our design to serve the entrance gate of the palace in the play. The entry and exit of the actors were worked out from behind that pillar. Finally, a painted canopy was suspended above the performance space like an umbrella, depicting various images of the Globe Theatre and the Elizabethan era. The major discovery during the process was to create a dramatic space by exploring the strength of the architectural design of the existing theatre. This unique transformation of a proscenium into an intimate traverse stage transformed the age-old Shakespearean style of presentation into an interactive and interpersonal experience both for the viewers and the actors.

THE VISUAL MOVEMENTS

Movement is an important phenomenon in art and design. It defines the living entity. There must be a constant movement in the stage space that would help glide our eyes, ears, body and mind through the rhythm of the compositions; otherwise it turns into a dead art form. While watching a play, we follow the movement of the sounds and visuals. Even a static image on stage creates internal movements through the spell of its energy. Therefore, the immovable props like doors, windows, pillars, staircases, trees, bench and other minor stuff also become integral to the performance. They help in the process of the emotional journey of the play. There are plenty of chances for a play to slip into boredom if it fails to create any visual movement. Often with less visual imageries, the performers make the play interesting through their performance skills. But with poor performances, the internal visual movement is not possible, in which case, no one can save the production from disaster.

Cinema is the best example to understand visual movements in which the movements are created through the craft of cinematography. The characters in a cinema often remain still as the camera moves in different angles creating the visual movements. While watching a movie, our eyes follow the camera movement. In every changing visual, it holds interest of the audience. Editing is another creative process that helps create visual movement in the film. It builds the dramatic graph of the story, alters the scenes, locales, moods, thoughts, actions and the psychology of the characters. It can bring the visuals into extreme close-up and gently blend them with different images without causing any discomfort to our eyes or any jarring effect, thus building the dramatic tensions smoothly.

Some cinematic effects can effectively be adopted into the context of theatre. Effects such as, close-ups, cut scenes, inserts, zoom, flashback, etc. create visual movements and dramatic tensions in a play. Stage lighting can also be a powerful tool to create close-ups and zooming effects into theatrical actions. Sometimes we emphasise on a particular visual or a character by highlighting it through lights. For example, in the play *Aadhe Adhure*, the monologue of Savitri can be highlighted and emphasised during her confrontation with Juneja. In this situation, one can lower down the general lights and highlight the central character through a special spot to bring her into focus. This effect can provide an impression of close-up. Coming back to the previous normal scene after the highlighted soliloquy seems to be like zooming out to the long shot again. This cinema-technique would enable to create visual movement in theatre by enhancing the viewing experiences.

In the play *Skandhagupta* (1984), the director, B.V. Karanth, incorporated 'insert' techniques to transform a text-centric play into a memorable visual experience. He split the scenes into smaller pieces, juxtaposed them with each other, inserted songs and music between the scenes and prepared, rather almost recreated, a performance text altogether. On the other hand, the imaginative design of Robin Das transformed the play into a spatial experience. The dramatic tension, created through various physical levels on stage and the entry and exit of the characters from all sides into the newly created space was to fabricate a visual movement of the performance.

Flashback is another technique to create visual movement in the composition. Though real time cannot be rolled back in theatre arts, it can be imaginatively interpreted. Slipping into the past memory and coming back to the present is a cinema technique which can be creatively adopted in theatre to enrich visual experiences. The theatrical version of the film *Rashomon*[4] is a good example of understanding the visual movements through the narrative of its presentation.

---

4   *Rashomon* is a Japanese film, directed by Akira Kurosawa in the year 1950. The plot is based on two short stories written by Aqutagawa. The screenplay of the film was adapted into a play in Hindi by Dr Ramesh Chandra Saha. The play was first performed by the Rangmandal Repertory at Bharat Bhavan Bhopal in the year 1983 and was directed by B.V. Karanth.

Sometimes, rendering of the text can also create the scenographic dramaturgy. Effective rendering of the text can formulate imaginary visuals in the audience's subconsciousness. It is a common practice in the popular narratives and folk theatres. Modern theatre can easily adopt this technique to initiate the visual movements in the contemporary presentations. There is also another way to form the scenographic dramaturgy by inserting images between the narrations. Parallel visual illustrations can be exercised along with the narrations; they would create visual movements in the space. A scene from the famous play *Chakravyuha* (1984)[5] reminds us of scenographic dramaturgy, created through parallel visual illustrations. In this production, parallel scenographic visual was created on stage prior to the text. In a sequence of the play, when Arjuna narrates the warfare technique to penetrating the Chakravyuha, and returned unharmed to his wife Subhadra, their unborn child Abhimanyu listens to the technique quietly from inside his mother's womb. During the conversation, Subhadra falls asleep in the middle, breaking the connection between the child and his father on this discourse, thus depriving him of learning the complete technique. This narrative scene was visualised along with the textual conversation between Arjuna and Subhadra. By dividing the performance space into two distinctive sections—one for textual narration between Arjuna and Subhadra and the other for the visual narration—the scenographic dramaturgy was created. While the text was being rendered on a higher level at upstage, the downstage was metaphorically transformed into Subhadra's womb through a group of chorus singers, who performed the rituals of the unborn baby. The delicate body movement of the chorus, with the help of the enchanting manjira[6]

---

5   *Chakravyuha*, a Manipuri play based on the episode of the *Mahabharata*, was written and directed by Ratan Thiyam. Chakravyuha is among the best 100 productions of the 20th century in the global context which achieved The Grand Fringe award in Edinburgh Theatre Festival in the year 1987.

6   Brass-made musical instrument

sound, Ratan Thiyam successfully created almost a divine atmosphere, surreal through the power of his visual perception.

Scenographic dramaturgy is the visual narration of the play that stays parallel with the text and often substitutes the text to a larger extent. In recent times, most of the Indian scenographers are trying to reduce the autocracy of the text by substituting with compensatory visuals. In the absence of the mother text these artists exploit the visual narrations, thus creating a visual dramaturgy for the spectators. In the comparatively recent production of *Tumhara Vincent*, (2015) a visual text, parallel to the verbal text, was fabricated as a compensatory parallel of the performance. In some sequences, the entire scene was transformed into visual narratives, supported by lights, stage props, masks, costumes, music and sound. In this regard, it becomes important to note that this two-hour-long play was designed through the interplay of various visual expressions while the actors used minimum verbal text. These dramatic visuals seek to provide the viewers the experience of viewing a series of three-dimensional paintings by Van Gogh.

AMBIGUITY OF THE SPACE

There always remains an ambiguity between the performance space and the dramatic space. While the former provides a space to perform, the latter is developed from within the play, expressed with the characteristics of certain locales. With individual distinctions and identity, they occasionally overlap and create ambiguity. While, in general, the performance space is physically transformed into various dramatic spaces with the change of sets and the props, in many occasions a bare stage is also transformed into different dramatic spaces at the time of presentation. At times, the space can be established through symbols with minimal stage or hand props. These are the common practices adopted in Indian theatre. But creating ambiguity in the space or by interchanging between dramatic space and performance space seems peculiar and is seldom practised. But the experience is unique. This bizarre activity breaks all the logics of theatrical illusions and makes theatre an immediate action between the actors and the audience.

Designing for *Khul ja Sim Sim*[7] (1999) was a great learning experience for me as well as for the TIE (Theatre-In-Education)[8] actors. The production process of this children's play opened for us a window for the 'flexibility of space'. Being the scenographer of this play, I designed a portable set unit considering the play to travel in different schools and teaching institutions. There were a few fragmental units of door and window frames, a painted scenery depicting the inside of a cave and a few vessels made of papier-mâché and thermocol, etc. These fragments are to be arranged and rearranged to establish various scenes. Along with all these materials, I prepared three large-size structural donkey masks to be worn by the actors in a particular scene. Wearing these masks, a few actors would perform the role of Donkey and carry bags loaded with gold coins (artificial props) into the house. But these masks were made larger than the actual size, impossible to enter through the doorframes on the stage. This posed a practical problem during the rehearsal. Reducing the size of the masks could solve this problem, but the director, seeing those large theatrical masks, was too fascinated enough to do away with these. He was rather ready to alter the compositions for that particular scene. With a humorous manner, Karanth narrated us the mystery of theatrical ambiguity in the space. He drew examples from various folkloric performances to

---

7   *Khul ja Sim Sim* is the Hindi version of *Ali Baba Chalish Chor* (Ali Baba and the Forty Thieves), based on a story from *The Arabian Nights*. This play for children was performed by the adult actors of the Theatre-in-Education Company, National School of Drama, in the year 1999. The play was directed by B.V. Karanth and the scenography was done by Satyabrata Rout.

8   Theatre in Education Company is a repertory that works to educate children through theatre. The company was established by NSD in the year 1989 headed by Barry John.

make us convince about the ambiguity of space. For him, theatre space is always interchangeable. One can break the logic of space, time and action whenever is required during the presentation—something we experience in our folk theatre. In jest, he told me to shift the doorframe for a while to let these donkeys enter into the space, (the house) and again to push it to its normal position in order to resume the scene as normal. Essentially, he wanted to bridge the gap between performance space and dramatic space. For him, a performance should provide a theatrical experience rather than logical explanations. During every show, three actors wearing large donkey masks, enter into the stage with bags full of gold coins. At the entrance of the house, they stop, confused, look at each other, remove their masks in front of the audience and lift the doorframe to enter the house. They put the frame back in its former position and wear the masks to become donkeys again. This unusual gesture of approaching the 'ambiguity of space' was accepted by the children as well as the adult audience with tremendous appreciation and laughter during the show.

In a similar situation, in the production of *Tumhara Vincent*, a frightened Tresteeg, an art dealer, unknowingly enters into the painting of the *Potato Eaters*, and starts talking to a peasant woman, a character in the painting. He tries to convince her about Vincent's unsocial mannerism. This absurdity in the midst of a high dramatic tension breaks the logic of the space and brings irony in the situation. At the same time, it alienates the sequence from the main action and creates humour. The sole purpose of it is to make the audience aware of watching a theatrical piece, a concept developed by Brecht.

THE AUDIENCE

In this book, we have elaborately discussed on various methods and the processes of space-making—conceiving and executing the ideas, and finally creating scenographic dramaturgy. In this contemporary time, when scenography has reformed the connotation of theatre and is engaged in bridging the gulf between the director and the designer, the responsibility of the scenographer is becoming multi-layered. We seem to have already talked about what Professor Robin Das pointed out as an important issue for contemporary theatre—'educating the audience', which means preparing the audience beforehand for the play. In today's theatre scenario, it becomes necessary to prepare the ground to elevate the general sensibility of the audience for this new experiment. The language of theatre in current times is not confined only to the written words, nor is it dependent on the acting and physical gestures in the conventional sense. The language of today's theatre is the integration and amalgamation of various expressions—acting, visuals, text, subtext, intra- and inter-disciplinary art activities, digital technology and the audience involvement and participation. The audience in a theatre come from different sections of the society who may or may not follow this unique language of theatre at the first instance. But with the help of the visual communication, they can slowly tune in to a particular presentation. This is one of the most challenging factors for the modern scenographers and directors—to educate the audience, to make them sensible and receptive to understand such experiment.

This is possible when the contemporary Indian productions would imbibe the magical power of presentation. Then only it can hold the interest of the audience and make them prepare for this challenge. The directors and scenographers, through their visual perceptions, can help the audience in their journey of experiencing the play. In a few experimental productions in the recent years, such as, *Rajdarpan*[9],

---

9   *Rajdarpan* was directed by Anamika Hakshar for the National School of Drama Repertory Company in the year 1994.

The Antigone Project[10] and *Midnight's Children*[11], the contemporary art expressions are fused together for presentations. These productions have the power to educate the audience to orient them for much abstract imageries of the performance design. In Ratan Thiyam's productions, one is amazed by the spectacular visuals unfolding one after the other as a series of paintings, thus narrating a story parallel to the verbal text of the play. Thiyam's 'Paint and Erase' method has been widely appreciated and his productions are universally comprehended, despite its usage of a regional language, i.e. Manipuri. However, 'visuals' need no footnotes of any sort to be accessible to the mass; it is a universal language that everyone can apprehend. The scenographers can make this universal language more profound for the spectators and invite them to participate in the work of art. They must allow the viewers to pass through their own life through the journey into theatre. In such a way, one can provide the audience with an experience of totality.

CONCLUSION

The ancient Chinese philosopher Confucius stated: 'I hear and I forget… I see and I remember… I do and I understand'. This statement is applicable to all streams of knowledge including theatre arts. Until the audience mentally, physically and spiritually get involved into the production, they would shy away from the aesthetic experiences and would not sustain the joy it lends. They are supposed to gradually wake up from their long night's slumber into the production, through the linking threads of the visual metaphors into the dawn of an aesthetic experience. And the director and the scenographer should ideally guide them in this quest for aestheticism.

---

10 *The Antigone Project* was jointly directed by Dr Anuradha Kapur and Dr Ein Lall for Vivadi theatre group, Delhi in the year 2003..

11 *Midnight's Children*, Salman Rushdie's novel, was adapted into a dramatic piece which was designed and directed by Abhilash Pillai for NSD students in the year 2005.

Still from the play: *Ismat Apa ke Naam* (1999). Story: Ismat Chugtai. Direction: Naseeruddin Shah. Scenography: Salim Arif. Group: Motley, Mumbai. Courtesy: Thyagrajan.

Quite often it is seen that an enthusiastic audience gradually withdraw from the experience of the play; it becomes difficult for them to get involved in the production anymore. In this case, the scenographers or directors fail to provide the linking source, an access to the theatrical vocabulary, through which the audience enter into the production by associating with their personal life experiences. Professor Robin Das was of the opinion that, 'Nobody creates a house like this, but this could be a representation and suggestion of a house.' A suggestion of the house is more potent than the real one, which forcefully or gently cajoles and trains the audience to view and understand the present atmosphere of a house and to appreciate the production, which would otherwise remain alien and inaccessible to the spectators. The biggest responsibility of the scenographer and the director is to allow the audience to go through such an experience, to have an access to the vocabulary of this new narrative.

References

i Brook, Peter. 2019. *The Shifting Point: Forty Years of Theatrical Exploration, 1946–87.* London, UK: Bloomsbury Academic. pp 4–5.
ii Howard-Reguindin, Pamela F. 2009. *What is Scenography?*. Abingdon, Oxon, UK: Routledge. p. 21.

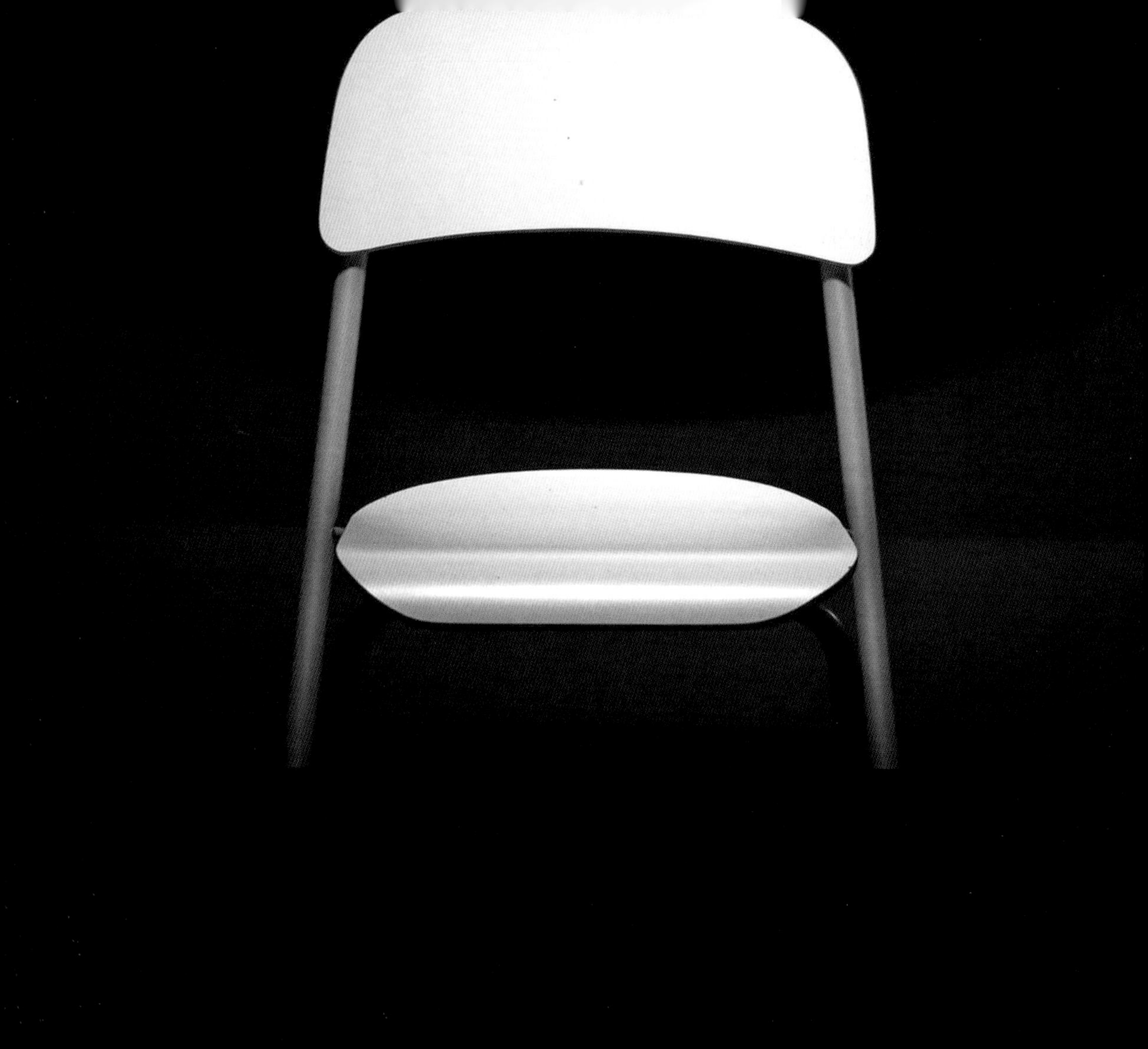

INTERVIEWS

TEACHING DESIGN: PROFESSOR H. V. SHARMA

(Professor H.V Sharma (1922–2011) was one of the finest teachers of theatre architecture and scenic design in India. Born and educated in Hyderabad, he had studied theatre at the National School of Drama, New Delhi, with a specialisation in scenic design and stagecraft. He taught theatre architecture and design at NSD until his retirement. Of the many things he learnt, painting, sculpture and music turned out to be his forte. He was conferred with the Sangeet Natak akademi Award for his contribution to stagecraft and design. Prof. Sharma left us on 5 October 2011.)

Rout: How did you come to teaching theatre design and what were your sources of inspiration?

Sharma: In 1958, Indian National Theatre (INT) organised a theatre design exhibition in Delhi. I came from Hyderabad to participate in this exhibition with a model of a portable theatre that could be assembled and dismantled within a few hours, suitable for travelling. After reviewing that portable theatre model, Mr Sattu Sen motivated me to join the Asian Theatre Institute (now, NSD) in Delhi as a student. By his advice, I left my teaching job in Hyderabad and joined NSD in 1959.

I owe to Sri Govardhan Panchal, a great scholar and teacher who inspired me at every stage of my career. In the beginning of my drama school days, he suggested me to read and understand the concepts of various design theories and discuss those ideas in the class by exchanging mutual knowledge. He became responsible to refine my knowledge and skills of theatre architecture and scenic design.

I learnt all the techniques of mechanical drawings from Professor Dev Mahapatra, a scenic designer and scholar from Odisha. Unfortunately, Professor Mahapatra did not give much importance to geometrical conventions. Since I was teaching mathematics in a high school, I tried to convince Mr Mahapatra about the role of geometry in building the foundation of all the drawings and forced him to include it in the syllabus. Since there was no teacher available to teach geometry, he asked me to teach this to my batchmates, and this is how I prepared myself for teaching design from the very beginning of my career.

I have already finished my training from the National School of Drama when Ebrahim Alkazi joined as the director of the School (1962). But he was regularly inviting me to teach scenic design and theatre architecture to the students. To make me understand the dramatic compositions in design, Alkazi introduced me to some of his rare collections of books and photographs of Western productions. In those days, Indian theatre was not evoked to such a state of professionalism. I started reading those books, keenly observed the photographs of all the great productions of the world, underwent a meticulous study on the paintings of the great masters to realise the nuances of theatre design and architecture. My real training for design started under the guidance of Mr Alkazi. With him, I understood the responsibility of a teacher towards the students.

Rout: So, according to you, what is the ideal method of teaching?
Sharma: I always believe in a teaching system that assimilates the

experiences of life. The process of learning should start from the fundamental issues and proceed further systematically; education needs a chronological development. Teaching is the mutual platform of understanding the dynamics of teacher, student and the subject. I remember, once a student asked me, 'Why all the ancient Greek theatres are found only in the north-west region of Greece?' The question was relevant and I didn't have an immediate answer. Mr Alkazi suggested me to go through a geographical map of ancient Greece. After a thorough inspection of the map, I discovered a range of mountains and hills in the northern and western parts of Greece; while the rest of the sides are surrounded by the sea. Since the Greek theatres were built inside the hills, they are only found in the northern and western region of the country. Teaching involves a lot of research, since a teacher has no right to pass wrong information to the students. Clarity comes through constant interactions with books and research. It has a direct link with the observation of life.

Rout: How do Indian arts differ from the Western arts and what must be the criteria of art in general?
Sharma: The foundation of design in Indian theatre is based on its vast cultural traditions. But unlike the West, we do not have the practice of archiving history and therefore, the *Natya Shastra* perhaps offers the only knowledge of the theatre-making, without providing any evidence and historical perspective of our ancient theatres and arts. It widens the scope for further additions, expansions and realisations. Indian arts are indicative and symbolic in nature. During the Renaissance, attempts were made in the West to explore the finer reality where the artist tried to envision the sublime inner beauty through physical dimension but not by the means of its socio-cultural and philosophical proportions. But art cannot be articulated through its physical embodiment; rather there should be a cry for a departure from 'known' to 'unknown'—from physical to spiritual. This

departure gave rise to Impressionism in the West that came as a symbolic representation of reality without a detailing and a literal accuracy, which was a common practice in ancient Indian arts. During 1901–11, the German dictators didn't allow the artists to express independently. Eventually, the artists found a different way of expressing themselves. And thus emerged 'German Expressionism'—an artistic expression that got articulated through symbolic representations and interpretations. No matter what, art must communicate to the people. If it fails to communicate, it becomes irrelevant and seizes to exist.

Rout: How does theatre design function in between 'stage design' and 'scenic design', and what is scenography to you?

Sharma: Theatre design, as a visual art, must be evaluated in the parameter of human emotions and intellect. We create a design through the expressions of colours, the line of direction, juxtaposition of elements, contrast, the centre of interest, sense of proportions, etc. All these elements and principles are also applied to visual arts. Aesthetics always exists in theatre design as well as in other forms of visual arts. The scenic visuals should appeal the eyes at a certain level of understanding. But, as a live medium that exists in a time frame, theatre design differs extensively from painting and other visual arts. Like a live entity, design, with the help of characters, situations, actions and interactions, becomes another character of the play that manipulates the actions and interprets them.

Stage design and scenic design were perceived with a different understanding in the early days. Fundamentally, stage design defines the space for the performance and prepares a ground for scenic visuals. It is a craft of making a space ready for the performance. But scenic design is related to the aesthetics of the visuals. Space, which we develop in scenic design, is not the performance space but the space defined by the play—the dramatic space, the locales where the characters live in. The geography of space, its historical authenticity, architectural conventions and the tradition of the performance can be included in the scenic design. But gradually both the terms have intermingled with each other to give rise to scenography—a complete making and viewing experience, responsible not only for the stage aesthetics but also for the performance. A great deal of exploration and experiments have been undertaken in Indian theatre to define the space in the recent years. With the departure from realism, the inner concept of design becomes more complex than the outer form.

(The interview was conducted on 10 January 2010)

THE WORLD OF SCENOGRAPHY: NISSAR ALLANA

(Dr Nissar Allana is a noted Indian scenographer, art director, light designer and theatre producer. His pursuit of scenography began at a time when stage design in India was in its infancy. At the beginning of his career in the 1970s, he was associated with the Schaubuhne Am Halleschen Ufer and had worked with the famous designers and directors like Karl Ernst Herrmann and Peter Stein, etc. in Berlin. Allana established a new sensibility in Indian scenography through an environmental theatre design. He has also curated 'Reinventing Ibsen in the 21st century', a theatre festival in India in 2008. He is currently the director of The Dramatic Art and Design Academy, Delhi, a training institute for acting and design.)

Rout: Please share a few things about your journey into theatre design.
Allana: It all started in the early 1970s when I travelled extensively in Europe. I spent almost six months in Germany watching different productions, though it was not my profession in those days. In Germany, I came in contact with The Berliner Ensemble and frequently visited the Deutsches Theatre and the Volksbühne Theatre established by Max Reinhardt, a renowned director of the West. In these theatres I saw the

productions of many eminent directors and designers that familiarised me with the Western theatre. I began developing a passion for theatre design which exposed me to many legendary practitioners including the famous designer Karl von Appen. The visual sensibility of Karl Von Appen inspired me to adopt scenography. Since I did not have much prior knowledge of theatre design, I had no other option than reading books on theatre and design. I studied the works of the great directors and scenographers like Robert Wilson and Ming Cho Lee, etc. Their ideas of exploring the space created interest in me.

Returning to India, I started my career as a designer in Mumbai. My first scenographic venture in India was *Man Equals Man* directed by Amal Allana in Mumbai in 1971. In *Aadhe Adhure* (1976), I tried to explore the possibilities of an intimate studio space at Rabindra Bhawan, Delhi, since an intimate space creates opportunities for establishing an interactive bond between the actors and the spectators. This intimacy of the space provoked me to design performances at the basement theatre of Shri Ram Centre for Performing Arts, New Delhi. That was the only intimate space available for experimental works during the 70s and 80s. Working in this small and intimate space, I discovered a novel way of spatial arrangements—develop a common space for the audience and the performers without discrimination. Eventually I engaged in creating space that reforms the relationships between the actors and the spectators, involving them in the performance.

Rout: Can you share your experience of designing *Cherry ka Bagicha* with Mr Richard Schechner?

Allana: Richard Schechner saw my design work in Amal Allana's production of *Aadhe Adhure* at NSD studio theatre at Rabindra Bhawan and asked me to design *Cherry ka Bagicha* a few years later. My interaction with Richard Schechner opened windows for environmental space design. Also, it changed my perception of design as a scenographer. As a scenographer, my prime responsibility was oriented for interactive spaces, pulsated with stage lighting. The amalgamation of space and lights works in two layers—firstly, it defines and specifies the space and secondly, it separates actors from the background.

Rout: How have Indian painted sceneries been influential for you and your practice?
Allana: The whole history of Indian miniatures and painted curtains has always motivated me to collect those antique old curtains and sceneries. I have a good collection of them. I developed an interest in the works of Indian scene painters. The space, which was adopted during the 19th century colonial theatre, was a 'hybrid space', complimented by declamatory performance styles whose source I found in the Marathi Natya Sangeet. This was the beginning of 'Neo-modernism' in Indian theatre. Western techniques crept into Indian theatre during the colonial period. Proscenium theatre and its stage techniques became popular and was widely adapted by the theatrical companies across the country. Indian scene painters such as Baburao Mistry, Fatehlal and P. S. Kale, etc. started exploring the technique of Western realism in their painted sceneries. Dharam Das Sur, a scenic designer and scene painter from the Bengal theatre, learnt perspective paintings and applied his skills in the Bengal stage which was totally a new technique for Indian theatre in those days.

The Indian style of scene paintings was blended with the European style by the influence of the legendary British painter William Daniell (1769–1837), whose efforts made the three-dimensional illusionistic painted sceneries a growing practice in the Indian theatre scenario. These painted sceneries were introduced to the company theatres which were gradually established in many parts of the country. These painted sceneries, had a deep impact on me and I wrote a book called *Painted Sceneries,* published by Theatre and Television Associates, Delhi in 2008, which was an extensive catalogue on the exhibition by the same name, at the Lalit Kala Akademi exhibition space.

Rout: Tell us about a few experimental works you have undertaken in the recent years.

Allana: I believe in the totality of space that brings holistic approaches in to the design. The transformation of space and the visual expressions with the changing actions dawned upon me through our classical performances. While designing *King Lear* (1979) for Amal Allana, at the Village Complex, Pragati Maidan, New Delhi, I explored the entire half an acre area as the performance space in which the action took place in four different locales while the audience used to sit in between in five different arrangements. The same concept I adopted for *Khamosh Adalat Jari Hai*, which was directed by Amal Allana and presented at Shri Ram Centre, New Delhi. In this production, I created a space within the space by breaking the concept of logical perspective and by flattening images as experienced in Indian miniatures. The spectators assembled in an octagonal space and the dramatic action occurred in the passages. While experimenting on the space design of this play, I fixed mirrors on the walls, which allowed the actions to reflect as a part of the performance. In this experiment, the spectators interacted with both of the spaces—'actual' and 'reflected'—by changing the physical attribution of space and also by challenging the convention of spectatorship. I was not interested in just the physical space, rather my experiment was to change the perception of the space and sound. When one actor speaks in the front and the other one from a corner and the third from behind, sound travels from various distances. Thus by altering spatial orientation, I tried to deconstruct the space and disorient the audience in order to suspend the action in time and space.

In the beginning of the new century, I experimented on painted sceneries by juxtaposing two- and three-dimensional spaces in the proscenium theatre. This was to separate the performers from the space while being an integral part of it. In 2007 I designed for the play *Nati Binodini*, based on the Bengali legendary actor Binodini's autobiography *Amar Katha*. I constructed an elevated and sloped glass-like platform made of transparent acrylic. It was 9 inches high in the front and 20 inches high at the back, to alter the floor of the performance area for this play. By lighting the glass floor from below, I tried to separate the actors from the rest of the spaces. To create verticality, I suspended few white strips from the fly gallery to create the impression of various locations by projecting appropriate painted sceneries on those white strips. While joined together, they formed a single large painting of the scene and for the next sequence, they were split to create broken images. Through these combinations, I tried to separate locales in different scenes—many layers of spaces, inside, outside and within the larger performance space. See, nobody would teach you the language of space, you have to understand it from various sources. The concept of the space is more philosophical than physical. My understanding of space came from Indian philosophy and Indian dances. All my design carries certain meanings in connection to the performances.

(The interview was taken on 18 January 2013 at his residence in Delhi)

FOR THE ART OF AESTHETICS: RATAN THIYAM

(Many a time Ratan Thiyam has been compared with some of the greatest directors of the world like Tadashi Suzuki, Peter Brook and Jerzy Grotowski. He has been experimenting on various theatrical forms for the last 45 years and successfully developed his own style of presentation. Spectacular and visually enriched, his performances profess a deep concern for society amidst the political turmoil in the contemporary world. He travelled across the globe with many of his productions that bear the testimony of Manipuri culture but are universal in their appeals. In October 2000, the *New York Times* critic Margo Jefferson hailed him as a 'genius'. Ratan Thiyam, the former director and chairman of the National School of Drama, is a Sangeet Natak Akademi Ratna and Padmashri by the Government of India.

Rout: What is national theatre to you and how are you contributing to the national identity while working in a regional level?

Thiyam: There is no such theatre called the 'national theatre' in India. Indian theatre carries hundreds of different theatrical expressions with multiple traditions, languages and cultures that bring variety and richness to the contemporary theatre practices. Working in a regional theatre at the extreme north-east corner of India, I too immensely contribute to the national theatre narratives through my Chorus Repertory Theatre Company. I found my roots in the native cultures of Manipur. At Chorus, my actors learnt Nata Sankirtan, Rasa lila, Pung Cholum, Thang-Ta martial arts, Shumang lila, etc. This was to orient them for the tradition and discipline. My actors also learnt Western theatre and contemporary acting methods in order to maintain balance between both the values—tradition and modern. After a rigorous practice of these disciplines for almost seven years, they gradually understood the deeper meaning behind these cultures and with them, I developed my style of presentation.

See, one needs deeper understanding to comprehend these traditional forms, their colours, music and rhythm in order to transcend theatre to a sublime aesthetic experience. I gradually realised the potential of these forms and developed insight to explore them in contemporary practices without losing their identity. These regional cultures have enriched our sensibilities by immensely contributing to our national identity. Therefore, Indian national theatre lies in its regional practices.

Rout: What is the purpose of art and how an artist creates their art?
Thiyam: Art is an extension of the eternal truth lying in the nature. We can never understand the complete meaning of art in a single life span. We are practising it only to live with its mysticism. In art, we must search for new meaning of life, every evening we must discover something new and each performance must open windows for a newer truth. Theatre differs from other forms of art, since it can only exist in the present context. This complex phenomenon is the only truth of this art form.

As a director, I often get bored of my own creations. Once my production opens for the audience, I try to alienate myself from it in order to be reborn in a different womb for a different creation. I start looking at the world like a new-born baby to learn new things, to interact with new wonders. This is the best possible way to keep yourself afresh. Theatre should be like a mirror where inner and outer image reflect at one point of time and space. If the image is ugly how can I face it? I would become insensible if that ugly image does not terrify me. In that case my experiment with truth would lead me to disaster.

Rout: What is aesthetics to you and how it is manifested in art?
Thiyam: The joy that vibrates the inner string of heart and gives solace to the conscious mind is the aesthetic experience. Aestheticism travels

from the conscious to the subconscious state of mind. At the moment of enjoying beauty, human feelings gradually spread into the mind and hits at the 'self'. At this point of union, springs out 'rasa'—the experience of blissful enjoyment. This is the aesthetics of art. Aestheticism in art can only be achieved through imagination, and needs to be connected with the experience of life. If an artist succeeds in creating the experience in the mind of the spectators, aestheticism is generated at that very moment.

Rout: How do you define 'Paint and Erase' method?
Thiyam: It is a concept developed out of my continuous practice on theatre visuals. I treat a performance space as a large three-dimensional canvas where my compositions are like paintings, expressed through a series of visual narrations. In each and every unit of a play, I try to paint something with actors, props, costumes and colours, and erase them. And then I bring up another unit and do the same again. But each unit adds some elements to the theme of the play. Then the impressions, overlaid as they are, one upon the other, ultimately thicken. In the process of crafting the scenes, each visual composition leaves behind a thin layer of impression in the mind of the spectators that helps them in linking the scenes together. The visual compositions, which are wiped out one after other in the performance space, leave deep impressions in the spectators' psyche and help them enjoy the aesthetics of the performance. The theatre space is the most flexible place in the world, where everything is fragile—time, space and action. In this space, nothing persists for a longer period of time. Each object, prop and design in the stage space changes its value and meaning along with the performers who use them. With the shifting of any visual element on stage, the meaning of the space changes.

Rout: How did you conceive the design idea for the play *When We Dead Awaken* and implement those ideas on stage with your actors?

Thiyam: Though fundamentally a realistic play, it inspired me to imagine in a dreamy atmosphere. I found elements of surrealism and expressionism in the text that led me to discover a suitable style for the production. In the play, I tried to create a unified space that is interpreted through actors, lights, costumes and props. I took a departure from the realistic structure of the text and explored, exaggerated and distorted surreal visuals for my dramatic compositions. These visuals turned to be the symbols and metaphors of the universal interpretations of dreams. The actors' realisation of a surreal environment and their adaptation to a strange and distorted design gave rise to weird physical behaviour in their movement, speech and thoughts. My experiment with the spatial rhythm and actors' physicality transformed an age-old realistic play into a surreal visual experience. But the biggest challenge was to transfer it into a suitable environment. One linking thread that I found in the memory of the protagonist was a sculptor who used to think of his dead wife. This idea provoked me to develop the ambience for the play, for which I have taken references from Salvador Dali. His famous work *The Persistence of Memory* was transposed into my design idea. At certain points, the design and the actors are fused with each other, inseparable—one exists for the other. The most unforgettable moment of the play was the rowing boat inside a lotus pond in which everything is on move—the boat, the lotus flowers, the fish and the flock of flying birds. The important factor in this composition was the fish swimming above the boat and the birds flying inside the deep water, whereas the boat sailed on the lower layer of the lotus pond. This surrealistic atmosphere broke all the illusion of realism and made it a 'dream play'.

I always interpret life the way I want. My each composition analyses the action, observes the next composition and guides the third. The spectators should understand the logic and concept behind each mood and atmosphere, its colours and the line of action. Then only, they can enjoy my production irrespective of the limitation of the regional Manipuri language.

(The interview was conducted at the Chorus Repertory Theatre, Imphal on 30 May 2011)

MEASURING THE SPACE: BANSI KAUL

(Among a few successful Indian artists who have enriched theatre through innovative ideas, philosophical pursuits and socio-cultural commitments, Bansi Kaul (1949–2021) is one. Graduated from the National School of Drama, New Delhi (1972), Kaul established his theatre group Rangvidushak at Bhopal in 1984. Kaul has a deep study on the clowning traditions of India, particularly Nata-kalabaji of Ujjain. He developed a synthetic training method for the actors out of this clowning tradition. An atmosphere of festivity and celebration dominates Kaul's design, connecting directly to the native folk traditions. He has been conferred with Sangeet Natak Akademi Award for play direction and Padmashree by the Government of India for his contribution to theatre.)

Rout: What are the sources of inspirations behind your design ideas?
Kaul: It is always linked with my childhood memories. In Kashmir, I have seen endless landscapes covered with white snow. When a flock of birds hop on the snow, they leave behind their footmarks on that white canvas. They seemed to me like floral patterns that have crept into my design time and again, and remained in my subconsciousness. The spirit of the community behaviour, celebration of livelihood and diverse shades of human relationships have always remained my inspirations. Even the ordinary house architecture of the hills and valley influenced me. As a child, I used to observe people doing rehearsals in the open spaces. I grew

interest in that working space more than the rehearsal itself. I imagined that rehearsal space as the performance, while the trees around represented the scenic visuals and the cattle grazing in the nearby field were my dancers. For many years, deep down it had remained a major consciousness behind my creations.

Rout: What does a space mean to you? How do you handle your space and actors?

Kaul: Space, for me, is an entity where human activities are to be realised. A performance space is like a piece of furniture—a dead log until it is utilised, acted and performed. It can be acknowledged only through the performance that makes the space a 'living entity' where a natural choreography is evolved out of an amalgamation of the space and the actors.

When an actor enters with certain gestures and treats the space physically or even through indicative actions, the potential of the space starts interacting with that actor and the audience as well. Sometimes when space and actors have different identities, the actors, instead of following the spatial rhythm, breaks it through their gestures, thus creating contradiction in the space—a dramatic conflict. I treat the space as a co-character, moving along with other characters of the play and often behaving in opposite manner—confronting the characters through a contradiction of its arrangements. This I observed in the hills. The terrace fields in the hills are neither rectangles nor squares, but have poetic curves in them. There are trails going down the hills to reach the destination through shortcut. When someone walks down the hills on these trails, he confronts the original curves of the hillscapes. Similarly, in confronting the space, my actors break the spatial rhythm of lines created through the design, resulting in the dramatic conflict.

The vastness of the northern Himalayan valley has perhaps subconsciously turned to be the motivation behind my affinity for larger spaces with multiple actions. They vividly echo in my performance design. Therefore, I am always in search of larger spaces other than the proscenium. When we did *Gadhon ka Mela* (1993) inside the rock-shelters of the Bhimbetka, we incorporated the entire shelters with huge boulders into the performance. The actors were excited in that unusual space. They climbed the boulders and jumped from one stone to the other, creating an impression of various levels and layers. Space never overshadows the actors if they know the craft of playing with it. Instead, it injects new energy and enhances their level of performance.

Rout: What is 'picking a space' and how does it help in defining the space?
Kaul: Imagine a piece of flesh lying on the ground. A kite from above jumps over it and flies away with that piece. Suddenly all our eyes would follow the movement of the bird. This is what I call 'picking a space'. The same principle can also be adapted to manipulating a space in theatre. An actor can suddenly take away the space to infinity like the kite and allow the audience to travel in different directions in that space. This happens in the hills—when you hear someone calling from the higher level, you look up to see the source of it. The perspective of sound in the space fascinates me from the very beginning. I try to apply the potential of sound in my design.

Stage blocking is the most non-creative exercise in theatre. Blocking prevents the actors from confronting the limitless space. Generally, a scenographer composes the space with various geometrical patterns and makes the actors walk, move, run, jump, climb and roll with these patterns. The actors should require full control over their body and mind to make and break these geometrical patterns whenever the text demands. In theatre, to demolish a wall, a bulldozer is not required, it can be done with a mere change of glance or even with a small gesture.

Indian performers have a tendency to go out of the frame, while the Western actors want to stay inside the box, within the frame. Indian actors are like warriors who resist the frame and finally come out of the proscenium to go in the midst of the audience. But by coming out of the framed space, one cannot claim to be an experimentalist; one has to change one's mindset. The actors need to know the exploration of the space.

Rout: What is soundscape in theatre and how it is codified in the context of performance space?

Kaul: The quality of the sound determines the nature of a space. Every different sound helps to imagine different spaces and their typical atmosphere. One can imagine the visuals through the perspective of sound. But it is only possible in a larger space, preferably open space but not inside a proscenium. The proscenium frame would not allow the sound to be expanded.

As a scenographer, our primary concern must be to create an experience out of the design through visuals and sound. One has to create layers of spaces for the actors to play within the space by creating an infinite distance in a finite measured space (the stage). Space can be measured in various dimensions and distances. It can also be measured through an actor's exploration of sound—low and high range of voice to establish far and near spaces. We can measure the space by volume and sound.

The realisation of space and its performance is an essential phenomenon that all the actors, as well as the audience, must understand. To comprehend the mystery behind the space, one has to think beyond the fourth wall of the proscenium. You may have observed how Indian folk and traditional theatres cleverly break the invisible wall in between the actors and the spectators to penetrate into the audience gallery and articulate with the spectators, thus intermingling both the spaces (actors' space and spectators' space) into one.

(The interview was conducted at his residence at Dwarka, Delhi, on 12 January 2010)

IRONY OF THE SPACE: ROBIN DAS

(Robin Das is an avant-garde theatre director and scenographer of our time. An accomplished caricaturist and academic of theatre and visual art, Das has developed a unique style by creating 'irony in the space' through intricate, multi-dimensional and provocative design. He studied theatre at the National School of Drama with a specialisation in design. After completion of his course in 1976, he started teaching at NSD till his retirement in 2015. A career spanning over 40 years, Das has done a number of ground-breaking productions for NSD. He has been conferred with the Sangeet Natak Akademi Award for his contribution to theatre design in the year 2001.)

Rout: Please tell me about your experiment with *Woyzeck*[1] as a designer.
Das: I designed an intimate space at Rabindra Bhawan for *Woyzeck* in 1976 for Ranjit Kapoor's diploma production when we were in the final year of the drama school. This was my first venture for theatre design. That was the time of illusionistic theatre in which realistic design for the plays was widely followed. But as a student designer I tried to break all these notions despite facing a lot of criticism by the fundamentalists. The architectural construction of the theatre basically did not leave any scope to execute my design idea for *Woyzeck*. The play had 16 different locales which needed to be employed in that small studio theatre. This practical problem was perhaps a big lesson for me at that time. The contradiction of the architectural space with the dramatic space compelled me to think for a suggestive design. That was the time when I was passionately influenced by the new document theatre, propounded by Appia and Craig. For me, the time consumed in the scene-changing is the 'dead time'. Moreover, the representation of locales through two-dimensional

---

1 *Woyzeck* is written by Georg Büchner, a German playwright of 19th century.

cut-outs seemed to be very pretentious. I was thinking of an interactive space in order to create a psychological atmosphere in the performance. I decided to create a formalistic design without any representation of specific locales to be expressed through a few horizontal and vertical lines—levels, frames, staircases, etc. That might have an abstract presence, but with the entry of the actors into the space by using these suggestive set units, the whole space would transform into the desired local.

I made a few sketches of the design, worked out the entry and exit of the actors, scene changing, shifting of the props, etc. After the execution of the design on the stage floor, it looked like an installation art, creating an essential atmosphere of the play as a whole but not with any specific scene depiction as described in the text. It was a suggestive and structural design which could convey meaning when it comes into action and when interacted by the actors accordingly and the mise-en-scène. This symbolic representation of space provoked many unseen images, through the actors' interaction with the space. More interestingly, the design challenged the actors to establish the desired locals since their identities in the space were vague. This new arrangement also challenged the audience to accept the space and connect the visuals with their experiences of life.

Indian performance has developed a theatrical language communicated through the actors' gestures and postures. These abstract gestures stimulate the audience and gradually educate them to understand the meaning behind those gestures. Similarly, in modern context, a scenographer creates certain symbols on stage which the viewers need to comprehend by drawing meaning out of the interactions of the actors with the space. The entire stage space or at least the nearby areas of the major action can be included with that action to enhance the scenic visuals. The rest can be taken care of by the performers through the spatial interactions. For me, scenography is not to create locales, nor even it is necessary to give a suggestion of the locale; it is to extract the inner core of the psychological atmosphere through the arrangements of space. It is an abstract target that needs to be evoked by the actors' interaction with the space, along with the scenographer's interpretations and the director's understanding.

Rout: What is your process of design and how do you create irony in the space?

Das: I often provoke my actors to improvise the scenes on a bare stage. I observe them quietly, remain out of sight and plan the scenes in terms of the stage requirements and draw a good number of freehand sketches. These rough sketches reflect various modes of compositions. With the help of these initial sketches, I work out on the practical issues—entry, exit, space distribution, local division, change of props and set units, etc. Occasionally, I convince the directors about the potential of space and its possible utilisation by the actors. While designing for *Barnam Vana* [2], I created an empty large space keeping the production design in mind. Once in the rehearsal, I found the actors doing the roles of Duncan and Banquo at one corner of the stage, while the whole space was lying empty. I quietly moved towards the space and told them, 'Why you two are so close to each other and talking in an inaudible voice! This is an open-air and the scene is inside a jungle with lots of trees around. Use the space and explore the atmosphere through your imaginative power. This will bring theatricality to your speech.' The next day when Karanth saw the scene, he was amazed by the compositional effect. Sometimes even the director insisted me to recompose the scene with the actors in perfect sync with the psychological atmosphere of the space.

I love to put myself into challenges. Occasionally, I go against the text and weave it through visual rhythms to create irony and contrast in

---

2   Hindi adaptation of Shakespeare's *Macbeth* by Raghuvir Sahay. It was directed by B.V. Karanth and designed by Robin Das in 1979.

the performance. This is to observe the actors, trapped in the network, and react to the situation. A space must carry certain amount of crazy psychological environment in which the craziness is not literal, but a double-layered theatrical presentation. It must carry the psychological images of the text from the point of view of the protagonist. My fascination for paintings, sculptures, caricature prepared the ground for my orientation for visual mediums.

I frantically work on my compositions to extract dramatic irony in each of the actions. This irony in the visuals creates contrast in the action, responsible for the dramatic tension and conflict, and is essential to create dimensions in the play. See, in the murder scene of Desdemona in *Othello*, we can surely bring a beautifully ornate bed, decorated with colourful flowers with delicate mosquito net accompanied by colourful curtains, hanging from the fly to project the murder as a counter action. This image would create contrast in the dramatic action and bring irony in to the situation. Of course, it may look unusual, the ambience and the action would contradict each other, but it would add a different dimension to the play.

(The interview was conducted on 5 September 2014 at the National School of Drama)

ACKNOWLEDGMENTS

First of all, I recall with gratitude B.V Karanth's words, 'In theatre, one should be a jack of all trades, master of one'. This statement has remained with me throughout my life and led me to dabble in all aspects of theatre, but specialise in one aspect—space and design.

I express my gratitude to all those well-wishers who provoked me to opt for design and direction when there wasn't any particular area of specialisation in my mind as I was studying theatre in the National School of Drama. However, I always had an inclination towards the visual medium, though it remained a domain far beyond my comprehension. My mentors at the National School of Drama moulded and chiselled me, waking me up into the sublime world of visuals. I am always indebted to my teachers at the drama school where I learnt the syllable of theatre craft and design. The memories of those days, when Prof. H.V. Sharma called me to his office at NSD and handed me a white canvas and a set of oil colours, asking me to draw along with him, still stands green in my mind. The feel of the texture of the canvas, the pungent aroma of the oil colours, the nervousness to make the first brush stroke across a blank canvas and learning painting from a master, this is a moment I cherish at every juncture of my life. Prof. H.V. Sharma is the one who taught me the art of pencil drawing, value of shades in colours, the fundamentals of theatre architecture, the *Natya Shastra* tradition and above all, the significance of observing the world around us. Prof. G. N. Dasgupta, who inspired me towards the world of visibility and taught me the role of lights in the total visual aesthetic, and Prof. Dev Mahapatra, from whom I learned the technique of stagecraft, are two great prodigies to whom I owe a lot. Another great master in the line is Tarsheem Lal, our *Bade-Guruji*, who tuned my eyes to see things in proportion and balance. I am grateful to all these mentors who had moulded me into what I am today.

During my quest for innovative ideas, I met Robin Das, a multi-faceted personality. As a student in drama school productions, I started off by assisting him and soon developed a passion for space and compositions. I have learnt a great deal from him, and I am, and will remain indebted to him forever.

After passing out from the National School of Drama, when I was struggling to find a suitable profession in theatre in the 1980s, I came across so many people, whose words have highly motivated me to become what I am today. It was Smt. Sheila Bhatia who led me to 'scenic design' through her mesmerizing Punjabi Opera, *Tere Mere Lekh*; an adaptation of Garcia Lorca's *Blood wedding*. I owe all my gratitude to her for being the cause of my first venture as a designer. Sri Amitabh Dasgupta, Prof. Barry John, Prof. D. R Ankur, Dr Nissar Allana, Sri Bansi Kaul and Sri Rajendra Gupta were the ones behind my choosing design as a career. It was Rajendra Gupta who invited me to Rangmandal at Bharat Bhavan for designing the space for his new production, *Rakt Parinaya* in 1984. The enchanting atmosphere of the art complex took me to another world, which held me back even after my assessment was over and I became a part of the Rangmandal family for the next six long years. My real training started when B.V. Karanth, the then director of the Rangmandal, offered me a job to look after the sets and lights for the Rangmandal productions. The days at Rangmandal made me understand the real meaning of theatre and what it means and does to the society! I am obliged to my guru B. V. Karanth, J. Swaminathan, Vijaymohan Singh, Alakh Nandan, Pravhat Ganguli and Sri Ashok Vajpayee for reposing trust on me and thrusting me into the vastness of art. I owe a bouquet of thanks to all the inmates and artistes of Rangmandal; late Javed Bhai, Raghuvir Hoola, late Pratap Saini, Jayant Deshmukh, Alok Chatterjee, late Ms Vibha Mishra, Jitu Shastri, Rajkamal Nayak, Saroj Sharma, Sanjay Mehta, Kamle, Mangilal, Gopal Dubey, to name a few.

I have been influenced by many Indian theatre directors. Among them, Habib Tanvir, K. N Pannikkar, E. Alkazi, B. V. Karanth, Prof. Raj Bisharia, Sri Prasanna, Sri Ratan Thiyam, Amal Allana, B. jayashree, Prof. Ram Gopal Bajaj, Prof. Mohan Maharishi and Dr Anuradha Kapur top the list. I grew up watching their plays. Their search for new vocabulary for Indian theatre every time enthrals me and flows in my blood as a committed theatre practitioner. I am indebted to these masters.

I learnt teaching theatre through practice. Motivating young generation towards meaningful and committed theatre and to find meaning of life out of that is my ultimate aim as a teacher. My students are always my driving forces in my journey into this sublime medium of truth. In fact, this book itself is an outcome of my constant interactions with the young Indian theatre practitioners. I acknowledge those young talents of India without whom this work would not have been possible.

I am obliged to Central Sangeet Natak Academy and its administrative staffs—Sri Jayant Kastuwar, Secretary, Kiran Bhatnagar, Deputy Secretary, Drama and Sri Vijay Kumar Singh, Programme Coordinator, for their kind financial support to carry initial field work for this research project.

My heartfelt gratitude to Ms Pamela Howard (OBE), one of the leading scenographers of international repute for writing the foreword of this book. From her only I came to know, she had already been to India with director John Russell Brown in 1974 with the production of *Candida* as the scenographer.

My special thanks to my professor at NSD and a great teacher, Sri Ram Gopal Bajaj, for his constant encouragement to write this book. I acknowledge Hina Khajuria, one of my students from Daulat Ram

College, Delhi, for her offer to be with me in the early stage of the manuscript. I thank Mr Bapi Bose, who happens to be one of my closest friends, for his frequent advices.

My special gratitude to those committed practitioners and theatre groups—Prof. K.S. Rajendran, Sauti Chakraborty, Anirudh Kuthwad, Rajesh Kr. Singh, Kanhaiya lal Kethwas, K. Ramaiyah, Chorus Repertory Theatre, Rang Vidushak, Naya Theatre, Circle Theatre Company, and those who have extended their hands by providing their production photographs for this book.

Last but not the least, I express my gratitude to my wife, Mitanjali, and my children for allowing me to live in my own world, completely detached from them, as I trod the paths to materialise my dream to bring out this book.

INDEX

A
Aadhe Adhure, 37, 39, 41, 249, 267, 274, 279
Abbas, Khwaja Ahmad, 30
Abhijnanasakuntalam, 102, 259, 268, 271, 277
Abhimanch Theatre, 355
abrupt value, 445, 447,
achromatic colours, 400
actor–object–space relationship, 482, 487–489
actors' space, 559
Adding Machine, 320, 321, 345, 347
additive colours, 401, 402, 403
Adima Kala Tanda, 493
Agra Bazar, 274, 277
Agrawal, Bharat Bhushan, 270
Agrawal, Pratibha, 61,
aharya abhinaya 57, 99
aisthetokos, 254,
Alakh Nandan, 565
Alana, Amal, 339, 548, 550, 566
Alekar, Satish, 274
Aleotti, Giovanni Battista, 161, 163
alienation effect, 300
Alkazi, Ibrahim, 36, 47, 189, 286, 390, 545
Allana, Nissar, 16, 28, 39, 136, 137, 223, 266
alley stage, 214
alternative theatre spaces, 40, 197, 200, 232
Amar Katha, 551
Amritamanthanam, 88, 187
Anaconda, 144, 147
Anagalli, Suresh, 41
analogous colours, 408– 409, 416
Ancient Greek Theatre, 65, 78, 166, 173, 454
Andha Yug, 38, 217, 272,393, 395, 415, 528
Andher Nagari Chaupat Raja, 244, 245
Angar, 34,
Angika, 58
Animal Farm, 41, 301, 302– 303
Ankur, D. R., 565
Annapurna A and B theatres, 139
Antarang theatre, 204, 206– 207
Antarang, 191
Anth–Anant, 41,
Antigone project,the 230, 539
Antigone, 37, 415,
Antoine, Andre, 165

Apparao, P.S.R., 87, 96
Appen, Karl Von, 343, 548
Appia, Adolphe, 23, 387, 455, 457, 512, , 560
apron, 164, 171, 172–173, 196, 202
Aranya Fasal, 274, 279
area of interest, 285, 335, 431, 464, 502– 506
arena stage, 209– 213, 331
Ashad Ka Ek Din, 36, 41, 249, 267, 346, 429,
Asian Theatre Institute, 32, 35, 543
Assimakopoulos, Panagiotis, 231
asymmetrical balance, 475– 477
asymmetrical shapes, 434
August Ka Khwab, 41, 326, 329, 357
Aurangzeb, 278, 431, 432
avant–garde theatre, 43, 224, 335, 560
Avartan theatre, 297
Azmi, Kaifi, 30

B
badi pala, 124
Bahirang, 189, 191–195
Bahumukh theatre, 219– 221
Bajaj, Ram Gopal, 318, 566,
Baji,392, 393, 498, 499
Baki Itihash, 211, 274, 279
Ballad of the Cosmo Café, the 282, 283
Bandit Queen, 144
Banham, Martin, 164
Banjh Ghati, 193
Barasch, Moshe, 260
Barba, Eugenio, 231
Barnam vana, 41, 191, 562
Basavalingaiah, C., 41, 303
Basi Khabar, 211
Basti Devatha Yadamma, 143
Bayreuth Festspielhaus, 161, 163
Begam ki Takia, 191
Beglar, J.D., 71
Belasco, David, 35
Bennewitz, Fritz, 523
Berliner Ensemble, 523, 547
Bhaduri, Sisir, 31
Bhand Pather, 112, 153
Bhandari, Manu, 313
Bhanja, Kavi Samrat Upendra, 123

Bharat Bhavan multi–art complex, 206
Bharat Rang Mahotsav, 53
Bharata muni, 37, 86– 91, 98, 187, 254
Bharati, Dharamvir, 37, 38
Bharatiya Natya Sangh, 36
Bhartendu Natya Akademi (BNA), 204, 208, 317, 321, 505,
Bhat, G.K, 73
Bhatia, Sheela, 276
Bhatnagar, Kiran, 566
Bhattacharya, Bijan, 30
Bhimbetka, 68, 70– 72, 528, 558
Bhishma, 143, 144,
Bhoma, 211
bhramyaman rangamanch, 144– 146
bhugruham, 142
Bibiena, Ferdinando Galli, 19, 22
bilaterally symmetrical design, 431, , 433, 473
Bisarjan, 31
black box, 401, 528
black curtain, 172, 419
Bloch, T., 72, 73
Blood wedding, 565
Boal, Augusto, 231
Bolton, Gavin, 232
Bose, Bapi, 40, 41, 266, 334, 343, 567
box set, 165, 203, 360, 516
Bread & Butter Theatre, 226
breathing space, 483, 507
Brecht, Bertolt, 13, 299, 300, 375, 523, 537
Breton, Andre, 322
Brihannala, 318
broken value, 447, 448
Brook, Peter, 13, 199, 226, 521, 522, 552
Brown, John Russell, 10, 120, 566
Brown, Percy, 75, 78
Buchner, Georg, 335, 560
Bury the Dead, 191, 335, 338

C

Candida, 10, 12, 566
Cardiff, Janet, 226
caturasra madhyama natyamandapa, 79, 98
caturasra, 68, 79, 80, 87, 91, 98
catwalk, 178, 179, 181, 214
Caucasian Chalk Circle, a, 260, 375
Cause–and–effect system, 290
centre of interest, 490, 491, 494, 499, 507, 546
centre stage, 68, 169, 356, 484, 492, 520
Cezanne, Paul, 284
Chakraborty, Souti, 315, 219
Cham dance, 153
chamara, 104, 124

Champaklal, Mahesh, 99
champu and chhanda, 133
Chand Badla Da, 277
Chandi Priya,143
Chandragupt, 273
Charan Das Choor, 274
chari, 102
Charlotte: A Tri–Coloured Play with Music, 351
Charpai, 274, 279,
Charvaka,318,
chatradharini, 107
Chatterjee, Alok, 566
Chattopadhyay, Kamaladevi, 35
Chaturvarna, 91
Chekhov, Anton, 222, 223, 291
Cherry ka Bageecha,41, 191
Chhau dance, 40, 112, 153
Chobey, Yogendra, 73, 75
Chorus repertory theatre, 259, 395, 481, 492, 552, 556, 567
Chote Shayad Bade Shayad,191
Choudhury, Khaled, 32, 33, 34
Circle theatre company, 334, 337, 567
Circulation Unit, 220
City Dionysia, 74
classical Indian theatre,100, 111, 154, 188, 301
Clowns and Clouds—a theatre–circus Project, 41, 229
Coalmines at Borinage, 305
Collins, Jane, 226, 528,
Commedia dell'arte, 115
company theatres, 29, 313, 549
compensatory images, 492, 499
complementary colours, 409, 410
computer–aided design and drafting system (CADD), 352
Comte, Auguste, 289, 290
Confucius, 539
contemporary plays, 273, 278
contradiction in the space, 557
conventional spectatorship, 225
Cook, Peter, 343, 375
Correa, Charles Mark, 191, 195, 206
counterweight system, 179, 181
Court Martial, 274
Craig, Gordon, 23, 24, 240
cross lights, 204, 428, 429
cubism, 295, 296, 380
Cunningham, Alexander, 71
cyclorama, 171–172

D

Dalcroze, Jaques, 23, 388, 512, 513
Dalvi, Jaywant, 313
Dance Like a Man, 274

Danton's Death, 37
Dard Aayega Dabe Paon, 277
darshak dirgha, 92
Das, Dhiren, 75, 114
Das, Manoranjan, 274
Das, Robin, 16, 40, 266, 337, 429, 462, 524, 565
Das, Sisir Kumar, 111
Dasgupta, Amitabh, 565
Dasgupta, G. N., 564
dasharupakam, 87, 99
Dattani, Mahesh, 274
dead space, 453, 454, 483
declamatory performance styles, 549
Deep, Gagan, 283
defined space, 49, 61, 242, 461, 483
Degas, Edgar, 284
Delhi Art Theatre, 276
Deshmukh, Jayant, 566
Deutsches theatre, 547
devised plays, 42
devised space, 225
Dhananjaya, 87, 88, 99,
dhanu jatra, 130– 134
dhola–maru, 152
Diderot, Denis, 167,
Dilli Chalo, 41
Dipak, Swadesh, 274
Divkar, V.V., 28, 136
Do Kashtion ka Sawar, 193
Dobuzhinsky, Mstislav, 166
Doll's house, a 272, 291, 292
drafting tools, 352, 364
Dramatic Art and Design Academy (DADA), 547
dramatic irony, 563
Dramatic Performances Act (DPA), 245
Dream Play, a, 326, 357
drishya–kavyam, 243
Drury lane, 164
duari, 115
Dubey, Gopal, 566
Dushyanta, 102
dussehra, 107, 126, 152
Dutt, Utpal, 30, 34
dvija, 266

E
Einstein: The Story Till 1905, 319
Ek Aur Dronacharya, 274, 275
Eklavya Uvaach, 53, 275
Elkunchwar, Mahesh, 274
environmental conflict, 268
environmental theatre, 130, 221– 224, 230, 547

Epic theatre, 300
Ernst, Max, 329
Euclid, 382
Euripides, 436, 529
eurythmics, 23, 388, 513
Evam Indrajit, 41, 61, 211, 274, 279, 297, 298
Experimental Theatre at NCPA, 220
expressionism, 296, 546, 555
extended scenes, 136
exterior space, 161
external conflict, 267

F
Fatehlal, 136, 549
fauvism, 296, 380
fire curtains, 175,
flexible theatre space, 218,
fly gallery, 137, 142, 174, 176, 178, 179, 184
foh light bars, 186
folding audience gallery, 218
formalism, 225
formalistic spatial design, 302
Forum theatre, 231, 232
found space, 200, 216– 218, 338,
fourth wall, 167, 196, 201, 202, 232, 559
fragmental Design, 319, 339
framed space, 161, 166, 167, 197, 516, 559
front elevation, 353, 357, 359, 373
Fujiyama, 41

G
Gadhon ka Mela, 40, 229, 528, 558
Gahana, 122, 123, 124
Galleria dell'Accademia, 460, 475
Gandharva, Bal, 31
Ganesh, 107, 159, 160
Ganguli, Pravhat, 565
gangway, 81, 116, 118, 120
Gannon, Martin, 282, 351
Gara ki Gaadi, 193
Garrick, David, 134
gauze curtains, 136, 164
Ghashiram Kotwal, 193, 245, 246, 277, 279
Ghosh, Sanchayan, 41
Gidwani, Asvin, 50
Globe theatre, 202, 531
Golovin, Aleksandr, 166
gopangana, 133
Gorky, Maxim, 315
grand curtain, 135, 174
grand drapery, 175, 176
Grant Road Theatre, 135

Greco–Roman theatre, 192
grid, 178, 180, 190, 213, 307
Grotowski, Jerzy, 46, 199, 230, 231, 232, 552
ground plan, 94, 157, 211, 353, 373, 441, 476
Gubbi Veeranna Nataka Company,139
Gudiya Ghar, 34
Guernica, 245, 248
Gupta, Rajendra, 565
Gurbax Singh hall, 284

H

Hakshar, Anamika, 538
half curtain, 25, 107
Hamlet, 23, 24, 135, 388, 530, 531
Hanamichi, 116
Hangal, A.K., 30
Hanush, 234, 279
Harishchandra, Bharatendu, 140, 244
Haritidevi, 79
hastadanda, 87, 91,
Hauptmaan, Gerhart, 165
Hayavadana, 56, 193, 249, 268,, 277, 323, 393
Heathcote, Dorothy, 232
Heer Ranjha, 277
hegemony of words, 267
Hellerau Institute, 513
Herrmann, Karl Ernst, 547
high–angle lighting, 204
holistic theatre, 100
Holst, Hans Peter, 291, 292
Hoola, Raghuvir, 566
horizontal sightline, 182, 183
hunting dance, 158
Husain, Master Fida, 139
Hussain, M.F., 237
hybrid space, 549
hyper–realism, 165

I

Ibsen, Henrik, 292, 547
Ikshvaku kings, 79
imaginary visuals, 58, 100, 104, 271, 491, 534
Impressionism, 380, 546
Indra Sabha, 139, 276
Indian classical theatre, 23, 159, 189, 300
Indian miniature paintings, 386, 419
Indian national theatre, 543, 553
Indian People's Theatre Association (IPTA), 29, 245
Indian ragamala paintings, 419
Indo–Greek theatre architecture, 67
inner rhythm, 25, 217, 224, 240, 255
inner space, 53, 491

interactive space, 230, 304, 338, 454, 506, 561
interior space, 161
internal conflict, 267
intimate space, 331, 548, 560
invisible space, 55, 56, 57
Ionesco, 269
Iphigenia at Aulis,436
irony in space, 40, 560, 562

J

Jai Pathala Bhairavi, 143
Jalan, Shyamanand, 34
Jana Natya Manch, 245
Jana Sanskriti, 245
Janta Rangmanch, 139
jarjara–dhvaja, 89, 104
Jataka Katha, 67, 79, 114
Jatra, 75, 112, 113– 122
Jawahar Kala Kendra, 376
Jefferson, Margo, 552
John, Barry, 232, 536, 565
Jokumara Swami, 277
Jones, Robert Edmond, 264
Jones, Steph, 58, 270
Julius Caesar, 41
Julus, 211
Juvarra, Filippo, 22, 23, 24

K

Kabhi Na Choden Khet, 191
kabuki theatre, 116, 196, 218
Kahan Kabir, 41
Kale, P. S., 28, 136, 137, 549
Kallol, 34
Kambar, Chandrasekhar, 274, 323,
Kamla, 279
Kamle, 566
Kansa–vadh, 130, 131
Kant, Immanuel, 254
Kapoor, Prithviraj, 30, 139, 204,
Kapoor, Ranjit, 335, 560
Kapoor, Sashi, 204
Kapur, Anuradha, 227, 539, 566
Karanth, B.V., 143, 206, 244, 533, 536, 565
Karmawali, 191
Karna katha, 275, 500, 501
Karnabharam, 271
Karnad, Girish, 37, 274, 275, 287, 323
Kartikeya, 159,
Kashmiri, Agha Hashar, 139, 276
Kastuwar, Jayant, 566
Katha Ghoda, 274

Kathakali, 10, 69, 154, 261, 417
Kathavachak, Radheshyam, 139, 276
kathputli naach, 152
Kaufman, Moises, 289, 299
Kaul, Bansi, 40, 229, 415, 520, 528, 556–559
Kaumudi Mahotsava, 74
Kelieh va Demneh, 66
Kendal, Geoffrey, 30, 34
Kendal, Jennifer, 204
Kethwas, Kanhaiya lal, 567
Khamosh Adalat Jari Hai, 274, 313, 346, 550
Khanna, Dinesh, 530
Khasakkinte Ithihasam, 229
Khayal, 112, 152
Khel Guru Ka, 416
Khol, 123, 124
Khubsurat Bala, 276
Khul ja Sim Sim, 536
Khutwad, Aniruddha, 315
Kichakvadha, 140
King Lear, 37, 191, 272, 550
King of the Dark Chamber, the, 461
Koipen Ek Phooluu Nam Bolo, 274
Konark opera, 121, 122
Koothambalam, 69, 82–85, 86
Korovin, Konstantin, 166
Krishna lila, 85, 13, 114, 152
Kumar, Anupam, 317, 318, 505
Kumarasambhavam, 418
Kunal, Kuldeep, 50, 275, 326, 384, 493
Kuritz, Paul, 67, 101, 222,
Kurosawa, Akira, 533

L

Laal Ghaas Par Neele Ghode, 41
Lady Macbeth Revisited, 230
Laila–Majnu, 139
Lal, Tarsheem, 565
Lalit Kala Akademi, 550
Lall, Ein, 539
Landscape at Arles, the, 305
Langula Narasingh Deva, 81
Lavakusa, 143
Lavender Mist, 294
Legend of Kashak, the, 528
Little Theatre Movement, 165
loading door, 177
lokadharmi, 113, 152
Lorca, Garcia, 13, 565
Lower Depths, the, 37, 291, 315, 346
Luminato festival, Toronto, 351

M

Ma Jolie, 295
Macbeth, 191, 249, 272, 388, 461, 481, 482, 562
Madhubani paintings, 382
Madhyama Vyayoga, 104
Mahabhashya, 65
Mahabhoj, 191, 313
Mahakavi Bhasa, 104, 270
Mahameghavahana Kharavela, 74
Mahanirvan, 274, 279
Mahapatra, Dev, 544, 564
Maharashtra Natak Mandali, 139
mahari nritya, 81
Maharishi Valmiki, 65
Maharishi, Anjala, 319
Maharshi, Mohan, 319
make–believe space, 57, 102
Malavikagnimitram, 193, 271
Man Equals Man, 548
mandapa vidhanam, 80, 85
Manet, Edouard, 284
Manganiyar Seduction, the, 230
Mangilal, 566
Manjira, 114, 124
mankha vidha, 65
Marathi natya sangeet, 549
Marx, Karl, 290
Mathur, Jagdish Ch., 274
Mathura Mangala, 133
Matigadi, 287
mattavarani, 76, 92, 93, 95
Matte Eklavya, 52, 53, 275, 384, 492, 493
Maya Bazar, 143
McAuley, Gay, 47
medieval European drama, 138
Meghadutam, 418
Meghdoot open air theatre, 47, 189–191, 223
Meher, Gangadhar, 123
Mehta, Sanjay, 566
Mena Gurjari, 191
Merchant of Venice, the, 50, 135
metaphorical space, 51, 160
method acting, 292
Midsummer Night's Dream, a, 268, 396, 397
Minerva theatre, 34
minimalism, 225
Mishra, Vibha, 566
Mistry, Baburao, 28, 136, 549
Mitra, Sombhu, 30, 32, 33, 34
Mitra, Tripti, 34
Mizhavu, 82
Mnouchkine, Ariane, 10, 226

mobile theatre, 121, 144, 145, 146, 147, 148
modern Kannada theatre, 286
Modi, Sohrab, 139
Mohenjo–daro, 441
Mohini, 89
Mohiniattam, 154
Moliere, 167
Monet, Claude, 284
monochromatic colour–scheme, 408
monochromatic colours, 400, 408
More Naina Rang Chadhe, 41, 397, 450, 526
Morris, Pam, 313
Moscow Art Theatre, 23, 24, 166, 291, 292
Mother Supreme, 274
Mr Puntila and His Man Matti, 191
Mrcchakatika, 278, 396
Mrigtrishna, 316, 317, 318, 505, 506
Mrityunjay, 275, 501
Mudrarakshasa, 271
Mudras, 90, 102, 103
Mukhashala, 81
Mukhyamantri, 191
Multi–tiered space, 118
multiple spaces, 225
Munch, Edvard, 329
Museo Reina Sofia, 248
Museum of Modern Art (MOMA), New York, 295, 324
musical plays, 276, 277
mythological plays, 274, 275

N

Nabanna, 32, 245
Nagamandala, 269, 323, 393
Nagari natak mandali, 216, 530,
Nagarjunakonda, 68, 79, 80
Namboodiri, Velanezhi Jathavedan, 83
Narasimhadev: I, 5oo
nata sankirtan, 552
Natamandira, 81, 82, 83, 85
Nati Binodini, 41, 551
National Gallery of Art, Washington DC, 294
National School of Drama Repertory Company, 189, 190, 223, 286, 287, 320, 390, 538
National Theatre of Great Britain, 10
national theatre, 543, 552, 553
Natya Shastra, 57, 85, 188, 243, 545, 564
Nautanki, 112, 152, 276
Nawab Wajid Ali Shah, 139
Nayak, Rajkamal, 566
Neel Darpan, 245
negative space, 255, 484, 487, 488, 502, 507,
Nehar, Casper, 343
net curtain, 53, 54, 136, 137
neutral space, 100, 104, 471, 483
Ninagawa, Yukio, 10
noh theatre, 196, 271, 301
non–objective style, 293
non representational style of design, 288, 296

O

object theatre, 152
objective realism, 312
obligatory image, 494, 495,
Odin theatre, 231
Odissi dance, 81
Oedipus Rex, 388
Olivier, Laurence, 521
Omar Khayyam, 277
open air performance space, 186, 187
open–air theatre, 73, 90, 157, 186, 337
opera, 22, 23, 121, 122, 161, 163, 276, 301, 432
optical phantasm, 263
oral tradition, 65
orchestra pit, 161, 164, 172, 173
Orpheus Hellerau, 388
Orwell, George, 302, 303
Otobo mask, 295,
outer space, 71, 491,

P

Padatik theatre group, 34
Padhi, Priyanka Mishra, 103
padya natakam, 141
pageant wagon, 202
Pagla Ghoda, 34, 269, 274, 323
paint and erase method, 461, 539, 554
pala, 112, 122– 126, 210
Panchal, Govardhan, 544
Panchatantra, 66, 346
panchkoshi yatra, 127
Pancika, 79
Panda, Daitari, 121, 122
Panicker, Kavalam Narayana, 256
para–psychological atmosphere, 329
parallel visual illustrations, 534
parikramya or parikrama, 24
Parker and Smith, 210, 264, 288, 510
parsi theatre, 29, 35, 134–140, 144, 273, 314
Parthasarathy, Indira, 274
Patel, Jabbar, 277
patra, 101, 301
Pavis, Patrice, 158
Peer Gynt, 41
periodical plays, 272, 273, 390

Pictorial or realistic design, 312–314
Pillai, Abhilash, 41, 227, 528, 539
Pipes, Alan, 240, 296, 385, 430, 444, 471
Pollock, Jackson, 294
Poor theatre, 231, 233
positive space, 483, 484, 487
post minimal art, 225
postmodernism, 296
Prasad, Jaishankar, 140
Prasanna, 286, 287, 566
prekshagriha, 88, 91, 95
Prem, Rameshwar, 274, 392, 498
presentational Style, 100, 289, 299–311
primary colours, 401, 402, 403, 404, 461
primitive theatre, 158, 186, 196
Prithvi theatre, 204, 205, 206
Prometheus Bound, 41
proscenium design, 157, 331
proskenion, 166
Psycho–physical theatre, 232
psychological atmosphere, 23, 56, 264, 288, 562
pung cholum, 552
Punjabi opera, 276, 565
Purulia chhau dance, 112, 153
Putul Khela, 34

R
radial balance, 477
radial symmetry, 477
Raghurajpur, 150
Rahman, Md. Sahidur, 284, 467
Rai, Madhu, 274
Raina, K. K., 340
Rajdarpan, 538
Rajendran, K.S., 431, 432, 567
Rakesh, Mohan, 25, 37, 274, 333, 337, 522
Raktakarabi, 33, 34
Ramayah, K.D., 52, 275
Ramcharitmanas, 127
Ramnagar ki Ramlila, 126, 127, 130
Rang Vidushak, 462, 567
Ranga Shankara theatre, 204
Ranga Yatra, 287
rangabhumi, 92
rangamandal, 16, 191, 193, 195, 206, 533, 565,
    rangamandapa, 67, 74, 80, 92
rangapatti, 25
rangapitha, 75, 76, 92, 93
rangasirsha, 76, 92, 107
rangmancha, 144, 149
Rangakalpa theatre group, 283
Ranigumpha, 67, 74, 76, 78,

Rao, Nageswara – Babji, 140
Rao, Rekandar China Venkata, 140
Rao, Vanarasa Govinda, 140
Rasa, 90, 99, 104, 107, 188, 254, 552, 554
Rashomon, 41, 42, 229, 528, 533
rasika, 90, 104, 188
Ratha, Kavisurjya Baladeva, 123
Rathbun, Marry, 382
Rabindra Bhawan, 47, 223, 337, 339, 548, 560
realistic design, 299, 312, 313, 314, 560
reciprocal units, 352
reflection of light rays, 403
regional theatre, 113, 552
Reinhardt, Max, 547
Rembrandt, 448, 449, 495, 497
Renoir, August, 284
representational design, 288,
representational style, 289–293, 304, 311, 312
Reth: Songs of the Sand, 50
revolving stage, 31
Rhinoceros, 269
rhythmic movements, 240, 431, 513
rhythmic space, 24, 510, 512, 514
Rice, Elmer, 345
Richard III, 135
right–angled triangle, 439
Ritusamhara, 415, 418
Roach, Joseph, 48
Romeo and Juliet and The Security Guard, 528
rotational symmetry, 431, 434
Roy, D.L., 31, 144
Royal Academy of Dramatic Arts, 36, 286
Royal Central School of Speech and Drama, 282
Royal Shakespeare Theatre Company, 521
Royal Theatre, 292
Rtih, 240
Rukmini Harana, 114
Russell Brown, John, 10, 120, 566
Rustam–O–Sohrab, 139, 276

S
Saha, Ramesh Chandra, 533
Sahani, Balraj, 30
Sahani, Bhisham, 274
Sahay, Raghuvir, 562
Saini, Pratap, 566
Samanta Singhara, Abhimanyu, 123
samavakara, 88, 98
Samudaya theatre group, 286
Sandhya Chhaya, 313
sanskrit theatre, 24, 24, 57, 58, 100, 111, 112
Saraswathi, A.R., 79

Sattavara Naralu, 277
Sawant, Sivaji, 275, 501
Sayan Bhaye Kotwal, 191
scale drawing, 352, 354, 359
scale model, 8, 10, 13, 373
scale unit, 354, 366, 373
SCENOFEST, 14, 351
scenographic dramaturgy, 519–522, 534, 535,
Schechner, Richard, 127, 223, 230, 548
Segan, Ved, 205
Selection of space, 330, 331
Sen, Satu, 32, 543,
Sen, Tapas, 34
Serra, Richard, 225, 226
Seurat, George, 284
shadow puppet theatre, 301
Shahjahan, 139, 273
shailaguhakara, 91
Shakespeare, 13, 37, 50, 135, 139, 154, 202, 521
Shakharam Binder, 279
Shakuntala ki Anguthi, 274
Shakuntala, 25, 26, 27, 41, 102, 105, 108, 260,
Sharma, H.V., 68, 79, 98, 431, 432, 532, 564
Sharma, M.N., 138, 142
Sharma, Saroj, 566
Sharvilak, 40, 41
Shastri, Jitu, 566
Shatabdi theatre group, 297
Shaw, George Bernard, 10
Shaw, Irvin, 335
Shesh, Shankar, 274, 275
Shila Sringar, 41
Shiv Purana, 159
Shri Ram Centre, New Delhi, 548, 550
shumang lila, 552
Shuturmurg, 34
sightline, 180, 182, 183, 184, 373, 384
Sikri, Surekha, 287
similarity symmetry, 432, 434,
Simov, Viktor, 166
Singh, Anila, 339
Singh, Manohar, 38, 339
Singh, Rajesh Kumar, 219, 227, 375
Singh, Vijay Kumar, 566
Singh, Vijaymohan, 565
single dimension, 382
Sircar, Badal, 61, 210, 231, 232, 269, 274, 297
siri palia, 122
Siri Sampige, 274
site–specific performance, 224, 225, 528
Sivaraman, Deepan, 41, 43, 227, 229, 258
Skandagupta, 218, 273, 528

skeletal design, 320, 321
skene building, 166
Sopanam theatre group, 257
space–group–symmetry, 434
spatial art, 55, 241, 242, 435
spatio–temporal art, 55, 241, 242, 243
Spinal Cord, 41, 43, 230
split–complementary colours, 410
Sri Venkateswara natya mandali, 140, 143
stage balance, 464, 471
stage geography, 168, 170
Stanislavsky System, 166
Stanislavsky, Konstantin, 23, 32, 166, 291, 292
state of blissfulness, 254
Stein, Peter, 547
storage shades, 177
storyboard, 343, 345, 346, 347, 349
Strindberg, August, 326, 357
structural design, 210, 287, 307, 320, 561
structural masks, 302, 303
stylisation, 100, 299, 312
Subhadramma, 140
subtractive colours, 401–404
Sudraka, 271
suggestive design, 286, 300, 314– 318, 319, 560
Sultan Razia, 139
Sun temple, 81, 83, 438, 500
Suno Janmejaya, 275
Sur, Dharam Das, 549
Surabhi nataka mandali, 140
surrealism, 322– 326, 380, 417, 555
Surya ki Antim Kiran se Pahli Kiran Tak, 274
Suzuki, Tadashi, 552
Swaminathan, J., 239, 565
Sydney Opera House, 432, 434
symmetrical balance, 473

T
Tagore, Rabindranath, 31, 32, 32
Tanvir, Habib, 30, 274, 566
Teatro Farnese, 161, 164
Teatro Libre, 165
Tempest, the, 10
temporal art, 241, 242, 243
Tendulkar, Vijay, 37, 246, 274
Tere Mere Lekh, 565
tertiary, 403, 404, 405, 417
The Clown and Clouds, The Circus–Theatre Project, 528
theatre of roots movement, 432
theatre of the oppressed, 231
Theatre Royal at Covent Garden, 164
Theatre–in–Education Company, 536

Therukoothu, 112, 154
Theyyam, 112, 154, 417, 439
third theatre, 231
Thirty Days in September, 274
Thiyam, Ratan, 16, 40, 256, 259, 275, 323, 566,
Tholu Bommalata, 140
Three Penny Opera, 260
Three Sisters, 41
thang–ta, 112, 552
thrust stage, 115, 116, 157, 192, 201– 204, 214, 218
Thrust theatre at BNA, 208
thumbnail sketches, 349
Thyagrajan, S., 315, 467
tint, 413, 417, 419, 420
Titus Andronicus, 521
Tolstoy, Leo, 291
tormentor, 174
Towards a Poor Theatre, 231, 233
transitional colour value, 445, 446
translational symmetry, 434, 435
Trojan Women, the,193
tryasra avara, 87
tryasra, 173, 174, 373
Tughlaq, 37, 38, 218, 273, 286, 287, 313, 388,
Tukke pe Tukka, 40, 41, 416
Tumhara Vincent, 41, 283, 302, 304, 305, 308

U
Ubu Roi, 41
Udayagiri hills, 67, 74
Uncle Vanya, 191
Understanding Brecht, 300
unified space, 473, 512, 555
unit of space, 101
upstage, 53, 54, 92, 107, 202, 205, 451, 468,
Urubhangam, 57, 58, 104, 259, 270, 271
Uttara Baokar, 339

V
vachika, 58
Vadakkunnathan temple, 83
Vajpayee, Ashok, 565
vajra, 89
value of colours, 444, 446, 447, 451
value of lines, 451, 452
Varadpande, M.L., 70, 75, 78
Varma, Kumara, 37
Varma, Raja Ravi, 26, 27, 245
Varma, Surendra, 37, 274
Vasa, Mahakavi, 58, 104, 270
vastu Shilpa, 88
vedika, 92, 107

Veer Abhimanyu, 276
Veera Brahmam Gari Charitra, 143
veshaghara, 116, 118, 119, 120, 124
Vijayan, O.V., 229
vikrista madhyama natyamandapa, 88, 91, 95,
Virasat, 274, 279, 313
virtual space, 373, 483
Vishakhadutta, 271
Vishnu Sharma, 67
Vishwakarma, 88
visual aesthetics, 19, 39, 59, 104, 157, 161, 166,
visual axis, 146, 184, 356, 357, 373, 465, 468
visual dialogues, 339, 454, 489
visual theatre, 9, 10, 40, 283, 307, 323, 326
visual weight, 435, 465, 467, 468, 471
Vivadi theatre group, 539
Volksbühne theatre, 547

W
Wagner, Richard, 161, 163, 164,
Waiting for Godot, 269, 272
Wakankar, V.S, 70
Walter, Benjamin, 300
wardrobe, 177
Warli paintings, 382, 439
warm colours, 405, 406, 407, 416, 417
Warner, Deborah, 226
Wheatfield and the Crows, 305
When We Dead Awaken, 323, 326, 461, 491,
Willis, Ronald A., 49
Wilson, Robert, 548
wing space, 138, 177, 178, 182, 331, 483, 523
Woyzeck, 335, 560
Wrights & Sites theatre, 226

Y
Yakshagana, 112, 154
Yamgatha, 191
yard (Globe theatre), 202
yavanika, 25, 59, 101, 104, 107, 108, 159
Yayati, 28, 275

Z
Zeami, 271
Zindegi aur Zonk, 462